Biblical Interpretation
in Ancient Israel

Biblical Interpretation in Ancient Israel

MICHAEL FISHBANE

CLARENDON PRESS · OXFORD

Oxford University Press, Walton Street, Oxford OX2 6DP

Oxford New York Toronto
Delhi Bombay Calcutta Madras Karachi
Kuala Lumpur Singapore Hong Kong Tokyo
Nairobi Dar es Salaam Cape Town
Melbourne Auckland Madrid
and associated companies in
Berlin Ibadan

Oxford is a trade mark of Oxford University Press

Published in the United States
by Oxford University Press Inc., New York

British Library Cataloguing in Publication Data
Data available

Library of Congress Cataloging in Publication Data
Fishbane, Michael A.
Biblical interpretation in ancient Israel.
Bibliography.   Includes index.
1. Bible. O.T.—Criticism, interpretation, etc.,
Jewish.   2. Bible. O.T.—Theology.   I. Title.
BS1186.F57 1984   221.6'0933   83–26797
ISBN 0–19–826699–5

5 7 9 10 8 6 4

Printed in Great Britain
on acid-free paper by
Biddles Ltd,
Guildford and King's Lynn

FOR MONA,
EITAN, AND ELISHA

נְהוֹרָא מְעַלְיָא

Preface

IN some respects, this book had its beginning in one of my earliest areas of interest in biblical studies — what I then construed as 'sub-surface culture', meaning those mental or cultural features in ancient Israel which are only indirectly indicated on the surface of biblical literature but which emerged to full view in post-biblical sources. More directly, the subject of this work on exegetical practices and traditions embedded in the Hebrew Bible first found expression in a lecture delivered in Jerusalem in 1973, at the Sixth World Congress of Jewish Studies, and subsequently published in the volume of *Proceedings*. Further clarification was achieved in the course of preparing essays for several publications from 1975 onwards. My decision to expand the topic into a full-length study came in the summer of 1977, when I enjoyed a stipend from the National Endowment of the Humanities, and during the subsequent sabbatical semester when I also received aid from the Memorial Foundation for Jewish Culture. Various drafts followed, and these were entirely reworked and expanded during the academic year 1981-2, when I held a visiting appointment at Stanford University on the Aaron-Roland Fund. I also received a research grant from this fund which provided for the typing of the final draft. I am grateful to Professor Van Harvey for making this money available to me, and to Ms Josephine Guttadauro for her expert typing. Support for earlier typing was provided by various research funds at Brandeis University, and I am particularly grateful to Professor Marvin Fox, Director of the Lown School of Near Eastern and Judaic Studies, and to Dr Marver Bernstein, past President of the University, for their kind offices in securing for me a substantial subvention which helped support this work in its final stages. Sincere thanks to the Mazur Family Fund for Faculty Research for its generosity.

It is out of the deepest gratitude that I extend my heartfelt thanks to Professor James Barr, Regius Professor of Hebrew at Oxford University, who exceeded the ordinary duty of a colleague by his interest in and support of this work. His acuity as a reader is well known, and I have benefited from it; his interest in the scholarship of a younger colleague is a debt which I happily acknowledge, and I can only hope to repay this to others in turn.

It is also my pleasure to acknowledge another virtually unpayable debt, and this of even longer standing, to my dear teacher and colleague, Professor Nahum M. Sarna, Golding Professor of Biblical Studies at

Brandeis University, who has been a faithful mentor and friend for nearly 20 years. It was from him that I first learned of the phenomenon of 'Inner Biblical Exegesis', and the term, which he used in his own excellent study of Psalm 89.

During my work on this book I have been assisted in sundry ways by various students of mine, particularly, Mr Bernard Levinson. I fully appreciate his conscientious and thoughtful efforts, his critical evaluations, and his alert help in locating discrepancies in the proofs. The usefulness of the book has been enhanced by the Subject Index which he has arranged and compiled: a time-consuming task which he performed with characteristic energy and analytical skill.

In its final stages, the careful and courteous professionalism of the editors and staff of the Oxford University Press was beyond praise. I am very thankful to them for their kind services, and to the Delegates of the Press for honouring me through this publication.

To Mona, whose presence is my abiding joy, and to Eitan and Elisha our sons, wide-eyed and wondrous, I dedicate this book, with love.

M. FISHBANE

Erev Rosh Hashanah, 5744
Brandeis University

I have been most gratified by the very positive responses to my work by many colleagues and friends—in long and reflective scholarly reviews, and in extensive conversations and correspondences. No scholar could hope for more than the serious, considered, and constructive comments of his peers.

In the present reissue, I could not hope to engage the issues raised by colleagues; nor could I hope to incorporate all the new observations of Inner-Biblical Exegesis that I have made since the initial publication. I have restricted changes in the text to reformulations of some infelicities and details, and have indicated some new interpretations in an Addendum. These latter are intended to nuance the present work, not to enlarge the corpus at random. I am grateful to the Press for this opportunity. In particular, heartfelt thanks go to Anne Ashby who has continued to extend to me every professional courtesy with grace, good humour, and efficiency.

M. F.

Hanukkah, 5748

Contents

Part Three. Aggadic Exegesis

Part Four. Mantological Exegesis

* An asterisk (*) in the outer margin of the text indicates that there is a
supplementary note in the Addenda

Abbreviations

Commentaries on the Bible – Series

AB	Anchor Bible, New York.
ATD	Das Alte Testament Deutsch, Göttingen.
BKAT	Biblischer Kommentar: Altes Testament, Neukirchen.
CB	Cambridge Bible for Schools and Colleges, Cambridge.
HAT	Handbuch zum Alten Testament, Tübingen.
HKAT	Handkommentar zum Alten Testament, Göttingen.
ICC	The International Critical Commentary, Edinburgh.
KAT	Kommentar zum Alten Testament, Leipzig, Gütersloh.
KeH	Kurzgefasstes exegetisches Handbuch zum Alten Testament, Leipzig.
KHAT	Kurzer Hand-Commentar zum Alten Testament, Tübingen.

Texts and other abbreviations

'Abod. Zar.	*'Abodah Zarah*
Akk.	Akkadian
Antiq.	Josephus, *Antiquities of the Jews*
Aram.	Aramaic
b.	*Babli*, The Babylonian Talmud
BCE	Before the Common Era
Bek.	*Bekorot*
Ber.	*Berakot*
Bik.	*Bikkurim*
B. Meṣ.	*Baba Meṣi'a*
B. Qam.	*Baba Qama*
CC	The Covenant Code (Exod. 21:1–23:19)
CDC	Cairo (Geniza text of the) Damascus (Document)
DN	Divine Name
'Ed.	*'Eduyyot*
Eg.	Egyptian
'Erub.	*'Erubin*
Esd.	Esdras
Giṭ.	*Giṭṭin*

Ḥag.	Ḥagigah
HC	The Holiness Code (Lev. 17–26)
Heb.	Hebrew
Ḥul.	Ḥullin
JB	The Jerusalem Bible
JE	Jahwist–Elohist narrative strand of the Pentateuch
Jub.	Jubilees
JPS	The Jewish Publication Society of America (Old Translation, 1917)
K	*ketib*
Ketub.	*Ketubot*
LH	The Laws of Hammurapi
LI	The Laws of Lipit Ishtar
LXX	The Septuagint Version
M.	*Mishnah*
Macc.	Maccabees
MAL	The Middle Assyrian Laws
Ma'aś. Š.	*Ma'aśer Šeni*
Menaḥ.	*Menaḥot*
MT	The Massoretic Text
NA	Neo-Assyrian
NB	Neo-Babylonian
NEB	The New English Bible
Ned.	*Nedarim*
NF	Neue Folge
NJPS	The New Jewish Publication Society of American Translation (1962–83)
NS	New Series
'Or.	*'Orlah*
OS	Old Series
OT	The Old Testament
P	The Priestly Writings
p	Pesher (commentary)
Pesaḥ.	*Pesaḥim*
PN	personal name
Q	Qumran
1Q, 2Q, etc.	numbered caves of Qumrań
1Q apGen.	*Genesis Apocryphon*
1Q H.	*Hodayot (Thanksgiving Hymns)*
1Q Isa.[a]	first copy of Isaiah

1Q pHab.	Pesher on Habakkuk
1Q S.	*Serek ha-Yaḥad (Rule of the Community, Manual of Discipline)*
4Q Flor.	*Florilegium* (or *Eschatological Midrashim*)
4Q Sam.[a, b]	first or second copy of Samuel
4Q Testim.	*Testimonia* text
11Q Melch.	*Melchizedek* text
11Q Torah	The Temple Scroll
Qidd.	*Qiddušin*
Rab.	*Rabbah*
Roš Has.	*Roš Haššanah*
RSV	The Revised Standard Version
Šabb.	*Šabbat*
Samar.	The Samaritan Version
Sanh.	*Sanhedrin*
Šeb.	*Šebi'it*
Šeqal.	*Šeqalim*
Sukk.	*Sukkah*
Syr.	Syriac
Ta'an.	*Ta'anit*
Tg.	*Targum*
Tg. Neof.	*Targum Neofiti*
Tg. Onq.	*Targum Onqelos*
Tg. J., Ps.-J.	*Targum Jonathan, Pseudo-Jonathan*
Tg. Yer.	*Targum Yerušalmi (I* and *II)*
TN	toponym
Tos.	*Tosephta*
Ug.	Ugaritic
Yebam.	*Yebamot*
yer.	*Yerušalmi*, The Palestinian Talmud
Zebaḥ.	*Zebahim*

Periodicals, serials, text editions, and reference works

AASOR	*Annual of the American Schools of Oriental Research*, New Haven
ABL	R. F. Harper, *Assyrian and Babylonian Letters*, Chicago, 1892-1914, cited by number.
AfO	*Archiv für Orientforschung*, Berlin: Graz.
AHw.	W. von Soden, *Akkadisches Handwörterbuch*, Wiesbaden, O. Harrassowitz, 1965-81.

AJSL	*American Journal of Semitic Languages and Literatures*, Chicaco.
AJS Rev.	*Association of Jewish Studies Review*, Cambridge, MA.
ALUOS	*Annual of Leeds University Oriental Society*.
An. Bib.	*Analecta Biblica*, Rome.
ANET	*Ancient Near Eastern Texts relating to the Old Testament*, 2nd edn., ed. J. B. Pritchard, Princeton, NJ, 1955.
An. Or.	*Analecta Orientalia*.
AOAT	*Alter Orient und Altes Testament*, Kevelaer.
Ar. Or.	*Archiv Orientálni*, Prague.
AS	*Assyriological Studies*, Chicago.
Asarhaddon	*Die Inschriften Asarhaddons, Königs von Assyrien*, R. Borger (*AfO* Beiheft 9), Osnabrück: Biblio-Verlag, 1967.
ASTI	*Annual of the Swedish Theolgical Institute in Jerusalem*, Leiden.
BA	*Biblical Archeologist* (New Haven), Ann Arbor.
BASOR	*Bulletin of the American Schools of Oriental Research*, New Haven.
BBB	Bonner Biblische Beiträge, Bonn.
BHT	Beiträge zur historischen Theologie, Tübingen.
Bib.	*Biblica*, Rome.
BR	*Biblical Research*, Chicago.
BSOAS	*Bulletin of the School of Oriental and African Studies*, University of London, London.
BZ	*Biblische Zeitschrift* (new series from 1957), (Freiburg i.Br.), Paderborn.
BZAW	Beihefte zur *Zeitschrift für die Alttestamentliche Wissenschaft* (Giessen), Berlin.
CAD	*Chicago Assyrian Dictionary*, Chicago, 1956–
CBQ	*Catholic Biblical Quarterly*, Washington, DC.
CS	*Cahiers sioniens*, Paris.
CTA	A. Herder, *Corpus des tablettes en cunéiformes alphabétiques*, Paris: P. Geuthner, 1963.
DBS	*Dictionnaire de la Bible, Supplément*, Paris.
DJD	*Discoveries in the Judaean Desert*, Oxford: The Clarendon Press.
Enc. Jud.	*Encyclopedia Judaica*, Jerusalem.
Enc. Miq.	*Enṣiqlopedia Miqra'it* (Encyclopedia Biblica; in Heb.), Jerusalem.
ETL	*Ephemerides Theologicae, Lovanienses*, Leuven.
FRLANT	Forschungen zur Religion und Literatur des Alten und Neuen Testaments, Göttingen.

HTR	*Harvard Theological Review*, Cambridge, MA.
HUCA	*Hebrew Union College Annual*, Cincinnati.
IDB	*Interpreter's Dictionary of the Bible*, ed. G. A. Buttrick, Nashville and New York.
IEJ	*Israel Exploration Journal*, Jerusalem.
Int.	*Interpretation*, Richmond, VA.
JANESCU	*Journal of the Ancient Near Eastern Society of Columbia University*, New York.
JAOS	*Journal of the American Oriental Society*, New Haven.
JBL	*Journal of Biblical Literature* (Philadelphia; Missoula), Chico, CA.
JCS	*Journal of Cuneiform Studies*, New Haven.
JEA	*Journal of Egyptian Archaeology*, London.
JJS	*Journal of Jewish Studies*, London.
JNES	*Journal of Near Eastern Studies*, Chicago.
JNWSL	*Journal of North-West Semitic Languages.*
JQR	*Jewish Quarterly Review*, Philadelphia.
JSOT	*Journal for the Study of the Old Testament*, Sheffield.
JSS	*Journal of Semitic Studies*, Manchester University Press.
JTS	*Journal of Theological Studies*, Oxford.
KAI	H. Donner and W. Röllig, *Kanaanäische und Aramäische Inschriften*, 3 vols., 1964, cited by inscription no.
KAR	*Keilschrifttexte aus Assur religiösischen Inhalts*, Leipzig.
Leš.	*Lešonénu*, Jerusalem.
LSS	Leipziger Semitische Studien, Leipzig.
MAOG	*Mitteilungen der Altorientalischen Gesellschaft*, Leipzig.
Maqlû	*Die assyrische Beschwörungssammlung Maqlû*, ed. G. Meier, *AfO* Beiheft 2, Berlin, 1937.
MGWJ	*Monatsschrift für Geschichte und Wissenschaft des Judentums*, Breslau.
MVÄG	*Mitteilungen der Vorderasiatisch(-Ägyptisch)en Gesellschaft* (Berlin), Leipzig.
Nov. Test.	*Novum Testamentum*, Leiden.
NTS	*New Testament Studies*, Cambridge.
NTT	*Norsk Teologisk Tidsskrift*, Oslo.
OLZ	*Orientalistische Literaturzeitung* (Leipzig), Berlin.
OTS	*Oudtestmentische Studiën*, Leiden.
PAAJR	*Proceedings of the American Academy of Jewish Research*, New York.
PSBA	*Processings of the Society of Biblical Archaeology*, Bloomsbury, London.
RA	*Revue d'assyriologie et d'archéologie orientale*, Paris.

RB	*Revue biblique*, Paris.
RÉJ	*Revue des études juives*, Paris.
RHR	*Revue d'histoire des religions*, Paris.
RIDA	*Revue international des droits de l'antiquité*, Louvain.
RLA	*Reallexikon der Assyriologie*, Berlin.
RQ	*Revue de Qumrân*, Paris.
SBLDS	Society of Biblical Literature Dissertations Series (Missoula), Chico, CA.
SBLMS	Society of Biblical Literature Monograph Series (Missoula), Chico, CA.
SBT	Studies in Biblical Theology, London and Naperville, Ill.
SJLA	Studies in Judaism in Late Antiquity, Leiden.
SNVAO	Skrifter utgitt ov Det Norske Videnskaps-Akademi i Oslo, Oslo.
SPB	Studia Post-Biblica, Leiden.
St. Theol.	*Studia Theologica*, Lund, Aarhus.
SVT	*Supplement to Vetus Testamentum*, Leiden.
TAPS	Transactions of the American Philosophical Society, Philadelphia.
TBü	Theologische Bücherei, Munich.
TLZ	*Theologische Literaturzeitung*, Leipzig and Berlin.
Toledot	Y. Kaufmann, *Toledot ha-Emunah ha-Yisra'elit*, Jerusalem and Tel Aviv, 4 vols., 1938–56 (in Heb.).
TSK	*Theologische Studien und Kritiken* (Hamburg, Gotha, Leipzig), Berlin.
TZ	*Theologische Zeitschrift*, Basel.
UF	*Ugarit-Forschungen*, Kevelaer.
UT	C. H. Gordon, *Ugaritic Textbook*, Rome, 1965, cited by text no.
VIO	Veröffentlichungen des Instituts für Orientforschung, Berlin.
VT	*Vetus Testamentum*, Leiden.
VTE	D. J. Wiseman, *The Vassal Treaties of Esarhaddon, Iraq*, 20, 1958, cited by line.
ZA	*Zeitschrift für Assyriologie*, Berlin.
ZAW	*Zeitschrift für die alttestamentliche Wissenschaft*, Berlin.
ZDMG	*Zeitschrift der Deutschen Morgenländischen Gesellschaft* (Leipzig), Wiesbaden.
ZNW	*Zeitschrift für neutestamentliche Wissenschaft*, Berlin.
ZTK	*Zeitschrift für Theologie und Kirche* (Freiburg i.Br., Leipzig), Tübingen.

Introduction

ONE of the most remarkable features of the great world religions is the emergence to independent dignity of traditions and commentaries which supplement the original authoritative teachings – be these latter the product of divine revelation or human wisdom. This phenomenon is not restricted to religious literature, of course, as the commentaries and super-commentaries to Aristotle in the Middle Ages, or to Freud in modernity, fully attest. But it is in the classical expressions of Judaism, Christianity, and Islam on the one hand, and Hinduism, Buddhism, and Confucianism on the other, that interpretation has become a cultural form of the first magnitude – transforming the foundational revelations of the first group and the metaphysical insights of the second, and determining the fateful historical paths of both. Indeed, far from simply being the fundamental mode whereby divine revelations and philosophical truths maintain their ongoing cultural value, human interpretation is also constitutive of what has been even more fateful and fundamental for our religious–cultural heritage: what Thomas Mann characterized, in another regard, as 'zitathaftes Leben'.[1] By 'zitathaftes Leben' I mean the dependence of the great religious–cultural formations on authoritative views which are studied, reinterpreted, and adapted to ongoing life. So much, it seems, is derivation – as opposed to radical innovation – a central ingredient of the human religious condition, that Gautama Buddha set his whole revolution of consciousness deliberately against it, only to have his followers turn him into a transcendent source of wisdom and his works into the subject-matter of exegesis.[2] Moreover, the exegetical orientation is also basic to the internal transformations of the historical religions. Significantly, the Teacher of Righteousness at Qumran, and Jesus, and Paul, and all the religious reformers that come to mind, presented themselves as the authentic *interpreters* of the religions which they represented.

Among the historical religions, none so much prizes 'zitathaftes Leben' as does Judaism, which casts the scholar and disciple of the wise

---

[1] See his 'Freud und die Zukunft', in *Gesammelte Werke* (Frankfurt-am-Main: Fischer, 1960), ix. 497.

[2] And yet it should be stressed that even the Buddha's apparent rejection of Brahmanic orthodoxy and the speculative tradition of the Upanishads did not repudiate entirely the ascetic and contemplative traditions of India. See E. Senart, 'Bouddhisme et yoga', *RHR* 42 (1900), 348.

as its central religious type, and God himself as their prototype.[3]
Complementing this attitude, the early rabbis actually portrayed their
God midrashically as a scholar of his own Torah and as subordinate to
the decisions made by the disciples of the wise![4] It is thus no under-
statement that the Jewish preoccupation with interpretation has proved
fateful to the historical course of Judaism, and to the religions and
civilizations influenced by it. In fact, the exegetical achievements of
Judaism (and Christianity and Islam) have proved so prodigious and
protean that the original hierarchical relationship of revelation to
exegetical tradition has been inverted for all practical purposes. Indeed,
it is a commonplace in traditional Judaism and Christianity (Roman
and Orthodox) to affirm that revelation is comprehensible only through
the authoritative tradition of interpretation. To the historically minded,
this transformation—and it occurred early—is nothing short of remarkable. The protest of the Reformers, '*sola scriptura*', stands out in sharp
relief against this background.

In view of these matters, and their religious–cultural significance for
Western civilization in particular, it has seemed fundamental to me to
investigate the following questions: When did the Jewish exegetical
tradition come to be formed? What literary and historical factors
contributed to its birth? Is the development of an exegetical tradition
in post-biblical Judaism solely the product of internal tensions—fostered
by competing sects with different claims on the biblical heritage, or do
its roots also go back to the biblical past itself? Are the independent
and religiously dignified compilations of oral traditions in early Judaism
solely the late product of theoretical study and practical need—fostered
by different exegetical techniques and social factors—or does the Hebrew
Bible also reflect the prehistory of those post-biblical phenomena
whose contents are so new and often 'unbiblical'?[5]

---

[3] Of the many essays which explore the religious and cultural dynamics of
interpretation in Judaism, two contributions of particular profundity are S.
Rawidowicz, 'On Interpretation', in *Studies in Jewish Thought*, ed. N. Glatzer
(Philadelphia: Jewish Publication Society, 1974), 45–80, and G. Scholem, 'Revel-
ation and Tradition as Religious Categories in Judaism', in *The Messianic Idea in
Judaism* (New York: Schocken, 1971), 282–303.

[4] For God as a scholar of Torah, cf. *b. Ber.* 8b, 63b; *b. 'Abod. Zar.* 3b; and for
God as subordinate to human exegesis, cf. the famous passage in *b. B. Meṣ.* 59b.

[5] Particularly pertinent here is the question posed by J. Barr: 'was the historical
and temporal continuity (between the Hebrew Bible and post-biblical Judaism)
also a logical and mental continuity?' See his 'Judaism—Its Continuity with the
Bible', *The 7th Montefiore Memorial Lecture* (The University of Southampton,
1968), 3. Seminal early attempts to provide a positive articulation of this question
may be found in I. L. Seeligmann, 'Voraussetzung der Midraschexegese', *SVT* 1
(1953), 150–81, and R. Bloch, in *DBS* v, ed. H. Cazelles (Paris: Letouzey and
Ané, 1957), 1263–81, s.v. 'midrash'. The present study will attempt to review the
issue more comprehensively on the basis of firm methodological criteria.

Since the paramount concern of the present work is exegesis found *within* the Hebrew Bible, the preceding questions are, to a certain extent, rhetorical and preliminary—but only to a certain extent, since these questions also set the gauge for a proper sighting of the relationship between the Hebrew Bible and its post-biblical offshoots *from the perspective of the history of exegesis.* Moreover, a critical perspective on the phenomenon of interpretation in early Judaism sets the initial contours for discerning and appraising the origins of that phenomenon within the Hebrew Bible. To be sure, factors pertinent to a phenomenon in early Judaism will not necessarily be appropriate to an earlier stage of that phenomenon unless they provide a critical opening to its problematics, and unless they contribute to an analysis of that first stage on its own terms. This proves to be the case, in fact, with respect to the following two factors which may be isolated as necessary *historical* components in the development of post-biblical Jewish exegesis: on the one hand, authoritative texts or teachings whose religious-cultural significance is fundamental; on the other, conditions to which these texts or teachings do not appear to be explicitly pertinent.

From the viewpoint of historical Judaism, the central task of exegetical tradition is to demonstrate the capacity of Scripture to regulate *all* areas of life and thought. However, this capacity is not at all manifest or self-evident. As a result, traditional Jewish exegesis first assumes the comprehensive adequacy of Scripture to be an implicit feature of its contents, and then sets its task as one of explication, as one which makes the comprehensive pertinence of Torah explicit and manifest. This fundamental task is achieved either by deriving new teachings *from* old—through one exegetical technique or another—or by legitimating existing social customs and laws (religious or civil) by means of secondary connections to Scripture. In this way, tradition assumes religious dignity through its exegetical association with revealed Scripture. It is therefore quite immaterial from this point of view whether these exegetical associations are established directly, via textual exegesis, or indirectly, via textual justification.[6] To be sure, those who labour in this garden will be aware of two distinct types of exegetical tradition: the one dignified by its verbal origins in Scripture, the other dignified by the religious community which lives by Scripture and whose customs can therefore be faithfully regarded as a form of non-verbal exegesis. But despite the fact that different Jewish sects valued the one type or the other, a notable feature of early Pharisaism is that it demonstrates

---

[6] On the early expressions of Scriptural derivation or attribution, cf. C. Albeck, *Mabo' la-Mishnah* (Jerusalem: The Bialik Institute, 1959), 25-62, and, recently, E. E. Urbach, 'The Exegetical Sermon as the Source of Halakha and the Problem of the Scribes', *Tarbiz*, 27 (1958), 166-82 [Heb.].

the inherent complementarity of both.[7] For the sages of this group, the exegetical attribution of Scriptural support for customary behaviours derived from 'Scriptural living' and the textual interpretation of Scripture collectively comprise a unified religious perspective. In this way, the ongoing value of Scripture is made explicit and the traditions themselves are reciprocally dignified.

One further dimension of these matters may be noted here briefly, and that concerns the remarkable attribution in certain groups of a revealed status to the human exegesis of implicit Scriptural meanings. The reason for this divinization of the content of exegetical traditions in ancient Judaism are multiple and can no longer be disentangled easily. What needs to be noted here is that this development cannot simply be explained as a consequence of rival systems of exegesis, but must be seen, just as surely, as a natural theological consequence of the notion that the contents of interpretation *are part of* the written divine revelation (implicitly or explicitly). In different degrees, both factors explain the emergence of the well-known Pharisaic chain of tradition which begins the tractate of *'Abot* and links its system of oral exegesis to a Sinaitic revelation parallel to the written, public one (though differentiated from it, of course, by being emergent over millennia).[8] An even earlier instance of this overall trend can be found in the so-called *Rule Scroll* of the Qumran covenanters, which refers repeatedly to an esoteric Torah of Moses and the exegeses of it practised by the Jews whom the sectarians considered unenlightened and rebellious.[9] All told, this divinization of exegesis in early Judaism is no less than a redivinization of it: for we shall have occasion to explore the oracular nature of the earliest records of legal exegesis in the Hebrew Bible.[10] In effect,

---

[7] The Sadduccees also had oral traditions and exegesis, but these had no ultimate authority and were never linked with the written Torah. See the dated but still standard essay by J. Lauterbach, 'The Sadducees and Pharisees', in *Studies in Jewish Literature, Issued in Honor of K. Kohler* (Berlin: G. Reimer, 1913), 176–98. Of much interest are those sources which not only note the significance of tradition among the Pharisees (e.g. *Antiq.* xiii. 297–8) but chart the significant transition towards its justification by exegesis. The famous encounter between Hillel and the elders of Beteira has recently been fully reanalysed by J. Fraenkel, 'Hermeneutical Problems in the Study of the Aggadic Narrative', *Tarbiz*, 47 (1978), 149–57 [Heb.].

[8] *M. 'Abot* i. 1 and parallels, on which see now M. Herr, 'Continuum in the Chain of Transmission', *Zion*, 44 (1979), 43–56 [Heb.]. This structure is also elaborated on in *b. 'Erub.* 54b, which probably reflects the system of study and repetition as developed by the earliest compilers of mishnaic traditions, like Aqiba. For this view, see J. Neusner, 'The Rabbinic Tradition about the Pharisees before AD 70: The Problem of Oral Transmission', *JSS* 22 (1971), 17.

[9] Cf. 1Q *S.* 5. 7–12, 8. 8–16, 9. 17, and CDC 3. 12–16.

[10] See H. H. Cohn, 'The Secularization of Divine Law', in his *Jewish Law in Ancient and Modern Israel* (New York: KTAV, 1971), esp. 7, 12, 17.

the humanization of interpretation which developed slowly at first in ancient Israel, and then proceeded more vigorously in the earliest centuries of ancient Judaism, was reversed as a matter of theological principle. What the individual sage would eventually innovate, went the ancient epigram, was already taught to Moses as oral Torah at Sinai.[11] With this transformation, the dignification of Jewish religious tradition was theologically complete. We must now explore its origins.

It is quite clear that, by the middle decades of the nineteenth century, the great representatives of the *Wissenschaft des Judentums* movement completely recognized the historical importance of discerning the earliest strata of Jewish exegesis. This awareness is particularly evident in the concerns of Zecharias Frankel critically to disclose Hasmonean and pre-Hasmonean halakhic regulations embedded in the Mishnah and other Tannaitic sources, and to distinguish traces of interpretation within the Septuagint.[12] The monumental work of this pioneer complements the studies of his contemporaries who traced the history of exegesis back into the biblical period. The general observations of Leopold Zunz, that the Book of Chronicles reflects a homiletical reworking of the Book of Kings,[13] come immediately to mind, as well as the stunning scholarship found in Abraham Geiger's *Urschrift und Übersetzungen der Bibel in ihrer Abhängigkeit von der innern Entwicklung des Judenthums.*[14] Geiger not only demonstrated that the major textual versions (the Septuagint, Targumic, and Samaritan recensions) reflect reworkings of the Hebrew Bible in the light of post-biblical social and theological concerns, but that the Hebrew Bible is itself the product (and source) of such reworkings. Despite the acid criticisms of some Jewish contemporaries,[15] Geiger's work convincingly shows 'that the history of the biblical text is interwoven with the history of the people, that the text itself, being a response to life, constantly adapted itself to the needs of the people, ... [and] that what the process of midrash and exegesis accomplished in a later age, was achieved through textual manipulation

---

[11] Cf. *M. Ḥag.* I. 5; *Sifra, Beḥukotai* viii, 12; *Kohelet Rab.* i. 29.

[12] *Vorstudien zu der Septuaginta* (Leipzig: Fr. Chr. Vogel, 1841); 'Die Essäer nach talmudischen Quellen', *MGWJ* 2 (1858), 30–40, 61–73.

[13] *Die gottesdienstlichen Vorträge der Juden* (1st edn., 1832; repr. Hildesheim: G. Olms, 1966, from Frankfurt-on-Main edn., 1892), 36–8. He also suggested other instances. M. Steinschneider gave broad currency to the position that 'the first germs of Midrash' are found in the Hebrew Bible in his decisive early survey of *Jewish Literature* (Hildesheim: G. Olms 1967; repr. of London edn., 1857), 2.

[14] (1st edn. 1857; repr.² Frankfurt-on-Main: Madda, 1928).

[15] Cf. S. L. J. Rapoport, *Naḥalat Yehudah* (*'Or Torah*), (Cracow: C. Budweiser, 1868).

in the period before the final stabilization of the biblical text'.[16]

Although these works bore fruit only very slowly and with abundant methodological confusions (to which my own study will make reference as necessary), the enduring and significant supposition of these 'Wissenschaftler' was that the content of tradition, the *traditum*, was not at all monolithic, but rather the complex result of a long and varied process of transmission, or *traditio*.[17] This supposition is, of course, the staple of the historical-philological method, whose primary concern in biblical studies has been to unravel the textual strands and documents of the canonical text, and to reorganize them into modern histories of Israelite religion and institutions. On such large matters no more need be said here. Nevertheless, it will prove beneficial briefly to focus on one branch of modern biblical studies which forms the wider methodological context for the present study and sets the framework within which the early Jewish exegetical dynamic of *traditum* and *traditio* finds its roots and incipient religious dignity.

In modern scholarship it is the method of tradition-history which has focused most intensively on the lively relationship between the traditions and their transmission in ancient Israel.[18] Fully appreciative of the long prehistory of many of the themes, legends, and teachings now found in Scripture, and the fact that over time these deposits of tradition were adapted to new situations and combined in new ways, the practitioners of this approach ideally seek to discern the components of a tradition-complex, to trace their origins or attribution to certain locales, and to show the profoundly new meanings which result as these materials were integrated into more comprehensive units. At each stage in the *traditio*, the *traditum* was adapted, transformed, or reinterpreted –be this by the use of old cult legends for retelling the life of a patriarch, or the integration of traditions into major literary complexes, like the Book of Genesis as a whole (with its diverse patriarchal materials and prehistorical prologue).Materials were thus detribalized and nationalized; depolytheized and monotheized; reorganized and reconceptualized.[19]

The integration and reworking of many types of tradition at many different times and places thus had the result of incorporating non-Israelite and local Israelite materials into a national corpus whose telling

---

[16] N. Sarna, 'Abraham Geiger and Biblical Scholarship', in *New Perspectives on Abraham Geiger; An HUC-JIR Symposium*, ed. J. Petuchowski (New York: Hebrew Union College Press, 1975), 25.

[17] I am indebted to D. Knight, *Rediscovering the Traditions of Israel* (SBLDS 9; Missoula: Scholars Press, 1975), 5, for this terminological distinction. Knight has used it primarily with respect to oral materials (cf. pp. 5-20). In the following I shall adapt these terms, with necessary modifications, to written sources.

[18] See the indispensable survey and analysis in Knight, op. cit.

[19] See, for example, G. Fohrer, 'Tradition und Interpretation im Alten Testament', *ZAW* 73 (1961), 1-30.

and retelling was a new basis for cultural memory. Accordingly, the movement from the small oral traditions (native and foreign) to the final written stage of Scripture is not only a process of tradition-building but of *Gemeindebildung* as well. Thus, the combination of northern and southern pastoral, warrior or cultic *legenda*, creates an authoritative and valued anthology of traditions and a sense of national identity. Comparable results arise from the adaptation of foreign mythic themes (like the primordial divine combat or the flood) to traditions leading to or expressive of Israelite history; or the incorporation of foreign *legenda* (like the destruction of Sodom) into the patriarchal narratives. When old mythic theomachies are subsequently reused to underpin purely historical narratives or hopes (as the motif of YHWH against the chaotic waters in Exod. 14-15, Isa. 11: 11-16, or 51: 9-11 suggests), or when foreign *legenda* are reused to illustrate national fate (as in Amos's reuse of the narrative of Sodom's destruction, 4: 11),[20] the remarkable capacity of tradition radically to transform a diverse inheritance and thereby *continually* to build up a sense of national history and destiny is fully attested.

All this is the proper background, I believe, for appreciating the development of inner-biblical exegesis and its post-biblical continuities in early Judaism and Christianity.[21] The dynamic we have just reviewed between *traditum* and *traditio*, characteristic as it is of traditions in ancient Israel, is also present in inner-biblical exegesis, but with one significant shift: whereas the study of tradition-history moves back from the written sources to the oral traditions which make them up, inner-biblical exegesis starts with the received Scripture and moves forward to the interpretations based on it. In tradition-history, written formulations are the final of many oral stages of *traditio* during which the traditions themselves become authoritative; by contrast, inner-biblical exegesis begins with an authoritative *traditum*. To be sure, the oral traditions would not be transmitted were they not, to some degree, authoritative in the first place. But the authority of these traditions is singularly assured by the very process of their transmission and final stabilization. Inner-biblical exegesis, on the other hand, takes the stabilized literary formulation as its basis and point of departure. Responses to it are thus interpretations of a basically fixed *traditum*, despite the somewhat fluid record of the most ancient biblical manuscripts and

[20] J. Wellhausen, *Die Kleinen Propheten*[4] (Berlin: W. de Gruyter, 1963), 80.

[21] In the past decade J. Sanders has frequently articulated the link between tradition-history and 'midrash' (by which is meant what is here called inner-biblical exegesis, as well as what post-biblical Judaism called 'midrash'). See his *Torah and Canon* (Philadelphia: Fortress, 1972), pp. xiii–xiv, and 'Adaptable for Life: The Nature and Function of Canon', in *Magnalia Dei*, edd. F. Cross *et al.* (Garden City: Doubleday, 1976), 531–60, esp. 534, 539–40.

versions. Accordingly, the movement from tradition-history to inner-
biblical exegesis — which is gradual and does not develop uniformly in all
genres — carries with it diverse methodological and historical-analytical
considerations, some of which require brief comment here.

To begin with, the dynamics we have begun to explore between
traditum and *traditio* in ancient Israel can be reformulated, without
distortion, as those between (increasingly) authoritative teachings or
traditions whose religious-cultural significance is vital (and increasingly
fundamental), and the concern to preserve, render contemporary, or
otherwise reinterpret these teachings or traditions in explicit ways for
new times and circumstances. This formulation is reminiscent of the
two factors which were considered earlier as 'necessary components in
the development of post-biblical Jewish exegesis', and is indicative as
well of the structural similarities which link tradition-history and inner-
and post-biblical exegesis. From a methodological point of view,
however, the task of discerning a particular *traditum* from its exegetical
reworking in the three broad areas just noted is dissimilar in the extreme.

Let us consider first the situation of tradition-history, which stands
at one pole of this spectrum. Although increasingly careful methods have
been devised over the last half-century — particularly among Scandinavian
scholars — in order to distinguish the *traditum* from the *traditio* in the
complexes of tradition which are analysed, the results remain largely
hypothetical and debatable since there are often no independent criteria
to determine the origins of the component traditions, their contours,
or their original independence from each other.[22] Even in the best of
circumstances, as the apparent reuse by Amos of the patriarchal tradition
regarding the destruction of Sodom, one may validly claim that Amos
drew independently from a fund of traditions quite distinct from that
found in Gen. 19. From this critical perspective, what seemed to be a
clear adaptation of an identifiable *traditum* is no longer the case: the
direct link between the particular Sodom *traditum* in Gen. 19 and that
in Amos 4: 11 is sundered. The pretextual *traditio* of Amos is thus no
longer recoverable with absolute certainty. Comparable difficulties
affect the length and breadth of the tradition-history programme.

It is for these and related reasons that Martin Noth was correct and
candid when he acknowledged in his own influential book, *A History
of Pentateuchal Traditions*, that the questions that tradition-history
generates can be more valuable than the tenuous results often achieved:[23]
for, he argued, it is unquestionably important to reorient oneself to

---

[22] This point has been frequently asserted in debates among the practitioners
of tradition-history, and by their critics. In general, cf. Knight's comprehensive
Rediscovering the Traditions, and the literature cited there.

[23] (Englewood Cliffs, NJ: Prentice Hall, 1972); cf. pp. 1, 3, 6, 65, 106, 110,
154-6, 163, 182, 227, 258.

Scripture as a complex of living traditions rather than as a pastiche of fixed written sources in the first instance. In the final analysis, however, the great methodological flaw of tradition-history remains. A *traditio* is inferred from a received *traditum*, and this 'recovered' *traditio* serves, in turn, as a principal means for isolating the components of that same *traditum*.

At the other pole, and in singular contrast to the preceding, early Jewish exegesis presents a happier situation. On the one hand, the relationship between an authoritative *traditum* and its *traditio* is often explicit and unmistakable by virtue of the host of citation formulae which appear—in Qumran sources, in the various Tannaitic materials, and in the New Testament itself.[24] Since the citations (which are recorded near or alongside the exegeses) can be checked against the received Hebrew Bible—contemporary manuscripts of which are also variously preserved—there can be no doubt about the origin of the *traditum*. The same holds true not only where the citation formula is simply 'as is written', or the like, without further ascription to 'the Torah of Moses' or 'the Prophets'. It also obtains where there are no citation formulae whatever and the *traditum* is embedded within the subsequent interpretation of it. Since we have a large register of explicit biblical citations in manuscripts from Qumran, there is a strong presumptive likelihood that what appear to be biblical allusions or phrases in the *Hodayot*-Psalms, for example, are in fact anthologized reuses of the vast biblical thesaurus, and not just terms picked from the spoken environment. For similar reasons, the register of nearly 400 apparent biblical allusions and phrases recorded by Solomon Schechter in his coedition of some Ben Sira fragments suggests that the Hebrew Bible was the pre-eminent *traditum* which underlies this wisdom text.[25] To be sure, appropriate criticisms have been made of over-hasty assumptions regarding the biblical origin of phraseology in Ben Sira.[26] But the case that numerous epigrams therein represent a new wisdom *traditio* of the biblical *traditum* as a whole cannot easily be dismissed. These factors also add to the likelihood that some passages in Ben Sira are actually implicit exegetical blends of several biblical sources (as is the case in 47: 2, 'for as fat is raised from the holy so is David from Israel', which cleverly combines Lev. 4: 8 and Ps. 89: 20 on the basis of similar

[24] Cf. the studies of B. Metzger, 'The Formulas Introducing Quotations in the NT and the Mishna', *JBL* 70 (1951), 297–307, and J. Fitzmyer, 'The Use of Explicit Old Testament Quotations in Qumran Literature and in the New Testament', *NTS* 7 (1960-1), 297–333.

[25] See *The Wisdom of Ben Sira, Portions of the Book of Ecclesiasticus*, edd. S. Schechter and C. Taylor (Cambridge: Cambridge University Press, 1899), 13–25.

[26] Solid cautionary considerations have been expressed by J. Snaith, 'Biblical Quotations in the Hebrew of Ecclesiasticus', *JTS* NS 18 (1967), 1–12.

terms in each).[27] Thus, whether a textual lemma is explicitly linked to a
commentary, or is implicitly incorporated into it, the biblical *traditum*
can be distinguished from its post-biblical *traditio* by means of objective
evidence. The isolation of the *traditum* from the *traditio* in such
exegetical historiographies as the Book of Jubilees and the *Liber Antiqui-
tatum Biblicarum* of pseudo-Philo presents no particular difficulties
from this point of view. The well-known general absence of explicit or
implicit biblical references in the Mishnah is a separate matter, and does
not affect the substance of the preceding remarks.

What now must be said of inner-biblical exegesis? The most obvious
issue from the viewpoint of *traditum* and *traditio* is that the Hebrew
Bible is a composite source, so that discerning the traces of exegesis
within this Scripture is not a matter of separating biblical (the *traditum*)
from post-biblical (the exegetical *traditio*) materials but of discerning
its *own* strata. The position of inner-biblical exegesis is unique among
the foundational documents of the Western religious tradition: neither
the Gospels nor Pauline writings on the one hand, nor the Quran on the
other, are quite like it. The dominant thrust of these documents with
respect to the Hebrew Bible is their proclamation that they have
fulfilled or superseded the ancient Israelite *traditum*. Theirs is an
innovative *traditio*, continuous with the Hebrew Bible but decidedly
something new, something not 'biblical' – if we may use that word for
the moment as indicating the ancient Israelite *traditum* which forms the
basis for the exegetical claims of Christianity and Islam. From this
perspective, the Tannaitic sources (followed by the Rabbis of the
Talmud), the Gospels and Pauline writings (followed by the Church
Fathers), and the Quran (followed by the Doctors of Islam) are three
post-biblical streams of tradition which are each based on the Hebrew
Bible but have each transformed this *traditum* in radically diverse ways.
Thus, while the Gospels occasionally comment upon themselves (as, for
example, Matt. 24: 15, which makes Scripturally explicit what is only
hinted at in Mark 13: 14), or include brief editorial remarks (also in
Mark 13: 14 and Matt. 24: 15), and while theological interpolations may
be found in the Quran as well (as the phrase 'for he is only one God', in
16: 51),[28] such are not the distinctive exegetical traits of these sources.

Textual comments and clarifications, scribal remarks and interpolations, and theological reactions and revisions are, however, among the
principal traits of the exegesis within the Hebrew Bible itself. How
each particular *traditum* can validly be distinguished from its *traditio* –
that is, the received text from the comments, clarifications, and revisions

[27] Schechter, op. cit. 31.

[28] Following J. Wansbrough, *Quranic Studies; Sources and Methods of Scriptural Interpretation* (London Oriental Series, 31; Oxford: Oxford University
Press, 1977), 28.

thereof—is thus the pressing and central concern of any critical study of this phenomenon. For this reason, each subsection of the following work will address itself to pertinent ramifications of this topic. For this reason too it must suffice to indicate at this point only those factors which bear on the continuum I have here tried to highlight which connects tradition-history to post-biblical exegesis. Thus, similar to the latter, where the Hebrew Bible cites itself before a new interpretation of the older text, whether that citation is complete or fragmentary, and whether its formulary refers to 'the Torah of Moses', 'the ordinance', or simply remarks 'as is written', there is usually no difficulty in distinguishing the *traditum* from the *traditio*.

At the other extreme, where possible cases of inner-biblical exegesis come closest to the phenomenon of tradition-history, one must exercise utmost caution, for reasons similar to those already stated. A good case in point is the literary topos, or scenic-compound, dealing with the 'Matriarch of Israel in Danger', repeated in Gen. 12:10-20, 20:1-18, and 26:1-16. In these sources, different patriarchs, matriarchs, foreign kings, and social settings are recorded; but the scenario and key terms remain basically the same. The real issue then is the overall relationship between the common type-scene and the manifest variations of language and circumstance. Focusing primarily on the latter, proponents of the documentary hypothesis have argued for separate sources as a way of explaining the differences. As against this view, first Samuel Sandmel, and then Klaus Koch in a more thoroughgoing way, have recently sought to advance the argument that the variations between each *traditum* reflect theological and moral revisions of the core tradition in Gen. 12:10-20.[29] Bothered by the lacunae in that source regarding Abram's motivations, the purity of Sarah, the role of God, and the responsibility of the foreign king, each *traditio*—so the hypothesis goes—reinterpreted the original *traditum* and transformed it in the light of its particular interests. But it is just this presumed relationship between *traditum* and *traditio* which is questionable. As in many other biblical cases, the topos here called the 'Matriarch of Israel in Danger' may derive from an oral scenario whose main outlines were current in ancient Israel; which are not reflected in Scripture *per se*; and which nevertheless generated wholly independent variations and transformations.[30] Certainly the

[29] See Sandmel's 'The Haggadah Within Scripture', *JBL* 80 (1961), 110–11, and Koch's *The Growth of the Biblical Tradition* (New York: C. Scribner's Sons, 1969), 123–5.

[30] Such a reservation derives from the existence in ancient Israel and elsewhere of formal scenario patterns which were not necessarily generically related. Cf. R. Alter, 'Biblical Type-Scenes and the Uses of Convention', *Critical Inquiry*, 5 (1978), 355–68, which builds upon R. Culley, *Studies in the Structure of Hebrew Narrative* (Philadelphia: Fortress, 1976), in the Israelite sphere, and upon W. Arend, *Die typischen Scenen bei Homer* (Berlin: Weidmann, 1933), in the Greek.

claim that Gen. 26: 1-16 is a moralizing interpretation of Gen. 12: 10-20 is not as convincing as the claim that the elaborate variations of this topos preserved in the Aramaic *Genesis Apocryphon* are dependent on the threefold *traditum* found in the Book of Genesis.[31] As we shall see, the principal cautionary considerations adduced here, that similar phenomena need not be exegetically related, has important implications for evaluating assumed textual-exegetical links in other biblical genres.

Between the two inner-biblical extremes just noted, between comparable traditions whose exegetical relationship is indeterminate and instances where citations are clearly linked to their interpretations, lie the great majority of examples of inner-biblical exegesis. In these latter cases, a nexus between the *traditum* and its *traditio* exists but must be analytically recovered and demonstrated in every instance. Or rather, it may be procedurally more correct to say the opposite: as and when a nexus between a given *traditum* and its exegetical *traditio* can be analytically recovered and demonstrated, then and only then are we confidently in the presence of examples of inner-biblical exegesis. This procedural way of phrasing the matter must also be stressed because methodological precision has not always been dutifully regarded in earlier studies.[32] For these reasons in particular an investigative-analytical approach will characterize each initial discussion of inner-biblical scribal, legal, aggadic, or mantological exegesis. Only as a spectrum of instances is firmly established will the larger questions—of comparison, synthesis, and evaluation—be taken up.

To rephrase the matter: once a *traditum* and its *traditio* are identified and isolated the relationship of the one part to the other may come under review—each case in its own right, as well as the many modes which a *traditum* and its *traditio* may assume in scribal, legal, aggadic, and mantological exegesis. Because there is no clear separation between lemmata, or textual references, and commentaries in the 'middle area' of inner-biblical exegesis we are discussing here, the problems of method cannot be avoided. For a variety of theological, stylistic, and historical reasons yet to be analysed, comments and interpretations are often interpolated into the *traditum*: sometimes annexing it; sometimes surrounding it; and sometimes, in fact, submerging it or constituting a new anthological form. Regarding the latter, cautions similar to those raised before regarding tradition-history are pertinent. In a manner

---

[31] Cf. 1Q *ap Gen.* xix. 14-xx. 34. See the text edition and commentary of J. Fitzmyer, *The Genesis Apocryphon of Qumran Cave I*[2] (Biblica et Orientalia, 18a; Rome: Biblical Institute Press, 1971), 58-67, 110-44.

[32] The work of A. Robert, and that of many scholars whom he influenced, is particularly prone to laxity and imprecision (see below, Chapter 10) despite Robert's often very exact definitions, as in s.v., *DBS* v (1957), 410-11, s.v. 'Littéraires (genres)', and in the conference résumé written in *ETL* 30 (1954), 283.

uncharacteristic of many scholars who have sought to identify instances of anthologized reuses of older 'scriptures', or of citations or adaptations from older historical and prophetic sources, S. Holm-Nielsen has discerningly remarked: 'Often what looks like a quotation may be due to coincidence. . . . It must be a matter of opinion whether in a context it may be supposed that there is a use of the Old Testament or an accidental agreement in diction.'[33] However, given the great historical significance of the matters under investigation, *which rest solely on the validity of the instances demonstrated*, such 'opinions' count for very little. For it makes all the difference—*all* and not some—whether a specific *traditum* has been reused or annotated; or whether, on the contrary, it either contains independent reflexes of common idioms or comments which are original to the particular composition or teaching.

The actual relationships between *traditum* and *traditio* in the Hebrew Bible, and their implications, add other typological and analytical considerations to those just considered. For if the phenomena of *traditum* and *traditio* constitute the master typology of inner-biblical (as of all) exegesis, and their isolation and clarification are its root analytical procedure, the relationships between *traditum* and *traditio* have produced a manifold of literary and historical types in the Hebrew Bible, and their analysis discloses the distinctive exegetical forms and features of ancient Israelite literature and culture.

Examples of inner-biblical exegesis cover the entire range of the Hebrew Bible, both in terms of the genres and the historical strata involved. It therefore occasions no surprise to learn that the relationships between *traditum* and *traditio* vary considerably. Scribes and legists are concerned with different issues; and the ways in which either of these two groups comments upon, resignifies, or renders contemporary an older document in the course of its *traditio* (and for the sake of its *traditio*) are distinguishable from the ways in which historians, preachers, and prophets do so. But it is not solely the concerns of each group which differ. Quite diverse, too, are the reasons why particular traditions (or laws or oracles) are reworked; the specific genres used or created; and the groups and times for which and within which the changes are made. Accordingly, there is nothing to be gained, and very much to be lost, by a restrictive perspective which limits the *traditum-traditio* relationship to one mould. Such a channelling of a protean form only obscures the rich dynamic between the two: indeed, sometimes a *traditio* functions for the sake of the *traditum* (by clarifying it, or adapting it to new considerations); and sometimes it functions for its

---

[33] See S. Holm-Nielsen, 'The Importance of Late Jewish Psalmody for the Understanding of Old Testament Psalmodic Tradition', *St. Theol.* 14 (1960), 17.

own sake, as a new and independent composition. Such a nuanced continuum of relationships between *traditum* and *traditio* may be observed in the Hebrew Bible, and in early Jewish exegesis as well. It would therefore be the height of folly to isolate only one dimension of this relationship in Jewish literature, and arbitrarily use it to regulate and evaluate the forms and features—indeed the very existence—of inner-biblical exegesis.[34]

Moreover, since the Hebrew Bible has an exegetical dimension *in its own right*, and this varies text by text and genre by genre, it also stands to reason that the Hebrew Bible is the repository of a vast store of hermeneutical techniques which long preceded early Jewish exegesis.[35] These have yet to be thoroughly investigated and systematized. Of immense interest, then, must be the types of exegetical reasoning that can be found in the received Massoretic text. This interest is not historical alone (in so far as these types are predecessors of rabbinic exegesis), but has an inherent concern with the ways ancient Israelite legists, or prophets, preachers, and scribes, resignified and explained their *traditum*. What were the stylistics of such exegeses, and what the logistics? How, in the diversity of cases, is exegetical technique related to literary form? Does inner-biblical exegesis manifest explicit or implicit analogies between texts; does it exhibit free or controlled associations among the materials; and does it focus on verbal contexts or isolated words? Or both? And so on.

At a broader level, the various types of exegetical style and reasoning give way to other typological factors. Let us, for the moment, return to the *traditum–traditio* distinction and view it in terms of the reformulation considered earlier, between authoritative texts or traditions and their reuse in new circumstances. From this perspective, the living tension in *traditum* and *traditio* between religious authority and its reinterpretation comes to the fore. How biblical culture maintained its sources of authority when these were not sufficient for new circumstances (as often in law and cult); when divine words had apparently gone unfulfilled as originally proclaimed (as in various promises and prophecies); or when new moral or spiritual meanings were applied to texts which had long since lost their vitality (or restricted this vitality to specific legal or cultic areas), are matters of the greatest interest.

[34] B. Childs succinctly criticized the work of A. Wright, *The Literary Genre Midrash* (New York: Alba House, 1967), as it pertained to biblical materials, from this general angle; see his essay 'Midrash and the Old Testament', in *Understanding the Sacred Text: Essays in Honor of M. Enslin*, ed. J. Reumann (Valley Forge, Pa: Judson, 1972), 50–52. Wright's work was subjected to a more far-reaching criticism with respect to rabbinic literature by R. Le Déaut, 'Apropos a Definition of Midrash', *Interpretation*, 25 (1971), 259–82.

[35] Already recognized by J. Sanders, 'Text and Canon: Concepts and Method', *JBL* 98 (1979), 28.

In different ways, then, the older *traditum* is dependent upon the *traditio* for its ongoing life. This matter is paradoxical, for while the *traditio* culturally revitalizes the *traditum*, and gives new strength to the original revelation, it also potentially undermines it. The reason for this lies in the fact of revelation itself. Where each particular *traditum* was believed to derive from divine revelation, recognition of its insufficiencies —inherent in the need for the interpretation of the *traditio*—decentralizes the mystique of the authority of the revelation.[36]

As we shall see, the acknowledgement of innovations, or their obfuscation, varies historically and by genre. In some sources there is recourse to new divine revelations to introduce innovations and interpretations; in other instances, new procedures or insights are incorporated into the formulation of the older revelations; and, most rarely, there is the actual acknowledgement in the latest historical strata of the Hebrew Bible that a human *traditio* had exegetically changed the divine *traditum*. Such, then, are the modalities of legitimating change in a culture which took the reality of divine revelations seriously, but soon perceived whole areas where they were not applied or incompletely applicable; and which just as soon realized that the supplementation and extension of these revelations *also* needed divine authority of some sort, direct or indirect. These vital issues are at the core of the *traditum-traditio* dynamic to be explored.

The issue of the stylistic forms found in inner-biblical exegesis raises the question of the social-historical setting of the reinterpretations themselves; just as the issue of the hermeneutical techniques employed raises the question of the circles within which the exegeses were produced or transmitted. These are all appropriate and necessary form-critical considerations to be addressed to each and every example of inner-biblical exegesis, and across the breadth of each genre and historical cross-section. It goes without saying that information concerning the procedures of such stable institutions as scribal craft, legal practice, or public education in the shrine (on festivals or occasionally), contributes to any understanding of the life-context in which exegesis functioned in ancient Israel, and in which certain forms of explanation were suitable. For modes of exegesis are just as much determined by social and historical settings as by the constraints of genre and circles of readership. One should add, of course, that whatever can be known of the procedures of unstable life-circumstances—like rivalries between priestly or lay groups —also greatly contributes to a historical understanding of the living pressures within which competing groups may cite (interpreted) Scripture against each other.

---

[36] Cf. my earlier reflections on these matters in 'Torah and Tradition', in *Tradition and Theology in the Old Testament*, ed. D. Knight (Philadelphia: Fortress, 1977), 275–300; and *passim* in 'Revelation and Tradition: Aspects of Inner-Biblical Exegesis', *JBL* 99 (1980), 343–61.

Unfortunately, much of this important information is lacking. Only rarely are we permitted to analyse or precisely to place exegetical 'facts' into the life-setting appropriate to them. Exemplary in this regard are the social and political rivalries recorded in the Books of Ezra and Nehemiah, which permit us to move analytically upwards from them to the exegetical contestations involved; also unique are the longings for the renewal of purification of the Temple detailed in post-exilic sources, which provide a fairly controlled context within which the renewal of older—and sometimes lapsed—prophecies also recorded in these texts may be explained. But these are the great exceptions. In the main, the analytical process is quite the reverse, involving first an examination of exegeses and then inferring downwards from them to the probable social or other occasions when and where these interpretations might have arisen. When or why a scribe or legist or historian would say thus and so, simply clarifying his *traditum* or radically renovating it, remains a matter of inference so long as the text does not precisely indicate its *Sitz im Leben*.

Thus, no matter how much we can say precisely regarding the forms and techniques of particular exegeses, or the internal dynamics of *traditum* and *traditio* in any instance, the need to infer the nature of the underlying social-historical context of such exegeses remains a function of the type of literature which we possess from ancient Israel. For example, there are legal corpora which incorporate legal exegesis, but there are rarely case summaries with stated situations, precedents, and interpretations; there are prophetic speeches which are pitched to specific audiences on specific occasions, but these latter are often of no help in clarifying why certain images or texts are reused; and there are historiographical accounts which clearly reuse older sources, but which frequently do so in a tendentious and non-historical manner. Moreover, we cannot exclude the distinct probability that many cases of exegesis in the Hebrew Bible are theoretical productions and arise out of inner-scribal processes of textual transmission, legalistic musings and generalizations, and diverse historiographical imaginings and biases. In such circumstances, the quest for a specific *Sitz im Leben* will be misguided and in vain.

The difficulty of recovering the social-historical contexts of inner-biblical exegesis also has considerable bearing on the larger typological distribution of this book into such categories as scribal, legal, aggadic, and mantological exegesis (Parts One to Four). From the point of view of the underlying institutions involved, this breakdown can be defended. For scattered information is preserved throughout the Hebrew Bible regarding scribes and their social positions and editorial tasks; regarding individuals acting judiciously or according to jurisprudence; regarding prophets and their disciples and amenuenses, and so on. To be sure, this

information hardly constitutes a precise social or historical understanding of the scribes and their craft, of legists and their deliberations,
or of prophets and their schools. But it is a basis. Beyond this, the basic
social–literary categories of this book, and the exegeses involved, may
be inferred from the preserved documents themselves—from the
received Massoretic text, in fact. Thus, we know that scribes existed
and that texts were transmitted and copied—for we have these texts
and references to copying activities. Scribal exegesis and its life-settings
may therefore be inferred from such indicia. Similarly, we have law
collections and know that legal practice existed from many references
in historical and prophetic sources. Accordingly, legal exegesis and the
contexts appropriate to it may be inferred from a detailed examination
of these various sources, separately and in conjunction. In some ways,
then, our approach to these matters follows a hypothetico-deductive
method (benefiting analogously from the procedures made famous
by Harry A. Wolfson in his work on medieval Jewish philosophy).[37]
First, a critical evaluation of the sources and processes under examination will be made with a view to the areas (social and literary) where
exegesis may be expected (because of the type of teaching or text
involved; or because of lacunae, contradictions, changing circumstances,
and the like). The results of these theoretical evaluations are then
reconceptualized as hypotheses and proved valid particularly in the
degree to which they generate the perception of instances of exegesis,
and so their analysis. The two steps just indicated (hypothesis and
verification) are not always formulated as such in the following pages,
but they everywhere contribute to the investigative reasoning at work.
Study of the traces of aggadic and mantological exegesis will proceed
from a comparable perspective but in ways appropriate to each.

In the main, each of the four parts of my study—the scribal, the
legal, the aggadic, and the mantological—will take the following pattern:
hypothetical and actual issues regarding the type of exegesis under
discussion will be treated first; then follows a detailed investigation of
exegetical examples with a strong concern for their types, styles, and
social–historical factors, wherever possible; and finally, a comprehensive
synthesis of the various examples will be offered in the light of the
initial questions posed of the material, the results achieved, and other
analytic considerations. Where the various discussions will not be able
precisely to locate the social or historical *Sitz im Leben* of specific
examples, the matters discussed will, in any case, disclose the mental
matrix within which inner-biblical exegesis operated and from which

---

[37] *Crescas' Critique of Aristotle* (Cambridge, Ma: Harvard University Press,
1929), 24–7.

early Jewish exegesis emerged.[38]

These twin factors, then, relating to the social and mental matrices of inner-biblical exegesis, indicate that two types of 'settings' may be anticipated from the outset. On the one hand, external historical determinants provide the social context for exegesis; on the other, exegesis arises from such purely internal factors as textual content and the 'issues' perceived therein by the tradents. Seen thus, the distinction just drawn between social–historical and mental matrices is not simply a function of the inadequate knowledge available to the modern investigator. It points just as much to distinct but correlative factors in the genesis and development of exegesis.

At the beginning of these introductory remarks I referred to that 'remarkable feature' of world religions whereby traditions emerge and supplement their foundational teachings. This issue—particularly in cases where divine revelations are succeeded by human interpretations—is of no passing cultural interest, and has served, in my mind, as generative of the work to follow. Cultures develop and change in any case; but they will just as certainly vary in the factors which inaugurate meaningful change, which guide it, and which justify it. Biblical Israel was set on its great course by transformative revelations. These served—at least in principle—to set Israel apart from the mythological civilizations round about her. They could have also turned into a closed and lifeless inheritance without the courage of the tradents of biblical teachings to seize the *traditum* and turn it over and over again, making *traditio* the arbiter and midwife of a revitalized *traditum*. The final process of canon-formation, which meant the solidification of the biblical *traditum* and the onset of the post-biblical *traditio*, was thus a culmination of several related processes. Each transmission of received traditions utilized materials which were or became authoritative in this very process; and each interpretation and explication was made in the context of an authoritative *traditum*. Further, each solidification of the *traditum* was the canon in process of its formation; and each stage of canon-formation was a new achievement in *Gemeindebildung*, in the formation of an integrated book-centred culture. The inner-biblical dynamic of *traditum–traditio* is thus culturally constitutive and regenerative in the most profound sense.

A second issue has been of fundamental significance in my mind, and was formulated earlier with respect to the origin of a religious

---

[38] For the notion of the mental matrix as a dimension of the *Sitz im Leben*, see R. Knierim, 'Old Testament Form Criticism Reconsidered', *Interpretation*, 27 (1973), 446, and D. Knight, 'The Understanding of "Sitz im Leben" in Form Criticism', *SBL Seminar Papers*, i, ed. G. MacRae (Cambridge, Ma.: Society of Biblical Literature, 1974), 109. The matter will be taken up below.

tradition endowed with religious dignity. Like the first—which asks, How does biblical religion renew itself?—this issue is deceptively naïve. It starts from the observation that when our biblical sources re-emerge after the dark Persian age which followed Ezra and Nehemiah, exegesis is in full swing with a commanding cultural presence and diversity. And so one is led to ask, Where did all this come from? What preceded the exegetical methods of the Teacher of Righteousness, Yose ben Yoezer, Nahum of Gimzo, and all their congeners? Jewish tradition has one answer, modern scholarship suggests another. In the first case, the exegetical tradition of the Torah of Moses was traced to Sinai according to Jewish (Pharisaic) tradition. In the second, the Alexandrian *oikoumene*, with its editing and exegesis of Homeric texts, and with its highly developed rhetorical and legal traditions, has been perceived by some modern scholars as the catalyst and shaper of the Jewish 'oral tradition'.[39] Neither answer seems particularly wrong, nor particularly right, for that matter.[40] and this suggests a third approach. Is it possible that the origins of the Jewish exegetical tradition are native and ancient, that they developed diversely in ancient Israel, in many centres and at many times, and that these many tributaries met in the exile and its aftermath to set a new stage for biblical culture which was redirected, rationalized, and systematized in the lively environment of the Graeco-Roman world? To ask the question this way is *almost* to answer it. What remains are the details, and it is to these that we now turn.

---

[39] The strongest argument for formal and terminological influence has been made by D. Daube, 'Rabbinic Methods of Interpretation and Hellenistic Rhetoric', *HUCA* 22 (1949), 239–65, and 'Alexandrian Methods of Interpretation and the Rabbis', *Festschrift H. Lewald* (Basel: Helbing and Lichtenholm, 1953), 27–44. S. Lieberman, *Hellenism in Jewish Palestine*[2] (New York: Jewish Theological Seminary, 1962), 56–68, has backed away from a genetic influence and restricted the borrowing to terminology.

[40] On the one hand, despite the theological comprehensiveness of its claim, the rabbinic tradition is reinforced by the ancient, historical exegetical tradition within the Hebrew Bible to be examined presently. On the other hand, despite the sharpness of the parallels, the temporal and spatial diffusion of the evidence from Graeco-Roman antiquity makes it difficult clearly to articulate the precise historical relationship of this evidence to the rabbinic materials. Moreover, it is hard to balance Daube's considered claim that 'philosophical instruction was very similar in outline, whether given at Rome, Jerusalem, or Alexandria' ('Rabbinic Methods', p. 257) with Lieberman's conclusion that 'the inhabitants of Palestine listened to the speeches of the rhetors, and the art of rhetoric had a practical value', although precise borrowing was restricted to terms. See his 'How Much Greek in Jewish Palestine?', in *Biblical and Other Studies*, ed. A. Altmann (Cambridge, Ma: Harvard University Press, 1963), 134.

PART ONE

SCRIBAL COMMENTS AND CORRECTIONS

1. Introduction. The Role of Scribes in the Transmission of Biblical Literature

INQUIRY into the diverse exegetical dynamics of *traditum* and *traditio* in the Hebrew Bible most properly begins with an analysis of scribal comments and corrections. There are two fundamental reasons for this. First, scribal practice provides the most concrete context for the transmission of a *traditum*. For while traditions and teachings were undoubtedly transmitted orally throughout the biblical period – and, of course, long afterwards, as the non-Scriptural oral traditions of early Judaism abundantly testify – it is only as these materials achieve a literary form that a historical inquiry can examine their continuities and developments. The basic role of scribes as custodians and tradents of this *traditum* (in its various forms) is thus self-evident. Scribes received the texts of tradition, studied and copied them, puzzled about their contents, and preserved their meanings for new generations. Whatever the origins and history of our biblical materials, then, they became manuscripts in the hands of scribes, and it is as such that we have received them.

The pivotal position of scribes as tradents of traditions also put them in a primary position with respect to their meanings. And this leads to the second reason for beginning an inquiry into inner-biblical exegesis with an examination of scribal comments and corrections. Scribes not only copied what came to hand but also responded in diverse ways to the formulations which they found written in earlier manuscripts. A fascinating record of these responses has left its traces in the Massoretic Text (MT), as we shall see, as well as in the other principal textual versions (like the Septuagint, Samaritan, and Peshitta texts).[1] Moreover – and this is central for present purposes – since these scribal comments are formally limited in scope but exhibit striking exegetical diversity,

---

[1] Geiger, as noted earlier (p. 6 n. 16), was among the first to give scholarly attention to this phenomenon. And indeed, while his evaluations are often tendentious, or based on problematic assumptions about early Jewish party contentions, and while his conclusions have often been revised in details, Geiger's massive compilation and the innovative angle of his scholarly vision are a bench-mark in critical biblical scholarship. In any event, his materials on changes and additions in the MT will not be reviewed in the present study.

they may serve as a typological prolegomenon to the interpretations found in inner-biblical legal and aggadic exegesis. Accordingly, the decision to begin with the phenomenon of scribal exegesis does not mean that this latter was always or only chronologically primary to the other types of exegesis to be examined. It only asserts that since it is a primary responsibility of scribes to transcribe the *traditum*, scribal practice is necessarily a primary locus for textual interpretation, and may therefore serve as a point of departure for an examination of exegesis within the Hebrew Bible as a whole. In sum, scribal practice evokes and marks out in the most historically concrete and literarily discrete manner the two constituent aspects of *traditio* discussed earlier: the transmission and reinterpretation of received texts and traditions.

The class of Jewish סופרים, or scribes, which emerges in the post-exilic period with a definable historical character, and whose tasks and procedures are abundantly referred to in canonical and extra-canonical rabbinical literature, had a major part in the epochal transformation of ancient Israel into ancient Judaism and ancient Israelite exegesis into ancient Jewish exegesis.[2] But these סופרים were not so much a new class or new beginning in ancient Jewish history as the heirs of a long and multifaceted Israelite scribal tradition, whose own roots in turn were struck in the soil of the great ancient Near Eastern civilizations. Fortunately, the available information regarding scribal practices in ancient Mesopotamia and Egypt, for example, is remarkably diverse and complete. This evidence begins in the third millennium BCE, with copies of old Sumerian school-texts, and continues throughout the second and first millennia in the several cultural areas of Mesopotamia, Egypt, and Syria (including materials from Ugaritic literature in the late second millennium and Akkadian text copies in the late first).[3] In Mesopotamia, for example, scribal activities included administrative, political, and didactic functions, together with the more routine tasks of copying, collating, and annotating manuscripts.[4] In ancient Israel, an equally multifaceted scribal class sprang to life to meet the needs of the burgeoning Judaean and Israelite monarchies, beginning in the tenth century BCE.[5] What particularly distinguishes these ancient Israelite

---

[2] See the re-evaluation of this class in Urbach, op. cit., and the earlier comments of E. Bickerman, *Ezra and the Maccabees* (New York: Schocken, 1947), 67-71.

[3] Conveniently summarized with full bibliography by J. P. J. Olivier, 'Schools and Wisdom Literature', *JNWSL* 4 (1975), 49-60.

[4] On the range of functions in Mesopotamia, see Olivier, ibid. 50-1.

[5] Cf. T. Mettinger, *Solomonic State Officials. A Study of the Civil Government Officials of the Israelite Monarchy* (Coniectanea Biblica, OT Series 5; Lund: Gleerup, 1971).

scribes from their international counterparts, however, is their involvement in religious activities and with religious texts, most noticeably from the last pre-exilic generations and thereafter, as we shall see.

The technical title סופר, meaning 'scribe', first appears in connection with the royal council established by King David at the outset of the United Monarchy (2 Sam. 8: 16-18 ~ 20: 23-5),[6] and appears in similar listings preserved for the dynasties of King Solomon (1 Kg. 4: 1-6),[7] King Joash (2 Chron. 24: 11-12), and King Hezekiah (2 Kg. 18: 18, 37). Thus the סופר appears as a stable component of the high royal bureaucracy for at least 300 years, from the beginning of the tenth to the seventh century BCE. However, the relative position of this court officer in these listings varies, and his relationship to the מזכיר, 'recorder' or 'secretary', is unclear.[8] As the priests, war commanders, major-domos, and tax officials noted in these lists were the heads of specialized sub-bureaucracies serving the royal administration, we may surmise that the סופר of these texts was the overseer of a diversified scribal network.[9]

Regrettably, no biblical sources describe the training of ancient Israelite scribes.[10] It may be assumed, however, that the skills taught in their various guild centres and schools (cf. 1 Chron. 2: 55) enabled these scribes to serve a variety of administrative and state functions. Some served the military and aided in conscription (2 Kgs. 25: 19 ~ Jer. 52: 25); others, Levites by lineage, served as overseers of the priestly

---

[6] Cf. 1 Chron. 26-7, esp. 27: 32-4.

[7] It has been argued by R. de Vaux, 'Titres et fonctionnaires égyptiens à la cour de David et de Solomon', *RB* 48 (1939), 401-3, that by the time of Isaiah (cf. 22: 16-22) the title *'al habbayît*, noted in 1 Kg. 4: 6, had absorbed the powers of *sôpēr* and *mazkîr*.

[8] For additional suggestions, see J. Begrich, 'Sōfēr und Mazkīr', *ZAW* 58 (1940-1), 1-29, and H. Graf Reventlow, 'Das Amt des Mazkir. Zur Rechtsstruktur des öffentlichen Lebens in Israel', *TZ* 15 (1959), 161-75.

[9] This biblical title would thus be equivalent to the title *rb spr* 'chief scribe' at Ugarit (e.g. UT 73, rev. 1.4), discussed by A. Rainey in 'The Scribe at Ugarit: His Position and Influence', *Israel Academy of Science and Humanities*, iii/4 (1968), 126-47. To date, this title appears only in cult-related texts. Whereas it is unknown in the Hebrew Bible, the Ugaritic title *lmdm* 'apprentice scribes' (cf. UT 62 = *CTA* 6. vi. 53-7) is paralleled in Isa. 8: 16.

[10] This contrasts sharply with what is known of the other ancient Near Eastern civilizations. On aspects of the ancient Mesopotamian curriculum, see B. Landsberger, 'Scribal Concepts of Education', *City Invincible*, edd. C. H. Kraeling and R. Adams (Chicago: University of Chicago Press, 1960), 94-102, and W. Hallo, 'New Viewpoints on Cuneiform Literature', *IEJ* 12 (1962), 22-3. For Egypt, see R. J. Williams, 'Scribal Training in Ancient Egypt', *JAOS* 92 (1972), 214-21. However, all judgements comparing the foregoing with the obscure situation in ancient Israel must be made with considerable caution. This applies, for example, to R. Whybray's suggestion that Prov. 1-9 constituted an ancient Israelite lesson-book for scribes, based on Egyptian models; see his *Wisdom in Proverbs. The Concept of Wisdom in Proverbs 1-9* (Naperville, Ill.: A. R. Allenson, 1965), 7.

rotations (1 Chron. 24: 6), or provided administrative services to the Temple and its upkeep (2 Chron. 34: 13; cf. Neh. 13: 13); and still other scribes served in the royal court, providing the king with diplomatic skill and sage wisdom. Trained in the forms and rhetoric of international diplomatic correspondence, and thus kept abreast of internal and external affairs, many of these court scribes – as individuals and as family guilds–were directly caught up in religious and political affairs affecting the nation as a whole.[11] Particularly exemplary of such involvements are the activities of the Shaphan scribal family during the final decades of the Judaean state.[12] In other cases, the professional court scribe was primarily a sage counsellor – a repository of traditional wisdom. Just such a personage was Jonathan, an uncle of King David, who was 'an adviser יועץ, a man of understanding מבין and a scribeסופר'.[13] There is no reason to doubt that this combination of traits reflects an authentic pre-exilic tradition, despite its unique articulation in the relatively late Book of Chronicles. What is certain, at any rate, is that this formulation draws from an international courtier vocabulary. Thus, in a striking parallel to our biblical source found in a contemporary Aramaic text, we find that one Aḥiqar, who served in the court of King Esarhaddon (680–669 BCE), and to whom the collection of ancient saws and epigrams are attributed, is also called 'a wise and skilled scribe ספר חכים ומהיר who gave advice עטה'.[14] The technical and official nature of this description is confirmed by the fact that Ezra the priest, the great teacher of the post-exilic restoration, is also called a ספר מהיר (Ezra 7: 6).[15] The fact that Ezra's title already occurs in Ps. 45: 2 as a frozen idiom suggests that this designation was known in the pre-exilic period as well, and was not simply a contemporary title conferred upon him

[11] 2 Kgs. 10: 1, 5 is particularly instructive. It refers to royal diplomatic correspondence (*sĕpārîm*, v. 1) sent to the princes, elders, and *hā'ōmĕnîm* of Ahab. Given this context, it is tempting to relate this word to the Akk. title *ummānu*, which recurs frequently in colophons listing scribes and scholars; cf. H. Hunger, *Babylonische und assyrische Kolophone* (Neukirchen and Vluyn: Butzon and Bercker Kevelaer, 1968), 292. 2, 409. 1, 471. 1, 519. 2. On *'āmôn* in Prov. 8: 30 see the discussion and literature in W. McKane, *Proverbs* (OTL; Philadelphia: Westminster, 1970), 356–8.

[12] See S. Yeivin, 'Families and Parties in the Kingdom of Judah', *Tarbiz*, 12 (1941/2), 241–67 [Heb.].

[13] 1 Chron. 27: 32. He is included in a list of Davidic officers; cf. vv. 33–4.

[14] A. Cowley, *Aramaic Papyri of the Fifth Century BC* (Oxford: Clarendon Press, 1923), Aḥiqar i. 3–4, 7, 12, ii. 35–6, 42–3, iv. 55, 61. A Babylonian text from 171 BCE. makes it clear that 'Ahuqar' was the PN given by the Aramaeans to Aba'enlidarli, a sage in the court of Esarhaddon; see H. Lenzen (ed.), *XVIII. vorläuf. Bericht über die Ausgrabungen in Uruk-Warka* (1962), 58. In the Aramaic version, Aḥiqar was placed in Sennacherib's reign.

[15] On rendering the word *māhîr* in this title as 'skilled' or 'expert', see E. Ullendorff, 'Contribution of South Semitics to Hebrew', *VT* 6 (1956), 195.

by later historians.[16]

In addition to their service in regional, national, and international capacities, ancient Israelite scribes were tradents of texts. Indeed, this activity was a constitutive characteristic of the ancient Israelite scribal class. Thus, in addition to copying texts, Israelite scribes were also responsible for maintaining, transmitting, and collating literary records. As this activity bears significantly on the exegetical activities to be considered in the next chapter, it deserves closer attention.

Details related to the scribal activities of collating, entitling, and indexing literary records can be deduced from a variety of biblical data. A general indicator of such activity is the recurrent references in the Books of Kings and Chronicles to the archives or records of the Northern and Southern kingdoms from which the 'historical' report is excerpted or derived (e.g. 1 Kgs. 11: 41, 14: 19, 29, 15: 7, 23; cf. 1 Chr. 9: 1; 2 Chr. 9: 29, 12: 15, 13: 22, 20: 34, 24: 27, 27: 7, 32: 32).[17] Such historical archives were maintained by court archivists or other guardians of the historical traditions. Some scribal practices may be deduced from the annotations to the priestly regulations found in the Books of Leviticus and Numbers. These records have both superscriptive titles (e.g. Lev.. 6: 2, 7, 7: 1, 11) and summary colophons (e.g. 7: 37-8, 11: 46-7, 12: 8, 15: 32-3, Num. 5: 29-31, 6: 21), which are well evidenced in other ancient Near Eastern documents.[18] Moreover, like the latter, these biblical regulations were often collated into short series or collections, for example the laws of sacrifice in Lev. 1-7 or the various laws on purity and impurity in Lev. 11-15.[19] Such annotations and collections, found in legal and prophetic literature, only make sense as formal conventions of an established scribal tradition.[20]

[16] Prov. 22: 29 provides another biblical occurrence of this language. The overall scribal–courtier context of this reference has been illumined by the Egyptian wisdom of Amenophis, with which it has been frequently compared. See H. Gressmann, 'Die neugefundene Lehre des Amen-em-ope und die vorexilische Spruchdichtung Israels', *ZAW* 42 (1924), 295, and F. Griffith, 'The Teaching of Amenophis, the son of Kanakht. Papyrus B.M. 10474', *JEA* 12 (1926), 224. It has been falsely assumed, however, that a title like *sōpēr māhîr* also occurs in an Egyptian hieratic papyrus, on which see the critique by A. Rainey, 'The Soldier-Scribe in *Papyrus Anastasi I*', *JNES* 26 (1967), 58-60.

[17] Cf. J. Gray, *I & II Kings* (OTL; Philadelphia: Westminster, 1963), 20-38.

[18] See M. Fishbane, 'Accusations of Adultery: A Study of Law and Scribal Practice in Numbers 5: 11-31', *HUCA* 45 (1974), 32-5 with notes, and 'On Colophons, Textual Criticism and Legal Analgoies', *CBQ* 42 (1980), 438-49.

[19] See A. Rainey, 'The Order of Sacrifices in Old Testament Ritual Texts', *Bib.* 51 (1970), 307-18.

[20] On Ezek. 43: 12 and related matters see M. Fishbane and S. Talmon, 'The Structuring of Biblical Books: Studies in the Book of Ezekiel', *ASTI* 10 (1976), 140-2. Also compare the comprehensive title in Jer. 46: 1, followed by the more specific ones in 46: 2, 48: 1, 49: 1. H. M. Gevaryahu, in 'Biblical Colophons: A

A closer examination of these assorted colophons appended to discrete legal texts, as well as those which close a series of texts, not only reveals a high degree of scribal professionalism but also, in fact, provides a clue to the manuscript traditions which these scribes have established and developed. The comprehensive cultic-legal colophon found in Lev. 14: 54-7, which concludes several instructions dealing with the detection and treatment of leprosy, is just such an instance. At first glance, the formulation of this colophon is merely a syntactical tangle. However, a comparison of this with the other summary lines which precede it, and with the several ritual instructions found in Lev. 13-14, has shown that the syntactical problem in the concluding and summarizing subscript is the result of a secondary interpolation introduced upon the insertion of additional instructions into the original text.[21] In another case, a close comparison of the colophon which concludes the laws of asylum in Josh. 20 with the preceding text allows the investigator to reconstruct the complex growth of this law, which has blended (and not successfully in some cases) diverse priestly and deuteronomic formulae and procedures.[22] In these and other cases, then, the colophon provides valuable evidence for a dimension of the ancient scribal craft and the textual history of legal instruction received and transmitted.

In a similar way, the levitical groups or singers responsible for producing a national anthology from the assortment of prayers salvaged from different shrines and guilds left traces of their work in concluding colophons and benedictions (Pss. 41: 14, 72: 18-20, 89: 53, 106: 48).[23] Here too the colophons and colophonic blessings indicate the conclusion of a specific literary limit or corpus, and reflect established scribal conventions. For example, the biblical expression in Ps. 72: 20 'the prayers of David, son of Jesse, are כלו completed' underscores the separate nature of the liturgical collection now found in Pss. 42-72, and corresponds to the expression *qāti* 'completed' found in cuneiform colophons.[24] Another similar term, תמו, 'completed', is used in Job

Source for the "Biography" of Authors, Texts and Books', *VT* 28 (1974), 42-59, has sought to identify superscriptions in prophetic literature (particularly) with colophons. An analysis of biblical and Mesopotamian materials makes this ascription unlikely.

[21] See my 'On Colophons', loc. cit. 439-43.
[22] Ibid. 443-6.
[23] N. Sarna has offered the suggestive view that the many Psalm titles reflect different guild associations in ancient Israel; see 'The Psalm Superscriptions and the Guilds', in *Studies in Jewish Religious and Intellectual History, presented to Alexander Altmann*, edd. S. Stern and R. Loewe (University, Ala.: University of Alabama, 1979), 281-300.
[24] Cr. in H. Hunger's collection, op. cit., *qāti* in 15.1, 19.1, 43.4, 109.1, and *ul qāti* in 87.2, 136.1. 144.2, 462.2.

31: 40 at the conclusion to the cycle of dialogues.[25] In like manner, the colophonic benediction in Ps. 72:18-19 (and 41:14, 89: 53, 106: 48) resembles features well attested in cuneiform sources.[26]

Finally, remarkable light is shed upon the diverse thesaurus of terms and the variety of technical procedures which comprised the ancient Israelite scribal craft by Eccles. 12:9-12:

(9) And besides that, Qohelet was a sage חכם . . . he אזן ordered and חקר examined [and]תקן fixed [or edited] many proverbs.

(10) And Qohelet sought to find choice sayings . . .

(11) The words of the sages are as prods, and [those of] the masters of the collections are like fixed nails . . .[27]

(12) And . . . עשות of the making [i.e., composing or compiling] of books there is no end . . .

On first view, there is nothing in these lines which invites close comparison with scribal colophons such as those we have reviewed previously:

25 Cf. *'ad hēnnâ* 'thus far', which concludes the Moabite oracles in Jer. 48: 47b (after the stereotypic closure v. 47a; cf. 49: 6, 39), and in 51: 64b, concluding Jeremiah's oracles as a whole. This 'colophon' undoubtedly originally followed v. 58, but was displaced with the inclusion of the curses in vv. 59-64a. The redundant *wěyā'ēpû* in v. 64a functions as a *Wiederaufnahme*, resuming v. 58 after the intrusion. Already H. St. J. Thackeray utilized 'introductory clauses and editorial notes' to index the history of the text of Jeremiah and the historical priority of the LXX to the MT; see his 'The Greek Translators of Jeremiah', *JTS* 4 (1903), esp. 254-9. Thackery notes the striking fact that the MT 'colophons' of Jer. 48: 47 and 51: 64 'coincide in the Greek with the close of the second group of foreign nations, and with the close of Jeremiah α respectively'. He thus infers that these notations originated with the LXX chapter arrangement, which is, accordingly, presumably older than the order preserved in the MT (p. 255).

26 For prayers and blessings in cuneiform colophons, cf. Hunger, op. cit. 13. 8, 323. 5, 328. 5-12, 332. 3, 338. 15-25. An additional element often found in cuneiform colophons is the blessing or curse designed to safeguard the tablet from destruction or tampering. See G. Offner, 'A propos de la sauvegarde des tablettes en Assyro-Babylonie', *RA* 44 (1950), 135-43. A different type of safeguard, warning the reader neither to 'add nor subtract' from the written version, is found in the Erra epic and has distinct biblical parallels, on which see my 'Varia Deuteronomica', *ZAW* 84 (1972), 350-2.

Note that some of the aforementioned colophons in the Book of Psalms were certainly in place by the Persian period. Indeed, it is striking that the original colophonic nature of Ps. 106: 48 was either forgotten or overlooked by the Chronicler. For in the process of anthologizing Pss. 105: 1-15, 96: 1b-13a, 106: 1, 47-8, respectively, into 1 Chron. 16: 8-36, the Chronicler integrated Ps. 106: 48 into his liturgical citation. He achieved this by adding 'let us say' to Ps. 106: 47 and pluralizing the communal response found in v. 48.

27 On reading *mērō'eh 'ehād* 'from one shepherd' as *kěmardē'a hād* 'as a sharp goad', and thus as an extension of the imagery, see H. L. Ginsberg, *Qohelet* (Tel Aviv: Neuman, 1961), 134 [Heb.].

for one thing, the comments are part of a series of epigrammatic phrases which laud the composer (or compiler) Qohelet and his scribal guild; for another, they do not reflect anything like a summary resumption of the topics or themes of the proverbs recorded. Such a negative conclusion would be hasty, however, and would overlook several formal and specific features of significance. Among these latter one must start with the fact that Eccles. 12: 9-12 is manifestly an addendum to the book. The immediately preceding line, 'Vanity of vanities, says Qohelet, all is vanity' (v. 8), is a precise and verbatim resumption of the opening line of the book in 1:2, and thus serves as an *inclusio* which formally frames the original composition—as so frequently in the Hebrew Bible. In addition to this formal marker, v. 9 itself opens with the words 'and besides that'; and it thus, at once, provides a syntactical transition to the ensuing summary of the scribal activities which Qohelet is engaged in, and identifies this as a supplement.[28] While there is no doubt that well-established technical terms are used in this summary, their precise sense is difficult to gauge on the basis of inner-biblical evidence alone. Thus, a brief side-glance at typical formulae found in ancient Assyrian and Babylonian colophons may provide a useful perspective.

šaṭirma uppuš u bari[29]	'written, composed, and collated'
ašṭur asniq abrēma[30]	'I have written, checked, and collated'
ašrā baria šalima[31]	'arranged, collated, intact'

The striking similarity between the preceding commonly repeated cuneiform references to the writing, composing, or collating of manuscripts bears on Eccles. 12: 9-12 in several important ways. First, in general terms, such parallels clearly indicate that the references to such activities in the addendum to the Book of Ecclesiastes are part of an established ancient Near Eastern colophonic pattern: texts were not

---

[28] These observations are commonly made in the commentaries. It is already stated by the medieval R. Samuel ben Meir (Rashbam). A synopsis of recent opinion is collected by R. Gordis, *Koheleth—The Man and His World* (New York: Schocken, 1968), 339 ff. Add Whybray, op. cit. 57.

[29] See Hunger, op. cit. 89.3. For *barû* 'to collate' see *CAD*, B, p. 117; also Hunger ('kollationert'). Since the verb has the sense 'to see' and the like, the translation 'checked' is suggestive; cf. E. Leichty, 'The Colophon', in *Studies Presented to A. Lee Oppenheim* (The Oriental Institute; Chicago: University of Chicago Press, 1964), 150, with citations of occurrences. It is significant in this regard that Ug. *t'y* (cf. Heb. *šā'āh* 'to look at', e.g. Gen. 4: 4-5) occurs in the colophon of *CTA* 6. vi. 53-7, discussed by M. Dieterich and O. Lorentz, 'Zur Ugaritischen Lexicographie', *UF* 4 (1972), 32-3.

[30] Hunger, op. cit. 328.16. For *šaṭāru* in Akkadian colophons, cf. Leichty, loc. cit.

[31] After *CAD*, B, p. 117; citing F. Köcher, *Keilschrifttexte zur assyrisch-babylonischen Drogen- und Pflanzenkunde* (VIO 28), 1. vii. 3.

simply summed up, but were often annotated with references to the scribal activities performed on it. This form-critical assessment suggests, moreover, that if such references in Eccles. 12: 9-12 are not stated tersely, but appear in a narrative style supplemented by epigrammatic praise of scribes (their activities and teachings), what we have, in fact, is a stylized variation of conventional scribal tasks well known in ancient Israel.

Recognition of the place of ancient Israelite scribal practices within the broader background of standard ancient Near Eastern activities has specific bearing on matters of vocabulary as well. For example, among the various terms found in the foregoing cuneiform formulae which have undergone a semantic transformation in their scribal uses, the verb *uppušu* is of particular interest. This Akkadian verb, which has been alternatively rendered as 'to compose' or 'to copy' a tablet (based on contextual usage and supposition), is formed from the stem *epēšu* 'to do' or 'to make'.[32] It thus bears close comparison with the Hebrew verb עשה used in the biblical expression עשות ספרים (Eccles. 12:12) and suggests that this latter is a technical phrase and should be rendered 'to compose' or 'to compile books', not to 'do' or 'make' them. The two verbs, *uppušu* and עשה, are thus interlinguistic variants and conjointly reflect a specialized international scribal vocabulary. Further and significant confirmation of this point can be had, in fact, since in some instances the Aramaic verb עבד 'to do, make' is also used in a precisely similar sense. Thus, a fifth-century BCE papyrus preserves the phrase עבדת...זי...ספרא, which, in the light of context and the foregoing discussion, must be rendered 'the letter (or document) ... which ... I have written'.[33]

Further examples of the use of Hebrew עשה in a technical scribal sense will be pointed out below; though the preceding may suffice to establish its conventional usage in Eccles. 12:12. Despite this, the paucity of our sources makes it quite impossible to know whether this term—or its congeners in Eccles. 12: 9-12—was restricted to Israelite scribes in the wisdom tradition, or whether these terms were also known or used by those bookmen who specialized in legal, cultic, liturgical, or prophetic materials. What appears certain, at any rate, is that Eccles. 12: 9-12 drew from a conventional stock of ancient Near Eastern scribal practices and vocabulary which long antedate the

---

[32] For 'compose' see Hunger, n. 29 above; for 'copy (a tablet)', see *CAD*, E, p. 232, and Leichty, loc. cit.

[33] For the text, see G. E. Kraeling, *The Brooklyn Museum Aramaic Papyri* (New Haven: Yale University Press, 1953), 9. 22. This parallel is already noted in Ginsberg, op. cit. 135.

Hellenistic period of its composition.[34] But not entirely; for this late biblical text also provides a remarkable indication that its scribal tradents had already absorbed technical terms shared by rabbinic and Alexandrian scribes of these times. Thus, although the basic meaning of the biblical Hebrew verb תקן is 'to correct', it is found with the developed scribal sense 'to edit' both in the contemporary Aramaic milieu to which 'Ecclesiastes' was so indebted and in rabbinic Hebrew.[35] It is therefore quite likely that the technical use of תקן in Eccles. 12:9 also means 'to edit' or 'arrange' in some sense, although it is unclear whether this development derives through an Aramaic or a rabbinic linguistic filter.[36] Indeed, the precise channel of influence upon this biblical verb is further complicated – even as the supposition of its scribal sense is correspondingly enhanced – by an analogous development in the surrounding world of Hellenistic scribes. For there, in that technical environment so influential upon the editorial and exegetical practices of the old rabbinic סופרים,[37] the verb διορθοῦν 'to correct' was used with the extended meaning 'to edit'.[38]

This review of assorted technical references to editorial activities among ancient Israelite scribes is derived from formal and linguistic comparisons with ancient Near Eastern colophons and colophonic terminology. Further information about scribal activities in ancient Israel can be deduced from other contexts. Prov. 25:1, Jer. 8:8, and Ezra 7:10-12 deserve particular mention in this regard. This is not so much for the technical information preserved in these sources – valuable though this is. Of even broader import is the fact that these three texts illustrate three striking conjunctions in ancient Israel between major episodes of scribal activity and major periods of national restoration. The latter two texts, moreover, also document the fairly unique involvement of Israelite scribes in religious activities· and movements noted earlier, as compared with the documented scribal activities known from ancient Egypt, Mesopotamia, and Canaan. A brief résumé of these three instances is therefore of interest in the present discussion.

[34] Quite possibly *ḥiqqēr* 'examine' should be compared to the uses of *barû* and *ṭ'y* in Akkadian and Ugaritic colophons, respectively (cf. n. 29). More speculative is the case of *ašrā*, in the Akkadian colophon cited above. It calls to mind *kātûb yōšer* in Eccles. 9:10 and, from the present comparative perspective, suggests that the Hebrew verse may indicate that 'Ecclesiastes sought to find choice sayings' which were 'well arranged' or 'properly written'.

[35] See Lieberman, *Hellenism*, 90 and n. 56.

[36] Thus, it is unnecessary to decide in this context whether the Book of Ecclesiastes was a translation of an Aramaic original (as does Ginsberg, op. cit.) or a species of late Hebrew influenced by contemporary Aramaic.

[37] See the Introduction and nn. 38-9, below.

[38] Lieberman, op. cit.

1. The collection of epigrams, gnomic utterances, and proverbial sayings preserved in the book of Proverbs are of complex and diverse origins. Some indication of this is readily apparent from the titles used to introduce the book's sub-units. Collections are accredited to Solomon (Prov. 1: 1, 10: 1, 25: 1), Agur (30: 1), and Lemuel (31: 1). In addition, there are references to the 'sayings of the wise חכמים' in Prov. 22: 17 and 24: 23. Among these superscriptions, that which opens the second collection of Solomonic proverbs in the Book of Proverbs is most instructive: 'These, too, are the proverbs of Solomon, which the men אנשי of Hezekiah, King of Judah, transmitted העתיקו' (25: 1). This text is a valuable witness to court-sponsored scribal activity in ancient Israel, although it is not certain whether the verb העתיקו indicates the transmission or transcription of literary sources.[39] The royal context referred to here is also striking, in so far as this witness to scribal activity and literary preservation in Judah occurs during the period which saw the destruction of the Northern kingdom and the dispersal of its literature. Such indications suggest that the literary processes reflected in Prov. 25: 1 may have been part of a larger religio-national restoration which had the preservation of Israelite literature and reform of the cult (2 Chron. 29-30) as its main elements.[40] But none of these considerations directly aid in the identification of these 'men of Hezekiah'. It may be surmised that they were more than royal scribes, and actually helped comprise those teachers of wisdom who consolidated at this time and against whom Isaiah fulminated (Isa. 5: 21, 29: 14). This possibility is supported particularly by the documented alignment between scribes and wisdom circles preserved in later biblical sources.[41]

2. The cult reform of Josiah in 621 BCE followed the revival of religious–national independence in Judaea, and took place approximately a century later than the reform and literary activities of Hezekiah and his court. It bears interesting witness to a new area of involvement of Israelite scribal circles. For up to this time there is scant record of the involvement of scribes with religious texts, or their interests in promoting religious concerns. Jer. 8: 8 indicates a changed situation.

---

[39] M. Weinfeld, *Deuteronomy and the Deuteronomic School* (Oxford: Clarendon Press, 1971), 161, n. 3, has proposed 'transmitted', comparing the Hebrew verb with Akk. *šūtuqu* (from *etēqu*; see *CAD*, E, pp. 390-1), while the sense 'transcribed' occurs in LXX ἐξεγράψαντο and rabbinic sources. Cf. L. Zunz, ' "verfassen und übersetzen" hebräisch ausgedrückt', *ZDMG* 25 (1871), 447.

[40] See H. Junker, "Die Enstehungszeit des Ps 78 und das Deuteronomium', *Bib.* 34 (1953), 346 n. 1. On the contemporary Near Eastern situation, note W. F. Albright, *From the Stone Age to Christianity* (Anchor Books. New York: Doubleday, 1957), 314-19.

[41] Cf. J. Fichtner, 'Jesaja unter den Weisen', *TLZ* 74/2 (1949), 75-9, and R. Anderson, 'Was Isaiah a Scribe?', *JBL* 79 (1960), 57-58.

Speaking some time after Josiah's reform and the publication of the Book of the Torah (cf. 2 Kgs. 22: 11, 23: 1-3), which scholarly consensus generally concedes to be the Book of Deuteronomy or some part thereof, the prophet cries out: 'How can you say "We are wise חכמים" and "The Torah of YHWH is with us"?[42] Truly, the pen [of the scribes] has worked עשה [i.e. composed or compiled] לשקר for naught; שקר in vain [have] the scribes ספרים [laboured].'[43] Despite the well-known syntactical tangle of these phrases,[44] the intent of the prophet's castigation and the addressees pilloried nevertheless seem quite certain. For the designation here most definitely refers to a determinate social group of persons representing traditional wisdom values (i.e., they are 'wisemen' or 'sages'), and not simply wise persons in general.[45] A possibility such as the latter would leave this denunciation without specific focus; whereas a definite social configuration is clearly indicated by the ensuing doom oracle which first mentions the חכמים (v. 9), and then adds also the prophets and priests who act falsely (v. 10). Oracular denunciation of or reference to these three groups is particularly common during this period (e.g. Zeph. 3: 3-4; Jer. 18: 18; Ezek. 22: 25-29) and undoubtedly reflects their marked social presence at this time.[46] The question 'How can you say "We are wise"?' is not, then, a

---

[42] It is generally agreed that this 'Torah of YHWH' is the Book of Deuteronomy. Cf. J. Skinner, *Prophecy and Religion; Studies in the Life of Jeremiah* (Cambridge: Cambridge University Press, 1922), 103; also J. Hyatt, 'Torah in the Book of Jeremiah', *JBL* 60 (1941), 381-96.

[43] On the technical usage of *'āśāh* in scribal contexts, see above, p. 31. For *laśśeqer* meaning 'in vain', cf. Kimḥi ad loc., who refers to 1 Sam. 25: 21. Similarly, LXX translates εἰς μάτην here (vs. ἄδικος or ψεῦδος for *šeqer* elsewhere).

[44] The present interpretation goes against the Massoretic phrasing and basically follows Y. Kaufmann, *Toledot ha-Emunah ha-Yisra'elit* (Jerusalem and Tel Aviv: The Bialik Institute and The Devir Co. Ltd., 1937-56), iii/2. 453 n. 54); although I have rendered the second phase as two parallel stichoi, and understand the *lāmed* of *laśśeqer* as serving double duty for *šeqer* in the second stichos (cf. the *Targum*).

[45] Whybray, op. cit., ch. 2 (and esp. p. 22), claims that the reference to *ḥăkāmîm* does not indicate a special class of wise men because special-class characteristics are lacking. This argument as its relates to Jer. 8: 8 and related sources ignores both the immediate context and the contextual associations with other classes, like the priests and prophets. See further below.

[46] Cf. also Isa. 29: 9-14, noted earlier (p. 33) and Ezek. 7: 26. Fichtner, op. cit. 21, and W. Zimmerli *Ezechiel 1-24* (BKAT 13/1; Neukirchen and Vluyn: Neukirchener Verlag 1969), 184, acknowledge that the *ḥākām* was part of a class, although Zimmerli suggests that Ezek. 7: 26 is itself a later adaptation from Jer. 18: 18. For other multiple class-listings, see Mic. 3 and Jer. 2: 8. The latter text lists priest, king, prophet, and *tōpśê hattôrāh*. It is not entirely clear, however, whether the latter are a separate group, somehow distinct from the priests who taught Torah (cf. Lev. 10: 10-11; Deut. 17: 8-12, 33: 10; Mal. 2: 6-7). The use of the stem *tpś* 'to hold' in the title may indicate a special skill (cf. Gen. 4: 22 and Akk. *ṣabātu*). Since the comparable Akk. noun *ṣibittu* is used to indicate a teaching

sarcastic rebuke as such so much as an ironic allusion to the social identity of those criticized.

Moreover, the marked impact of wisdom ideology and style on the Book of Deuteronomy – indeed its substantive claim to be a teaching of wisdom which will make those who heed its provisions 'a wise and knowledgeable nation' (Deut. 4:6) – gives good reason to suppose that the claim ascribed to the חכמים in Jer. 8:8, that they 'have' the Torah, alludes to their considerable influence on its final form and promulgation.[47] But the Book of Deuteronomy also bears the strong imprint of scribal traditions, as M. Weinfeld has most recently and cogently argued.[48] The combination of these two influences on the Book of Deuteronomy supports and underscores the striking semantic linkage in our text between חכמים and the 'vain' or 'useless' work of the ספרים, and suggests that the scribes referred to here were identical with these sages (or followers of the wisdom tradition).[49] Indeed, there would be little reason to make the neutral statement that the work of scribal copyists was for naught; but there would be every point to mock the work of scribes who had invested the Torah with their particular ideology. The חכמים who are also ספרים in Jer. 8:8 are thus an earlier and Biblical reflex of the aforementioned designation of Aḥiqar as a ספר חכים – a sage-scribe, a scribe of and in the wisdom tradition.[50] What characterized the סופרים חכמים of the Hebrew Bible is their involvement with Torah.

Just what brought these Israelite groups of sage-scribes to the fore at this time is difficult to say. They presumably took advantage of the cultural vacuum created by the renewal of Judaean independence after

(which is 'held') in nearly contemporary Sargonid inscriptions (see S. Paul, 'Sargon's Administrative Diction in 2 Kng. 17:27', *JBL* 88 (1969), 73-4), it is possible that *tōpśê hattôrāh* means 'teachers of the Torah'. This terminological clarification does not, unfortunately, clarify the relationship of these teachers to the priests.

[47] Cf. Weinfeld, op. cit. i. 3, ii. 1. The centrality of priests and Levites in the administration and teaching of Deuteronomy may therefore only indicate different *originating* circles. Thus, von Rad's form-critical assessments in *Studies in Deuteronomy* (Studies in Biblical Theology, 9; London: SCM, 1953), chapters I and V, may be correct with respect to core elements which underlie the book, but not with respect to the text as it has been redacted by wisdom groups.

[48] Op. cit., *passim.*

[49] The identification of the scribes and sages in this passage is by now virtually agreed among commentators, although the ways they reach their conclusions vary somewhat. Compare, for example, K. Marti, *Der Prophet Jeremia von Anatot* (Basel: Detloff, 1899), 18ff.; P. Volz, *Das Buch Jeremiah* (KAT; Leipzig: A. Deichert, 1922); H. Cazelles, 'A propos d'une phrase de H. H. Rowley', *SVT* 3 (1960), 29; P. de Boer, 'The Counsellor', ibid. 61; W. Rudolph, *Jeremia* (HAT; Tübingen: J. C. B. Mohr, 1947), 52; Kaufmann, op. cit. 278; Weinfeld, op. cit. 158.

[50] Above, p. 26 and n. 14.

Assyria's collapse, and the cultic elevation of Jerusalem as the dominant national-royal shrine after the fall of Samaria, to propagate their adjustment of old wisdom traditions to the ancient, sacred teachings of Moses —a foretaste of Ben Sira centuries later. In this venture they would have found common cause with reformist priestly families who also saw in these circumstances a historical opportunity to increase their power and revenues. These several factors may explain the dual presence of Hilkiah the priest and Shaphan the scribe in the events which surrounded the 'finding' of the Torah of Moses in the days of Josiah (cf. 2 Kgs. 22:8, 10, 12). But be this as it may—and it must remain speculation— the fact remains that Jeremiah presupposes scribal involvement with the Torah but *does not* condemn the composition itself. His remarks are pitched against the sage-scribes, its promulgators, who claimed that 'the Torah of YHWH is with us'. If, then, Jeremiah accused this group of having 'worked for naught' this is not because of the inherent falsity of the teaching but because of the insincerity of their piety.[51] For as the prophet himself says, their work is futile since they have 'despised the word of YHWH' (v. 9) which they claim to teach and represent.

3. A final example of the conjunction of national revival, religious reform, and scribal involvement in religious-literary activities in ancient Israel occurs almost two centuries later, during the post-exilic restoration. Biblical sources report that in the mid-fifth century BCE, most probably during the reign of Artaxerxes I,[52] Ezra, a priest (Ezra 7:11-12,21; Neh. 8:2, 9) and a 'skilled scribe ספר מהיר' (Ezra 7:6, cf. vv. 11-12, 21), returned from the Babylonian exile and 'set his mind to study לדרש the Torah of YHWH, and to "do" לעשת [or, "compose"] and to teach ללמד law and ordinance in Israel' (Ezra 7:10). This compact designation of Ezra's activities reflects his large-scale programme of interpreting, compiling, and teaching the pre-exilic Torah traditions to the community which returned from exile. As Ezra's interpretative activity will be subjected to detailed analysis in a later chapter, it must suffice here to underscore Ezra's combination of scribal, priestly, and exegetical

---

[51] The misinterpretation of *lašseqer* in Jer. 8:8, and perhaps other reasons (cf. Kaufmann, op. cit. iii/2. 463 n. 4), led Marti and others to speak of the falsity and forgery of the teaching. Most recently, W. Rudolf, op. cit., has translated the passage: 'Jawohl! Siehe in Lüge hat "es" verwandelt, der Lügengriffel der Schreiber', and similarly in J. Bright, *Jeremiah* (AB 21; Garden City, NY: Doubleday, 1965), 60. In all this, the suggestion of H. Gressmann, 'Neue Hilfsmittel zum Verständnis Jeremiah', *ZAW* 43 (1925), 145-7, is intriguing. He proposed that in vv. 8-9 Jeremiah was actually citing a popular critique of the sages and their Torah work which fell into disrepute after Josiah's death, and that the prophet upbraids the people for this attitude (v. 10).

[52] The precise date remains a crux; see J. Bright, *History of Israel*² (Philadelphia: Westminster, 1972), 392-403, and the literature cited.

roles. While he apparently functioned as a local administrator in the far-flung Achemaenid empire, Ezra's knowledge and role as a (priestly) סֹפֵר put him in a unique position to satisfy the dominant contemporary Persian policy of reviving and restoring local legal traditions.[53] What is more, his particular political mandate provided the occasion for an intensification and renewal of earlier scribal and literary activities. Since Ezra the Scribe not only returned from Babylon with a knowledge of the ancient law, but also as head of an established retinue of levitical interpreters (Neh. 8:1-8), there is little to support Schaeder's oft-cited claim that Ezra's work as a 'Schriftegelehrter' was a new activity.[54] The many examples of legal exegesis to be studied below will provide further support to this claim that Ezra inherited a venerable Israelite tradition of scribal and textual scholarship.

The preceding review of the social-historical evidence concerning ancient Israelite scribes in the Hebrew Bible, and the objective indications of their work as tradents, compilers, and copyists of the *traditum*, may serve as a prolegomenon to our inquiry into those instances where the scribes altered their text-copy or added to it in one way or another. For there is no doubt that the technical competence involved in copyist activities made biblical scribes — individually and as members of schools — more than mere passive tradents. They were, in fact, both students of and even believers in the materials which they transmitted, and so were far from simple bystanders in matters relating to their clarity, implication, or application. It is thus squarely within the function of scribes as copyists and transmitters of texts that their annotations and exegeses take shape and are given form. Involved in the factual *traditio* of the *traditum* (in its many parts), scribes responded to what came to hand and adjusted it or supplemented it as they saw fit or were allowed. The 'annotative' *traditio* of biblical scribes is thus a product of the 'copyist' *traditio* of the ancient *traditum*: it is here that ancient Israelite scribal comments and corrections find their life-context and occasion.

---

[53] E. Meyer, *Die Entstehung des Judentums* (Halle: Niemeyer, 1896; Hildesheim: Olms, 1965), 70-1, cites the instance of Darius' permission to the Egyptian high priest of Sais to reorganize the college of ἱερογραμματεῖς and the cult of his temple. In these colleges sacred books were composed or copied; see A. Gardner, 'The House of Life', *JEA* 24 (1930), 157. It should also be noted that upon his accession Darius assembled 'the wise among the adversaries, the priests and scribes' of Egypt and requested a collection of their known laws. This was completed in 503 BCE. See F. Altheim, 'Das Alte Iran', in *Propyläen-Weltgeschichte* (Frankfurt-on-Main and Berlin: Ulstein, 1962), ii, 171. On these matters, see further below, p. 107.

[54] So H. Schaeder, *Esra der Schreiber* (Beiträge zur historischen Theologie, 5; Tübingen: J. C. B. Mohr, 1930), 39-49; esp. p. 42.

A full discussion of the purely technical aspects of the scribal copyists in ancient Israel need not detain us in this context; nor, too, the natural errors of hand and eye whereby scribes have misidentified letters, blended distinct words, skipped words and lines, or even created ligatures of separate letters.[55] Such matters are well enough known. What claims our attention here, however, is the fact that when manuscripts containing such errors were recopied many mistakes were retained unchanged—thus leaving manifestly 'difficult' if not absurd readings—or were retained together with their (putative) corrections, and this despite the anomalous or redundant readings produced. The fact that the problematic letters or words were not deleted attests as much to the growing authoritative character of the biblical manuscripts as to the fact that our MT, despite its authoritative çharacter, is not a 'clean' or 'corrected' text-copy, but rather a compound of errors, corrections, and supplements. This observation could easily be expanded on the basis of the well-established phenomenon of 'synonomous readings', or 'wirkliche Varienten', whereby the MT is shown to reflect distinct manuscript traditions which have been interpolated into one master manuscript (now our MT) during the long process of editing, comparing, and collating manuscripts.[56] However—and this is what bears on the present study—in so far as there is no attempt in these technical collations or manuscript conflations to change the text substantively, such scribal activities are quite distinct from those additions which are due to a real or perceived lack of clarity of the words of the original text, or which are due to assorted theological considerations.

While both types of interpolations—the correction of errors and the collation of manuscript variants, on the one hand, and the clarification or explication of words, on the other—are secondary additions to the *Vorlage* before the scribes, the second set reflects definite exegetical procedures. In these latter cases, the texts were not simply recopied and corrected: they were also interpreted. It would, however, be a vain pursuit to inquire as to which corrections and clarifications are the work of individuals and which bear the imprint of scribal schools. For one thing, there is not the slightest scrap of objective evidence which

---

[55] On the latter, see the classic compilations by F. Delitzsch, *Die Lese- und Schreibfehler im Alten Testament* (Berlin and Leipzig: W. de Gruyter, 1920). Of distinct value is the brief study by R. Weiss, 'On Ligatures in the Hebrew Bible (נו = ם)', *JBL* 82 (1963), 188–94, now usefully expanded on the basis of private notes in the posthumous collection of his writings, *Studies in the Text and Language of the Bible* (Jerusalem: The Magnes Press, 1981), 3–19, where the essay appears in Hebrew.

[56] See S. Talmon, 'Synonymous Readings in the Old Testament', *Scripta Hierosolymitana*, 8 (1961), 335–83; and cf. B. J. Roberts, *IDB*, iv. 190.

would guide such an endeavour. For another, even if, here and there, idiosyncratic comments were smuggled into the manuscript copies and escaped the eye of the master scribes or archivists, such comments would undoubtedly have been caught and evaluated in the social filter of generations of copyists tradents, and students. And finally, one must hasten to add a third factor working to regulate such matters: the very religious authority of the texts themselves. The aura of the textual contents, if not, of course, that of its authors and mediators, would have particularly served to discourage permissible innovations and textual tampering. Indeed, the remarkably limited nature of these tendentious or intentional additions, given the long history of textual transmission, and concerning which our study will provide a typological sampling, is presumptive proof of this inner-cultural 'censorship', so to speak.

But how, considering the preceding factors, may the various explications and annotations occurring in the Hebrew Bible be recovered? The scholarly task is difficult and halting, for these scribal additions have been incorporated into the transcribed text with few identifying features. Accordingly, recourse to comparable scribal practices in ancient Near Eastern documents is of limited value. In ancient Mesopotamia, for example, lexical explications and annotations known as *ṣâtu, šūt pî*, and *maš'altu* commentaries were kept separate from the main text, as was the more interpretative *mukallimtu*-commentary, and were often put in special collections.[57] In so far as explications or glosses were incorporated into the body of a text, they were routinely separated from the text by means of a special double wedge-mark. This formal mode of explication is a recurrent phenomenon in cuneiform sources, and is well known from the West Semitic glosses to the El Amarna letters.[58] A third scribal technique used for lexical explication was the interlinear gloss. Many early cuneiform texts, in particular, use such a mode of annotation,[59] and, recently, one such interlinear gloss has been noted in Ugaritic sources.[60] These formal and conventional factors isolate scribal annotations in a clear and objective way.

The breadth of the foregoing techniques found in cuneiform sources,

---

[57] See G. Meier, 'Kommentare aus dem Archiv der Tempelschule in Assur', *AfO* 12 (1937-9), 237-40, for discussions of the *ṣâtu* and *mukallimtu*. Regarding the question and answer format of the *maš'altu* commentary, see Y. Elman, 'Authoritative Oral Traditions in Neo-Assyrian Scribal Circles', *JANESCU* 7 (1965), 19-32.

[58] Cf. P. Artzi, 'The Glosses in the El-Amarna Tablets', *Bar Ilan Annual*, 1 (1963), 24-57 [Heb.], and F. M. Th. Bohl, *Die Sprache der Amarnabriefe* (LSS 5/2; Leipzig: J. C. Hinrichs, 1909).

[59] For Akkadian examples, see *RLA* 431, 433-4, s.v. 'Glossen'.

[60] S. Loewenstamm, 'Eine lehrhafte ugaritische Trinkburleske', *UF* 1 (1969), 74, has favoured the view that *lhm* (in RS 24. 253) is explained by interlinear *bmṣd* (after line 7).

which aid in the identification of scribal explications, cannot be matched, however, by the available evidence from ancient Semitic, non-cuneiform scripts. One comparable instance is that of early copies of Ben Sira preserved in the Cairo Geniza, which indicates updated lexical equivalents of the older lexical forms of the text in the margin.[61] However, few other parallels are available. Thus, the interlinear elements found in 1Q Isa*ᵃ* are generally—if not entirely—examples of manuscript corrections and duplicate readings rather than cases of actual explication.[62] Similarly, enterprising attempts to find parallels in the Hebrew Bible to the cuneiform gloss indicator must be judged inconclusive. For example, it has been proposed that the Massoretic *pěsîq*, which is a Massoretic vertical line frequently found in printed Hebrew Bibles, is often a 'note-line' indicating glosses in the biblical text.[63] However, even where a close examination of the textual context of the *pěsîq* suggests that a particular instance serves as a gloss-marker, this is but one of its many (and frequently obscure) functions.[64] Moreover, it must be strongly stressed that there is no assurance that the *pěsîq* preserves old Israelite traditions of scribal glosses rather than later interpretations of Massoretic origin. And finally, since many of the proposed examples are either strained, or subject to alternative explanations, they run the risk of circular argumentation. One could hardly conclude from this evidence, therefore, that the *pěsîq* was a routine, technical gloss indicator used by the ancient Israelite scribes. Other proposals of scribal markers are even more problematic; so that whatever their intriguing value in isolated cases, they must be used with sceptical caution and

---

[61] See W. Caspari, 'Über die Textpflege nach den hebräischen Handscriften des Sira', *ZAW* 50 (1932), 160–8, ibid. 51 (1933), 140–50.

[62] As against S. Talmon, 'Aspects of the Textual Transmission of the Bible in the Light of Qumran Manuscripts', *Textus*, 4 (1964), 101–25.

[63] Cf. the evidence and evaluation of H. Fuchs, *Pesiq, ein Glossenzeichen* (Breslau: H. Fleischmann, 1907).

[64] The conceptual imprecision and schematic nature of Fuch's typology and analyses tend to obscure the diversity and significance of the phenomena. More methodological precision is necessary. Fuchs is therefore best when he develops Praetorius' older notion that the *pěsîq* marks abbreviations (cf. '*Pāsēq*', *ZDMG* 53 (1899), 684 f.), on the basis of comparisons with the LXX. In this regard one may note occurrences of the *pěsîq* at or near manuscript variants interpolated into the MT and missing in the LXX (e.g. Prov. 25: 19–20a, on which see I. L. Seeligmann, 'Indications of Editorial Alteration and Adaptation in the Massoretic Text and the Septuagint', *VT* 11 (1961), 102). Another type shows the occurrence of the *pěsîq* at or near intrusions which reflect late rabbinic notations concerning the triennial lectionary cycle (e.g. Pss. 49: 14 and 81: 6, on which see A. Guilding, 'Some Obscured Rubrics and Lectionary Allusions in the Psalter', *JTS* NS 3 (1952), 41–55). Thus, even in the best of cases, the *pěsîq* is not simply a *Glossenzeichen*.

hardly suggest objective or conventional scribal practice.[65]

The virtual absence from the Massoretic text of scribal marginalia, interlinear notes, or vertical gloss-markers, thus require a historian to rely on internal *textual* criteria for the identification of glosses. But here too the situation is far from straightforward. Whereas vast quantities of textual glosses have been proposed over the centuries, rarely have they been subjected to comprehensive criteria of validation or analysed as to their methods and principal features. The few attempts which have been made to collect glosses in one or several biblical books, to systematize them, to provide a typology of their forms and techniques, and to deduce their hermeneutical procedures, all prove more valuable in the breach than in the fulfilment of their proper goals. They more readily serve to indicate the potential methodological dangers involved in such a line of inquiry – particularly the tendency to isolate glosses on the basis of implicit and subjective criteria – than provide the objective basis upon which this cultural phenomenon can be established. Thus the commentator decides, according to individual stylistic tastes, and frequently without systematic recourse to inner or comparative textual factors, that a given work or phrase is redundant, explicative, or otherwise represents a secondary interpretation added to the text.[66] This is unfortunate. For failure to establish objective and verifiable criteria gives way to other imprecise and arbitrary procedures. Thus, one finds transcription errors confused with explications, glosses presumptively located at a considerable distance from the word assumed to be explained, and so forth.[67] The classifications which result from all such

[65] Of interest, in this regard, is F. Perles's contention that the *maqqēp* often reflects an abbreviation-marker. See his *Analekten zur Textkritik des Alten Testaments* (Munich: T. Ackermann, 1895), 36-8; and cf. my 'Abbreviations', *IDB Suppl.* 3-4.

[66] The idiosyncratic nature of the analyses, and the failure to deal systematically with these issues in conjunction with the technical terms used by the Israelite scribes (on which see below, pp. 44-55) are the principal weaknesses of the study made by G. R. Driver, 'Glosses in the Hebrew Text of the Old Testament', in *L'Ancien Testament et l'orient* (Orientalia et Biblica Lovaniensia, 1; Louvain, 1957), 123-61.

[67] K. Freedy, 'The Glosses in Ezekiel i-xxiv', *VT* 20 (1970), 130, properly criticized Fohrer's systematization in 'Die Glossen im Buch Ezechiel', *ZAW* 63 (1951), 33-53, as 'meaningless' for using the term 'gloss' to indicate loosely any type of comment, and for classifying as glosses cases which are actually scribal errors. However, although Freedy's classification seems more precise, it is entirely dependent on his new definitions (cf. pp. 144, 146 regarding editorial or exegetical glosses). His method of analysis, moreover, is often problematic, particularly the recurrent claim that a so-called gloss refers to a word several verses earlier (e.g. pp. 131-2 on Ezek. 1: 9a, 11a; p. 141 on Ezek. 1: 15a and 24: 27a). Among other problematic features of his treatment, the use of later rabbinical hermeneutical terms to explain supposed glosses found in the MT is hazardous, anachronistic, and highly misleading. Besides giving the impression of systematic procedures

analyses are consequently of little theoretical or practical value.

It is presumably the underlying exegetical attitude and presupposition of text-critics which has been at fault all along. Over the centuries, modern textual analysis has been principally concerned to establish the 'original' text, which is deemed 'authentic', and to weed out the scribal addenda and annotations, which are considered secondary and therefore 'inauthentic'. This attitude has thus greatly misprized the independent value of these additions; and, given the great analytical potential of scribal glosses both to serve as indices to the ongoing lexical and theological revisions of the MT and to recover the underlying hermeneutical processes whereby biblical texts were clarified or resignified in the course of their study and transmission, must be reversed.[68] Glosses must be perceived as 'authentic' in their own right; they must be analysed with all due precision; and they must be prized as valuable cultural facts. Indeed, well over half a century ago, P. Volz voiced his hopes for a new text-critical project which would utilize such an insight and benefit from it.[69] But his call has gone largely unheeded, partially, it would seem, because of a lack of a critical methodology which could be used as an investigative tool and standard of evaluation. The ensuing discussion will therefore seek to trace some critical path into the remarkable trove of inner-biblical scribal exegesis.[70]

For procedural reasons it is well to recall here the methodological principle which emerged in the course of the Introduction, wherein the importance of establishing clearly stratified sources for the analysis of inner-biblical exegesis was duly stressed. Accordingly, three means will be employed in the following typology and analysis of inner-biblical scribal exegesis to distinguish between the received text, the *traditum*, and the scribal annotations addressed to it, the *traditio*:

1. The easiest and most explicit means of recognizing scribal comments is where they are formally indicated through technical terms in

when there are none, the examples brought forward are frequently little more than scribal lapses. This criticism also pertains to Fohrer's remarks, op. cit. 44–8, and to the more elaborate project of I. Willi-Plein, *Vorformen der Schriftexegese innerhalb des Alten Testaments* (BZAW 123; Berlin: de Gruyter, 1971).

[68] The point is well made by J. Sanders, 'Text and Canon', 6–7. Cf. the newer trends exemplified by Sanders's own article, and the earlier study by D. Barthélemy, 'Problématique et tâches de la critique textuelle de l'Ancien Testament', in his *Études d'histoire de texts de l'Ancien Testament* (Göttingen: Vandenhoeck and Ruprecht, 1978), 365–81.

[69] Cf. his 'Ein Arbeitsplan für die Textkritik des Alten Testaments', *ZAW* 54 (1936), 108–9.

[70] Among earlier studies, the work of I. L. Seeligman, 'Investigations on the Transmission of the Massoretic Text of the Bible, I, *Tarbiz*, 25 (1955–6), 118–39 [Heb.], and op. cit. (n. 64), 201–21 is of particular value. But these *animadversiones* do not attempt a typological or analytical overview of the phenomenon.

the MT. By such formulaic signalling devices, the primary text is set off from the remark which explicitly bears upon it.

2. Scribal comments may also be isolated by comparing parallel texts *within* the MT, or *between* the text of the MT and its versions (for example, the LXX or Samar.), to show their degree of variance from each other. Such comparisons disclose scribal comments when one or more of the parallel texts contain a paraphrase or other exegetical remark bearing on the shared text.

3. A third means of isolating scribal comments relies on a more subjective text-critical judgement. To provide maximal control, the present study will restrict inquiry to manifestly redundant and disruptive features in the MT *which are also explanatory in nature*. In this way, these features may be distinguished from redundancies which reflect conflated readings based on synonymous manuscript variants, scribal dittographies, or parallel literary strands.

To be sure, these several methodological criteria must be considered as minimal, not maximal, types. There is no doubt that other valid methods may be devised for the isolation of scribal glosses in the Hebrew Bible. These can always be added, however, once the broad outlines of a typology of scribal exegesis and its hermeneutical procedures are established along the most cautious lines.

2. Lexical and Explicative Comments

A. THE USE OF DEICTIC ELEMENTS

THE recognition of explanatory words or phrases in the Hebrew Bible is facilitated by the formulaic use of pronouns like הוא or היא 'it is', demonstrative pronouns like זה 'this (means)', and even particles like את 'namely', to introduce them. Such deictic, or indicative, elements are part of a broad range of explicit exegetical terms found in biblical texts of various genres and periods. Their standard use in connection with the interpretation of dreams, visions, and oracles, for example, constitutes a fixed feature of the inner-biblical mantological tradition.[1] That is, these deictic elements comprise integral parts of the literary presentation of a dream or vision and its interpretation, so that they are, in fact, constitutive of this genre. A full examination of this exegetical feature will be undertaken in a later chapter.[2] It is noted here to contrast the peculiarly scribal use of the deictic elements in the discussion to follow, where terms like הוא or זה are not primary exegetical features, but rather indicate secondary annotations of words, persons, and places. As such, they disrupt the original literary piece, and are not constitutive of it or its genre. Indeed, such deictic elements indicate the *traditio* of the scribes, not their *traditum*.

The Formulaic Use of הוא and היא

1. The concern of biblical scribes to provide themselves or their readers with accurate geographical information about old locales mentioned in the texts—toponyms whose names have been changed or whose identities have been obscured with time—is manifested in various ways. For example, the territorial outline of the tribe of the Benjaminites in Josh. 18:13 states: 'And the boundary runs southwards to Luz, to the slope of Luz . . .' The topographic sequel to this description, recurring as a fixed stylistic pattern in the other boundary descriptions of this document, is the phrase 'and the boundary continues down to . . . TN'. However, in Josh. 18:13 this continuity is interrupted by another

---

[1] See M. Fishbane, 'The Qumran Pesher and Traits of Ancient Exegesis', in *Proceedings of the VIth World Congress of Jewish Studies*, i (Jerusalem, 1977), 97–114, with parallels from the ancient Near East.

[2] Chapter 15, below.

clause, 'it is הִיא Beth El', which stands in apposition to the preceding toponym, Luz. In this way, the reader is informed that Beth El is the contemporary name for the ancient city called Luz.[3] In a similar way, the name of the ancient Canaanite toponym 'Valley of Shawe', mentioned in Gen. 14 (v. 17), is contemporized by the explanation 'it is הוא the Royal Valley', which is actually an interdialectical Hebrew translation of the older designation.[4] As such, Gen. 14:17 is one of several translation-glosses found throughout the Hebrew Bible introduced by deictic elements, although asyndetic translation-glosses occur as well.[5] In other instances, concern for historical accuracy led to the annotation of toponymic anachronisms, introducing these latter with deictic elements. Thus, 1 Chron. 11:4 reads 'And David and all Israel went to Jerusalem – this is הוא Jebus . . .'

Patronymic and other personal identifications are also frequently clarified by the ancient Israelite scribes, in the light of their knowledge of other inner-biblical traditions or in their attempt to establish a clear

[3] Cf. vv. 14, 28, which introduce toponymic glosses by means of the pronoun *hî'*. Both glosses in Josh. 18:13-14 interrupt the stereotyped formulations of the older boundary list. Cf. the contemporizing identifications in Gen. 23:2, 19. These are syntactically disruptive and apparently contradictory. This problem is resolved in Gen. 35:27. The toponymic glosses with *hî'* in Josh. 15:8-10, 13, 49, 54, 60 deserve special note: they interrupt the stylistic form, are contemporizing versions (v. 15 does not use *hî'* but a fuller, paraphrastic form), and indicate a fairly systematic procedure. On this last point, the glosses in the two parts of the list parallel each other (v. 10 is an isolated case; *snh* in v. 49 is an indubitable corruption of *spr*). Only certain cities, therefore, were glossed – and twice, at that (see vv. 9 and 60; vv. 13 and 54; vv. 15 and 49; and cf. vv. 8 and 63).

The contemporizing of date formulary shows an interesting development. In 1 Kgs. 6:38 and 8:2 the names (*bûl*; *'ētānîm*) of Canaanite months (*yeraḥ*) related to the agricultural cycle are correlated by the deictic term *hû'* with the corresponding Israelite month (*ḥōdeš*) in ordinals. In a later historical stratum, influenced by Babylonian month-names, the ordinal enumeration of months is correlated by the deictic term *hû'* with these originally foreign designations (*nîsān*; *'ădār*; etc.); cf. Esther 2:16, 3:7, 8:12.

[4] A. Wieder, 'Ugaritic–Hebrew Lexicographical Notes', *JBL* 84 (1965), 160-2, has effectively demonstrated that Ug. *ṯwy* means 'to rule', as does Heb. *šwy* in Ps. 89:20. The TN 'Royal Valley' is mentioned alone in the later 2 Sam. 18:18. Cf. also the TN gloss with *hû'* in Gen. 23:19.

[5] Esther 3:7, 9:24 explain that the *pûr* (deriving from Akk. *pūru* 'lot') means Heb. *gōral* 'lot' by means of the deictic pronoun *hû'*. An asyndetic translation gloss occurs in 1 Kgs. 11:19, where Heb. *haggĕbîrāh* (a senior lady of the harem, often the mother of the heir apparent) explains *taḥpĕnês*, deriving from Eg. *t. ḥmt. nsw* 'the wife of the king'; cf. J. Gray, *I & II Kings* (rev. edn.; SCM; London: McKay, Chatham, Eng., 1970), 282. A second instance is in Prov. 22:21, where Aram. *qōšṭ* is explained by 'words of truth'. A final example is in Ezek. 19:9, where Heb. *sûgar* (related to Akk. *šigaru* 'neckstock') is explained by Heb. *ḥaḥîm* 'shackles'. For comparable Mesopotamian phenomena, see C. Frank, 'Fremdsprachliche Glossen in assyrischen Listen und Vocabularien', *MAOG* 4/1-2 (1928-9), 36-45.

textual meaning. Equivocations in the Esau–Edom genealogy in Gen. 36 give some insight to these procedures. Thus, the superscription in this genealogy, 'And these are the generations of Esau, הוא that is Edom', with its continuous reference to the name Esau alone in vv. 2, 4, 6, suggests that the identification of Esau with Edom in v. 1 is a secondary scribal clarification which parallels the identification of the two in the birth narratives of Gen. 27: 25, 30. In fact, the pleonasm 'that is Edom' is repeated at the conclusion of the opening section of the genealogy ('and Esau dwelt by Mt. Seir; Esau, הוא that is Edom'), where it is even more syntactically awkward and disjunctive than in its first occurrence, and again. after the colophon to the list of the sons of Esau in v. 19. Whether these patronymic annotations, like the toponymic ones discussed earlier, simply reflect the historical penchant of the scribes who copied these historical manuscripts, or reflect a time when even genealogies and boundary lists were 'public' texts for lay audiences who would need such clarifications, cannot be determined.

2. In addition to the preceding annotations, where the original text is, in any case, clear, scribal tradents occasionally supplemented indeterminate textual references with explicatory comments. An example of this concern to clarify ambiguous subject matter in a text can be found in the conclusion to Ezek. 31. In this taunt-song, the prophet Ezekiel is commanded (v. 2a) to address 'Pharaoh, King of Egypt, and his horde המונו' with the query, 'אל־מי דמית בגדלך to whom are you comparable in your greatness?' (v. 2b). This question is insidious and ultimately rhetorical, of course, since without pause the prophet launches his tirade with an extended metaphor of a wide-branched and deeply rooted cedar-tree. This tree is identified with Assyria, so that the natural figure becomes concrete through a well-known historical entity.[6] However, because of its pride, this tree (Assyria), compared to which none was finer in all the garden of Elohim (v. 3), was toppled. Thus, all who depended upon its sustenance—both birds and beasts—

---

[6] Although MT 'aššûr (Assyria) is also found in the versions, it has been commonly emended to ta'ǎšûr 'cedar', on the presumption that the historical reference is not original; cf. W. Zimmerli, *Ezechiel 25-48* (BKAT 13/2; Neukirchen and Vluyn: Neukirchener Verlag, 1969), 748, with earlier literature. J. Bewer, 'Textual and Exegetical Notes on the Book of Ezekiel', *JBL* 72 (1953), 164-5, suggested that 'aššûr is a secondary insertion (possibly by the prophet) intended to give an example of a world power, and accordingly noted Ezek. 32: 18-32, where Assyria is the world power Pharaoh will see when he descends to šĕ'ôl. But the similarity of Ezek. 32: 18-32 to Ezek. 31, the unanimity of the versions, the fact that mî in 31: 2, 18 refers to royal personages, and the fact that Pharaoh is never identified with cedar in Ezekiel (cf. 29: 3, 32: 25), combine to argue for the authenticity of the MT. On these points I follow J. Joüon, 'Notes philologiques sur le texte hébreu d'Ézéchiel', *Bib.* 10 (1929), 309 n. 1.

were wanting (vv. 10-14). As a final ignominy, this tree was cast into the realm of Sheol, where it joined many other trees (monarchies) similarly disposed (vv. 15-17). This lamentable end is repeated at the end of the taunt, in a phrase which returns the focus of the piece to Pharaoh, i.e. Egypt (cf. 'אל־מי דמית ... בגדל' to whom are you comparable ... in greatness?' (v. 18a)).[7]

The result of this shift in v. 18a back to the second-person address first formulated in v. 2 (after the extended third-person figure in vv. 3-17)[8] does more than simply refocus attention on Egypt; it also serves to draw the analogical conclusion of the figure. 'To whom are you comparable?' Pharaoh is again asked. To Assyria? But even mighty Assyria, the superior tree in the garden of Elohim, was cut low by Nebuchadnezzar the Babylonian (v. 12; cf. 28: 7), so how, then, could Egypt presume to withstand this same foe?[9] 'You will [also] be brought down [like Assyria] to the netherworld,' runs the response, 'together with the other trees of Eden, and lie with those slain by the sword' (v. 18b; cf. vv. 16-17). From this conclusion it thus appears that the original rhetoric of 'To whom are you comparable?' has hidden the seeds of its irony throughout the extended figure of the tree. To whom is Egypt comparable? – to Assyria, implies v. 3 and its sequel; no, not even Assyria, implies the repetition of this question in v. 18a. 'To whom are you comparable', Pharaoh? – to nothing but hewn trees and slain bodies in the nether world!

But for all the force of this ironic conclusion, and the signal (by verbal repetition and the use of the second person singular) that the reference to this question is Egypt, neither Pharaoh nor Egypt is mentioned in v. 18a, and this leads to an ambiguity, subsequently corrected by a later scribe, who wrote: 'הוא this refers to Pharaoh and all his horde וכל המונו, oracle of YHWH' (v. 18b). The deictic particle in this addendum manifestly refers to the person addressed by the question in v. 18a; and by repeating the language of v. 2a ('Pharaoh ... and his horde') in v. 18b, the scribe has further reinforced the fact that the person queried in v. 18a is the same as the one addressed in v. 2b – Pharaoh. Verse 2 first states, 'Speak to Pharaoh, king of Egypt, and his horde', and then asks, 'to whom are you comparable in your greatness?'

---

[7] *běgōdel* in v. 18a is missing in LXX Mss.

[8] In addition, vv. 3-17 are distinctively in the perfect tense. Nevertheless, the recurrence of the stems *gdl* (vv. 4, 7) and *dmy* (v. 8, twice) integrate the language of this unit with keywords in the frame, vv. 2, 18a.

[9] The observation that 31: 12 refers to Babylon, as indicated by 28: 7, was made by W. Eichrodt, *Ezekiel* (OTL; Philadelphia: Westminster, 1970), ad loc.; Y. Hoffmann, *Prophecies Against the Nations in the Bible* (Tel Aviv: Tel Aviv University Press, 1977), 148 n. 59 [Heb.], adds 30:10-11 and 32:11-12. My formulation of the prophetic rhetoric as an *a fortiori* argument follows Hoffmann, p. 148.

Verse 18, by contrast, first asks the question and then, via the scribal annotation, answers it.[10] With this addendum the ambiguity in the conclusion of the figure is removed, and a stylistic envelope is formed which frames the tree metaphor in chiastic fashion:

A 'Speak to Pharaoh . . . and his horde' (v. 2a)

   B 'To whom are you comparable in your greatness?' (v. 2b)

      C Tree Figure (vv. 3–17)

   B[1] 'To whom are you comparable in . . . greatness?' (v. 18a)

A[1] 'This refers to Pharaoh and all his horde' (v. 18b)

Formulaic Uses of את

1. The divine command in Hag. 2: 4–5 from Haggai to Zerubbabel, the post-exilic overlord of Judaea, to Joshua the High Priest, and to the remnant of the nation, to rebuild the Temple has long proved troublesome to interpreters. For after the charge to these leaders and the people to 'be strong . . . and build [the Temple], for I am with you', and before the parallel motivation 'for my spirit is with you, do not fear', there is the following comment: 'את הדבר the promise which I made with you when you left Egypt' (2: 5aα). This remark is difficult for stylistic and syntactic reasons. First, it interrupts the two motivation clauses 'be strong' and 'do not fear', so often used as a hendiadys in commands to individuals to embark on a new and dangerous task.[11] In the present context, in fact, these two motivations are linked with two other motivation clauses—'for I am with you' and 'my spirit is with you'—which also recur in similar commission scenarios.[12] The fact that these four standard expressions combine to form a chiastic pattern here ('be strong'; 'I am with you'; 'My spirit is with you'; 'do not fear'),

---

[10] Zimmerli, op. cit. 76, argued that v. 18b is not 'überflüssig' but original and necessary, so as to clarify the reference with respect to Egypt. This is also basically the point of G. A. Cooke, *The Book of Ezekiel* (ICC; Edinburgh: T. and T. Clark, 1936), 344, and has an earlier reflex in the perceptive comment of R. Eliezer of Beaugency, *Kommentar zu Ezechiel und den XII Kleinen Propheten*, i (Schriften des Vereins Mekize Nirdamim³, 4; Warsaw, 1909), p. 53 = fos. 154[b]–155[a] [Heb.].

[11] e.g. Deut. 31: 6–8; Josh. 1: 9; Jer. 1: 8, 18; 2 Chron. 20: 17. A critical discussion of this formulary, with form-critical implications for several biblical texts, particularly Isa. 7, can be found in M. Fishbane, 'The "Sign" in the Hebrew Bible', *Shenaton. An Annual for Biblical and Ancient Near Eastern Studies* 1 (1975), 217–24 [Heb.]. This formulary has well-known ancient Near Eastern parallels; see ibid. 218 n. 18, with literature cited.

[12] Cf. Exod. 3: 12; Deut. 20: 4, 31: 8; Josh. 1: 9; Judg. 6: 12; Jer. 1: 8, 19, 15: 20; 2 Chron. 20: 17. The notion that God's spirit serves as a guiding agent in difficult ventures appears in other late texts; cf. Isa. 63: 11; Dan. 9: 20.

which is interrupted by the aforementioned clause in 2: 5aα, suggests that the latter is a secondary intrusion.[13] This observation is reinforced by the awkward syntax, since the comment 'the promise which I made with you . . .' *begins* with the particle את, whose routine function in biblical Hebrew is to introduce a direct object.

Nevertheless, various proposals have been advanced to interpret the particle את in Hag. 2: 5aα as a regular accusative marker. But these are unconvincing. For one thing, it is highly unlikely that 'את הדבר the promise' is the object of the preceding verb עשה (interpreted as 'do' or 'fulfill'—not 'build'), since the issue of the oracle is unquestionably a charge to rebuild the Temple, and no such promise was made during the exodus. Such an attempt to routinize the את-clause in v. 5aα would also be hard pressed to explain the occurrence of the motivation 'for I am with you' between the verb and its object, as well as the unique use of עשה (as 'fulfill') in this context. For such reasons it has also been proposed that את הדבר is the object of the following relative clause ('which I . . .'), and precedes the object in this case—after the manner of *attractio inversa*.[14] But while this syntactic construction in itself has the merit of emphasizing the promise which forms the basis of trust in God's new command, such a solution does not take adequate account of the manifestly disruptive nature of this clause in this particular context. Indeed, the syntactic explanation of 2: 5aα cannot be dissociated from its larger textual environment. It is therefore far simpler to regard הדבר as a regular nominative introduced by the particle את, used here as elsewhere in the Hebrew Bible in a substantive or explicative sense.[15] One may thus interpret the commission in Hag. 2: 4-5 as follows: '. . . for I am with you . . . namely/that is to say, [in accordance with] the promise which I made with you when you left Egypt . . .' Accordingly, a later scribe has added the theological explanation that God would be with the leaders and people of post-exilic times in their new task just as he was with their forefathers, when he promised to be with them during the exodus (cf. Exod. 3-4, 6, 23: 20-33). If the scribe has a more precise biblical text or tradition in mind here, we cannot

---

[13] P. Ackroyd, 'Some Interpretative Glosses in the Book of Haggai', *JJS* 7 (1956), 167, has noted the syntactic interruption but not the chiasm or the standard formulae—which reinforce his observation.

[14] Cf. Ackroyd, loc. cit., following J. Blau, 'Zum angeblichen Gebrauch von *'et* vor dem Nominative', *VT* 4 (1954), 11-12.

[15] Such a sense for *'et* has been noted by G. R. Driver in *Alttestamentliche Studien* (Festschrift F. Nötscher), edd. H. Junker and J. Botterweck (Bonn: P. Hanstein, 1950), 57. For other cases of *'et* in a secondary gloss, see the example to follow and the well-known Isa. 7: 17b. For *'et* introducing an explicative original to the text, one may note Exod. 1: 14b; Neh. 9: 19b.

say.[16] What is certain is that 2: 5aα is an attempt to specify more precisely the exact condition of the promise made to Zerubbabel and his colleagues. It may be added that the secondary nature of the את-clause in v. 5aα, proposed here on the basis of internal stylistic considerations, is confirmed by its absence from the LXX and minor versions. Had this more difficult, explicative clause been original, it is unlikely to have been deleted by later tradents.

2. Isa. 29: 9-11 provides another example of pleonastic comments inserted into the text by means of the deictic particle את.

(9) Be astonished and dazed, revel and be blinded – you that have drunk, but not from wine; that totter, but not from drink;

(10) For YHWH has poured over you a spirit of stupefaction; He has closed your eyes, את *the prophets*, and cloaked your heads, *the seers*.

(11) All prophetic visions have become as a sealed book for you . . .

The object of the denunciation beginning in v. 9 is unspecified; but in so far as the people of Judaea have been the object of scorn throughout the chapter, and no new subject has been introduced, it is reasonably certain that the reference is to the people of Israel. It is they who are drunk and totter, and who cannot fathom the import of the prophetic visions given to them. From this point of view, the phrases 'את the prophets' and 'the seers' are problematic, and reflect a shift in subject from the people to the prophets. Moreover, since these two phrases have a syntactically distinct, appositional relationship to their preceding clauses—the first is actually introduced by the particle את *after* a clause ending in an object; and since the initial sentences also form a distinct and coherent chiasm (literally, 'He has closed your eyes ~ your heads He has cloaked'), it is very likely that Isa. 29: 10 preserves two secondary scribal interpolations.[17] Presumably a motivating concern of these annotations was simply to elucidate the literary figure of closed eyes.[18] The result, however, was to transform a national oracle of condemnation into a rebuke of false prophets. Tendentious motivations cannot, therefore, be entirely excluded. But whatever their origin and aim, the

---

[16] The speculation of Ackroyd, that the reference is to the crossing of the sea, is not convincing. See loc. cit., and his *Exile and Restoration* (OTL; Philadelphia: Westminster, 1975), 161. More suggestive, to my mind, is the possibility that Exod. 15: 17 was read in the post-exilic period as a promise that the people would (re)settle the land and (re)build the sanctuary. Significantly, Hag. 2: 22 gives an eschatological reading of Exod. 15: 4.

[17] Already S. D. Luzzatto, *Il Profeta Isaia, volgarizzato e commentato* (Padua: A. Bianchi, 1855, 1967), 337–8.

[18] The theological idea and the imagery are strikingly similar to the famous paradox in Isa. 6: 9–10.

annotations in v. 10 were made relatively early, for the LXX presupposes such an awkward text. In this latter version the problematic grammar and syntax found in the MT is thoroughly normalized and the condemnation of false prophets further extended.[19] In this manner the LXX – and even its Lucianic revisor, who, it seems, sought to improve upon his Greek version without even consulting the MT itself – has added to the tissue of revisions which has accumulated around Isa. 29: 10.[20]

But the foregoing is solely a text-critical evaluation. From the viewpoint of the exegetical *traditio* involved, the textual strata represented by the MT and LXX reflect continuous rereadings of the original oracle. This striking transformation of an oracle against the people into one against the prophets not only demonstrates the theological character of the scribal reading of this text (or whatever school tradition it gives expression to), but also shows the extent to which scribal annotations introduce a new pedagogical authority *into* the received *traditum*, so that this latter 'teaching' contends with and *even tries to neutralize* the original textual reading. The scribal *traditio* has thus transformed the *traditum* and subjected it to its own concerns and viewpoint. Accordingly, the preceding example from Isa. 29: 9-10 succinctly underscores a paradoxical dimension of the scribal *traditio*: namely, the fact that the *traditum* which it receives is not the *traditum* it transmits, for this latter is now the bearer of multiple authorities for new generations of readers and interpreters. That this paradox is not always perceived by later readers is a measure of the scribes' success: *their* interpretations have become the *traditum*.

Formulaic Uses of זֶה

1. As suggested earlier, the scribal comment in Hag. 2: 5aα explains the basis of trust in the divine oracle commissioning the restoration of the first Temple. Up to the time of Darius (Hag. 2: 1), the people did not consider the time to be propitious for its rebuilding (v. 2). Perhaps the reason for the initial delay was similar to that reflected in the vision of Zechariah – two months later – wherein perplexity is expressed as to whether the seventy-year Jeremian oracle of divine wrath and destruction (Jer. 25: 8-12) had come to pass (Zech. 1: 12-15). Zechariah's *angelus interpres* tells him in YHWH's name that the time of doom has passed and that the advent of grace and (Temple) restoration is nigh (Zech. 1: 16-17). No such reason or explanation is found in the prophecies of

---

[19] So H. W. Hertzberg, 'Die Nachgeschichte alttestamentlicher Texte innerhalb des Alten Testaments', in *Werden und Wesen des Alten Testaments*, edd. P. Volz, F. Stummer, and J. Hempel (BZAW 66; Berlin: Töpelman, 1936), 114.

[20] See I. L. Seeligmann, *The Septuagint Version of Isaiah. A Discussion of its Problems* (Mededeelingen en Verhandelingen van het Voorziatisch-Egyptisch Genootschap 'Ex Oriente Lux', 9; Leiden: E. J. Brill, 1948), 19.

Haggai.[21] Indeed, the prophet speaks a divine oracle which implies that a proper attentiveness to the poor agricultural yield and general economic travail should have been sufficient indication to the people of divine disfavour for the unbuilt Temple, and that YHWH was warning them thereby (Hag. 1: 6–11). In an ironic allusion to David's words to the prophet Nathan prior to the building of the first Temple, and to his own words stated earlier, YHWH has the prophet Haggai ask the people 'Is it the [propitious] time for you to dwell in panelled homes while this House [Temple] is in ruins?' (Hag. 1: 4; cf. 2 Sam. 7: 2). Thereupon, the Lord commanded and encouraged the people and its leadership to restore his Temple (Hag. 1: 13–15; 2: 1–5).

In the context of these restoration oracles, Haggai asks: 'Who of you remains who saw this Temple in its first glory? And how do you see it now? It is not like nothing in your eyes?' (2: 3). From this prologue the prophet turns to an oracle guaranteeing divine support in the enterprise of Temple rebuilding. However, it is important to stress that the despair and nostalgia in Haggai's words to those who had lived in Judaea prior to the exile is not a mere rhetorical flourish devoid of all historical substance. The fact is that the same mood is reflected in the historiographical report in Ezra 3, which also refers to the initial laying of the Temple's foundations by the post-exilic 'community of the exile'.[22] It is there reported how 'the builders וְיִסְּדוּ laid the foundations of the Temple of YHWH', and how the clerics performed liturgical festivities at this occasion (vv. 10–11). The joy was mitigated, however, since 'many of the priests, Levites, heads of patriarchal clans, and elders who had seen the first Temple בְּיָסְדוֹ when it was founded–זֶה הַבַּיִת–with their eyes, cried loudly' (v. 12), so that the attending crowd had trouble in discerning the trumpets of joy for all the wailing (v. 13).

This report cited from Ezra 3: 12 is syntactically awkward. The relative clause 'who had seen the first Temple when it was founded' is separated from its adverbial modifier 'with their eyes' by the words זֶה הַבַּיִת, and the relationship of this latter clause to its context is uncertain. Since the occurrence of a demonstrative pronoun in a nominal clause (translating זֶה הַבַּיִת 'this is the Temple') appears to be contextually problematic after the preceding relative clause, some ancient versions and modern interpreters have preferred to construe זה as a

---

[21] According to Ezra 4, esp. vv. 23–4, the reason was entirely political. When the conditions changed in the days of Darius, Haggai and Zechariah began to prophesy (Ezra 5: 1–3). The lapse of nearly seventy years since the Judaean exile was undoubtedly considered providential and provided the conditions for the renewal of prophecy after the exile. On these prophetic correlations, see M. Fishbane, 'Revelation and Tradition: Aspects of Inner-Biblical Exegesis', *JBL* 99 (1980), at 356–8, and below, Part Four.

[22] J. Bright, *History of Israel*[2] (Philadelphia: Westminster, 1972), 367, has argued that Ezra 3 is contemporary with Haggai.

demonstrative adjective with its modifying noun הבית (translating 'this Temple').[23] But such an explanation is against all grammatical form and makes no apparent sense in the present context. Finally, and not completely unrelated to the solution of this grammatical problem, one must note the inherent ambiguity of the form בְּיָסְדוֹ (literally 'when *it* was founded') at the outset of Ezra 3:12, whose received vocalization permits the manifestly absurd interpretation that the elder folk who cried had actually seen the foundation of the first Temple, half a millennium earlier! To resolve this latter point, many moderns, following the LXX, have 'corrected' בְּיָסְדוֹ to the nominal form בִּיסֹדוֹ.[24] On this basis, the text is reconstructed (or restored) to mean that the elders only saw and remembered the first Temple 'when it was on its foundation'. But however suggestive, this solution does little to clarify the problematic sense of the words זה הבית, and actually adds to the overall syntactic difficulties.

A more integrated solution to the several grammatical and syntactic problems of this passage was offered by Ibn Ezra. He perceived the aforementioned historical ambiguity in בְּיָסְדוֹ 'when it was founded', and remarked that זה הבית 'has been linked to בְּיָסְדוֹ' in order to indicate that the pronominal suffix 'it' refers to the second Temple – not to the first. In this syntactic observation Ibn Ezra was undoubtedly correct, and, although he does not indicate his understanding of זה הבית, he has pointed the way to a historical assessment of the text from the perspective of scribal practices in ancient Israel. For in so far as זה הבית is grammatically inappropriate and syntactically disruptive in its MT context, sense may be readily restored once it is recognized that it is a secondary scribal gloss which has been introduced to clarify the ambiguity of MT בְּיָסְדוֹ and to stress its proper semantic reference.[25]

---

[23] Syr., *Tg. Ps.-J.* RSV, and NEB blend the phrase 'this house/temple' with the foundation-laying which precedes it; JPS blends it with what follows, and constructs the paraphrase 'when this house was before them'. W. Rudolph, *Esra–Nehemia* (HKAT 20; Tübingen: J. C. B. Mohr, 1949), 20, ignores *zō't habbayit* completely.

[24] LXX ἐν θεμελιώσει αὐτοῦ is probably an attempt to solve the apparent historical anomaly. Besides MT v.12, the verbal form of the stem *ysd* recurs in vv. 6, 10–11. The Syr. reads *bkbdw* for *bysdw*. It is unlikely that this is the original text, as suggested by C. H. Hawley, *A Critical Examination of the Peshitta Version of the Book of Ezra* (New York: AMS Press, 1966; reprint of New York: Columbia University Press, 1922), 30, after J. Bewer, *Der Text des Buches Ezra* (Göttingen, 1922), 46. The textual 'solution' in the Peshitta may be influenced by Hag. 2: 7, 9.

[25] The demonstrative pronoun *zeh* thus responds to *bĕyāsdô* and means 'this [preceding] means/refers to the [present] Temple'. Among moderns, the solution advanced here has also been noted by the *Preliminary and Interim Report of the O.T. Text Project* of the United Bible Societies (Stuttgart: United Bible Societies, 1977), ii. 501f.

The pronominal suffix of 'when *it* was founded' is thus explained to indicate 'זה הבית, this refers to the [present, second] Temple'.

Accordingly, those people who had survived the exile and recalled the glory of the second Temple when the foundations of the second Temple were being laid cried out and raised an awesome din. The popular despair arising from this inevitable comparison is reflected, as noted earlier, in the prophecies of Haggai. Indeed, it is highly significant, and indicative of the matters discussed here, that the oracle of confidence in rebuilding the Temple addressed to Zerubbabel and others in Hag. 2: 4-5 at once follows Haggai's reference to this despair (2: 3) and precedes the pointed promise: 'the glory of this latter Temple will surely exceed that of the first [one] – says YHWH of Hosts' (2: 9).

2. The exacting scrutiny to which the biblical text was subjected by ancient Israelite scribes went beyond the clarification of historical and semantic ambiguities. Of particular interest in this regard are those which reflect ancient reading traditions whose meaning has been obscured by modern interpreters, but which the present focus on scribal practices may help to reconstruct. Just such an instance is found in Ps. 68: 9. Referring to the appearance of God before the people in the previous verse, most recent commentators have tended to interpret the phrase זה סיני in this verse as an ancient divine epithet, and so read: '(Elohim, when you come forth before your people ...) the earth trembled, yea the skies melted before Elohim – זה סיני the One of Sinai – before Elohim the God of Israel.' The consensus for this interpretation has derived from the authority of W. F. Albright, who construed MT *zeh Sinai* as **zû Sinai*, a divine appellation with attested parallels.[26] Albright made this suggestion in the context of a study which went on to claim that Ps. 68 as a whole is nothing short of a catalogue of the title lines of ancient Hebrew poetry, and so also rejected any attempt to see meaningful relations between the various stichoi.[27]

A closer examination of both the context and imagery of the opening lines of Ps. 68 suggests, however, that this evaluation of the text is misleading, and that the psalm was actually read in biblical antiquity as containing a series of consecutive historical references. Thus, one may note that the text refers successively, from v. 8 to v. 13, to the exodus (v. 8a), the desert wanderings (v. 8b; cf. Deut. 32: 10), the settlement in the land (v. 10), and finally to the Temple and its royal splendour

---

[26] See W. F. Albright, 'A Catalogue of Early Hebrew Lyric Poems (Psalm 68)', *HUCA* 23 (1950-1), i. 20, and the earlier observation in 'The Names *Shaddai* and *Abram*', *JBL* 54 (1935), 204 (postscript).

[27] Loc. cit. 1-39.

(vv. 13-15).[28] Within this contextual sequence, v. 9 reports that, upon YHWH's appearance in the desert, the earth quaked and the heavens melted. Now such volcanic and storm imagery is quite commonly found in the Hebrew Bible to convey the sense of a divine advent in general (cf. Nah. 1: 5; Jer. 10: 10) and the Sinaitic theophany in particular (cf. Exod. 19:18, 20:18; Joel 4: 6).[29] It is therefore readily conceivable that a later glossator-scribe read the particular imagery of Ps. 68: 9 within its particular historico-geographical context as an allusion to the Sinaitic revelation – and so interrupted the a~ab parallelism ('before Elohim ... before Elohim, God of Israel') with the specifying comment: זה סיני 'this [earthquake caused by Elohim] refers to [the theophany of] Sinai'.

Another consideration in Ps. 68 would have reinforced the annotator's perspective. For it could hardly have gone unnoticed that if vv. 8-15 describe a movement from Sinai to Zion, vv. 16-18 reflect just the reverse perspective. The orientational standpoint there is Mt. Zion itself, the new 'mountain of Elohim' which 'Elohim has desired for his dwelling' (vv. 16-17). And it is from this new summit that the psalmist describes the rivalry of other mountains which YHWH passed over when he 'came from Sinai [to Zion] in holiness' (v. 18),[30] there to establish the seat of his eternal dominion (v. 17). Indeed the mention in v. 18 of the abandonment of Sinai would certainly have brought the earlier geographical descriptions in the psalm to sharpened focus, and reinforced the view that the convulsing of the earth at the time of the divine advent in the desert was nothing if not a reference to the great Sinaitic theophany; and so it is now remarked in the text. The scribal annotation 'this is Sinai' in v. 9 is, therefore, of great historical value in revealing or suggesting some of the inner-textual dialectics whereby ancient Israelite readers understood this passage, and in cautioning modern critics to look to inner-biblical exegetical comments as an ancient guide to textual meaning – if not simply as a stage in the history of interpretation.

B. SCRIBAL COMMENTS WITHOUT DEICTIC ELEMENTS

The preceding examples of lexical, toponymic, or patronymic clarifications, and textual contemporizations or identifications, are marked,

[28] The sequential coherence of Ps. 68 is also evident from its larger context: in brief, vv. 2-7 emphasize the military-redemptive powers of YHWH; vv. 16-18 go on to reflect the glory of Zion (see below); vv. 19-25 return to the theme of a god of might, which leads to a national (vv. 26-9) and international (vv. 30-6) glorification of YHWH.

[29] For this, and its wider ancient Near Eastern context, see the valuable study of S. Loewenstamm, 'Earthquakes at the Time of Theophany', *'Oz le-David* (Jerusalem: Qiryat Sepher, 1964), 508-20 [Heb.].

[30] Reading *bā' missinay baqqōdeš*, with many moderns.

as noted, by deictic elements. These formulaic indicators permit a relatively objective identification of the scribal comments involved. However, such an isolation of scribal comments and the traditions which underlie them becomes much more complicated where these deictic formulae are absent. Nevertheless, the existence of such unmarked comments in the various genres and strata of the Hebrew Bible strongly indicates that this form of annotation was also a conventional feature of ancient Israelite scribal exegesis, and therefore requires discussion in the present context. Following the pattern of the preceding section, the following sampling will be restricted to lexical, syntactical, and grammatical items. Unlike the preceding section, however, inner-biblical scribal comments without deictic markers will be recovered on the basis of a comparative methodology, primarily utilizing parallel traditions within the Hebrew Bible as a control. Two concluding instances will suggest that a cautious comparison of textual redundancies and pleonasms in any one text may prove equally valuable in uncovering the living scribal traditions of ancient Israel.

A common feature of normal linguistic development is the change in meaning of words and phrases, and the development of syntactic structures, over time. Such transformations can be isolated easily by the investigator and provide objective indices to the relative dating of, or relationship between, texts. Just such changes characterize, for example, many differences between words and phrases found in the priestly writings and their equivalents in the prose of late historiography —and this despite the vast differences which may obtain between the two contexts and contents.[31] Of a similar type, but set upon a narrower methodological basis, is the substitution of words in texts of different periods which, however, transmit the same content. The scribal mechanics of such lexical revisions can be hypothetically reconstructed, given the fortunate survival of certain exemplary types. For example, when the scribal copyists of early Ben Sira manuscripts annotated older terms found in their master copy, they put the updated variants in the margin. Thus, marginal ישלם glosses textual ישיב 'pay; recompense' in 32:13, and תפעל glosses תעשה 'do' in 33:10.[32] Such contemporizing of vocabulary is easy to detect because both variants are preserved in the same manuscript. It is when scribes deleted older words and replaced them with newer equivalents that the modern exegete must resort to inner-textual parallels and manuscript variants in order to detect the phenomenon.

---

[31] Cf. A. Hurwitz, 'The Evidence of Language in Dating the Priestly Code', *RB* 81 (1974), 24–56.

[32] Cf. W. Caspari, 'Über die Textpflege', *passim*.

1. The detection of inner-biblical examples of this scribal phenomenon is particularly dependent upon such methodological procedures. Thus, a relatively ambiguous word like עֲנוֹתוֹ in 2 Sam 7: 10, an imprecise word like חפצך in 1 Kgs. 5: 22, or an obscure nominal form like מוּפָז in 1 Kgs. 10: 18, are substituted by בלתו 'destroy him',[33] צרכך 'your requirements', and טהור 'pure', *in the parallel inner-biblical version*: 1 Chron. 17: 9, 2 Chron. 2: 15 and 9: 17, respectively.[34] Comparable to these variations occurring between the Books of Samuel–Kings and the Books of Chronicles are those which may be registered between the MT and certain Qumran manuscripts, for example. Thus, the obscure phrase יהלו אורם in Isa. 13: 10 is replaced in 1Q Isa[a] by the simpler and more common יאירו אורם 'their light will shine'; and the *hapax legomenon* שֹׁבֶל 'hem' in Isa. 47: 2 is simplified by the synonym שולים in 1Q Isa[a].[35] *

It should be obvious, of course, that designating the above changes as scribal comments is a loose characterization. For if, on the one hand, the above-mentioned changes in the Ben Sira and Qumran manuscripts reasonably testify to their being the product of scribal tradents in the narrow sense, the inner-biblical examples do not as readily support this supposition. One may suppose, in fact, that the changes in the Books of Chronicles are simply one more piece of evidence for the large-scale historiographical revision of Samuel–Kings which this work – in part – undoubtedly represents. How can one be certain that the shift from מוּפָז to טהור, for example, is to be separated from the overall contemporizing trends of the Books of Chronicles and viewed as evidence of an isolated scribal change? The weight in favour of the interpretation that the foregoing substitutions are independent scribal 'events' appears to lie solely in the fact that such rewordings are not systematic, but random and isolated occurrences – much as one would expect from scribal, as against authorial, changes. Nevertheless, this difficulty of completely separating scribal from compositional changes must be borne in mind as an inherent factor in the present analyses. The next example exhibits this range of ambiguities more fully.

[33] Cf. G. Yalon, *Qiryat Sepher*, 27 (1951), 174 [Heb.]; but cf. the text-critical point raised by Seeligmann, 'Studies', 127–8.

[34] Among other examples, note the several changes between 2 Sam. 6: 14, 16 and 1 Chron. 15: 27, 29, respectively. Among the changes in 2 Sam. 6: 16 ~ 1 Chron. 15: 27, *bûṣ* replaces *bad*, although it usually replaces *šēš*; cf. A. Hurvitz, 'The Usage of *šš* and *bwṣ* in the Bible and its implications for the Date of P', *HTR* 60 (1967), 117–21. Possibly *gĕdílîm* 'twisted fringes' in Deut. 22: 12 is a simplification of *ṣíṣít* in Num. 15: 38. Also, cf. Obad. 6 and Jer. 49: 10.

[35] The situation can also be reversed: thus, the archaic 4Q Sam[b] 20: 34 *wayyiphaz* 'he sprang up', which is also reflected in the LXX (and cf. LXX 1 Sam. 25: 9), has been 'simplified' in the MT reading *wayyāqām* 'he arose [quickly]'. Cf. K. McCarter, *1 Samuel* (AB 8; Garden City, NY: Doubleday, 1980), 339.

2. Apart from lexical substitutions, an analysis of parallel biblical texts, or a comparison of alternate recensions of a set piece, is particularly helpful in detecting scribal annotations *added to* the original reading but unmarked by any deictic element. In the following — extended — example from Lev. 19: 19 and Deut. 22: 9–11, formal stylistic features and comparative analysis serve to distinguish the lexical comment from the text in each of its several stages of development. We may start with the injunction in Lev. 19: 19:

Do not mix-breed your cattle;   בהמתך לא־תרביע כלאים
do not mix-seed your field;   שדך לא־תזריע כלאים
and do not put on a mixed garment.   ובגד כלאים שעטנז לא יעלה עליך

This prohibition rhythmically and formulaically prohibits the mixture of seeds in various conditions: whether in natural breeding, in the domestication of grains, or in the manufactured use of its by-products. The keyword of this cadenced unit is כלאים 'mixtures', and its exact meaning has operative force for each of the three prohibitions — since the precise constitution of the various mixtures would have to be comprehensible for the injunctions to be effective. As these injunctions are quite general in nature, and therefore subject to inevitable qualifications or clarifications, the requisite interpretations would thus have had to accompany the teaching and transmission of these legal injunctions, possibly prior to the planting and breeding season, or on other occasions. In fewer instances, these qualifications or clarifications would have entered the very formulation of the law and been preserved in its subsequent transcriptions. Just such a situation is reflected in Lev. 19: 19c, where the rhetorical cadence of the law is disrupted after the phrase 'mixed garments' by the word שעטנז, which follows in apposition. At some point, therefore, in the course of the teaching or transmission of the law of prohibited mixtures as formulated in Lev. 19: 19, the precise constitution of a mixed garment needed specification or clarification. The now obscure term שעטנז was introduced to serve that purpose.[36]

The preceding suggestion is indirectly supported by the parallel biblical recension of the injunctions against mixtures. Deut. 22: 9–11, as the deuteronomic recasting of Lev. 19: 19, is also a tripartite series of prohibitions against mixtures subdivided into the categories of cattle, fields, and garments:

---

[36] S. R. Driver, *Deuteronomy* (ICC; Edinburgh: T. and T. Clark, 1895), 253, observed that *ša'atnēz* may mean 'woven falsely', comparing LXX κίβδηλος and Coptic *saht + nudj*. This view was first advanced by A. Knoebel, *Exodus und Leviticus* (KeH; Leipzig: S. Hirzl, 1857), 511. For an alternative proposal, see the view of W. F. Albright cited by T. O. Lambdin, 'Egyptian Loan Words in the Old Testament', *JAOS* 73 (1953), 155.

(9) Do not sow your vineyard
with mixed seeds (lest you
forfeit[37] the full-
growth, the seed which
you sow, and the produce
of the vineyard).

(10) Do not plough with an
ox and an ass together.

(11) Do not wear שעטנז,
wool and flax,
together.

לא־תזריע כרמך כלאים

פן־תקדש את המלאה
הזרע אשר תזרע ותבואת
הכרם

לא־תחרש בשור־ובחמור יחדו

לא תלבש שעטנז
צמר ופשתים יחדו

However, closer examination of this topical similarity between Lev.
19:19 and Deut. 22:9-11 reveals notable variations in style, language,
and content. For example, the syntactical sequence of negative verb +
object in Deut. 22:9-11, which has adjacent parallels in Deut. 22:,4-5,
differs from the object + negative verb pattern which occurs in Lev.
19:19 and elsewhere in the Holiness Code (Lev. 19:9-10). Other
variations, as the deuteronomic use of 'vineyard' for 'fields' or mixed
ploughing instead of mixed breeding, suggests that a common legal
model has been variously adapted by different legal draftsmen in
different socio-historical circumstances.[38] Particularly notable in the
present context is the formulation of the law of mixed garments in
Deut. 22:11. Like the lexical gloss in Lev. 19:19c, that in Deut. 22:11
is also appositional. However, whereas the word שעטנז in Lev. 19:19c
is a lexical gloss *explaining* the phrase 'mixed garments', it occurs in
Deut. 22:11 as the basic or primarily legal term, and is itself *explained*
by the pleonastic phrase 'wool and flax'.[39] What remains uncertain is
whether this clarification (i.e. 'wool and flax') was intended to translate

---

[37] The verb *tiqdaš* here implies the forfeiture of the crop (cf. NEB), although
whether it is forfeited to the shrine or merely from use (cf. *Sifre* Deut. 230) is
debatable. *Tg. Yer. I* ('liable for burning') reflects a variant halakhic view of the
proper praxis.

[38] The deuteronomic shift to 'vineyard' is a significant variation, on which see
immediately below. On the other hand, the variation between breeding and
ploughing may be less severe, owing to a *double entendre*; for ploughing is a
common Near Eastern euphemism for sexual intercourse. Cf. Judg. 14:18, and S.
Kramer, 'Cuneiform Studies and the History of Literature: The Sumerian Sacred
Marriage Texts', in *Cuneiform Studies and the History of Civilization* (TAPS 107;
Philadelphia: The American Philosophical Society, 1963), 494 f. (UM 29-16-37: *
32-42, and comment) and 506 (Ni 9602; *obv.*, col. ii. 17-31).

[39] For a similar instance where a lexical explication clarifies a technical legal-
cultic term, compare Deut. 14:6 with its parallel and source in Lev. 11:3. After
the common phrase the deuteronomic regulation has the added remark *šĕtê
pĕrāsôt* 'of two parts'. Presumably this is a gloss which clarifies what the expression
šōsaʿat šeraʿ adds to *mapreset parsāh*, i.e., that the hoof is split in two.

שעטנז, or whether it is a paradigmatic legal instance, including but not restricted to such a mixture. The same question obtains with respect to the legal application of the preceding verse, since it is not certain whether the prohibition of mixed ploughing should be restricted to 'an ox and an ass', or whether this is but a simple case in point, really forbidding *all* mixed ploughing.

3. In the light of the lexical clarification of the legal term שעטנז in Deut. 22:11, the expansion to the preceding law in v. 3, treating the prohibited sowing of a vineyard with mixed seeds, invites closer scrutiny:

Deut. 22:9 (a) Do not sow your vineyard with mixed seeds –כלאים
        (b) lest the full-growth המלאה: be forfeit:
        (c) the seed which you sow and the produce of the vineyard.

As is evident, the relationship between the initial law in (a) and the continuation in (b) and (c) is one of prohibition and warning. With characteristic acuity, the medieval exegete R. Moses ben Naḥman (Nachmanides) suggested that the entire formulation of Deut. 22:9 ((a), (b), and (c)) is an explanation of the law of כלאים in Lev. 19:19.[40] That law only referred to a prohibition against the mixture of seeds in 'fields', allowing one to infer, in Nachmanides' words, that such a prohibition was applicable to 'every sown area'.[41] Accordingly, Nachmanides argued, Deut. 22:9 was 'added here [to specify] that were one to sow a vineyard with mixed seeds he would forfeit the seed sown and the produce of the vineyard'. Ultimately, this perception is correct in its interpretation of the meaning of Deut. 22:9; however, as formulated, the historical and exegetical dynamics within Deut. 22:9 *itself* are bypassed.

Several considerations require a reconceptualization of Nachmanides' position. First, it is both notable and puzzling that the initial legal prohibition in (a) was not sufficient to make the case against sowing a vineyard with other seeds, hence requiring the continuation now found in (b) and (c). Second, the indication of forfeiture in (b) for the infraction of the law in (a) is formulated with the word 'full-growth', and not with clause (c) which stands in apposition to (b). Accordingly, whereas the text in Deut. 22:9 syntactically joins (b) with (c), Nachmanides follows (a) with (c). The result is that the relationships between (a) and (b), and between (b) and (c), are not clarified. Furthermore, as the particle פן 'lest' in (b) is not characteristic of this series of laws, but is a characteristic stylistic element of the Book of Deuteronomy as a whole, where commandments or warnings are frequently continued by

---

[40] Indeed, he sees various explanations in the 'deutero-nomos' of Deut. 22; cf. his comments on 22: 1, 6, 8–11.
[41] Among moderns, cf. S. R. Driver, op. cit. 252.

paraenetic cautions and clarifications introduced by the particle פֶן,[42] one must ask: what is the precise relationship of (*b*) to (*a*), and what might explain it? By means of this explanation the relations between the strata in Deut. 22: 9 emerge.

The opening prohibition in (*a*) is prima facie clear; but for it to be obeyed all unspecified elements would have to be understood. For example, (*a*) does not state whether violation of this prohibition invalidates the yield of the vineyard, the produce of the seed sown in the vineyard, or both. It is undoubtedly to resolve these basic questions that the explicatory paraenesis in (*b*) is addressed: If one were to sow a vineyard with mixed seeds the 'full-growth' thereof would be forfeited, or invalidated for lay use. But all this presupposes that the archaic and rare term מלאה 'full-growth' was well known to the farmers to whom the law was addressed, and remained so. However, at any point when either of these conditions was not met, the questions raised about the meaning of (*a*) are applicable to (*b*) as well.

The question as to the meaning of מלאה is not an idle one, for the inner-biblical evidence has resulted in a full spectrum of contradictory interpretations since antiquity. According to the evidence of Exod. 22: 28, as interpreted by the LXX and early rabbinic tradition,מלאה referred to the first fruits of cereals or grains (i.e. dry goods) and not to the yield of the vat (or vine).[43] On this view, מלאה in Deut. 22: 9b would refer only to the produce of grains, corn, and the like which had been sown among a vineyard, but not to the produce of the vineyard itself. However, according to Num. 18: 27, priestly tithings which may be drawn from the vats are called מלאה, in contrast to the cereals and the like stored in silos. Such a view results in an opposite interpretation of Deut. 22: 9b to that just stated; i.e., only the vintage would be invalidated by the different seeds sown in a vineyard, not the yield from the seeds.

Since at some point the precise sense of מלאה had thus become problematic in ancient Israel, the early paraenesis in (*b*) was itself supplemented by the asyndetic clause 'the seed which you sow and the product of the vineyard' in (*c*). As in Deut. 22: 11, the clarification in v. 9c is in apposition to the term to be explained. It is now unambiguously stated that the invalidated מלאה includes *both* the yield of the seeds sown *and* the product of the vineyard. This inclusive interpretation of the word מלאה was first noted by R. Saadia Gaon and then Nachmanides himself in relation to Exod. 22: 28.[44] To be sure, this

---

[42] Cf. Deut. 4: 16, 23, 6: 12, 15, 7: 22, 25, 8: 11, 12, 9: 28, 11: 16, 12: 13, 19, 30, 15: 9, 19: 6, 20: 5-7, 22: 9, 25: 3, 29: 17;

[43] Cf. *M. Tem.* iv. 1 and Ibn Ezra.

[44] Saadia is cited by Ibn Ezra, so his view was known in Spain. This may be Nachmanides' chain of tradition. However, an old Palestinian tradition under-

interpretation is implicit in Nachmanides' aforementioned comments
on Deut. 22: 9; but since he understood (*a*), (*b*), and (*c*) as an integrally
formulated explanation of Lev. 19: 19, their syntactical and hermeneutical interrelationships were not a problem for him.

Reconstructed, Deut. 22: 9*b* + *c* thus reflect several layers of reflection and clarification of the prohibition formulated in v. 9*a*–so as to
make the law fully comprehensible to those who heard it or who had to
teach it. It was presumably a common practice in ancient Israel to
exploit all arable land by sowing grain among the olive-trees or grape-
vines. Such a practice, though undoubtedly motivated by the exigencies
of limited arable land, was proscribed. One may safely presume that
this prohibition did not originate from theoretical ritual considerations.
The entirely practical agronomic concern that over-cultivation of a
circumscribed area eventually results in the premature exhaustion of
the arable soil would have been the more urgent consideration.[45]

To sum up the preceding considerations: one can clearly perceive the
secondary scribal character of the lexical comments in Lev. 19: 19 and
Deut. 22: 9, 11 on the basis of their appositional nature. These addenda
stand in marked contrast with the replacement of כלאים by שעטנז in
Deut. 22: 11, or the inclusion of the motivation clause in Deut. 22: 9,
as noted above. Both of these latter instances reflect the organic reformulation and articulation of the law in new times by new tradents
and are not disruptive of the law's syntax. Moreover, as much as the
explicatory interpolations in Lev. 19: 19 and Deut. 22: 9, 11 indicate
that a *traditum* cannot be separated from its *traditio*–indeed, that the
traditum is constituted by its *traditio*–these examples bring to new
sharpness the significant fact that scribes incorporate their own understanding of the *traditum* (or that of the oral tradition round about
them) into the *traditio* of it. Hence, the received divine teachings are
supplemented and focused by human comments grafted upon it.
The result, of course, is paradoxical; for the *traditum* is rendered thereby
a composite of multiple levels of authority. But since the preceding
lexical comments attest to the perception that 'Scripture' required

stood *mĕlē'ātô* as *bišlēmûtô* 'in its totality'; cf. *Gen. Rab.* 14: 7 in the edition of
J. Theodor and Ch. Albeck, *Midrasch Bereshit Rabba*[2] (Jerusalem: Wahrmann
Books, 1965), 130 and notes. Among moderns, an inclusive interpretation of
mĕlē'āh was proposed by Y. Kutscher, 'Re the Biblical Lexicon', *Leš.* 21 (1956–7),
253 f. [Heb.]; M. Haran, *Enc. Miq.* iv. 975, limited its sense to the yield of vats
and thereby missed both the extent of the gloss in v. 9 and the exegetical strata.

[45] In the light of the remarkable system of mixed sowing positively reported
in Isa. 28: 23–29, one may wonder if Lev. 19: 19 is a reaction to such practices
and, further, whether Deut. 22: 9 is a further attempt to narrow that law to more
reasonable proportions (i.e. Deut. 22: 9 would thus not be an expansive explication, stating that 'fields' included 'vineyards', but a restrictive comment on Lev.
19: 19, stating only that vineyards may not be sown with seeds for cereal grains).

proper interpretation for its understanding and performance, these interpretations – the scribal addenda – were necessarily regarded as 'Scriptural' in an extended, hermeneutical sense, and so were read together with the received *traditum*. Since the oral *traditio* has thus become part of the written *traditum*, one might even say that the human *traditio* is nothing less than a 'revelation' of the true import of the divine *traditum*. Thus, though they appear to derive from different sources, the two are complementary and – so their conjoint preservation attests – ultimately one.

4. An examination of the biblical record reveals other dimensions of the scribal enterprise and its scholarly traditions. In addition to the inevitable tasks of copying, checking, and clarifying texts, and no doubt in conjunction with these processes, fixed though unusual orthography would be carefully noted for the instruction of scribal apprentices and, of course, for the preservation of accurate manuscript traditions. Such annotations are among the well-known writing and reading traditions preserved in rabbinic and Massoretic sources, though many may be presumed to derive from biblical antiquity.[46] It is thus particularly fortunate when such instances of attentiveness to scribal detail are preserved in the MT itself. The phrase חסד ואמת מן ינצרהו 'grace and truth מן will protect him' in Ps. 61: 8b is an instance of such ancient Israelite scribal activity. This clause concludes a third-person invocation (vv. 7–8a), wishing that the subject of the Psalm be granted 'days beyond those of a king'. However, the literal meaning of this conclusion is an ancient crux due to the problematic nature of the graph מן. Problematic or little sense is achieved whether one vocalizes these letters as the partitive מִן 'from' or as the Aramaic interrogative מַן 'who'.[47] The emendations proposed by modern commentators are likewise of little help in resolving the syntactic and semantic difficulties. Indeed, they rather compound them.[48] Quite different is the forgotten remark of

---

[46] Cf. the material in S. Frensdorff, *Das Buch Ochlah W'ochlah (Massorah)* (Hanover: Hahn, 1864), and *Massorah Gedolah*, i. *Manuscrit B. 19a de Leningrad*, ed. G. Weil (Rome: Pontifical Biblical Institute, 1971). And see J. Barr's 'A New Look at Kethibh-Qere', *OTS* 21 (1981), 19–37, for a critique of earlier views and a fresh proposal. He gives several indications that many later traditions presuppose biblical antiquity.

[47] The MT is vocalized *man*; the LXX reads an interrogative (τίς). Clear uses of Aram. *mān* 'who' in the MT are in Aramaic passages; cf. Ezra 5: 3–4, 9; Dan. 3: 6, 11, 15, 4: 14, 22, 29, 5: 21. Elsewhere, it is commonly supposed that the obscure *min-yĕqûmûn* in Deut. 33: 11b should be repointed *man-yĕqûmûn* 'whoever will rise up'.

[48] e.g. C. Briggs, *The Book of Psalms* (ICC; Edinburgh: T. and T. Clark, 1907), ii. 28, offers the emendation *yĕmîn* 'on the right hand'; the NJPS 'appoint' presumably understand the letters as an apocopated Piel imperative of *mnh*.

Julius Fürst, recently revived by J. Weingreen.[49] Fürst reported that
'some say' that מן 'stands for' (i.e., is an acronym for) the grammatical
comment מָלֵא נוּן (*plene nûn*). He does not elaborate. Presumably the
reader is thereby advised, or the scribe merely notes, that the verbal
form preserves a *prima nûn* in a closed unaccentuated syllable of the
future tense. This proposal has inherent probability – quite apart from
the fact that acronyms can be adduced in other scriptural contexts.[50]
Removal of the annotation restores an immediate and natural grammatical sense to the passage ('grace and truth will protect him').

The proposal that מן in Ps. 61: 8b is of a secondary scribal nature
may be reinforced on comparative grounds, for the annotation is missing
both from the lesser Greek manuscript variants and from the nearly
exact MT variant found in Prov. 20: 28, חסד ואמת יצרו־מלך 'grace and
truth will protect a king'. Indeed, the reason for the absence of מן from
this last passage is the clue to its occurrence in Ps. 61: 8b. For while
the third person masculine plural of the stem נצר is regularly written
plene nûn (ינצרו; cf. Deut. 33: 9; Ps. 78: 7, 105: 45; Prov. 5: 2), it is
written without the *nûn* in bound and suffixed forms (cf. Ps. 25: 21,
40: 12; and Prov. 20: 28) *except* in Ps. 61: 8b.[51] Accordingly, ancient
Israelite scribes clearly recognized the orthographic anomaly of ינצרהו|
and their comment was inserted in order to call attention to this feature
and to preserve it. This record of inner-biblical scribal professionalism
is thus of considerable cultural interest, for it provides a glimpse of the
training and concerns of ancient Israelite scribes otherwise unknown.

5. Where scribal glosses cannot be apprehended on the basis of
deictic elements, inner-biblical parallels, or text versions, one may still
isolate exegetical interpolations through a cautious recognition of
disruptive redundancies where these are also explanatory in nature.
One case in point is Gen. 30: 38, which describes the actions of Jacob
when he breeds his flock through some sort of sympathetic magic:

(*a*) And he set up the staves which he peeled in the troughs ברהטים,
(*b*) in the water trays to which the flock would come to drink לשתות
(*c*) before the flock; and they went into heat as they came to drink.

Various attempts have been made to clarify this passage, whose
language is both obscure and prolix, and whose syntax is certainly

---

[49] Cf. J. Weingreen, 'Rabbinic-Type Glosses in the Old Testament', *JSS* 2
(1957), 160, referring to Fürst's *Hebräisches und Chaldäisches Handwörterbuch
über das Alte Testament* (1857), 753 (s.v. *mnh*). The same solution was proposed,
apparently independently, by F. Perles, *Analekten*, 20.

[50] Cf. F. Perles, *Analekten*, 20 f.

[51] Of the *plene* forms, Deut. 33: 9, Ps. 78: 7, and Prov. 5: 2 have a *sillûq* and
are pausal; Ps. 105: 45 is only pausal.

garbled. Among these proposals, Wellhausen's decision to delete the phrase denoted above as (*b*), 'in the water trays to which the flock would come to drink', still remains the most widely accepted solution.[52] The chief exegetical virtue of this proposal is that it recognizes the redundancy of the content found in (*b*) with that found at the end of (*a*). Wellhausen considered this redundancy a textual gloss. From the analytical perspective adopted here, one may nuance this observation and suggest that, in fact, element (*b*) is an extended scribal comment on the word ברהטים 'in the troughs'.[53] On this view, the assumed original text ((*a*) + (*c*)) indicated where the staves were set up ('in the troughs before the flock . . .') – as would be expected.

Another example of an unmarked pleonasm in the Hebrew text which serves to specify the meaning of a preceding clause may be found in the description of the garments of the priesthood, in Exodus 29. In this chapter we are informed that Aaron and his sons are first brought to the entrance of the Tent of Meeting, and both are then washed (v. 4). After that, Aaron is robed in the special vestments of his high office and annointed to divine service (vv. 5-7); following him, his sons are likewise robed in their more simple garments (v. 8). The text then continues: 'And you shall gird them [with a] belt, *Aaron and his sons*, and put mitres on their heads: and the priesthood will be theirs as an eternal statute; and you shall consecrate Aaron and his sons' (v. 9). From this passage it may easily be seen that the italicized words *Aaron and his sons* interrupt the description of the final features of the cultic costume of Aaron and his sons, and were apparently introduced by a scribe because of the shift in v. 9 from the separate descriptions of Aaron and his sons in the previous verses. Evidently not satisfied that the plural pronoun 'them' sufficiently indicated that the reference was to Aaron *and* his sons – previously (though separately) mentioned – the careful annotator removed all possible doubt and redundantly specified *
that those who would be so attired and crowned were none other than 'Aaron and his sons'.

[52] See his *Die Composition des Hexateuchs und der historischen Bücher des Alten Testaments*[3] (Berlin: G. Riemer, 1899), 39 f.

[53] It also seems that the phrase *maḥśōp hallābān 'ăšer 'al-hammaqlôt* 'the white exposure on the staves' in the previous verse, Gen. 30: 37, is a paraphrastic explication of the confusing *pĕṣālôt lĕbānôt* 'white strips'.

3. Pious Revisions and Theological Addenda

A. SCRIBAL CORRECTIONS

ALONG with the scholarly annotations of textual obscurities which arose in the long course of study and transmission, tendentious corrections are also in evidence in the Hebrew Bible. Such corrections arose as an antidote to original words or expressions which appeared to be impious or improper to later scribes and readers. As a result, words, letters, and syntax were variously manipulated. Traditions regarding such intentional scribal corrections go back to antiquity. It is a phenomenon attested both among the Alexandrian grammarians and copyists, and in contemporary rabbinic sources.[1] However, because both early and later Jewish sources list different numbers of such changes,[2] because the employed terms — כנה 'euphemism' and תקון 'correction' — are so divergent in their implications, and because of the inconclusiveness of the ancient versions, the reliability of this tradition has been recurrently denied.[3] A new turn in the discussion has been offered by S. Lieberman. He accepted the veracity of the tradition on comparative and inner-textual grounds, and argued that the diverse terminology actually

---

[1] See the comparative evidence adduced by S. Lieberman, *Hellenism in Jewish Palestine* (New York: Feldheim, 1950), 36 f. and notes.

[2] The various lists of corrections preserved in rabbinic literature in comments on Exod. 15: 7, in Massoretic lists, and other sources, are presented and annotated in C. D. Ginsburg, *Introduction to the Hebrew Bible* (KTAV reprint; New York, 1966), 347–67; and see the more recent works of W. McKane, 'Observations on the Tikkune Sop^erim', in *On Language, Culture, and Religion: In Honor of Eugene A. Nida*, edd. M. Black and W. Smalley (The Hague: Mouton, 1974), 53–77, and C. McCarthy, *The Tiqqune Sopherim and Other Theological Corrections in the Massoretic Text of the Old Testament* (Orbis Biblicus et Orientalis, 36; Fribourg: Universitätsverlag, and Göttingen: Vandenhoeck and Ruprecht, 1981). The oldest list is found in the *Mekhilta, Beshalaḥ* 6 (to Exod. 15: 7); see the edition of H. Horowitz and I. Rabin, *Mechilta d'Rabbi Ismael* (Jerusalem: Bamberger and Wahrman, 1960), 135.

[3] See the overall comments of W. E. Barnes, 'Ancient Corrections in the Text of the Old Testament (*Tiḳḳun Sopherim*)', *JTS* 1 (1900), 387–414. Barnes's tables (393–401) give a thorough tabulation of the pertinent traditions and variations. His overall conclusion is 'that the *tiḳḳun* tradition is not Massoretic (i.e. textual) but Midrashic (i.e. exegetical or, more accurately, homiletic)'; see p. 413.

reflects the different school traditions of R. Joshua and R. Joḥanan.[4] Lieberman further suggested that the corrections were made, with one exception, for the honour of God.

Like textual and lexical comments, theological corrections or revisions reflect an intense preoccupation with authoritative text-traditions on the part of generations of tradents and schoolmen. But even more than textual annotations, theological changes underscore the fact that those persons most responsible for maintaining the orthography of the texts tampered with their wording so as to preserve the religious dignity of these documents according to contemporary theological tastes. However, the rabbis did not have to look to the neighbouring Alexandrian scribes for motivation. They were themselves heir to an older, native tradition. Thus, not only do the old rabbinic lists preserve considerable older biblical traditions of scribal corrections, but there are also examples of theological corrections in the MT unattested in rabbinic literature. Many of these more ancient examples may be recovered by means of attention to significant theological variations between parallel texts within the MT itself or between the MT and its principal versions.

1. Most rabbinic sources and Massoretic lists record that 1 Sam. 3:13 contains a תקון of the scribes. In this verse God tells Samuel that he had rejected the priestly line of Eli 'because his sons cursed להם themselves'. The use here of an ethical dative in a reflexive sense is most unlikely syntactically.[5] More importantly, such a statement bears no connection with the impious action of these sons in 1 Sam. 2:12-17, where it is stated that 'they did not know YHWH' (v. 12) and 'despised . . . the offering of YHWH' (v. 17) when they misappropriated priestly emoluments in excess of their due, prior to the sacrifice. Thus, solely on syntactical and contextual grounds one is led to suppose that להם is a deliberate scribal correction of the divine name אלהים.[6] It was introduced so as not to use the divine name in connection with a curse. As noted, this correction is listed in old rabbinic sources. Its authenticity and pre-rabbinic origin, however, are clearly indicated by

---

[4] Op. cit. 28–35. See his reference to Barnes, p. 29 n. 7. Most recently, C. McCarthy, op. cit. 120, 197, 247, has endorsed Barnes's basic contention (see n. 3 above), while conceding three genuine corrections (in 1 Sam. 3:13; Zech. 2:12; Job 7:20).

[5] Cf. Ginsburg, op. cit. 354.

[6] Rashi speculated that 'it should have read *lî*'. The Massoretic list printed by Ginsburg, op. cit. 351 n. 2, gives the reading *lô*. The forced grammatical speculation of S. R. Driver, *Notes on the Hebrew Text of the Book of Samuel* (Oxford: The Clarendon Press, 1890), ad loc., which retains *lāhem*, is not convincing.

the reading Θεόν 'god', preserved in the LXX.[7]

In a similar way, the Lucianic recension of the LXX confirms the presence of other euphemistic theological revisions unattested in rabbinic texts. These תקונים may be detected on inner-textual grounds as well. Thus, twice in Nathan's rebuke of David for killing Uriah the Hittite and taking his wife the MT mitigates the harsh theological tone of the corresponding passages in LXX[L] and 4Q Sam[b], and twice contradicts its context. In 2 Sam. 12: 9 the king is rebuked with the words 'why have you contemned *the oracle of* YHWH' in connection with his past murder and theft. As there is no reference to a divine oracle (or word) at the outset of the David–Bathsheba pericope, and the verb 'contemn' recurs in v. 10 with the Lord as object, the absence of the phrase 'the oracle of' from LXX[L] undoubtedly reflects the original reading of the passage, whereas its presence in the MT is theologically tendentious. It softens the harsh tone of the original critique.[8] A similar case can also be made for the occurrence in the ensuing v. 14 of the phrase 'the enemies of' ('you have despised *the enemies of* YHWH'): the reference to enemies is irrelevant and intrusive in the personal rebuke delivered by Nathan, and the words are also missing in LXX[L]. Here again David's impropriety against the Lord has been mitigated by a scribal alteration of the MT.[9]

One may suppose that the types of theological sensibility reflected in these foregoing corrections were probably fairly common in ancient Israel. And indeed a close inspection of parallel versions to other passages in the Books of Samuel, or to the Book of Job, for example, often reveals slight variations where the MT subverts or deflects the theological tone of the passage evidenced by archaic Hebrew manuscripts

[7] Cf. Ginsburg, op. cit. 354, and D. Barthélemy, 'Les Tiqquné Sopherim et la critique textuelle de l'Ancient Testament', *SVT* 9 (1963), 293f. In contrast to such corrections, the use of *qallēl* 'to curse' with a DN frequently led to the euphemistic substitution or formulation *bārēk* 'to bless'. Cf. Job 1: 11, 2: 5, 9, and cf. Exod. 22: 27 with its citation in 1 Kgs. 21: 10, 13. The ironic use of *bērēk* in Ps. 10: 3 was misunderstood by later tradents, who inserted the word *ni'ēṣ* 'despised'. The *pěsîq* following does not so much indicate the gloss as require a pause before the DN. The verb *ni'ēṣ* before a DN could occasion a 'correction'; cf. the discussion on 2 Sam. 12: 14, following, and nn. 9–10 below.

[8] One may note that while *bāzîtā* 'you have contemned' in v. 9 is separated from the direct object, 'YHWH', by the periphrasis, the repetition of the judgement in v. 10 simply states 'because you have contemned me (*bězîtānî*)'–i.e. YHWH. Verse 10 thus further confirms the reading in LXX[L].

[9] A tendentious revision of v. 14 was already suspected by Geiger, *Urschrift*, 267, though without manuscript evidence. 4Q Sam[a] has the variant alteration 'the oracle of YHWH'. On this phrase in 2 Sam. 9: 9, see D. Barthélemy, *Les Devanciers d'Aquila* (*SVT* 10; Leiden: E. J. Brill, 1963), 139.

(like 4Q Sam*ᵇ*) or various recensions of the LXX.[10] In fact, many other MT passages seem to give witness to just this phenomenon, although the comparative evidence is lacking for their verification.[11] In sum, then: ancient Israelite scribes did not simply transcribe their materials but altered them significantly at various points.

2. A corollary to scribal corrections concerned with preserving divine honour are those changes which remove apparent pagan elements from the text. Quite well known in this regard is the MT 'reading' בני ישראל 'people of Israel', found in Deut. 32: 8. On the surface this phrase easily comports with the content. One would not necessarily expect or suspect a problem. However, as late as medieval times a tradition was preserved among the authoritative commentators that angels or divine beings are referred to here.[12] The veracity of this tradition need not be doubted—for both the LXX at this point, and now a manuscript fragment found in the caves of Qumran, indicate that the original reading was בני אל 'divine retinue'.[13] Since one can hardly

[10] For example, MT 1 Sam. 2:17b states, regarding the sins of Eli's sons, that 'the men despised the offering of YHWH'. The reference to 'men' is redundant; cf. the reference to the same individuals as 'youths' in v. 17a. 4Q Sam*ᵇ* and LXX are without 'men', and this is a superior reading to the MT, which has undoubtedly introduced the 'corrective addition' after *ni'ăṣû* 'despised', just as in 2 Sam. 12: 14, noted above. Similarly, David's self-directed imprecation in the MT, LXX*ᴸ*, *Targ.* and Vul. 1 Sam. 25: 22 oddly mentions 'the enemies of David'. The periphrasis with 'enemies', missing in LXX*ᴬᴮ* and Syr., was probably intended to soften David's curse by his own life (cf. the periphrasis 'the enemies of' in 2 Sam. 12:14, above), although such was the normal formulation (cf. 1 Sam. 20: 13). See also the curse formulation in 1 Sam. 29: 4, and the clarifications of Kimḥi ad loc., and 1 Chron. 12: 19. Similar circumlocutions are found in rabbinic literature. Cf. *b. Ber.* 28a, 63b; *b. Yoma* 72b.

Several *tiqqûnîm* cluster in the MT of Job, e.g. (*a*) cf. *'ālay* in MT 7: 20 with the LXX (*'ālêkā*); the *tiqqûn* is already noted in the *Mekhilta*; cf. n. 3 above; (*b*) cf. *pî* in MT 9: 20 with the LXX (*piw*); (*c*) cf. *'immādî* in MT 9: 35 with the LXX (*'immādô*); (*d*) and cf. *'ăkazzēb* in MT 34: 6 with the LXX (*yikazzēb*).

[11] Note, for example, the perceptive insight of R. Gordis on Hos. 4: 15, in his 'Studies in the Relationship of Biblical and Rabbinic Hebrew', *L. Ginzberg Jubilee Volume* (New York: Jewish Theological Seminary, 1945), 195-7, that YeHuDaH is a euphemistic correction of YHWH. As a parallel instance, the absence of the first-person pronouns in 1Q p Nah. ii.10-11, citing the biblical lemma Nah. 3: 5 (cf. MT), suggests a scribal correction at Qumran to obscure direct divine involvement in the punishment which is forecast. On the other hand, I am inclined to suppose that 1Q pHab. v. 3 suggests that the *tiqqûn* recorded in several Massoretic lists for Hab. 1: 12 (*nāmût* for *yāmût*) is presupposed.

[12] Cf. Ibn Ezra, and the earlier *Tg. Yer. I*; also Ben Sira 17: 17, Jub. 15: 32.

[13] Cf. P. Skehan, 'A Fragment of the "Song of Moses" (Deut. 32) from Qumran', *BASOR* 136 (Dec. 1954), 12. The LXX reads ἄγγελοι θεοῦ in v. 8 and v. 43; and *běnê'ēlîm* may be presumed in 4Q Deut. 32 on the basis of spacing and the parallel stichoi (cf. Skehan, 12-15). On other aspects underlying the original text of Deut. 32: 8-9, see Barthélemy, op. cit. 295-302.

imagine that this *lectio difficilior* is a transformation of 'people of Israel', it stands to reason that our MT preserves a theologically motivated scribal correction. It is not reflected in the old rabbinic lists.

Such a concern to eliminate pagan references is not without parallels in the Hebrew Bible. Thus, an analysis of several old liturgical settings shows how references to the pagan 'gods' and their assemblies have been transformed: sometimes by substituting national formulae; and sometimes by orthographic changes of one sort or another.[14] In a related vein, one can still detect a theological sensitivity to the fact that the divine name Elohim is a collective plural, originally meaning 'gods'. As in later rabbinic times, when there was recurrent concern to emphasize the unity of the creator, and to leave no room for any biblical support to heretical speculations of divine multiplicity ('that they . . . do not say: "there are many powers in heaven" '—*M. Sanh.* iv. 5), ancient Israelite scribes were attentive to ambiguous formulations and 'corrected' such potential trouble-spots. Thus, in the case of Exod. 32: 4, 23, where the divine name Elohim is used with a plural verb, and the subject is clearly the God of Israel, later tradition cited the passage in a normative theological way—changing 'אלהיך your gods who העלוך took you up from Egypt' to 'אלהיך your God who העלך took you up . . .' (see Neh. 9: 18).[15] In other instances—still detectable—the aforementioned ambiguity of the term אלהים led to scribal qualifications, not orthographic changes. A notable instance is Exod. 22: 19, 'Whosoever sacrifices to אלהים will be put to death: save to YHWH alone.' The general context of apostasies in this context indicates that the legal norm was formulated against idolatrous worship, and that the syntactically disjunctive phrase 'save to YHWH alone' is a tendentious scribal addition designed to clarify any ambiguity in the word אלהים. A comparison of the major versions, like the Samaritan, reinforces this

---

[14] For the change in Ps. 7: 8, and the relationship between Pss. 29: 1-2 and 96: 7-8, see R. Tournay, 'Les Psaumes complexes', *RB* 56 (1949), 47–55; and on the relationship between Pss. 97: 9 and 99: 2, see I. L. Seeligmann, 'A Psalm from Pre-Regal Times', *VT* 14 (1964), 81 n. 1. Cf. also the suggestions of A. Gonzales, 'Le Psaume lxxxi', *VT* 13 (1963), 301 n. 1, on Exod. 15: 15, 2 Kgs. 24: 15, Ezek. 17: 13, 31: 11, 32: 21. On the likely change of the pagan DN *'azaz 'ēl* 'mighty god' to the more neutral *'ăzā'zēl* (Lev. 16: 8, 10), signifying the open country (cf. Lev. 16: 21–2), see H. Tawil, ''Azazel the Prince of the Steppe: A Comparative Study', *ZAW* 92 (1980), 58–9.

[15] As is clear from the context, it is the disappearance of Moses 'who took us up from Egypt' that prompts the popular request 'to make us gods who will go before us' (v. 1). The phrase *kî zeh mōšeh hā'îš* in this passage has long been a crux resisting grammatical clarification. In the light of the earlier discussion of deictic particles (above, pp. 51–5), one may recognize here that *zeh mōšeh* is a clarifying gloss. The original passage presumably read 'make us gods for . . . the man who took us up'; and subsequently the ambiguous 'the man' was glossed 'this is/ refers to Moses'.

estimation. For in this latter source the reading 'Whosoever sacrifices to אלהים אחרים other gods will be put to death' occurs, but with no qualifying 'save to YHWH alone'–so that it is most reasonable to conclude that the word אחרים is a theological qualification parallel to that found in the MT.[16]

The striking fact about such theological changes as the foregoing is their non-systematic nature. Indeed, in many instances a word was left intact in one place though changed elsewhere. This inconsistency suggests that many of these changes were the product of isolated scribes or scribal schools. It is thus rare to find even fairly systematic revisions of these theological trouble-spots, such as one can regularly find even in such so-called 'vulgar' or popular textual traditions as the Samaritan.[17] A partial exception occurs in the reference to 'shrine of Ashtoret' in 1 Sam. 31:10 and 'their idols' in 2 Sam. 5:21, which are changed to 'shrine of their gods' and 'their gods' in 1 Chron. 10:10 and 14:12 respectively. Similarly, it has often been suggested that the theophoric בַּעַל element in biblical personal names has been changed to בֹּשֶׁת 'shame'.[18] Traces of this apparently tendentious shift linger, in fact, in single passages. Thus, Jer. 11:13 preserves two distinct scribal layers with its reading 'altars for בֹשֶת, altars to burn incense to בעל'. Similarly, Hos. 9:10, reflecting the Pentateuchal tradition concerning Israelite worship of the local Ba'al during their sojourn at Shittim (cf. Num. 25:1,3), preserves two scribal levels as well when it reads '. . . they came to Ba'al Pe'or and defected to בשת, and became detestable שקוצים like that to which they became consecrated'. This use of the term שקוצים to refer to paganizing activity is undoubtedly an allusion to a common biblical euphemism used to characterize foreign gods (cf. שקוץ in 1 Kgs. 11:5, 7).[19] With this in mind, and recalling its association with בעל and בשת in Hos. 9:10, there is further support for the old view that the improbable reference to a שקוץ (מ)שֹׁמֵם ('the abomination which makes desolate') in Dan. 11:31, 12:11 is itself a sarcastic correction from an

---

[16] Alternatively, it is speculated that the Samar. reading *'ĕlōhîm 'ăhērîm yāḥorām* is original and that the MT qualification became necessary after the haplography of *'āḤēRim* to the following *yāḤoRaM* in the MT *Vorlage*. Cf. M. Noth, *Exodus* (OTI; Philadelphia: Westminster, 1962), 186; but the view is well established in the commentaries. LXX^A is a more composite tradition.

[17] Cf. Gen. 20:13, 31:53, 35:7, and Exod. 22:8, where the MT retains a plural verb with *'ĕlōhîm*, but the Samar. consistently renders a singular form. Weiss, *Studies* (op. cit. above, p. 38 n. 55), 75–186, has collected considerable evidence to counter the view that Samar. was unsystematic in its revisions.

[18] See already A. Geiger, 'Der Baal in den hebräischen Eigennamen', *ZDMG* 16 (1862), 728–32.

[19] Note, however, that v. 8 retains the term *'ĕlōhîm* for the pagan gods (also the LXX). By contrast, the MT at v. 33 has *'ĕlōhê* while the LXX changes it to 'abomination'.

* original בעל שָׁמֶם 'Ba'al of the heavens'.[20]

3. Concern for theologically problematic statements also resulted in textual corrections. Such an instance is evident when one compares 2 Sam. 8:18 and 1 Chron. 18:17. The first text records the fact that 'Benayahu, son of Jehoiada, and (–ן) the Cerethites and the Pelethites, and the sons of David were priests'. This statement is altogether puzzling, since neither Benayahu nor David was a priest, and since the Cerethites and Pelethites were Aegean mercenaries. The Chronicler was clearly aware of the theological difficulties involved in having David's sons reckoned as priests, and so replaced the word 'priests' with the paraphrase 'first by the side of the King'. The tendentious nature of this revision holds even if this paraphrase might be an accurate translation for a rare technical usage of 'priests'.[21] The Chronicler also replaced the
* conjunctive 'and (–ן) the Cerethites' with 'over (על) the Cerethites', and so further mitigated the offensive implications of 2 Sam. 8:18. The result is that Benayahu the warrior is now recorded as head of the mercenaries, while David's sons serve as his right-hand men. The historical and theological differences between these texts make it more likely that 1 Chron. 18:17 is a correction, not an alternative version, of 2 Sam. 8:18.

4. Another series of tendentious corrections are those concerned with the religious deportment of royalty. Thus, when the prophet Ahiyah sought out Jeroboam for an oracle near the end of Solomon's reign, Ahiyah cited the word of God that while the united Kingdom would be taken from Solomon (1 Kgs. 11:31), one tribe would remain 'for him', for the sake of David and Jerusalem (v. 32).[22] However, the reason given for this censure of Solomon in v. 33 is odd: 'because *they* abandoned me and [*they*] prostrated themselves to Ashtoret, god of the Sidonians, to Cemosh, god of Moab, and to Milcom, god of the people of Ammon, and [*they*] did not go in my ways . . . like David his father.' The plural verbs used in this passage are improbable, given the singular references to Solomon in vv. 31-2, at the end of v. 33, and in the ensuing vv. 34-6. Moreover, Ahiyah's oracle follows almost verbatim that already given to Solomon himself in vv. 11-13. Solomon is charged there (in the singular!) with not having obeyed the covenant, since he built open-air sanctuaries and altars for the gods of the Sidonians, Ammonites, and Moabites (vv. 5, 7-10). Given the unexpected and awkward use of the plural verbs in v. 33, together with the prior

[20] E. Nestle, 'Zu Daniel', *ZAW* 4 (1884), 284.

[21] LXX αὐλάρχαι suggests some tradition 'intepreting' *kōhănîm* as 'chiefs of the court', or the like.

[22] For the likely historical background and motivation for this oracle, see A. Caquot, 'Ahiyya de Silo et Jeroboam Ier', *Semitica*, 11 (1961), 17-27.

recitation of the oracle to Solomon in the singular, there can be little doubt that the plural verbs in v. 33 are a deliberate correction to obscure the culpability of King Solomon. This inner-textual conclusion is reinforced by the fact that the LXX and other versions preserve singular verbs throughout the verse.

5. A similar theological correction of singular to plural verbs can be noted by comparing 1 Kgs. 3: 4 with its parallel in 2 Chron. 1: 3. As above, the import of the change is to dilute the individual ritual impropriety of Solomon. Thus, the historical notice in the Book of Kings, that 'the King went וַיֵּלֶךְ to Gibeon to slaughter there, for כִּי it was the great high place . . .', clearly indicates that Solomon engaged in non-centralized worship outside of Jerusalem. This act bore no cultic impropriety in Solomon's day; it was, however, decidedly problematic for later theologians. The post-exilic deuteronomic historians who sought to project their notion of cult centralization back into the post-conquest period, and who wished to see Solomon as the chief protagonist of such a process, were understandably perplexed by this old stratum of tradition even though they felt compelled to preserve it. This perplexity is clear from the ambivalent praise with which these historians introduced this tradition: 'Solomon loved YHWH, following in the ordinances of David his father – except that he continued to slaughter and burn incense at the high places' (v. 3).[23]

The Chronicler took an even more decisive approach than the deuteronomic historians. Citing his sources about Solomon's attendance at the high place in Gibeon (1 Kgs. 3: 4), the Chronicler elaborated upon these records and indicated that all the people participated in this event: 'Solomon, and all the congregation with him, went וַיֵּלְכוּ to the high place in Gibeon – for כִּי there was the Tent of Meeting of Elohim, built by Moses, the servant of YHWH, in the desert . . . as well as the bronze altar, which Bezalel b. Uri b. Hur had built in front of the

---

[23] The qualifying clause ('except that . . .') is in close proximity to the similar expression used regarding the people's worship at high places 'because a temple to the name of YHWH had not yet been built' (v. 2). However, it is striking that the latter justification is not applied to Solomon. The language criticizing illegitimate cultic practices is of the same stereotypic cast as that used against the people *after* the Temple was established (e.g. 2 Kgs. 12: 4, 14: 4, 15: 4, 35). These latter expressions usually follow references to the actions of an immediate royal ancestor, although sometimes the royal ancestor David is mentioned (cf. 1 Kgs. 14: 3); they are syntactically complete, with subject and object, and they deal with cultic behaviour. Given the attempts to mitigate the royal actions of Solomon, 1 Kgs. 15: 3–5 is of interest: following the standard repertory of elements, v. 5b adds the *moral* observation (irrelevant to the cultic context) that David did right 'except in the matter of Uriah the Hittite'. The clause is missing from the LXX, and undoubtedly reflects a later censure of David.

Tabernacle of YHWH.' With these changes and expansions the Chronicler sought to present the actions of Solomon in a somewhat favourable light.[24]

The full extent of the Chronicler's literary subtlety and theological inventiveness (if not daring) is only alluded to in the preceding example.[25] Indeed, the purpose of our discussing the shift from a singular (in 1 Kgs. 3:4) to a plural verb (in 2 Chron. 1:3) is not so much to suggest how the Chronicler reworked his historical sources as to highlight the peculiarly *scribal* nature of the shift from singular to plural in the earlier example, 1 Kgs. 11:33. For it is clear that scribal alteration in 1 Kgs. 11:33—as determined from its MT context and the LXX—is of an isolated and disruptive nature; whereas the verbal shift in 2 Chron. 1:3 is part of a more expansive revision by the Chronicler of 1 Kgs. 3:4. Notably, the Chronicler has both altered the verb in question and expanded upon his source, stating that 'Solomon, *and all the congregation with him*, went . . .'. By contrast with this expansion, 1 Kgs. 11:33 gives witness to a meagre and unsystematic revision. It is just this element which marks the change as the work of a scribe—not a historiographer.

B. PIOUS AND THEOLOGICAL REACTIONS

If the preceding examples reflect unsystematic corrections of a fairly fixed scribal agenda—a particular concern for divine and royal honour is reflected, as well as a concerted interest in excising or changing certain references to the 'gods' and their shrines—there is another type of scribal feature which deserves mention: *ad hoc* theological interpolations motivated by context and content. For in the process of *traditio*—be that acts of transcription, instruction, or recitation—it was inevitable that the content of the *traditum* would occasionally elicit such pious and theological reactions as are now scribally incorporated into the received text. These responses are varied, differ in theological subtlety and scope, and commonly give expression to dominant strands of

---

[24] Since the researches of S. Hermann, 'Die Königsnovelle in Ägypten und Israel', *Wissenschaftliche Zeitschrift der Karl Marx Universität* (gesellschafts- und sprachwissenschaftliche Reihe, 3, 1954-5), 51-62, the opinion has solidified— with revisions (cf. M. Weinfeld, *Deuteronomy and the Deuteronomic School*, 250-2)—that Solomon's dream in 1 Kgs. 3, upon which the Chronicler draws, is a literary topos. It therefore deserves note that the Chronicler seems to have preserved the preliterary reasons that Solomon goes to Gibeon: to offer sacrifices, to receive divine assurances, *and to be crowned king* (2 Chron. 1:8, 11-12, and esp. v. 13). The record in 1 Kgs. 4:1 that Solomon became king has been displaced from the Gibeon event by the tale of wisdom in 3:16-28—and so the original *Sitz im Leben* of the event is obscured.

[25] Other examples of cultic-legal changes will be discussed in Part Two, below.

biblical religious values. Among the latter one may include comments dealing with personal fate,[26] national salvation,[27] or the observance of the Torah.[28]

These brief considerations bear on an interpolation found in the Blessing of Moses, Deut. 33. In fact, this interpolation is of particular interest here in the light of the earlier discussion of the toponymic remark found in Ps. 68: 9. In that context, it will be recalled, scribes or scribal tradition correctly perceived the historical sequence and geographical itinerary in Ps. 68: 8-13 and identified the storm imagery in v. 9a – occurring between allusions to the exodus and the desert wanderings, on the one side, and the land settlement on the other – as 'Sinai', the mountain of the theophany. With the increasing significance which the dominant textual tradition of the Sinaitic theophany in Exod. 19 must háve imposed upon biblical culture, together with the fact that this theophany tradition was but the prelude to the revelation of divine laws and commandments (Exod. 20-3), one can easily understand that biblical scribes and tradents would be quick to locate references to this monumental Sinaitic event in any text which offered the slightest clue. In this way they could draw older traditions into the orbit of the ideologies of Sinai and Torah which developed at a later time.

These reflections illuminate the case of Deut. 33. For this Blessing of Moses, which refers to an ancient assembly of the Israelite tribes and its leaders,[29] begins with the remark (v. 2):

(*a*) YHWH has come from Sinai, and shone from Seir for them;
(*b*) he has appeared from Paran, and arrived from the desert of Qadesh.
(*c*) At his right hand: a fiery stream – for them.

Now it is clear from this opening stanza that ancient Israel was heir to old theophanic traditions which describe a divine advent from the south:[30] indeed the toponymic references hardly leave this in doubt. And since, moreover, there is nothing in this description of the overall *mise-en-scène* of the Blessing which would remotely suggest that Sinai is to be particularly distinguished from the other desert and mountain

---

[26] Cf. Num. 23:10b, and the comment of P. Haupt in J. A. Paterson, *The Book of Numbers* (Sacred Books of the Old Testament, 4; Leipzig: J. C. Hinrichs, 1900), 57.

[27] Cf. Gen. 49: 18, and the rationale in *Gen. Rab.* 98: 14.

[28] On Pss. 78:10 and 105:45, see I. L. Seeligmann, 'Cultic Tradition and Historiographical Creativity in Scripture', in *Religion and Society* (The Historical Society of Israel: Jerusalem, 1964, 59-61 [Heb.].

[29] Cf. the discussion of I. L. Seeligmann, 'A Psalm from Pre-Regal Times', 75-92.

[30] e.g. Judg. 5: 4. The similarity of v. 5 to Ps. 68: 9, including the gloss *zeh sînay*, is notable. The geographic itinerary in Ps. 68: 8-13 suggests that the gloss occurred there first.

locales mentioned, or that the occasion is one of lawgiving or covenant-making (and indeed the liturgy reflects the *settled* nature of the tribes in the land *to which* the ancient desert-storm god now comes), it is certain that the great Sinaitic theophany is not involved.[31] For later rabbinic thought, on the other hand, it was inconceivable that the reference to Sinai in v. 2 was simply a geographic reference among others—part of a divine advent topos, in fact—and not an allusion to the great moment of the Sinaitic revelation.[32] Their sensibility was directed to this view by the fact that Sinai was the first of the locales mentioned, and was reinforced by an interpretation which sprang from this view: for they interpreted the enigmatic אשדת 'fiery stream' as אש דת 'fiery law'.[33]

But howsoever fanciful and tendentious this interpretation may appear through historical hindsight, there can be no doubt that it reflects an authentic 'reading' of the *traditum* from a 'torahistic' perspective: for a precisely similar attitude is already embedded in the received text by an ancient Israelite glossator. Thus, in v. 4—following the description of the divine advent with his holy entourage (vv. 2-3) and before the description of the Israelite tribal assemblage and their proclamation of divine kingship (v. 5)—we find 'Moses commanded the Torah to us; an inheritance of the congregation of Jacob.' The secondary nature of this striking remark is not in question. For one thing, the notion of a Mosaic lawgiving is entirely out of keeping with the temporal context and concern of this ancient piece; for another, the passage disrupts the immediate scenario-context, describing the divine advent and the national assembly; and, finally, the verse is stylistically distinct, being formulated in the first person plural, whereas the surrounding context is in the third person singular and plural.

Much more than the identification of the tremulous imagery in Ps. 68: 9 with Mt. Sinai, then, where at least the context is supportive of this attribution, the scribal addition in Deut. 33: 4 is a theological *tour de force*—a forceful theological intrusion—which contemporizes the neutral topographic imagery of v. 2 in the light of developing (but independent) covenantal-nomistic concerns. The nature of the scribal annotation in Deut. 33: 4 also suggests that the remark may not derive from scribal circles in the strict sense, but may just as much owe its

[31] Cf. Seeligmann, loc. cit. 78-80.

[32] Cf. *Sifre Deut.* 343 (Friedmann, 142b). See, too, the interpretation of v. 3bβ, *yiśśā' middabrōtêkā*, ibid. (Friedmann, 143b); and cf. Rashi, Ibn Ezra and Ramban, ad loc.

[33] e.g. in *b. Ber.* 6a, *b. Soṭa* 4b. See the discussion and review of modern opinions in L. Blau, 'Zwei dunkle Stellen im Segen Moses (Dt. 33: 2-3, 24-25)', in *Jewish Studies in Memory of G. Kohut*, edd. S. Baron and A. Marx (New York: The Alexander Kohut Memorial Foundation, 1935), 95-6.

origin to the ongoing liturgical recitation and teaching of this Blessing long after the pre-monarchic tribal confederation which it describes. From this perspective, the scribes were the means whereby the oral *traditio* of this text was incorporated into the *traditum*. However, the possibility remains that the rhetors and teachers of this Blessing were, in fact, its scribal tradents as well. Be this as it may, the comment in Deut. 33: 4 is a truly remarkable witness to the living exegetical tradition of ancient Israel, which adapted this ancient Blessing to later ideological realities. Significantly, the LXX and the Greek text of Ben Sira 24: 23, which quotes this verse, show an even later contemporizing exegesis of Deut. 33: 4 when they translate קהלת יעקב 'congregation of Jacob' with κληρονομίαν συναγωγαῖς Ιακωβ. In this way they brought the ancient tribal 'congregation'—which inherited the Mosaic Torah—into line with the 'synagogue of Jacob', established many centuries later.[34]

[34] See also Seeligmann, 79 n. 1.

4. Conclusions

A. In comparison with the records and traditions available from Mesopotamia and Egypt, the extant testimonies to scribal activity preserved in the Hebrew Bible are meagre and difficult to evaluate. Nevertheless, ancient Israel had a long and multifaceted scribal practice. The intent of the preceding analyses has been, therefore, to call attention to this long history and its diverse aspects, while giving particularly close attention to a typology of the exegetical content, concerns, and techniques of the scribes of ancient Israel.

The official political and bureaucratic role of scribes is attested in biblical sources beginning with the royal council established by David (2 Sam. 8: 16-18~20: 23-5).[1] This role is complemented by the particular involvement of diverse groups of scribal tradents in the transmission of the several major genres of ancient Israelite literature (for example, the cultic-legal, the historical, the wisdom, and the liturgical, among others). There is certainly no evidence that only scribes from the priestly guilds transcribed and transmitted Torah-instructions; or that only scribes from within prophetic or wisdom circles worked on their corresponding materials. In fact, scribes from the wisdom tradition were manifestly involved in the transmission of Torah-texts (cf. Jer. 8: 8); and there is evidence suggesting that prophetic groups and attitudes were involved in the shaping and composition of historiographical literature.[2] Nevertheless, it is reasonable that those groups most familiar with certain types of literature would have had primary involvement in their transmission, and in the development of distinct stylistic features. Thus, the colophon formulary of the cultic-legal material (e.g. x‑ל התורה זאת, x‑ה תורת זאת) is easily distinguished from the colophon formularies found in prophetic (cf. הנה עד), liturgical (cf. כלו), and wisdom literature (cf. תמו).[3] Similarly, the title formulary – the superscriptions – of the different biblical genres also

---

[1] Above, pp. 25.

[2] In addition to the dominant role played by the fulfilment of prophecies in the Books of Kings, discussed by von Rad, 'The Deuteronomic Theology of History in *I & II Kings*', in *The Problem of the Hexateuch and other Essays* (New York: McGraw Hill, 1966), 205-21, and the interventionist role of prophets in Chronicles, on which see Part Three below, note the reference in 2 Chron. 26: 22 to a royal chronicle composed by a prophet and the interpolation of references to prophetic sources in the formulaic notices found in 2 Chron. 32: 2, 33:18.

[3] Above, pp. 27-9 and notes.

shows clear stylistic distinctions not explainable solely by the different contents of the materials transmitted.

From such evidence one can reasonably assume that different scribal circles developed their own specialized vocabularies and technical procedures within the larger framework of a common scribal enterprise.[4] By the same token, one may also assume that such scribal networks were closely affiliated with certain institutional groups—like the priests, prophets, or sages—if they were not, in fact, distinct components within them. For not merely the aforementioned interest to preserve certain sources, but also the technical competence to annotate specialized materials, would certainly derive primarily from those groups most interested in their accurate preservation and comprehension. Nevertheless, it is noteworthy that no stratum of biblical literature—including its most technically esoteric cultic prescriptions—ever records anything resembling the comments in comparable Mesopotamian ritual-ceremonial texts which state that they are 'secret', or are for 'initiate-scholars' only.[5] One may therefore assume that the natural tendency for scribes to specialize, and for certain groups to train their own scribes, would account for the variations in ancient Israelite scribal vocabulary and for the scribal expertise manifest in various technical genres.

Certain technical features, like the copying, checking, and collation of manuscripts, were undoubtedly part of the standard repertoire of all scribal groups. Accordingly, textual variants found in different or better manuscripts, from the same or different scribal traditions, were incorporated into the standard school recensions of all genres at all times.[6] Although this record of ancient Israelite copyist activity is embedded unmarked in the *traditum* transmitted, it is often easily enough detected and objectively validated by manifest stylistic redundancies in the MT and by comparison with the principal versions.[7] In a few special instances, however, detailed records of these scribal processes are

---

[4] That there are many remarkable reflexes of cuneiform formulae in biblical contexts we have seen in detail; cf. above, pp. 30–2. On Jer. 32: 10–14 and similar scribal-legal traditions in Mesopotamia and Qumran, see my remarks in *HUCA* 75 (1974), 34. Of further interest is the biblical reuse of colophonic terms in new stylistic formulations. Cf. my remarks on Deut. 4: 2, 13: 1, and Jer. 26: 2 in 'Varia Deuteronomica', 350.

[5] For representative texts and terms, see R. Borger, 'Geheimwissen', *RLA* iii. 188–91, and *CAD*, N, ii. 276 f., M, ii. 166.

[6] Two major types of this phenomenon are synonymous and double readings, on which cf. S. Talmon, 'Synonymous Readings' (above, p. 38 n. 56), and 'Double Readings in the Massoretic Text', *Textus*, 1 (1960), 144–84. A third type is the conflation of variants, on which see R. Gordis, *The Biblical Text in the Making* (augmented edn.; New York: Philadelphia: KTAV, 1971 [1st edn., 1937]), 41–3, and 'The Antiquity of the Massora in the Light of Rabbinic Literature and the Dead Sea Scrolls', *Tarbiz*, 27 (1958), 24–6 [Heb.].

[7] For example, see the studies in the previous note.

actually preserved in the Hebrew Bible. This is the case with respect to the addendum to the Book of Ecclesiastes (12: 9-12) studied above, which articulates a particularly detailed description of the type of scribal activity which could have transpired in wisdom schools—if not more broadly—at any time.[8] But although these activities were ongoing, and were, in the main, routine in nature, they were undoubtedly intensified during periods of historical crisis or national-religious renewal—like the retrieval of the cultic and historical literature of the north after the fall of Samaria, the reuse of old manuscripts and traditions during the promulgation of the Book of Deuteronomy during the Josianic cult reform, or the transmission of pre-exilic texts after the return to Zion. Such periods of copying and transmission would have been prime occasions for the correction of orthographic and textual details, and for incorporating into the master texts speculations, annotations, and assorted marginalia which had accumulated in the normal course of text study.[9]

The occurrence of scribal exegesis and textual alterations varies in quantity and occasion from genre to genre and from issue to issue; but there is no indication that any type of style is restricted to any particular genre or to any particular issue. Indeed, the deictic or indicative elements הוא, היא, זה, and את introduce comments in a variety of genres; and their function varies in accordance with the matter to be explained. Thus, הוא or היא may contemporize a toponym in a historical text (e.g. Gen. 14: 7; Josh. 18:13), or clarify an obscured reference in prophetic discourse (cf. Ezek. 31:18b); זה may clarify an obscure textual reference in a historical text (cf. Ezra 3:12), or clarify the implicit antecedent in a liturgical text (Ps. 68:9); and את may introduce new specifications in prophetic oracles (Hag. 2:5a), or simply mis- or reapply them (cf. Isa. 29:10). Where deictic elements are not found, the new comment is simply juxtaposed to the textual element to be explained; although, as noted, the frequency of this device suggests that it was a fixed part of annotative conventions.

---

8 See above, pp. 29-32.

9 We may actually have scribal comments on their copying poor manuscripts. Two examples may be singled out. The first is that of J. Bewer, 'Some Ancient Variants in Hosea with Scribe's or Corrector's Mark', *JBL* 30 (1911), 61, who offered an intriguing solution to the old text problem in Hos. 9:13, with his speculation that *ka'ăšer rā'îtî* 'as I have seen', is an old copyist's comment. In a similar way, F. E. Peiser, 'Obadiah 6-7', *OLZ* 20/9 (1917), 278, proposed that *'ên tĕbûnāh bô* does not mean that Edom is without wisdom, but is a scribal remark that the text is incomprehensible. Apart from the contextual merit of these proposals, it is notable that, apparently unknown to either author, both types of comments occur in Akkadian texts. Cf. the gloss NU IGI (= *ul āmur*) 'I cannot read [it]' (e.g. 4 R 53. ii. 32; see *RLA* iii. 438) and the remark *ul idî* 'I cannot understand [it]'. On this last, cf. F. Köcher, 'Ein akkadischer mediziner Schülertext aus Boğazköy', *AfO* 16 (1952-3), 48. 9, and the comment on p. 53.

In all the aforementioned cases, then, the formal hermeneutical method is straightforward: explanations elicited by obscurities *within* the text are secondarily *added to it*. The hermeneutical issues involved, on the other hand, can be inferred only from the result. To do this, one must first hypothesize the textual problem or concern presumably felt by the ancients on the basis of their recorded comments. These concerns evidently range from straightforward toponymic annotations (e.g. Gen. 14: 7) to considered proto-Massoretic observations (cf. Ps. 61: 8b). In some cases, the comments are undoubtedly based on genuine semantic analyses (e.g. Ezra 3:12); in others, they appear to reflect an established lexical tradition rather than a purely philological deduction (cf. Lev. 19:19; Deut. 22:9). The solutions or comments in each case are thus *ad hoc* and contextual. This type of exegesis does not require more.

Ancient Israelite scribes were also involved in theological corrections or modifications of their received texts. According to early rabbinic traditions stemming from the Tannaitic period, corrections wrought in the MT for the sake of 'divine honour' are found in all the textual genres. As noted, some of these rabbinic traditions can be corroborated on the basis of variants found in the ancient versions; other examples not attested in these traditions can be deduced from contextual analysis and corroborated by the evidence of the major and minor versions, as well as the Qumran manuscripts. A notable feature to emerge from the MT cases of scribal changes identified above is the preponderance of corrections or additions found in non-Pentateuchal literature: both those intended to mitigate references to the divinity in contexts recording oaths or curses, and those introduced for the sake of 'royal honour'.

In these various instances, the hermeneutical techniques vary from changes of personal pronouns to periphrastic and often contradictory supplementations. Thus, like the lexical and semantic exegeses referred to earlier, the techniques found among the theological corrections are straightforward; and, again like the lexical and semantic exegeses, the hermeneutical issues underlying the theological corrections are subject to inference in every case. Nevertheless, it would be quite accurate to say that the theological corrections are not motivated by grammatical or verbal ambiguity but by a perceived theological dissonance between the wording of the received *traditum* and the religious values and sensibilities of the reader or tradent. Indeed, the entirely remarkable result is that the attitudes of the *traditio* have qualified or modified this *traditum* for all future generations. And the degree to which this scribal *tour de force* has imposed itself on the *traditum* is clearly reflected in the fact—and not this one alone—that changes introduced to preserve the pious quality of the textual artefact were often achieved at the expense of semantic and grammatical sense. One may propose that in some cases the *traditum* was read according to the received orthography while the euphemistic *traditio* was kept apart, as an oral exegesis; in other cases, perhaps, the orthographic *traditum* was retained but the text was read according to the *traditio*; and in still other cases, those which now constitute our MT, the euphemistic *traditio* became the orthographic *traditum* as well. These possibilities may serve to suggest the sequential reality for some changes, and, at the same time, the larger synoptic situation.

To be sure, all lexical and theological corrections in the MT are not exhausted by the several examples reviewed above. The foregoing have been presented because they can be methodologically verified in one way or another. Many other cases are deeply embedded in the *traditum* beyond scholarly recall; while still others are embedded in the text in an undistinguishable way, although the dim ray of ancient tradition often searches them out. To take one example: according to a very old rabbinic tradition, the conjunctive *waw* was removed by scribes in five places in Scripture so as to restore readings preserved among the scribes themselves.[10] Clearly the conjunctive *waw* was added to the original *waw*-less *traditum* by later scribes in order to alleviate thorny semantic and syntactic ambiguities: for it was often disturbingly unclear whether a given clause was to be construed with what precedes or follows it. The authenticity of this particular tradition can be partially verified by a comparison of the MT with the Samar. readings in the five afore-mentioned MT cases; for in all of the cases the Samar. has a 'simplifying' reading with a *waw*. Furthermore, in three of the instances the LXX has the conjunctive καί. If this feature is not simply an inner-Greek development the old *traditum* recalled by the rabbis may be preserved here as well. Even more striking, however, are those instances where 1Q Isa.*a* differs from the MT also by reason of a conjunctive *waw* apparently inserted to resolve an issue of semantic ambiguity.[11] As against these 1Q Isa.*a* readings, the *lectio difficilior* of the MT is to be preferred.

The variations between texts within the MT, and between it and the versions and Qumran manuscript fragments, are thus valuable aids in the discernment of scribal comments and corrections, and attest to different scribal readings and exegetical traditions at different times. By the same token, the diverse LXX expansions to Isaiah,[12] or the LXX

---

[10] These are the *'itûrê sōpĕrîm* listed in *b. Ned.* 37b. Of the five passages, four – Gen. 18: 5, 24: 55, Num. 31: 2, and Ps. 68: 26 – involve the adverb *'aḥar*; the fifth text is Ps. 36: 7. Note the reason given for the insertion of the *waw* in the medieval *Aruch Completum*, ed. G. Kohut (New York: Pardes, 1926), vi. 189.

[11] See A. Eliner, 'Ambiguous Scriptural Readings in Isaiah in Light of the Qumran Scrolls', *Publications of the Israel Society of Biblical Research*, i, S. Dim Volume (Jerusalem: Qiryat Sepher, 1958), 280–3 [Heb.].

[12] See J. Ziegler, *Untersuchungen zur Septuaginta des Buches Isaias* (Münster in Westfalen: Aschendorffschen Verlagbuchhandlung, 1934), 103–75.

expansions to Jeremiah,[13] are also more often evidence for the intrusion or exegetical and ideological traditions than indicative of real textual variants. Moreover, as evidence for living school traditions, the MT scribal features discussed above reciprocally indicate the development of an authoritative text. For despite the fact that the various scribal changes and additions reflect a period of notable manuscript fluidity and scribal freedom, these addenda and explications were interpolated into authorized text copies. Both points are significant: Israelite scribes did not simply transcribe textual materials believed to be divinely revealed or otherwise authoritative; they intensively studied them and left us a record of their *traditio* in the received *traditum*.

There need be little doubt that the intimate acquaintance of the ancient Israelite scribes with textual minutiae bearing on orthographic details and verbal and syntactic sense increased over time—owing to their own competence and associations with priests and legists—and contributed to the development of those exegetical methods which required exact knowledge of the full scope of the *traditum* for intra-textual correlations, combinations, and harmonizations. Our biblical sources do not permit us to grasp—save by inference—the full organic movement from technical scribal competence to comprehensive textual knowledge, and from there to the role of the scribes in the development of textual exegesis in its diversity of techniques and concerns. Nevertheless, some documentary traces do exist. For example, it will be recalled that Ezra, a leader of the post-exilic restoration, was both a priest and a scribe, and that his retinue of interpreters were clerics as well (cf. Ezra 7: 1-6; Neh. 8: 1-9). This is significant: for, as we shall have occasion to remark in the next Part, the exile provided those priestly literati who were expert in matters of cultic purities and sancta (cf. Lev. 10: 8-11), or specialists in the diagnosis of contagions (cf. Lev. 11-15), the great occasion to consolidate their traditions and become conversant with textual ambiguities and contradictions. The inevitable alliance between these priests and scribes who were (also) the custodians of the *traditum* would have stimulated a cross-fertilization leading to true exegesis (the interpretation of ambiguities, the clarification of obscurities, the reconciliation of variations, etc.). To be sure, no *terminus a quo* can be set for such processes; their origins were even pre-exilic, as the evidence of the next Part will indicate. Nevertheless, the centrality of a priest-scribe (Ezra) at the beginning of the restoration period—one who was also a master exegete and the leader of exegetes—should not pass unnoticed in its pivotal and symbolic significance for later, more fully documented trends. For if our inner-biblical evidence

[13] Cf. A. W. Streane, *The Double Text of Jeremiah* (Cambridge: D. Bell, 1896), 18-19, 21, etc.

is allusive and incomplete, early Tannaitic sources are much more specific. In fact, an examination of these old rabbinic records clearly shows a clear line of historical developments from scribes who were professional copyists[14] – sustained by the Temple treasury and most probably priests[15] – to exegetical activities designated as 'teachings of the scribes'.[16] Indeed, it has been acutely noted that this early hermeneutical activity of the ancient Jewish bookmen developed from their precise textual knowledge of Scripture, and that their precise textual observations subsequently influenced the exegetical techniques of the rabbinic sages – a distinct class which began to interpret Scripture with an eagle eye for its scribal minutiae.[17]

B. Despite the high degree of professionalism found in ancient Israelite scribal practice, it is nevertheless quite noticeable that scribal comments – with and without deictic elements – are unsystematic in character.[18] One would be hard pressed to know why in any case this is so – i.e., why a certain type of comment appears only in one place rather than another; or why one type of revision or correction was not systematically carried through in the same text or cluster of texts. Certainly, as suggested earlier, the occasional nature of these comments is strong presumptive evidence for their *scribal* nature. Had these comments actually been the work of a more comprehensive historiographical revision, as we may here generally characterize Chronicles' relationship to Samuel-Kings, more systematic procedures might be expected. At the same time, the unsystematic nature of scribal changes – as, for example, the simplification or contemporization of terms via a

---

[14] According to the later pseudo-etymology in *b. Qidd.* 30a, the scribes 'were called *sōpĕrîm* because they used to count all the letters of the Torah'.

[15] Cf. *yer. Šeqal.* iv. 2 and *b. Ketub.* 106a. Of further interest in this regard is the exegesis of priests noted in the *M. Šeqal.* vi. 6, xi. 4. A contemporary, Jonathan ben Uzziel, translated 'priest and prophet' as 'priest and scribe'. Cf. Isa. 28: 7, Jer. 18: 18. On the γραμματεῖς τοῦ ἱεροῦ in the letter of Antiochus III (in *Antiq.* xii 3. 142), see E. Bickermann, 'La Charte Seleucide de Jérusalem', in *Studies in Jewish and Christian History* (Leiden: E. J. Brill, 1980), ii. 59–60.

[16] On this term, cf. *M. 'Or.* iii. 9. The records indicate that the scribes taught Scripture and some Mishna (cf. *M. Ned.* ix. 2; *M. Qidd.* iv. 13). On the whole line of development noted here, with an exhaustive review of the sources, see E. Urbach, 'The Exegetical Sermon', 166–82.

[17] This is the significant conclusion reached by E. E. Urbach, op. cit., esp. 178–82. As indicated here briefly, I see no reason to restrict this observation to the post-biblical era. Much pertinent evidence will be considered in Part Two.

[18] I do not understand how one could conclude otherwise. The estimation of J. Koenig, 'L'Activité herméneutique des scribes', *RHR* 144 (1962), 162, that scribal revisions are an 'activité méthodique', is hardly justified by the evidence reviewed above or by his few examples (even granting the validity of his interpretations).

(more or less) synonymic counterpart—in one text, like the Books of Chronicles, without the corresponding correction in the parallel Books of Samuel-Kings, is evidence for *local* text recensions and scribal practices that were restricted in scope. Scribes who revised or annotated Chronicles were thus, evidently, not involved in scribal revisions of other—even parallel—historical sources.

The intrusion of scribal comments into the *traditum* may serve to refocus a related consideration: the relationship between scribes and composers (or authors). It was suggested above that the random nature of written lexical exegesis suggests scribal as against authorial activities. This said, it also bears comment that the boundary-line between scribes and authors is often quite difficult to draw in biblical literature, and, in some cases, involves precarious judgements. For if, on the one hand, the affiliation of scribes with groups for whom certain texts were a speciality or prerogative would explain the expert knowledge of scribes in somewhat esoteric areas, it would also explain the readiness of these scribes to incorporate certain interpretations into the authoritative text. Many scribes undoubtedly saw themselves as the cultural allies of the composers—teachers of their meanings and reporters of their teachings —and so composers in a derivative sense. And if, in fact, the scribes also belonged to the institutional groups which composed and taught these texts, and therefore regarded their addenda as part and parcel of the larger guild composition, there would be additional reason to consider the demarcation between scribe and author somewhat artificial.

Whether the one or the other of these two options is true, and how, it is of pertinent interest here to note that in a number of areas one may plot a continuum between purely scribal-redactional procedures on the one hand, and authorial-compositional ones, on the other. To take one example: a careful analysis of many biblical texts shows that one means whereby interpolations of new material entered the original *traditum* is the verbatim (or very similar) repetition after a distinct sequence of material of the words in the original text which immediately preceded the break.[19] In cases where there are clear generic and thematic differences between a continuous text and a sequence of material within it, as, for example, the occurrence of a genealogy in a historical narrative (cf. 2 Sam. 3:1-6), or a visionary oracle in a narrative with different promises (cf. Gen. 15:13-16), there is presumptive likelihood that a scribe or scribal redactor has added new material *after the fact*. However, such types as these shade off very rapidly into those literary

---

[19] This is the so-called *Wiederaufnahme*, first isolated as a textual phenomenon by H. Weiner, *The Composition of Judges II 11 to 1 Kings II 46* (Leipzig: J. C. Hinrichs, 1929), 2, and by C. Kuhl, 'Die "Wiederaufnahme"—ein literarisches Prinzip?', *ZAW* 64 (1952), 1-11.

intrusions which appear to have been incorporated *at the time of a text's revision.* An example is the conquest account and prophetic scenario found in Judg. 1:1-2:5. These texts interrupt a repeated notice of Joshua's death (Josh. 24:29-33 and Judg. 2:6-9)—but nevertheless appear to be part of a larger compositorial redaction of the materials rather than an isolated interpolation. The indistinct boundaries between scribal and authorial activities suggested here are even more obscured, however, when the material is of the same genre (for example, law; cf. Lev. 24:10-24, esp. vv. 17-21), until in the end one is presented with a situation such as the repeated notice of the sale of Joseph by tradesmen to Potiphar in Egypt (cf. Gen. 37:36 and 39:1). In this latter case the repetition frames the distinct story of Judah and Tamar and serves such highly authorial functions as regulating narrative tempo, introducing separate—though morally related—scenes, and creating a synchronous time-perspective. One may say that the only point on this spectrum—of phrases repeated at the beginning and end of a text—where an authorial feature is clearly distinguishable from a scribal one is when an *inclusio* is involved.[20] The latter is manifestly a stylistic device which frames a text and marks its own integrity: it does not mark off another literary unit.

These several reflections on the continuum and relationship between scribes and authors in ancient Israel add another dimension to the *traditum–traditio* dynamics traced here. For if scribes were allied—formally or functionally—with composers, sharing with them a diversity of knowledge, concern, and technique, the status of the *traditio* which slightly modifies the authoritative *traditum* must be postulated accordingly. Thus, if scribes and authors are considered to be radically distinct, so that authors only compose texts and scribes only copy them, the occasional emending activities of the scribal *traditio* in the MT would produce a *traditum* with multiple levels of authority.[21] However, in contradistinction, if scribes and authors cannot always or productively be distinguished in the Hebrew Bible, an emending *traditio* (whose primary concern is—in any event—the faithful transmission of the text)

[20] The frequent ambiguity in assigning the 'intrusion' to a scribe or an author extends to parallels of this phenomenon in ancient Mesopotamia. One will note that the *Wiederaufnahme* in the Vassal-Treaties of Esarhaddon is in an official, bilateral legal document. Cf. D. J. Wiseman, 'The Vassal-Treaties of Esarhaddon', *Iraq* 20 (1958), col. i. 1, 11–12 + 41-5. The technique is also found in New Testament sources. See the texts referred to by J. M. Robinson, 'The Johannine Trajectory', in *Trajectories Through Early Christianity*, edd. J. M. Robinson and * H. Koester (Philadelphia: Fortress Press, 1971), 244 f.

[21] I owe this expression to F. Bowers, though I have adapted it for present purposes. See Bowers's 'Multiple Authority: New Problems and Concepts of Copy-Text', in *Essays in Bibliography, Text, and Editing* (Charlottesville: University of Virginia Press, 1975), 447–87.

does not so much interrupt the *traditum* with material of independent authority as simply supplement or adjust it. Viewed in this way, the *traditum* dominates the *traditio* and conditions its operations. And to the extent that the scribal *traditio* makes the *traditum* lexically more accessible, theologically more palatable, or materially more comprehensive, its operations are intended to reinforce the authority of the *traditum* and to serve it. Even those scribal remarks which contradict the manifest *traditum*, one might add, confirm the dominating presence of the *traditum* in their attempts to provide alternatives to it. Thus, scribal exegesis derives from the *traditum*, articulates and underscores its content, and ultimately shares in its composition. From this perspective, the *traditio* of scribal exegesis simply brings obscure or problematic dimensions of the *traditum* to the level of textuality. It neither alters nor rivals the centrality and authority of the textual artefact.

Thus far, the *traditum-traditio* dynamic has been viewed from the perspective of the *traditio*, the active mode. It presupposes, however, a certain status of the *traditum*. For whether the *traditum* prohibits modifications or permits them is a decisive precondition for the type of scribal *traditio* which may be carried out, and for whether its annotations can be marked in the text itself. Nor is this matter completely unrelated to the author-scribe relationship indicated above. For the tendency to draw excessively determinate distinctions between scribes and authors is rooted in excessively determinate notions of what the authoritative status of the *traditum* meant in ancient Israel. If an authoritative *traditum* does not mean a fixed, unalterable account, but rather the overall traditional version in a very definite formulation, there would be latitude for a scribe to modify aspects of the *traditum* —whether in its local, popular recensions or in its more official ones. Indeed, under these conditions, a scribe who was concerned with transmitting the *traditum* to the community of faith for observance and memory would want that *traditum* to be properly understood and regarded: and so textual features which seemed opaque or impious would be commented upon or changed. The scribe would then be a co-author of the *traditum* to which his *traditio* is allied.

Naturally enough, a complex gradient of stages must be envisaged in these matters. On the one hand, an oral *traditum* would be undoubtedly more flexible and receptive of variations than a written one; on the other, even a written *traditum* is more easily altered in the Hebrew Bible when it is reconceptualized and stylistically recast *in toto*. For confirmation, one need but recall the degree to which the materials in the books of Exodus-Numbers are subject to modification via the reformulating *traditio* of them in Deuteronomy, or how much the historical record in Samuel-Kings is transformed by the reformulating *traditio* of them in Chronicles. An obvious major reason for this is that

the written form of the *traditum*, and its textual context, impose
certain inevitable restraints on the *traditio* which copies it and might
want to modify its *particular formulation in situ*. Hence, when the
traditum is recontextualized into a new version of it, significant modifications are more prone to occur. But however this may be—and it is
remarkable how little of this seems to have taken place overall—the
traditum was certainly more fluid in ancient Israel than in post-canonical
times. Given this textual fluidity, the ancient Israelite scribes had access
to the very formulation of the *traditum*; and, by virtue of this, were
participants in its composition.

In conclusion, scribal exegesis makes one particularly aware, at even
the most rudimentary of textual levels, that a *traditum* always exists by
virtue of its *traditio*; and that it is compounded of the *traditio* of its
many tradents. Indeed, for such scribal tradents a *traditum* is *their
traditio* of it: they share in its composition, and they are subservient to
its authority. Moreover, for such scribal tradents the *traditio* arises
within a given *traditum*, and exists for the sake of that *traditum* which
now embodies it. The two, the *traditum* and the *traditio*, are thus one:
entwined and inextricable. The great paradox in all this, of course, is
that the textual *traditum* received *by* faith (i.e., of the scribes) is not the
one given *for* faith (i.e., of the community). Indeed, the *traditum* of
the people is the *traditio* of its scribes. In fact, the people only have a
particular scribal traditio. To be sure, all this is the more paradoxical
when the *traditum* is not simply the composite record of historical
memory but teachings which have been attributed to divine revelation.

The complex degree to which these several matters obtain in biblical
literature—at once the necessity of the *traditum-traditio* dynamic and
its paradoxical aspects—will be seen in the succeeding three Parts of
this study. There the *traditum-traditio* dynamic will be explored
through such more substantive and theologically significant genres as
law, *aggadah*, and mantology. It is to the first of these three—law—
that we now turn.

PART TWO

LEGAL EXEGESIS

5. Introduction. The Scope and Content of Biblical Law as a Factor in the Emergence of Exegesis

1. Students of biblical law have long noted that neither any one collection of laws, nor all of them together (the *mišpāṭîm* ordinances of Exod. 21:1-23:19; the so-called Holiness Code of Lev. 17-26; and the laws of Deut. 12-26), sufficiently cover the numerous areas required for an operative and positive law code.[1] Thus, not only are there substantive lacunae in such vital areas as marriage, death, and contracts, but even in areas where legal interest is articulated, such as the area in private law concerned with damage to property, it is notable that our received biblical materials ignore direct damage to another's property and focus exclusively on damage indirectly caused—like a pregnant woman accidentally struck while others were brawling (Exod. 21:22), or a field ravaged by roaming cattle (Exod. 22:4).[2] While such lacunae are apparently surprising from the modern point of view, it is vital to bear in mind, as D. Daube has argued, that the 'conspicuous absence of simple, direct damage is not accidental, nor should it be explained away by postulating rules which have got lost. The answer is that many ancient codes regulate only matters as to which the law is dubious or in need of reform or both.'[3]

But that is not all. Anyone approaching the biblical legal materials with an interest in detailed statements concerning legal process or the constitution of the courts will find great gaps and contradictory comments; indeed, sanctions necessary for legal enforcement are often vague and non-juridical. Thus, the apparently precise formula used with regard to capital punishment, מות יומת 'he will be killed [by court order]', often leaves the manner of death unspecified,[4] and, to further complicate matters, may actually be construed in an optional sense, i.e.

---

[1] Cf. Y. Kaufmann, *Toledot*, i/1. 48, 73-7.

[2] See below, pp. 94f.

[3] 'Direct and Indirect Causation in Biblical Law', *VT* 11 (1961), 257; and cf. id., 'The Self-Understood in Legal History', *Juridical Review* 18 (1973), 126 f.

[4] On this phrase, see J. Milgrom, *Studies in Levitical Terminology*, i (Berkeley: University of California, 1970), 5-6.

'he *may* be killed'.[5] In other cases there is no formal indication of court enforcement, so that legal sanctions appeal either to a subjective state of moral sensibility (e.g. Exod. 22: 24; Deut. 15: 18, 24: 11, 13) or to an extra-legal threat of divine punishment (e.g. כָּרֵת).[6]

In addition to these and related gaps in the scope and enforcement of biblical laws, frequent lacunae or ambiguities in their legal formulation tend to render such laws exceedingly problematic—if not functionally inoperative—*without interpretation*. The following two instances are exemplary.

(*a*) Exod. 21: 22 deals with the case of a pregnant woman hit by brawling men and the assignment of penalties based on damages.[7] The phrasing of the case suggests that we are dealing with an instance of unintentional battery involving culpability.[8] However, due to its complicated redactional history, the two result clauses which describe the consequences of the injury are semantically ambiguous.[9] The first of these clauses, וְיָצְאוּ יְלָדֶיהָ, follows the casuistic condition 'if men are brawling and strike a pregnant woman', and may be construed in two ways: either it specifies the *immediate* result of the blow ('so that her children come out'), or it indicates the *eventual* result of the pregnancy ('when her children come out'). On the first possibility, the childbirth is caused by the blow; on the second, the woman naturally comes to full term.

---

[5] Cf. M. Buss, 'The Distinction between Civil and Criminal Law in Ancient Israel', in *Proceedings of the VIth World Congress of Jewish Studies*, i (Jerusalem, 1977), 56.

[6] See S. Loewenstamm, *Enc. Miq.* iv. 330–2 s.v. *'kārēt'* [Heb.]. For *kārēt* as 'premature death', cf. M. Tsevat, 'Studies in the Book of Samuel', *HUCA* 32 (1961), 197–201. On *yāmût*, see Milgrom, op. cit. 7.

[7] The law is formulated with the penalties of talion (vv. 23b–25), and this unit has been interpolated into a law dealing with injuries to a slave (vv. 20–1, 26–7). Two principles were apparently at work: (1) the juxtaposition of a case of indirect damages with laws dealing with direct injury (also vv. 18–19); (2) the verbal association with the law of talion and with the conclusion of the law of harm to servants. Torts and talion have also been spliced into the legal case in Lev. 24: 10–23 (vv. 17–21; note the catchword *yûmat* and the chiastic *inclusio*: capital offences; reparations for torts against animals; talion for injuries to persons; reparations (*re* animals); capital offences)—on which see below, pp. 100–2.

[8] The accidental factor has never been a difficulty. Indeed, this may be a third reason for the law's interpolation here (see above, n. 7): it will be noted that the sequence in vv. 12–13 is intentional—accidental homicide (v. 14 qualifies v. 13); while in vv. 18–27 the sequence is intentional—accidental bodily injury.

[9] A thorough discussion of the problematics of the law and reconstruction of its redactional history, together with a full bibliography, can be found in B. S. Jackson, 'The Problems of Exod. 21: 22–5 (Jus Talionis)', *VT* 23 (1973), 271–304. And see the critique by S. E. Loewenstamm, 'Exodus 21: 22–25', *VT* 27 (1977), 352–60.

The solution to the preceding ambiguities is further complicated by the succeeding result clause, ולא יהיה אסון, which follows the reference to childbirth. Aside from temporal ambiguities ('and there be no calamity'), it is syntactically and grammatically unclear whether the object of the 'calamity' is the foetus or the pregnant mother. Three legal perspectives are possible. A construction emphasizing damage to the child would deal either with a premature delivery consequent to, or a full-term birth subsequent to, accidental roughness affecting the mother but without foetal damage. Alternatively, focus on the child could indeed be concerned with foetal damage: either the 'calamity' was an immediate miscarriage or it involved a stillbirth at full term. Either way, a significant implication of the preceding interpretations is that the unborn child would be considered viable *in utero* and entitled to legal protection and benefits (v. 22).[10] However, from a legal perspective construed with respect to the pregnant mother (viz., *she* suffered no 'calamity'), the foetus would be without legal rights and its status irrelevant to this case of damages.

A third theoretical position lies between the two preceding legal constructions and argues that the first result clause ('her children come out') deals with the foetus and involves an arbitrated or imposed settlement of damages;[11] whereas the second result clause ('and there be no calamity') deals exclusively with the mother. Accordingly, if there is a miscarriage consequent to a blow, but not resulting in damages to the mother, there would be a settlement *for the child*; but if the mother was injured, there would be a stipulated scale of *talion* punishments imposed. There is a presumptive likelihood in favour of this interpretation—given the present legal sequence of Exod. 21: 22-5,[12] and ancient Near Eastern legal parallels.[13] Even so, it is still unclear whether damages payable upon injury to the mother would cancel those made for the miscarriage or whether there is to be a double penalty for double damages (i.e., the miscarriage being construed as a

[10] On the legal status of the foetus in Jewish law, see S. Rubin, 'Der "nascituurus" als Rechtssubjekt im talmudischen und römischen Rechte', *Zeitschrift für vergl. Rechtswissenschaft*, 20 (1907), 119–56. Cf. also the recent discussion of M. Weinfeld, 'The Genuine Jewish Attitude Towards Abortion', *Zion*, 42 (1977), 129–42 [Heb.].

[11] By the husband or court decision—for the law preserves traces of its evolution from self-help to judicial procedure. The latter involved *pělîlîm*, or an 'objective assessment' (Loewenstamm), of the husband's claims. On the verb, cf. H. Yalon's remarks on the Talmudic stem *plpl* in *Tarbiz*, 6 (1935), 223–4 [Heb.].

[12] Jackson, loc, cit. 297-301, has argued that the talion formulary is an addition to the *Urgesetz* of Exod. 21: 22 and radically transformed its meaning.

[13] Cf. the Sumerian law UM-55-21-71, iii. 11. 2′–13′, discussed by M. Civil in *Assyriological Studies in Honor of B. Landsberger* (AS 16; Chicago: University of Chicago Press, 1965), 4–6; LH 209–14; and MAL A 50-2.

damage to the child, not the mother).[14]

In view of these several considerations, it is quite clear that the present instance of *aberratio ictus* is thoroughly dependent upon legal exegesis for its viability. There is virtually no feature of its present formulation and redaction which is entirely unambiguous and self-sufficient.

(*b*) Another example of legal ambiguity requiring exegetical elucidation may be recognized in Exod. 22: 4. The case involves a situation in which a person releases cattle to graze or roam in a field or vineyard and the cattle subsequently consume or destroy an adjacent field.[15] The result clause stipulates that 'he will pay the best of his field and the best of his vineyard'. But this formulation leaves it uncertain whether the tortfeasor (damageor) must make compensation from his property or from that of his neighbour (the damagee).[16] A preliminary determination of this matter would, however, be but a first step in the clarification of this law. There are other, derivative issues. For example, if the standard of compensation were to be made on the basis of 'the best' of the damagee's field, how would a just assessment be made if that field had, in part or whole, been damaged? Conversely, if reparation was to be made from or by a field of the damageor, would not justice require a graduated or comparative penalty according to whether the neighbour's field was ruined in part or whole (for whether best or worst had been destroyed is now unknown)?[17]

The perplexing ambiguities raised by the formulation of this case thus clearly require exegesis. The diversity of interpretations in the earliest and classical rabbinic legal literature is sufficient testimony to the complex and confusing nature of this law even to its most intimate inheritors. It is therefore highly significant that exegetical clarifications have been interpolated into the LXX and Samar. versions, the antiquity

[14] MAL A 50 admits double penalties; but the principle is rejected in early Jewish law, for which see *Mekhilta D'Rabbi Shim'on* (Rashbi), edd. J. Epstein and E. Z. Melamed (Jerusalem: Mekitze Nirdamim, 1955), 276, and *b. Ketub.* 35a.

[15] The basic sense of the verb *bi''ēr* ('to destroy') is clear enough, although the mode (consumption or trampling) is not (cf. LXX ad loc.; Isa. 5: 5; Ben Sira 36: 26). Confusions have arisen due to the threefold usage of the stem *b'r* in v. 4, and the usage in v. 5 to mean a fire. Accordingly, *Tg. Neof.* and other Palestinian Targums have interpreted v. 4 as dealing with a fire. The correction of *yib'eh* in v. 4 of Samar. and 4Q 158 seems designed to distinguish between v. 4 and v. 5; for the Hebrew verb *bā'āh* means 'to destroy' (in some sense; cf. Isa. 64: 1; *M. B. Qam.* i. 1).

[16] This question has been debated since early rabbinic times. A convenient collection of the opinions can be found in E. Bickerman, 'Two Legal Interpretations of the Septuagint', in *Studies in Jewish and Christian History* (Leiden: E. J. Brill, 1976), i. 216-17 and notes.

[17] Cf. Bickerman, op. cit. i. 215, 218, and especially A. Toeg, 'Exodus 22: 4: The Text and the Law in the Light of the Ancient Sources', *Tarbiz*, 39 (1970), 226-8 [Heb.].

of which is now fully confirmed by a fragment found at Qumran.[18]

In consideration of the variety of issues just posed – regarding which the foregoing cases are but two examples among many – there need be no reasonable doubt that the preserved written law of the Hebrew Bible is but an expression of a much more comprehensive oral law. Such an oral legal tradition would have both augmented the cases of our collections and clarified their formulations to the scope and precision necessary for viable juridical decisions. Accordingly, the biblical law collections may best be considered as prototypical compendia of legal and ethical norms rather than as comprehensive codes. Even if jurists made quasi-statutory, analogical, or referential uses of some of these ordinances, the publication of agglomerate collections primarily served to make available digests of the divine requirements for 'justice and righteousness' which served as the contractual basis for the Israelite covenant. The received legal codes are thus a literary expression of ancient Israelite legal wisdom: exemplifications of the 'righteous' laws upon which the covenant was based.[19]

To a limited extent, the ancient Near Eastern law collections provide some comparative basis to these observations. For there is a growing consensus among students of cuneiform law that such corpora were not codes at all, but rather prototypical collections of cases produced by various kings in order to publicly announce or advertise their adherence to 'justice and right'.[20] In fact, the available evidence suggests that the so-called 'Legal Codes' are typologically comparable to royal testaments and have developed from earlier royal enactments dealing with temporary remissions and their eventual publication as edicts.[21] Being stylized collections of typical cases, there is no question that these 'codes' were ever intended to be comprehensive in their scope or sufficiently precise in their formulations.[22] The literary and non-legislative character of

[18] These interpolations are discussed by Bickermann and Toeg, loc. cit.; and while Toeg has convincingly argued for the authenticity of such supplementation based on comparative models, Bickermann's point concerning the impact of Alexandrian law on the LXX formulation is not disproven. 4Q 158 is probably proto-Samaritan; cf. R. Weiss's review of J. Allegro, *Qumran Cave 4* (Oxford: The Clarendon Press, 1968), in *Qiryat Sepher*, 45 (1970), 61.

[19] Cf. S. Paul, *Studies in the Book of the Covenant in the Light of Biblical and Cuneiform Law* (Leiden: E. J. Brill, 1970), 36–41, and B. Jackson, 'From *Dharma* to Law', *American Jl. of Comparative Law*, 23 (1975), 493–4.

[20] F. R. Kraus, 'Ein zentrales Problem des altmesopotamischen Rechtes: Was ist der Codex Hammurabi?', *Genava*, 8 (1960), 289–90.

[21] J. J. Finkelstein, 'Ammiṣaduqa's Edict and the Babylonian "Law Codes"', *JCS* 15 (1961), 100–4.

[22] See above, nn. 20–1. The typicality of the laws does not mean, of course, that their origin may not also reflect actual litigation; on which see R. Yaron, *The Laws of Eshnuna* (Jerusalem: The Magnes Press, 1969), 69. But compare B. Jackson, 'From *Dharma*', 498.

these collections is further indicated by the fact that neither the Laws of Hammurapi nor the other legal corpora are cited as precedents in the many legal dockets and protocols which have been preserved,[23] by the fact that there are no adjurations stating that judges or officials must heed these collections, and by the recurrent legal topoi chosen for illustration —often of bizarre cases—when one could have expected a greater variety.[24] It therefore comes as no surprise that, despite the integrated and developed traditions of law in ancient Mesopotamia, new legal collections are not exegetical revisions of earlier ones, and that a body of legal exegesis has not been discovered as yet.

These remarks point to inherent limitations in a comparison between the ancient Near Eastern and biblical legal corpora. For while the biblical corpora are, as noted, also incomprehensive in scope and frequently imprecise in formulation, the fact remains that the biblical collections are presented as divine revelation and the basis for covenantal life. The priests must teach these laws (e.g. Lev. 10: 10-11; Mal. 2: 7); the judges are enjoined to follow them (e.g. Deut. 16: 18-20; 2 Chron. 19: 6-10); the kings are held accountable to their enforcement; and the prophets repeatedly exhort their observance. In addition, the covenantal laws are the basis for many citations, precedents, and cross-references— as we shall see.[25] Accordingly, despite the fact that the biblical legal corpora are formulated as prototypical expressions of legal wisdom, *the internal traditions of the Hebrew Bible present and regard the covenantal laws as legislative texts*.[26] The significant result of these observations is that the various legal collections in the Hebrew Bible were each subject to repeated exegetical revision; that the later collections reflect (in many places) that they are (in part) exegetical revisions or clarifications of earlier ones; and that the biblical legal traditions developed a body of legal exegesis preserved in non-legal texts. Where the scope of the received law(s) was incomprehensive, it was supplemented so as to include other vital areas of social-religious life; where the formulations of the received laws were incomprehensible or ambiguous, for all practical purposes, their verbal or semantic sense was qualified; and finally, where the received laws were sufficient for

[23] See G. R. Driver and J. C. Miles, *The Babylonian Laws* (Oxford: The Clarendon Press 1952), i. 53, 401. H. Saggs, *The Greatness that was Babylon* (New York: Hawthorne, 1962), 210, has suggested that LH 8 is the precedent for the penalty in a legal text from 528; see H. Figula, 'Lawsuit Concerning a Sacrilegious Theft at Erech', *Iraq*, 13 (1951), 95–101 (esp. p. 100 n. 2).

[24] See J. J. Finkelstein, *The Ox That Gored* (TAPS 71/2; Philadelphia: The American Philosophical Society, 1981), 19 and n. 11.

[25] Below, p. 106 and ch. 6.

[26] This intermediate position must be stressed: for there is a tendency to regard the biblical law corpora *either* as 'statutory' (in some sense) *or* as ideal (literary) products. Cf. Jackson, loc. cit., and the literature cited.

certain circumstances, but required modification or expansions in the light of new considerations, they were appropriately emended so as to make them viable once again.[27]

The evidence for the foregoing assertions is complex and diverse. Fortunately, typological, generic, and stylistic distinctions may be discerned. These will permit a close analysis of the remarkable processes of inner-biblical legal exegesis and ensure a methodologically sound stratification of the materials involved. Typologically, a broad spectrum exists which spans revelations which are overtly recognized to be incomplete and are subject to new (exegetical) revelations, to revelations which are supplemented by human exegesis which is not explicitly distinguished from the former, to human exegetical materials which are subsequently validated by their re-presentation as part of divine revelation. Generically, the legal exegetical materials are incorporated in folk narratives, in historiographical narratives and annals, and in the Pentateuchal and historiographical collections of legal corpora or résumés. And stylistically, the exegesis is variously presented legalistically, through oracular formulations as well as historiographical references and stylizations. These latter are variously indicated by citations, by technical formulae, or not at all.

Unfortunately, the historical interrelationships between the foregoing types, with their generic and stylistic variations included, are not so easy to isolate. This pertains, for example, to the question as to whether the phenomenon of new oracular revelations which supplement existing laws is basically earlier than the exegeses found in the legal corpora, or whether the difference between the two is largely a question of genre — and so more indicative of the different procedures used by the priests (for example, their mantic techniques) as against those of the jurists and legal draftsmen (for example, their lapidary or annotative style). Consideration of this matter must await full analysis of the evidence.[28] It is not, in any case, decisive at this point. Moreover, since the phenomenon of legal revelations supplemented by new legal revelations explicitly acknowledges the insufficiency of the legal norms or traditions available to the judge or decisor (whether in scope or nuance), and explicitly distinguishes between the older, incomplete law and its new, *ad hoc* exegetical supplements, it will be expedient to begin our investigation of inner-biblical legal exegesis from this point. The fact that the examples of this phenomenon constitute a definable genre, and are presented as the oldest post-Sinaitic legal exegesis — the historical fact and literary form of which (not the literary style) is

---

[27] See the examples below, pp. 98–105, and in the various chapters in Part Two.
[28] See pp. 234–65, 273–6.

confirmable cross-culturally[29] — are further reasons to begin with these materials.

2. The pericopae of Lev. 24:10-23, Num. 9:6-14, 15:32-6, and 27:1-11 contains four *ad hoc* legal situations set during the period of the desert wanderings. In each case, judicial adjustments are added to the covenantal law by means of a new divine oracle. Lev. 24:10-23 deals with the case of one who 'pronounced . . . the [divine] Name in blasphemy'; Num. 9:6-14 deals with a case of persons 'impure consequent to contact with a corpse'; Num. 15:32-6 deals with a case in which some Israelites 'seized a man gathering wood on the Sabbath day'; and Num. 27:1-11 deals with a grievance put forward by the daughters of Zelophehad who were to be deprived of their patrimony because their father had no male heir. Each of these four situations required a legal decision, and so were brought to Moses. Unable to deal with them on the basis of his knowledge of the law, Moses referred them to God, who provided the oracular adjudication in each case.[30]

The specific covenant laws which may underlie the preceding cases, and the reasons why these latter present judicial difficulties, are not stated, and must be inferred in each instance. We shall present them according to their degree of clarity:

(*a*) The inheritance issue facing the daughters of Zelophehad is explicit: in so far as inheritance rights existed in ancient Israel only for male heirs, the danger existed that ancestral property would become alienated (יגרע) if no natural sons existed.[31] The core of the grievance is thus of wide ethnic import — as the daughters were well aware (27:4). This realization, together with their shrewd introduction of the inheritance issue with a reference to the support their father Zelophehad

[29] Cf. the discussion on the antiquity of oracular legal decisions (not just exegesis) in the Hebrew Bible, below, pp. 102, 133 n. 74, 227-8, 236-8. For the present, note the broad cross-cultural evidence reviewed by H. Cohn, 'Secularization of Divine Law', *Jewish Law in Ancient and Modern Israel* (New York: Ktav, 1971), 17-22. For ancient Egypt, see A. M. Blackman, 'Oracles in Ancient Egypt', *JEA* 11 (1925), 249-55, ibid. 12 (1926), 176-85.

[30] Note especially the terminology in Num. 9:8 and 27:5, which has parallels in other oracular–omen scenarios. For *šāmaʿ*, cf. Ps. 85:9 (*re* Lev. 10:20, see below, p. 227; for *qārēb*, cf. Exod. 22:7 (and see below, pp. 237 f) and Josh. 7:14, 16-18 (also 1 Sam. 14:41-2).

[31] Two issues must be separated: inheritance based on the agnatic principle of blood kinship and the concept of inalienable property. In some legal systems these are distinct; they converge implicitly in Num. 27:1-11, and explicitly in Num. 36 (on which see § 4, below). The issue of inalienable paternal property is at stake in 1 Kgs. 21:3; cf. Jer. 32:6-15. The institution of levirate marriage attempts to solve the converging issues of property and blood kinship when only sons are considered heirs (cf. Deut. 25:5-10).

gave Moses' contested leadership during the Korah affair (27: 3), undoubtedly helped allay any timidity they might have had in requesting a reconsideration of customary legal practice. The divine ruling given to the daughters was favourable: they were deemed the legitimate inheritors of their father's estate (v. 7).[32] The divine *responsum* is then reformulated as a new law for all Israelites (vv. 8-11).

(*b*) The issue presented by the case in Num. 9: 6-14, in which impure men came to Moses at the time of the paschal feast, is less straightforward. When the men ask 'Why should we be debarred (נגרע) from bringing YHWH's sacrifice at the designated time, together with the rest of the Israelites?' (v. 7), the issue is not whether impure members of the Israelite *ethos* could participate in paschal sacrifice. While no explicit Pentateuchal rule deals with the subject of impurity and the paschal sacrifice, the editorial-narrative remark that these persons 'were not allowed to sacrifice the paschal-offering' is undoubtedly based on an analogical extension of the explicit biblical legal principle that persons who have become impure due to contact with corpses are unable to share in sacrificial rituals or touch holy things (cf. Lev. 22: 3-6; Num. 5: 1-4, 6: 9-11, 19: 11-13; also Hag. 2: 11-13). Why, then, did these persons beseech Moses? The clue would seem to lie in their use of the verb נגרע—also used by the daughters of Zelophehad in their grievance—which means to be 'cut off' or 'separated'. Accordingly, what is at issue for these men is their fear that failure to participate in the paschal ritual *at its appointed time* would somehow debar them from ethnic status. Since this ritual was regarded as basic, but no contingency provision was made in the earlier legislation for mitigating circumstances (cf. Exod. 12: 1-20, 43-50), the law required amendment. The new oracular ruling permits a person defiled by a corpse to sacrifice the paschal-offering precisely one month later, 'in the second month, on the fourteenth day of the month, at twilight' (v. 11). 'But any person who is [ritually] clean . . . and [yet] fails to perform the paschal offering [on time] will be cut off from his people, because he did not bring the sacrifice of YHWH *at its appointed time* (v. 13).[33]

(*c*) Num. 15: 32-6 presents the situation of a person caught *in*

[32] Diverse customs and laws may have been in local effect; thus, Job 42: 15 permits daughters to be coheirs with the sons. But I see no reason to assume that the daughters of Zelophehad only wanted a portion of the paternal inheritance (i.e. as coheirs), as argued by B. Jackson, 'Human Recognition and Divine Knowledge in Biblical and Tannaitic Law', *Shenaton ha-Mishpat ha-'Ivri*, 16-17 (1979-80), 65 [Heb.]. For comparative evidence of daughters inheriting without and after sons, see Z. Ben-Barak, 'Inheritance by Daughters in the Ancient Near East', *JSS* 25 (1980), 22-33.

[33] The fear of loss of full ethnic status would seem to be confirmed by the punishment of divine excision (*kārēt*; cf. n. 6 above); in the meantime, the guilty would bear their guilt (v. 13b).

flagrante delicto while gathering wood on the Sabbath day. The accused is therewith put in bond (וינחו אתו במשמר) 'because there was no ruling (לא פרש) on how to deal with him'.[34] The oracular ruling, given by God, was death by stoning. But the punishment does not clarify the nature of the crime—which remains unclear. Inasmuch as the narrative itself reports that the judicial problem was how to deal with the individual, one might assume that the issue was whether the act of gathering wood on the Sabbath constituted work—for the prohibition in the decalogue simply states that one 'shall do no manner of work' on the Sabbath (Exod. 20: 10), and does not indicate what would actually constitute such an offence. Accordingly, early rabbinic tradition and many moderns have tried to determine the precise nature of the work involved.[35] However, since the adjudication specifically mentions only the punishment of 'stoning', it is entirely possible that the only real legal issue was the precise manner of death—not whether the act was a violation of the Sabbath rest.[36] This interpretation is all the more likely given that the punishment of death for Sabbath violation listed elsewhere in the Pentateuch is also imprecise (Exod. 31: 14-15).[37] In any event, some feature of the Sabbath laws needed clarification and supplementation: and this was provided by the divine oracle.

(*d*) The case of a blasphemer in Lev. 24: 10-23 provides another situation wherein an offender was caught *in flagrante delicto*. Like Num. 15: 34, the accused was put in bond (וינחהו במשמר) 'while they besought a ruling (לפרש להם) by YHWH's decision' (v. 12). The ruling given, first with respect to the immediate case (v. 14) and then

---

[34] The verb *pāraš* is used with a comparable sense in Lev. 24: 12. For the uses of *parāsu* in Akkadian contexts, see von Soden, *AHw*. 831.

[35] Cf. *b. Šabb.* 96b, where the crime is assumed to be the uprooting of shrubs, and, though warned, the perpetrator continued his action (cf. *b. Sanh.* 41a). This would suggest that the law dealt with a case of outright defiance. This may, in fact, be the case, and explain the position of this case after Num. 15: 30; see G. Gray, *Numbers* (ICC; Edinburgh: T. and T. Clark, 1903), 182, and below. Nevertheless, it must be stressed that the *particular* crime is *not* indicated.

[36] J. Weingreen, 'The Case of the Woodgatherer (Num XV 32-36)', *VT* 11 (1966), 362-3, has argued that the crime was not at issue, but rather the question was whether the gatherer of wood showed intent to desecrate the Sabbath (i.e. light a fire). This is a presumptive interpretation. Moreover, Weingreen's view that the ruling involves a 'secondary' restriction (as in rabbinic law) to prevent Sabbath desecration is anachronistic. Cf. the criticism of A. Phillips, 'The Case of the Woodgatherer Reconsidered', *VT* 19 (1969), 125-8.

[37] Cf. *b. Sanh.* 78b, and medievals like Rashi. Note that Exod. 31: 14 has both capital punishment (*yûmat*) and *kārēt* (also the case of the Moloch worshipper, Lev. 20: 1-5), which raises the question whether the second is a later mitigation of the first, or whether we have a conflated text reflecting different punishments. See the quite different solution of Milgrom, op. cit. 6 n. 10, and Loewenstamm, op. cit.—that God promises intervention if the community does not act. But there are no syntactic grounds for this harmonization.

reformulated as a norm for Israelites and strangers (vv. 15-16), was death by stoning. The reason why this case constitutes a *novum* requiring a divine resolution is not given. Several alternatives are defensible. First, the fact that the person who is accused of blaspheming 'the Name' (v. 11, i.e. YHWH)[38] is of mixed parentage must have raised the question as to whether the normative covenantal prohibition 'Do not blaspheme Elohim nor curse a prince of your people' (Exod. 22: 27) was applicable to the non-Israelite.[39] A second and not unrelated interpretation of this case arises from the fact that the hortatory injunction upon which the case is based ('Do not blaspheme Elohim') lacks any reference to a specific punishment. Accordingly, the key legal issue may well have been the mode of punishment. But even presuming that this latter was known (in the tradition) with respect to cases involving native Israelites,[40] the fact remains that it needed precise legal specification with respect to the non-Israelite 'stranger'. Indeed, an indirect confirmation of this interpretation is provided by the restatement of the case in casuistic terms in Lev. 24: 15-16: for the statement 'if a person blasphemes his god[s] he will bear his sin, but if he blasphemes the Name [of] YHWH he will be put to death' indicates that a distinction could be drawn between the non-application of Israelite jurisprudence in cases where a non-native blasphemed his own god(s) and its legitimate application where such a one blasphemed the Israelite god (within areas of Israelite jurisdiction). The formulation in v. 16 thus states that in such cases where a non-Israelite blasphemes YHWH he shall be stoned to death just like the native Israelite ('the stranger is like the native').[41] If this casuistic reformulation is not in fact a key to the juridical conundrum at issue in this case, it is at the very least an ancient (and normative) interpretation of it. At all events, the case in

---

[38] 'The Name' is used euphemistically here; v. 16aα is presumably older. A euphemistic–pious interpolation of this sort occurs in Deut. 28: 58, where the deuteronomic expression 'to fear YHWH, your God' (Deut. 6: 24, 10: 12, 14: 23; cf. 17: 19, 31: 13) is interrupted by the phrase 'this great and awesome Name' followed by the original *nota accusativi, 'et*, here used appositionally; cf. pp.48-50).

[39] Cf. M. Noth, *Leviticus* (OTL; Philadelphia: Westminster, 1965), 178-80. Nachmanides considers this to be the issue, but from a very different perspective.

[40] e.g. orally. This would explain the clear indication of stoning in 1 Kgs. 21: 10, which is based on Exod. 22: 27 – unless this punishment is derived from our case; but the verb *rāgam* is used in Lev. 24: 16, *sāqal* in 1 Kgs. 21: 10. For stoning as the punishment for sedition, especially where the offence puts the community in jeopardy, see Finkelstein, *The Ox*, 26 f. and n. 4.

[41] This point is made twice, in vv. 16 and 22. The principle of analogical extensions will be treated below. Here it may suffice to note that this repetition is of the nature of a *Wiederaufnahme*, which highlights the interpolation of several laws, including talion, in vv. 17-21. The result of this redaction is a stylistic chiasm: vv. 13-14 (A); vv.15-16 (B); v. 17 (C); v. 18a (D); vv. 18b-20 (talion; E); v. 21a (D'); v. 21b (C'); v. 22 (B'); v. 23 (A').

Lev. 24:10-13 once again indicates that whatever the received legal norms may have been at the time of the event described, they were inadequate and required an *ad hoc* oracular supplement.

3. The four preceding cases dealing with *ad hoc* oracular *responsa* are preserved in a fairly patterned literary form: (i) a case is brought to Moses (Lev. 24:11; Num. 9:6, 15:33, 27:2); (ii) the law is unknown and God is consulted (Lev. 24:12; Num. 9:8, 15:34, 27:5); (iii) a divine decision is given to Moses for the case in hand (Lev. 24:13-14; Num. 15:35, 27:6-7) and/or as an ordinance for all Israelites (Lev. 24:15-16; Num. 9:10-14, 27:8-11); and (iv) a compliance formula is used which states that the law was enacted (Lev. 24:23; Num. 15:36), or was to be enacted (Num. 9:14, 27:11), 'as YHWH commanded Moses' (Lev. 24:23; Num; 15:36, 27:11). The patterned nature of the cases is further indicated by the fact that all the rulings are given by some mantic means; that the verbal stem פרש recurs in cases (iii) and (iv), together with the use of the similar term משמר regarding the temporary incarceration of the person seized *in flagrante delicto*;[42] that the verbal stem גרע recurs in cases (i) and (ii); and that the compliance formula is exactly reiterated in cases (i), (iii), and (iv). Accordingly, whatever their original context and formulation, such ancient legal oracles have been recast in a highly stylized manner. It is tempting to speculate that the original context of these old oracles was somehow related to the tradition recorded in Exod. 18, whereby the divine oracle was sought as the court of last resort (vv. 19, 26). But however much this latter preserves an ancient mantic kernel, comparative evidence suggests that neither the present text of Exod. 18, nor the particular legal organization projected therein, is primitive. In fact, precisely similar structures of adjudication, of legal bureaucracy, and of moral requirements for judges are paralleled in Hittite, Mesopotamian, and Egyptian sources throughout the second and first millennia.[43] A somewhat more 'primitive' oracular-juridical situation is reflected in Exod. 33:7. But any link between it and the stylized desert scenarios just reviewed is without documentary foundation.

Two further factors contribute to the present view that several literary and historical strata are embedded in our texts: in all cases but that of the wood-gatherer, the oracular *responsum* is formulated in the precise casuistic style of the Pentateuchal priestly ordinances ('if a

[42] Num. 15:32 actually uses the verb *māṣā'*, meaning 'to catch' or 'seize in the act' in several biblical laws (with corresponding Mesopotamian parallels); cf. my remarks in *HUCA* 45 (1974), 26 n. 4.

[43] The comparative evidence has been collected by M. Weinfeld, 'Prince and Judge in the Hebrew Bible and the Ancient Near East', *Proceedings of the VIth World Congress of Jewish Studies* (Jerusalem, 1977), i. 73-89 [Heb.].

man' (איש איש/אדם כי)[44] and presents a law *more comprehensive th*
the situation called for by the original oracular situation. Thus, the law
dealing with a person who blasphemes YHWH specifies that the same
law pertains to the Israelite as to the non-Israelite 'stranger' (Lev. 24:
16); and, as noted, it also notes that if a stranger blasphemes his own
god(s) he simply has to bear his guilt: Israelite jurisprudence does not
apply. If the first element of the law, which deals with the native
Israelite, is somehow implicit in the *ad hoc* situation, the second
element, which deals with the stranger, is not, and is the product of a
secondary legal specification. Similarly, the law permitting a second
(deferred) occasion for the performance of the paschal-sacrifice for
persons defiled by a corpse is extended in Num. 9:10 to persons away
'on a distant journey'. In v. 14 both provisions are extended to the
stranger as well. It may be that the amendment of the law to include
those on a journey is a concession to traders forced to be outside
Canaah during the month of Nisan and so unable to perform their
religious-ethnic duty; and that the general impurity believed to obtain
in other lands may have provided the analogy with the law dealing with
impurity contracted from corpses—so that a ritual deferral extended to
those in the latter state was extended to those in 'impure' lands.[45] In
any event, the extension of both laws to the stranger deserves some
note. Since conditions were formulated in Exod. 12:48 for the conversion of strangers via circumcision, so as to enable them to participate
in the paschal-offering, it may be concluded that the stranger to which
reference is made in Num. 9:14 is a circumcised proselyte. It is this fact
which permits him to defer the paschal-offering—if impure or on a
journey—*just like* the native Israelite.[46]

Finally, the law permitting daughters to inherit their father's patrimony when no brothers exist is extended—in the casuistic reformulation
of it—to other contingencies: where no daughters exist (Num. 27:9),
paternal uncles were to have priority of inheritance (v. 9); in their

---

[44] The legal codes have different formulary: the priestly Holiness Code characteristically has: noun (twice) + relative pronoun (*kî/'ăšer*) + verb, over against
the Covenant Code and Deuteronomy, which have: conjunction (*kî*) + verb +
noun (once).

[45] Cf. Josh. 22, esp. v. 19, also Amos 7: 17.

[46] It has been well noted that the Priestly Code preserves many indications of
secondary extensions of the law to the 'stranger'. Cf. P. Grelot, 'La Dernière
Étape de la rédaction sacerdotale', *VT* 6 (1956), 174–89. The reasons for this were.
undoubtedly varied, and not necessarily broadminded. For example, extending
the law to strangers would be one way to regulate their behaviour and guarantee
that no ritually impure person was resident in the land. See M. Weber, *Ancient
Judaism* (Glencoe, Ill.: The Free Press, 1952), 337f., and cf. M. Smith, *Palestinian
Parties and Politics that Shaped the Old Testament* (New York: Columbia University Press, 1971), 178–82.

Legal exegesis

absence, first the paternal grand-uncles and then the next closest relative in the same line of descent were to be considered eligible (vv. 10-11). The technical elaboration of the rules of agnatic descent added to this case are formally similar to the legal extensions in the other two. In all three of them later legal draftsmen reformulated an old legal *responsum* which was received by tradition and incorporated it into matters perceived to be analogous or otherwise related—on the basis of pure legal speculation or practical legal tradition. We are thus witness to the ongoing work of a trained legal bureaucracy which reused old cases by amending them and reformulating them as normative precedents. A double process is at work: on the one hand, there is the transformation of older *ad hoc* rulings into fixed, permanent norms. This must have happened repeatedly in the course of early Israelite history and helps explicate the growth and development of normative legal formulations from custom and legal tradition.[47] On the other hand, the derivative and secondary matters which accumulated through living experience of the law were accorded new authority—on the basis of their representation as a divine revelation set in the immediate aftermath of the original oracular situation.

4. The diversities of content, form, and promulgation thus suggest that the casuistic legal formulations in cases (i), (ii), and (iv) are historically later than the *ad hoc* oracles which introduce them. If these oracular scenarios were merely fictive accounts used to introduce selected legal precedents, it would be difficult to explain why the case narratives are so opaque and incomplete, and why just these cases were chosen for emphasis outside the legal corpora.[48] Nevertheless, there *is* one instance where the historical nature of an *ad hoc* oracular situation may be questioned—and that is the narrative found in Num. 36, a text which presupposes the casuistic formulation of the inheritance law of Num. 27: 8-11 and its problematics.

Num. 36 follows a series of diverse passages which constitute addenda to the present Book of Numbers.[49] In 36: 2 the family heads of the

[47] See B. Jackson, 'From *Dharma*', 504 f. This valuable insight was made with specific reference to the case of the daughters of Zelophehad by D. Amram in his generally overlooked study, *Leading Cases in the Bible* (Philadelphia: J. Greenstone, 1905), 112.

[48] The historical reality of inheritance procedures at the time of the original land division may be the *Sitz im Leben* for the case of Zelophehad's daughters; cf. Josh. 17: 3-6, where, however, it refers to the 'older' legal precedent set in the desert wanderings. Lev. 27: 1-11 is notably without a practical *Sitz*, although there may be a loose contextual link to the issues of inalienable property found in Lev. 25: 23-55.

[49] Inner-Pentateuchal evidence suggests that the announcement of Moses' death and transfer of leadership to Joshua in Num. 27: 12-23 – after the daughters

Gilead clan approached Moses and cited the earlier divine legislation designed to keep clan property within the paternal line of descent. The clansmen now contend that even this new divine ordinance is insufficient, in so far as patrimonial property could still become alienated from the clan if daughters without brothers were to marry outside their tribe. As they state, with deliberate allusions to the language used by the daughters of Zelophehad in Num. 27: 3-4, exogamy would mean that property 'would be separated (ונגרעה)' from the paternal inheritance and transferred to the new husband and his tribe – a situation which even the jubilee provisions, whose primary intent was to prevent the perpetual alienation of immovable property, could not counteract (vv. 3-4).[50] In the face of this problem, Moses gives a new divine dispensation (v. 5a; cf. Lev. 24: 12) which acknowledges the legitimacy of the elders' grievance (v. 5b), and states that the daughters of Zelophehad 'may marry any one they wish *provided that* they marry into a clan of their father's tribe' (v. 6). Through the instrument of this new provision, clan property would be protected. This text concludes, like the other pericopae outlined above, with a compliance formula (v. 10), and records the marriages of the daughters of Zelophehad to their paternal cousins (v. 11).

What is extraordinary about the case in Num. 36: 6-9 is not simply that the new divine ordinance of Num. 27: 6-11 also proved insufficient. The remarkable fact from a legal standpoint is that this second *responsum*, requiring the daughters to marry a paternal relative, produces a veritable legal fiction.[51] For if the daughters of Zelophehad must marry into their father's family – in this case their cousins, for paternal uncles were forbidden by law (cf. Lev. 18: 14) – the inheritance would necessarily revert to just those males who would be in line to inherit if the father had no children whatsoever (*per* Num. 27: 9-11). Accordingly, the ruling in favour of female inheritance provided by the first adjudication (Num. 27: 8) is functionally subverted by the *responsum* in Num. 36: 6-9 – *even though* its specific provisions remain valid (27: 9-10). Inheritance of property is thus retained as a male prerogative. As a rule of law, then, the law of Num. 27: 8-11 remains in force; but it has been so operationally transformed by the new decision of Num. 36: 6-9 as to be of little if any practical significance.

of Zelophehad pericope in vv. 1-11 – was an early conclusion to the Book of Numbers: for it is precisely this scenario which is recapitulated in Deut. 32: 48-52 and 34: 7-9, after the incorporation of the deuteronomic tradition. In a parallel fashion, the death notice of Joshua in Josh. 24: 28-31 is editorially recapitulated in Judg. 2: 6-10 *after* the interpolated materials in Judg. 1: 1-36, 2: 1-5.

[50] This factor was part of the 'unwritten' law; it is not mentioned in the laws of the jubilee in Lev. 25: 23-55.

[51] The classic discussion of legal fictions is H. S. Maine, *Ancient Law*[2] (New York: H. Holt and Co., 1877), ch. 2, esp. pp. 24-25, 29.

5. The preceding five legal pericopae explicitly acknowledge instances when the covenantal law required supplementary clarifications or amendments.[52] Comparable supplementations and explications can be identified in the Pentateuchal legal corpora. However, in these cases there is no formal or explicit distinction between the older rule or norm and the new exegesis or ruling.Indeed, the genre of the legal collections (Exod. 21:1-23:19; Lev. 17-26; Deut. 12-26) largely obscures the inner development and supplementation of its laws. Innovations are incorporated into the prevailing corpus with only occasional traces betraying its growth. For this reason analysis of the exegesis in these legal collections will be preceded by an analysis of legal exegeses in the narrative historical sources: for in this latter genre the strata of law and exegesis can be fairly easily identified due to their frequent citation of, or reference to, authoritative legal texts. Thus, for example, the Books of Kings, Chronicles, Ezra, and Nehemiah frequently refer to what 'is written (כתוב)' in the Torah of Moses or of YHWH, or the like, in connection with literal (1 Kgs. 2: 3; 2 Kgs. 14: 6; Ezra 9:11; Neh. 8:14, 13: 1; Jer. 17: 21-2; cf. Lam. 1: 10) or abbreviated citations (Ezra 3: 2; Neh. 10: 35, 37; 1 Chron. 15:15; 2 Chron. 31: 3). There are many other references to written texts which are not cited verbatim (e.g. 2 Kgs. 23: 21; Ezra 3: 4; Neh. 7: 5; 2 Chron. 35: 26; cf. Dan. 9: 1. 12: 9), as well as references to the fact that a ritual has been done 'as is written' (Ezra 3: 4; 2 Chron. 23:18, 35:12; cf. ibid. 30: 5) or 'as *per* the statute' (Ezra 3: 4; Neh. 8: 18). And finally, the textual citations in the narrative histories frequently employ technical terms or formulae in their citations, like לאמר 'saying' (2 Kgs. 14: 6; 2 Chron. 25: 4; Ezra 9: 11), אשר 'that' (Neh. 8:14-15, 13:1), כ(אשר) plus the stem צוה 'as . . . commanded' (Jer. 17:11; Ezra 9:11; 1 Chron. 15:15; Lam. 1:10).

The combined effect of these textual references, citations, and citation formulae is thus formally to distinguish the inherited legal sources from their reinterpretations, and so greatly to facilitate the identification and analysis of the exegetical processes involved. In addition, because the narrative histories are descriptive accounts of political and religio-cultural events they frequently bring to the forefront the dynamic relationship which obtains between laws and social processes, in consequence of which the laws are reinterpreted or transformed. This dynamic is also largely obscured in the Pentateuchal legal corpora, where the *Sitz im Leben* of its legal exegeses must often be inferred.[53]

---

[52] For two other possible instances, see below, p. 133 n. 74, and pp. 227 f.
[53] See below, *passim*.

6. Legal Exegesis with Verbatim, Paraphrastic, or Pseudo-citations in Historical Sources

A. CONCERN WITH THE MEANING AND APPLICATION OF THE LAW

THE historical record preserved in the Books of Ezra and Nehemiah, and their factual and literary interrelationship, is of well-known complexity.[1] Despite this, these sources remain of immense importance for their detailed witness to ancient biblical legal exegeses. Indeed, these latter constitute a major dimension of the activities of its chief protagonists. As noted earlier, Ezra's official position was that of a religious scribe who was given official Persian permission to reconstitute the post-exilic Palestinian community on the basis of its ancestral Torah.[2] Thus, the Judaean 'community of the exile' which returned from Babylonia benefited from a Persian policy which encouraged the regeneration and reworking of native legal and religious traditions. The foundation for this policy was solidified during the reign of Darius I: he permitted the returning Jews to restore their sacral worship,[3] encouraged the compilation of native Egyptian laws, and sent one Oudjahorresne to restore the colleges of the Temple scribes.[4] Parallel to this foreign policy, Darius and his successors promulgated, compiled, and codified native Persian laws as well.[5]

It is within the framework of this policy of support for non-Persian cults that Artaxerxes I, in his seventh year (458 BCE), authorized Ezra to lead a group of exiles back to Judaea and to implement 'the law of your God' (Ezra 7: 14). It is now quite clear that this Persian policy was

---

[1] See the succinct review and evaluation of the evidence and its problems in M. Smith, *Palestinian Parties and Politics*, 119-27, with previous literature cited.

[2] Cf. the two ordinances of Cyrus in Ezra 1: 2-4, 6: 3-5. These have been carefully reevaluated by E. Bickerman, 'The Edict of Cyrus in Ezra', in *Studies in Jewish and Christian History*, i (Leiden: E. J. Brill, 1976), 72-108.

[3] Ezra 6: 1-12.

[4] See above, p. 37, n. 53. To this add: H. Cazelles, 'La Mission d'Esdras', *VT* 4 (1954), 118-19, 123-6; G. Posner, *La Première Domination perse en Égypte* (Bibliothèque d'étude . . . de l'Institut Français d'Archéologie Orientale, 9; Cairo, 1936), 22.

[5] See above, p. 37, n. 53. To this add: A. T. Olmstead, 'Darius as Lawgiver', *AJSL* 51 (1935), 247-9; F. Altheim and R. Stiehl, *Geschichte Mittelasiens im Altertum* (Berlin: W. de Gruyter, 1970), 95-103.

not free of political self-interest. Precisely at this time, in 458, Egypt was in the midst of a revolt, supported by Athenians who were also fighting along the Syro-Palestinian coast.[6] It was thus of importance that the Persians maintain a land bridge and buffer in its Western empire: accordingly, official support of native autonomy and the consequent indebtedness of the Judaeans (both those who had remained after 587/6 and those allowed to return) was a skilful political move. Ezra was told to appoint judges and magistrates who would adjudicate cases on the basis of this law for 'all who know the laws of your God' (7: 25), and to 'instruct those who did not know [them]'. Thus, 'Ezra set his mind to inquire of the Torah of YHWH, and לעשׂת to make and teach law and ordinance in [the community of] Israel' (7: 10).[7]

Ezra arrived in Jerusalem in early August 458 and set about to fulfill the royal firman through a series of public teachings of Torah.[8] On the first day of the seventh month (2 October), during the Rosh Hashanah convocation (Neh. 7: 17–8: 1), Ezra began reading the Torah to the people with the aid of levitical 'instructors' (8: 4, 7–9). The nature of this instruction is summarized in Neh. 8: 8. The Levites 'read from the book of the Torah of Elohim מפרשׁ ושׂום שׂכל ויבינו במקרא'. Even though the precise meaning of the preceding terms remains in question, the way these activities are referred to leaves little doubt that they express developed and well-known exegetical procedures. The first term, מפרשׁ, is related to an old Semitic verb used to denote a legal decision, and it is in this basic sense in which it was used in Lev. 24: 12 and Num. 15: 34.[9] The verbal stem also occurs in the Aramaic text of Ezra 4: 18, though with the more developed sense of a report read explicitly or precisely before the king. Such a lexical expansion was arguably influenced by Persian courtier customs of declaiming records and by Iranian terminology.[10] The latter evidence suggests that מפרשׁ in

---

[6] Cf. Smith, op. cit. 123 and nn. 114–15.

[7] Cf. the verb *'āśāh*, above, pp. 30 f. The nature and extent of Ezra's legal activities are discussed by H. Cohn, 'Legal Studies in the Book of Ezra', *Zer li-Geburot* (Z. Shazar Jubilee volume; Jerusalem: Qiryat Sepher, 1973), 371–401 [Heb.].

[8] For the calendric conversions, see R. Parker and W. Dubberstein, *Babylonian Chronology* (Brown University Studies, 19; Providence: Brown University Press, 1956). The present argument is not substantively affected by accepting the later date of 428 BCE.

[9] Above, pp. 100–2. On the verb itself, see W. von Soden, *AHw*, s.v. *parāsu*. The biblical term has been studied by I. Heinemann, 'The Development of Technical Terms for the Interpretation of Scripture', *Leš.* 15 (1947), 108–15 [Heb.].

[10] See H. H. Schaeder, *Iranische Beiträge* (Schriften der Königsberger Gelehrten Gesellschaft, Geisteswiss. Kl., 6/5; Halle: Niemeyer, 1930), 199–205, and H. J. Polotsky, 'Aramäisch *prš* und das Huzvaresch', *Le Muséon*, 45 (1932), 273–82. H. Rabin has compared such a 'diglossic translation' with the origins of the Targums; see his 'The Translation Process and the Character of the Septuagint', *Textus*, 6 (1968), 17–18.

Neh. 8: 8 indicates that the Torah was 'read out explicitly'. Such a lection undoubtedly involved care for exact pronunciations, intonation, and phrasing, so as to make the units of the piece and its traditional sense readily comprehensible.[11] These aspects of the declamation of Torah were complemented by the other two expressions which follow: שום שכל 'gave the sense' and ויבינו במקרא 'and they expounded the recited text'. Both these terms are explicitly exegetical, and indicate the addition of clarifications and interpretations to text where intonation and phrasing and traditional meanings were not sufficient.[12]

1. A detailed instance of the exegetical proceses involved at this time is presented in the scenario of levitical activities reported for the second day of the convocation. On this occasion, the lay and religious leaders assembled with Ezra 'to find the sense of (להשכיל אל) the words of the Torah' (Neh. 8: 13), which concerned the festival of Tabernacles and its modes of celebration. During the course of the lection the instructors 'found it written (וימצא כתוב) in the Torah, which YHWH had commanded through Moses, that אשר "the Israelites must dwell in booths [tabernacles] during the festival on the seventh month"' (v. 14). Immediately thereafter, word was sent to all Israelites throughout the countryside and in Jerusalem to go to the mountains and collect twigs of five species of trees, 'to build booths, as was written (לעשת סכת ככתוב)' (v. 15). The Israelites complied with this proclamation based on the cited text, and built booths 'each one on his roof, and in their courtyards, and in the courtyards of the Temple of Elohim, and in the broadways of the Water Gate and the Ephraim Gate' (v. 16).

Given the repeated stress on the 'written' law, and the use of the idiom וימצאו כתוב . . . אשר 'they found it written . . . that', which is elsewhere used before quotation,[13] it has been argued that the phrase

---

[11] According to Heinemann, loc. cit. n. 9, the verb *pāraš* did not take on an exegetical sense until post-biblical times. In any event it maintained the sense of explicit or careful pronunciation well into Tannaitic times; cf. *M. Sanh.* vii. 5; *M. Šeqal.* i. 5. It is conceivable that *mĕpōrāš* in Neh. 8: 8 may have meant '[read out] section by section' in the light of Akk. *pirsu*. For this term see E. Leichty, 'The Colophon', *Studies Presented to A. Leo Oppenheim* (Chicago: University of Chicago Press, 1964), 159; and cf. the remark of P. Haupt, 'Midian und Sinai', *ZDMG* 63 (1909), 516.

[12] See M. Gertner, 'Terms of Scriptural Interpretation: A Study in Hebrew Semantics', *BSOAS* 25 (1962), 22-3.

[13] The idiom without *'ăšer* 'that' occurs in Neh. 7: 5, before the citation of the genealogy in vv. 6-68, and in Dan. 12: 1, before the (covert) citations from Isaiah in vv. 2-3 (see below, Part Four). The full citation formula is found in Neh. 12: 1, before the citation from Deut. 23: 4-7 in vv. 1b-2. S. Lieberman has noted that the idiom 'to find written' is found in those Tannaitic passages reporting on the three Torah scrolls found in the Temple Court; see his *Hellenism in Jewish Palestine*, 21-2, with sources. Lieberman further notes that the idiom here has

in Neh. 8:14 is a verbatim citation from Lev. 23:42 ('you must dwell in booths for seven days'); and that the proclamation in Neh. 8:15 to gather species of trees for the festival is a reference to the comparable injunction found in Lev. 23:40.[14] On this basis it would seem that the levitical instructors 'made sense' of the ancient Tabernacles' law and issued a directive that the people comply with it. They presumably did little more than specify or clarify the plain sense of the law as stated in Scripture.

In his monumental study of Israelite religion, Y. Kaufmann argued that Lev. 23:39-42 functioned in Neh. 8:14-17 in yet another way. On the basis of the fact that Lev. 23:39-42 refers to booths in one's locale (but not to a centralized pilgrimage), while Deut. 16:13-15 only stresses a pilgrimage to Jerusalem (and does not refer to the building of booths), Kaufmann claimed that Neh. 8:14-17 is a legal blend: the feast would be celebrated in Jerusalem, as *per* the deuteronomic law, but the people were allowed to build booths in the city by way of concession to the levitical tradition.[15] Kaufmann's argument is untenable. If Neh. 8:14-17 depends upon the Pentateuchal law in Lev. 23:40-2, one cannot explain (1) why Neh. 8:14 is not more specific about the context and time of gathering the species (cf. Lev. 23:39-40); (2) why the proclamation calls for five species (Neh. 8:15) when Lev. 23:40 refers to four somewhat different ones; and (3) why the proclamation states that the species were used 'to build booths', when Lev. 23:40 specifically states that the twigs were to be used as part of a ritual of rejoicing 'before YHWH'. Moreover, (4) Kaufmann's basic assumption that the command to rejoice 'before the Lord' and 'celebrate ... to YHWH' in Lev. 23:40-1 refers to non-shrinal celebrations is incorrect. There is good reason to assume that these instructions are technical references for pilgrimages to local *shrines*: similar expressions occur in Exod. 23:14, 17, 34:23, and Deut. 16:15-16. Thus, pilgrimage celebrations at a shrine were not an innovation of the deuteronomic law, but were deeply rooted in Israel's most ancient cultic tradition.[16] The deuteronomic innovation was simply the restriction of all festival pilgrimages to the central shrine in Jerusalem.

Kaufmann's argument that Neh. 8:14-16 reflects a blend of Penta-teuchal law also presupposes a deuteronomic component. However, the

the same technical sense as εὕρομεν γεγραμένον 'we have found written', used by the scholiasts on Homer.

[14] Cf. Y. Kaufmann, *Toledot* iv. 327-9; J. Licht, *Enc. Miq.* v. 1042, s.v. '*sukkôt, ḥag hassukkôt*'.

[15] Kaufmann, loc. cit.

[16] Cf. N. Raban, 'Before the Lord', *Tarbiz*, 23 (1952), 1-3 [Heb.], and M. Haran, 'The Idea of Centralization of the Cult in the Priestly Apprehension', *Beer-Sheva Annual*, 1 (1973), 114-21 [Heb.].

fact is that Deut. 16:13-15 is not cited in Neh. 8:14-16.[17] This leaves the inference that Deut 16:13-15 is there referred to dependent on the assumption that Neh. 8:16 prescribes the erection of booths only in Jerusalem. But this is hardly the plain sense of the text. Aside from the fact that the convocation took place in Jerusalem, there is nothing to indicate that the proclamation to gather tree species and erect booths was either restricted to those people then in Jerusalem or that booths had to be set up there. Indeed, the proclamation was sent to Judaeans 'in all their cities *and* in Jerusalem' (v. 15); and the national compliance recorded in v. 16 indicates that the people 'built themselves booths: each one on his roof, *and* in their courtyards, *and* in the courtyards of the Temple of Elohim, *and* in the broadways of the Water Gate and the Ephraim Gate'. There is no reason to infer from these texts that booths built on private roofs and in private courtyards had to be only in Jerusalem.

Although Neh. 8:14-17 is neither a citation and enforcement of the exegetical plain sense of Lev. 23:39-42, nor a harmonistic blend of it and Deut. 16:13-15, the levitical instructors nevertheless engaged in legal exegesis. A close comparison of the citation in v. 14 (to 'dwell . . . in booths') with the proclamation in v. 15 (to 'build booths' *out of* local tree species) suggests that the latter is an interpretation of the former based on an etymological exegesis of the noun 'booths'. Faced with a legal prescription to build סכות, but with no indication as to its manner of construction, the levitical instructors apparently started with the fact that the noun סכות is derivable from the verbal stem סכך 'to cover over [with branches]'. On this basis they interpreted the Torah command to dwell in booths as implying that one must dwell in 'branched' shelters—hence the directive to go to the forests and hills to gather representative tree species wherewith to build the booths.[18] Given the exegetical procedure involved, it is furthermore striking that both the cited text (which says 'dwell') and its interpreted implementation (which reads 'build') are described as 'written' in the Torah (vv. 14, 15). The interpreters apparently felt their exegesis to be implied in the written Scriptural passage read on the second day of the seventh month. It was in this way that they 'made (exegetical) sense' of it.

Post-biblical exegesis reflects comparable difficulties in comprehending and determining how to implement the laws of the Tabernacles festival. The injunction in Lev. 23:40 to 'take' the species and 'rejoice before YHWH' was considered basic to its implementation—though its

---

[17] The use of *śimḥāh* in Neh. 8:17 and *śāmēaḥ* in Deut. 16:14-15 is no proof of deuteronomic borrowing. The verb is also found in Lev. 23:40.

[18] Cf. N. H. Tur-Sinai, *Ha-Lashon weha-Sepher* (Jerusalem: The Bailik Institute, 1955), iii. 79.

precise sense remained ambiguous. Thus, 2 Macc. 10: 6-7 reflects an interpretation of the law whereby one should take the species in one's hands as a festival bouquet and rejoice with them. Quite different is the interpretation reflected in Jub. 16: 30 f, which traces to Abraham the custom of putting tree bowers around the altar as one walks round it on each day of the festival. While the mode of implementation and celebration recorded in 2 Macc. 10: 6-7 was continued as the standard rabbinic interpretation,[19] it is possible that the custom preserved in the Book of Jubilees is of biblical origin, and is reflected in the exhortation found in a pilgrimage psalm: 'Bedeck the festival with [willow-] branches at the corners of the altar' (118: 27).[20] Such festivities were undoubtedly related to even older Israelite celebrations which took place amid the vineyard bowers at harvest time (cf. Judg. 21: 19-22).

2. In addition to the interpretation of Neh. 8: 14 in v. 15, it is possible that v. 18 preserves a more implicit instance of legal exegesis. The narrator records that Ezra 'read from the book of the Torah of Elohim each day, from the first day to the last; and they [the people] celebrated the festival [of Tabernacles] seven days and a solemn convocation on the eighth, in accordance with the ordinance כמשפט'. This reference to a daily Torah reading during Tabernacles—presumably paralleling the ritual of daily sacrifices prescribed for this period[21]—has no explicit biblical support. If this festival lection is not merely an *ad hoc* innovation, there is good reason to regard it as an exegetical deduction based on Deut. 31: 10-13, which commands that the Torah be read and taught on the festival of Tabernacles every seven years.[22] Inasmuch as this commandment helps account for the general situation of Ezra's Torah reading and teaching on Tabernacles, it is also likely

---

[19] See Albeck, *Mabo' la-Mishnah*, 22.

[20] Cf. the interpretation in *b. Sukk.* 45a, where Ps. 118: 27 is cited. According to *M. Sukk.* iv. 5 the altar processional was accompanied by a recitation of Ps. 118: 25 on all seven days; on the last day, additional willow-branches were set up by the altar. Jub. 16: 31 takes an interesting compromise position with respect to the use of the species: the boughs and willows were used to build the booths, whereas the palm-branches and fruits were decked around the altar.

[21] The Tabernacles' sacrifices specified in Num. 29: 1-38 are referred to in Ezra 3: 4 (note *kakkātûb* and the catch phrase *běmispārām kěmišpāt*). What is more, the preceding annotated list of sacrifices in Num. 28 is referred to as well: the daily offerings noted in Num. 28: 1-8 are mentioned in Ezra 3: 3b; the new moon, festival, and free-will offerings listed in Num. 28: 11-15, 28: 16-31 (+ 29: 1-38), respectively, are mentioned in Ezra 3: 5. Num. 28-9 has thus been 'used' historiographically to give a synopsis of post-exilic piety and conformity to the Pentateuchal laws of sacrifice. This priestly sequence is also referred to in 2 Chron. 31: 3, and referred to 'as is written in the Torah of Moses'.

[22] While the phrase 'at the conclusion of seven years' is clarified in context to mean the sabbatical release year, *M. Sukk.* vii. 8 prescribes the lection on Tabernacles of the eighth year', i.e. 'at the [actual] conclusion of seven years'.

that Ezra interpreted the command in Deut. 31:10 to read the Torah בחג in a distributive sense; i.e., to read it '*during* the festival' and not just 'on' its opening day. Significantly, the expression בחג is also used distributively in the text cited in Neh. 8:14 ('the Israelites must dwell in booths *during* the festival'; and cf. Lev. 25:20). This verbal repetition may thus have been the basis for an exegetical analogy between the two passages: בחג in Deut. 31:10 was interpreted in the light of בחג in Neh. 8:14, with the result that the lectionary practice referred to in Neh. 8:18 found textual support in the Torah of Moses.

To be sure, the custom of reading the Torah during the festival week may not be an (exegetical) innovation of Ezra's post-exilic convocation in 458, and may well have had its origins in exilic worship. Consideration of this point reopens the old query as to the origin of the synagogue.[23] For what is particularly noticeable with regard to the events described in Neh. 8 is the variety of features which reflect established congregational worship: there is a public gathering; the Torah is opened before the throng (v. 5); a hymn of blessing with a communal *responsum* and genuflection precede the recitation of the Torah (v. 6); and then the Torah is read out and interpreted by well-trained levitical personnel (v. 8). Thus, for all the apparently impromptu character of Ezra's convocation, the presentation of the ceremonies involved appears based on established practice: so that there is a presumptive likelihood that the entire service, or its several parts, developed during the Babylonian exile. Certainly the custom of reading and studying the Torah under levitical guidance would have formed a sound basis for communal worship in the exile, in the absence of sacrifices and the disinclination (in some circles at least) to recite Psalm liturgies of the Temple service (cf. Ps. 137:1-4). In addition, the fact that the Levites appear in Neh. 8:8 with fully developed exegetical procedures further suggests a prehistory for such instruction. The need to explain the Torah and teach its laws to the exiles would conceivably have been of paramount importance in a Jewish worship service in the diaspora; and the need to evaluate, sift, and harmonize the many legal traditions of the exiles would have helped sharpen the exegetical skills of the Levites.[24] Thus, whether during the exile or thereafter, exegesis filled the gap between inherited traditions and their accurate or adequate comprehension.

---

[23] Cf. W. Bacher, *Hastings Dictionary of the Bible*, iv, s.v. 'synagogue'.
[24] S. Smith, 'The Priestly Source ("P") and the Pentateuch', in *The Cambridge Ancient History*, vi (New York: Macmillan and Cambridge University Press, 1927), 193-9, correctly focused on the importance of integrating the national traditions during the exile.

B. CONCERN WITH THE COMPREHENSIVENESS AND SCOPE OF THE LAW

Exegetical Precedents for Exclusion from the Community in the Post-exilic Period

Ezra's role as a teacher and administrator of the Torah of YHWH was publicly demonstrated during Rosh Hashanah 458 and the interpretations regarding the festival of Tabernacles which he oversaw at that time (Neh. 8). The returning 'community of the exile' was formed with Torah and its exegesis at its living centre:[25] it was a community which 'sought YHWH' (Ezra 6: 21); and this, under Ezra's aegis, meant strictly speaking that they 'sought the Torah of YHWH' (Ezra 7: 10). It was this orientation and its consequent behaviour which set the 'community of the exile', and those who joined them, apart from the 'impurities' of the local population (Ezra 6: 21). Two factors in the incipient and developing self-definition of the 'community of the exile' thus emerge. The community was concerned with a ritual *ethos* based on the Torah; and it was concerned with a ritualized ethnicity, reinforced by a sense of the impurity of those who did not adhere to its particular praxis and modes of purity. Both factors intermingle, but each has its distinct articulation. Torah study and its interpretation, as found in Neh. 8, demonstrate the concern with *ethos*. The proliferation of concern for proper lineage in the post-exilic period demonstrates the obsession with ethnicity.

Shortly after the events of the festival of Tabernacles (Neh. 8), and an accounting of the 'community of the exile' (Ezra 8), Ezra was informed by his princes that 'the people of Israel, and the priests, and the Levites have not נבדלו separated themselves from the people of the land' (9: 1). Upon hearing this news, Ezra went into a state of mourning and contrition, together with 'all who חרד trembled at the teachings of the God of Israel' (9: 4). 'While Ezra was praying and confessing . . . a very great crowd of Israelites gathered about him . . . and wept bitterly' (10: 2). It was from within this expanded group that one Shechania ben Yeḥiel made the proposal to expel all foreign wives and their offspring 'according to the advice' of Ezra[26] 'and those who חרדים tremble at the command' of God—so that 'the Torah [law] be followed' (v. 3).[27] This

---

[25] The designation *běnê haggōlāh* 'community of the exile' appears to be the title of the pious returnees; cf. Ezra 4: 1, 6: 19-21, 8: 35. For 'congregation of the exile' cf. Ezra 10: 8.

[26] Reading *'ădônî* 'my lord', for MT *'ădônay* 'the Lord'—a pious correction.

[27] The designation 'those who trembled at the teaching/commands' of the Lord in Ezra 9: 4, 10: 3 seems to refer to a pious subgroup among the returnees. They are referred to again in Isa. 66: 2, 5, together with those called the 'poor' and 'humble in spirit' (see Isa. 66: 2, and cf. 57: 15, 61:1). Other designations

recommendation was undertaken forthwith: the nation was gathered in Jerusalem and told to banish its foreign wives (vv. 7-11). The people appeared willing to comply with this directive, but, as the infractors were many, it took three months for the lists to be drawn up and the priests, Levites, gate-keepers and laity located (vv. 13-43).[28] But here the text breaks off, ominously (v. 44): for it is not at all clear that the foreign wives of those listed were actually evicted from the community --as the faithful had sworn to do (in 10: 3-5).[29]

The events in the ensuing days of the procuratorship of Nehemiah, when intermarriage was still very widespread, underscore the ominous nature of the precipitous close of the Book of Ezra. But before turning to these events, it is well to note that Ezra wished to establish a 'pure' community based on the Torah ('and let the Torah be followed', 10: 3) and had the community actually swear a pact to this end (vv. 3, 5). However, the prickly question is, Where in the Torah is there any indication of a provision dealing with the expulsion of foreign wives (and the dispossession of their children)? There are, to be sure, frequent admonitions in the Pentateuch and historical books prohibiting intermarriage between the invading Israelites and the native, autochthonous Canaanite population (cf. Exod. 34: 16; Deut. 7: 3; Josh. 23: 12-13; Judg. 3: 5-6). But what has this to do with the post-exilic situation? On what possible basis could a legal precedent be established or formulated so as to exclude foreign wives? The clue lies in the way the princes articulated their complaint to Ezra (9: 1-2) and in the way Ezra reflected upon these words in the course of his ensuring prayer.

The text of Ezra 9:1-2 is straightforward: 'Neither the people of Israel nor the priests and Levites have separated from the peoples of the land, and their abominable practices—the Canaanites, the Hittites, the Perizzites, the Jebusites, the Ammonites, the Moabites, the Egyptians, and the Amorites. They [the Israelites] have taken [from these nations] their daughters for themselves and for their sons in marriage, so that the זרע קדש holy seed has become mixed among the peoples of the land.' Nevertheless, on closer inspection, it is perfectly clear that the princes' complaint is not straightforward: it is a deliberate allusion to Deut. 7, wherein the Israelites are prohibited to intermarry with the

include the 'servants' (65: 8-9, 13, 15, 66: 14), the 'faithful' (57: 13), the 'chosen ones' (65:9, 15), 'the people of *hesed*-loyalty' (57:1), and 'the mourners [of Zion]' (57:18, 61: 2-3).

[28] The natural period referred to was from 29 December to 27 March 457. S. Mowinckel's rearrangement of the material is both unnecessary and tendentious; cf. his *Studien zu dem Buche Ezra-Nehemia* (SNVAO 2/7; Oslo, 1965), iii. 8ff.

[29] The MT in 10: 44 is obscure: it seems simply to note that the men had wives and children. 1 Esd. 9: 36b corrects this troubling lacuna in the light of Ezra 10: 3, and reads 'they sent them away with their children'.

local population (v. 3) – 'the Hittites, the Girgishites, the Amorites, the Canaanites, the Perizzites, the Hivites, and the Jebusites' (v. 1). And just as the princes refer to Israel as a 'holy seed', the command of Israelite separatism in Deut. 7: 6 is justified 'because you are a *holy* nation to YHWH, your God'.

The leaders of the returning 'community of the exile' thus wanted to impress upon Ezra the similarity between their situation and that of the first Israelite settlers during the conquest of Canaan. But they also wanted much more: for they added one factor which remarkably transforms the textual allusion to Deut. 7:1-3, 6. They added the names of the Ammonites, the Moabites, and the Egyptians to the old Pentateuchal list. The mention of these nations, which are never included among the roster of autochthonous Canaanites, is of some moment – not just because the Ammonites were the contemporaneous enemies of the returnees, but because they, *and* the Moabites, *and* the Egyptians are the population groups explicitly prohibited from entering the 'congregation of YHWH' in Deut. 23: 4-9! Add to this the fact that LXX manuscripts and 1 Esd. 8: 68 read Edomites for MT Amorites at Ezra 9:1 (the Edomites being the fourth of the four prohibited groups mentioned in Deut. 23:4-9), and there can be little doubt that the reference by Ezra's princes to the intermarriage law in Deut. 7:1-3, 6, *with the notable addition of just those peoples mentioned in Deut. 23: 4-9*, is an intentional exegetical attempt to extend older pentateuchal provisions to the new times.[30] The old list of autochthonous peoples mentioned in Deut. 7: 1 is thus updated to include the Ammonites and Moabites – the former a contemporary enemy, and both of them groups with whom the returnees intermarried (cf. Neh. 13: 23).

Ezra's response to the princes confirms the hypothesis that Ezra 9:1-2 is an exegetical blend of Deut. 7:1-6 and 23: 4-9. In Ezra 9: 11-12 he specifically cites the following words – which he claims were commanded by God to his servants the prophets: 'The land which you are coming to inherit is a polluted land, polluted by the abominations of the peoples of the land . . . so now, do not give your daughters to their sons, and do not marry their daughters to your sons; and do not ever seek their peace or favour . . .'. In this manner, Ezra makes clear how he understood the words of the princes and, most probably, how the princes actually intended them. His citation from the 'prophets' mentions the 'peoples of the land', their 'abominations', and the old prohibition of intermarriage.[31] These key elements allude verbally

---

[30] The reading 'the Edomites' is thus to be preferred. Cf. Kaufmann, *Toledot*, viii. 291-3.

[31] Verse 11 uses a standard citation formula, 'which you [God] commanded . . . saying'. What is striking is Ezra's statement *to God* that the teachings were commanded 'through your servants, the prophets'. Why the plural? Does this

and thematically to the statement by the princes in Ezra 9: 1 and
to their own allusion to Deut. 7: 1-3. Even more specifically, the phrase
הארץ אשר אתם באים לרשתה 'the land which you are coming to inherit'
is a verbatim allusion to כי יביאך ה' אלהיך אל־הארץ אשר־אתה
בא־שמה לרשתה 'when YHWH, your God, shall bring you to the land
to which you are coming to inherit [it]' from Deut. 7: 1. But it is
particularly his citation of the clause 'do not seek their peace or favour
for ever' which makes clear that Ezra also understood Ezra 9: 1 in the
light of Deut. 23: 4-9. For this clause is a fairly close citation from
Deut. 23: 7, and concludes the prohibition of allowing the Ammonites
or Moabites into the Israelite 'congregation' ('do not seek their peace or
favour all your days, for ever'; Deut. 23: 7).[32]

Accordingly, the mechanism for prohibiting intermarriage with the
Ammonites, Moabites, etc. was an exegetical extension of the law in
Deut. 7: 1-3 effected by means of an adaptation and interpolation of
features from Deut. 23: 4-9. Notably, the textual blend appears in both
Ezra 9: 1 *and* 9: 11-12. By means of this new association, the contents
of Deut. 23: 4-9 were reinterpreted *with respect to intermarriage*, and
the subsequent legal move — expulsion — follows quite logically: people
who were legally barred from admission to the 'congregation of YHWH',
but had somehow gained access, were to be expelled. Perhaps Ezra
himself had some form of exclusion in mind in the course of his prayer;
but he does not say as much. It was left to Shechaniah, therefore, to
hit upon banishment as a means to solve the communal crisis (Ezra
10: 2-3)[33] although he judiciously left the details to Ezra and his
associates (v. 3). So seen, Shechaniah's remark that 'the Torah be
followed' is presumptuous: for what this strictly means is that the
interpretation of the Torah *as developed in this circle of exegetes* was
to be followed. This last point also applies to Shechaniah's remark that
the children of these foreign wives be sent out as well. Since there is
no ordinance in the Torah to this end, it was presumably inferred that,
in so far as the Ammonites and the Moabites were excluded from the
congregation of Israel through the 'tenth generation . . . for ever' (Deut.
23: 4), and the progeny of the Edomites and the Egyptians were to be

reflect a notion that the legal teachings were communicated through *several*
inspired individuals?

[32] The variations are minimal: Ezra 9: 12 has *tidrĕšû . . . 'ad 'ôlām*; Deut. 23: 7
has *tidrōš . . . lĕ'ôlām*. The prohibitions themselves probably reflect injunctions
from different historical periods. On this, see K. Galling, 'Das Gemeindegesetz in
Deuteronomium 23', in *Festschrift A. Bertholet*, edd. W. Baumgartner *et al.*
(Tübingen: J. C. B. Mohr, 1950), 176-9.

[33] He says *lĕhôṣî'* 'to cast out'. The Akkadian cognate is used in divorce
proceedings; cf. the texts in C. H. Gordon, 'Hos 2: 4-5 in the Light of New
Semitic Inscriptions', *ZAW* 54 (1936), 278-80. The technical biblical legal term
appears to be *šillaḥ*; see Deut. 24: 3-4 and Jer. 3: 1 (cf. Deut. 21: 14).

excluded to the third generation (vv. 8-9), the children of the banished foreign wives were to be similarly excluded. But the exegesis underlying this decision is nowhere stated.

Taking all this into account, it is, nevertheless, altogether remarkable that no provisions for purification or conversion were extended either to the foreign wives or to their offspring—even though the circumcision of males was an ancient means of incorporating non-Israelites into the community of Israel (cf. Gen. 34:14-16; Exod. 12:48),[34] and, more importantly, even though from earliest times a 'woman's description follows her father's or husband's', i.e., naturalization of foreign women was achieved by marriage.[35] The absence of such provisions should not necessarily be ascribed to a policy of uncompromising separatism on Ezra's part—although this possibility cannot be rejected out of hand, given Ezra's concerns and the overall polemics then taking place in the post-exilic community. Since the earliest days of the Return from Exile, and into the days of Ezra's successor, Nehemiah, foreigners were systematically excluded by the 'community of the exile' from a share in the building of the Temple and the reconstruction of the walls of Jerusalem (cf. Ezra 4:2-5; Neh. 3-4). This position is contradicted by the anti-exclusivist manifesto of Trito-Isaiah, who stated that 'foreigners (בני־נכר) will build [the] walls' of Jerusalem (60:10) and will offer acceptable sacrifices to the Lord on his throne (60:7, 61:5-6). On one occasion, at least, this prophet even forecast that the בני־נכר who will join the community, and the eunuchs who will observe the Sabbath, will have a special place in the new Israel: by their faithful service the eunuchs will achieve an everlasting memorial in the Temple and walls of Jerusalem (56:5); and because of their pious behaviour the foreign converts will not be separated (stem: בדל) from the congregation of Israel (v. 3), and will even serve as officiants in the Temple. Indeed, says the Lord, their offerings 'will be acceptable upon my altar' (vv. 6-7).[36] This possibility is vigorously rejected in the reflex of these

---

[34] Cf. the discussion by C. Tchernowitz, *Toledot ha-Halakha* (New York: printed privately, 1945-53), iii. 108. The language of Gen. 34:16 recalls the formulary in Exod. 34:16, Deut. 7:3, Judg. 3:5, Ezra 9:12 (cf. v. 2), and Neh. 13:25. Certainly Deut. 21:10-14 could have served as a precedent for the domestication of foreign women—but this was far from Ezra's or Shechaniah's interest. See below.

[35] See D. Daube, *Ancient Jewish Law* (Leiden: E. J. Brill, 1981), 3-5.

[36] The polemical substratum is particularly evident in the terms used. For example, in Isa. 56:3, 6-7 foreigners will not be separated (*habdēl*) but 'will draw near (*nilwîm*) to YHWH to serve him (*lĕšārtô*). However, in Num. 18:2 the Levites 'will be drawn near *(wĕyillāvû)*' to the priests and serve with them (*wîšarĕtûkā*); and Deut. 10:8 states that the Lord 'separated (*hibdîl)*' the Levites 'to serve him (*lĕšārtô*)'. Divine service is here considered an exclusive prerogative of sacral groups.

post-exilic debates found in Ezek. 44: 7.[37] In this latter passage, the prophet condemns the Israelites for having brought 'בני נכר, uncircumcised in mind and body' into the Temple (v. 8). For this offence, the laity lost its ancient right to perform sacrifices (vv. 11-12).[38]

It is not unlikely that with his campaign against intermarriage Ezra chose his side in the debate. As a priest he was certainly concerned that the priestly and levitical lineages, in particular, be kept pure—and it will be recalled that both priests and Levites were involved in intermarriage (Ezra 10: 18-23). Indeed, Ezra does not even hint at the possibility, as did Ezekiel, a near-contemporary priest-prophet, that some time in the future (of the New Temple and Restoration) non-natives who had undertaken the burden of the law, and their children, would be permitted to inherit land like native Israelites (47: 22).[39] If, then, Ezra is so unyielding towards foreigners and their progeny, perhaps another reason for his position may be found—both in the particular choice of terms in his prayer (Ezra 9: 6-15), and in the parallelism which he draws there between the impurities of the autochthonous Canaanites and those of the contemporary 'peoples of the land'.

In the same citation of the ancient prophets in which he refers to Deut. 7: 1-3 and 23: 4-9, Ezra states that the land which the Israelites will inherit is polluted (נדה היא) with the abominations (תועבת) of the native settlers of the land (Canaan), and filled with their impurities (טמאתם).[40] This set of terms and ideas is also found in Lev. 18; so much so, in fact, that it appears that Ezra 9: 11 is a deliberate reference to them. In Lev. 18 the ancient Israelites are told that when they come to Canaan they should not follow native practice (v. 3): for the natives have rendered both themselves and their land impure (טמא; vv. 23-30) with abominations (תועבת; vv. 26-30), which include intercourse with females 'in [the state of] the pollution of her impurities בנדת טמאתה' (v. 19) and the practice of incest between children and their parents (vv. 6-7)—the latter being *precisely* the outrage practised by the daughters of Lot, who conceived and bore (the eponymous ancestors of) Ammon and Moab (Gen. 19: 31-8)![40b] From this point of view, the textual blend in Ezra 9: 11-14 of citations from Deut. 7: 1-3 and 23: 4-9, and of allusions to Lev. 18, gives further exegetical basis to Ezra's prohibition of intermarriage between the 'community of the exile' and the 'peoples of the land'—both the real and putative (Ammonites and

---

[37] It was also rejected in Qumran circles. The verb *lĕšārtô*, used in Isa. 56: 6 with respect to foreigners (cf. preceding note) was deleted in 1Q Isaᵃ Tendentious corrections are evident in the LXX as well. Cf. M. Weinfeld, 'Universalism and Separatist Trends in the Period of the Return to Zion', *Tarbiz*, 33 (1964), 240-1 [Heb.]. [38] See below, pp. 138-43.

[39] This is an eschatological reversal of Lev. 25: 45-6. [40] Ezra 9:11.

[40b] The phrase *'erwat 'ăbîkā wĕ-* ('the nakedness of your father and') in Lev. 18: 7, which is anomalous with the sequel, may well have been added in the light of Gen. 19: 31-8.

Moabites) descendants of the ancient Canaanites. It also goes some way to explain his failure to provide any means whereby the foreign wives or their offspring (present or future) might be incorporated into the polity of Israel. For Ezra, the genealogies of the Ammonites and Moabites—peoples now included among the ancient Canaanites and, like them, stained by incest in their lineage—were impure 'for ever'. Purification or conversion was thus unthinkable: for they would contradict explicit *and exegetically developed* deuteronomic law.

It bears mention that, although the offspring of incest are not stigmatized in Lev. 18, ancient rabbinic tradition labelled such persons ממזר.[41] The textual collocation of the prohibition of incest in Deut. 23: 1 with the prohibition in v. 3 against allowing the ממזר to ever enter the 'congregation of YHWH' was decisive in this regard. Given the blend of texts in Ezra 9: 11-12 from Deut. 23: 4-6 (regarding Ammonites and Moabites) and Lev. 18 (regarding incest), it seems less than coincidental that the ממזר is permanently prohibited from entering the community of Israel *just after* the prohibition of incest (v. 1) and *just before* the exclusion of the Ammonites and Moabites from the community 'for ever' (vv. 4-6)![42] Accordingly, if the textual redaction of Deut. 23: 1-9 does not already presuppose the exegetical understanding that the Ammonites and Moabites were excluded permanently from the community of Israel as an instance of the prohibition of the offspring of incest (i.e. as a contextual inference from the general to the particular), then it appears that this is an exegetical conclusion drawn by Ezra himself—given the particular elements which he chooses to blend in his citation from the ancient 'prophets' (Ezra 9: 11). As noted, Ezra's manifest goal was to expunge (i.e. 'separate') genealogical impurity from the post-exilic 'community of the exile'. Since the Ammonites and Moabites were doubly tainted—because of the incest in their own past, and by virtue of their (exegetical) association with the ancient Canaanites (who had similar practices)—they could not be allowed to sully the 'holy seed' of Israel. And so they were expelled from the

[41] In Tannaitic times there was great controversy over the definition of a *mamzēr*. See *M. Yebam.* iv. 13. According to the later Amoraic tradition in *b. Yebam.* 49a, R. Aqiba derived his rule (that a *mamzēr* was the child of any forbidden marriage) from the proximity of Deut. 23: 3 to v. 1. For this reasoning, see the earlier discussions in *Sifre Deut.* 248 (on Deut. 23: 1) and *Midrash Tannaim*, 144, ed. Hoffman (on Deut. 23: 1). On this and related matters, see A. Büchler, 'Family Purity and Family Impurity in Jerusalem before the Year 70 CE', in *Studies in Jewish History* (Jews College Publications, NS 1; London: Oxford University Press, 1956), esp. 75-82.

[42] C. Carmichael, *The Laws of Deuteronomy* (Ithaca: Cornell University Press, 1974), 173f., correctly observes that the legal sequence of Deut. 23: 1, 3 + 4-6 should be seen in relationship to Gen. 19 and so provides a contextual explanation of the word *mamzēr*. He fails, however, to note the bearing of this redactional sequence upon the exegesis in Ezra 9: 11-14.

community – through a combination of exegetical blends, te
allusions, and formal parallels.[43]

In his concern with ethnic and genealogical sanctity, Ezra was a man
of his times. Nehemiah, his successor, was also concerned that the 'seed
זרע of Israel' separate itself (stem: בדל) from all 'foreigners (בני נכר)'
(Neh. 9: 2). Similarly, the post-exilic prophet Malachi (2: 11) censured
the nation for desecrating 'the holiness (קדש) of YHWH' – that is, the
people of Israel – 'by marrying בת אל נכר 'daughters of a foreign god'. He
goes on to criticize their divorce of Israelite women (vv. 14, 16), since the
consequence is that they have not produced a 'godly seed' (זרע אלהים,
v. 15).[44]

It is clear from these texts that a corporate holiness is attributed to
Israel, and, as such, is vulnerable to pollution and desecration. But the
idea was not born amid post-exilic squabbles: it is already found in
pre-exilic Pentateuchal traditions. As indicated, the notion of a 'holy
seed' found in Ezra 9: 2 is derived from Deut. 7: 6. This latter text
addresses the need for ethnic exclusivism 'because you are a עם קדוש
holy nation to YHWH', who 'chose you . . . to be his עם סגלה special
people'. There is no qualification to this status; it is unconditional.
Indeed, this theological feature of Deut. 7: 6 is clearly evident in the
citation of it in Deut. 26: 18-19, 'And YHWH swore to you this day
that you would be his special people עם סגלה *as he had said* . . . that
you would be a holy nation עם־קדש to YHWH . . . *as he had said*.' The
unconditional nature of Israelite holiness is even more sharply underscored when the promise referred to in Deut. 26: 18-19 is compared
with an earlier version of it in Exod. 19: 5-6. The holiness of Israel is
portrayed there as contingent upon covenantal obedience: '*If* you
hearken to my commandments . . . *you will be* סגלה special to me . . .
and be for me a kingdom of priests and a holy people גוי קדוש.'[45]

This portrayal of Israel as a priestly–holy people can be discerned in
two instances of exegetical transformation which help illumine the
deuteronomic tradition and ideology to which the post-exilic teachers
were heir. The first example involves a comparison between Lev. 21:

---

[43] Reconsideration of the status of the Moabites and Ammonites was a major
post-exilic preoccupation: the genealogical legitimacy of the Moabites is the
theme of the Book of Ruth; the conversion of the Ammonites is the sub-plot of
the Book of Judith; and the Book of Tobit is an apology for the Samaritans and
Ammonites. Quite unexpectedly, it now appears that the latter is of Samaritan
provenance; cf. J. Milik, 'La Patrie de Tobie', *RB* 73 (1966), 522-30.

[44] Verse 15 is a notorious crux. The context suggests that the offspring of
proper ethnic marriages are 'godly', not 'desecrated'.

[45] Or 'priestly kingdom', following W. Moran, 'A Kingdom of Priests', *The
Bible in Current Catholic Thought*, ed. J. L. McKenzie (New York: Herder and
Herder, 1962), 7-20.

5-6 and Deut. 14: 1-12:

Lev. 21: 5-6	*Deut. 14: 1-2*
They [the priests] shall not make their heads bald . . . and shall not lacerate their skin; they shall be holy to their God . . .	. . . do not cut yourselves nor make your forehead bald for the dead; because you are a holy nation to YHWH, your God . . .

Both texts deal with mourning rituals. But whereas Lev. 21: 5-6 is part of a law for holy priests alone, the injunction in Deut. 14: 1-2 has been extended to the entire nation.[46] . The deuteronomist has thus inherited a priestly notion of corporate sanctity and extended it without condition to the whole people, as a religious fact of their being: 'you *are* a holy nation to YHWH.'[47]

The preceding example is reinforced by the repetition of the formula of corporate holiness in Deut. 14: 21, at the end of the aforementioned pericope. The people are told: 'Do not eat any carcass; give it to the stranger who lives in your gates, that he may eat it; or you may sell it to a foreigner—because you are a עם קדוש holy nation to YHWH, your God. . .'. Like Deut. 14: 1-2, the Israelites are told to refrain from certain unholy deeds because *they are* themselves holy; and, like Deut. 14: 1-2, v. 21 reflects the notion of corporate holiness found in Deut. 7: 6. By contrast, the priestly recension of this law in Lev. 17: 15 forewarns both the native and resident stranger against eating carcasses and ripped carrion, lest they *become* impure. Similarly, in the version of this law found in the Covenant Code, the people are told: '*You shall be* a holy people אנשי־קדש to me: do not eat ripped carrion from the field; throw it to the dogs' (Exod. 22: 30). What is particularly striking about this formulation is that the people are enjoined *to become* holy; i.e., their status of holiness is not unconditional. Thus, just as the didactic-hortatory formulations concerning the holiness of Israel found in Exod. 19: 5-6 and Deut. 7: 6 are to be contrasted, in that the first presents Israel's conditional holiness whereas the second stresses the unconditional nature of Israelite sanctity, so too may the motivations attached to the law of ripped carrion in the Covenant Code and the Deuteronomic law be similarly contrasted: the one dealing with con-

[46] For the practice, cf. Isa. 22: 12; Jer. 41: 5, 47: 5, 48: 37; Mic. 4: 14.

[47] Thus, in priestly circles only the priests were inherently 'holy'; the people were *conditionally* so (cf. Lev. 11: 44-5, 19: 2, 20: 7, 26), just as in the JE tradition, reflected in Exod. 19: 6, 20: 30. The lay Israelite could, however, achieve a parapriestly status while a Nazirite (Num. 6: 5). The notion that '*all* the congregation *is* holy' was a priestly anathema (cf. Num. 16: 3). Presumably the deuteronomic extension of the priestly notion of corporate holiness to the entire nation is itself a specimen of inner-biblical exegesis, building on the phrase 'You will be to me a kingdom of priests/priestly kingdom'.

ditional, the other with unconditional, holiness.

Quite evidently, then, it is the deuteronomic notion of corporate holiness which underpins the remarks of Ezra's associates in Ezra 9: 2, and which helps clarify the ideology of this 'community of the exile'.[48] Ezra regarded the community of the Return as heir to the holy status of the pre-exilic community of Israel. But in the choice of terminology there is the trace of a further exegetical echo, and the hint of other contemporaneous polemics: for the phrase זרע קדש recalls the prophecy of Isaiah of Jerusalem, centuries earlier, that Israel would be destroyed by its enemies down to the stump of its זרע קדש 'holy seed' (6: 13).[49] Is it not this planting, this remnant of the people of Israel, that Ezra and his colleagues sought to nurture? Like the contemporary anonymous prophet Trito-Isaiah, Ezra anticipated a new rooting of Israel in her land (Isa. 61: 3); but, unlike Trito-Isaiah, who foresaw a day when all Israelites would serve as priests (61: 6), a 'זרע seed blessed by YHWH' (61: 9; cf. 65: 23), Ezra wished to restore Israel along more restricted lines. For him, they would be heir to the old covenant community, heir to the old designation 'kingdom of priests'. The nation would be priestly; but not everyone would be a priest.

The nature and definition of the renewed Israelite 'kingdom of priests' thus set brother against brother in the post-exilic period. And if, as one may conclude from the evidence, disputes over older definitions and group membership were among the stimuli fostering the development of exegesis, and if, more broadly speaking, the linchpin of these disputes was the rival claims to inherit and interpret the pre-exilic Torah traditions, then a new turn in Israelite religious history has emerged. The development may be characterized as follows: the new community of Israel was a community of communities, a variety of Judaisms, each one laying claim to the received pre-exilic Torah traditions—*through their separate and separating interpretations of them.* The full scope of this characterization will emerge through other instances of post-exilic legal exegesis.

Further Exegetical Precedents for Exclusion from the Post-exilic Community

1. The policy of expulsion based on the exegesis of Deut. 23: 4-9

---

[48] While emphasizing conditional holiness for the nation, the priestly substrate of ideas (cf. previous note) cannot be totally excluded: note especially Lev. 20: 26, 'you shall be holy to me . . . and (*'abdil*) I shall *separate you from the nations*'.

[49] J. Sawyer, 'The Qumran Reading of Isaiah 6, 13', *ASTI* 3 (1964), 111-13, has plausibly argued that this phrase in v. 6bβ was originally a scribal comment on v. 6bα. It is notably absent in the LXX (although it is not clear if this is by homoeoteleuton or simply a different manuscript tradition). Another nationalist interpretation of Isa. 6: 13 – besides Ezra 9: 2 – is *b. Ketub.* 112b.

continued into the years of Ezra's successor, Nehemiah. Ezra, it seems, was not altogether successful in his avowed programme of expelling foreign wives from the 'community of the exile'. We have already indicated the ominous termination of his actions—and the recording of them—in Ezra 10. One can well imagine that resistance to Ezra's programme was due to various motives, not least of these being the deliberate rejection of Ezra's social-religious authority, on the one side, and, on the other, the undoubted emergence of a counter-exegesis. It is intriguing to speculate how the husbands of the Ammonite and Moabite women justified their actions on the basis of the religious and Scriptural claims made against them. As the 'offenders' (from the viewpoint of the 'community of the exile') included priests and Levites, there were undoubtedly included among them persons versed in the law and capable of meeting the challenge of Scriptural exegesis. Thus, it may be assumed that the Book of Ruth, with its concluding genealogical validation of marriages between Israelites and Moabites, on the basis of Davidic precedent, was a product of such religious polemics. The later rabbinic justification of this legal matter, based on the Scriptural 'fact' that Deut. 23: 4-7 only prohibits the admittance of Ammonite and Moabite *males* into the 'congregation'[50]—i.e., the common masculine plural is used, and so there was room to claim that females were not *expressly* prohibited—may well have had its forebears in the early restoration period as well.

In any event, Nehemiah records in his memoirs that the expulsion of foreign wives and other foreign elements was a priority item during the days of his procuratorship in Judaea, and was one of the corner-stones of his religious pact with those members of the 'community of the exile' who remained devoted to the principles of purity and separatism (Neh. 10: 30-1). Nehemiah refers to these episodes of expulsion as troublesome times for himself and the community. When referring to the matter of foreign marriages between Judaean men and Ashdodite, Ammonite, and Moabite women,[51] Nehemiah recalls: 'I contended with them and cursed them; I whipped[52] them and bruised them; and I forced them to swear: "We shall not marry our daughters to their sons, or take any of their daughters in marriage for ourselves or for our sons"'

---

[50] *b. Ketub.* 7b; cf. *M. Yebam.* viii. 3.

[51] The asyndetic juxtaposition of 'Ammonites, Moabites' after the reference to the Ashdodite women of the Judaeans in Neh. 13: 23, and the consecution in v. 24, which refers to 'their children' speaking Judaean and Ashdodite (not also Ammonite and Moabite), suggest that 'Ammonites, Moabites' is a tendentious addition—as in Ezra 9: 1 (for 1 Kgs. 11: 1-2, see below).

[52] Cf. Deut. 25: 2-3. The similarity between Neh. 13: 25 and Isa. 50: 6 suggests a stock pairing of verbs. Accordingly, a degree of hyperbole in Nehemiah's words cannot be excluded.

(Neh. 13: 25). The language of this oath recalls that of the oath in Neh. 10: 31, and the formulations of the prohibition of intermarriage with local foreign women found in the deuteronomic law (Deut. 7: 3) and in the deuteronomistic historiography (Josh. 23: 12). This allusion to older textual precedents, particularly those referred to by Ezra himself (cf. Ezra 9: 12), is notable – since Nehemiah goes on to refer to Solomon as one who sinned before the Lord by marrying foreign wives (vv. 26-7).

At first glance, it would seem that the relationship between Nehemiah's condemnation of foreign marriages in the post-exilic period and the precedent of the sins of Solomon in the early monarchy are only formal and exhortatory in nature: both Solomon and the post-exilic people sinned by marrying foreign wives, and so equally contemned their covenant with YHWH. But the links go much deeper; for Neh. 13: 25 is a deliberate reference to 1 Kgs. 11: 1-2, which records Solomon's marriage with foreign wives. In addition to the Egyptian daughter of Pharaoh, he married Moabite, Ammonite, and Edomite women, among others. According to the text, these latter were 'among the peoples concerning which YHWH told the Israelites: "Do not enter them [viz., their community], and they shall not enter לֹא־יָבֹאוּ among you [viz., your community]."' These remarks, together with vv. 3-5, reflect a more elaborate theological explanation of Solomon's sins than that found in vv. 6-7, which is undoubtedly the primary historical notice.[53] To be sure, v. 1 picks up the reference to Solomon's worship of the gods of Sidon and Ammon mentioned in v. 6, and is thus faithful to the received historical tradition; but by linking Solomon's sins with foreign marriages, and thereby deriving the penchant for idolatry from such associations, the deuteronomistic historian harks back to an old pentateuchal theme particularly reflected in Deut. 7: 3-4. What is more, and certainly more significant, is the fact that when the deuteronomistic historian records Solomon's covenant infidelity through intermarriage he *does not* recite the old list of autochthonous Canaanite nations found in Exod. 34: 11 or Deut. 7: 1. He rather lists precisely those four nations – Ammonites, Moabites, Egyptians, and Edomites – included in Deut. 23: 4-9 and interpolated into Ezra 9: 1! This use of Deut. 23: 4-9 is further underscored by the pseudo-Pentateuchal citation ('concerning which YHWH told you') 'do not enter them, and they shall not enter among you'. For although there is no such citation found in the Pentateuch, it finds its nearest parallel in Deut. 23: 4, where the phrase 'לֹא־יָבֹא בְ shall not enter [the community]' is used regarding the censured Ammonites and Moabites.

The evidence suggests, therefore, that 1 Kgs. 11: 1-2 (+3-4) reflects

<hr />

[53] Cf. J. A. Montgomery, *The Book of Kings* (ICC; Edinburgh: T. and T. Clark, 1951), 231-2.

an early post-exilic exegetical expansion of the old Canaanite population
roster to include the Ammonites, Moabites, Egyptians, and Edomites
which interpreted the idiom in terms of intermarriage! Indeed, this
very same weave of deuteronomic sources by the deuteronomistic
historian lies behind the hortatory warning found in Josh. 23:11.
Presumably, then, Ezra and his associates inherited a species of legal
exegesis which served to support their separatist programme; this interpretation is implied in Neh. 13: 23-7 as well. From a perspective sceptical
of the historical reality described in Ezra-Nehemiah, it could be argued,
of course, that all that is involved is a historiographical *use* of deuteronomic traditions and exegeses, and that neither Ezra and his associates,
nor Nehemiah, was personally involved in the reuse of these traditions.
But little is to be gained from such a supposition, for present purposes,
since the facticity of the exegetical *achievement* cannot be doubted—
whoever executed it. Such a supposition is seriously weakened, moreover, by the fact that the exegeses are depicted neither explicitly nor
programmatically. This would be expected if the interpretations were
merely literary fictions and without historical basis.

2. The allusion to Deut. 23: 4-9 in Neh. 13: 23-7, in which Nehemiah
refers to the expulsion of foreign women, is indirectly strengthened by
the explicit use of that Pentateuchal source in Neh. 13:1-3, also in
connection with the expulsion of foreigners. On the occasion of the
dedication of the completed walls of Jerusalem the Torah was read
publicly (Neh. 12: 27, 13: 1a), and 'it was found written' there that
'neither an Ammonite nor a Moabite may ever enter the congregation
of Elohim; for they did not greet the Israelites with food and water [on
the Israelites' march to Canaan, Deut. 23: 5a]; and he [viz., the Moab-
ites] hired (וישכר) Balaam to curse him [viz., Israel]—but [Elohim]
turned the curse into a blessing' (Neh. 13:1b-2). In response to this
lection the Israelites 'separated (ויבדילו; or, 'removed') every foreigner
(ערב) from Israel' (v. 3). The precise historical occasion of this episode
and the specific identity of the ערב have long been a scholarly crux.
(Is the event, for example, another allusion to the expulsion of foreign
wives or is a different expulsion described?) Equally in need of a solution
is the question why Deut. 23: 4-7 was chosen as the special lection for
the celebrations; or why it is referred to by the celebrants.

A brief inspection of the events described in Nehemiah's memoirs
reveals the reason why Deut. 23: 4-7 was read during the convocation
and the exegesis which underlies the popular response to its recitation.
It will be recalled that Sanballat, Tobiah (the Ammonite), and the
Ammonites, among other persons and groups, were particularly bother-
some to the builders of the walls of Jerusalem (cf. Neh. 3: 33-4: 2).
On one occasion, in fact, Sanballat and Tobiah hired (stem: שכר) a

false prophet to try to trick Nehemiah into entering the shrine and have him killed (6: 7-14). They were foiled in this plot, however, even as 'Elohim foiled their plot' (4: 9) and spoiled their curse (cf. 3: 36) on earlier occasions.[54] From this review it is clear that Deut. 23: 4-7 was read because its contents (which refer to Ammonites, a hired prophet, a divine reversal, and exclusion from the community) and its language (cf. שכר) so precisely parallel the contemporary historical circumstances (the antagonism of the Ammonities, the hiring of a prophet, the divine reversals, and .the exclusion of foreigners entering the community through intermarriage). And despite the historiographical presentation of the events, which makes it appear that the people responded spontaneously to the Pentateuchal text, it is also reasonable to assume that Deut. 23: 4-7 was read on the occasion of the dedicated walls because it had been reinterpreted long before as an analogical precedent for the exclusion of foreigners—especially Ammonites—from the community.

Neh. 13: 1-3 is followed by Nehemiah's recollection that when he returned to Jerusalem after a brief hiatus at the Persian court he found Tobiah the Ammonite ensconced in the Temple, and promptly evicted him—bag and baggage (v. 7). Nehemiah may have simply recalled this event after his report of the eviction of other foreigners (v. 3b). But one must mark well the astonishing fact that Nehemiah reports that he—a layman—entered the Temple precincts forbidden by law and evicted Tobiah (cf. 6: 11)![55] One can hardly imagine that he did so entirely without warrant; and since no Scriptural warrant is known it is likely that he justified his acts exegetically. Deut. 23: 4-7 would have fitted the bill quite well. But the only basis for this inference is the redactional juxtaposition of Neh. 13: 1-3 and 4-8—and this is hardly evidentiary proof.[56] Nevertheless, if it is true that 'Nehemiah, if challenged, would almost certainly have justified his contradiction of the High Priest by appeal to some written law code *interpreted* according to the traditions of his party', then 'here is the first conspicuous instance of the clash between priestly authority and pious layman's traditions of scriptural interpretation'.[57] This gives an unexpected twist to the new dimension of Israelite religious history observed above

---

[54] The matter was an old one: for it is reported that during the reigns of Cyrus and Darius 'the people of the land' disturbed the returnees' building by 'hiring (*sōkĕrîm*)' dissemblers to confuse them (Ezra 4: 4-5).

[55] The injunction that a layman may not encroach upon the sacred precincts of the shrine is a recurrent feature of the priestly corpus; cf. the discussion of J. Milgrom, *Studies*, 5-59, with previous literature cited.

[56] That this sequence is not entirely random is suggested by the parallel sequence of Neh. 13: 23-7 (the eviction of foreign wives) and 13: 28 (the banishment of a priest). As with 13: 1-3, the legal precedent in vv. 23-7 is ultimately Deut. 23: 4-7.

[57] M. Smith, *Palestinian Parties*, 133-4.

regarding Ezra and his exegetical procedures. The new community of Israel was a series of communities of Torah interpretation; so much so, in fact, that lay exegesis could challenge old textual and priestly authority.

But one must quickly add here that the preceding is but one aspect of the clash between priestly authority and pious laymen in the post-exilic period. Trito-Isaiah, it will be recalled, forecast a time when all Israelites would serve as priests (Isa. 61: 6), and when even foreigners would serve in the shrine (56: 6-7, 60: 7, 66: 18-21)—including those whose genitalia were maimed, in apparent flagrant violation of priestly (cf. Lev. 21: 16-23) and non-priestly law (cf. Deut. 23: 2). Indeed, such allowances are so revolutionary and so contradictory to ancient practice that they can hardly have been justified by exegetical means alone. Proof for this lies in the fact that these various innovations—particularly those stated in Isa. 56: 1-7—are presented as new divine teachings, remarkably transforming the ancient Pentateuchal revelations and regulations. In this way post-exilic priestly authority was challenged by the laity from two distinct sources: human exegesis and divine revelation. Which of these two was the greater challenge and the greater cause of separatism in early post-exilic Judaea is impossible to say. But it was unquestionably exegesis which was the revolutionary principle overall. The fact that laymen could reinterpret or challenge priestly rules of purity was the great inheritance of Nehemiah; and the remarkable proliferation of these interpretations of the nature and enactment of the ancient rules of purity was the hallmark of early Jewish sectarian exegesis, as it was of Pharisaism triumphant.[58]

There are other indications that Deut. 23: 4-7 enjoyed exegetical reuse in the post-exilic community. As we have seen, the term 'congregation of YHWH' in Deut. 23: 4 was appropriated by the 'congregation of the exile' to serve their separatist inclinations. The operative legal clause, 'they shall not enter', was undoubtedly understood in a prescriptive and adjudicatory sense. However, this was not the only way this clause was employed. In Lam. 1: 10 the eulogist laments the destruction of Jerusalem: 'The enemy spread out his hand against all her beauty; when the nations—concerning whom you had commanded: 'they shall not enter your congregation'—saw [this] they entered her sanctuary.' In this passage, the law cited from Deut. 23: 4-7 is redirected to God himself. The very nations whom he had prohibited the Israelites from accepting into their community have now ravaged Jerusalem.

---

[58] For the early Pharisaic *havûrāh*, cf. J. Neusner, *Fellowship in Judaism* (London: Valentine and Mitchell, 1963); and, more broadly, see id., *The Idea of Purity in Ancient Judaism* (Leiden: E. J. Brill, 1973). For comparative issues, see J. Baumgarten, 'The Pharisaic-Sadducean Controversy about Purity and the Qumran Texts', *JSS* 31 (1980), 157-70.

Nevertheless, one must point out that the citation is utilized in an expansive sense. It refers to *all* the ravaging nations which besieged Jerusalem, and does not single out those of Deut. 23: 4-9.[59]

An even later use of Deut. 23: 4-9 in the Dead Sea Scrolls is particularly instructive for the way it interweaves a number of features which were exegetically attached to it already in the earlier, biblical period. 4Q Flor. deals with the rebuilding of a pure Temple in the *eschaton*.[60] Col. i. 1-2 opens with a citation from 2 Sam. 7: 10-14, regarding the Temple which David's heir will build. Added to this text is the following comment: 'this refers to the [future] temple, into which shall not enter [one with smashed testicles or cut penis for] ever,[61] nor an Ammonite, a Moabite, a bastard, a בן נכר foreigner, nor a stranger for ever, because my holy ones are there' (i. 3-4). The comment clearly cites the language and various prohibitions of Deut. 23: 2-7.[62] In so far as the Qumran sect often identifies itself as the realized embodiment of the repurified temple and Israelite community in the *eschaton*, it can be inferred that the phrase 'congregation of YHWH' in Deut. 23: 2-4 was taken to refer both to the sectarian community and to the future Temple. Moreover, it is striking that col. i. 4 also expands upon its biblical source by adding the בן נכר and the stranger to the list of those prohibited from entering the New Temple. It is thus evident that Deut. 23: 4-9 was again exegetically reused by a post-exilic group to cut off contact with those Israelites and non-Israelites who did not meet its requirements of ethnic purity. Col. i. 4 of 4Q Flor. thus brings to stark articulation tendencies inherent in the separtist exegesis of Deut. 23: 4-9 recorded centuries earlier.[63]

The Sabbath Law in Nehemiah 13: 15-21 and Jeremiah 17: 19-27

We have had occasion to note that two of Nehemiah's reformist activities referred to in chapter 13 are also mentioned in the covenant-pact of Neh. 10: thus the 'community of the exile' separated itself from the peoples of the land in Neh. 13: 3 and 10: 29; and the people forswore intermarriage in Neh. 13: 25 and 10: 31. But the parallelism between Nehemiah's *ad hoc* measures and the pact is more replete: Nehemiah's reform of the practice of impounding persons and property

---

[59] Cf. D. Hillers, *Lamentations* (AB; Garden City, NY: Doubleday, 1972), 25.

[60] J. M. Allegro, *DJD* (Oxford: Clarendon Press, 1968), v, *Florilegium* 174, pp. xix-xx and 53 f.

[61] This reconstruction not only fits the spaces available but fills out the citation from Deut. 23: 2-7 (as noted below). The reconstructions of Allegro's *editio princeps* (n. 60) and of Y. Yadin, *IEJ* 9 (1959), 96, can therefore be dismissed. [62] Cf. the preceding note.

[63] One may also note that, just as Ezra 9: 1-2 juxtaposes the Ammonite and Moabite to the 'holy seed' of Israel, so col. i. 3-4 juxtaposes the same peoples to 'my [*or* his] holy ones'. Cf. n. 43 above.

for failure to meet loan agreements (Neh. 5:1-14) is paralleled by the
oath to release property and loans on the sabbatical year (10:32); the
reform of tithe donations and collections (13:10-13) is paralleled in
detail in the pact (10:38-40); the purifications of priestly rotations (13:
29-30) and the regularization of yearly wood- and firstfruit-offerings
(13:31) are paralleled by the institutionalization of these practices by
means of the rules set forth in the covenant itself (10:35-7); and finally,
Nehemiah's concern for vigilance in observing the Sabbath rest (13:14-
22) is paralleled by the people's vow: 'we shall not buy any of the
wares or foodstuffs which the people of the land bring to sell on the
Sabbath' (10:32).

In the light of this striking overlap between the reform measures
mentioned by Nehemiah in his *memorabilia* (5:1-14, 13) and the
enactments which formed the substance of the new covenant, one may
infer that the pact of Neh. 10 was a subsequent ratification and codification of the *ad hoc* measures discharged by Nehemiah during the
course of his procuratorship.[64] In this regard, the striking similarity
between Nehemiah's reforms and pact, on the one hand, and ancient
Mesopotamian royal practice, on the other, requires brief comment
here. Just as several Mesopotamian kings instituted a series of temporary
reforms at the outset of their reign in order to alleviate inherited
socio-economic inequities, and these measures were subsequently
reformulated as a royal (*mīšarum*) edict,[65] so Nehemiah instituted a
series of reforms during his procuratorship to redress economic
pressures affecting laymen and clerics, and these too were substantially
re-embodied in the *'āmānāh* pact (Neh. 10).[66] To be sure, considerable
time had passed between the *mīšarum* edicts of ancient Mesopotamia

[64] M. Smith, 'The Dead Sea Sect in Relation to Ancient Judaism', *NTS* 7
(1961), 350 n. 3, has argued against this relationship on the grounds that the
markets closed in Neh. 13:19-21 are still open in 10:32, and that the tithes
brought to Jerusalem by the laity in 13:11-12 are collected locally by the Levites
in 10:39. These arguments are not decisive. First, on general grounds, the multiple
parallels between Neh. 10 and Nehemiah's reformist activities cannot be overlooked; and second, regarding the specific text, Neh. 10:32 is a promise not to
retreat from the sabbatical reforms which preceded it, and 10:38-9 is actually an
(exegetical) reformulation of the *ad hoc* measure in 13:11-12. Smith's interesting
comparison of the reforms of Nehemiah with those of the 'tyrants' of the Greek
city-states (*Palestinian Parties*, 136-44) is nothing but a formal parallel of reforms
(like those of ancient Mesopotamia); there is no reason to align Nehemiah more
with the Aegean *oikoumene* than with other Persian satrapies.

[65] Cf. Finkelstein, loc. cit. (above, p. 95 n. 21), and see n. 67 below.

[66] Significantly, except for the ban on intermarriage (10:31), all the other
issues relate to economic matters affecting the people, the clerics, or the Temple.
That many of the economic reforms also served the self-interest of Nehemiah's
party, and enhanced the role of the Levites and the Temple, does not change
matters.

and the *'āmānāh* agreement of Neh. 10, from post-exilic Judaea under the Persians. There are, in addition, significant internal differences between the two types of document.[67] Nevertheless, the foregoing historical analogy between the actions of Mesopotamian kings and Nehemiah remains of considerable interest because of the *formal* explanation it suggests for the relationship between Nehemiah's *ad hoc* reforms and the legal compact which issued from them.

Of the various issues noted in the *memorabilia* and pact. the concern for Sabbath obedience in the post-exilic community was of singular concern for Nehemiah. Indeed, he regarded its desecration as a chief reason for the destruction of Jerusalem and the exile (13: 18). Nehemiah condemns the treading of vats on the Sabbath, as well as the loading of such produce on beasts of burden for transport and sale to the Tyrians in Jerusalem on that day (13: 15-16). This denunciation exceeds in its details, but generally echoes. the oath taken in 10: 32, where the covenanters forswear purchase on the Sabbath of wares brought into Jerusalem by the 'people of the land'.[68]

While he does not say as much, it is none the less clear that Nehemiah bases his fomulation and condemnation on Jer. 17: 19-27: first, because Jer. 17: 21 contains the only other biblical reference aside from Neh. 13: 15-16 which prohibits the transport of goods to Jerusalem on the Sabbath;[69] and second, because Nehemiah's explanation in Neh. 13: 18, that *such* Sabbath desecration caused the exile, is found elsewhere only in Jer. 17: 27.[70] Significantly, the Jeremian passage poses the doom of exile for Sabbath violation as a conditional threat, whereas Nehemiah

---

[67] Neh. 10 is a compact signed and sealed by the procurator, princes, and clerics, and also sworn to by laymen, other clerics, and cult personnel (vv. 1, 29-30); it refers to the (written) Torah (vv. 30, 35, 37), deals with religious issues separately and in relation to economic ones (cf. the preceding note), and includes exegetical features (see below). For characteristics of the *mišarum* edicts, see F. R. Kraus, *Ein Edikt des Königs Ammi-Ṣaduqa von Babylon* (Studia et Documenta ad Iura Orientis Antiqui Pertinentia, 5; Leiden: E. J. Brill, 1958), and J. J. Finkelstein, loc. cit. (above, p. 95 n. 21), 91-104.

[68] Both chapters refer to 'bringing' (*měbî'îm*) goods to Jerusalem for sale (stem: *mākar*) there (10: 32, 13: 15-16, 19-20). Neh. 13: 15 uses the verb *'ōměsîm* to speak of the act of loading produce, and vv. 15, 19 use the noun *maśśā'* to refer to such loads or burdens (of produce). This contextual usage bears significantly on the meaning of *maśśā'* in Jer. 17: 21; cf. below and n. 73.

[69] Cf. the preceding note.

[70] Moreover, if Jer. 17: 21-2 was based on Neh. 13: 15-17 it would be difficult to explain the absence from Jeremiah of the references to selling found in Neh. 13: 15-16, 20, or of any mention of the Syrians or pedlars (13: 16, 20). It is thus far more likely that the dependency is reversed and that Nehemiah's reference to selling is an (exegetical) expansion. See A. Rofé, 'Studies in the Composition of the Book of Jeremiah', *Tarbiz*, 44 (1974-5), 14 n. 41 [Heb.].

considers it as realized.[71] In this way both passages echo the emphasis placed on the observance and desecration of the Sabbath in late Judaean and early post-exilic sources.[72]

The prohibition of Sabbath labour, sales, and porterage for sales found in Jer. 17: 21-2, upon which Neh. 13: 15-21 is based, is a remarkable instance of inner-biblical legal exegesis. In it the general Pentateuchal prohibition of Sabbath work is expanded in new ways, and the entire result is presented as Sinaitic in origin!

Deut. 5: 12-14	*Jer. 17: 21-2*
Heed the Sabbath day to sanctify it – as YHWH, your God, commanded you: six days you may labour and do all your work, but the seventh is the Sabbath of YHWH, your God; do not do any work . . .	Be heedful *and do not bear a burden on the Sabbath day*[73] *and bring it into the gates of Jerusalem; and do not take any burden from your homes* on the Sabbath day; do not do any work; you shall sanctify the Sabbath day, as I commanded *your forefathers*.

The foregoing comparison makes it quite clear that the Jeremian passage is based on the deuteronomic version of the Decalogue. This is certain for two reasons: first, both Jer. 17: 21 and Deut. 5: 12 use the verb שמר 'to heed', whereas the Decalogue in Exod. 20: 8-11 uses the verb זכר 'to remember'. Second, both Jer. 17: 22 and Deut. 5: 12 refer to the Sabbath command as given earlier to the ancestors. But here lies a significant difference: in Deut. 5: 12 the reference is simply to the earlier citation of the command in Exod. 20: 8; whereas its recurrence in Jer. 17: 22 follows two prohibitions not found in either Exod. 20: 8-11 or Deut. 5: 12-14. In this new context, the statement 'as I commanded your forefathers' does not simply refer to the general prohibition of

---

[71] Rofé, loc. cit. 13-14, has strongly argued that the threat of exile may belong to the deuteronomic expansion of Jer. 17: 21-2, which has stylistic, structural, and idealogical parallels in Jer. 21: 1-5. By contrast, M. Greenberg, 'The Sabbath-pericope in Jeremiah', '*Iyyunim be-Sepher Yirmiyahu* (Jerusalem: Israel Bible Society, 1971), 23-51, considers the 'threat of exile' motif to be authentic. But it is obvious, in any case, that even a historical stratification of Jer. 17: 19-27 does not disprove that this pericope was *received* by Nehemiah (or the 'historians') in its present form.

[72] e.g. Isa. 56: 2, 4, 6, 58: 13-14; Ezek. 20: 12-24 (cf. Exod. 31: 13). These texts will be reconsidered in later discussions.

[73] C. Tchernowitz, op. cit. 113-17, has argued that the prohibition '*al tiś'û maśśā* means 'do not barter', not 'do not bear a burden'. But (1) cf. n. 68 above; (2) note that Neh. 13: 19-20 differentiates bringing a *maśśā'* and selling goods (*mimkār*); and (3) the fact that the prohibition in Jer. 17: 21 against taking a *maśśā'* to Jerusalem is supplemented in v. 22 by the prohibition against taking a *maśśā'* – clearly a burden! – from one's home. It is unlikely that the same legal context would use the noun *maśśā'* in such different ways.

labour derived from the decalogical command, but is expanded to include a prohibition against bearing burdens into Jerusalem on the Sabbath, and one against removing a burden from one's home on that day. The effect of this interpolation into the deuteronomic citation is transformative. Not only has the original Sabbath law been expanded and made more comprehensive, but the innovations have been raised to the level of Sinaitic prohibitions, and thereby legitimized.

The new teaching is thus authorized around a pseudo-citation from the Pentateuch ('as I commanded'): for it is nowhere stated there that one is forbidden to bear burdens into Jerusalem on the Sabbath, or to take them from the private to the public domain. These secondary restrictions thus serve two purposes. They explicate aspects of the general decalogical command against labour on the Sabbath day, and so restrict behaviour—by requiring that any and all burdens remain in the home—as to curtail any opportunity for the transport of goods to Jerusalem.[74] While such transfer of goods would seem to be for the sake of sale, it must be noted that this particular element is not mentioned in Jer. 17: 21-2. The fact that it is detailed in Neh. 13: 15-16 (and 10: 32) has prompted the view that Jeremiah forbade the transfer of burdens to Jerusalem for storage only, and that it was Nehemiah who exegetically applied this prohibition to sales.[75]

---

[74] These restrictions have a formal parallel in Exod. 16: 11-30, which deals with Sabbath regulations concerning the manna. Although this text is contextually pre-Sinaitic, it clearly presupposes the laws of the Sabbath and their elaboration: for while it was prohibited to leave manna from one day to the next, and manna so retained was spoiled, the people went to Moses on a Friday with a double portion and asked how the Sabbath portion might be preserved from ruination (v. 22). Moses then gave a divine ruling on permissible pre-Sabbath preparations (vv. 23-6), but some people still went looking for manna on the Sabbath (v. 27), which prompted YHWH to reformulate his law in v. 26 and add 'no one may leave his home on the Sabbath' (v. 29). As in Jer. 17: 21-2, the second restriction ensured obedience of the first, and, thereby, of the Sabbath day. The recourse by the elders to Moses in v. 22 and his subsequent announcement of new divine legislation, also have strong similarities with the desert pericopae studied above, pp. 98-105. And see below, p. 227, for yet another possibility.

Although, in context, Exod. 16: 29b simply prohibits leaving one's home to collect the manna (so Rashi, Ibn Ezra, and others), it was already reinterpreted in early rabbinic literature as the basis for curtailing movement on the Sabbath; cf. *Mechilta d'Rabbi Ismael, Beshalaḥ,* edd. Horowitz-Rabin, v. 170. Isa. 58: 13 served as an early textual support for this exegetical innovation in CDC xiii. 20-1, Jub. 50: 12, and *Lev. Rab.* 34: 16, in *Midrash Wayyiqra Rabba²,* ed. M. Margulies (Jerusalem: Wahrmann Books, 1972), 814 [Heb.]. In the light of the *inner*-biblical expansions of the Sabbath law in Jer. 17: 21-2 just discussed, it is striking that the *post*-biblical prohibition of sabbath travel has been interpolated into LXX Jer. 17: 21 ('and do not go out of the gates of Jerusalem').

[75] Rofé, op. cit. 14, suggested that Jeremiah's innovation was to expand the prohibition of Sabbath work in 'fields' (Exod. 23: 12) to transport for 'storage'.

As noted, the pseudo-citation in Jer. 17: 21-2 gives the exegetical
expansion to Deut. 5: 12-14 Sinaitic, and so revelatory, status. Even
more remarkable is the fact that the teaching given by Jeremiah is
itself a divine revelation ('thus says YHWH', v. 21a), so that it is YHWH
who putatively cites himself and his ancient teachings. The claim is made
that the people have not heeded the old Sabbath commands (cited in
vv. 21-2), and so are advised to obey the Sabbath laws (as formulated)
lest doom and destruction befall Jerusalem (vv. 24-7). In sum, such a
revelation by the Deity which presumptively cites regulations hitherto
unrecorded as known and ancient is most remarkable. It points, at the
very least, to the need in ancient Israel to camouflage and legitimate
its exegetical innovations. Similar needs and comparable techniques
will be recorded in succeeding discussions. Indeed, inner-biblical legal
exegesis contains many other instances whereby the old revelation is
misrepresented to one degree or another; but there is none like Jer.
17: 21-2 where exegetical innovations are so brazenly represented as a
citation of the old revelation by YHWH himself.

The Passover Law in 2 Chronicles 35: 12-13 and the Superfluity of Pentateuchal Sources

The preceding discussions of legal exegesis have been organized
around texts with verbatim, paraphrastic, or pseudo-citations (cf. Neh.
8: 14-17, 13: 1-3; Jer. 17: 21-2). Each contains some technical formula
indicating the quoted nature of the text. But although the citations are
indicated and explicit, the exegeses themselves are not; these are implicit
and indirect, and often actually obscure the innovations by representing
them as part of the text-citation. This was the technique used in Jer.
17: 21-2, where the new material was incorporated into an older source.
Similarly, the citation from the 'prophets' in Ezra 9: 11-12 is rooted in an
older exegetical inclusion of the Ammonites and Moabites among
references to the autochthonous Canaanite population such as is found
in Ezra 9: 1-2, which itself derives from Deut. 7: 1-6. In this latter
instance, an outdated prohibition was given new authority and force by
incorporating independent material into it.

Such blending or supplementation of laws as appears in Ezra 9: 1-2
and Jer. 17: 21-2 suggests a creative but dependent relationship to
authoritative sources in the post-exilic period. Several uncited text-
blends will be discussed below. For the present, mention may be made
of Neh. 10: 32b. This text is part of the compact sworn in Neh. 10:
1-40, and its contents are represented as Scriptural (cf. v. 30). The

To this, one may compare the view of A. Phillips, op. cit. 127-8, that Num. 15:
32-6 shows an expansion of Sabbath prohibitions from 'occupations' (Exod. 23:
12, 34: 21) to 'domestic work'. But this interpretation of Num. 15: 32-6 is not
self-evident; cf. pp. 99-100 and notes.

people swear: 'ונטש we shall abandon [the land on] the שביעית seventh year as well as משא כל־יד all loans.' This statement combines the law of sabbatical land release in Exod. 23: 11, 'you shall release ונטשתה and abandon it [the land] in the השביעת seventh [year]', with the law in Deut. 15: 1-2, which only refers to debt release: 'every lender shall release משה ידו his loan' (v. 2).[76] Neh. 10: 32 does not resolve the textual contradiction inherent in these two versions of the sabbatical law. Neither is rejected. Instead both Pentateuchal sources are blended and harmonized to create a law more comprehensive than either was independently.

Such attentive uses of older Torah sources by post-exilic scholars were not limited to the blending of complementary laws. Being products of different regions and periods, the laws of the Pentateuch are often in manifest contradiction. For example, in Exod. 12: 9 the Israelites are instructed: 'Do not eat [the paschal meat] raw or מבשל במים בשל boiled in water, but [eat it] צלי־אש roasted through and through.' However, the law in Deut. 16: 7 is in outright contradiction to this regulation. It commands: 'ובשלת You shall boil it and eat it at the place which YHWH, your God, shall choose.' A striking attempt to resolve this ritual contradiction is found in 2 Chron. 35: 12-13. After noting that the paschal slaughter was performed 'as written in the Book of Moses' (v. 12), the Chronicler states: 'ויבשלו הפסח באש כמשפט then they boiled the paschal-offering in fire, according to the law' (v. 13).

On the face of it, the logic of this ritual statement is absurd, since one does not boil meat *in* fire; and the attribution that the ritual was done 'according to the law' is presumptuous, since there is no 'law' to which the preparation refers. Bothered by the incomprehensible phrase 'they boiled the paschal-offering in fire', and its apparent variation from the received Pentateuchal traditions, many ancient and modern interpreters have argued most extraordinarily that the verb in 2 Chron. 35: 13a must mean 'roast', on the basis of the assumption that the same verb in Deut. 16: 7 *also* means 'roast'.[77] This argument is

---

[76] The original III–h/y form of the verb *nšh* occurs in other early sources, e.g. Exod. 22: 24 and Deut. 24:10–11; but it is also found in later redactions, e.g. 2 Kgs. 4: 1, and recurs in Neh. 5: 10–11. (On the other hand, the later III–' form predominates in Nehemiah; cf. also 5: 7, *maššā'*, and *nōši'ym*.) In this light, there is strong support for the old view of A. Geiger, 'Ein alter Fehler in Nehemia 5, 11', *Jüdische Zeitschrift für Wissenschaft und Leben*, 8 (1870), 226–7, to emend *ûmě'at hakkesep* in Neh. 5: 11 to *ûmaššat hakkesep*. Cf. Deut. 24: 10.

[77] Cf. C. Albeck, *Mabo' la-Mishnah*, 9 [Heb.], who claims that 2 Chron. 35: 13 explicates (by mentioning fire) the more terse phrasing in Deut. 16:7. He is preceded by an old tradition; cf. *Mechilta, Bō'*, vi, which cites 2 Chron. 35: 13 as proof; *b. Ned.* 49a; and Ibn Ezra *ad* Exod. 12: 9 and Deut. 16: 7. In *M. Pesaḥ.* vii. 1 R. Aqiba responds to a view which claims that the 'roasting' of the paschal

both tendentious and circular, and attempts to suggest that neither 2 Chron. 35: 13 nor Deut. 16: 7 contradicts the injunction in Exod. 12: 9 – to roast the paschal-offering. The argument also ignores the plain fact that 2 Chron. 35: 13b goes on to state that the Levites 'boiled (בשלו) the holy things in pots and jugs'. This usage makes perfectly natural sense, and is paralleled by 1 Sam. 2: 13-14, where cultic personnel also boiled meat in similar containers. From these comparable contexts it is certain that בשל means 'boil' in 2 Chron. 35: 13a as well.

An unprejudiced examination of the plain sense of the Chronicler's text makes it clear that 2 Chron. 35: 13 is, in fact, a textual blend of the two aforementioned Pentateuchal laws prescribing the paschal-offering.[78] The word אש 'fire' has been taken from Exod. 12: 9, and the verb בשל 'boil' has been derived from Deut. 16: 7; hence the peculiar formulation 'they *boiled* the paschal-offering in *fire*'. Evidently, the Chronicler knew the two distinct sets of ritual norms, and, regarding both as authoritative traditions, preserved them by an artificial, exegetical harmonization. This he tendentiously called 'the [ancient] law'. Commentators who do not recognize this fact simply compound one (modern) harmonization with another (earlier, biblical) one.[79] In fact, however, the Scriptural harmonization in 2 Chron. 35: 13 and its later – rabbinically inspired – one are clear corollaries of one and the same principle: that the Pentateuchal Torah of Moses is integral and indivisible. The antiquity of this perception is thus of considerable note in the overall growth of biblical exegesis.

Verses 7-9 provide another indication that the Passover ceremony described in 2 Chron. 35 has drawn upon diverse Pentateuchal sources. It is there stated that Josiah donated to the people 'sheep—lambs and goats - for all the paschal-offerings . . . and cattle', and that the secular leaders and Levites donated '[sheep] for the paschal-offerings . . . and cattle'. At first sight it appears that the use of sheep and cattle is merely in compliance with the law in Deut. 16: 2, which permits both types, as opposed to the law in Exod. 12: 5, which permits only sheep.[80] However,

---

lamb was to be done on a spit by stating that it was 'like a form of boiling', since the entrails were cooked from within. For modern reflexes of the view that *baššēl* in 2 Chron. 35: 13 means 'roast', cf. the RSV and JPS translations.

[78] Cf. the earlier assertion by M. Z. Segal, *Parshanut ha-Miqra*'[2] (Jerusalem: Qiryat Sepher, 1971), 6.

[79] Albeck, op. cit., remarked that when Scripture wants to use the verb *bašēl* for 'boiling' rather than for 'roasting' it adds 'in water' (so Exod. 12: 9 vs. 2 Chron. 35: 13, which adds 'in fire'). But it is unlikely that ritual texts would use an ambiguous word needing such modification – especially since no modification is found in Deut. 16: 7, and there already was a precise term for 'roasting' in Exod. 12: 9 (there distinguished from *baššēl* + 'with water').

[80] Starting from the assumption that the two Pentateuchal prescriptions are not contradictory, rabbinic tradition assumed that the mention of cattle in

once it is observed that the formulation in Exod. 12: 5 is specifically 'lambs and goats' it becomes clear that 2 Chron. 35: 7 has conflated the language of the two Pentateuchal sources. Once again, the Chronicler was heir to differing recensions of the cultic law and sought to preserve both in his historical source.

A third example of integrated Pentateuchal traditions in 2 Chron. 35 pertains to the sacrifice itself. Whereas the paschal-offering is described in Exod. 12: 3-4, 7 as a local clan ritual, the deuteronomic law states that 'you shall slaughter the paschal-offering . . . at the place which YHWH shall choose' (Deut. 16: 2). The key difference between these two rules is that in the deuteronomic version the layman must perform the rite at the central shrine, in Jerusalem; but since the Israelite was required to perform the sacrifice in both texts there was no unresolvable contradiction between them. A more severe problem arises, however, in 2 Chron. 35: 6, 11, where it is recorded that the paschal-offering was not done by lay individuals, but by the Levites. Although the distinctive nature of the paschal-offering as a lay ritual was compromised, an accommodation was nevertheless achieved with the patriarchal rites stipulated in Exod. 12: the Levites only performed the sacrifice; thereafter they apportioned the slaughtered animals *to* the local clan heads for distribution to the people. Thus, the ritual was performed in Jerusalem—as *per* the deuteronomic law (though now with the Levites playing a central role); but the clan heads retained the right to disburse the slaughtered meat to their family groupings—as *per* the local ritual custom of Exod. 12: 4.

1. Although it is stated in 2 Chron. 35: 12 that the paschal slaughter was performed 'as written in the Torah of Moses', it is remarkable that none of the Levitical activities just described have any Pentateuchal basis: neither their role in the paschal slaughter, nor their role in aiding the priests in sprinkling the blood of the paschal-offering (v. 11), nor again their role in performing the burnt offering (v. 12). Paschal slaughter, blood daubing, and the sacrifice of burnt offerings were originally lay performances.[81] Initial traces of the elevation of levitical activity

Deut. 16: 2 referred to a distinct 'festival' sacrifice; cf. *Mechilta, Bō'*, iv (Rabin–Horowitz, p. 13); *Sifre Deut.* 129; *b. Pesaḥ.* 70b; and Ibn Ezra and Ramban *ad* Deut. 16: 2. This tradition is followed by Albeck, op. cit. On this traditional view, the two types of animals mentioned in 2 Chron. 35: 7-9 would be interpreted as those in Deut. 16: 2.

[81] Regarding the role of the laity in paschal slaughter and blood daubing, see Exod. 12: 3-7. On the lay role in burnt offerings, see Lev. 1: 2-13 (regarding cattle and sheep); but note that the priests sprinkle the blood (vv. 5, 11; cf. v. 15 for bird offerings). For the priestly role in sprinkling blood in other sacrifices, cf. Lev. 3: 2, 8, 13, 4: 6-7, 17-18, 25, 30, 5: 9, 6: 20, 7: 2, 14.

can be found elsewhere in post-exilic sources. For example, priests and
Levites performed the paschal-offering in both Ezra 6: 20 and 2 Chron.
30: 15-18; although only .the latter text acknowledges that this was an
innovation, by noting that it was a (temporary) necessity due to the
widespread priestly impurity which followed the rites of Temple
purification during Hezekiah's reign.[82] These various levitical activities
are, however, strikingly transformed into permanent law in 2 Chron.
35: 6, 12, and justified as part of the written Torah of Moses. The
sacrificial burning of the fat of the slaughtered animals described in
2 Chron. 35: 14 is also a cultic innovation without Pentateuchal basis.
It awaited the skill of later rabbinic exegesis for its textual derivation
and justification.[83]

2. The transfer of cultic responsibilities from the laity to clerics is
also a theme of Ezek. 44: 9-16. In this respect, a notable difference is
discernable between the mode of authorizing inner-cultic changes in
2 Chron. 35: 6, 12, where, as noted, levitical activites are justified as
part of the written Torah of Moses,[84] and the justification of levitical
activities in Ezek. 44: 9-16, which rests on a new divine oracle. In
another respect, however, it must be stressed that such oracular pronouncements regarding ritual rules were not exceptional in the post-
exilic period, as can easily be observed from a host of passages attributed
to Trito-Isaiah, particularly chapter 56.[85] Indeed, the fact that the
oracle in Isa. 56 permits all strangers, בני הנכר, to serve in the shrine,
while that in Ezek. 44 restricts cultic roles to certain groups *because* the
בני־נכר came into contact with the holy office of sacrifices, suggests
that we have here hit upon a live post-exilic issue:[86] both sides are
concerned with the Temple and the involvement of the בני־נכר, and
both sides invoke a new divine word to advance their case. To be sure,
this comparison yields remarkable proof of the belief in post-exilic
times that YHWH could reveal new laws and even abrogate older
legislation. But there is much more to Ezek. 44: 9-16 which bears on
the present discussion. For analysis shows that this later text is not just
a new divine word for a new historical situation, but is an *exegetical
oracle* as well. It does not impute a later ruling to an early divine word,
as does Jer. 17: 21-2, but utilizes the language of an older Pentateuchal

---

[82] 1 Chron. 23: 32 (cf. Num. 18: 3-5) is another example of the Chronicler's
pro-levitical tendency. See the reasoned observations of J. Milgrom, *Studies*,
82-3 n. 307.

[83] See *Sifre Num.*, *Koraḥ*, 118; and, in the edition of H. S. Horovitz, *Siphre
D'he Rah* (Jerusalem: Wahrmann Books, 1966), 139f. Also cf. *b. Zebaḥ*. 37a.

[84] Immediately above.

[85] Above, pp. 118, 123, and in the following discussion.

[86] Also perceived by Zimmerli, *Ezechiel*, ii. 1134, 1126.

ruling in order to reach an entirely new conclusion. A juxtaposition of the pertinent passages will bear this out.

Num. 18: 1-7, 22-3	*Ezek. 44: 9-16*
1. Then YHWH said to Aaron: 'You, your sons, and your descendants together, will bear the guilt of the shrine תשאו את־עון המקדש[87] . . . and the guilt of your priesthood.	9. Then the lord YHWH said: 'No foreigner בן־נכר . . . may enter my shrine מקדשי . . .
2. And also draw your brethren of the house of Levi . . . nigh הקרב to you, and they will join you וילוו and serve you וישרתוך . . .	10. except the Levites who separated from me, when Israel went astray . . . after their idols, and bore their sin ונשאו עונם . . .
3. And they shall guard . . . the watch משמרת . . . ושמרו of the Tabernacle . . .[88]	11. And they shall be stewards משרתים in my shrine . . . [and] they shall slaughter the holocaust and meat offerings for the people . . .
4. And they shall be joined to you ונלוו . . .; but the stranger זר shall not draw nigh to you. . .	12. since they served ישרתו them [the Israelites] before their idols . . . and [so] bore their guilt ונשאו עונם . . .
22. The Israelites shall no longer draw nigh to the Tabernacle [lest they] bear sin [and] die;	14. Thus I have appointed them guardians of the Temple-watch שמרי משמרת for all its work לכל עבדתו.
23. But the Levite shall perform עבד the work of the Tabernacle . . .'	15. But the levitical priest, the sons of Zadok . . . will draw nigh יקרבו to me to serve me לשרתני . . .
	16. And shall guard . . . my watch ושמרו את משמרתי

At first glance, one is struck by the numerous terminological and thematic links between these two passages. Both texts establish a priestly and levitical hierarchy to guard against the encroachment of improper groups into the graded domains of the shrine, and to perform the requisite cultic services. Moreover, the hierarchies established in both texts are the product of a prior crisis: Num. 18 is the result of the Korahite rebellion and Israelite fear of approaching the Tabernacle (cf. Num. 17: 27-8); Ezek. 44 is the result of the paganization of the Temple (vv. 9-12).[89] However, it is the disjunctions between them

---

[87] See the discussion in Milgrom, *Studies*, 22-32.

[88] Op. cit., esp. 8-16.

[89] In Ezek. 44: 6 reference is made to the *merî* 'rebellion' of Israel (the LXX reading, *bêt hammerî*, is preferable); at the conclusion of the Korahite affair, Num. 17: 25, the rebels are called *bĕnê merî*. Cf. also the laws of Num. 18: 8-20 in Ezek. 44: 28-30.

which are of more immediate interest: for they indicate just how Num. 18:1-7, 22-3 was reused in Ezek. 44:9-16. In Num. 18 Aaron's tribe and clan (the Kohathites) are told that they must bear the guilt of the shrine (v. 1; i.e., they must bear responsibility for improper priestly, levitical, or lay encroachment).[90] The levitical brethren are enjoined to serve the priests and be in charge of the work in the shrine (vv. 2-4); and they are, moreover, warned that no stranger (זר, i.e., non-priest)[91] may join them (in their activities) and that they must bear responsibility for non-levitical (v. 4) or lay (vv. 22-3) encroachment. The common Israelite is barred, therefore, from the inner sanctum. By contrast, the situation in Ezek. 44 is quite different. Here the laity is condemned for having allowed foreigners, בני־נכר, to serve them in their sacrifices (vv. 6-7), and for actually appointing them as guardians of the shrine (v. 8). And, further, certain Levites are also condemned for having assisted the Israelites in this illicit worship (v. 12). For these reasons a series of far-reaching cultic changes are announced. Since the laity allowed foreigners to serve in the cult, they are barred from making sacrifices—even though this contradicts established practice (cf. Lev. 1:5, 3:2, 8, 13, 4:24, 29, 33).[92] Their lay role is now taken over by Levites, who are themselves punished for their role in the illicit cultic practices by being barred from the priesthood. This latter right is assigned exclusively to those levitical priests who did not transgress, the sons of Zadok.

It will be noted that the exegetical transformations in this divine oracle range from the oblique to the direct, from the redirection of passages to the replacement of older words by new ones. For example, in Num. 18 the lay Israelites were forbidden to draw nigh (יקרבו) to the shrine (v. 22) to serve as its officients; only the Levites could so draw nigh (הקרב, v. 2). There is no censure in this fact: it is simply a pro-scription designed to protect the Israelites against divine wrath for cultic infractions (cf. Num. 17:27-8, 18:5b, 22-3). The role of the Israelite in lay slaughter is, however, in no way compromised. In Ezek. 44:10-14, on the other hand, the Israelites are replaced in the very performance of lay slaughter for reason of their improper admittance of the בני־נכר into the shrine. Only the sons of Zadok could draw nigh

---

[90] According to Num. 3:38, 18:5a the Aaronid tribe guards the most sacred objects during the encampment; while according to Num. 4:4-15 the Kohathites guard them in transit. Milgrom, op. cit. 24, n. 79, is correct to differentiate between Aaron's tribe and clan here (on the basis of *wĕgam* in 18:2).

[91] On this word, cf. Milgrom, op. cit. 5, and the literature cited in n. 6.

[92] If Ezekiel's reform was institutionalized, its effectiveness was but episodic; for the laity performed the ritual slaughter of sacrifices in the later second Temple. Cf. *Antiq.* iii. 9. 1 and *M. Zebah.* iii. 1.

(יקרבו, v. 15) to the shrine.[93] This change of Israelite status is undoubtedly a pretext, however, even though it appears to be theologically
grounded and divinely sanctioned. For the change in Israelite status
affects, as noted, other cultic roles—principally the emergence of the
sons of Zadok to exclusive clerical pre-eminence. This latter is textually
effected by a manifest terminological addition, as a comparison of the
language of Num. 18: 2-3 with Ezek. 44: 15-16 makes clear.[94] Such a
blatant exegetical transformation suggests that the theological faults of
the Levites and Israelites are actually matters of subordinate significance
in the present document, and that the exclusive elevation of the
Zadokites to the priesthood is the primary issue. Indeed, just as the
Korahite rebellion was the occasion for the emergence of the cultic
hierarchy propounded by Num. 18, one may reasonably regard Ezek.
44: 9-16 as a document of theological propaganda for the priestly line
of Zadok, subsequent to the shrinal improprieties which occurred due
to lay and levitical laxity.[95]

This said, it may nevertheless be the case that the Zadokites rode to
power on a platform which condemned the involvement of foreigners
in the cultic service, and that this was the catalyst to their supercession
over the less zealous Aaronids in their midst. That this factor is also of

---

[93] Note the exegetical redirection of the key verb *qārēb*. Milgrom, op. cit.
83-5, has suggested further that Ezek. 44: 14 exegetically recasts Num. 18: 4a
(though a variant text is possible, cf. p. 83 n. 310), that Ezek. 44: 11 paraphrases
Num. 16: 9bβ to justify the innovation of ritual slaughter (p. 84 n. 315), and that
Ezek. 44: 14 exegetically recasts Num. 4: 26b (p. 85 n. 317). To call the latter
two instances examples of 'midrashic technique' is, however, too strong.

[94] The key verbs of Num. 18 — *qārēb, šārēt,* and *šāmar* — all recur in Ezek. 44:
14-15, but the sons of Zadok constitute the new element (although, of course,
the locution 'the levitical priests, the sons of Zadok' immediately derives from
Deut. 18: 1, 'the levitical priests, *all the tribe of Levi*' – thus reversing the de-
hierarchizing thrust of the deuteronomic ideology). In this regard, it has been
suggested by, among others, H. Gese, *Der Verfassungsentwurf des.Ezechiel* (BHT
25; Tübingen: J. C. B. Mohr, 1957), 57-69, that the passages restricting the
priesthood to the Zadokites are a late stratum in Ezek. 40-8. But this does not
affect the point made here. Of comparative interest is the interpolation inserted
into MS B of Ecclesiastes, Ben Sira (51: 120 (+ ix) (cf. *RB* 9 (1900), 52f.), which
reads: 'Give thanks to him who elects the sons of Zadok to be priests.' See J.
Trinquet, 'Les Liens "sadocites" de l'Écrit de Démas, des manuscrits de la Mer
Morte, et de l'Ecclésiastique', *VT* 1 (1951), 287-92.

[95] In addition to purity concerns and fears of cultic contamination, which
would explain the banishment of the laity, other motives may have been at work.
Milgrom, op. cit. 85 n. 316, suggests that Ezekiel's programme may have sought
to provide country Levites employment in the Temple in the wake of the Josianic
reforms. M. Haran, 'The Law-Code of Ezekiel xl-xlviii and its Relation to the
Priestly School', *HUCA* 50 (1979), 65, sees the 'limitations of the priesthood to
Zadok's descendents . . . as an outcome of the tremors which took place in the
temple service during the reigns of Manasseh and Josiah, that is, as an effort to
restrict the right to the Jerusalem priests alone'.

basic importance, and led to the Zadokites' counter-exegesis of precisely the same theological document – Num. 18 – which had given the Aaronids their own legitimacy, can be seen from another bit of exegesis in Ezek. 44. In this case, as in the latter, a remarkable substitution can be observed: whereas Num. 18: 3, 7 states that the זר, or (non-priestly) stranger, cannot encroach upon the shrine, the social element singled out by Ezek. 44 is the בני־נכר (vv. 7-9). This change in terminology is hardly fortuitous. As indicated earlier, it was precisely in the post-exilic period that a great debate raged over the participation of foreigners, בני־נכר, in the society and the cult.[96] In Isa. 60, for example, it is stated that the בני־נכר will build the walls of the new Jerusalem (v. 10) and offer acceptable sacrifices to the Lord (v. 7). The issue is dealt with again in Isa. 60: 10-11, 66: 21, especially 56: 1-8. Indeed, in Isa. 56, when the prophet forecasts that the בן־הנכר will not be excluded from the community of YHWH (v. 3), he also states (in v. 6) that these people will join (נלוים) and serve the Lord (לשרתו) and will offer acceptable sacrifices to him (v. 7). The use of these technical terms in this context makes it altogether clear that Num. 18 is also the text alluded to by Trito-Isaiah (cf. Num. 18: 2, 4). Accordingly, Ezekiel's use of it, and, in particular, his reference to the בני־נכר, has its *Sitz im Leben* in debates over the cult which dominated the post-exilic scene.[97]

If it was necessary earlier to speculate concerning the counter-exegesis that may have been invoked by those husbands who wished to reject Ezra's interpretation of Deut. 23: 4-7, Ezek. 44 and Isa. 56 provide explicit testimony of contesting exegesis of one common Scripture: Num. 18.[98] On this evidence, there need be no doubt that already from the earliest historical stages of social dissension in post-exilic Israel, when different groups had different visions – some more

---

[96] This contemporary issue of cultic purity undoubtedly underlies the divine investiture of the post-exilic priest Joshua, who is admonished in Zech. 3: 7 to 'guard my watch (*mišmartî tišmōr*)' and to 'guard my courtyards (*tišmōr 'et ḥăṣērāy*)'.

[97] The fact that Ezekiel does not always seem to utilize the P source as we now have it, and thus reflects (in some cases) an indirect, and perhaps 'epigonic' relationship to P material (as argued by Haran, op. cit., esp. 62, 66-7), does not change matters in this case. Something like our present Num. 18 was clearly a pivotal and known document in post-exilic times (and cf. other uses of Num. 18 in Ezek. 44, in n. 89 above).

[98] As for the possibility that Deut. 23 also evoked exegesis and counter-exegesis in this particular debate, it may be noted that Ezek. 44:6-7 censures the Israelites for having brought (*bahăbî'ăkem*) foreigners and uncircumcised males into the shrine. Indeed, Zimmerli, op. cit. 1126, already noted the fact that the form of Ezek. 44: 9, which states that the foreigners 'may not enter (*lō' yābô'*) my shrine', is similar to the exclusionary formula in Deut. 23: 2-4 (*lō' yābō'*) whereby non-Israelites and those with maimed genitalia could 'not enter the congregation'. Could it be that Ezek. 44: 6, 9 is an exegetical application of this Pentateuchal

restrictive, some less—of the future, ideological programmes were established and contested (at least on one level) via Scriptural exegesis. Moreover, the very fact that the divine oracles in Isa. 56 and Ezek. 44 are also exegetical is of major import. It suggests that, at least in the circles represented by these texts, a divine oracle was not in and of itself able to ensure a new social-theological reality, but had to appropriate and reutilize texts which had become authoritative in one way or another. What, then, is remarkable and of historical moment in Ezek. 44 is its witness to the fact that the *traditum* of Num. 18 could not be simply set aside—even by its divine author, in a new oracle—but had to be revised by means of a reinterpreting *traditio*.

passage to exclude such types (parallel to Ezra's use of it, analysed above, pp. 115–20), and that Isa. 56: 7, which announces that YHWH will bring (*hăbî'ôtîm*) the foreigners and the uncircumcised to perform holocaust and meat sacrifices (cf. Ezek. 44: 11!), is a rebuttal of these exclusionist claims *on the basis of the same text*?

7. Legal Exegesis with Covert Citations in Historical Sources

In contrast to the legal exegeses discussed above, the examples to be considered in this chapter are without citation formulary and do not separate the exegeses from the traditions or sources commented upon.[1] The absence of these two features considerably complicates the recognition of additional examples of inner-biblical legal exegesis cited in a covert or implicit manner. So as to isolate those cases from the contexts in which they are presently embedded, at least the following two methodological guidelines are pertinent: (*a*) to observe the clustering of legal terms in non-legal contexts, and to correlate them with legal formulations and prescriptions found in the Pentateuch; and (*b*) to be sensitive to prolix formulations, tendentious explanations, and exceptional legal circumstances. These two perspectives are often complementary. Their conjunction, in fact, makes it easier to identify covert legal (and ritual) comments in the historical sources than in the law corpora—for the clustered presence of legal language in a historical discourse, or the shift in style or focus in a historical description to legal considerations, is more easily differentiated than the unmarked intrusion of new legal terms into older prescriptive rules. It is for such reasons that legal exegesis embedded covertly in the historical narratives will be studied before similar material in the Pentateuchal law collections.

Several distinct types of covert legal exegesis in historical sources will be treated. In some instances, the historical narratives reflect primary attempts to explain or expand upon issues found in the Pentateuchal legal texts; in other instances, the historical narratives simply preserve traditional legal exegesis not otherwise articulated in the Hebrew Bible; and in still other instances, later historical narratives comment upon legal issues included in yet earlier historiography. Each of these sub-types reflects different exegetical processes, different exegetical functions, and different relationships with the primary Pentateuchal legal sources. Their common denominator is that they are embedded in historical narratives without citation formulary and without consecutive or complete allusions to the original Pentateuchal laws.

---

[1] The previous discussion of the exegetical reuse of Num 18 in Ezek. 44 (pp. 138–43) is the exception to this generalization.

A. CONCERN WITH THE MEANING AND APPLICATION
OF THE LAW

On Counting the 'ōmer: the Interval between Passover and Pentecost

Ambiguity in the meaning of prescribed Pentateuchal rituals presents immediate problems, for observance of the law hinges on its understanding. The meaning of the phrase ממחרת השבת in Lev. 23:11, 15 illustrates this issue. After the laws of Passover are given (Lev. 23: 4-8), there follows an ordinance regulating the first wave-offering of the newly grown stalks (vv. 9-14). The law prescribes that 'when you [the Israelites] come into the land which I [YHWH] give to you, and you reap its harvest, you shall bring the first sheaf (*'ōmer*)[2] of your harvest to the priest; and he shall wave[3] the sheaf as an acceptable offering [for you] before YHWH: the priest shall wave it on the ממחרת morrow of the שבת .'

The significance of the proper understanding of the phrase 'on the morrow of the שבת' is plain: this was the date *from which* the interval of seven complete weeks to the festival of Pentecost was to be counted (v. 15). As this prescription follows the ordinance of the Passover (vv. 4-8), as noted, it is natural to assume that the phrase 'on the morrow of the שבת' somehow refers to the period after the paschal rite. But when? What is the precise meaning of the word שבת? Because of the significance of the matter, and the textual ambiguity, a wide range of interpretations was offered in antiquity, reflecting the different exegetical postures of post-exilic Judaism. These various interpretations shall be briefly outlined below—in order to illustrate just how diverse exegesis of the phrase 'on the morrow of the שבת' could be, and to provide a framework against which the earlier inner-biblical exegesis of this passage, in Josh. 5: 10-12, can be appreciated.

Three legal schemata can be distinguished, depending on whether the word שבת is interpreted to refer to the Sabbath day, to a seven-day period, or to the Passover festival itself:

1. The view that שבת refers literally to the Sabbath day is found in the Dead Sea Scrolls. The Qumran calendar is based on a solar cycle which begins its annual computation on Wednesday of the first month, since it was on the fourth day of the week that the solar light was

---

[2] For *'ōmer* and its probable origin as an 'armful' of grain, see G. Dalman, *Arbeit und Sitte in Palästina* (Gütersloh: C. Bertelsmann, 1933), iii. 18, 46-52, 58-60, 62-6.

[3] This is the *tĕnûpāh*-offering, most probably an elevation rite of 'dedication'; see J. Milgrom, 'The Alleged Wave-Offering in Israel and in the Ancient Near East', *IEJ* 22 (1972), 33-8

created (Gen. 1:14).[4] Accordingly, the festival of Passover on the fifteenth day of the first month also falls on a Wednesday. Since the Qumran calendar goes on to record that Pentecost falls on the fifteenth day of the third month—a Sunday—it is clear that the seven-week interval calculated between the two commenced on the twenty-sixth day of the first month. For this to be so, the phrase ממחרת השבת had to be understood to mean 'from the morrow of the [first] Sabbath-day' *after* Passover.[5] Seven complete weeks from the morrow of the last Sabbath day of the Passover week (the twenty-sixth of the first month) would thus be the fourteenth day of the third month—a Saturday—and the morrow of *that* Sabbath day would be the Pentecost, the conclusion of fifty days of counting (cf. Lev. 23:15-16). It was in this way that a solar calendar could be followed and the Pentateuchal law—which required the onset of the *'ōmer* and the Pentecost to occur 'on the morrow of the שבת'—observed. The Book of Jubilees reflects a similar reckoning.[6] The Boethians, however, interpreted differently: they began counting the interval from the morrow of the first Sabbath occurring *during* the festival week.[7]

2.   The foregoing attempts at a literal interpretation are complemented by the exegesis of Lev. 23:11 found in the Syriac Peshitta. The troublesome phrase is rendered there by a paraphrase בתר יומא אחרנא, meaning 'after the last day [of the festival]'. On this view, שבת meant a seven-day period or 'week'. The basis for such a view is not hard to find. for the biblical text itself states that one should count 'seven שבתות', i.e. 'seven sabbaths' or 'seven weeks'.

3.   Other interpretations of the phrase ממחרת השבת were less literal. Early Pharisaic scholars understood שבת as a figure for the first festival day and began counting towards Pentecost 'from the morrow of the [first] festival day ממחרת יום טוב'; that is, from the sixteenth of the first month, Nisan.[8] This interpretation recurs in Josephus,[9]

---

[4] For a review of the Qumran evidence in the light of the manuscript on the priestly courses, and a review of earlier discussions, see S. Talmon, 'The Calendar Reckoning of the Sect from the Judean Desert', *Scripta Hierosolymitana*, 4 (1958), 169–76.

[5] Loc. cit. 174–6.

[6] Jub. 15:1, 16:13, 44:1-3. See the discussion of C. Albeck, *Das Buch des Jubiläen und die Halacha* (Berlin: Hochschule für die Wissenschaft des Judentums, 1940), 16, and also D. Barthélemy, 'Notes en marge de publications récentes sur les manuscrits de Qumran', *RB* 59 (1952), 200.

[7] *Tos. Roš Haš.* i. 15; *M. Menah.* x. 3; *Tos Menah.* x. 23; *b. Menah.* 65a–66a; and cf. the scholion *ad Meg. Ta'an.* 1 (see *HUCA* 8–9 (1931-2), 276–7). The Sadducean and Samaritan counting began on the first Sunday *after* the festival.

[8] *b. Roš Haš.* 13a; *M Menah.* x. 3; *Seder Olam*, xi; and Ibn Ezra *ad* Lev. 23: 11. Cf. also C. Albeck, *Mabo' la-Mishnah*, addendum to *M. Menah.* x. 3.

[9] *Antiq.* iii. 10. 5.

Philo,[10] and the Septuagint. The latter, in fact, inserted the pleonasm τῇ ἐπαύριον τῆς πρώτης 'after the first day' into its version to authorize the exegesis involved. This interpretation was explicitly rejected by the Boethusians.[11] The Karaites, on the other hand, understood the word שבת as a figure for the Passover festival, but restricted its meaning more literally to the evening of the festival, when the paschal-offering was made.[12] On this view, the phrase was taken to mean 'on the morrow of the paschal festival'; that is, the fifteenth day of the month of Nisan.

As the wave-offering and the Pentecostal calculation were undoubtedly enacted in ancient Israel, there must have been contemporary interpretations which established the meaning of ממחרת השבת for all practical purposes. Indeed, an indication of just such exegesis may be found in Josh. 5:10-12. These verses appear in the context of a general presentation of the Conquest traditions as a reiteration of the exodus: for one thing, Joshua is promised by YHWH that 'I shall be with you as I was with Moses' (Josh. 3:7), and is even instructed (like Moses, in Exod. 3:5) to take off his sandals inasmuch as the ground upon which he was standing was 'holy' (5:13-15); for another, the Lord dried up the Jordan waters 'just as [he] did at the Red Sea' (4:23).[13]

The presentation of the Conquest as a new exodus pertains to the chronology of events as well. The time of the crossing of the Jordan was the tenth day of the first month (4:19)—the time enjoined by Exod. 12:3 as the beginning of paschal celebrations. It is therefore not surprising to learn that the Passover rite was performed as soon as the people came into Canaan:

> Then the Israelites encamped at Gilgal and performed the paschal-offering on the fourteenth day of the month, at evening, on the plains of Jericho. And they ate unleavened bread and parched corn from the produce of the land on the morrow of the Passover, on that very day. And the manna ceased 'from the morrow', when they ate from the produce of the land ... (Josh. 5:10-12)

Examination of this passage shows that it contains unmistakable and detailed allusions to Lev. 23:10-14, such that Josh. 5:10-12 was undoubtedly understood as a fulfilment of its prescriptions. According to Lev. 23:10, 15, the law of a post-Passover wave-offering is incumbent from the beginning of the Conquest. The Israelites are enjoined to make sure that no new bread or parched corn (קלי) be eaten from the land's yield 'until that very day', that is, until the wave-offering was waved ממחרת השבת (vv. 14-15). Correspondingly, Josh. 5:10-12 occurs after

[10] *de Special. Legibus* ii. 162.
[11] Cf. *M. Menah.* x. 3.
[12] Hadasi, *Eshkol Hakofer*, 42a, 85b ff.
[13] For a full discussion of this typology, see below, pp. 358-60.

the Conquest, and notes that the people ate bread and parched corn (קלי) from the land's yield only 'from the morrow of the Passover ממחרת הפסח'. Only then, 'on that very day', did the desert manna cease. The phrase וישבת המן ממחרת 'and the manna ceased on the morrow' is an unmistakable allusion to the Pentateuchal expression ממחרת השבת in Lev. 23:11.

In all this one might suppose that Josh. 5:10-12 is nothing but another of the many instances in the Book of Joshua in which either Joshua, or the people, or both together, fulfill ancient Pentateuchal prescriptions.[14] However, on closer inspection, it is clear that Josh. 5: 10-12 reflects an inner-biblical exegesis of Lev. 23:10-14 which is decidedly different from the standard rabbinic, and most of the non-rabbinic, interpretations of the phrase 'on the morrow of the שבת' reviewed above.[15] Specifically, Josh. 5:12 states that the people ate the produce 'on the morrow of the Passover'. By substituting this phrase for the Pentateuchal 'on the morrow of the שבת' a new exegetical sense for the latter is implicitly proposed. Since the word 'Passover' in Josh. 5:12 could only refer to the specific paschal sacrifice which took place on the fourteenth of the month, at nightfall (Lev. 23: 5), the plain sense of the phrase must be 'from the morrow of the paschal-offering', namely, on the fifteenth day of Nisan.

Support for this view comes from a surprising source. Rabbi David Kimḥi, in his comment on Josh. 5: 11, also understood the phrase ממחרת הפסח quite literally, and offers proof by referring to Num. 33: 3.[16] This reference is of considerable significance, for it is not found in either a prescriptive or descriptive legal rule, but rather occurs as an innocent time-reference in an old itinerary report. There it is recorded that 'They [the Israelites] travelled from Ramses on the first month; on the fifteenth day of the first month, on the morrow of the paschal-offering (ממחרת הפסח), the Israelites haughtily left Egypt in the sight of all the Egyptians.'[17] The phrase 'morrow of the פסח' is thus

---

[14] For examples, note Josh. 8: 22-9, 10:1, 28-40, 11: 8-15, 20-1 (fulfilling the *ḥērem* law of extermination, Deut. 7: 2), 8: 30-5 (fulfilling the prescription of altar-building, inscriptions, and cultic blessings and curses, Deut. 27: 4-26), 8: 8-29, 10: 25-7 (fulfilling the law of hanging, Deut. 21: 22-3). For Josh. 9, see below, p. 206f.

[15] Maimonides actually used Josh. 5: 10-12 as a proof-text in his anti-Karaite polemic, *Hilkhot Temidin u-Musaphin*, halakha XI. H. Albeck, *Mabo' la-Mishnah*, 5, follows the traditional Jewish view, interpreting Josh. 5: 10-12 in the light of the *rabbinic* interpretation of Lev. 23:11.

[16] Cf. the comment of Malbim *ad* Josh. 5: 11, which also cites Num. 33: 3.

[17] Exod. 12: 41-2, 50-1 offers further confirmation, since it is recorded there that the exodus did not take place until 'that very day'; i.e., *after* the 'night of watching' that followed the paschal-offering.

expressly equated with the fifteenth day of Nisan. Accordingly, it may be reasonably assumed that Josh. 5:10-12 implicitly cites the cultic-legal situation of Lev. 23:10-16, and interprets the phrase as referring to the fifteenth day of Nisan *and to this day only*.

The obvious question must now be posed: If the foregoing argument is valid, how can we explain the use of the term to indicate the onset of the paschal-feast at mid-month? Or, in other words, why would a term indicating a heptad, or the Sabbath day, be applied to a mid-month festival? If the concern was to stress the fact that the feast was at the end of the *second* week, why was the ordinal number not noted? And if the reference was to the Sabbath day itself, then all sorts of problems arise as to *which* Sabbath day is actually referred to. All these problems are resolved once it is realized that the term שבת used in Lev. 23:16 actually preserves an ancient and precise terminology.

The linguistic similarity between Hebrew שבת and Akkadian *šapattu* has long been noted; and its pertinence for the biblical institution of the Sabbath has been a matter of common consent as well.[18] Since the term *šapattu* occurs as one of several days of ill omen in ancient Meso-potamia, during which a variety of activites were proscribed, biblical שבת was considered to be a transformed use of this old astrological term for a 'rest day': the term and status of the day as one of special character were retained, but the astrological associations were truncated and given new religious significance within the week. The issue takes an entirely new turn in the light of evidence which further demonstrates that the *šapattu* was used as a technical term for the full moon at mid-month.[19] Thus, the sequence *arḫu . . . šapattu* refers to two lunar phases: the first, new moon phase, and the latter phase of the full moon on the fifteenth of the month.[20] Comparatively viewed, this sequence strikingly clarifies the biblical parallelism שבת ~ חדש found in 2 Kgs. 4:23, Isa. 1:13, Amos 8:5. and Hos. 2:13. This latter must not, therefore, be assumed to mention the new moon and the Sabbath day, but rather to indicate two distinct lunar phases. The corollary juxtaposition of כסה ~ חדש means the same thing in Ps. 81:4 and

---

[18] Cf. Th. Pinches, 'Šapattu, the Babylonian Sabbath', *PSBA* 26 (1904), 51-6. and J. Meinold, 'Die Entstehung des Sabbats', *ZAW* 29 (1909), 81-112, 'Zur Sabbatfrage', *ZAW* 48 (1930), 121-38.

[19] See H. Zimmern, 'Sabbath', *ZDMG* 58 (1904), 199-202 (and his revision of Pinches, loc. cit.).

[20] See W. G. Lambert and A. A. Millard, *Atra-ḫasis: The Babylonian Story of the Flood* (Oxford: The Clarendon Press, 1969), 56-7 (i. 206), and *CAD*, A, s.v. *arḫu*. For a recent full review of lunar festivals in ancient Mesopotamia and Israel, see W. W. Hallo, 'New Moons and Sabbaths: A Case-Study in the Contrastive Approach', *HUCA* 48 (1977), 1-18.

Phoenician texts.[21]

The bearing of all this on the meaning of the phrase ממחרת השבת in Lev. 23:11, 15-16 is obvious. Since the term preserves its old technical sense of 'full moon' in this ritual text, the counting of the *'ōmer* began 'on the morrow of the full moon' in the first month and terminated 'on the morrow of the full moon' in the third month, i.e. on Pentecost, seven full weeks and one day later. Although indications of new-moon celebrations are meagre in ancient Israelite ritual texts,[22] the striking onset of all three pilgrimage festivals in priestly sources on the fifteenth day of the month points to some significance still accorded to lunar— and especially full-moon—phrases in ancient Israelite religion.[23] In this light, references to the celebration of the Passover in the deuteronomic tradition are of some pertinence: for it has been proposed that the command in Deut. 16:1 'to observe the חדש of Abib' and perform the paschal rites at that time actually refers to an ancient custom of celebrating the holiday on 'the new moon of Abib'.[24] Be this as it may,

[21] Aquila (ἐν πανσελήνῳ) and Jerome (*in medio mense*) have preserved this ancient meaning of *kese'* (cf. LXX). The Phoenician parallelism is found in the Larnax Lapēthos 2 inscription; see G. A. Cooke, *A Text-Book of North Semitic Inscriptions* (Oxford: The Clarendon Press, 1903), 82-3 (29.12). Also, cf. Prov. 7:20.

[22] Indications of ceremonies connected with the new moon are found in Num. 10:10, 28:11-15. The new moon of the seventh month clearly had a ritual character distinct from regular new moon celebration; cf. Num. 29:1-5 and v. 6. The early celebration of this day as a New Year is still doubtful.

[23] In many Ur III documents there were special observances only for the new moon, the first crescent (7th day) and the full moon (15th day); whereas the third crescent (21st day) was not especially marked (cf., however, the neo-Babylonian *ḫitpu*-offerings at Uruk, marked for the 7th, 14th, 21st, and 28th days of the month); see Hallo, op. cit. 6-8. The Ur III evidence has an interesting biblical parallel in the purification ceremonies and offerings at the new moon, first crescent (7th day), and (evening of) the 14th day (i.e. the 15th; cf. Exod. 12:6), mentioned in Ezek. 45:18-21.

[24] According to H. L. Ginsberg, 'The Grain Harvest of Leviticus 23:9-22 and Numbers 28:26-31', *PAAJR* 46-7 (1979-80), i. 146 f., following A. B. Ehrlich, *Randglossen zur hebräischen Bibel* (Leipzig: J. C. Hinrichs, 1908), i. 312f. In asserting that the earliest legislation for a grain harvest festival in the old cultic calendars (Exod. 13:4, 23:15, 34:18; Deut. 16:1) was also linked to a lunar phase, Ginsberg provides indirect support for our present contention regarding the phrase 'morrow of the *šabbāt*' in the HC (Lev. 23:11, 15-16). His own view, however, is to stress that since *šabbātôt* means 'weeks' in Lev. 23:16b, and *šabbāt* must refer to a day in vv. 11, 15, 16a, the latter references must be glosses (p. 146). But this position sidesteps (i) the conjunction of the ancient lunar meaning of *šabbāt* with the prescribed date of the grain festival (cf. Lev. 23:5-6); (ii) the question as to why one should wait for the morrow of the *šabbāt* and not the morrow of the *miqrā' qōdeš* itself; (iii) the reasonable coexistence of two different technical meanings for *šabbāt* in the same text (for a third, cf. v. 32; this refers to the tenth day of the month); (iv) the correlation of grain harvests with lunar phases on the old pilgrimage calendars; and (v) the strong attestation of inner-biblical exegetical tradition itself (Josh. 5:11-12).

it bears note that after the celebration of the paschal meal, the פסח,
in the evening (16: 6a), the ancient Israelite is told to return to his
dwelling-place 'in the morning' (v. 7b). The distinction noted here
between the evening paschal rites and the morning onset of the agricultural rituals of the new grain parallels the sequence in the priestly ritual
sources of the Pentateuch *and* in Josh. 5: 10-12.

In conclusion, those ancient interpreters who saw in the word
שבת in Lev. 23: 11 a reference to the day of the Passover festival (the
Pharisees), or only to the evening onset thereof (the Karaites), have
paradoxically preserved the original sense of the mid-month lunar term:
for they did not interpret it either as the Sabbath day or as a reference
to the week. The fact that neither the rabbinic nor the non-rabbinic
discussions ever indicate the lunar meaning of the term suggests that by
their time its original meaning had long since fallen into obscurity, and
that references to it in Lev. 23: 10-16 were interpreted inner-biblically
and in terms of current usage. To be sure, the desuetude of the lunar
meaning of the term שבת may also have been due to powerful theological motivations, similar to those which actively transformed the word
into a weekday blessed by the Creator.[25]

Josh. 5: 10-12 preserves eloquent witness to the fact that the old
lunar sense of the term שבת was once current in priestly circles and was
the basis for ritual calculations towards Pentecost. Whether Josh. 5:
10-12 also preserves the standard priestly oral interpretation of Lev.
23: 10-16, or whether it rather reflects new exegesis, cannot be known.
What is significant, however, is that Josh. 5: 10-12 preserves a covert
exegetical clarification of the practical ritual sense of Lev. 23: 10-16;
and that it does so in the context of a descriptive historical narrative
which purports to be a fulfilment of the prescriptive command of
proper ritual procedure 'when you come into the land'.

Clarification of Solomon's Celebration of the Feast of Tabernacles: 2 Chronicles 7: 8-10

When the ancient Chronicler studied his historical sources, he
occasionally came upon passages of considerable legal confusion or
incomprehensibility. In such cases he felt compelled to resolve or
elucidate the matter in as satisfactory a way as possible. 1 Kgs. 8: 65-6
is a case in point. As presently formulated, this text is perplexing: for
the procedure by which Solomon celebrated the feast of Tabernacles in
conjunction with the newly dedicated Temple altar is so unclear as to

---

[25] Gen. 2: 1-3; Exod. 20: 11; cf. Exod. 16: 29. Zimmern, op. cit. 202, raises
the possibility that the term *šapattu* influenced the Israelites in two of its meanings—as full moon and as first lunar phase, the latter of which was transformed
in the Sabbath institution.

indirectly cast aspersions on his piety and knowledge of the ritual law.

The report in the Book of Kings states that 'Solomon performed the festival [i.e. Tabernacles] at that time for seven days . . . seven days and seven days: [a total of] fourteen days. On the eighth day he sent the nation [home] . . .' The problem with this historical report is as follows: if the first seven days constituted the feast of Tabernacles, then the eighth day of solemn assembly is not mentioned (as *per* Lev. 23:36, 39; Num. 29:35; or Neh. 8:18); whereas if the second seven days constituted the week of Tabernacles, then the eighth day was not observed at all. To be sure, there are biblical sources like Deut. 16:15 which only refer to a festival heptad, and such may explain Solomon's practice in the Book of Kings.[26] But however this be, it is nevertheless certain that the Chronicler knew of a festival octave. Only this assumption adequately explains his whole exegetical procedure in 2 Chron. 7:8-10.

The Chronicler tried to harmonize his knowledge of the law of a festival octave with the historical record preserved in the Book of Kings by regarding the phrase 'on the eighth day he sent the nation [home] . . .' in 1 Kgs. 8:66 as an ellipsis. Thus, after his verbatim citation of 1 Kgs. 8:65a in 2 Chron. 7:8 ('Then Solomon performed the festival at that time for seven days; and all Israel was with him—a huge throng from Lebo-hamath to the watercourse of Egypt'), the Chronicler undertook to provide a paraphrastic rendition of the troublesome ritual passage as a means of resolving its confusions. Instead of merely recording that the festival Temple dedication and Tabernacles were celebrated 'seven days and seven days: [a total of] fourteen days; [and] on the eighth he [Solomon] sent the people . . . and they returned to their dwellings happy and glad of heart'—as in 1 Kgs. 8:65b-66, with all its afore-mentioned problems—the Chronicler states: 'And they performed a solemn assembly on the eighth—for the dedication of the altar took seven days and the celebration of the festival took seven days. Then, on the twenty-third day of the seventh month he [Solomon] sent the people to their dwellings happy and glad of heart' (7:9-10). Quite evidently, the Chronicler interpolated his harmonistic exegesis *into* his received source: between the phrases 'on the eighth' and 'he sent the people' of 1 Kgs. 8:65b-66 the latter-day historian inserted his ritual explication.

Underlying the foregoing exegesis is the Chronicler's interpretation of his historical source in such a way that the seventh day of the altar dedication *coincided with* the first day of the week of Tabernacles.[27] Only in this way could he understand how Solomon could observe the

[26] Cf. J. Gray, *I & II Kings*, 219.

[27] Cf. M. Segal, *Parshanut ha-Miqra'*, 6 f. and I. H. Weiss, *Dor Dor we-Doreshaw* (Berlin: Platt and Mitikus 1923), i. 25.

day of solemn assembly and *then* release the crowd (i.e. the eighth day of 1 Kgs. 8: 66 was interpreted to be the day *after* the final assembly). As the feast of Tabernacles commenced on Tishri 15, the eighth day of assembly fell on the twenty-second of that month. Accordingly, when the Chronicler states Solomon released the crowd on the twenty-third of Tishri, there was no ritual problem: it was already the day of—or, perhaps, the sunset following—the completion of the total festival period. A comparable contemporary regard for the sanctity of this eight-day period (i.e. the week of Tabernacles plus the additional day of assembly) is evidenced in Neh. 9: 1, which describes the people gathering for penitence on the twenty-fourth day of Tishri, one full-day interval after the conclusion of the festival octave (Neh. 8: 18).

Such attentiveness to the formulations of earlier biblical materials, as evidenced by 2 Chron. 7: 8-10, is noteworthy. It continues the scribal tradition of comprehending ambiguities in the received textual corpus, and of interpolating insertions therein—though with the significant difference that the Chronicler rewrote his historical source. Of course, it is as unclear here as in Josh. 5: 10-12 whether the exegesis merely articulates a traditional explanation or actually innovates a new interpretation. In either case, the ultimate purpose of the harmonistic exegesis would seem to be to demonstrate that 1 Kgs. 8: 65-6 *only appears* to contradict priestly ritual prescriptions; so that, in fact, there is no real legal problem—it being the task of exegesis to make this clear.

To be sure, there is a distinct difference between the harmonistic exegesis found in 2 Chron. 7: 8-10 and that noted earlier regarding 2 Chron. 35: 12-13. For in the latter text the issue was one of resolving two manifestly contradictory rituals. Nevertheless, it may be argued that there is an important point of contact between the two cases, since both reflect exegetical resolutions of problematic traditions such as generally characterize post-exilic biblical sources. Indeed, this scholastic character of the exegeses points to an important new dimension. With the growth of exegesis, and its techniques, the context of exegesis is not only the juxtaposition of new life-circumstances with older laws *but also the scholarly study and comparison of texts (or received laws) in their own right*. Such developments are not solely characteristic of historiographical reworkings of older sources; they also occur in juridical materials, as we shall see. Such developments are, moreover, particularly characteristic of the growing text-culture which was post-exilic Israel, and are significant harbingers of the exegetical forms and thinking of early Judaism.

B. CONCERN WITH THE COMPREHENSIVENESS AND SCOPE OF THE LAW

The Passover Law in 2 Chronicles 30

As noted earlier, both this chapter and 2 Chron. 35 allow the Levites to sacrifice the paschal-offering. But whereas 2 Chron. 30: 16-17 suggests that this ritual procedure was but a temporary ruling owing to the impurity of many Israelites, this action is normalized in 2 Chron. 35: 6 by its ascription 'to the word of YHWH, through Moses'.[28] No such justification is accorded the levitical involvement in the sprinkling of blood (2 Chron. 35: 11), even though this activity is also presented in 30: 16-17 as one of the rites performed by the Levites owing to lay impurity.

The reason for this lay impurity and inability to perform the paschal slaughter is presumably due to the people's contact with non-YHWHistic cult objects when they dismantled slaughter and incense sites and threw them into the Kidron river upon their arrival in Jerusalem for the Passover celebrations (2 Chron. 30: 13-14).[29] Similarly, during the earlier purification of the Temple, the priests also cast out the impure cult-objects brought into the Temple by King Ahaz, and gave them to the Levites, who threw them into the Kidron river (2 Chron. 29: 12-19). As the Levites purified themselves quicker than the priests, they were able to assist the priests in their slaughter of the many animals brought by the people to celebrate this event (29: 31-4, esp. v. 34). And, because of the continued impurity of the priests, as well as the absence of the people from Jerusalem, it was decided in royal council to postpone the Passover celebration to the next month (2 Chron. 30: 2-3). It was during the intervening period that the masses came up to Jerusalem and defiled themselves, so that the Levites had to assist them in their paschal-offerings.

However, the matter is far more complex than would appear at first sight. The decision to perform the Passover festival in the second month could not have simply been 'because the priests had not purified themselves sufficiently' (v. 3); for it is expressly stated in 2 Chron. 29: 17 that the Temple was not completely purified and dedicated until 'the sixteenth day of the first month'—that is, more than a day *after* the paschal-offering. Why, then, were the continued impurity of the priests and the fact that 'the nation had not assembled in Jerusalem' singled out (30: 3) as reasons for the postponement of the Passover? And on what legal grounds was such a decision made? J. Myers has argued that Hezekiah wanted to reunify the north and south in a national festival,

---

[28] Above, p. 138.
[29] Cf. the later reasoning of R. Aqiba in *M. 'Abod. Zar.* iii. 6.

and so deliberately followed the northern calendar—set one month later than the southern (cf. 1 Kgs. 12: 32-3)—as an overture of reconciliation.[30] An ancient rabbinic tradition also argues that Hezekiah's celebration of the Passover in the second month follows northern practice.[31] But such assumptions are inherently unlikely, given the contempt for Jeroboam's act of impiety recurrently expressed in the Judaean-biased Book of Kings;[32] given the Chronicler's excessive interest in presenting Hezekiah as a pious king;[33] and finally, given the Chronicler's scrupulous deletion of historical notices favourable to the north while also adding several hostile ones (cf. 2 Chron. 13, 19: 2f., 25: 7, 20).[34]

To appreciate the issue and legal exegesis involved, the case of Num. 9: 1-14 must be recalled.[35] In that pericope, people defiled by corpses approached Moses in the wilderness and complained of their inability to participate in the paschal-sacrifice. Moses addressed this problem to God and was provided with divine legislation on this and a related point. He was instructed that persons defiled by contact with corpses, or away on a journey, were permitted to celebrate the Passover one month later, at nightfall on the fourteenth day of the second month. A close comparison of this ruling with the language and provisions found in 2 Chron. 30 reveals that the divine ruling in Num. 9: 6-13 served as the basis and authority of the decision made by Hezekiah:

Num. 9: 6, 9-11, 14	*2 Chron. 30: 2-3, 25*
There were men defiled by corpses and so were unable to perform the paschal-sacrifice at that time (ולא־יכלו לעשׂת־הפסח ביום ההוא). Then YHWH said to Moses, saying, 'Speak to the Israelites as follows: If a man is defiled by a corpse or away on a journey —either now or in your future	Then the king consulted with his princes and the entire assembly in Jerusalem to perform the paschal-sacrifice on the second month, as they were unable to perform it at that time (לא יכלו לעשׂתו בעת ההיא) since the priests had not sufficiently purified themselves and the nation had not yet gathered

[30] *2 Chronicles* (AB 13; Garden City, NY: Doubleday, 1965), 178; and cf. W. Emslie, 'The First and Second Book of Chronicles', *The Interpreter's Bible* (New York and Nashville: Abingdon, 1954), 524, 541.

[31] *yer. Pesah.* ix. 1, 36c.

[32] Cf. 1 Kgs. 13: 34, 14: 16, 15: 30, 34, 16: 19, 26, 31; 2 Kgs. 3: 3, 10: 29, 31, 13: 2, 6, 13: 11, 14: 24, 15: 18, 28, 17: 22.

[33] See, particularly, the discussion of H. G. Williamson, *Israel in the Books of Chronicles* (Cambridge: Cambridge University Press, 1977), 120-30.

[34] This point is now well established; for an early, seminal discussion, see the remarks of W. M. de Wette, *Beiträge zur Einleitung in das Alte Testament*, i. *Kriticher Versuch uber die Glaubwürdigkeit der Chronik mit Hinsicht auf die Geschichte der Mosäischen Bücher und Gesetzgebung* (Halle: 1806), ch. II.

[35] Cf. the analysis above, pp. 99, 103.

generations—he may perform the
paschal-sacrifice: let him do it on
the second month . . . and if a
stranger (גר) dwells among you
. . . let there be one law among
you for both stranger and native
alike.'

in Jerusalem . . . and all the
Judaeans, priests and Levites,
Israelites and strangers (גרים) . . .
rejoiced [during the Passover
celebration].

Verbal and structural similarities clearly link Num. 9: 6-14 and 2 Chron.
30: 2-3, 25. In the Pentateuchal passage men 'unable to perform the
paschal-sacrifice on time' due to corpse defilement received an oracular
decision through Moses permitting all Israelites and strangers in such
a situation, or away on a journey, then or in the future, to postpone
the feast by a month (vv. 6, 9-11, 14). In 2 Chron. 30: 2-3, 25 a comparable situation obtained: due to continued priestly defilement and
the absence of the majority of the people from Jerusalem those already
assembled 'were unable to perform it [the paschal-sacrifice] at that
time'. As a result, the event was postponed by a month so that all the
Israelites and strangers participated in its celebration (v. 25).

One may go further. The foregoing similarities of style and content
suggest the exegetical dependence of 2 Chron. 30: 2-3, 25 on the
prescriptive formulation of Num. 9: 6, 9-11, 14. In both cases the
paschal-sacrifice could be delayed to the second month if there was an
'inability' to perform it at the proper time; in both cases the 'inabilities'
involve impurity and distance; and in both cases the ruling applies to
the stranger as well as to the native. But despite this congruence between
the two texts the following differences may be noted: Num. 9: 6
addresses the cases of lay defilement for a lay ritual and distance from
a local shrine whereas 2 Chron. 30: 3 describes the situation of priestly
defilement for a national ceremony and distance from Jerusalem.
Additionally, the Pentateuchal case deals with lay defilement by contact
with a corpse, but the post-exilic situation deals with priestly defilement
through contact with impure cult-objects. Given these discordances,
one can easily see that 2 Chron. 30 is not an outright application of
Num. 9. Nevertheless, the linguistic and structural concordances do
point to some analogical relationship between the texts—one which is,
in short, exegetical.

The precise nature of the exegesis performed in 2 Chron. 30: 2-3 can
only be inferred. The king and his councillors wanted to celebrate the
Passover festival; but the date had already passed. They searched
Scripture for an analogy broadly suitable to their situation of defiled
priests and a population scattered far from the central shrine. Num. 9
admirably fitted the bill. It not only touched on defilement and physical
distance from a shrine, but included an operative clause most pertinent

in encouraging the analogy: for Num. 9:10 prescribes this case as applicable 'now or *in your future generations*'. How, then, was the Pentateuchal issue reapplied to the new situation? The issue of defilement was easily generalized from a private to a public matter and so extended from physical to cultic contact by analogy. The reapplication of the aspect of physical distance from the shrine may have been helped, on the other hand, by more precise textual considerations. The authorities may well have understood the phrase 'on a distant journey (בדרך רחקה)' in Num. 9:10 in the light of the Pentateuchal use of similar phraseology to indicate distance from God's one chosen place —Jerusalem (cf. Deut. 14:24). Since the concern in 2 Chron. 30:3 was distance from Jerusalem, such an exegetical application of the Pentateuchal law is not unlikely.[36]

The combination of the foregoing factors produced the exegesis and present formulation of 2 Chron. 30: 2-3. As we have suggested, recourse to such a procedure was dictated by the desire to have a national Passover celebration, while faced with forbidding realities. The actual impurity of the priests, and the absence of the people from Jerusalem, were convenient pretexts in this situation. The king and his councillors conveniently disregarded the fact that the Pentateuchal law deals with cases of defilement and distance which make it impossible to perform the paschal-sacrifice *on time*, whereas in 2 Chron. 29-30 the whole affair is a *post factum* consideration; i.e., these chapters describe a situation *after* the proper time for the sacrifice had passed. It is striking that no reference is made to the defilement of the shrine. But the reason is clear enough. If such had been done, there would have been no legal grounds for having the Passover festival postponed to the second month. And it was just this that Hezekiah and his councillors were determined to do (v. 2).

2 Chron. 30 is an important text—for the significant examples of legal exegesis which it contains and for the procedural information which it provides. As recorded, 'the king ויועץ consulted with his princes and the entire קהל assembly in Jerusalem'. Significantly, no

---

[36] If this supposition is correct, we have biblical forebears of the latter rabbinic exegetical procedure called *gĕzērāh šāwāh*, or analogy based on linguistic similarities. Broad structural analogies were called *heqēš*. On these matters, see below, p. 249. For this distinction between the two hermeneutical terms, cf. S. Lieberman, *Hellenism*, 58-62. The Chronicler understood *bĕderek rĕḥōqāh* in Num. 9:10 in relationship to centralization of worship in Jerusalem. Similar technical language was used in the legal qualification (due to centralization) found in Deut. 14:24 (cf. Deut. 12:21, 19:8). The question therefore arises whether *bĕderek rĕḥōqāh* in Num. 9:10—itself a legal addition (see above, p. 103)—also reflects this later cultic reality.

recourse is made to sacerdotal figures or to a divine oracle. It is rather to an informed laity that the king turns. For, indeed, amendments to the Torah appear in 2 Chron. 30 to be the result of discussion and consultation by an assembly of notables. While we do not know the precise make-up of this particular assembly, all indications point to its association with kings (1 Kgs. 12: 3; 1 Chron. 13: 2-4; 2 Chron. 23: 3, 29: 23, 30: 2, 23) and to its advisory function (cf. 1 Chron. 13: 2; 2 Chron. 30: 1, 23).[37] Perhaps a type of (semi-) institutional *jurisconsultus* may be envisaged. Indeed, after the consultation in 2 Chron. 30: 2 there was another meeting of the assembly. At this time they again decided—through consultation (וַיִּוָּעֲצוּ)—to extend the Passover festival an additional seven days (v. 23; cf. v. 22).[38] No biblical precedent is invoked for this act; and none is subsequently added.

One can hardly determine if the scenario in 2 Chron. 30 is historically accurate, or if it is only a historiographical *tour de force*.[39] From the point of view of the exegetical procedures reflected in the document, however, a final determination is not necessary: for much may be learned from it about the processes of inner-biblical legal exegesis in post-exilic Israel. As noted, 2 Chron. 30 reflects the temporal extension of an older Pentateuchal law, its reapplication on the basis of general (topical) and specific (linguistic) analogies, and its generalization to include the entire nation of Israel. Indeed, the covert use of the Pentateuchal law, the unspecified application of exegetical procedures, and the natural relationship between the king and his councillors in these matters, all suggest that such elements were neither out of the ordinary nor invented for this particular historical text. Accordingly, there is good reason to assume a firm historical reality in the processes reflected in 2 Chron. 30—although there is greater likelihood that this reality is closer to the post-exilic period of the Chronicler than to the eighth-century reign of King Hezekiah.

It bears note that other events in 2 Chron. 30 reflect the social and

---

[37] This usage of the term *qāhāl* is not restricted, of course, to such official or semi-official groups; for it repeatedly recurs in the post-exilic sources of Ezra-Nehemiah and Chronicles broadly to denote the social-religious organization of Judaea. Cf. *Enc. Miq.* vii. 69-70.

[38] The phrase *wayyō'kělû 'et hammô'ēd* 'they ate the festival' (!) in v. 22 is impossible. Kimhi corrects the reading by assuming an ellipsis ('they ate the *sacrificial meat* of the festival'); the LXX corrects it in another—more tendentious—direction by reading καὶ συνετέλεσαν τὴν ἑορτὴν τῶν ἀζύμων 'and they completed (*wayyěkallû*) the Passover festival'.

[39] Myers, for example, equivocates (op cit. 176): while he refers to the general scholarly position 'that the Chronicler transferred to Hezekiah some of the religious celebrations of Josiah', he sees 'no reason to believe that [the Chronicler] invented the story itself'. But he does not perceive the exegesis involved. Cf. my evaluation below.

legislative reality of post-exilic Israel as well. Indeed, a Persian ambience can be detected in the fact that Hezekiah sent out letters (אגרות) informing the nation of his decision (30: 1). Not only is אגרת a Middle Persian loan-word found in biblical (e.g. Neh. 6: 17, 19) and Babylonian sources of this period,[40] it is also used in Neh. 2: 7-9 and Esther 9: 26 in connection with official correspondence from the Persian chancellery. Moreover, as we know from other biblical sources reflecting a Persian milieu (cf. Esther 1: 19-22, 3: 13-15, 8: 5-14, 9: 20, 29; Ezra 10: 7; Neh. 8: 15; 2 Chron. 24: 9), as well as materials preserved from the Achaemenid archives, royal edicts and laws were commonly publicized by written and oral messages sent throughout the provinces of the realm.[41] Accordingly, if the foregoing serves to support the possibility that 2 Chron. 30: 2-3 depicts an actual historical phenomenon, one may also discern here the traces of a royal concilium dealing with exegetical matters that parallels the consortium of sacerdotal officers who taught and interpreted Torah in the same post-exilic period (cf. Neh. 8). Whether the one or the other prefigures the 'Great Assembly' of early Jewish sources – whose own origin is sadly obscured – can only be surmised. At any rate, what deserves final note here is that 2 Chron. 30 – even more than Neh. 13: 7-13 – depicts laymen reinterpreting the rules of purity which affect the Temple, its practices, and its personnel. The cultural transformation involved is nothing short of remarkable.

The Stones of the Temple in 1 Kings 6: 7

In the preceding case a Pentateuchal source was covertly cited and extended in various analogical ways. The notice in 1 Kgs. 6: 7 provides a comparable instance. For here, too, a Pentateuchal law has been embedded in a historical source; and its ancient prescriptions have been deliberately reworked and analogically extended to accommodate a new circumstance.

According to 1 Kgs. 6: 7, 'the Temple during its building (בהבנתו) was built with blocks of undressed stone (אבן שלמה), quarry-hewn; but neither hammer, saw, nor any iron (ברזל) implement was heard in the Temple during its building.' This descriptive statement is clearly based on the old Pentateuchal law found in Deut. 27: 5-6, which prescribes that a slaughter site (מזבח) must be made (תבנה) of blocks

---

[40] Of the various words for letter (e.g. *unnedukku, ṣi'pu, šipru, egirtu), egirtu* is late (cf. Aramaic *'iggerâ*). See *RLA* ii (1938), 62-3. For *egirtu* in NA and NB sources, see *CAD*, E, pp. 45-6. According to B. Landsberger, *MAOG* 4 (1928-9), 315, *egirtu* is a loanword in the Persian empire.

[41] Cf. the discussion and evidence of E. Bickermann, loc. cit. (p. 107 n. 2), 104-8.

of undressed stone (אבנים שלמות) upon which no iron (ברזל) has
been wielded. In fact, this law actually rearticulates the more ancient
provision recorded in Exod. 20: 22, which states that 'when you build'
a slaughter site it must not be of hewn (גזית) stones upon which a sword
has been wielded.

The complementary Pentateuchal prescriptions of Exod. 20: 22 and
Deut. 27: 5-6 thus provide for the construction of outdoor slaughter
sites with natural blocks of stone.[42] In themselves, of course, there is
nothing exceptional in these ancient prescriptions – the latter of which
undoubtedly reflects the old Shechemite stratum of the Book of
Deuteronomy,[43] and has links with the ritual erection of stones at
Gilgal (Josh. 4: 19-24; cf. 24: 25-6).[44] Moreover, being ancient and
pre-monarchic, there is also nothing prescribed in Exod. 20: 22 and
Deut. 27: 5-6 which pertains to the Temple; just as there is nothing
contradictory in the fact that the foundation of the Temple of Jerusalem was built with hewn stones (גזית, 1 Kgs. 5: 31~1 Chron. 22: 1).
Nevertheless, the compiler-redactor of the Book of Kings felt otherwise,
and interrupted the architectural description of the Temple and its
balconies with the aforementioned deuteronomic citation in 1 Kgs.
6: 7 (cf. vv. 5-6, 8).[45] Indeed, with this interpolation, the ancient
historian actually reveals his motivating presuppositions and establishes an exegetical bridge between two originally unrelated entities.

Quite evidently, the recontextualization of Deut. 27: 5-6 into 1 Kgs.
6: 7 serves explicit notice that an analogy between the Pentateuchal
laws of open-air slaughter sites and the Temple was perceived in biblical
antiquity. But this analogy was hardly homologous, inasmuch as the
deuteronomist's historical sources also record that the building blocks
for the Temple were hewn in a quarry outside the Temple area (cf.
1 Kgs. 5: 31-2). For this reason, the analogical link between the laws
of slaughter sites and the Temple – introduced by the interpolation –
required an exegetical adjustment. This was done by a tendentious
rereading of Deut. 27: 5-6. Since the latter prescription syntactically
separates its two operative clauses – distinguishing between the positive

[42] It is possible that *'ăbānîm šělēmôt* does not mean 'whole stones', in the
sense of being uncut, but rather 'unblemished stones' or the like. This is, at any
rate, the interpretation of *Tos. Meg.* iii. 5; and of Maimonides in *Hilkhot Beit
ha-Behirah*, ch. I, halakha 14-15.

[43] See, most recently, the concise comments in A. Rofé, 'The Strata of the
Law about the centralization of worship in Deuteronomy and the history of the
deuteronomic movement', *SVT* 22 (1972), 221-6.

[44] Cf. C. Steuernagel, *Das Deuteronomium*[2] (HKAT; Göttingen: Vanderhoeck
and Ruprecht, 1923), 347. For an expanded discussion, see also E. Nielsen,
Schechem[2] (Copenhagen: G. Gads, 1959), 295 ff.

[45] This interruption was already pointed out by Kimḥi, though his interest was
quite different from the view developed below.

command to build slaughter sites from 'blocks of undressed stone' and the negative command not to wield an iron tool — it was entirely possible to introduce the following exegetical qualification: iron could be used to cut the building bocks of the Temple, *but not within its sacred precincts*. It is presumably such reasoning which underlies the reworking of the deuteronomic passage in 1 Kgs. 6: 7, which states that the Temple was built of hewn stones, but that no iron tool was heard in the Temple during its construction. The result is an exegetically qualified analogy: as with the open-air slaughter sites, it was also forbidden to use stones hewn with iron implements in the building of the Temple (thus the exegetical analogy, the result of the Pentateuchal interpolation); but unlike the practice in the slaughter sites, such stones were permitted in the Temple — except for the altar — if they were hewn elsewhere (thus the exegetical restriction, the result of the respecification of Deut. 27: 5-6).[46]

It is, of course, impossible precisely to determine the latent processes of exegetical reasoning utilized by the historian. But, based on the textual interpolation and its peculiar formulation, there is little doubt that an exegetical analogy was at once conceived and qualified — an analogy which served, in some respects at least, formally to extend the prescriptions of the old deuteronomic law to the new reality of the Temple. It is thus of considerable interest that precisely the double exegetical process just reviewed — of analogical extension plus qualification — is recorded in the most ancient non-biblical commentary on the subject. Indeed, the old Tannaitic scholars unwittingly retraced the same analogistic-harmonistic path of the yet more ancient biblical exegete on the subject — the historian of 1 Kgs. 6: 7.[47] In the final analysis, one may add, the result of the restriction was less harmonistic than fictive; for the qualification essentially undermined the analogical extension of the laws of altars to the Temple for which very purpose it was introduced. In legal theory, then, the deuteronomic prescription was accorded extensive applicability; in reality, on the other hand, it only applied — now as before — to the altar, and to it alone.[48]

The preceding remarks indicate how Deut. 27: 5-7 was reinterpreted and made more comprehensive by a reflective ancient Israelite historian. Other historians, however, found this Pentateuchal law confusing and in need of clarification. For upon analysis it is clear that these verses are composite: vv. 5-6 are drawn from Exod. 20: 22 and have been interpolated into their present context. They break up the narrative sequence

[46] Cf. Albeck, *Mabo' la-Mishnah*, 5, and the earlier formulation of Weiss, *Dor Dor*, 25.

[47] See *Mechilta de Rabbi Ishmael*, edd. Horowitz-Rabin, *Jethro*, ch. XI, *ad fin.*

[48] On a comparable legal fiction, cf. the discussion of Num. 36, above, p. 105.

and introduce an outright dilemma. In Deut. 27: 2-4 God commands
Moses, the elders, and the people to set up large stones, plaster them,
and write upon them 'all the words of this Torah upon crossing the
Jordan' (v. 3). This instruction is recapitulated in v. 8 ('and you shall
write on the stones all the words of this Torah . . .') after the interpolation of vv. 5-7, which command that an unhewn altar be set up for
sacrifices. However, while v. 8 literally resumes the command of v. 3,
and therewith brackets the secondary (or parenthetical) material,[49]
it is possible unequivocably to conclude that the 'words of this Torah'
were to be written solely on the altar-stones mentioned in vv. 5-6, and
not on the free-standing stelae, as suggested by vv. 2-4. And, indeed,
this latter is precisely how the text was understood in Josh. 8: 31-2.
Complying with the Pentateuchal command to set up an altar upon
crossing the Jordan, Joshua wrote the words of the Torah on the *stones
of the altar*. In other words, later tradition read Deut. 27: 5-7 together
with v. 8, so that the stones in the latter verse were not understood to
recapitulate the reference to the stelae, in vv. 2-4, but rather to refer to
the stones of the altar just described.[50]

[49] On the *Wiederaufnahme* see above, p. 85 n. 19.

[50] It is quite likely that Josh. 8: 31-2 reflects the deliberate intent of the
Wiederaufnahme of Deut. 27: 8 – which wished both to preserve older traditions
of combined stelae and altars, such as are also found in Exod. 24: 4, and, at the
same time, to obscure the cultic significance of free-standing stones, or stelae,
which to him were forbidden (cf. Deut. 16: 22). On the authority of this theological attitude, the word 'stela' in MT Exod. 24: 4 has been replaced by 'stones'
in LXX and Samar.

8. Legal Exegesis and Explication in the Pentateuchal Legal Corpora

A. INTRODUCTION

THE law collections in the Pentateuch present a distinct context for inner-biblical legal exegesis. In contrast to the legal exegeses embedded in the historiographical materials, the analytical separation of laws from their subsequent exegesis is more problematic. This is due to two principal factors: (*a*) there are few technical terms which formally introduce exegetical expansions or clarifications of the biblical laws, so that these latter must be isolated mostly by contextual considerations; and (*b*) there is no sharp distinction in genre, style, or terminology which would serve to highlight the exegetical strata, since the legal comments are formulated in a parlance largely similar to that of the laws themselves. The net effect is that the inner growth and clarification of the laws are often obscure – if not actually obscured. Such obfuscation may, of course, be directly due to the inherent tendencies of legal conservatism, in so far as legal conservatism prefers to give the impression of a unified, harmonious, and comprehensive law corpus. But such tendencies would only reinforce the basic theological framework of the laws themselves: all three collections are presented as the word of the Lord from Sinai. In the Covenant Code (Exod. 21: 1-23: 19) the *mišpāṭîm*-ordinances are given by God to the people through Moses at Mt. Sinai (cf. Exod. 20: 22, 21: 1, 24: 12); in the priestly laws of the Holiness Code (Lev. 17-26) the teachings are severally spoken by God to Moses, and the whole is summed up with the remark that 'these are the laws, and ordinances, and teachings which YHWH set between himself and Israel, through Moses on Mt. Sinai' (Lev. 26: 46; cf. 27: 34); and, finally, in the Book of Deuteronomy the entire corpus is presented as a recapitulation by Moses of 'all that which YHWH commanded him' (Deut. 1: 1) at Sinai (v. 6).

Since all the laws are presented as one integrated teaching from one specific historical moment, there would appear to be no reason to have citations within the Pentateuchal legal corpora. However, closer analysis of the deuteronomic materials shows a repeated concern to refer to earlier traditions and legislation; and, indeed, to distinguish these latter from the innovations of the deuteronomic teachings. Thus, D. Z. Hoffmann pointed out many years ago that whenever Deuteronomy refers to its own teachings it uses the participial expression אשר אנכי מצוה which I command' (4: 2, 40, 6: 2, 6, 7: 11, 8: 1, 11, 10: 13, 11: 8, 13, 22, 27, 28, 12: 14, 28, 13: 11, 19, 15: 5, 19: 9, 27: 1, 4, 10, 28: 1, 13, 14, 15, 30: 2, 8, 11, 16).[1] By contrast, J. Milgrom has convincingly demonstrated that whenever Deuteronomy refers to its sources in the Tetrateuch it uses a citation formula in the perfect tense, כאשר צוה/נשבע/דבר which/as [he] commanded/swore/promised' (1: 11, 19, 21, 2: 1, 14, 4: 5, 5: 12, 16, 28-29, 6: 3, 19, 25, 9: 3, 10: 5, 9, 11: 25, 12: 21, 13: 18, 15: 6, 18: 2, 19: 8, 20: 7, 24: 8, 26: 15, 18, 19, 27: 3, 28: 9, 29: 12, 31: 3, 34: 9).[2] These textual references make it perfectly clear that Deuteronomy was heir to earlier JE and P traditions.[3] Nevertheless, it is striking that there is only one demonstrable case from this rich ensemble of instances where the citation formula functions exegetically – and even this instance requires close scrutiny.[4]

Deuteronomy's citation of Tetrateuchal sources may thus be viewed as a formal witness to the fact that the deuteronomic corpus reused earlier laws. In fact, a close comparison of the deuteronomic laws with those of the Covenant and Holiness Codes reveals that Deuteronomy also explained and expanded older legal materials *without* identifying them by citations or other formal means. Deut. 22: 9, it will be recalled, clarified the terminology and meaning of the law of mixed seeds from Lev. 19: 19 in precisely this way. Other examples of this type, showing exegetical developments between the Covenant and Holiness Codes, or between strata of any of the legal corpora themselves, will be discussed below. Instances of inner-biblical legal exegesis which are preceded by technical formulae will be treated separately.

Taken as a whole, the foregoing types of legal exegesis reflect normal processes of lawyerly handling of the laws: a concern with scrutinizing the content of laws for real or anticipated deficiencies; a concern with contradictions among the inherited cases; a concern with making the law comprehensive and integrated; and a concern with making the law workable and practicable. In the main, such concerns characterize a living legal setting, such as is identified in Deut. 17: 8-12, for example,

---

[1] *Das Buch Deuteronomium* (Berlin: Poppelauer, 1913), vol. i, *passim*.

[2] 'Profane Slaughter and a Formulaic Key to the Composition of Deuteronomy', *HUCA* 47 (1976), 3-4. In deuteronomic compositions, cf. Josh. 1: 2-3.

[3] Ibid. 4-13.

[4] Cf. ibid. 7-9, where Milgrom claims that the citation formulation in Deut. 20: 16-17, regarding the antiquity of the *ḥērem* (extermination) injunction, can be verified by Saul's actions against the Gibeonites (1 Sam. 21: 1, 22: 7). But this view is hardly necessary, and ignores the exegetical thrust of the deuteronomic passage, on which see below, pp. 199-200.

where judges decide the law locally but may bring exceptional cases to the High Court in Jerusalem for special analysis and inquiry.[5] The results of these and other investigations were incorporated into the received legal sources. Once in place, these developments of the typical cases in the law collections served—together with the older stratum of materials—as guides to future legal practice. At the same time, it should be realized that these various explanations and elaborations may also have been stimulated by a developing legal scholasticism—one which studied the received laws independently of practical cases, compared them one to the other, and even resolved the inevitable lacunae and contradictions. This professional study of legal sources would have grown up while Israel lived on its own land, with its own legal and paralegal institutions; and would have developed considerably during the exilic period, when the Judaeans lived in an alien legal environment with only their legal traditions as an 'institution' by means of which they could establish or maintain some measure of autonomy. These matters will require further elucidation. For the present it is simply important to recognize that the exegeses now found in the legal sources of the Pentateuch are the result of many possible types of circumstance.

There is one final type of material which is related to the foregoing and requires separate comment. This is the collection of laws sworn to in Neh. 10. Indeed, like the Pentateuchal law collections, Neh. 10 is not merely a source of early Jewish legal exegesis but *an exegetical source in its own right.*[6] There are weighty reasons for keeping a discussion of the laws and exegeses in Neh. 10 separate from a discussion of the laws and exegeses in the law collections. The laws in Nehemiah are not found in the Pentateuch, but rather within a historiographical narrative; they are manifestly not Sinaitic, but rather refer back to those laws; they make no pretence to be a collection of comprehensive norms, but rather serve as a reformulated digest of issues mostly related to Nehemiah's reforms; and lastly, the laws in Neh. 10 are not meant for all Israel, but rather for a small sectarian group which wished to be separate from the 'peoples of the land' (and other Israelites). Nevertheless, these considerations are not decisive. Neh. 10 is a legal document with a list of laws, and is formulated in legal terms. These factors alone serve to align it closer generically to the Pentateuchal law collections

---

[5] The phrase in v. 8, *kî yippālê' mimměkā dābār*, suggests that either the case was exceptional, or somehow beyond discernment (cf. the stem *pl'* in Gen. 18: 14, Deut. 30: 11, and Ps. 131: 1). The combination of priests and magistrates in the Jerusalem court is a deuteronomic innovation, and most likely reflects two independent judicial institutions (sacral and civil) with different terminologies and procedures; thus C. Steuernagel, op. cit. ad. loc., followed by M. Weinfeld, *Deuteronomy and the Deuteronomic School*, 235.

[6] Cf. the discussion below, pp. 213–6, for examples and literature.

than to the laws incorporated into the Books of Ezra-Nehemiah and Chronicles. In addition, although Neh. 10 presents citations putatively deriving from the Torah of Moses (vv. 35, 37; cf. v. 30), just like Neh. 8:14, 13:1, and 2 Chron. 35:12-13, such citation techniques are included in the legal sections of the Book of Deuteronomy as well (cf. 12:21, 13:18, 15:6, 18:2, 19:8, 20:7, 24:8). And, finally, the weaving together of Pentateuchal laws, as in Neh. 10:32b,[7] is found both in contemporary historiographical narratives (e.g. 2 Chron. 35: 12-13) and in the Pentateuchal legal corpora themselves.[8] Considered thus, there is justifiable reason to consider the legal exegeses in Neh. 10 in conjunction with the law collections, and not with the post-exilic historiographies. The considerable stylistic and formal differences between the exegeses in Neh. 10 and the Pentateuchal law collections, together with their implications and typological relationship, will require separate comment.

B. EXPLICATIONS AND GLOSSES

1. Our earlier discussion of the phrase ממחרת השבת in Lev. 23:11 indicated that the Syriac Peshitta interpreted the noun שבת as a seven-day period, or week. This exegetical option appears in rabbinic sources as well, but was rejected. It was also suggested in the earlier discussion that the interpretation found in the Syriac version may have biblical legitimacy, in so far as Lev. 23:15 states that one should calculate 'seven complete שבתות'. The phrase in Lev. 23:11 would thus seem to suggest that the noun שבת also meant 'week' in the biblical period.

A comparison of Lev. 23:15 with Deut. 16:9 supports this observation. Whereas the priestly text states 'you shall count [pl.] . . . seven שבתות', the formulation in Deut. 16:9 reads 'you shall count [sg.] . . . seven שבעות'. The two prescriptions show both a traditional formulation ('you shall count') and a significant variation (שבתות vs. שבעות). This latter clearly points to the fact that שבתות could mean שבעות, or 'weeks', in some cases.

Another source leads to the same conclusion. Lev. 25:8 specifies the calculation and extent of the jubilee institution, concerning which the context deals at length:

(a) You shall count seven שבתת of years—
(b) seven years, seven times—
(c) so that the days of the seven שבתת of years shall total forty-nine years.

---

[7] Cf. pp. 134 f above.
[8] On this see below, pp. 228-30.

The abrupt syntax and redundant specifications suggest that section (*b*) constitutes a secondary elucidation of the opaque phrase 'seven שבתת of years'. Presumably the author of the interpretation now inserted into the MT understood שבתת to mean 'weeks', or seven-day units. Thus 'seven שבתת' would mean 'seven heptads', or forty-nine years. In sum, the explicatory gloss attempts to render an obscure formulation comprehensible and, thereby, to safeguard the observance of the divine law.

It may be added that the explication in Lev. 25: 8 is not necessarily a professional scribal achievement totally unconnected with the life of the community: for it appears that the jubilee laws in Lev. 25 were elsewhere disrupted by an instructional comment. After a sequence of prescriptions regulating the sabbatical and jubilee years, and prohibiting sowing, reaping, and pruning during these periods (vv. 1-13), the law turns to compensation for sales (מִמְכַּר) of land during a jubilee period and exhorts the Israelites not to victimize each other in such matters (vv. 14-15). The natural legal-thematic continuation of the foregoing is vv. 23-4, which announce the principle of inalienable patriarchal land and the possibility of its redemption. These verses are at once a link to vv. 14-19, since the sale (תִּמְכַּר) of property is again mentioned, and a transition to vv. 24-55, since they anticipate the issue of land redemption. However, it is also apparent that between vv. 14-19 and vv. 23-4 + 25-55 there is a new topic—one which is tied thematically to the regulations concerning land use during fallow periods spelled out in vv. 11-12.

Verses 11-12 state that in the jubilee year 'you may not sow, and you shall not harvest the self-sown crop, and you may not gather in the grapes from the unpruned vines . . . [but] you shall eat [only] what comes directly from the fields'. This regulation has an implicit problem: if one could not plant either in the forty-ninth year (a sabbatical period, v. 4) or in the fiftieth year (a jubilee period, v. 11), how could one eat on the first year of the *new* sabbatical cycle (three years later)? That such a problem was anticipated in the biblical period is certain: for a solution is presented in vv. 20-2 which anticipate and resolve this difficulty. Verses 20-2 state: 'And if you [should] ask, "What are we to eat during the seventh year, since we may neither sow nor gather our harvest?"—I [YHWH] have ordained that my blessing-produce for you in the sixth year [of a sabbatical cycle] shall produce a harvest for three years: you may sow in the eighth year, but you must eat of the old harvest until the ninth year; [indeed] you must eat of the old [crop] until the [new] harvest is gathered.'[9] At first glance, the ruling

---

[9] It is vital to note that although the question in v. 20 is posed with respect to the seventh, sabbatical, year—clearly the original concern—it is answered in vv. 21-2 with respect to the sabbatical and jubilee years; for otherwise there would be no reason even to refer to the eighth year. If the latter were the first year of a

in v. 22 (permitting sowing in the eighth – or jubilee – year but prohibiting use of the yield) is simply an outright contradiction of the law in vv. 11-12 (prohibiting sowing in the jubilee but permitting what comes directly from the fields). On closer examination, however, it is clear that Lev. 25:11-12 was retained in such a way as to make the law livable: one could sow the land in the jubilee year (*contra* Lev. 25:11) but not eat of its yield during that period (*per* Lev. 25:12). Verse 22 specifically states that 'you may sow in the eighth year, but you must eat of the old harvest until the ninth year'.[10]

To observe the law, one must first understand it. This was the purpose of the explicative legal gloss in Lev. 25:8. However, even if the law was comprehensible it was not always practicable. This was the situation of the law in Lev. 25:11-12, which imposed a recognizable hardship on an agricultural community. This law not only prescribed a sustained fallow period but so restricted sowing as to impinge upon times of permissible land use. This is one reason for assuming that a reaction to the law in vv. 11-12 came from the living community, rather than from a professional group of scribes or legal annotators. These latter may, of course, have given the popular reaction its legal formulation, and even helped find a workable solution to the difficulties involved; but it is unlikely that the issue originated with them. Moreover, the fact that the query in vv. 20-2 anticipates the people's difficulty with the law, and proposes a new solution, is another reason to see the origins of the reaction to vv. 11-12 in a living community.[11] The law was imposed upon the people, but they were not altogether powerless before it: through interpretation and exegesis the teachers of the law responded to the people's own response to the law and transformed its demands. Even more significantly, the people's response to

new sabbatical cycle, why call it the eighth year, and why be concerned over sowing and eating?

[10] M. Noth's comment, *Leviticus* (OTL; Philadelphia: Westminster, 1965), 188, that 'the mention of the "ninth year"... must be an addition... [which] probably came in through a secondary reckoning by spring years', apparently misses the point; for the whole issue presupposed by the solution in vv. 21-2 is that one could not eat produce planted during the sabbatical and jubilee years (i.e. years 7 and 8 of the previous cycle), but only thereafter, at the beginning of the new cycle (or the ninth year since the onset of the previous one). Hence the reference to three years. An appreciation of the problems involved is found in the commentary of A. T. Chapman and A. W. Streane, *The Book of Leviticus* (CB; Cambridge: Cambridge University Press, 1914), 140. Nevertheless, it is quite possible that the phrase *following* 'ninth year' is a secondary annotation, specifying precisely when eating the new crop was permitted.

[11] Anticipatory questions seem to have been part of the cultic and paraenetic repertoire of different traditions in ancient Israel. Cf. Deut. 7:17, 18:21. See also A. Soggin, 'Kult-ätiologische Sagen und Katechese in Hexateuch', *VT* 10 (1960), 341-7.

the difficulty of the law is now presented *as part of* the divinely given Mosaic law, so that this law is represented as one which anticipates problems and corrects itself. It was in this way, among others, that the entire Mosaic law attained the status of a comprehensive collection of norms by early rabbinic times. The record of this development is one of the remarkable features attested by inner-biblical legal exegesis.

2. Lev. 20:10 offers a quite different example of legal explication from that found in Lev. 25:8 or 20-22. Lev. 20:10 neither explains difficult legal terms nor works out a practical compromise of difficulties inherent in the law. It rather provides an instance of legalistic precision, where a detail is added to the law in order to explicate its exact scope and application.

Lev. 20:10 contains a list of forbidden sexual unions. Many of these prohibitions appear in Lev. 18:16-23, in comparable or slightly different formulations. Among these latter laws, v. 20 formulates a proscription of adultery in apodictic terms: 'you shall not have sexual intercourse with the wife of your countryman...' The technical terminology for adultery is not used here. But it is in fact used in Lev. 20:10, which formulates the law in casuistic terms: 'If a man commits adultery (ינאף) with another woman—[if he] commits adultery (ינאף) with his neighbour's wife—both the adulterer and the adulteress shall be killed.'[12] On the one hand, this latter formulation shows an elaboration of the terse apodictic formulation found in the Decalogue: 'Do not commit adultery (לא תנאף)' (Exod. 20:14); but it does not add any significant information. Adultery is, *per definitionem*, sexual intercourse with another man's wife (or vice versa). On the other hand, the law in Lev. 20:10 is prolix. The protasis is uncharacteristically repeated before the apodosis. This stylistic anomaly had led to various emendations of the passage, with either the one or the other protasis deleted as a dittography. However, such solutions totally miss the mark. The second protasis clause—'if a man commits adultery with his neighbour's wife'—is rather to be considered a legal explication of the first, so that adultery is not prohibited with any woman, but precisely with the wife of one's neighbour, i.e. another Israelite (cf. Lev. 18:20). The initial formulation of the law has thus been restricted to manageable ethnic proportions. One may assume that such a reformulation of the scope of the law arose in the natural course of handling received cases.

---

[12] M. Noth, op. cit. 150, may be correct to see the reference to the women in v. 10bβ as an addition, since the punishment *môt yûmat* is in the singular. In that case, one may conceive an exegetical harmonization with Deut. 22:22. On the other hand, the punishment formula may have been a frozen expression irrespective of the number of subjects. In Lev. 13:29 and Num. 6:2 (cf. Num. 30:1; Deut. 23:22) the phrase 'or a woman' appears pleonastic with the masculine verb.

Alternatively, it may have arisen in the course of attempts to promulgate or specify punishable cases of adultery.

C. LEGAL EXPANSIONS WITH INTRODUCTORY FORMULAE

Formulae with או and כל

1. In comparison with the Massoretic Text, a notable feature of the Samaritan version of the Pentateuchal *mišpāṭîm* (Exod. 21:1–23:19) is that it regularly adds the phrase '[or] any animal' to ordinances mentioning oxen or sheep (cf. Exod. 21:28, 29, 32, 35, 36, 22:3, 23:4, 12).[13] It is uncertain whether this supplement actually innovates an extension of the law, or whether it merely makes explicit an older oral tradition which interpreted the mention of specific animals (like oxen or sheep) as typical instances of livestock in general.[14] In any case, it may be supposed that a more literal reading of the law was maintained where penalty sanctions imposed the specific compensation of oxen or sheep (as in cases of torts, theft, and deposits).[15]

Exegetical tendencies similar to the foregoing Samaritan annotations can already be noted in the MT. Given the clear-MT tendency in the *mišpāṭîm* to mention specific items or typical animals in each situation,[16] the generalized reference to '[any] loss' in Exod. 22:8 must be considered a deliberate addition to the regulation. An analysis of the role of this particular supplementation to the overall rule will be considered below. For the present, of further introductory interest is the case of deposits found in Exod. 22:9. The protasis opens: 'If a man gives his neighbour an ass, או or an ox, או or a sheep, וכל[17] or any
* animal, to guard . . .' The stylistic shift from specific to general cases, with the accumulation of examples climaxed by the phrase 'or any animal', suggest that this latter is a secondary addition. Were the cumulative category 'any animal' part of the original legal formulation, the

---

[13] Cf. D. Daube, 'Zur frühtalmudischen Rechtspraxis', *ZAW* 50 (1932), 148. Note the same tendency in LXX Exod. 20:17.

[14] Significantly, Samar. thus reflects an early stage of rabbinic halakha which generalized the biblical mention of oxen or asses to all animals in cases of torts, damages, and injuries; cf. *Mechilta d'R. Ismael, Mišpāṭîm*, edd. Horowitz–Rabin, 280; *Mekilta de-Rabbi Shim'on*, edd. Epstein–Malamud, 178; *M. B. Qam.* v. 7; *Tos. B. Qam.* vi. 18 (p. 355, Zuckermandel); *b. B. Qam.* 54b; and Rashi *ad* Exod. 21:28, 33.

[15] Hence Samar. Exod. 21:37 does not generalize; and this is also the situation in rabbinic law, as Daube, loc. cit., has noted. Cf. *M. B. Qam.* vii. 1.

[16] Thus, Exod. 21:28–32, 35–6 (ox), 23:5 (ass), 21:34 (ox or ass), 21:37 (ox or sheep), 22:8 (ox; ass; sheep).

[17] Also Samar.; but a Qumran manuscript reads *'ô kol* (see *DJD* v. 158, p. 5). On the variation *wĕ-/'ô*, cf. my remarks on Num. 5:13,30, in *HUCA* 45 (1974), 31.

specific series would have been legally redundant and empty. Alternatively, one may suppose that a law of deposit which was originally formulated with respect to two or three typical animals was later supplemented by the comprehensive category 'any animal'. Since this generalizing expansion does not add a new principle to the law, it probably reflects a later scholastic concern to make precise and explicit what any jurist would (or should) have easily inferred by analogy.[18]

In the foregoing cases the אוֹ-formula is part of a series of objects which now fall under the purview of the rule. In other instances that formula does introduce an addition to the original subject of the protasis. Thus, a comparison of the casuistic vow formulary in Num. 6:2, '[any] man (אִישׁ) or woman (אוֹ אִשָּׁה) who will make a vow', with that found elsewhere in the Pentateuchal legislation, '[any] ˙person (אִישׁ) who vows' (Num. 30:3; Deut. 23:22), suggests that in the former case the אוֹ-clause is a legal supplement concerned to include the female. Indeed, this secondary character of the אוֹ-clause is further suggested by the failure of the later draftsman or interpolator to change the original grammatical formulation of the law, which remains in the masculine singular.[19] Similar grammatical inconsistencies may be found in the Samaritan Pentateuch as well, also in conjunction with legal supplements.[20] It may be supposed, therefore, that Num. 6:2 was originally formulated with the general designation אִישׁ, like its Pentateuchal parallels, and simply meant 'anyone'. However, with time, and a more literal reading of the word אִישׁ as 'man' alone, or simply a concern to make the original meaning precise for all concerned, the expansionary construction אוֹ אִשָּׁה was added.[21] If the latter is the case, the expansion would be in the manner of an 'empty phrase'—which

---

[18] On the other hand, the phrase *wĕkol-mĕlaktekā* 'and all your work' in Exod. 20:9 would seem to be a formulation designed to give particular emphasis to the comprehensive prohibition of Sabbath work; thus A. Phillips, *Ancient Israel's Criminal Law* (New York: Schocken, 1970), 69, who says that in comparison with Exod. 23:12, 20:10 refers to all types of occupations. Going even further, J. Milgrom, *Studies*, 80-1, n. 297, notes the recurrence of the above phrase in P regarding both the Sabbath and the Day of Atonement (cf. Lev. 23:3, 28; Num. 29:7); P also speaks of a 'sabbath of sabbaths' (cf. Lev. 23:3, 21). He concludes that *kol mĕlaktekā* prohibits any activity, as against occupational activity, designated by the general P phrase *mĕleket ˁăbôdāh* (*re* Exod. 12:16, see below, pp. 197 f). On the other hand, I find it unlikely that 'any activity' entails, in biblical times, what rabbinic halakha called *šĕbût*, as contended by A. Goldberg, '*Shibuth* and *di-oraitha* with respect to Sabbath Labor', *Sinai*, 46 (1959), 181-9 [Heb.].

[19] These variants suggest that Num. 6:2 is a bit different from Lev. 13:29, where the *'ô 'iššāh* clause with a masculine singular verb may only reflect a frozen mode of expression, as occurs elsewhere; cf. above, p. 169 n. 12, and also Exod. 21:28-9.

[20] Cf. Samar. Exod. 21:28-9, 32, 36, 23:12.

[21] Regarding Deut. 15:12, see below, p. 211 n. 99.

adds nothing to the law itself, but merely articulates what any lawyer would have invariably inferred. Of just this sort is the אֹו‎-clause in Num. 35:18, which repeats v. 17 verbatim except for one variation (the agency of a stone causing death is extended to a wooden implement).[22] Here, again, no new legal principle is introduced, and the expansion merely gives written expression to what could be inferred, or to the existing oral interpretation. At the same time, the nascent or underlying scholastic tendencies of ancient biblical legists are clearly attested.

2. The scholastic nature of the legal generalization 'any animal' in Exod. 22:9, dealt with above, can be put into wider perspective by a review of the preceding rules in vv. 6-8. The formulation of v. 6, 'If a man gives his neighbour silver or utensils to guard', so closely parallels the protasis of v. 9, 'If a man gives his neighbour an ass, or an ox . . . to guard', that it is clear that vv. 6-12 comprise a related series of cases dealing with bailment. The deposit of chattels (or inanimate objects) is treated first, in vv. 6-7, and the deposit of livestock (or animate goods) follows thereafter, in vv. 9-10. Moreover, the similarity between the two cases of bailment extends to the parallel apodoses as well, both of which require a formal oath (vv. 7a and 10b). In v. 7a the oath is undertaken by the bailee to aver that a deposited item has been stolen and not misappropriated by him. Similarly, in v. 10 the bailee swears that the death, impairment, or loss of the deposited animal is not the result of a personal fault, but rather the result of an external agency (like the earlier case of theft).

Between the foregoing two parallel cases of bailment, more specifically *after* the bailee's oath, the following rules are found: 'Concerning every case (עַל־כָּל־דְּבַר‎) of [property] contestation;[23] concerning an ox, concerning an ass, concerning a sheep, concerning a garment, [or] concerning any (עַל־כָּל‎) kind of loss, [regarding] which he [viz., the owner-depositor] may indicate, "This is it",[24] the [disputed] matter of the two of them [viz., the depositor and the bailee] must be brought before God . . .' (v. 8). Quite certainly, this material is structurally

---

[22] See B. Jackson, *Essays in Jewish and Comparative Legal History* (SJLA 10; Leiden: Brill, 1975), 151f. Cf., too, his discussion of Exod. 21:31, pp. 150f.

[23] Following L. Köhler, 'Archäologisches. Nr. 22; zu Ex 22: 8', *ZAW* 46 (1928), 218, who renders *pešaʿ* here as 'Bestreitung', or even 'Eigentumsanfechtung'. The RSV renders 'breach of trust'; the NJPS has 'charge of misappropriation'.

[24] So, Rashi ad loc. For *kî* as a demonstrative, cf. J. Muilenberg, 'The Linguistic and Rhetorical Usages of the Particle *kî* in the Old Testament', *HUCA* 32 (1961), 136. Jackson's counter-argument, op. cit., 158f., that if the object is 'it' (rather than 'he'), then there is no need for an ordeal, is not to the point: for the ordeal is to resolve the claim of the depositor that the item identified in the possession of the bailee is, in fact, the item originally deposited with him. On this, cf. J. Morgenstern, 'The Book of the Covenant, Part II', *HUCA* 7 (1930), 111.

distinct, even as it is stylistically distinguished from the surrounding *mišpāṭîm*.[25] Moreover – and this is central – the general formulation, 'concerning every case of contestation', extends the subject of bailment beyond its original confines. Thus, if, as appears on first view, the contestation referred to in v. 8 is related to the preceding situation of bailment, then the concern of the legal generalization would be to extend permissible bailment to the much larger domain of livestock (cf. v. 6). But such cannot be the case here, since it will be recalled that the deposit of livestock with a bailee is manifestly dealt with in vv. 9-10, the original legal complement to vv. 6-7. Accordingly, one must conclude that v. 8 reflects the intrusion of a different legal concern, one that pertains to all cases of disputed property when a depositor claims to identify a given object in the bailee's possession as his own (after the bailee had claimed that it was stolen from his household). In this situation (v. 8b), as in this mini-series of rules dealing with bailment (vv. 7b, 10), the cases were subject to divine adjudication.[26] The net result is that the original legal issue of bailment and its contestations is expanded beyond the inanimate objects specified in v. 6 to the animate objects of v. 8a. Such specifications are manifestly designed to add reasonable precision to the formulation of the rule. After the generalization at the beginning of v. 8a, however, the enumeration of asses, oxen, sheep, and garments is somewhat superfluous.

Within the broad framework of bailment and its contestations, the phrase at the end of v. 8 '[or] concerning any kind of loss',[27] requires special consideration. Like the preceding rule of property contestations, it is a comprehensive formulation using the technical term כל. However, by contrast, the inclusion of the category of losses at the end of v. 8 is formally discontinuous with the property disputes enumerated just before; for an entirely different set of legal issues regarding agency and responsibility is at stake. In the first situations, where a deposit is missing, the bailee is charged with misappropriation, thus suggesting that the bailee acted with malice aforethought. In the matter of losses, some type of irresponsibility or negligence on the part of the bailee is assumed. Accordingly, it may be proposed that the phrase 'concerning any kind of loss' is a later legal stratum now related to the earlier issues of contested deposits. With its addition, cases of disputed losses are subject to oracular adjudication just like other bailment disputes. Presumably, different punishments were administered in the different cases, depending upon whether the bailee was assumed to have acted

---

[25] It is neither casuistic in form nor specific in concern – the characteristic features of the surrounding cases; cf. J. Morgenstern, loc. cit. 110f.

[26] On this procedure here, and earlier views, see B. Jackson, op. cit. 240-3.

[27] Cf. Köhler, loc. cit. 216f. The Hebrew phrase corresponds to Akk. *mimmašu ḥalqam* 'whatever is lost', in LH 125.

with intent (theft) or not (negligence). In any event, it is notable that the later legal annotator has supplemented the original rules of bailment with a generalized reference to losses *after* an earlier addition specifying objects which a depositor might allege to have been misappropriated. Given this complex and highly stratified series of rules in Exod. 22: 6–8, one may justifiably conclude that property claims were recurrent in ancient Israelite civil jurisprudence, and that the ancient legists were faced with a full spectrum of instances. Our text presumably reflects practical responses to such cases – it being rather doubtful that the two sets of legal generalization found in v. 8 are merely the product of a theoretical legal scholasticism.

3.   The Pentateuchal rules regarding the taking of interest reflect another series of legal expansions and generalizations of direct pertinence to the exegetical processes here under review. Among the various formulations, that in Exod. 22: 24 'If you lend money [lit., silver] to my people the needy among you,[28] do not act as a נשה lender to them [lit., him]; do not exact נשך interest from them [him]',[29] would appear to be the most concise and hence the most original. But this is not the case. In fact, the reduplicated apodosis in v. 24b, formulated in the plural and treating the distinct topic of interest, suggests that the phrase 'do not exact interest from them' is a secondary, explanatory expansion.[30] It was presumably introduced to clarify, or specify, what it meant to act 'as a נשה'. This observation is confirmed by the fact that the general exhortation in v. 24a is immediately followed in v. 25 with a specific elaboration of not acting 'as a נשה'–for the Israelite is told that if he takes a pledge in hand he must return it at nightfall. In short, the legal draftsmen appear manifestly concerned to specify the injunction found in v. 24a, and do so with the same second person singular grammatical form.[31]

---

[28] This reference to the needy now appears to clarify the preceding clause, and may be viewed either as a natural development or one undertaken in the light of other rules dealing with loans to indigents (cf. Lev. 25: 35). J. H. Schorr, *He-Halutz*, 3 (1856), 92, long ago supposed that 'my people' (*'my*) is the result of a scribal confusion with 'needy' (*'ny*). The MT is thus witness to a double reading, deriving from two text traditions. For the LXX, see below, n. 38.

[29] On this particular type of interest, see the many views collected by E. Neufeldt, 'Prohibitions Against Loans at Interest in Ancient Hebrew Laws', *HUCA* 26 (1955), 355–7.

[30] Ibid. 366.

[31] The very clear rule in v. 25 is itself supplemented by a motivation–explanation clause in v. 26. Of immediate interest in the light of the lexical glosses studied earlier (ch. 2) is the opening clause, v. 26, *kî hî' kĕsûtōh lĕbaddāh hî' śimlātô lĕ'ōrô*. As the Massoretes pointed it, the first part is to be translated 'for it is his only covering'. That the unvocalized consonants *lbdh* could be read otherwise is

The secondary nature of Exod. 22: 24b, and further evidence of intra-Pentateuchal exegeses of the laws of interest, can be seen by a comparison of two passages from the deuteronomic laws: Deut. 24: 10-18 and 23: 20-1a. In the first of these, Deut. 24: 10-18, it is clear that its legal agendum has been derived from, and closely modelled upon, the legal code in Exod. 22: 20-6. This relationship is supported by the fact that Deut. 24: 10-11 only deals with loans (כי־תשה)–not with matters of interest. Moreover, the deuteronomic formulation even seems to provide its own explanation of how one should not 'act like a נשה' when it enjoins the Israelite not to enter the home of the borrower in order to seize a pledge. The independence of this explanation from the original formulation of the law in the Covenant Code is verified by the fact that only the explanation given in Deut. 24: 12-13 (that the lender must return a security deposit–if taken–at nightfall) is found in Exod. 22: 25. Exod. 22: 24-5 has no reference to the proper decorum of a lender when seizing his pledge. These several considerations indicate that Deut. 24: 10-18, particularly vv. 10-11, derive from Exod. 22: 20-6, particularly vv. 24-5; and that the original version of Exod. 22: 24-5 spoke both of a lender (נשה) and the misuse of security pledges, but not about loans with interest.

By contrast, the second of the two aforementioned deuteronomic passages, Deut. 23: 20-1a, does refer to interest, נשך, but not to security pledges–just like the formulation in Lev. 25: 25-7, with which it is formally related in other respects as well.[32] Thus, when the deuteronomic rule in 23: 20 states 'Do not make loans to your fellow Israelite [lit., 'your brother'], neither loans of silver nor loans of food: [even] anything which you might loan כל־דבר אשר ישך', it is clear that the reference to loans of silver and food derives from the regulation in the Holiness Code not to loan one's fellow Israelite (lit., brother) silver or food at interest (Lev. 25: 35-7).[33] This overall legal dependency of

---

confirmed by the second part of this phrase, which means 'it is the garment for his skin'. Here *śimlātô* 'his garment' gives a more common synonym for *kĕsûtôh*, and *lĕ'ōrō* 'his skin' shows that *lbdh* was read *lĕbadôh* 'his skin' (cf. Job 18: 13). The second clause is thus stylistically redundant for a legal regulation and appears to be a lexical gloss. The oppression which v. 26 has in mind is articulated in Isa. 3: 6-7.

[32] Neufeldt, loc. cit. 367, has observed the chiastic nature of v. 37, and acutely suggested that it 'is a quotation from a much older moral code which had poetical structure'. He compares Prov. 22: 22 and 23: 10. In fact, the original formulation probably concluded at v. 36a (cf. v. 43b, and the redundancy of v. 36b with v. 35bβ).

[33] On the meaning of *tarbît*, as a type of interest distinct from *nešek*, see the discussion by Neufeldt, loc. cit. S. Loewenstamm, *JBL* (1963), 78-80, advanced the view that *nešek* and *tarbît* do not indicate two *types* of interest on loans paid, but rather refer to the *content* of the loans (e.g. silver or victuals). Deut. 23: 20 has levelled the distinction.

Deut. 23: 20-1a upon Lev. 25: 35-7 is further confirmed by several instances of exegetical revision: (a) the prohibition in Lev. 25: 35-6 against exacting interest on loans made to one's fellow Israelite is first taken over literally in Deut. 23: 20 *and then realistically clarified in v. 21a* so that interest on loans to foreigners is explicitly permitted;[34] (b) the social condition of indigency which Lev. 25: 35 articulates prior to its prohibition of loans at interest is expanded in Deut. 24: 20 to include all situations—a much more radical matter, in so far as there would henceforth be little inducement for speculative or profiteering loans which might finance new areas of the economy;[35] and (c) whereas Lev. 25: 35-7 and Deut. 23: 20a only refer to silver and food as typical goods which were lent, and against which interest was customarily exacted, Deut. 23: 20b adds '[even] anything which you might loan'. This comprehensive designation, using the formula כל, is clearly an addition to the legal stratum from which the deuteronomic rule has been modelled, and presumably derives from one of the following two possibilities. Either the analogical extension to 'anything which you might loan' merely reflects the concern of a scholastic annotator or draftsman to make the deuteronomic rule precise and comprehensive, and so incorporates the oral exegetical *traditio* into the legal *traditum* derived from the Holiness Code, or else the extension reflects a time when the formulation of silver and food was not regarded as a merism circumscribing typical loans,[36] but was rather interpreted quite literally, thereby necessitating an addendum which would render the prohibition comprehensive once again. If, on the first possibility, the expansion be considered a legistic redundancy, it would be, on the second, an instance of careful and cautious legal draftsmanship.

Deut. 23: 20-1a and 24: 10-11 thus derive from two legal sources— the Holiness and Covenant Codes, respectively—and exhibit a variety of exegetical revisions of them, including one which uses the formula כל.[37] From this perspective, the grammatical redundancies and inconsistencies noted earlier with respect to the mention of נשך in Exod. 22: 24b appear in a different light. Verse 24b is not just a secondary

---

[34] Lev. 25: 35b has also been exegetically expanded with the addition of the *gēr wĕtôšāb*. The inclusion of these social types disrupts the reference to *'āḥîkā* and the singular verbs.

[35] This is a good instance of Utopian economics, designed to minimize in-group class divisions, being, on a practical level, inhibitory and counter-productive. If it is not simply idealistic, it also invites infractions and fictitious circumventions via alien middlemen. Such impractical, Utopian legislation is actually a characteristic feature of Lev. 25 as a whole. Cf. the discussion of N. Soss, 'Old Testament Law and Economic Society', *Journal of the History of Ideas*, 34 (1973), 323-4.

[36] Cf. A. M. Honeyman, '*Merismus* in Biblical Hebrew', *JBL* 71 (1952), 11-18.

[37] The *kol*-formula is not, of course, necessarily secondary to the overall deuteronomic revision of the HC rule.

clarification of v. 24a, but one which harmonizes the original rule prohibiting a lender to treat a compatriot 'as a נשׁה' with the later prohibition against exacting interest found in the deuteronomic laws. This deuteronomic prohibition against interest, itself derived from Lev. 25: 35-7, was thus secondarily incorporated into the Covenant Code at Exod. 22: 24b by a later revisor. The result is that, at present, Exod. 22: 24 is both the source of one deuteronomic rule and the beneficiary of another; in totality it is a harmonization of two independent Pentateuchal rules within the Pentateuch itself.[38] Formally, such legistic activity is comparable to the blending of diverse Pentateuchal rules in the historiographical literature, such as was evidenced in 2 Chron. 35: 12-13. Other instances of intra-Pentateuchal legal harmonizations will be discussed in a later chapter of this section.

The כן־תעשׂה Formula

1. Pentateuchal legal expansions are marked by technical formulae other than אוֹ and כל. The phrase כן־תעשׂה is such a one. It serves to introduce additions to various biblical legal regulations—demonstrating continued legistic reflections on the Pentateuchal rules, so as to provide for new and related contingencies, or to explain, accommodate, or adjust the received regulations on a given topic. In the three examples which follow, the first shows a deuteronomic expansion of a regulation in the Covenant Code; the second an expansion in the Holiness Code of a regulation in the Covenant Code; and the third an expansion within the Covenant Code itself.

As is generally recognized, Deut. 22: 1-2 takes over the old regulation of Exod. 23: 4.[39] This latter enjoins that if an Israelite should happen upon his enemy's ox or ass wandering, he should return it to him (השׁב תשׁיבנו לו). By contrast, the deuteronomic rule deals with the same case but is more complexly formulated and more nationalistic in focus. Deut. 22: 1 states that if one should see (תראה) the ox or sheep of a compatriot cut off from the herd or flock, it is necessary to return them (השׁב תשׁיבם); and Deut. 22: 2 goes on to require that the aforementioned animals be retained until they are claimed by their owner—whether known to the finder or not—and then returned (והשׁבתו). Thus, as is apparent, the deuteronomic version is at once indebted to the older regulation in Exod. 23: 4 and has broadened it in several directions: whereas the older rule spoke simply of encountering the

---

[38] LXX[B] to Exod. 22: 24a appears to reflect a further exegetical harmonization, since it reinterprets *'ammî* 'my people' as τῷ ἀδελφῷ 'to the brother', in clear conformity with the use of *'āh* 'brother' in Lev. 24: 35-6 and Deut. 22: 20-1.

[39] Cf. S. R. Driver, *Deuteronomy*, ad loc.

animals,[40] Deut. 22:1 speaks of witnessing (lit., seeing, being aware of)
straying animals;[41] whereas the older rule simply specified the ox of
one's enemy, the formulation in Deut. 22:1 speaks comprehensively
about a fellow Israelite, without regard for personal sentiments; and
whereas the older rule makes no provision for the retention of the
items, Deut. 22:2 is articulate and precise on the matter.

The preceding developments comport with general deuteronomic
interests in specifying and generalizing aspects of its inherited legal
tradition. However, it will be noted that none of the changes in Deut.
22:1-2 is accompanied by a technical formula, which is not the case
with Deut. 22:3, which states: ‘וכן תעשה and you shall do likewise for
his ass, and you shall do likewise for his garment, and you shall do likewise for every loss of your compatriot . . .’ This formulation can be
considered additional to vv. 1-2 for several reasons. First, with respect
to the overall legal consecution and tradition of the passage, it may
be observed that Deut. 22:1-4, like its source in the Covenant Code,
deals first with the issue of returning lost animals (cf. Deut. 22:1-2 and
Exod. 23:4), and then advises the Israelite to help an animal suffering
under an imbalanced load (cf. Deut. 22:4 and Exod. 23:5).[42] Nothing
whatsoever is mentioned in Exod. 23:4 about lost garments or other
lost objects. Accordingly, when Deut. 22:3 follows up the reference to
returning certain animals (in v. 2) with the formula ‘and you shall do
likewise’, a supplementary list of encountered animals, and then also
formulaically adds the topic of lost garments and goods, there can
be little doubt that these latter clauses supplement and expand the
topic dealt with in v. 1. Were v. 3 part of the original formulation of
the regulation, its proper conceptual position would have been *after* v. 1
(which enumerates the overall situation of seeing stray or lost animals)
and *before* v. 2 (which specifies the duties and responsibilities of the
finder). As it stands, the list in v. 3 is isolated and entirely after the fact.

It will be furthermore observed that v. 3 is also conceptually supplementary to the items mentioned in v. 1. For if the addition of an
ass in v. 3 may be considered a natural addition to the list of animals
mentioned in v. 1, and thus an attempt to be as comprehensive about
this category as possible, the added reference to lost garments is of a

---

[40] It is possible that the clause ‘or (*ŏ*) his ass’ in Exod. 23:4 is secondary,
since the verb is singular (cf. Deut. 22:1). ‘Ass’ is added in Deut. 22:3a (see
below), and this may explain the addition here.

[41] The word *niddāhîm* is used here, thus proving that Ezekiel's rhetorical reuse
of this topos in Ezek. 34:4 (with the expression *lō' hăšēbōtem* ‘you did not
return [them]’) derives from the deuteronomic version of the rule.

[42] Driver, op. cit. 250, suggested that the change in language may be an instance
of linguistic simplification. His point is reinforced by the old observation of
Rashi, that *'āzab* can mean ‘raise up’. Cf. Neh. 3:8.

different nature: it expands the scope of the rule from animate to inanimate goods. Moreover, it is also clear that the legist(s) involved in these supplements were concerned to specify that the rule involved losses *of any sort* – for this is the manifest intent of the generalizing formula 'כל־אבדת אחיך every loss of your compatriot', which follows the reference to lost garments. Such an addition is clearly of a positive legal nature: it closes a perceived gap in the law as it expands its scope to embrace movables in general–not just livestock or work animals.[43] If, nevertheless, these significant specifications and expansions are tacked on after v. 2, and not interpolated into v. 1, it may be considered certain that the formulation of the regulations in vv. 1-2 was already fixed. As in other notable cases, so also this supplementation of a finalized legal formulation was achieved by an addendum – not an interpolation.[44] The result, to be sure, is that the supplement is the more noticeable and striking. However, as in the cases noted earlier, the addendum is remarkably transformed by its present contextualization: for it is now represented as part of the original divine law. No distinction is drawn between laws believed to be divine and those legistic additions known to be human in origin. Thus, if the legal *traditio* is signalled by addendum formulae, it is also completely normalized as part of the official divine laws. In this manner, the legal *traditio* has become legal *traditum* – in fact and in authority.

2.   Exod. 23:10-11 preserves an old rule regulating agricultural activity for the sabbatical year: 'You shall sow your land for six years and reap its yield, but [during] the seventh you shall let it lie fallow and abandon it; let the poor of your nation eat thereof, and let the beast of the field eat what they leave over. You shall do likewise with regard to your vineyard and your olive grove.' As one can readily see, the law is bifurcated. The critical stipulation regarding the release of sown fields (agriculture) is extended only in v. 11b to vineyards and olive groves (viticulture). Moreover, this latter clause, introduced by כן־תעשה, is awkwardly related to the main law. Not only does the present formulation put the issue of non-sown produce *after* the complete statement of how the unused yield should be treated, but the

---

[43] The draftsman of v. 3 has also been careful to repeat the moral exhortation not to disregard (*hit'allēm*) lost goods which present themselves to view (cf. vv. 1, 4). It is likely, moreover, that this latter verb has technical legal connotations. Thus, the stem *'ālam* is used in a reflexive sense by the deuteronomic draftsmen to convey the sense of intentional disregard, and in the Niphal form by priestly legists to indicate unintentional disregard or oversight (cf. Lev. 5: 2-4) as well as unintentional lack of witness (Lev. 4: 13, 5: 13). See also Eccles. 12: 14.

[44] See D. Daube, *Studies in Biblical Law* (Oxford: The Clarendon Press, 1947), ch. 2.

very use of the frozen formula 'you shall do likewise' leaves unclear precisely what is forbidden for such produce. For example, it is unclear if one may prune in the seventh year, but not reap; or if one may eat from the vine if one does not prune it. Accordingly, while the initial addendum was geared to foreclose exegetical ambiguity by creating a more comprehensive law, the result is of little practical value. Too much remains unspecified.

Undoubtedly here, as is often the case with traditional rules, the ambiguities of interpretation were supplemented and resolved by oral exegesis. It is thus of particular note when such exegetical supplements are actually preserved and incorporated into the written text. Such, indeed, appears to be the case in Lev. 25: 3-7—for a close inspection of it reveals it to be an expanded exegetical revision of Exod. 23: 10-11. Several indicators support this contention. Not only did the draftsman of Lev. 25: 3 take over Exod. 23: 10-11a quite precisely; he also incorporated the addendum referring to vineyards (v. 11b) *into* it ('You shall sow your fields for six years, *and you shall prune your vineyards for six years*, and reap its yield'). This new formulation is clearly awkward, and betrays its interpolated nature: the law for fields and vineyards is repeated separately, and the pronoun of the final phrase ('*its* yield') undoubtedly reflects the form found in Exod. 23: 10, where the antecedent is singular and not plural, as in Lev. 25: 3. But despite this awkward and problematic syntax, the result of the incorporation of the addendum from Exod. 23: 11b into the main body of Lev. 25: 3 is the normalization of that exegetical supplement. The formula 'you shall do likewise' is therefore no longer necessary.

The reuse of Exod. 23: 10-11 is further indicated by the way it is cited and exegetically expanded upon in Lev. 25: 4-7. Thus, whereas Exod. 23: 10-11 simply states that fields and groves must lie fallow, Lev. 25: 4b-5a gives precise details on this matter, and seeks fully to resolve many of the queries regarding the use of fields and crops during fallow periods suggested above ('you shall not sow your field nor prune your vineyards; you shall not reap the aftergrowth of your harvest nor gather the grapes of your untrimmed vines'). Further, whereas Exod. 23: 11a simply mentions that 'disadvantaged' people may eat the abandoned food, Lev. 25: 6 enumerates them and even includes the landholder in the list; and whereas Exod. 23: 11a simply notes that 'beasts' may graze on the abondoned land, Lev. 25: 7a stresses that domesticated cattle may do likewise. All this gives clear witness to a determined exegetial venture.[45] Whether these exegetical elaborations are the result of a rational exegesis rooted in legal tradition and procedure,

---

[45] Noth, *Leviticus*, 185, observed some overlaps in the content of these two legal passages, and also the more detailed nature of Lev. 25: 4-7, but overlooked their precise *exegetical* relationship.

or whether liturgical recitation and explication were a contributing factor, cannot be determined.

3. Another example where the formula כן־תעשה introduces an exegetical expansion into a fixed biblical law is suggested by Exod. 22: 28-9. This text-sequence preserves an old cluster of laws dealing with the donation of firstlings to God. After noting the donation of produce (28a), the text continues: 'You shall give me your first-born son [28b], *you shall do likewise for your ox and your sheep* [29a]; seven days he will stay with his mother, [but] on the eighth you shall give him to me [29b].' Some commentators construe the italicized passage with what follows, and translate 'it will stay' for 'he will stay'.[46] In this manner they implicitly distinguish between a law for first-born humans, who were explicitly redeemable in the other versions of the law of first-born, and the law for first-born oxen and sheep which, as eatable (i.e. holy) animals, had to be slaughtered (cf. Exod. 13: 12-13, 34: 19-20; Num. 18: 15). The pronoun 'it' is thus presumed to refer to the clean animals and not to the human males, despite the fact that its putative antecedent (ox and sheep) is plural. Other commentators emend 'he will stay' to 'they will stay' in the final clause, and thereby unify the law by obscuring the precision of its received formulation.[47]

A reconsideration of the phraseology of this cultic rule suggests that the preceding interpretations are either harmonistic or misleading—or both. Whether the italicized clause, 'you shall do likewise for your ox and your sheep', is primary or secondary, there is no prima-facie reason not to interpret it as indicating that both first-born human males and their animal counterparts were to be donated to the Lord. For one thing, there is no articulated differentiation there between types of animals, some of which were to be donated and some of which not (as *is* found in Exod. 13: 12-13, 34: 19-20, Num. 18: 15); for another, there is no indication that the humans were to be treated in a manner different from the pure or impure animals, by means of a monetary substitution for their lives. Accordingly, there is no *textual* reason for assimilating the interpretation of Exod. 22: 28-9 to those articulations of the law where redemption by compensation *is* envisaged and

---

[46] Cf. RSV.

[47] Cf. NEB. H. Holzinger, *Exodus Erklärt²* (KHAT; Tübingen: J. C. B. Mohr, 1900), ad loc., reads *bĕkôr miqnêkā* 'the firstling(s) of your cattle'—but this emendation is precluded on general principles, given the use of the latter phrase in general formulations of the regulation (see below), and on specific contextual grounds, since it vitiates in advance the *kēn-taʿăśeh* clause which includes the *miqneh*. The rendition of JB, 'the first-born', is ambiguous in its reference, but essentially correct.

specified,[48] and where the unclean ass may be redeemed by a sheep or unceremoniously killed (cf. Exod. 34: 20). But does this mean that Exod. 22: 28-9 has preserved a biblical law which prescribes and sanctions the donation of first-born human males to the God of Israel, in apparent flagrant contradiction of those legal formulations which prohibit such a practice, together with the thunderous rebuke of such practices by the prophets and the patriarchal narratives themselves (Gen. 22)?

To answer this question a formal comparison of Exod. 22: 28-9 with the other Pentateuchal prescriptions regulating the handling of the first-born of a human womb is necessary. In this respect, a particularly noticeable formal feature of the various prescriptions is the recurrence of the generalized statement that all first-born—humans and animals— are to be donated to YHWH. The most austere formulation is found in Exod. 13: 1-2, where all firstlings are required to be donated to YHWH, with no qualification or mitigating circumstance specified. By contrast, Exod. 13: 12-13, 34: 19-20, and Num. 18: 15-18 all articulate general- ized formulations which are subsequently qualified by particular means of redemption.[49] In Exod. 13: 13 and 34: 20 the Israelites are simply told to redeem human first-born, whereas in Num. 18: 16 the price of compensation is explicitly stated. Comparably, there are generalized formulations in Num. 3: 12-13 and 8: 16-19 as well, although in these two instances the qualifications announce that the Levites are to be devoted to divine service in (vicarious) compensation for the first-born males of Israel. It is thus obvious even from this brief summary that the rules governing redemption of first-born humans have a diverse background which incites speculations regarding their development. For the present, what requires notice is the point that the existence of the unqualified rule in the preceding cases, and particularly in Exod. 13: 1-2, where it remains without any qualification what- soever, would be hard to explain if the qualifications were original.[50]

---

[48] As, for example, M. Weinfeld, 'The Worship of Moloch and of the Queen of Heaven and its Background', *UF* 4 (1972), 154. On the inner-biblical example of Neh. 10: 37, see below, pp. 213-6.

[49] Cf. the formal stratification of G. Brin, 'The Literary Composition of the Laws Dealing with the Sanctity of the First Born', *Tarbiz*, 46 (1977), 5 and *passim* [Heb.].

[50] The problematic nature of Exod. 13: 1-2 is also recognised by the modern traditionalist D. Z. Hoffmann, *The Book of Leviticus* (Jerusalem: Mossad HaRav Kook, 1953), ii. 270 [Heb]. Remarkably, R. Samuel ben Meir (Rashbam) inter- preted v. 2 as an instruction to work the animal firstlings in sacred domains— thereby implicitly recognizing that the ensuing section of 'redemption' is a later stratum, and also remarkably bypassing the standard rabbinic position which viewed these laws from the 'general rule' (*binyān 'āb*) of redemption of human firstlings stated in Exod. 13: 13. Thus, the rabbis saw Exod. 13: 2 as a 'generalization in need

Far from having a series of cultic rules formulated after the style 'general-particular', where Exod. 13:1-2 is a problematic exception, it would appear that successive legal strata have been preserved: an ancient, categorical rule which states that all first-born—humans and animals alike—belong to YHWH; and subsequent qualifications and justifications which permit modes of redemption for persons and for asses (unless these latter were killed). From this perspective, the unique formulation found in Exod. 22:28-9, which subsumes persons and animals into one undifferentiated cultic-legal category, reflects the older of the two strata just delineated.

Beyond the foregoing stylistic-historical stratification, Exod. 22:28-9 may itself be further differentiated into two literary strata: an original formulation which prescribed the dedication of first-born human males to the Lord, and an analogical extension of this to include first-born animals and thus harmonize it with the other Pentateuchal formulations. Quite apart from the preceding documented comparisons, which show that the formulary כן־תעשה is used in the legal corpora to introduce extensions, several syntactic and semantic considerations lead to this conclusion. First, the phrase 'you shall do likewise for your ox and sheep' (29a) disrupts the syntax linking vv. 28b and 29b. Indeed, the inclusion of a manifest extension to the opening prescription *before* a complete statement of the law regarding first-born males (which all agree extends to v. 29b) is legally obtuse. One would naturally expect the discussion concerning animals to occur after the completed statement of the law regarding humans which introduces the cultic rule. Moreover, the shift from 'you shall do likewise for your ox and sheep' to '*he* [lit.] will stay' is grammatically awkward: the two pronouns in v. 29b ('he'; 'him') are in the singular, as contrasted with the plural antecedent ('ox and sheep'). It would thus appear that 'he will stay' refers back to the human first-born, in v. 28b.[51] This latter point is reinforced by a comparison with Lev. 22:27. Admittedly, this priestly text does not deal with firstlings; but it is concerned with the sacral donation of oxen and sheep and, in this regard, stipulates that they must 'remain *beneath* their mother for seven days, but will be acceptable as a donation-offering from the eighth day onward'. The preposition

of particularization' (cf. *b. Bek.* 19a, *Tanḥuma, Bo'*, xi). Among moderns, G. von Rad, *Old Testament Theology* (New York: Harper and Row, 1965), ii. 394 n. 10, saw the particularization of Exod. 13:2 in vv. 11-15; and cf. B. Childs, *The Book of Exodus* (OTL; Philadelphia: The Westminster Press, 1974), 203.

[51] Still sensing the incompleteness of the MT form (as interpolated) with the other Pentateuchal rules, the LXX added the further harmonization καὶ τὸ ὑποζύγιόν σου) 'and your ass' to v. 29b. This interpolation of an interpolation betrays itself since 'and your ass' is added to the ox and sheep—unredeemables—and not to the human firstling—a redeemable—as elsewhere.

'beneath' used in this prescription is certainly most appropriate in this formulation concerned with animal young, in contradistinction to the preposition 'with' found in Exod. 22: 20b. This latter term seems more appropriate with respect to human young, which, it is argued, is its true subject.

We are thus returned more forcefully to the earlier query. Does this mean that Exod. 22: 28-9 has preserved a regulation which prescribes and sanctions the donation of first-born human males to the God of Israel? Recalling the failure of Exod. 22: 28-9 to provide any *written* comment differentiating the treatment of human first-born from their animal counterparts (regardless of how the *oral* biblical tradition may have eventually harmonized this formulation with the other Pentateuchal versions), and recalling the occurrence of generalized statements (sometimes, like Exod. 13:1-2, with no subsequent qualification) that all first-born belong to YHWH, the answer must be affirmative – although qualifiedly so, since it is not always clear precisely what form the donation took. One reason for this uncertainty lies in the diversity of terminology: sometimes the language is inconclusive, as in the prescription to 'dedicate (קדש)' all first-born males to YHWH (Exod. 13: 2); at other times the language is only slightly more precise, as in the phrase 'and you shall transmit (והעברת) every first-born of the womb to YHWH' (Exod. 13:11), or in the use of the verb נתן 'to dedicate/ donate' when referring to the Levites' permanent status as sacral devotees in vicarious substitution for the first-born of Israel (cf. Num. 8:16, 18, 18: 7).[52] On the other hand, however, there are references which are strikingly precise, as in the phrase 'every first-born of the womb – of all kinds – which they [the priests] will sacrifice (יקריבו) to YHWH – be it human or animal – will be yours [as perquisites]: however (אך), you shall surely redeem the human male . . .' (Num. 18:15). This clear use of sacrificial terminology in a general statement regarding human and animal first-born (only subsequently – with אך – qualified) is a sign of the most vestigial cultic custom regarding human first-born in ancient Israel which we have been investigating.[53] One may imagine that many Israelites preserved the old custom as an expression of excessive piety *long after* the permission to redeem human first-born males had substituted new, divinely sanctioned, procedures.

This speculation, as well as other reasons why the practice may have continued, is inconclusive. The reasons are manifold. Principally, the evidence is insufficient and the various historical strands intertwine.

[52] On this latter term in these passages, with Akkadian analogues, see E. A. Speiser, 'Unrecognised Dedication', *IEJ* 13 (1963), 69–73. But, as in Exod. 22: 28b, it is not always clear which form the 'giving' took – for there the same verb is used for men and animals. Cf. Childs, op. cit. 479f.

[53] On *'ak* as a technical exegetical term, see below, pp. 185, 197–8.

One may at least note from Ezekiel's criticism in Ezek. 16:21 and 23:39 that first-born were sacrificed in fact;[54] and from 23:39 that the practice was believed to have had some official standing by those who performed it. Why else would they 'come to my sanctuary' without perceiving, as does the prophet, that they are defiling it? Under divine inspiration, Ezekiel himself seems to offer an explanation for what he too undoubtedly perceived as a most puzzling matter. His explanation, in fact, does not stop short of implicating the God of Israel. In Ezek. 20, after a reported divine rebuke of Israel's historical past, when the people rebelled against YHWH in the wilderness, YHWH states, through the prophet, that instead of destroying the people there and then he swore to exile them in the future, and, so as to ensure this event, 'I gave them laws which were not good and ordinances by which they could not live; and I polluted them through their [sacral] donations, *when they transmitted/devoted* (בהעביר) *every first born*, in order to destroy them . . .' (vv. 25-6). The juxtaposition of the bad laws with the donation of first-born (clarified, we may add, by the just-noted explicit references to child sacrifice) has suggested to many interpreters that the law of the human first-born was 'bad' because it was abused or misinterpreted — to the people's doom and the fulfilment of the divine oath.[55] Perhaps, as already suggested, this misunderstanding was simply the result of excessive piety; or perhaps the reason has a more semantic basis. For it is, in fact, quite possible to interpret the prescription in Exod. 13:13 and 34:20 (to redeem the first-born human male) in an optional sense; i.e., 'you תפדה *may* redeem' your human first-born, if you choose. This construing of the verb is particularly suggestive in the light of the fact that the preceding clause of both texts clearly uses תפדה in just such an optional sense with respect to the ass (i.e., one may redeem the ass with a sheep, *or* have its neck broken). From this perspective, the unqualified statement in Exod. 13:2 may have been interpreted (in the light of the other recensions of the law) as allowing for a choice between two possibilities: redemption or donation to YHWH (whatever form that took). If this be so, then the later priestly version of the cultic rule, which uses the emphatic formula אך פדה תפדה *'however*, you *must surely* redeem' in Num. 18:15, must be seen as an inner-cultic rebuke of such an option.

---

[54] The language is explicit and unqualified. Note particularly the ritual sequence of 16:21: 'you slaughtered (*tišḥăṭî*) my sons, and donated them (*tittnîm*) by transmitting them (*bĕhaʿăbîr*).' The verb *šāḥaṭ* in 16:21 and 23:39 is also used in Isa. 57:5 (as part of a complex ritual (vv. 5-8)). The verb *zābaḥ* is clearly used with respect to bloody sacrifices of children offered by some Israelites to Canaanite deities in Ps. 106:37-8. Jer. 19:5 has 'to burn (*liśrōp*) their sons in fire as holocaust-offerings to Baʿal'. Also see Isa. 30:33.

[55] Cf. Zimmerli, *Ezechiel*, i, ad loc. On this passage as a prophetic fulfilment of transgressions, see next note.

Beyond these various hints of vestigial cultic practices regarding the existence of sacrifice of the first-born Israelite male, the unofficial practice of child sacrifice apparently continued throughout ancient Israelite history and was due to a variety of factors. On the one hand, there was noticeable contamination from local Canaanite practices (cf. Lev. 18: 21,[56] Isa. 57: 3-11) and from the neighbouring Aramaean states. Indeed, there seems to have been an increase of such practices (or variations thereof) in the eighth to seventh centuries, during the reigns of Kings Ahaz and Manasseh. Significantly, this period is marked by Israelite contacts with the neo-Assyrian empire (particularly via the adjacent Aramaean states), where related practices are attested and may have been revitalized.[57] On the other hand, popular Israelite piety certainly kept these practices of firstling dedication alive in various native forms. Thus one may note that Ḥiel of Bethel sacrificed his first-born son in order to lift the ban on the city of Jericho (1 Kgs. 16: 34; cf. Josh. 6: 26), and also note the actions and attitudes condemned in Mic. 6: 6-7 and Jer. 7: 31. While of an entirely different sort, it should certainly not go unnoticed here that Hannah vowed to donate (verb: נתן) her first-born son (Samuel) to the Lord (1 Sam. 1: 11). Although Samuel was not the first fruit of her womb — and so what we have is, at most, a votary offering — he was the very much desired first son. Her act is thus a weakened popular variant of extreme privative donations in the Israelite cult.

On the basis of the textual strata and vestigial terminology found in the Hebrew Bible, it may be possible to propose a reconstruction of the major phases of the cultic rules dealing with the first-born human males in ancient Israel. In such a hypothetical reconstruction, the earliest stratum would certainly be the general statement found in Num. 18: 15, which refers to the sacrifice of all first-born males. Whether the apodictic rule in Exod. 22: 28-9 (and 13: 2) refers to the same behaviour (as a requirement or an option), or simply refers to a donation to the shrine (verb: נתן), cannot decisively be determined. If this latter is the case with respect to Exod. 22: 28-9 (as it is in Num. 8: 16, 18), then we may assume that the donation of the body of the first-born humans to YHWH would have taken the form of some sort of (lay) menial work in the Temple, on its land-holdings, or in some more private arrangement with the revenues going to the

---

[56] The links between Lev. 18 and Ezek. 20 are striking. Lev. 18: 5 commands laws for one to 'live by' (wĕhay bāhem). If, however, the Israelite 'donates to transmit' his seed to Moloch (tittēn lĕha'ăbîr, v. 21), the land will be polluted (tāmē') and exile will result (v. 25). Compare the same terms and concepts in Ezek. 20: 23-6, 30-1.

[57] See the balanced re-evaluation of the evidence by M. Cogan, *Imperialism and Religion* (SBLMS 19; Missoula, Mont.: Scholars Press, 1974), 77-83.

Temple.[58] The livestock, on the other hand, would have been counted among the Temple revenues, to be sacrificed to YHWH and to provide emoluments for his priestly personnel.

In time, we may assume, the donation of persons to the shrine(s) or shrinal holdings was replaced by a vicarious monetary atonement, and with this practice the desacralization of the first-born male was complete. Several factors must have contributed to this process. For one thing, there is certainly no reason to deny that strong theological motivations were a major element in the condemnation of child sacrifice. Alongside it, however, socio-economic considerations were undoubtedly at work. The sacrifice of first-born human males would have substantially deprived the *ethnos* of a major source of workers and progenitors. Similarly, the donation of all first-borns to the shrine (probably as an early interpretation of the neutral verb נתן) would have wrought havoc on the economic stability of local clans for whom all forms of manual labour were vital. Thus, while the priests would have benefited from such an arrangement (whereby they received a fixed supply of lifelong serfs), popular sentiment would never have tolerated it for very long, and so we may reasonably suppose that the introduction of financial compensation is not so much an indicator of the financial power of the clergy as a compromise measure between it and the laity. Under the terms of the new arrangement, the socio-economic welfare of both groups was taken into account: the families of a first-born son would be required to pay a fixed sacral tax of five shekels shortly after the birth of the child, and then, ever after, be quit of all special sacral claims upon his body or produce.

D. LEGAL EXPANSIONS WITHOUT INTRODUCTORY FORMULAE

Careful examination of individual laws in the biblical legal collections, and comparison of different recensions of a particular law, indicate that legal supplementation, either by interpolation into the biblical text or by amendment of it, was a standard procedure of the official draftsmen or unofficial annotators of the ancient Israelite legal corpora. The recurrence of this phenomenon together with expansions marked by legal formulae indicates that such was one of the various modes of supplementing fixed rules and their phraseology — though there is no internal evidence which allows one to determine why in a given instance one technique was preferred over another, and whether these latter

[58] Cf. Rashbam *ad* Exod. 13: 2 (and n. 50 above). The *nĕtînîm* were another class of humans 'donated' to menial work in the shrine. On the latter, see M. Haran, 'The Gibeonites, the Nethinim and the Sons of Solomon's Servants', *VT* 11 (1961), 159–69.

reflect individual or periodic idiosyncrasies as against being the product of school traditions. At any rate, the absence of fixed formulae complicates the methodological recognition of the phenomena, so that it is necessary to resort to a comparativist perspective – inner-biblical and extra-biblical – to achieve some measure of analytical control. In what follows, three broad types will be distinguished, with examples from each: unmarked interpolations of a substantive legal nature inserted into the text; unmarked amendments of a substantive legal nature added to the conclusion of a text; and unmarked explanations of the substantive legal content incorporated within the text. Formally distinct, these three types nevertheless overlap and combine in actual texts.

1.   Among the stylistic patterns of the *mišpāṭîm* of the Covenant Code, and in fact clustered together at one point, is the formulation that if a person does a certain act or behaves in a certain way 'he shall be put to death' (cf. Exod. 21:13, 15, 16, 17).[59] The formulation is characteristically terse. Of marked quality, therefore, is the somewhat more prolix character of Exod. 21:16, 'And if one steals a person and sells him, ונמצא בידו and he is found [or 'seized'] with him [lit., in his hand],[60] he shall be put to death.' This law clearly applies to a situation of theft of a person and his sale. In its original formulation this was the extent of its provisions. This is proved by the clause 'and [or] he is found with him', which is secondary in nature: for it follows the phrase 'if one steals . . . and sells' rather than preceding the selling, as one would expect if an original sequence of alternatives were at hand. If the victim were sold, he could not be found with the thief; and if the victim were found with the thief he could not have been sold at the same time.[61] The illogical and syntactically disruptive placing of this clause bears witness, therefore, to its interpolated character even as it disturbs the simplicity of the legal stylistic pattern of which it forms a part. The supplement may thus betoken a historical development of the laws of evidence in such cases, as Daube has suspected,[62] so that, at first, a person was liable to the charge of theft of persons only in situations where there was an attempted sale, while later ancient Israelite law admitted mere possession of a missing person as evidence for the charge.

---

[59] Verses 13–14 are qualifications of v. 12, and thus part of this legal unit.

[60] In many biblical cases *nimṣā'* is equivalent to Akkadian *ṣabātu* 'to seize'. See my remarks in *HUCA* 45 (1974), 26, and S. Iwry, '*whnmṣ*': A Striking Variant Reading in 1Q Isa*ᵃ*, *Textus*, 5 (1966), 33–43. For *ṣabātu* in LH, see cases 129. 42–6, 130. 61–3, 131. 71–3, 132. v. 83–vi. 3, 155. 77–9 (and cf. 151. 29–31, 42–3, 50–1); for another biblical instance see Exod. 22: 3.

[61] Cf. Daube, *Studies in Biblical Law*, 95.

[62] Ibid.

Significantly, the illogical positions of the clause 'and [or] he is found with him' clearly bothered the legal draftsman of the deuteronomic corpora, who was dependent upon this rule from the older *mišpāṭîm* of the Covenant Code just as he was dependent upon its materials in many other cases. This deuteronomic formulation, in Deut. 24: 7, reads, 'If a person ימצא will be found [caught][63] stealing one of his Israelite compatriots, treating him like an article of trade,[64] and sells him, that thief shall die . . .' The consistent use of the terminology of Exod. 21:16, as well as the very topos of the law, make it clear that the deuteronomic draftsman had the parallel formulation in the Covenant Code as his inheritance.[65] Of particular interest here, however, is the legal normalization of the disruptive phrase ונמצא בידו. The deuteronomic draftsman reconceptualized the entire sequence and reinterpreted this troublesome phrase, which originally indicated the possession of the stolen persons,[66] as indicating the broad temporal context wherein a thief might be caught with the stolen person *in flagrante delicto*. Presumably this latter was understood to refer not merely to the act of stealing itself but to the time-period wherein the person was still 'found with' or 'in the hand of' the thief. This legal situation is thus distinct from that of sale, which follows. It must of course be stressed that the formulation of the deuteronomic draftsman reflects how he interpreted the received materials from Exod. 21:16, not how that formulation with the problematic phrase was understood by the original annotator. Nevertheless, the deuteronomic interpretation, with its regularization of the sequence and meaning of Exod. 21:16, does strongly underscore the secondary disjunctive nature of ונמצא בידו. A parallel instance was discussed above, where it was noted that the addendum to Exod. 23:10-11a in v. 11b was normalized in the exegetical revision of it in Lev. 25: 3-7, together with the omission of the legal formula which originally introduced that supplement.

2. In his discussion of 'Codes and Codas' in biblical law, D. Daube made the significant observation that, whether due to factors of 'laziness', 'undeveloped legal technique', 'writing on stone', 'oral transmission of the law', or 'regard for tradition', there are 'several examples in the Pentateuch'—as in the ancient Roman statute *lex Aquila* —'of the method . . . of new provisions being joined to an existing code as an appendix

---

[63] See n. 60 above.

[64] Cf. Daube, *Studies*, 95, and the earlier view of *Tg. Onq.*

[65] *Contra* Daube, loc. cit., who apparently sees no relationship between the two cases.

[66] i.e. *běyādô* need not literally be 'in his hand', as Jackson, *Theft*, 46, rightly notes regarding Exod. 22: 3; for biblical and rabbinic evidence, see his p. 46 n. 6 and p. 92 n. 5.

instead of being worked in properly'.[67] In addition to the examples adduced by Daube,[68] and of a more readily identifiable nature, is one which occurs at the conclusion to the laws dealing with the commitment of accidental sins by the community and the individual and their modes of ritual reconciliation. This latter unit is found in Num. 15: 22-9, and has, since antiquity, been compared with the similar laws found in Lev. 4,[69] with a full spectrum of views on the relative priority in time of the first or second of these two sources,[70] and even analyses which concede little analytical merit to either of these two approaches.[71] This controversy cannot lightly be dismissed, despite the complexity of the received evidence, both because of the unmistakable similarities which can be observed between Lev. 4 and Num. 15: 22-9 and because of the arresting inter-textual implications which hang in the balance. The strong similarity between the two sources consists primarily in their common concern with accidental transgressions committed both by the community and by the individual, although Lev. 4 extends its purview to similar transgressions committed by the high priest and the prince of the congregation (vv. 3-12, 22-6), as well as more elaborate ritual specifications. As regards the latter, many of the cultic and terminological divergences between Lev. 4 and Num. 15: 22-9 have been noted by previous investigators, as, for example, the requirement in Num. 15: 24 of a bull for the holocaust-offering and a he-goat for the purification-offering[72] in cases of accidental transgressions, as against the specification of a bullock for the purification-offering in the parallel situation in Lev. 4: 14; or the fact that each paragraph of Lev. 4 refers to accidental transgression committed 'from among all the commandments (מכל המצות) which one shall not do' (cf. vv. 2, 13, 22, 27), while Num. 15: 22 introduces the whole with the more comprehensive

---

[67] *Studies*, 77.

[68] Ibid. 78-99.

[69] Cf. the view of Aaron b. Elia in his commentary *Keter Torah ad* Num. 15: 22ff., where the latter unit is justified because it deals with 'positive', not 'negative', commandments. For this, see the ensuing discussion.

[70] For the recent view that Lev. 4 is the latest, see R. Rendtorff, *Die Gesetz in der Priesterschrift* (Göttingen: Vandenhoeck and Ruprecht, 1954), 14-17; for the view that Num. 15: 22ff. is the latest, cf. K. Elliger, *Leviticus* (HAT 1/4; Tübingen: J. C. B. Mohr, 1966), 58, and also G. B. Gray, *Numbers* (ICC; Edinburgh: T. and T. Clarke, 1912), 179.

[71] For example, D. Kellermann, 'Bemerkungen zum Sündopfergesetz in Num 15, 22 ff.', in *Wort und Geschichte, Festschrift für K. Elliger*, edd. H. Gese and H. P. Rüger (AOAT 18; Neukirchen and Vluyn: Neukirchener Verlag, 1973), 107-13, emphasized in Num. 15: 22 ff. three distinct strata, all earlier than Lev. 4, which the text variously supplements.

[72] For this meaning of the *ḥaṭṭā't*-offering, see J. Milgrom, 'Sin-offering or Purification-offering?', *VT* 21 (1971), 237-9. The relations between Lev. 4 and Num. 15 pose a special problem (see Milgrom, 238; and cf. *M. Zebaḥ.* i. 1).

and far-reaching statement, 'And if you unintentionally transgress and do not do any of [lit., all] these commandments (כל המצות האלה) which YHWH spoke to Moses.'

These and other differences may be noted; their discussion and resolution will be taken up in this and successive parts of this chapter and the next. For the present it must be noted that a detailed comparison of the sequence and language of the two sources under review (Lev. 4 and Num. 15: 22-9), such as that undertaken by A. Toeg, conclusively demonstrates that Num. 15: 22-9 is based on Lev. 4: 13-21, 27-31: for not only can one observe a precise terminological correspondence in the consecution of these two sets of legal materials (cf. Lev. 4: 13 and Num. 15: 22-24aα; Lev. 4: 14 and Num. 15: 24aβ-bβ; Lev. 4: 20b and Num. 15: 25-6; Lev. 4: 27a and Num. 15: 27a; Lev. 4: 28b and Num. 15: 27b; and Lev. 4: 31b and Num. 15: 28), but, more importantly, Num. 15: 22-9 is characterized by a variety of exegetical expansions which supplement the skeletal frame which it shares with Lev. 4.[73] The following example offered by Toeg, in which the italicized words reflect the homiletical explications, illustrates this point.

Lev. 4: 20b	*Num. 15: 25-6*
Then the priest will expiate them, that they be forgiven.	Then the priest will expiate *all the congregation of Israel*, that they be forgiven: *for it was an accidental transgression; and they brought their offering as a gift to YHWH;*[74] *and their sin-offering to YHWH for their accidental sin*; that *all the congregation of Israel, and the stranger dwelling among them* be forgiven, *for the nation had transgressed accidentally.*

As is evident, Num. 15: 25-6 clarifies the expiation rite and the divine forgiveness. It also provides a more substantive expansion to the law in so far as it now includes the stranger among the residents of the land for whom the legislation is applicable. This addition of a provision which includes the stranger is a matter of frequent occurrence in the priestly sources; although it quite often betrays the fact that it is a legal afterthought or addendum to the received legal tradition, either by following the law—as in the threefold repetition of this injunction in Num. 15: 14-16—after determining the applicability of the law for the

---

[73] 'Numbers 15: 22-31—a Halakhic Midrash', *Tarbiz*, 40 (1960-1), 1-20 [Heb.]. While Toeg builds on Kellermann's supplementation theory (note 71), his study constructs a more unified and penetrating literary analysis.

[74] Hebrew *'iššeh* is most likely related to Ug. *'wš*; see C. H. Gordon, *Ugaritic Textbook* (Rome: Pontifical Biblical Institute, 1965), 354, no. 117.

native (v. 13; cf. v. 2),[75] or by being interpolated into a received legal formulation despite the manifest syntactical and grammatical difficulties which result, as in Lev. 25: 35b, or by interweaving it with other expansions, as in the present instance. The cultural and legal implications of this particular expansion will occupy a later discussion. What is of note here is that the homiletical expansions which include the stranger in Num. 15: 25-6 are thus part of several variations on the more formal articulation of the law in Lev. 4, and strongly combine to establish the relative priority of this latter text to Num. 15: 22-9. In turn, this leads to the conclusion that Num. 15: 30-1, which is formally linked with the preceding verses but deals with intentional transgression, is an amendment or supplement to the older legal provision dealing with unintentional transgression only, in the *clausula finalis* manner identified by Daube.

The distinctiveness of Num. 15: 30-1 has often enough been observed —both in terms of its unique phraseology referring to intentional transgressions,[76] and its particular penalty of כרת.[77] It is not, to be sure, the simple fact of this penalty in connection with intentional transgression—as against ritual expiation for unintentional errors— which arouses attention; but rather the fact that the application of this penalty is so unique, governed as it is by the opening verses: 'And if you unintentionally transgress and do not do any of these commandments which YHWH spoke to Moses [v. 22]: all that which YHWH commanded you through Moses, from the day on which YHWH commanded and forward, for [all] your generations' (v. 23). In the light of this protasis, which remarkably differs from Lev. 4 by applying the rules of unintentional transgressions to *all* the commandments (כל המצות) —that is, each and every one of them—and not just those which are negative prohibitions ('from among all the commandments which one shall not do'), one must construe the addendum as invoking כרת for any wilful transgression of *any* of the commandments, and not just for the transgression of particular ones, as is the rule elsewhere (cf. Gen. 17: 14 for violation of the law of circumcision; Exod. 31: 14 for violation of the laws of Sabbath; Lev. 18: 29 for violation of the laws of permissible sexual intercourse). The simultaneous elevation of the law of unintentional transgressions to a level of such comprehensiveness

---

[75] M. Buber, *Darko shel Miqra'* (Jerusalem: The Bialik Institute, 1964), 283, understands v. 14 as a homiletical component, which meets the need to include the stranger among the people through a direct address: *haqqāhāl* 'O Congregation! . . .' (cf. the more oblique formulations in vv. 14, 16).

[76] Cf. Toeg, loc. cit. 18-19.

[77] On this term, see above, p. 92 n. 6. For thematic and terminological reasons, Tsevat, 'Studies in the Book of Samuel', 202f., has suggested that the legal pericope in 1 Sam. 2: 30 presupposes Num. 15: 30-1.

undoubtedly reflects a revolutionary attitude towards the law and its scrupulous performance, in so far as this penalty raises all the commandments to the same level of significance. And lest the comprehensive formulation 'And if you unintentionally transgress and do not do any of these commandments' (v. 22a) be obscure, or ambiguously imply that the reference of 'these' is the previous set of commandments in Num. 15: 3-21, a later glossator—or perhaps the preacher himself— adds the clarification, introduced by the deictic particle אֵת, '*all* the commandments which YHWH commanded you' (v. 23a).

This comprehensive regard for all the commandments is recorded in the addendum, too (v. 31), which explains the reason for the severe penalty of כרת 'because [that person] has despised the word of YHWH and violated מִצְוָתוֹ his commandment'—each singular commandment, therefore, and not only specific ones or the entire ensemble of divine commandments. Given the revolutionary seriousness of this addendum, one is led to conclude that it is the core element of the entire preaching and the reason for the very repetition of Lev. 4. Indeed, the expansion of an older law dealing only with unintentional transgression of negative prohibitions to the unintentional transgression of every one of the commandments, and the corresponding transfer of the penalty of כרת from specific transgressions to the wilful and high-handed violation of any particular commandment, is a quantum development. However, whether this new attitude of severity for all the minutiae of the law is merely the product of a new religious scrupulosity on the part of a post-exilic community, newly dedicated to the ancestral traditions and their unmitigated obedience, or whether such a monumental and apparently unrealistic advocacy of the penalty of כרת for wilful transgression of any of the commandments is a desperate appeal to divine sanctions on the part of a minor satrapy in the Persian commonwealth, which was without certain political constraints that might restrain the wilful disregard of group norms at the transitional time of national restoration, is a matter of speculation.

However, what is not a matter of speculation is the remarkable transformation of religious ideology which the preacher gives expression to regarding the nature of the divine law: its many commandments are put on the same plane; they are each of equal significance with respect to their wilful violation, so that the burden and fullness of the whole is now attached to each particular part thereof—*multum in parvo*. What is also not a matter of speculation is how this ideology is set forth and authorized. And, in fact, this matter is no less revolutionary and remarkable than the preceding. For it will be noted that in contra-distinction to those cases of human legal *traditio* where an interpretation is interpolated into the *traditum* and receives its authority thereby, and in contradistinction to another derivative mode, at the other end of the spectrum, whereby materials are incorporated into the *traditum* and given authority by means of an introductory ascription of the material to divine authority (as occurs for example in Num. 15:1-2a and 17-18a, in the phrase 'Then YHWH spoke to Moses as follows: Speak to the Israelites, and say to them')—in contradistinction to these two modes, Num. 15:22-3 *does not* indicate who speaks 'And if you unintentionally transgress any of these commandments which YHWH spoke to Moses: all that which YHWH commanded you through Moses . . .' Clearly YHWH is not the speaker, for he is referred to in the third person in the relative clauses of vv. 22b and 23b; nor is Moses the speaker, and for the same reason. The speaker is thus neither YHWH nor Moses but —*mirabile dictu*—a preacher of the law of YHWH as given to Moses. That this preacher did not simply preach the law of Lev. 4 is clear in the explanations which are added, the expansion of the law to include the stranger, and the addition of provisions dealing with intentional transgressions and an entire ideology pertaining thereto. But nowhere does the preacher adjust his legal *traditio*—revolutionary as it is—to a divine speaker's words or authority; and nowhere does he make use of the preaching authority of Moses, as does the deuteronomist routinely.

Nor will it suffice to maintain that the authority of the new teachings beginning 'And if you unintentionally transgress' derives from vv. 17-18a, and the latter's reference to YHWH's command to Moses, because, as noted, the relative clauses in vv. 22b and 23b imply a third person— the preacher himself. Accordingly, neither can the contents of Num. 15:22-31 be passed by, nor its method of presentation. Num. 15:22-31 is a legal homily by a preacher, who interprets and supplements his legal *traditum* with a revolutionary *traditio* of it. The human voice of the legal exegete of Num. 15:22-31 breaks through the imposing context in which the teaching has been redacted; it breaks through the awesome weight of teachings and traditions which have been attributed to the divine, or marked by its authority, and betoken the revolutionary significance of human exegesis to change the divine revelation and to adapt it to new circumstances. It further betokens another style which contributed to the emergence of exegesis; a style whose full significance is only to emerge in early rabbinic literature: *the exegetical-legal discourse.*[78]

3. Another variation on the exegetical-legal discourse can be found in Exod. 34:11-26. By contrast with Num. 15:22-31, which is from first to last a legal discourse, Exod. 34:11-26 is more complex. It

---

[78] Toeg, loc. cit., has pointed to the second-person address and the didactic discourse style of the piece in its several parts, but did not draw the more radical implications noted above. On the rabbinic halakhic discourse, cf. E. Urbach, 'The Exegetical Sermon'.

begins with a homiletical, hortatory prologue—which contains exhortations not to make covenants with the autochthonous Canaanite population, and to be removed from their modes of worship and women (vv. 11-17)[79]—and continues with a series of ritual rules—which stress the observance of the three agricultural pilgrimages, the Sabbath, and assorted sacrificial and cultic obligations (vv. 18-26). This pattern of a prologue (which emphasizes historical events, divine zeal, and the prohibition against making gods of cast metal) followed by stipulations is, of course, remarkably similar to the pattern known from the Decalogue (Exod. 20: 1-14). However, even closer literary affinities with earlier sources can be noted by a more concentrated look at the prologue and stipulations separately. Thus, on the one hand, the homiletical prologue is clearly overlaid with a variety of exhortations and promises which betray an extremely close topical and linguistic similarity with the unified discourse found in Exod. 23: 20-33; so much is this the case, in fact, that it would appear that Exod. 23: 20-33 is the source for Exod. 34: 11-16 (cf. Exod. 34: 11 and 23: 21, 23; 34: 12a and 23: 32; 34: 12b and 23: 33; 34: 13 and 23: 24b; and 34: 12a and 23: 24a). On the other hand, it is also clear that the stipulations in Exod. 34: 18-26 are built on the pattern of the old pilgrimage calendars and their stipulated rules, such as may be found in Exod. 23: 15-19. Indeed, given the precise similarity between Exod. 23: 15-19 and 34: 18, 21b, 22-3, 25-6, and between Exod. 23: 20-33 and 34: 11-16, there can be little doubt that the original contextual contiguity of the pilgrimage rites and the hortatory discourse in Exod. 23: 15-19 and 20-33 was seized upon by the speaker of Exod. 34: 11-26, though reworked and inverted to suit the new circumstances.

An even closer inspection of the pilgrimage pattern of Exod. 23: 15-19, and its reuse in Exod. 34: 18-26, will serve to disclose the modes of legal exegesis employed in the discourse. Thus, whereas Exod. 23: 15-16 first refers to the three pilgrimage festivals (the festivals of unleavened bread and of cutting and reaping), then indicates that all must be present at the shrine of YHWH three times a year (v. 17), and then articulates various ritual provisions from the various seasons (vv. 18-19), this clear pattern is exegetically and homiletically disrupted in Exod. 34: 18-26 at several points. Thus, between the command to visit the shrine three times a year and the various ritual provisions (Exod. 34: 23; 25-6) there is an extended exhortation not to covet (חמד) one's property and possessions during those ritual occasions when one is required to be present at the shrine, some distance from

---

[79] For a thorough discussion of this unit, and earlier views, see F. Langlemet, 'Israël et "l'habitant du pays"; vocabulaire et formules d'Ex xxxiv 11-16', *RB* 76 (1969), 321-50, 481-507.

home (v. 24).[80] Further, between Exod. 23:15a, 'Observe the festival of unleavened bread: for seven days you must eat unleavened bread, as I commanded you for the season of the month of Abib, for at that time did you leave Egypt', and 23:15b, 'and you shall not see me empty-handed', Exod. 34:19 has inserted the rules pertaining to the donation of animal and human first-born and the provisions for their redemption. Such an interpolation is manifestly exegetical and of considerable interest; for while it is striking that there are references to the donation of animal and human firstlings in Exod. 13:1-2, 11-16, both before and after references to the celebration of the festival of unleavened bread (vv. 3-10), such that there is a clear redactional attempt to bring the two matters into some type of association, there is no explicit attempt whatever in Exod. 13:1-16 to bring the issue of first-born donations and the festival of unleavened bread into a *seasonal* relationship. But this is precisely what the exegetical interpolation in Exod. 34:19 does. Whether this application of the donation of animal and human firstlings (and their redemption) to the season of the festival of unleavened bread is a free theological attempt to link different types of redemption (ritual and historical), or whether it is derived either from an interpretation of the redactional juxtaposition of these two items in Exod. 13:1-16, or from an oral tradition and practice which had motivated the aforementioned redaction, the fact remains that the particular contextualization of the laws of first-born *into* the law of the unleavened bread as found in Exod. 34:19 not only conjoins these two events temporally but explains the injunction 'you shall not see me empty-handed' *in terms of* a specific mode of fulfilment: the donation of firstlings (or their redemptive equivalent) to the shrine.

It is probably because of the reference to the seven days of the festival of unleavened bread (v. 18) that the discourse turns, associatively, to the Sabbath (v. 21). It is not, however, the first half of the verse, 'You may labour six days but on the seventh you shall rest', which arrests attention; for this basically follows the form and language of the Decalogue (Exod. 20:9-10). It is rather the second half of the verse, 'you shall rest during ploughing [i.e. seed-time] and reaping', which is striking. Such a formulation, juxtaposed as it is to the official Sabbath rule, obviously serves to emphasize that the Sabbath was to be

---

[80] The inclusion of Sabbath rules among pilgrimage ones, plus this striking homiletical reference to the verb *ḥāmad* in v. 24, strike me as further indications of the influence of the Decalogue. In addition, the reference to expanded borders (*wĕhirḥabtî 'et gĕbûlekā*) in v. 24 seems to be an interpolation: it supplements the concise formulary of Exod. 23:17-18, and it is enclosed by a *Wiederaufnahme*. Moreover, the phraseology of Exod. 34:24 is strikingly comparable to Deut. 19:8a (cf. Deut. 12:21, 14:24), and may reflect a deuteronomic redaction of Exod. 34:11-26 (cf. v. 13 and Deut. 12:3).

observed precisely in those periods when it was likely to be violated. Indeed, the seasonal pressures of an ancient – as of any – agricultural community were such that the ploughing and reaping seasons were of vital significance. If the requisite work were not accomplished, famine and starvation might result. Both because many people undoubtedly violated the Sabbath rest during such period, and also because the more heedful would have wanted to know if such an economic and health necessity temporarily overruled the law, a ruling was necessary. Just such a clarification, designed to make the Sabbath law more comprehensive in the case of this problem, can be found, then, in Exod. 34: 21.

E. LEGAL RESTRICTIONS WITH INTRODUCTORY FORMULAE

1. The phenomenon of legal restrictions added to a text requires special comment, for these are not so much restrictions which naturally clarify or circumscribe the application of a general principle, and so arise organically with it, as a secondary legal response to a given formulation in the light of new legal situations or perceptions. Thus, it was noted earlier that ancient Israel had – or inherited – general formulations concerning the donation of firstlings to the shrine. Indeed, the phraseology in Num. 18:15a, which informs the priests that 'everything (כל) which breaks the womb [i.e. first-born], of all (כל) flesh which shall be sacrificed to YHWH, both human and animal, is yours', is a radical, comprehensive, and unmitigated proclamation. The term כל is used twice; sacrificial terminology is employed and unqualified; and no distinction is introduced regarding humans and animals. It is only in Num. 18:15b, which states 'however (אך) you shall surely redeem human firstlings and the firstlings of impure animals', that restrictions are made. This qualification (and its sequel) thus exegetically modifies the initial generalization here as elsewhere, although in the case of Exod. 13: 2 the older demand remains starkly unmitigated. Were the restrictions primary, neither the independent generalizations nor the diversity of modifications which are found could readily be explained. It is rather the authoritative – if troublesome – *traditum* which required adjustment in the light of later cultic rules and sensibilities.

In another instance, the commandment in Exod. 12:15 requiring the Israelite to eat unleavened bread for seven days, and to rid his home of this substance as well, is followed by the general remark: 'And you shall have a sacred convocation on the first day and on the seventh; no manner of work (כל־מלאכה) shall be done among you' (v. 16a-bα). In this formulation the phrase כל־מלאכה would appear to be comprehensive. Indeed, elsewhere in priestly regulations כל־מלאכה appears to be a more severe category than מלאכת עבודה – the first being used regarding work on the Sabbath and the Day of Atonement (Lev. 23: 3,

28; Num. 29: 7), which are also exclusively referred to as days of special rest (שבת שבתון), and the second being used regarding work on the festivals (Lev. 23: 7, 8, 21, 25, 35, 36; Num. 28:18, 25, 26, 29:1, 12, 35). It has accordingly been proposed by J. Milgrom that כל־מלאכה refers to *all* activities while מלאכת עבודה refers to occupational work only.[81] However this may be, Lev. 23: 7-8 and Num. 28: 25, 28 prohibit work on the first and seventh days of the festival of unleavened bread by means of the phrase מלאכת עבודה, *not* כל־מלאכה, which is used in Exod. 12: 16a.

It may be an awareness of this discrepancy which prompted the qualification of the phrase כל־מלאכה in Exod. 16: bβ, which states 'however (אך) that which a person would eat, that only may one do' (יעשה; cf. לא יעשה, v. 16bα). With this qualification כל־מלאכה was restricted so as to permit the preparation of food. If מלאכת עבודה was itself understood to be a more limited designation than כל־מלאכה, permitting certain work like food preparation but not occupational work,[82] then the restriction in Exod. 12: 16bβ is an exegetical attempt to normalize the formulation in Exod. 12: 16a-bα and adapt it to actual practice. On the other hand, it is equally reasonable to suppose that these various formulations existed independently, and that the restriction introduced into Exod. 12:16 is a practical and limited exegetical response to an actual legal formulation and its problems. Faced with a harsh and unmitigated formulation, the draftsman qualified it. What is not stated, of course, and inevitably required the decision of later rabbinic authorities, was whether cooking on the first and seventh day could be done with a new fire or whether one was only permitted to use a fire ignited before the onset of each of the days of sacred convocation.

2. At the conclusion of the account of various sacrifices found in Lev. 6:1-7:21 there is an appendix with matters only indirectly related to the preceding specifications of sacrificial procedure. These matters include the prohibition from eating the fat of oxen, sheep, and he-goats (vv. 22-5), or from eating the blood of birds and animals (vv. 26-7). The penalty for disobedience in both cases is כרת. In fact it may be that this penalty is the associative reason for the very occurrence of these provisions at this point; for the preceding paragraph, dealing with the shared-offering, invokes the penalty of כרת for anyone who eats this particular sacrifice in a state of ritual impurity. This aside, the provisions in the appendix are of inherent interest, particularly

---

[81] *Studies*, 80-1, n. 297.

[82] The rabbinic designation for such work for creaturely enjoyment or need is *mĕleket hanā'āh*. See Nachmanides' comment on the prohibition from doing work (*mĕleket 'ăbôdāh*) on the first and seventh days of the festival of unleavened bread in Lev. 23: 7, and the comments of Ibn Ezra and Rashbam *ad* Deut. 16: 6.

the first, which prohibits the eating of certain fats. The prohibition against certain fats in vv. 23 and 25 shares a similar stylistic pattern with the following prohibition against blood in vv. 26-7: a comprehensive negative commandment (לא . . . כל) is first set forth (vv. 23 and 26) and followed by the similar statements that whosoever (כל) would eat of the prohibited substances would be subject to כרת. However, this precise symmetry between the two provisions is broken by v. 24, which also interrupts the consecution of vv. 23 and 25. Verse 24 states 'However (ו) the fat of carrion which has died naturally or been ripped to death may be used for all work (כל־מלאכה); but you may in no wise eat it.' It is obvious that this passage is an exegetical restriction of the general norm enunciated in v. 23, prohibiting the Israelite from eating of the fat of certain (clean; i.e. permissible) animals. One may still not eat of the fat of such animals, or even of the fat of carrion (prohibited in any case), *but* one may utilize the fat of the latter for work (to grease objects, for example) or (presumably) utility (to make tallow, for example). This exegetical concession is thus of practical significance. It undoubtedly reflects a consideration which arose out of the necessities of life and the concern for an economy to utilize all its resources. Verse 24 may thus be a *responsum* to a living problem subsequently formulated by a draftsman and incorporated into the *traditum*. Once again the *traditio* bends and adjusts its *traditum* to new concerns. It was in this way that the frequent priestly comment that a rule was an 'eternal statute for [all] your generations' was fulfilled in practice— and perhaps also liberally interpreted.[83]

3. In the previous two instances, restrictions have been introduced by legal draftsmen to modify a prior generalization or to circumscribe its validity and applicability. In this process two terms—אך and the particle ו—were used from among the technical exegetical vocabulary of ancient Israelite draftsmen. Another phrase, which appears to have had a particular resonance among deuteronomic draftsmen and their legal tradition, is כן־תעשה. Its use was discussed earlier in connection with cases of analogical extensions of a law. However, it was also employed to circumscribe a received law and adjust it to new circumstances.

In his study of the old law of putting the Canaanite population into workforces, A. Biram pointed to an inconsistency in the formulation found in Deut. 20:10-18.[84] Verses 10-14 state that if a Canaanite city responds favourably to an Israelite overture of peace, its people may not be destroyed—but they may be exploited as a workforce (vv. 10-11).

[83] Clearly, *raq* in Deut. 20:20 introduces a qualification of v. 19, but it is less certain whether this is a later exegetical stratum.
[84] See 'The Corvée', *Tarbiz*, 23 (1952), 138 [Heb.].

However, if the Canaanites choose to fight, then all males are to be slain (v. 13). All this is a straightforward rule. But a logical problem arises with vv. 15ff. The speaker continues: 'you shall do likewise כן תעשה' *only* to the far-off cities, but all persons living in the cities of the promised inheritance must be killed (v. 16). The explanation given is that the Canaanites must be exterminated by the Israelites, as they had been commanded to do (v. 17).

Now it is obvious that the law from v. 15 on, introduced by 'you shall do likewise', is in manifest contradiction to the preceding siege law, and betrays an attempt by the draftsmen to harmonize it with the deuteronomic law of extermination. The initial stratum of Deut. 20: 10-18, vv. 10-14, dealt with siege and destruction in the context of an Israelite overture for peace. No reference was made there to a ban of extermination (חֵרֶם) imposed on the autochthonous population; and, indeed, the permission for slaughter only extended to the males. All this is overturned, however, in vv. 15-17. By means of the phrase כן תעשה – which links the two sections – the initial law was exegetically transformed and restricted to 'distant cities', whereas 'every person' in the promised inheritance must be put under the ban of extermination.

The need to redefine the parameters of the first law is undoubtedly due to the addition of the law of חרם to an older siege law. This latter had apparently achieved some authoritative status, so that it was retained and modified – not deleted. The latter point may also help explain why the equally ancient war law pronouncing on how female captives would be taken and domesticated (Deut. 21: 10-14) – a law totally contradictory to the later חרם legislation – was retained. The reason that no qualifying clause is added to it suggests that the requisite qualification was deemed *already* introduced in Deut. 20: 15. To the harmonistic and pious temperament of the deuteronomist, Deut. 21: 10-14 could thus be contextually interpreted as applicable to those enemies outside the land, and to them alone.

The formulation in Deut. 20: 17, which cites the law of חרם ('For you shall surely exterminate them: the Hittite, the Amorite, the Canaanite, the Perizzite, the Hivite, and the Jebusite'), is intended to recall an older law. This is the force of the concluding formula, 'as YHWH, your God, commanded you'. Indeed this quotation is surely intended to recall the first formulation of the law of חרם in Deut. 7: 1-2. It states there that when the Israelites come into the land they shall defeat 'the Hittites, the Girgashites, the Amorites, and Canaanites, the Perizzites, the Hivites, and the Jebusites'. It goes on to exhort them: 'you shall surely exterminate them.'

The Exegetical Relationship Between Deut. 7 and Exod. 23: 20-33

The adjustment in Deut. 20: 10-18 of an old siege law to later rules of חרם is of much interest, since the very rule of חרם is cited in Deut. 20: 17. Moreover, its source in Deut. 7: 1-2 is itself a supplement to an older law. This can be seen by a detailed comparison of Deut. 7 with Exod. 23: 20-33. The numerous and precise topical and verbal correspondences that exist between these passages make it quite clear that Deut. 7 is dependent upon Exod. 23: 20-33 (cf. Exod. 23: 20, 23 and Deut. 7:1; Exod. 23: 24 and Deut. 7: 5; Exod. 23: 25 and Deut. 7: 12-13, 15; Exod. 23: 26 and Deut. 7: 14; Exod. 23: 27 and Deut. 7: 23; Exod. 23: 28 and Deut. 7: 20; Exod. 23: 29-30 and Deut. 7: 22; Exod. 23: 22 and Deut. 7: 2; and Exod. 23: 33 and Deut. 7: 26).[85] Indeed, this series of correspondences even extends to the very structure of Deut. 7. For if we detach the manifestly homiletical speeches found in Deut. 7: 6-11–a unit which contains such manifestly deuteronomic themes as the holiness of the people of Israel, its election by God, and the individual retribution by God–it will be observed that the topic sequence of commands to destroy the autochthonous population and its idols followed by themes of blessing and health (vv. 12-16) is the very sequence found in Exod. 23: 23-6 in similar terms.[86]

These topical and verbal correspondences, significant as they are, prove less illuminating, however, than the difference between the two texts–which prove that Deut. 7:1-26 is a deuteronomic expansion of its Exodus source. Among the deuteronomic expansions are several of exegetical significance.

1. Certainly the most significant difference between the two documents is the reference to the extermination of the local population in Deut. 7: 1-2 after the reference to their coming into the land and before the command to destroy idolatrous altars (v. 5). This is a distinctly deuteronomic sequence. Its parallel in Exod. 23: 20-4 is, by contrast, without any such extermination law. Indeed, the command 'to destroy them' in Exod. 23: 24 seems to refer to 'their gods . . . their practices . . . [and] their sacred pillars'. But even if this command actually refers to the people, there is no indication that this means total extermination. Accordingly, the later injunction to rout the inhabitants, so that they do not dwell in the land, and also not to make covenants with them or marry them (vv. 31-3), is a realistic warning. As long as the Canaanites were alive, they and their practices were a religious threat. By contrast, when Deut. 7: 2-3 commands to exterminate them, *and also* neither to make covenants with them nor to intermarry with them, it is clear that

---

[85] Cf. also the comments of N. Lohfink, *Das Hauptgebot. Eine Untersuchung literarischer Einleitungsfragen zu Dt 5-11 (An. Bib.* 20; Rome: Pontifical Biblical Institute, 1963), 172-85.

[86] There is also a close chiastic connection between Deut. 7: 1-6 and 12-16. See N. Lohfink, op. cit. 181-2.

the two commands are contradictory. Enemies, once exterminated, cannot be married. The חרם law thus shows itself, from this viewpoint as well, to be a *later and more radical element* in the passage.[87]

2. A second distinguishing feature between the two texts concerns the matter of intermediaries. In Exod. 23: 20 God states that he is sending 'a messenger . . . who will bring you to the place which I have prepared for you' (i.e. the promised land; cf. v. 23). Just this reference to an intermediary is missing from Deut. 7: 1, where, however, the same verb is used and the same nations are mentioned as in Exod. 23: 20, 23. This is a deliberate omission in line with the theological perspective of the Book of Deuteronomy.

But if the messenger of Exod. 23: 20 is ignored in Deut. 7: 1, he resurfaces in Judg. 2: 1-5. In Exod. 23: 29-30 (and correspondingly in Deut. 7: 22) the Israelite people are told that the invasion and banishment of the autochthonous peoples will be gradual, so as to allow them to slowly settle the land and not be overrun by wild beasts. Since these Canaanite peoples will be present in the land, the Israelites are cautioned not to enter into a covenant with them—for they will be a religious snare to them. This statement is tendentious, and undoubtedly arose from a need theologically to explain and justify the gradual and partial invasion. However, it is to be stressed that this explanation is stated positively. It does not say that the failure of complete conquest was a punishment inflicted upon the Israelites owing to their failure to fulfill the covenant. This latter point becomes all the more significant in the light of Judg. 2: 1-5, where Exod. 23: 29-30 is referred to—and transformed. In Judg. 2: 1-5 the messenger says that *because* the Israelites have made a covenant with the inhabitants of the land, and not destroyed their cult places (v. 2), *therefore* 'I will not banish them from before you . . . and their gods will be a snare to you' (v. 3). This transformation of an ancient source into a conditional prescription is remarkable. The incomplete and long-term conquest now finds firm theological support. By contrast, a later deuteronomic historian, without recourse to the 'messenger' theme in Judg. 2: 1-5, confirmed this divine judgement in his own language (Judg. 2: 12, 20-1) and offered another explanation (v. 22).

3. A third feature distinguishes Exod. 23: 29-30 from Deut. 7: 22. In Exod. 23: 29-30 God states that 'I will not drive them [the Canaanites] out in one year lest the land become desolate and the beasts of the field overwhelm you; little by little will I drive them out . . .' By contrast, Deut. 7: 22 also follows up the reference to the fact that God

---

[87] See already G. Hölscher, 'Komposition und Ursprung des Deuteronomiums', *ZAW* 40 (1922), 170f. n. 4.

will defeat the nations 'little by little' with the statement that 'you will not be able to wipe them out quickly, lest the beasts of the field overwhelm you'. Both passages clearly indicate divine sovereignty during the conquest, anticipate a gradual settlement, and justify this latter by reference to the wild beasts from which God would protect his people. But whereas Exod. 23: 29 assertively states that 'I [God] will not drive them out', Deut. 7: 22 states that *you will not be able* (לא תוכל) to wipe them out'. Both comments are undoubtedly *post factum* rationalizations. But the variation in phraseology is of significant interest.

To appreciate the force of the phrase 'לא תוכל כלתם you will not be able to wipe them out' in Deut. 7: 22, one must observe that the conquest list found in Judg. 1: 1-36 indicates that in many cases the invading people 'did not dispossess (לא הוריש)' the local population (vv. 19, 21, 27-33). In only one case is the reason for failure to dispossess the Canaanites attributed to inferior Israelite armament (v. 19). The basic force of the other uses of the formula לא הוריש is to state that this was an intentional failure to wipe out the population. And indeed, just this point is explicitly made in v. 28: 'Later, when the Israelites became strong, they put the Canaanites into workforces, but did not dispossess them.' Clearly the old editor of this conquest list is concerned to explain why the promised land was not completely conquered. He did so by attributing the failure to a deliberate violation of older injunctions which commanded the removal of the nations of Canaan.

By contrast an entirely different explanation for the failure to conquer the land can be found in (the earlier) Josh. 14-18. Here the issue is not that the Israelites were unwilling to dispossess the Canaanites, but that 'they were not able (לא יכלו) . . . to dispossess them (להורישם)' (cf. Josh. 15: 63 with Judg. 1: 21, and Josh. 17: 12 with Judg. 1: 27).[88] This explanation of the Israelites' *inability* to complete the promised conquest is illumined by the prognosticative remark found in Deut. 7: 22: 'you will not be able (לא תוכל) to drive them out.' Such a prognostication would retrospectively serve to justify the 'later' Israelite failure fully to enact the original religious command totally to exterminate the resident Canaanite population immediately upon entering the land.

[88] Apart from the fact that Judg. 1: 21, 27 appears to be a tendentious revision of the explanation given in Josh. 15: 63, 17: 12, another indication that Judg. 1 is a reworking of Josh. 14-18 can be seen in the fact that, in connection with his emphasis on Judah (given its priority of position in the list, and the majority of verses it is given: vv. 1-20 for Judah, only vv. 27-36 for all the northern tribes), the composer of Judg. 1 ascribes the conquest of Jerusalem to Judah (v. 8) but the failure to settle it to the Benjaminites (v. 21), as against the tradition in Josh. 15: 63 where the Judahites are charged with *not* being able to settle it Jerusalem. Were Josh. 15: 63 the later tradition, it is unlikely that a compiler of the Judahite traditions (in ch. 15) would have changed the blame from the Benjaminites (Judg. 1: 21) to the Judahites!

Further Exegesis of the Rules of חרם

1. The historical judgement that the Israelites were 'not able' to exterminate by חרם all the existing autochthonous groups in the promised land is also embodied in a historical notice found in 1 Kgs. 9: 20-1, explaining that Solomon put all of these people into forced labour of some sort. But just as the explanation found in Josh. 15: 63 and 17: 12 concerning the Israelites' failure to dispossess the Canaanites was replaced by the more condemnatory judgement found in Judg. 1: 21-7 and elsewhere, so was 1 Kgs. 9: 20-1 rejected by a later historian. Indeed, to him, the notion that somehow 'the Israelites were unable (לֹא יָכְלוּ)' to vanquish the Canaanities by חרם was theologically problematic. In citing 1 Kgs. 9: 20-1, therefore, the Chronicler revised this estimation of the events and simply said that 'the Israelites did not obliterate (לֹא־כִלּוּם)' the local population (2 Chron. 8: 7-8). The change is subtle but momentous; it is theological and no mere scribal error.

2. There is little reason to doubt that originally the imposition of חרם in war was *ad hoc* and related to a vow (cf. Num. 21: 1-3). Undertaking the vow of חרם was thus neither a requirement nor a necessity in all war situations. Undoubtedly the varieties of piety and duress predetermined the nature of each vow and account for their varying scope as regards the destruction of cities, people, and possessions. Instructive of the types of vows that might be undertaken is a comparison of the national vow found in Num. 21: 1-3 and Jephtha's personal vow found in Judg. 11: 30-1. In both language and circumstance there is a striking similarity between the two. Thus, in the first case, after the Canaanite king of Arad heard of the Israelite approach and attacked them, and made off with considerable booty (Num. 21: 2), 'Then Israel made a vow to YHWH, and said: "If you give this nation into my hand then I shall exterminate (וְהַחֲרַמְתִּי) their cities"' (v. 3). Similarly, Jephtha during a battle against the Ammonites, and in precisely similar words, 'made a vow to YHWH, and said: "If you give the Ammonites into my hand then whatsoever emerges from my home towards me when I return in peace from the Ammonites will be for YHWH, and I shall raise it up as a holocaust offering."'

Neither of the foregoing vows reflects the absolute and unconditional requirements of the rules of חרם imposed by the Book of Deuteronomy, in 7: 5, 25-6. The emergence of this commandment from earlier sources is not entirely certain, since there is nothing precisely like it in earlier materials. Nevertheless, there are some circumstantial grounds for the view that the development of the rule of חרם against the Canaanites and their possessions is itself an exegetical product. According to M. Greenberg, the injunction of חרם in Exod. 22: 19 against an

Israelite who has sacrificed to a foreign god has been combined with the law of expulsion in Exod. 23: 20-33 against the Canaanites to produce a rule of חרם against all idolators, their possessions and cult-objects— both Israelite (Deut. 13: 13-19) and Canaanite (Deut. 7: 5, 25-6) alike.[89] Additional support for this argument lies in the fact—noted earlier—that the speech in Deut. 7 has been strongly influenced by Exod. 23: 20-33.

Whatever its exact origin, the formulation of a norm proscribing absolutely the use of the possessions and ritual objects of the Canaanite 'idolators' rendered some old historical records theologically problematic, and required their exegetical resolution. For example, it is quite clear from 2 Sam. 5: 21 that David, after routing the Philistine in battle, 'carried off' (וישאם) the idols left by the enemy. This apparent non-compliance with חרם prescriptions on the part of pious King David clearly bothered the Chronicler. Since, in his view, it was David who established the Temple protocol, and was thus a man of piety and ritual knowledge, the transgression could not be overlooked. The Chronicler, therefore, in 1 Chron. 14: 12 effaced the fault and read: 'they burnt . . . in fire (וישרפו . . . באש)'—an act fully in accordance with the Pentateuchal norm (Deut. 7: 25). Whether the Chronicler deliberately reworked the original text,[90] or whether out of naïve or troubled piety he interpreted the verb וישאם in the light of an obscure verbal stem meaning 'to ignite' or 'burn',[91] cannot be determined. What can be determined, however, is that the Chronicler has reformulated the phraseology of his received text so that the piety of David's actions (to him) would be clear and explicit (for all). As far as the instance in 2 Sam. 12: 30 is concerned, wherein it is reported that David was crowned with the gold crown of the Ammonite god Milcom after the battle at Rabah—an outright infraction of Deut. 7: 25-6—the Chronicler is embarrassingly silent.

The old warnings not to make a covenant with the inhabitants of the land have a clear polemical thrust (Exod. 23: 32, 34: 12). They seem distinctly designed to prevent attraction to Canaanite religious practices. The phrase used in these old warnings is 'do not make a treaty with them (להם)'. As long ago noted by Begrich, such a phrase reflects a contractual arrangement in which the Israelites are the dominant party.[92]

---

[89] See his article in *Enc. Miq.* viii. 348 f., s.v. *'ḥĕrem'* [Heb.].

[90] Cf. the formulation of Seeligmann in *Tarbiz*, 25 (1955-6), 121.

[91] See M. Cogan, *Imperialism and Religion*, 166, n. 2, who notes the use of the noun *maś'ēt* as 'fire' in Judg. 20: 38, 40, Jer. 6: 1, Zech. 4: 10, and *KAI* 194. Kimḥi, in his comments on 2 Sam. 5: 21, interprets this noun as derived from an old verb *nāśā'* 'to set fire'—and also notes Nahum 1: 5 and Job 32: 22. Kimḥi may have been influenced by rabbinic usage, as in the expression *maśśî'în maśśû'ôt* 'ignite torches' (*M. Roš Haš.* ii. 2-3).

[92] J. Begrich, 'Berit', *ZAW* 60 (1944), 1-11.

A comparable legal relationship is envisaged by Deut. 20:10-14, so that it is not impossible that this passage also reflects those kinds of treaties prohibited by Exod. 23:32 and 34:12. In any event, the innovation of a law of total חרם changed matters considerably. Now such treaties were, if not impossible (cf. Deut. 7:1-2 *prior to* vv. 3-4), then totally reconceptualized so as to pertain only to distant, non-Canaanite peoples (cf. Deut. 20:15-18). An interesting example of such a harmonization between the older reality and the later חרם requirements can be found in Josh. 9, a literary-historical source.

Scholars have long laboured over the possible strata of this complex text, and various positions have emerged.[93] As a result, most commentators now agree that the treaty between the Israelites and the Gibeonites (called Hivites in Josh. 9:7 and Amorites in 2 Sam. 21:2) reflects an old and authentic tradition stemming from the early conquest period. Such was the reality of this covenant that its violation in the time of Saul was clearly the basis of a vendetta shortly thereafter (2 Sam. 21:3ff.). In Josh. 9:3, 9-10 the reason given for this treaty is the fear of the Gibeonites who sued for peace before the invading Israelites. This too many be an authentic historical record. But what is of more interest is the way the pious deuteronomic historian of the Book of Joshua has harmonized this tradition of a treaty with Canaanites with the reality (for him) of the חרם law, which he assumed to be in force at that time.

To resolve the legal-historical contradiction of how pious Joshua and the princes could have made a treaty with the Canaanites—especially when he elsewhere presents Joshua as fulfilling the חרם (cf. Josh. 10: 35, 37, 11:12-14), punishing its violators (Josh. 6:17-7:25), and even obeying other deuteronomic laws (cf. Josh. 8:29, 10:26, and Deut. 21: 22-3)—the historian made use of a legal exegesis known to him. Thus, when the Gibeonites came and sued for peace they stated that they came from a distant land (9:6), in apparent anticipation of the Israelite reaction which is concerned that these people are in fact from the local area (v. 7). The reason for this Israelite concern lies in the *received* law of Deut. 20:14-18, which made an exegetical distinction between near and far-off cities, and legislated that the חרם was in effect only in local territories. As indicated earlier, the need to make this particular distinction was due to the fact that an older law permitting peace treaties with the autochthonous Canaanites was supplemented by a later rule of חרם (Deut. 20:10-14 *plus* vv. 15-18). The distinction between near and far-off cities—articulated by the Gibeonites and implicitly acknowledged by the Israelites—presupposes this very

---

[93] See the thorough study of J. Liver, 'The Literary History of Josh IX', *JSS* 8 (1963), 227-43, with previous literature cited.

deuteronomic supplementation, and so presents us with the amusing situation of Canaanites *using the biblical law so as to circumvent it!*[94] In reality, it is the historiographer of the Book of Joshua who has cleverly utilized the legal subdivision in Deut. 20:10-18 for his own harmonistic purposes. He could not ignore the reality of the treaty made with the Gibeonites, but neither could he ignore the חרם law and the implication that the original settlers did not follow it. The result is a blatant anachronism.

To circumvent the law, the Gibeonites produced 'proof' that they were indeed from far away (9:11-14), whereupon the duped Israelites made a treaty with them (v. 15). The force of this treaty was such, in fact, that subsequent exposure of the mendacity of the Gibeonites could not revoke it. Indeed, the divine law of חרם was actually suspended in this case (v. 18). Nevertheless, owing to popular turmoil, a legal compromise was imposed: the Gibeonites would thenceforth be hewers of wood and drawers of water for the congregation and for the shrine (vv. 21, 23, 27). This compromise may in fact conceal an exegetical dimension. Unable to kill the Gibeonites, Joshua and the princes made them 'servants'—thereby applying to them the *consequences* of the law which they had themselves cited (Deut. 20:11).

3. A final group of examples may be adduced to indicate another way in which the later rule of חרם was worked into earlier sources. This type is more blatant than the preceding ones, where either the legal supplement was obscured through a reconceptualization of the law (Deut. 20:10-18), or an older reality was reworked to harmonize it with a later law (Josh. 9). In Deut. 2:34-7 and 3:4-7 a new phrasing of a historical event, emphasizing the fulfilment of the חרם, is placed after an earlier one which does not—and with no attempt to camouflage the contradiction between them. As S. Loewenstamm has acutely observed, these two passages utilize the formula 'at that time', which functions repeatedly in Deut. 1-9 to introduce a variety of historiographical supplements.[95] In his discussion, Loewenstamm noted how the formula 'at that time' introduces a supplement to the first battle report. What must be added here is that the historical sources which the deuteronomist cites before his supplementation of the references to the חרם are derived from the battle reports of the Book of Numbers, which do not mention compliance with the rules of חרם. Thus, Deut. 2:33 and 3:3 simply say that Kings Sihon and Og and their nations were

---

[94] Not perceiving the exegetical link, Liver, loc. cit., in his otherwise admirable analysis claims that the Gibeonites' ruse is confused; for why else, he wonders, would the Gibeonites ask for a covenant if they came from far away?

[95] 'The formula *bā'ēt hāhî'* in Deuteronomy', *Tarbiz*, 38 (1968), 99-104 [Heb.].

'smitten' in battle, as do Num. 21:23-25 and 34-5. No mention is made in these latter sources of the rules of חרם.

Accordingly, even though the rules of חרם were only first enunciated in Deut. 7:5, 25-6, the pious deuteronomic historian undoubtedly wanted to stress that the rules of חרם were in force and were practised from the very beginning of the conquest. His harmonistic intentions are thus betrayed by the composite and anachronistic nature of the received text. If his supplementation is not simply tendentious, then it may reflect his belief that the older military records implied the practice of חרם, even if they did not say so; so that his addendum merely served to make this practice explicit. But even if this latter assumption is the case, and the deuteronomist wished to show that the rules of חרם were in effect from earliest times, then it is still the case that he is dependent on rules *other* than those found in Deut. 7:25-6: for Deut. 2:35 and 3:7 clearly indicate that the Israelites did not destroy the cattle of the destroyed cities, but rather plundered it as booty.

These matters permit the reconstruction of an old problem. For the anomaly has long been noted that while Samuel instructs Saul to smite the Amalekites and all their possessions with a total חרם (1 Sam. 15: 2-3), Saul claimed to have 'fulfilled the word of YHWH'—even though the king of the Amalekites and all the Amalekite cattle were saved. Certainly, it would seem that Saul could not be either that brazen or that disingenuous if he had heard the חרם formulation of 1 Sam. 15: 2-3. But now, on the basis of the recognition of the great variation in older—including deuteronomic—sources regarding the severity and actual practice of the חרם, it may be proposed that Saul did believe himself to have fulfilled the commandment properly, and the manifest anomaly between the specifications recorded in 1 Sam. 15: 2-3 and Saul's response is really the product of Judaean prophetic or court circles wishing to discredit Saul and provide a historical pretext for his fall from divine grace and the transfer of royalty to David (cf. 1 Sam. 15: 26-9, 16: 1-3, 11-14). These circles, presumably, took over an older narrative about Saul and his wars—a narrative which also, presumably, reported Saul's fulfilment of a חרם commandment—and reworked it in the light of the harsher rules of חרם which had developed. The disingenuous reaction of Saul is thus authentic and part of the older narrative stratum; while the outraged reaction of Samuel, on the other hand, bears the signature of a later hand which transforms Saul the Benjaminite into a self-incriminating, impious liar, unworthy to wear the mantle of kingship.

F. COMPARISON OF LEGAL CASES WITH FORMULAE

In the course of drafting, studying, and analysing legal texts and cases, the ancient Israelite legists were naturally drawn to make comparisons among like and unlike legal or ritual situations. Biblical sources do not exhibit an abundance of such instances but the identifiable cases adequately prove that processes of legal comparison and cross-indexing did occur. These latter, in turn, give valuable witness to the oral legal *traditio* which is not always preserved in the *traditum* but which developed alongside it and for its sake. In fact, enough of this legistic activity is preserved in the *traditum* to suggest a spectrum of types that was undoubtedly more abundant in the living legal tradition. This spectrum ranges from simple shorthand references to texts developed or treated elsewhere, to an assorted series of instances—of varying specificity and analogical development—which are exegetical in nature, instructing one how to interpret and apply related, nearly similar, or obscure cases and actions. The modes of incorporating these additions into the legal *traditum* vary between lapidary references in ritual and historical documents, additions to a unit of related cases in the law corpora, and interpolations into fixed legal formulations.

The Formula כמשׁפט

1. In the drafting of ritual sources, shorthand cross-references were occasionally employed, although it is difficult to determine whether this is due to laziness, conservation of space, or traditional formulation —since these cross-references are inconsistently employed overall. Nevertheless, some patterns are clear. Thus, on some occasions, the performance of the holocaust-offering is not simply referred to but, as in Lev. 5: 10 and 9: 16, also marked by the notice that it be done כַּמִּשְׁפָּט, according to the ritual specifications given in detail in Lev. 4: 3-17, 6: 2-6. In other cases, as in Num. 15: 24, it is the meal- and libation-offerings related to the holocaust-offering of cattle (v. 24aα) which are to be performed כַּמִּשְׁפָּט, according to the specifications detailed earlier in the chapter, vv. 8-12 (cf. vv. 5b-7, for sheep). Similarly, while in Num. 28: 5-7, 13-14, 20-1, 28-9, 29: 9-19, the details of the approp- riate meal- and libation-offering are given, it is recorded in Num. 29: 6 that the 'monthly holocaust-offering and its meal-offering, and the daily holocaust-offering and its meal-offering' are to be performed כְּמִשְׁפָּט, according to the ritual rules specified in Num. 28: 3-8, 11-15. The same type of shorthand reference is found in connection with the Tabernacles festival and the final day of assembly: first, the details of the meal- and libation-offering are given in the ritual account of the first day (Num. 29: 14-16); after that, the specifications of each of the succeeding days are condensed and related to the opening expansive formulation by means of the formula כַּמִּשְׁפָּט (Num. 29: 18, 21, 24, 30, 33). In non-ritual texts one may also note the same lapidary style.

Thus, in Ezra 3: 4 it is stated that the people 'performed the festival of Tabernacles as is written; each daily holocaust-offering according to its number, כְּמִשְׁפָּט, according to the rule of each day'. The reference here is to Num. 29: 12-38, even as the sequence of offerings noted in Ezra 3: 5 (daily, monthly, sacred occasions, and votary) precisely accords with the contents of the remainder of that Pentateuchal ritual calendar (cf. daily offerings, Num. 28: 3-8; monthly offerings, 28: 11-15; offerings for sacred occasions, 28: 9-10, 16-29; 11 + 12-38; and votary offerings, 29: 39). And finally, the Chronicler in his architectural description of the Temple, refers to ten golden lampstands made כְּמִשְׁפָּטָם (2 Chron. 4: 7), according to the specifications found in 1 Kgs. 7: 49-50, not, in fact, according to the Pentateuchal prescription preserved in Exod. 25: 32 (where a six-branched candelabrum is mentioned).[96]

2. In the preceding instances, the shorthand cross-references to other rules by means of the formula כְּמִשְׁפָּט seems to have been largely the product of priestly legists or their derivatives. In the two instances to follow, cases from the *mišpāṭîm* of the Covenant Code utilize the formula כְּמִשְׁפָּט with clear exegetical intent; but, as against the priestly usage, כְּמִשְׁפָּט in such cases does not mean 'according to the ritual rule' but 'according to the civil rule (or norm)'. Of further interest is that the inner-textual cross-references in the Covenant Code are not lapidary, and thus primary, shorthand features, but rather secondary interpolations which further clarify or explicate the case at hand. Thus, in Exod. 21: 7-8, 10-11, there is described a situation which involves the sale of a daughter as a handmaid and the specific circumstances regarding her maintenance and manumission by her new master. Amidst this consecution of issues and conditions, however, there intervenes the possible situation that 'if he [the master] designates her[97] [the handmaid] for his son, he [the master] shall treat her כְּמִשְׁפַּט הַבָּנוֹת according to the rule of daughters-in-law [i.e. as a free-born woman]' (v. 9).[98] Unfortunately, the precise implication of this analogical reference is

---

96 Also cf. the tendentious use of *kᵊ'ammišpāṭ* in 2 Chron. 35: 13, where different Pentateuchal rituals are actually blended. See the discussion·above, pp. 135-7.

97 Heb. *yā'ad* is a technical term for marriage; cf. Akk. *uddû*, and the comments of S.·Paul, *Studies in the Book of the Covenant in the Light of Cuneiform and Biblical Law* (*SVT* 18; Leiden: E. J. Brill, 1970), 54.

98 The phrase 'to treat according to the rule of daughters (*kᵊmišpaṭ habbānôt ya'ăśeh*)' appears to have a technical cast; and, indeed, a remarkably similar linguistic expression is found at Nuzi, in the phrase *ša ki-i mārat [A]r-ra-áb-ḫi ip[u]-ša-aš-ši* 'she shall treat her as a daughter of Arrapha'. See E. A. Speiser, 'One Hundred New Selected Nuzi Texts', *AASOR* 16 (1936), 42. 21-2. In his 'Nuzi Marginalia', *Or*, 25 (1956), 14, Speiser regards this latter as 'an officially recognized and legally protected designation'. In the preceding document, moreover, this 'official designation' is explicated by *ana amti^ti la ú-ta-ar-ši* 'she shall not

not known; but a later draftsman or legal annotator has clearly wanted to specify another rule regarding the ownership and maintenance of a handmaid. The result is that the main case – of a handmaid designated to a son – is to be interpreted in the light of the rules of daughters-in-law as regards the former's personal status. The handmaid of a man is thus *de jure* a daughter-in-law if she is given by that man (her master) to his son, and she is then subject to all the established rights and protections pertaining to daughters-in-law. Without so much as explicitly indicating it, the effect of the interpolated analogy is to articulate one of the special circumstances whereby a handmaid may be manumitted.[99]

In another instance, later in the same collection, a series of cases moves in descending order from the case in which an ox kills a freeman or -woman, and the penalties pertaining thereto (21: 28-30), to the case in which an ox kills a servant or handmaid, and the penalties pertaining thereto (v. 32), to cases involving damage to animals (vv. 33-4), particularly the injury of one's ox by a neighbour's (vv. 35-6), and the penalties pertaining thereto. Such a graded cluster of laws – proceeding from freemen to slaves etc. – is found elsewhere in the *mišpāṭîm* of the Covenant Code (cf. 21: 18-21) and in the Laws of Hammurapi.[100] It is thus not a particularly special feature. However, what is notable in the aforementoned series is the phrase in v. 31 – beginning with the supplementary formula אוֹ (vs. אִם in other qualifying phrases, vv. 29-30) – which states that '[if an ox] should gore a [freeman's] son or daughter, it [the ox] shall be treated כמשפט הזה as in this [i.e. the previous] rule'. This latter specifies that the ox which gores and kills a freeman or -woman must be killed, and so, too, its

return to [the status of] a slave girl', a phrase also analogous to the topos in Exod. 21: 9, which deals with a handmaid, *'āmāh* (v. 7), and her new status as a free person. Cf. Paul, op. cit. 55.

[99] Indeed, Exod. 21: 8-11 deals with special circumstances, since the case opens with the stipulation that the handmaid 'shall not be manumitted like male slaves' (v. 7; cf. vv. 1-6). Of related interest is the addendum to Deut. 15: 12-17a, the deuteronomist's reworking of Exod. 21: 1-6. After referring to a situation where a slave rejects manumission and becomes a permanent slave through the ritual boring of the ear, it is stated 'even so shall you do (*ta'ăśeh-kēn*) to your handmaid' (v. 17b). This variation of the standard *kēn-ta'ăśeh* clause is an interpolation, for the case continues in the masculine singular (v. 18), used elsewhere ('or (*'ô*) a female slave', v. 12, is also an addition). The juxtaposition of v. 17b to issues regarding the rejection of manumission seems designed to elaborate on what is unstated regarding handmaids in Exod. 21: 7-11. More radically, the subject of the clause is not the rejection of manumission as such, but rather the extension to the handmaid of the same procedures granted the slave earlier (vv. 12-14) – and so a thorough rejection of Exod. 21: 7.

[100] Cf. B. Jackson, *Essays*, 144-5, who also notes Exod. 21: 12-17 + 18-19, and vv. 22-3 + 26-7; and LH 200-1, 207-8, 218-19/20. Larger clusters are found in LH 196-9, 209-13, 215-17, 221-3.

owner if the latter had been warned of the animal's vicious nature and if the owner was not able to arrange an agreed price for his vicarious self-atonement.

Now it has long since been noted by D. H. Müller,[101] and subsequent commentators following his lead,[102] that the clause in Exod. 21: 31 is of a polemical nature intending precisely to regulate the penalties in a case where an ox gores and kills a freeman's son or daughter because of a legal tradition in the Laws of Hammurapi which permitted forms of vicarious penalties when minors were involved.[103] This interpretation has been properly parried with the observation that the allusion in Exod. 21: 31 cannot be to the Laws of Hammurapi or other collections in so far as no case of vicarious penalties is known from that material involving goring, and in so far as there is no inner-biblical evidence that vicarious penalties existed which the clause in v. 31 seeks to counteract.[104] However, these observations are more valuable as qualifications of Müller's basic point than as indicating that v. 31 is simply an 'empty phrase' which states the obvious out of some desire for completeness.[105] The fact is that it is quite out of keeping with the biblical corpora to address cases to minors. The rules are normally formulated in terms of adults, even in cases of murder, manslaughter, or theft of persons (Exod. 21: 12-14, 16). It would have been particularly apropos to formulate a case regarding kidnapping, for example, if this had been conventional drafting procedure. But this does not appear to be the case. Accordingly, the specific reference to children in v. 31 stands out unmistakably, so that one must presuppose some customary practice in which the goring of a freeman's son or daughter was subject to penalties different from those imposed upon the goring and death of adults. Presumably there may have been occasions where the owner of such an ox offered minors of his own household in vicarious recompense for his own or ox's life if his ox killed the minors of another freeman. Such practices are now explicitly proscribed. Henceforth, the freeman's children are analogous to adults in cases involving their goring to death by a vicious ox, so that that ox and its owner are entirely subject to the penalties of the latter situation.[106] As in the case

---

[101] *Die Gesetze Hammurapis und ihr Verhälthis zur mosäischen Gesetzgebung sowie den XII Tafeln* (Vienna: Verlag der Israelitisch-Theologischen Lehranstatt, 1903), 166-9.

[102] e.g. Daube, *Studies*, 167; U. Cassuto, *Book of Exodus* (Jerusalem: Magnes Press, 1967), 194 f.; J. Porter, 'The Legal Aspects of the Concept "Corporate Personality" in the Old Testament', *VT* 15 (1965), 365 f.

[103] Cf. LH 116, 210, 230.

[104] Jackson, op. cit. 150.

[105] Ibid. 151.

[106] As noted, v. 29 states that both the vicious ox and the owner must be killed; while v. 30 notes that 'if a ransom be set (*yûšat*) for him (the owner), he

of Exod. 21: 9, so also in this case the analogous extension of one rule to another reflects the ongoing exegesis of ancient Israelite legists concerned to interrelate the known legal rules and to correlate established legal structures and procedures.

The Formula ככתוב

As with the formula כמשפט, the expression ככתוב is used as a shorthand formula to indicate conformity with the 'written' rules of the Torah. Thus, it is recorded in Ezra 3: 3, 5 that the returnees to Zion built an altar 'to raise up holocaust-offerings upon it, ככתוב as written in the Torah of Moses, the man of God'; and then they 'celebrated the festival of Tabernacles ככתוב as written: each day the holocaust-offering according to its number, כמשפט according to the ritual for each day' (cf. Num. 29: 12-38). Similarly Yehoiada, in 2 Chron. 23: 18, re-established the priestly and levitical courses set up by David, that they (the cultic officiants) might 'raise up holocaust-offerings to YHWH as written in the Torah of Moses'. This reference to the priestly and levitical courses established by David is, of course, an inner-textual allusion to 1 Chron. 23, which notes, at its conclusion, that the priests and Levites were to 'raise up holocaust-offerings to YHWH; for the Sabbaths, the new moons, and sacred occasions, according to their number and rule' (v. 31). The specification for the holocaust-offering is given in Lev. 1: 3-17; while the rule for its performance on Sabbaths, new moons, and sacred occasions is again according to the sequence recorded in Num. 28-9.

Even more striking among these post-exilic shorthand allusions to Pentateuchal sources is the reference to the 'wood-sacrifice' in Neh. 10: 35, which the priests, Levites, and Israelites were to bring to the Temple yearly, on special occasions 'as written in the Torah'. No such Pentateuchal commandment is known. In addition, later on in the covenant oath of Neh. 10, one's attention is called to the self-adjuration 'to bring the firstlings of our sons and animals ככתוב בתורה as is written in the Torah, and the firstlings of our cattle and flock to the Temple of our God: to the priests who serve in the Temple of our God' (v. 37). The question immediately presents itself, What does ככתוב בתורה mean here?—particularly as it is found only *after* the reference

shall pay his life's redemption (*pidyōn napšô*) according to whatever is set (*yūšat*) for him'. It seems that v. 30 betrays another attempt to counteract the possibility of vicarious talion; for the phrase '*his* life's redemption' redundantly interrupts a concise protasis and apodosis formulation using *yūšat* – a technical term for self-help (cf. Exod. 21: 22b, and above, p. 93 n. 11)—and shifts the weight of meaning from any ransom (possibly vicarious talion) to ransom only for the life of the owner of the vicious ox.

to 'the firstlings of our sons and animals', and is thus apparently distinct from the next clause which refers to 'the firstlings of our cattle and flock'. Further, what is special about the first phrase, and is there not a redundancy between 'animals' in v. 37a and 'cattle and flock' in v. 37b? To deal with these questions a wider textual perspective is needed.

Upon examination, it is clear that Neh. 10: 36-9 constitutes a coherent subunit in the oath, designating a variety of donations to the Temple for the priests and Levites. Thus, 'the first growth of our field(s) and the first growth of every fruit of every tree' is to be brought to the Temple (v. 36); the human and animal firstlings are to be brought to the Temple and its priesthood, as noted (v. 37). In addition, 'the choicest of our dough, and the heave-offering, and the first fruit of . . . the wine and oil' are to be brought to the Temple and its priesthood, and the tithe is to be given to the Levites (v. 38). These Levites are further formally appointed to apportion a tithe of the tithe for the Temple and its priesthood (v. 39). Reviewing these donations, it is manifest that the contents of Neh. 10: 36-9 are dependent upon the contents of Num. 18, where, too, various heave-offerings (v. 8) are specified for donation to the Temple and its priesthood. This includes choice oil (v. 12), the first growth of the field (v. 13), human and animal firstlings (v. 15), tithes given to the Levites (v. 21) and tithes of the tithe given to the priests (v. 26).

This topical concordance between Num. 18 and Neh. 10: 36-9 extends to a close linguistic similarity: in phrases, in technical terms, and even in isolated verbs. There is thus no reason to deny that Num. 18 has served as the basic Pentateuchal source for the draftsman of Neh. 10: 36-9, even though Neh. 10: 36-9 emphasizes the transmission of the offerings to the Temple and Num. 18 does not; and even though Neh. 10: 38 refers to an offering of the 'choicest of our dough' and Num. 18 does not. For if this draftsman has added a reference to the 'choicest of our dough' from Num. 15: 20-1, this was only to co-ordinate all known prescriptions of priestly emoluments and revenues in one place; and if the draftsman has also given special attention to the Temple in Neh. 10: 36-39 this was due to his stake in the ideology of centralization which characterizes the post-exilic sources of Ezra-Nehemiah and Chronicles, and to their concern with the status and maintenance of Jerusalem, its Temple, and its cultic personnel.[107] In the light of these elements it is striking to note that, in his report of

---

[107] Contrast the more tendentious view of Kaufmann, *Toledot*, viii. 334-5, that Neh. 10: 36-9 is an exegetical blend of priestly and deuteronomic components, the latter represented by emphasis on the Jerusalem Temple and the view that *rē'šît* ('choice' crops) in Neh. 10: 38 refers to Deut. 26: 2. This last is especially unlikely. Compare *rē'šît* with *yiṣhār* and the verb 'to bring' in Num. 18: 13 and Neh. 10: 38.

Hezekiah's centralization of cultic worship in Jerusalem, the Chronicler stated that Hezekiah sought to re-establish the portions of the priests and Levites and thus proclaimed that all Israelites bring their first fruits to Jerusalem (2 Chron. 31: 4-12). An examination of the technical terms used in this narrative suggests that—like the draftsman of Neh. 10: 36-9—the historiographer had Num. 18 in mind;[108] and this, in turn, invites the speculation that the Chronicler in the Persian period wished to present to his contemporaries the anachronistic image of popular Israelite support of Pentateuchal regulations concerning the Temple and its clerics from pre-exilic times. The account in 2 Chron. 31 would thus be generally contemporary with the covenant-oath found in Neh. 10: 36-9, and reflect similar historical exigencies. The significant difference between the two texts would, accordingly, be that the first is a propaganda document presented as history, while the second reflects actual circumstances and the binding commitment of some returnees in the post-exilic period to support the Temple and its priesthood.

On the basis of the verbal and topical dependency of Neh. 10: 36-9 upon Num. 18 just reviewed, it is possible to find a solution to the problems of Neh. 10: 37 stated earlier. For in the context of an enumeration of the gifts and revenues which are the priests' due, Num. 18: 15a first notes—by way of a general formulation—that all human and animal firstlings are to be given to YHWH. It then qualifies this pronouncement in vv. 15b-17a, with the statement that both human firstlings and the firstlings of 'impure animals' must be redeemed (variously), but the firstlings of oxen (cattle) or sheep and goats (flock) must be sacrificed. Since Neh. 10: 36-9 utilizes Num. 18 overall, it stands to reason that it also refers to its prescription about human and animal firstlings. Accordingly, when Neh. 10: 37 states that 'human and animal firstlings' are to be treated 'as is written', while cattle and flock are to be brought to the Temple, it is certain that the phrase 'as is written' is but a shorthand allusion to Num. 18: 15b-16, and means that both human and *impure* animal firstlings are to be treated—that is, redeemed—in accordance with established Pentateuchal procedure. The odd use of 'animals' in Neh. 10: 37a over against the reference to cattle and flock in v. 37b is thus clarified. Since the latter are pure animals and were required to be slaughtered, the simple reference to 'animals' together with human firstlings in Neh. 10: 37a must mean that these 'animals' are in that category of animal firstlings which shared a fate similar to that of humans—a category designated 'impure animals' in Num. 18: 15.

Given the terse phraseology which characterizes the covenant in Neh. 10, the draftsman apparently felt that an expansion of the types

---

[108] Note especially the phrases in vv. 5-6, 12, and the verb 'to bring'.

of redemption for human and impure animal firstlings was inappropriate
– and so this entire exegetical complex was simply alluded to by the
formula ככתוב בתורה. For those who knew the Pentateuchal law of
firstlings, most specifically that found in Num. 18: 15-16, the proper
interpretation of Neh. 10: 37 was beyond doubt.[109] Somewhat more
surprising is the fact that this latter refers only to 'animals' in general
and not specifically to asses, as in Exod. 13: 13 and 34: 20. Since Num.
18: 15 also refers to 'impure animals' in general, and does not refer to
asses, it is doubtful whether 'animals' in Neh. 10: 37 is an exegetical
expansion of the Pentateuchal prescription. It is, on the contrary, more
likely that the isolated reference to asses in Exod. 13: 13 and 34: 20
was meant all along as a paradigm example of impure animals, and that
Num. 18:15 and Neh. 10: 37 merely make this sense explicit. Thus, if
Num. 18: 15-17a serves to clarify Neh. 10: 37a, both serve to clarify
the formulation of the law regarding the redemption of asses in the
Book of Exodus.

The Formula כאשר . . . כן

Another formula occurs in our Pentateuchal sources which served
as exegetical shorthand for ancient Israelite legists: the formula כאשר
. . . כן 'just as . . . so'. It functions somewhat differently in ritual and
legal sources. In ritual texts the formula (or its abbreviation כאשר) is
found simply referring to earlier ritual details – indicating that one
ritual must be performed 'as' or 'like' another. By contrast, in legal
sources the formula reflects a marked advance in legistic reasoning, for
it serves to indicate that one case must be understood in the light of
another. It may be added that in ritual sources the formula is of a
lapidary nature, forming part of the original narrative account but
functioning as an abridged reference to a procedure previously described.
The example from legal sources is an interpolation into the *traditum*,
serving to guide its very interpretation. It is not part of the original
legal formulation.

1. Towards the end of the sacrifice for the errant priest recorded in
Lev. 4: 9, the cultic officiants to whom the document was originally
addressed are told to raise up a holocaust-offering of the fat of the
bullock (sacrificed in v. 8) כאשר just as [the fat] is raised up from the

109 This inner-biblical conclusion is also reached by Kaufmann, op. cit. viii.
334–5, and Tchernowitz, *Toledot ha-Halakha*, iii. 132–4. By contrast, B. Eerdmans,
'Ezra and the Priestly Code', *Expositor*', 10 (1910), 313, claimed that the phrase
'as is written in the Torah' in Neh. 10: 37a concludes the original formulation, as
in v. 35, and that v. 37b is a 'repetition' of the first 'part of the verse' and 'must
be of younger origin'.

whole-offering' (v. 10)—a procedure reported in Lev. 3: 3-5, although the precise praxis is not described. Variations of the phraseology found in Lev. 4:10 occur in the same textual position in connection with the bullock (v. 31) and lamb (v. 35) sacrificed for errant individuals. Given the precise nature of these texts, such variations are occasionally surprising but not in any real respect consequential. Of a far more distinctive nature, by comparison, is the comment found in Lev. 4: 20, which comes towards the end of the description of the sacrifice for the errant congregation. Like the others, it follows a reference to the raising up or removal of the fat of the sacrifice, and states that 'he [the priest] will do to the bullock—כאשר just as he did to the bullock of purification[110] כן so will he do to it . . .'. The reference here is to the bullock previously described in Lev. 4: 4-12, sacrificed for the errant priest. The comment is designed to compare both procedures—although the phraseology is muddled and reflects some tampering.[111] In order further to be certain that the bullock of the congregation be treated in all respects like the bullock sacrificed for the expiation of the priest, the ritual narrative first refers to the burning of the bullock outside the camp (v. 21aα) and then specifies that the priest deal with it 'כאשר as he burned the first bullock' (v. 21aβ). This shorthand reference is to the details found earlier, in vv. 11-12.

2. An entirely different perspective on the כאשר . . . כן formula emerges from its singular occurrence in the biblical legal corpora. This instance appears in a distinct series of civil cases in the Book of Deuteronomy, and serves to evoke a comparative legal situation which serves exegetically to clarify one of the cases in the original series.

The pertinent instance deals with the rules governing attempted rape in the countryside (Deut. 22: 25-7). These occur within a varied collection of norms of sex and marriage (Deut. 22: 13-29).[112] In terms of its scope and references this collection forms an integral unit—even though one might have expected that the statement against incest (23:1), the rules of marriage and remarriage (24:1-4), and the rules exempting newly-weds from military service (24: 5-6) might have preceded 23: 13-19, or at least have been more formally integrated with it. In any event, Deut. 22:13-29 deals with cases of false and true

---

[110] For this meaning, see J. Milgrom, loc. cit. (n. 72 above).

[111] Cf. Noth, *Leviticus*, 41, who also proposes that v. 20b may have been the original conclusion, subsequently transferred from v. 12, the end of the first section.

[112] A thorough form-critical and redactional analysis of Deut. 22 has recently been undertaken by P. Merendino, *Das deuteronomische Gesetz* (BBB 31; Bonn: P. Hanstein, 1969), 257-74, without, however, attention to the legal exegesis to be developed below.

accusations of lost virginity (vv. 13-21), intercourse with a married woman (v. 22), intercourse with a betrothed woman in the city (vv. 23-4) and the countryside (vv..25-7), and intercourse with an unbetrothed woman (vv. 28-9). Linking these laws are not only common phrases ('remove the evil', vv. 21, 22, 24) and common penalties (e.g. death for both male and female, vv. 22, 24), but the more substantive issue of evidence. Both in the case of the accusation of false virginity and the cases in which the couples are seized *in flagrante delicto*, the common root is מצא (vv. 17, 20, 22, 23, 27) 'to seize, come up on, or find the operative legal conditions or principals'.[113] This structural link between the various sex laws is, in turn, joined to the significant variable of public versus private occurrence. Actions which are private or unseen must be proved publicly; and acts which are public (i.e. potentially visible) must be found or witnessed—and not simply attributed or asserted. There is thus an attempt here by the law to circumvent circumstantial or false accusations (cf. the עלילת דברים of v. 14).

All this sets the stage for the issue at hand. Deut. 22: 23-4 deals with the seizure and rape of a betrothed virgin in the city, while vv. 25-7 envisage a similar occurrence in the countryside. The penalties in these two instances differ remarkably, however. Whereas rape in the city renders both the woman *and* the rapist culpable if the woman did not shout for help (v. 24), responsibility for rape in the field belongs solely to the male; for while there is no way to determine if the woman called for help, biblical law grants her this presumption (v. 27).[114] Thus, the woman is protected in the absence of tangible evidence that she protested against the rape and was forced against her will. To this extent the laws of vv. 23-4 and vv. 25-6 are structurally similar. However, the absence of such evidence and the necessity of relying on a common-sense presumption clearly bothered some ancient Israelite legists, as is indicated by the explanation added to vv. 25-6 which further justifies the exculpation of the women raped in the field without witnesses. Between the statement of the women's guiltlessness in v. 26a and v. 27a, which explains this in terms parallel to the preceding case (i.e. her presumed call for help), is the comment of v. 26b: '—for כאשר as a man will rise up against his fellow and smite him, כן so is this case.'

Verse 26b clearly intrudes upon the syntax and formal structure of vv. 26a and 27a, and compares this case of rape to premeditated murder. In both cases a stronger person overpowers a weaker one who is forced and non-consenting. The analogy, introduced and concluded

---

[113] On this meaning in biblical laws and LH, see above, pp. 188 f and n. 60.

[114] A reflex of this legal topos can be observed in Gen. 39: 10-13, on which see H. Jacobson, 'A Legal Note on Potiphar's Wife', *HTR* 69 (1976), 177.

by a formulaic expression (*'for as* . . . [just] *so* is this case'), is derived via Deut. 19:11, which occurs in the framework of rules governing premeditated murder and asylum.[115]

Deut. 22:26b	*Deut. 19:11*
for as a man will rise up against (יקום . . . על) his fellow (רעהו) and murders him (נפש) . . .	and if a person hates his fellow (רעהו), and lying in ambush for him rises up against him (וקם עליו) and smites him mortally that he die (והכהו נפש ומת) . . .

As is evident, the analogy interpolated into Deut. 22:26b is a citation from another known Pentateuchal rule in order to elucidate the problem of rape in the field without witnesses. It also adds a further dimension to the fact that only the male is punished because the female is presumed to have protested. The force of the legal analogy is to suggest that the male is a molester with malice aforethought, while the woman is a victim of physical violence and is not a consenting party. Since her physical well-being was threatened, and since she could not have taken protective precautions, her innocence and resistance are presumed beyond doubt. Accordingly, the ancient Israelite legists started out with a common-sense notion of a 'normal woman' in treating this case — much like modern legal notions of the 'reasonable person' — but soon saw fit to bolster their reflections by adducing comparable legal circumstances. The interpolation of their considerations into the legal *traditum* is thus but another indication of the living legal *traditio* of ancient Israel which circulated orally and was relied upon for concrete judicial determinations. This *traditio* has hereby become part of the *traditum* for all time.

In the long course of the development of biblical jurisprudence, then, ancient Israelite legists began to think comparatively of one legal situation in terms of another. Such legal reasoning moves from specific case to specific case; from particulars to particulars, and not from particulars to general principles or propositions. In Deut. 22:25–6 we are thus presented with a valuable historical witness to the ways in which legal corpora and cases were utilized in the ancient Near East — a witness only dimly reflected outside ancient Israel.[116] As an example of com-

---

[115] Cf. my discussion of this Pentateuchal rule in *CBQ* 42 (1980), 443–6.

[116] It would appear that one particular case is interpreted by comparison with another in LH 7, 9, 11, 13. Thus, it is stated in LH 7 that a person who has purchased items, or received them for safekeeping, from another's son or slave without witnesses or contact — *a-wi-lum šu-ú šu-ra-aq* 'that man is a thief' (vi. 55–6) — shall be put to death. My attention was drawn to this method of drafting jurisprudence by D. Daube, 'Some Forms of Old Testament Legislation, *Oxford Society for Historical Theology* (1945), 40, 42.

parative legal reasoning, Deut. 22: 25-6 is also a forebear of the more abstract types of legal thinking found in early Jewish sources. These types include the deduction of general principles from disparate cases, and are not limited to correlating the latter.

G. COMPARISON OF LEGAL CASES WITHOUT FORMULAE

The detailed examination of earlier sources by legists—be they draftsmen or annotators—was bound to produce the various expansions and restrictions noted above, as well as the comparison of cases for the sake of explicating one of them. In addition, as the variety of legal sources accumulated through study and collation, legal tradents would necessarily become aware of the incompleteness of some sources compared with their parallels elsewhere, and of contradictions between sources which derived from different periods or locales. The solution of these tradents was often to create a legal blend of the sources to which they were heir, as in the earlier noted case of Neh. 10: 32b, which combines different Pentateuchal rules regarding land and economic release on the Sabbatical year; or in the case recorded in 2 Chron. 35: 12-13, also considered earlier, regarding the harmonization of different rules pertaining to the sacrifice of the paschal-offering. Clearly such developments in post-exilic historical sources reflect determined and deliberate attempts to correlate disparate laws of Moses, and thereby imply their synthetic relationship. The concern was thus apparently to establish explicitly in certain cases—and by means of the redaction together of the diverse legal corpora, implicitly—the overall complementarity of the received Mosaic traditions.

The foregoing tendency towards unifying the strands of Scripture is well marked in other post-exilic literary deposits, like the Samaritan version of the Pentateuch. For example, in its recension of Exod. 20: 18-26, the account of the public witness of divine power on Sinai followed by certain altar regulations, the sequence known from the MT breaks off after v. 18 and inserts the parallel description found in Deut. 5: 24-7. Following this interruption the text resumes with Exod. 20: 19-22a; but, thereupon, another interpolation occurs from the parallel account in Deut. 5: 28-9, together with an addition from the deuteronomic promise of a future prophet (Deut. 18: 18-22). It is only with the termination of this large insertion that the original text-sequence resumes and concludes with Exod. 20: 22b-26.[117] The result is a harmonized text-blend whose redactional unity asserts the mutual relationship and authority of the different Pentateuchal traditions on

---

[117] On this redaction, cf. the analysis of J. Tigay, 'An Empirical Basis for the Documentary Hypothesis', *JBL* 94 (1975), 333-41.

one topic. In other cases the blend is more interpretive in nature, as where Deut. 3: 21 is inserted after Num. 27: 23 and Deut. 3: 23-4 is inserted after Num. 20: 13. Since in both cases the source in the Book of Numbers is more terse than the parallel account in the Book of Deuteronomy, the combination of the parallel texts reflects a harmonistic tendency which attempts to clarify Scripture by Scripture, in a manner which anticipates the later hermeneutical dictum of the rabbis: 'words of Scripture which are poor [i.e. unclear] in one place are rich [i.e. explicatory] elsewhere.'[118] This practice of narrative blending is also found in proto-Samaritan versions found at Qumran,[119] and has reflexes in the Septuagint as well. For example, the striking diversity in the rules of theft of persons as formulated in Exod. 21: 16 and Deut. 24: 7 was considered at some length earlier. These divergences are remarkably obscured in the LXX recension of Exod. 21: 16, however, for this version has conflated the two Pentateuchal rules by inserting features from Deut. 24: 7 into Exod. 21: 16.[120] Since the deuteronomic formulation is the fuller of the two, the effect of the interpolation is to normalize the ruling in Exod. 21: 16 and to minimize the differences between the two Pentateuchal versions of the same rule.[121]

The exegetical procedure of harmonization and correction (or supplementation) of one text in the light of another has several notable reflexes in the Pentateuchal ritual texts. They indicate a spectrum of modes whereby ancient Israelite tradents of the ritual rules came to terms with varied traditions on certain subjects. In some cases, the formulation of one text was clarified or developed by comparison with another which was interpolated into it without technical formulae; in other cases, the formulation of one text was harmonized and corrected by comparison with another text which was subsequently interpolated into it without technical formulae; and, in still other cases,

---

[118] *yer. Roš Haš.* iii. 5.

[119] See P. Skehan, 'Exodus in the Samaritan Recension from Qumran', *JBL* 74 (1955), 182-7.

[120] LXX Exod. 21: 16 reads 'Whosoever steals a person, *an Israelite, and treating him harshly*, sells him . . .'. The italicized phrases derive from Deut. 24: 7. For evidence that *hit'ammēr* in Deut. 24: 7 involves an economic misuse of another's personal status (i.e., that the abducted person is treated harshly *by being sold*), see the use of *tgr* in the Targums; also Daube, *Studies*, and M. David, 'Hit'amēr [sic] (Deut. 21: 14, 24: 7)', *VT* 1 (1951), 219-21.

[121] Cf. also the inclusion of Exod. 17: 16 at LXX Isa. 48: 21 and Deut. 14: 1bβ at Lev. 21: 5aα. An interesting blend for the sake of halakhic exposition appears at the end of Jub. 4: 32 (cf. vv. 3, 31-2), where Lev. 24: 19 is cited to explain why Cain was not just killed 'measure for measure'—a basic rabbinic principle— but by the very manner in which he killed Abel. This jurisprudence is also found in 11Q *Torah* lxi. 11-12; and it is considered by *yer. Sanh.* xxiv. 2 (*ad fin.*), but rejected as a halakha.

the formulation of one text was harmonized and corrected by comparison with another text and the results were recorded as a special legal appendix. Examples of each of these three types are thus instructive for their witness to ancient Israelite scholastic preoccupations with diverse rules believed to stem from one authority, and for their attestation of the diversity of hermeneutical procedures which had developed or were resorted to under such conditions.

1. An example of the first type—in which the formulation of one text was clarified or developed by another which was interpolated into it—occurs in the context of the prescriptions governing guilt-offerings, in Lev. 5. In vv. 18 and 25-6a the guilt-offering appropriate for the situation is described by a fixed formula, stating that the offender must bring 'a pure ram from the flock, בערכך לאשם valued by you [the priest] according to the guilt, to the priest; and he shall make atonement thereby . . . and he [the guilty person] shall be forgiven'. As against this formulation—in two successive paragraphs—the language of Lev. 5:15-16 is more prolix and convoluted, stating that the offender must bring 'a pure ram from the flock, בערכך valued by you *in sheqels of silver, according to the sheqel of the sanctuary*—לאשם for the guilt-offering . . . and the priest shall make atonement with the ram of the guilt-offering, and he [the offender] shall be forgiven'.

A comparison of the formulation in Lev. 5:18 and 25-6a with that in vv. 15-16 makes it quite clear that the technical expression בערכך לאשם has been artificially divided in the latter case, and that a secondary phrase—derived from Lev. 27:25—has been interpolated.[122] The result is a transformation in the sense of the passage. In the first cases, vv. 18 and 25-6a, the ram required for expiation is established at a value equivalent to the guilt involved; whereas in the case of vv. 15-16 the rate of exchange is established in accordance with the currency standard used in the sancuary. Minimally, this passage simply explicates the meaning of the word בערכך 'valued by you', so that it is still a living ram which serves as expiation. But this interpretation does not explain why the phrase בערכך לאשם was disrupted and the 'gloss' not placed elsewhere. It also fails to consider the new syntactical sense established by the interpolation.

These several problematic points suggest that a more extensive interpretation of Lev. 5:15-16 is required. Since the offence in Lev. 5:14-15 requiring expiation involves the unintentional desecration of sancta, the interpolation of a phrase from Lev. 27:25 into vv. 15-16 may have been designed to bring about a total reinterpretation of the ritual praxis. Just as the redemption of sancta in Lev. 27 (vv. 13, 15, 19,

---

[122] B. Jackson, *Theft*, 172.

27, 31) had to be by the holy monetary standard (v. 25), so now infractions of sancta were also to be expiated by that standard. In other words, proper expiation could be made by a monetary payment of the established amount.[123] This exegetical result is certainly revolutionary. But despite the muddled syntax of Lev. 5: 15-16, and the fact that the original *traditum* was not deleted (so that the passage continues to speak of a sacrifice), the plain sense of the interpolated passage ('a pure ram from the flock, valued by you in sheqels of silver ... for the guilt-offering') would seem to support the preceding exegesis. Perhaps the additional fact that both Lev. 5: 16 and 27: 13, 15, 19, 27, 31 all add a surcharge of one-fifth of the value – of the ram of expiation, in the first case, or the redeemed sancta, in the second – may have been an added factor which brought these ritual procedures into comparative association. Moreover, the absence of references to sancta in Lev. 5: 17 and 20-4 'further explains the absence of the interpolation in these two cases. Thus, if Lev. 5: 15-16 does not simply make its praxis explicit in the comparative light of Lev. 27: 25, it has actually introduced a remarkable reinterpretation of it.

2. Another type of legal comparison of cases without formulae involves the perception by ritual legists that the formulation in one source is incorrect when compared with others, and must be exegetically corrected or harmonized in their light. The passage in Num. 15: 24 is of special interest in this regard. As will be recalled, it was argued earlier – following Toeg – that Num. 15: 22-31 is a diverse exegetical reuse of Lev. 4.[124] It was also noted that earlier commentators had been led to different estimations of the relationship between these two texts, including the view that they are parallel but unrelated documents, on the basis of several substantive differences between them. One of these is the difference between Lev. 4: 14 and Num. 15: 24. For whereas Lev. 4: 14 prescribes 'a bullock for the purification-offering', Num. 15: 24 requires 'a bullock for the holocaust-offering . . . and a he-goat for the purification-offering'. While the mention of a holocaust-offering before the purification-offering in Num. 15: 24 is unusual, and inverts the general norm, more pressing is the unusual reference in Lev. 4: 14 to a bullock for the purification-offering. If Num. 15: 22-31 is a reworking of Lev. 4, how may such discordances be understood?

In his penetrating analysis of Num. 15: 22-31, Toeg also offered a satisfying and notable solution to these problems.[125] He suggested that, faced with an outright contradiction between his sacrificial system and

---

[123] Cf. ibid. 172 n. 3.
[124] Above, pp. 190-3.
[125] See loc. cit. (n. 73 above) 8 f.

that found in his source in Lev. 4:14, and also not willing either to
correct or ignore that source, the composer of Num. 15 produced a
harmonizing exegesis. Reading Lev. 4:14 in the light of his sacrificial
system, he understood 'a bullock for the purification-offering' in Lev.
4:14 as an elliptical and compressed formulation only apparently in
contradiction with his own system. Breaking down the phrase he took
the initial word 'a bullock' as an elliptical allusion to the more normal
'a bullock [for the holocaust-offering]', and the concluding phrase 'for
the purification-offering' as an elliptical allusion to the more normal
'[and a he-goat] for the purification-offering'. By thus adding a suffix
to the first clause and a prefix to the second, the legal exegete of Num.
15:22–31 produced his own v. 24 ('a bullock for the holocaust-offering
. . . and a he-goat for the purification-offering'); and by being dependent
upon the *traditum* of Lev. 4:14 he could not present the purification-
offering before the holocaust-offering, but was constrained to invert
their order. One may assume, moreover, that because the exegetical
orator of Num. 15:22–31 took Lev. 4 as an authoritative *traditum* he
did not feel that his exegesis added anything that was not latent in the
text. The surface contradiction between Lev. 4:14 and his own ritual
system was thus only an apparent contradiction, not a substantive one;
and it was the honourable task of exegesis in a world of sacred texts to
show that explicit discordances were, in truth, merely the surface
manifestations of deeper, implicit harmonies. Harmonistic exegesis thus
serves to make the implicit explicit. As the many teachings of God
through Moses were increasingly seen as one continuous discourse, or,
otherwise put, as readers came increasingly to read (or hear) the many
teachings of God through Moses as one continuous document (or
discourse), such processes were inevitable.

Despite its unusual character, Toeg's interpretation of Num. 15:24
cannot be dismissed as a modern *tour de force*, for, as he has elsewhere
established, a comparable hermeneutical procedure can be observed in
the Samar. and LXX to Exod. 22:4.[126] As noted at the outset of our
discussion of legal exegesis, this rule, which deals with damage caused
by grazing animals to adjoining fields, is both unspecific and highly
ambiguous regarding the assessment of the reparation penalty.[127] It is
this ambiguity which the aforementioned versions eliminate by their
interpolation of a clarifying clause. As with the reinterpretation of Lev.
4:14, the interpolation in Samar. and LXX takes the original text as an
elliptical formulation, and adds a suffix to the first clause and a prefix
to the second. A similar exegetical technique is found in rabbinic
sources—a technique called חסורי מחסרא והכי קתני, which roughly

---

[126] See his discussion, loc. cit. (p. 94 n. 17 above) 229 f.
[127] Above, p. 94.

translates as 'there is something missing here and one should read [the Mishnah] as follows'.[128] And in such cases there often enough follows a quite radical reinterpretation of the Mishnah under discussion. But like the case in Samar. and LXX Exod. 22:4, and against Num. 15:24, such exegetical interpolations were often purely rational reconstructions of a text and not formulations based on other textual sources.

In view of these considerations, the exegetical harmonization found in LXX Lev. 9:19 is thus of particular note. For, having noted that the ritual texts in Lev. 3:3b-4, 9b-10, 14b-15, 4:8b-9, and 7:2b-4 all refer formulaically to 'the fat המכסה which covers the entrails, and the two kidneys with the fat upon them . . . and the lobe of the liver', but that Lev. 9:19 had the uniquely condensed formulation 'והמכסה and the covering, והכליֹת and the kidneys, and the lobe of the liver', the Greek translator interpreted the latter phrase in the light of the former, longer versions and expanded his rendition of Lev. 9:19 so as to conform with the normal ritual formulary. On its own terms, the phraseology of Lev. 9:19 is simply a dense contraction of the fuller lapidary description – indicating merely the principal organs, not their fatty parts. Indeed, as we shall have occasion to indicate more fully in the next example, a notable feature of Lev. 9, when compared with the preceding ritual descriptions on the same subject in Lev. 6-7, is its compressed and abbreviated nature. Thus, whether for reasons of stylistic habit, or because of a lapse into brevity, the priestly legists who formulated Lev. 9:19 would have had no doubt as to its full meaning. By contrast, the later Greek translator had to make sense of the language of Lev. 9:19 – both for his own purposes, and for the audience to which the LXX was presumably originally presented as a simultaneous translation of the weekly Torah lection.[129] When compared with the formulations in Lev. 3:3b-4, 9b-10, 14b-15, 4:8b-9, and 7:3b-4, Lev. 9:19 was, then, only apparently discordant: for it could be regarded as an elliptical rendition of them. The translator made sense of his Hebrew original in precisely this way, and thus added an exegetical elaboration which made the implicit sense of Lev. 9:19 fully explicit. In so doing, the Greek translator has not only interpreted one Scriptural passage by another, and thereby indicated the harmony of related Pentateuchal passages; he has also given further proof that the treatment of compressed phraseology as ellipses in need of paraphrastic elaborations was an established hermeneutical technique whereby ancient Israelite and early Jewish legal exegetes made sense of difficult texts.

---

[128] Cf. the discussion in J. N. Epstein, *Mabo' le-Nusaḥ ha-Mishnah*[2] (Jerusalem and Tel Aviv: Magnes and Devir, 1964), ii. 626-44, also 645-70. Also see above, pp. 152 f.

[129] Cf. E. Bickermann, 'The Septuagint as a Translation', *Studies*, i. 172.

3. The final type of inner-biblical comparison of legal texts without formulae to be considered is stylistically different from the preceding two; for in it the legists did not resort to interpolation or paraphrase but rather set the proper legal meaning apart as an appendix. A singular case in point is Lev. 10:12-20. In the words of a recent commentator, M. Noth, this unit constitutes an appendix to chapter 9 of 'regulations ... which a later writer found missing, or incorrectly carried out'.[130] According to the received account, the ritual prescribed and performed in Lev. 9 are for the people's part in the priestly investiture ceremony (Lev. 8-9), and employ ritual praxes fully articulated in the preceding descriptive ritual texts of Lev. 6-7. However, while Lev. 6:9-11 precisely permits Aaron and his sons to partake of 'the remainder' of the people's meal-offering—'gifts of YHWH'—and to 'eat' them as 'wafers' in a 'holy place' (this being a 'statute' for all generations), Lev. 9:17 is entirely silent regarding what is to be done with this remainder; and, further, while Lev. 7:30-4 permits Aaron and his sons to eat of the 'breast which is waved' and the 'thigh which is heaved' from the people's shared-offering (this being a 'statute' for all generations), Lev. 9:21 is also entirely silent regarding what is to be done with such ritual meat.

Later priestly tradents were clearly aware that Lev. 9:17 and 21 contained lacunae in comparison with the formulations in Lev. 6:9-11 and 7:30-4, respectively; for, following an account of the death of Aaron's sons Nadab and Abihu for a ritual impropriety (Lev. 10:1-2), and ritual instructions related to that and general occasions (vv. 6-7, 8-11), an independent speech of Moses to Aaron and his surviving sons presents a series of instructions related to Lev. 6:9-11 and 7:30-4. Specifically, the priests are told to partake of the remainder of the meal-offering (Lev. 10:12-13) and the breast and thigh of the shared-offering (Lev. 10:14-15) in precisely the same language as that used in Lev. 6:9-11 and 7:30-4. Moreover, fully to underscore the fact that these instructions refer to the earlier prescriptions, Moses twice adds a citation formula at the end of each instruction. He adds 'for so was I commanded' to the first, and 'just as YHWH commanded' to the second—even though the praxes in Lev. 9 also carry the divine imprimatur (v. 7). In this way the priestly legists speaking through Moses indicate that the praxes of Lev. 9:17 and 21 must be supplemented in the light of other established procedures. Since there was no out-and-out contradiction between the two sets of instructions, one may assume that the legistic annotators added their comments in Lev. 10:12-15 in order to avoid any impression that any of the practices recorded in different places in Scripture were contradictory.

[130] *Leviticus*, 87.

A third matter in the divine instruction of Lev. 9 caused more consternation, however; for one could not simply state that the text was merely a briefer version of others recorded elsewhere. Indeed, while Lev. 9:15 states that the people's purification-offering was to be performed 'like the first one'—that is, like Aaron's offering in vv. 8-11 —in which the animal's meat parts were not eaten but rather burned outside the camp, Lev. 6:17-23 prescribes an entirely contradictory procedure. There the expiating priest may eat of the offering in a 'holy place' (cf. v. 17), unless 'its blood has been brought into the Tent of Meeting to provide atonement for the sanctuary' (v. 23). In such circumstances as the latter, the purification-offering 'may not be eaten' and must 'be burned'. In the light of this blatant contradiction, the instructions in Lev. 10:12-15 continue with the report that 'Moses inquired regarding the goat of the purification-offering and found that it had been burned' (v. 16a). This was, of course, the procedure prescribed and carried out according to Lev. 9:15. However, upon learning of this state of affairs, Moses became angry and asked why the priests did not eat the purification-offering in a 'holy place' (v. 17a), for, he continued, 'if its blood was not brought into the inner sanctuary, you [priests] may eat it . . . as I commanded'. By this final citation formula, and the language which precedes it, it is clear that Moses is citing Lev. 6:17-23 and, on that basis, rebuking the priests for their practice in Lev. 9:15 (which he had also commanded, in vv. 1-2, 7!). To this rebuke Aaron retorts that while he had indeed performed the purification-offering of the people in conjunction with the investiture rites, his sons Nadab and Abihu had died and, being in mourning, he felt it inappropriate to eat of the purification-offering. As there was apparently no known ruling dealing with such a state of affairs, Aaron asks Moses 'will YHWH approve?' (v. 19b). This latter is undoubtedly a request for a divine oracle, as in Lev. 24:10-14, Num. 9:6-8, and 27:1-5, where, too, cases were presented to Moses and adjudicated by divine oracle because no known ruling was at hand. And, indeed, the obscure sequel in Lev. 10:20, 'וישמע and he heard', may confirm this: for since Aaron asks for YHWH's response, and since the verb 'to hear' is used in Num. 9:8b (ואשמעה) as a technical term indicating the receipt of an oracular response, one may safely assume that וישמע means that *Moses* 'heard' *YHWH's response*, and that the ensuing approval is YHWH's and not that of Moses.

What can be the meaning of this strange scenario, in which Aaron responds to Moses' rebuke that he would have followed the procedure in Lev. 6:17-23 had not his sons died? For is it not altogether obvious that Aaron had completed the ritual before his sons' death and that the ritual which he performed is also the command of YHWH through Moses? Indeed, all this must have been perfectly obvious, and confusing

to the priestly tradents who had easily disposed of the differences
between Lev. 6: 9-11 and 7: 30-4, and Lev. 9: 17 and 21 respectively.
But what could be the solution here, especially since, for the tradents,
Lev. 6-7 was the more authoritative document? What they did was to
harmonize the ritual traditions by obscuring the temporal difference
between the performance of Lev. 9: 15 and the death of Aaron's sons in
10: 1-2, and by overlooking the fact that Lev. 9 was also a document
which tradition had sanctioned as divinely authoritative. The dialogue
between Moses and Aaron suggests the way in which the legists reinterpreted their materials: they assumed that the death of Aaron's sons
occurred sometime before the burning of the purification-offering of
the people and that Aaron acted on his own initiative. That is, although
it appears that Aaron is divinely instructed in Lev. 9: 15 not to eat of
the offering, and to burn it outside the camp, this episode is rather an
ad hoc ritual action undertaken by Aaron with no explicit divine
sanction. By having Moses request a divine oracular *responsum* on the
affairs, and by having the oracle approve *ex post facto* of Aaron's
action, the legists could mitigate the contradictions involved and even
produce a new ruling regarding the propriety of priests eating of the
purification-offerings while in the state of mourning. The fact that the
legists had to forcibly distort the divine authority of Aaron's actions in
Lev. 9: 15 shows, at the very least, that their exegetical *tour de force* is
hardly disingenuous or naïve. Faced with two *tradita* of established
authority, and clearly unable to delete either one of them, the legists
resolved their contradictions by invoking a third situation which would
support both. Quite certainly, as suggested earlier, it was only the onset
of a historical situation that required all received *tradita* to be maintained
and, where possible, explicitly harmonized, that encouraged the development of such hermeneutical processes, and their support.[131] That
historical situation, and its underlying reality, will be discussed below.

H. EXEGETICAL RECOMBINATION OF LEGAL SOURCES

Apart from the comparison of disparate legal cases in order to clarify
one rule by another, or in order to harmonize and resolve their contradictory nature, ancient Israelite legists also compared cases of some
topical similarity and brought them into new exegetical combinations.

---

[131] A Rofé, *Mabo' le-Sepher Debarim* (Jerusalem: Aqadamon Press, 1975),
20f., has offered another plausible example of such late theoretical harmonizations in his suggestion that the contradiction between Lev. 17:1-7 (which
prohibits profane slaughter in the land) and Deut. 12: 13-19 (which permits
profane slaughter in the land) is resolved by Deut. 12: 20-8 (which permits
profane slaughter *after* the period when the boundaries of the land have been
expanded as divinely promised).

For example, the regulations in the Covenant Code include two entirely
distinct rules dealing with food: one, Exod. 22: 30, which is an isolated
rule which adjures Israelites to refrain from eating ripped carcasses; and
a second, Exod. 23: 19, which concludes a series of cultic prescriptions
– related to the pilgrimage festivals – with a prohibition against boiling
a kid in its mother's milk in conjunction with the feast of ingathering,
the feast of Booths.[132] These rules thus appear in separate sections of
the *mišpāṭîm*; but they are combined as one rule in Deut. 14: 21:

Exod. 22: 30, 23: 19	*Deut. 14: 21*
And be a *holy people to Me*; *do not eat* ripped carrion; throw it to the dogs . . . Bring the first of your produce to the shrine of YHWH; *do not boil a kid in its mother's milk.*	*Do not eat* any carcass; either give it to the stranger . . . or sell it to the foreigner: for you are a *holy nation to YHWH*, your God; *do not boil a kid in its mother's milk.*

The recombination of separate rules in Deut. 14: 21 is also a transformation of them by the infusion of various characteristic features
of deuteronomic ideology; for example, gifts to strangers, and the
representation of Israel's holiness in unconditional and nationalistic
terms. Of greater exegetical significance, however, is that the recombination of disparate rules from the Covenant Code is appended to a
digest of rules on permitted and forbidden foods derived from the
Priestly Code (Lev. 11).[133] This juxtaposition has not only created an
anthology of rules without regard for their original context, it has also
substantially transformed the meaning and application of the rules from
the Covenant Code – particularly Exod. 23: 19. For whereas this latter
was originally a prohibition against boiling a kid in its mother's milk
during a pilgrimage festival rite, its combination with a digest of food
regulations has exegetically transformed this special festival regulation
into a general food regulation as well. One is now prohibited from
boiling a kid in its mother's milk just as one must observe whether fish
have scales and fins, and whether mammals chew the cud and have
cloven hooves.

The full practical ritual implications of the exegetical transformation
of Exod. 23: 19 by its reuse in Deut. 14: 21 are not stated. Thus, there
is no way of determining whether the 'kid' in 'a kid in its mother's
milk' is now also a paradigm case for all permitted animals, and whether

---

[132] For the meaning of this prohibition and the reason for its association with
the feast of Booths, see M. Haran, 'Seething a Kid in its Mother's Milk', *JJS* 30
(1979), 24-35.

[133] On this deuteronomic digest, see W. Moran, 'The Literary Connection
between Lev. 11: 13-19 and Deut. 14: 12-18', *CBQ* 28 (1966), 271-7.

the 'mother's milk' is a paradigm case for all milk (or its derivatives). It is sufficient to recognize that the prohibition of Exod. 23:19 has been desacralized in Deut. 14:21, and that it no longer simply pertains to pilgrimage rites but to profane eating habits as well. The full practical ritual implications of this fact, together with an interpretation of the phrase 'a kid in its mother's milk' as a paradigm expression prohibiting the combination of edible animals and milk products, only appear in written form in the Mishnah.[134] The oral tradition of which it is an expression was undoubtedly of greater antiquity.

[134] *M. Ḥul.* viii. 1, 4.

9. Conclusions

A. From the outset of this Part it was observed that gaps and obscurities in the ancient Israelite legal *traditum* were conducive to the rise of exegetical solutions of a legal *traditio*. The observable fact that the biblical legal corpus is neither comprehensive in scope, nor altogether detailed with respect to the rules which do appear, meant that supplementation, amendment, and clarification were required if the legal *traditum* was to function in some way as a body of living jurisprudence. To be sure, the biblical legal corpora, like their ancient Near Eastern counterparts, are — formally speaking — literary achievements embodying cases exemplary of the wisdom and authority of the lawgiver (human in ancient Mesopotamia; divine in ancient Israel).[1] Moreover, as with the ancient Near Eastern legal materials, there is virtually no explicit evidence in ancient Israel that jurists used the rules preserved in its legal corpora as precedents or guides in the handling of specific cases.[2] Nevertheless, the concrete historical existence of these great legal collections, and their diverse inner- and cross-cultural connections in ancient Mesopotamia and Israel, attest to a shared legal *Tradentenkreis* of remarkable scope;[3] so that if only certain cases are singled out in the Covenant Code or the Laws of Hammurapi, for example, it can be safely assumed that an oral legal tradition supplemented the gaps and obscurities in various ways. Indeed, the preservation in ancient Israel of a complex and diverse exegetical *traditio* fully attests to an intense preoccupation with the legal *traditum* by legists and schoolmen, and suggests how its rules were handled in concrete circumstances. The incorporation of comments into the corpora *in relation to specific formulations* thus shows that such formulations were considered unclear by the legistic and scholarly tradition which studied and applied them.

Further perspective on this matter can be had by recalling in this context the legal proverb *in claris non fit interpretatio*, which may be rendered 'where the text is clear there is no room for interpretation'.[4] Indeed, the ambiguity latent in this very pithy phrase is sufficient to 'clarify' the problem raised by legal formulations which are variously

---

[1] See above, pp. 95 f.

[2] For implicit cuneiform examples, cf. above, p. 96, n. 23, and below, pp. 233 f.

[3] Cf. the comments of P. Koschacker, 'Keilschriftrecht', *ZDMG* 83 (1936), 32.

[4] See the discussion in G. Tedeschi, 'Insufficiency of the Legal Norm and Loyalty of the Interpreter', *Proceedings of the Israel Academy of Sciences and Humanities*, 1/3 (1967), 1-22.

obscure or over-generalized. For, at one extreme, the proverb can be construed to imply that the meaning of a rule (or case) is never fixed, and that every recourse to its language requires new — though loyal — interpretations. On this view, the problem of the clarity and meaning of legal materials does not first arise when the formulation is plagued by lacunae, solecisms, or opaqueness. Since the application of a rule (or case) to a new context is never a precise equation, adequate knowledge of the words, syntax, or social topoi of a rule rarely removes the need to determine its precise semantic emphasis or pertinence (i.e. its scope and intent) to the situation at hand. Quite naturally, social circumstances must be taken into account by a legist or jurist handling a case, so that legal reasoning based on a particular rule will regularly be inductive and synthetic; or, in the words of one commentator, the text of a statue or rule 'should be construed to mean that which the legislator would himself have expressed if he had been in possession of all the relevant facts which the court finds to exist at the time of rendering its decision'.[5] And yet, even if one would not wish to dispute the essential point made by Oliver Wendell Holmes, that 'general propositions do not decide concrete cases',[6] one would also not wish to be so sophistic as to assume that because all legal rules must be interpreted they do not have any meaning in and of themselves.[7]

For obvious reasons, the horns of this theoretical dilemma in legal hermeneutics were bypassed in our discussion of inner-biblical exegesis, and attention was restricted to cases where the exegesis of incomprehensive or incomprehensible legal formulations is expressly and explicitly preserved in the Hebrew Bible. Hence the pertinence of the proverb *in claris non fit interpretatio* for present purposes is just this: *were* the text clear there would be no *need* for the interpretations of it now recorded in the biblical *traditum*. From this vantage-point the assumption that gaps and obscurities of legal formulation give rise to exegetical solutions is fully justified by the evidence; and this evidence, in turn, provides valuable testimony to the legal *traditio* of ancient Israel. As seen, this *traditio* surfaces in the remarkably broad literary spectrum of legal corpora, legal orations, oracular *responsa*, prophetic discourse,

---

[5] E. Brunken, 'Interpretation of the Written Law', *Yale Law Journal*, 25 (1915), 135, with italics deleted; cf. p. 129. On 'gaps in the law', see J. Stone, *Legal System and Lawyer's Reasonings* (Stanford: Stanford University Press, 1964), 188, 192.

[6] An *obiter dictum*; see *Lochner* vs. *New York*, 198 US 45 (1905), 76. Cited in Tedeschi, loc. cit. 3.

[7] As to the measure of force which may be attributed to a legal rule, see H. L. Hart, 'Positivism and the Separation of Law and Morals', *Harvard Law Review*, 71 (1957–8), 593, who distinguishes between the 'core' and 'penumbra' of a rule. Regarding the core, Hart denies all creativity to the interpreter.

narrative histories, and priestly proclamations. And as a witness to the professional circles which took a vibrant and ongoing interest in the meanings and interpretations of the covenantal rules of the Pentateuch, this spectrum is of redoubled value—even though mere fragments of the concern of these virtuosi is preserved, so that a delineation of these circles is always more approximate than precise in any given case. This paucity of data makes it impossible, furthermore, to know why, for example, just the instances of exegetical annotation in the legal corpora have been preserved, or why exegesis was not more consistently carried out in the historiographical materials.

But these limitations in the received record of the Hebrew Bible should not obscure the remarkable wealth of data which can be ferreted out. By contrast, despite the superabundance of legal materials from ancient Mesopotamia—such that enthusiasts have exulted with the proclamation *ex oriente lex!*—we are left almost totally in the dark as to how ancient Mesopotamian legists and jurists interpreted their cases. Rarely does a trial docket indicate how a known statute was handled or interpreted;[8] and rarely, too, are the interpretations of these circles incorporated into the major legal collections. Among the limited evidence for the latter it is possible to point to two examples involving the law collections of Lipit Ishtar (LI) and Hammurapi. In one instance, involving the case of a man who has married a second time and the proper disbursement of his inheritance to children of both marriages upon his death, it is clear that LH 167 has taken over the topos and language of LI 24 and provided paraphrastic elaboration.[9] The version in LH 167 does not add anything substantive to the earlier material, but simply articulates the case more fully, by providing explicit statements about the first marriage and the father's death. By contrast, a comparison of LI 10 with LH 59 shows that the attempt to make the earlier material more explicit involves the addition of a clause which deliberately removes any ambiguity in the interpretation of the case. Thus, whereas LI 10 flatly states: 'If a man cut down a tree in the garden of [another] man, he shall pay half a mina of silver', LH 59 records: 'If a man has cut down a tree in a man's plantation *without [the knowledge of] the owner of the plantation*, he shall pay half a maneh of silver.' Since it is quite unlikely that LI 10 was understood to mean that a penalty was imposed even when the owner agreed to the cutting down of his tree, the draftsman of LH 59 has simply made what

---

[8] Cf. the example proposed by E. Szlechter, 'L'Interprétation des lois babyloniens', *RIDA* 17 (1970) 107–14; also the proposal on p. 115.

[9] Szlechter, loc. cit. 114, refers to this case but cites it as article 29; cf. S. Kramer, *ANET* 160.

was implicit in LI fully explicit in his version.[10] Indeed, one might add that LH 59 has preserved and recorded the oral tradition of ancient Mesopotamian legistic circles. Such an outcropping on the barren surface of the preserved evidence betokens, as do its cogeners, the rich vein of legal exegesis which sustained ancient Mesopotamian law.[11]

B. Among the objective marks of a tradition of legal exegesis, its patterns of law-finding or legal development, on the one hand, and its stylistic patterns with their technical terms, on the other, take pride of place. The former show distinct procedures which vary under the auspices of different professional groups (e.g. priestly or non-clerical legists) and within the framework of different social institutions (e.g. legal oracles or practical and theoretical legal scholarship); the latter indicate diverse networks of training and practice. In the course of their historical development and diffusion, both factors naturally interpenetrate and yield a spectrum of types under the impact of different social configurations. For example, a patriarchal social order, rooted as it is in forms of individual authority and status, will self-evidently tend to produce more personal, *de facto*, and idiosyncratic styles of legal decision-making and interpretation than more complex bureaucratic orders, where the presence of codes of law and cadres of legists tends to cast legal decision-making and interpretation into more impersonal, *de jure*, and routinized moulds. By the same token, the available recourse to divine revelations (of law) within different social orders will vary and be a decisive variable in the spectrum of legal decision-making and interpretation produced. For while the procedures involved in the production of oracular *responsa* are usually regularized, their legal results are irregular and unpredictable, and tend to be manifest in social configurations dependent upon divine (and human) legal interventions. In such cases, the role of deliberative reason is nil, and thus in marked contrast with those social configurations where legists or decisors work with a divinely revealed legal *traditum* which must constantly be reconsidered or reinterpreted in new historical circumstances. The rational role of such legists or decisors is, moreover, usually but one expression among many whereby the cultural forms of a complex society are constantly subject to human modification and rethinking.

The preceding social-scientific assertions are much more than

---

[10] B. Jackson, *Theft*, 47 n. 4. For an example from the Hittite laws, see case 47 and its later version (*ANET* 191).

[11] A brief discussion of these matters can be found in G. Boyer, 'De la science juridique et sa méthode dans l'ancienne Mésopotamie', *Semitica*, 4 (1951-2), 5–11. Of interest is his view that *šarāqu* and its derivatives in LH 6-10, 14, 253, 255, 259–60 are used to characterize aspects of the will. Also, cf. above, p. 219 n. 116.

matters of mere theory and hypothesis, however; for they may be corroborated by the historical content of a broad diversity of legal systems the world over – that of ancient Israel included. Indeed, a consideration of such matters has an obvious bearing on any attempt to comprehend the forms and patterns of inner-biblical legal exegesis as fully as possible. Naturally, the fruit of such labours is inextricably connected with the analytical strength and suppleness of the model used for such a reconceptualization of the historical data. For present purposes, the conceptual model provided by Max Weber in his researches into the history of law in economy and society sets a standard of theoretical perspicuity and practical utility for the student of ancient Israelite law and legal exegesis.[12] Ranging over a voluminous array of materials, Weber observed the tendency of law to move through a series of stages, each of which reflects a certain mode of lawmaking, authority, and social structure – all in a complex interaction. Isolating various theoretical 'ideal-types', Weber perceived a fairly regular movement from (i) charismatic legal revelation (by prophetic or mantic individuals), to (ii) the empirical creation or finding of *ad hoc* laws (by social notables), to (iii) the imposition and systematization of laws (by secular or theocratic powers), to (iv) the systematic and even theoretical elaboration of laws (by persons with developed legal training).[13] Now, while these four types may be strongly correlated with certain types of individuals (as noted), and the increasingly bureaucratized and complex social configurations of which they are part (the first two dominate patriarchal and tribal organizations; the second two figure in monarchical and highly specialized societies), such a schematization is methodologically heuristic. Indeed, in Weber's words, an ideal-typical 'construction is merely a technical aid which facilitates a more lucid arrangement and terminology, and which make[s] it possible to determine the typological locus of a historical phenomenon'.[14] No society has to evolve through each of these stages in just this way, or without the possible persistence of (or even devolution to) earlier stages along the way. In fact, no society will ever have these types in a pure form: their theoretical purity is merely a rational tool for the investigator, not a criterion for historical actuality.[15]

[12] See the materials collected in M. Weber, *Law in Economy and Society*, ed. M. Rheinstein (Cambridge: Harvard University Press, 1954).

[13] For a discussion and elaboration in relation to biblical law, see below.

[14] *From Max Weber: Essays in Sociology*, edd. H. H. Gerth and C. W. Mills (New York: Oxford University Press, 1946), 324.

[15] Cf. also the comment of R. Bendix, *Max Weber: An Intellectual Portrait* (New York: Anchor Books, 1962), 410 n. 55, that '. . . pure types [are used] to sort out the constituent elements of each empirical constellation and to illustrate areas of possible tension . . .'

Having said all this, it is nevertheless true – and the Hebrew Bible is no exception – that the empirical record of world legal systems shows a remarkable tendency towards rationalization in the law, such that the modes of lawmaking or law-finding may be charted along a four-staged 'irrational–rational' continuum: (i) the 'formally irrational'; (ii) the 'substantively irrational'; (iii) the 'substantively rational'; and (iv) the 'formally rational'.[16] Without any attempt to provide a total exemplification, the following paragraphs will try to define and correlate these four modes of rationality with the preceding types and social stages, as they bear on the making and finding, but particularly on the exegesis and reinterpretation, of rules and cases in the Hebrew Bible. Thus, the present discussion will not examine other factors of interest or even pertinence to a full consideration of rationalization in biblical law – as the movements from self-help to court-centered jurisprudence, or the developments in the nature of witnesses and evidence. The principal concern will be rather to utilize Weber's dynamic model as a means of setting inner-biblical legal exegesis within a *typological continuum* of biblical law.

1. *Lawmaking and law-finding which are 'formally irrational'*. Such a modality occurs, according to Weber, 'when one applies in lawmaking or law-finding means which cannot be controlled by the intellect, for instance when recourse is had to oracles or substitutes therefor'.[17] In such cases, the means are highly formalized with respect to the procedures involved; but the conclusions are beyond rational control, in so far as a supernatural response is mediated through these formal procedures. Thus, the ways in which the legal questions are asked, as well as the overall scenario, tend to be precise, routinized, and controlled, whereas the *responsa* are subject to the independent divine will or the random 'fall' of the lots.[18] In the Hebrew Bible an interesting range of examples occurs which illustrate how new laws were made or found by such procedures in ancient Israel. Certainly the repeated recourse to Moses in the desert, in the cases of blasphemy (Lev. 24: 10-23), defilement at the time of the Paschal feast (Num. 9: 1-14), gathering wood on the Sabbath (Num. 15: 32-6), and grievance of the daughters of Zelophehad (Num. 27: 1-11), are exemplary in this regard. In these cases, Moses cannot solve the legal situation on the basis of the inherited (oral or written) *traditum*, and so turns to a divine oracle for adjudication.

From the perspective of the biblical narrative formal procedures such as those preserved in the foregoing cases were intended to be

[16] Weber, *Law in Economy*, 63-4.
[17] Ibid. 63.
[18] Ibid. 73-4, 77-9, 228.

understood in the light of Exod. 18. There, a judicial hierarchy is established in which Moses oracularly inquires of God only in those instances when the lower decisors or magistrates could not solve the problem at hand (vv. 19-20, 26). However, in so far as the pattern of judicial stratification and the emphasis on pious and ethical judges in Exod. 18 reflect, as noted, patterns and emphases known from Egyptian and Mesopotamian documents and their bureaucratized judiciaries,[19] one may assume that the judicial matters presented in Exod. 18 do not reflect the earliest tribal traditions of ancient Israel. Indeed, the presentation of Moses as a charismatic chieftain burdened by a judicial overload, and in need of relief in the form of a new judicial structure (vv. 13-23), must reflect a later socio-historical shift from tribal to more complex national patterns--wherein the sacred leader could no longer be approached personally in each and every case. The interventions of the leader were rather replaced by a bureaucratic configuration and restricted to those situations in which the ancient oracular questions and *responsa* were required.

In addition to the preceding, where laws were supplemented or reinterpreted by oracular means, judgements through divine lots were also part of the oldest social-legal situation—and reflect a similar modality of legal rationality. In such ancient records as Josh. 6-7 and 1 Sam. 14: 36-44, a highly formal set of binary questions is posed, although the answers are 'irrational' since they, like oracles, are divinely derived, and thus not the product of human reason. Such ancient modes of legal decision-making and law-finding were not entirely eclipsed in later developments of the legal system of ancient Israel— for they are reflected in the form of ordeals employed in those cases where witnesses or evidence were insufficient to permit the formal court system to resolve a case through human reason.[20] Thus, 'formally irrational' procedure are found embedded in the Covenant Code, in Exod. 22: 8, 10, and in the priestly legislation, in Num. 5: 11-31. While the technicalities of these latter two instances are not entirely clear, it is evident that divine authority is appealed to (whether via óracles or the ordeal of handling sacred objects, as in Exod. 22: 8, 10,[21] or whether

[19] Above, p. 102.

[20] Cf. Weber, *Law in Economy*, 91.

[21] Different viewpoints on the biblical procedure have been adopted: cf. Morgenstern, *HUCA* 7 (1930), 112-13, who viewed the procedure as an ordeal, and Graf, 'Was bedeutet der Ausdruck: vor Gott erscheinen, in den Gesetzen des Pentateuch? Ex 21, 6, 22, 7. 8', *ZDMG* 18 (1864), 309-14, who viewed it as an oracle. Recently, O. Lorentz, 'Ex. 21. 6; 22. 8 und angebliche Nuzi-Parallelen', *Bib.* 41 (1960), 173, has considered the procedure an oath. For cases from Nuzi of oaths before the gods where sufficient evidence was lacking for the judges to render a decision, see A. Draffkorn, 'Ilāni/Elohim', (*JBL* 76 (1957), 216-24. Remarkably, *hā'ĕlōhîm* in Exod. 22: 7-8 is functionally similar to *ilāni*, the

via the mantic–magical means referred to in Num. 5:11-31)[22] in the event of a judicial stalemate. From a typological viewpoint, such procedures are not substantively different from the recourse to divine oracles or lots. All three resort to a divine *responsum* where the case had no precedent in the *traditum*, or where the normal 'rational' procedures of judicial inquiry were stalemated or otherwise inadequate. The different mechanisms are presumably a function of the different social groups entrusted with law-finding and lawmaking.

In the light of the foregoing data, there need be no doubt that recourse to a divine *responsum* was a feature of biblical lawmaking and law-finding, particularly in its earliest stages. In most cases the utilization of a mantic procedure served situations where the law was non-existent or the evidence obscure. It is thus of interest to recall here that the ancient legal tradition has preserved at least two instances, in Num. 9 and 36, where an older law was inadequate and had to be reinterpreted or amended. Earlier, reasons were given to suppose that the sophisticated solutions found in these cases—particularly the use of a veritable legal fiction in Num. 36—reflect resolutions of a later legal age, now anachronistically legitimated by divine oracle. But even if one would hardly expect such subtle legal resolutions from oracles, it is nevertheless fundamental to acknowledge that the biblical writers *do* present these cases as paradigmatic instances of new divine lawmaking and exegesis. Hence, the existence of these remarkable 'exegetical *responsa*' in the context of narrative of Israel's desert sojourn may actually bear precious historical witness to the diversity of 'formal irrationality' in ancient Israelite legal praxis.

2. *Lawmaking and law-finding which are 'substantively irrational'*. Such a modality is a further move along the continuum towards rational, human legal decisions. According to Weber, 'lawmaking and lawfinding are "substantively irrational" . . . to the extent that decision is influenced by concrete factors of the particular case as evaluated upon an ethical, emotional, or political basis rather than by general norms'.[23] That is to say, to the extent that legal decisions are *ad hoc* they are not based on any 'rule-orientation', but rather on a perceived 'sense of justice' which is often 'guided by the "pragma" of objective and subjective interests'.[24] Decisions are thus made from case to case in accordance with the way injustice is perceived by the adjudicators; and these decisions are legitimated to the extent that the contending parties are

'gods' before whom such oaths were taken at Nuzi. The exceptional plural pointing of the divine decision in v. 8 of the MT (*yaršiʿun*) is 'corrected' in the Samar.

[22] Cf. Fishbane, *HUCA* 45 (1974), 37-9.
[23] Weber, *Law in Economy*, 63.
[24] Ibid. 75.

brought to an amicable or imposed resolution of the claims involved.[25]

The legal mechanism of substantive irrationality thus relies on the concrete case at hand, but the procedures are not formal: for in the sense that there is neither a fixed mode of inquiry nor a fixed mechanism for legal solutions, all depends on the parties involved. This does not mean that reason or ratiocination is absent from such a legal process. By 'irrational' Weber means in this type that there are no public, verifiable norms or rules of thought. Each case is resolved as the adjudicating party, or the contending parties, see(s) fit; so that while each decision may be rationally derived or defended, it is nevertheless inherently subjective, individual, and *sui generis*.

There are diverse instances in the Hebrew Bible of cases where the contending parties themselves work out mutually satisfying resolutions without recourse to violence (e.g. Gen. 26: 26-31, 31: 44-54). In other instances of 'substantive irrationality' a mediating third party—a requested or sought-after arbiter—makes the decision with respect to the case at hand. Two well-known cases in point are the decisions of Abram in the case of the contending shepherds (Gen. 13: 7-12), and of Solomon in the case of the contending mothers (1 Kgs. 3: 16-28). Since there is no recourse to fixed norms, each resolution depends on the clever, unpredictable, and hence arbitrary will of the 'judge'. Justice depends on the grace or whim of the acknowledged authority (leaving completely aside issues of enforcement and constraint).[26]

One may assume that Deborah (Judg. 4: 5) and Samuel (1 Sam. 7: 16) also functioned as legal mediators of this type in the ancient period of settlement. Popular recourse to such figures would reflect a social reality of a local, tribal sort, in which legal norms either did not exist or had no public character. Nevertheless, as is evident in the instance of Solomon's wisdom, such types of legal intervention undoubtedly retained a strong hold long after a more complex social order arose with its concomitant needs for a more normative legal administration. This is probably due to inherently conservative attitudes with respect to the law and figures of charismatic authority. It is thus a secular parallel to the appeal to divine ordeals in order to resolve intractable cases long after the formalization of such judicial procedures as witnesses and evidence in ancient Israel (cf. Exod. 22: 8, 10; Num. 5: 11-31).

According to Weber, war or national danger are contexts particularly supportive of 'substantive irrationality', in so far as these circumstances

---

[25] Cf. Ibid. 76.

[26] Despite this, one must bear in mind that an adjudicator will wish to avoid the charge of bias by disregarding 'in a later case a norm which he has consciously used as his maxim in an early situation', and so on. Cf. ibid. 74. Such conformability to past standards develops 'rational norm-formation' with basically irrational mechanisms of adjudication.

often forced or required the emergence of new laws or decisions.[27] Two significant instances may be adduced. The first case is found in 1 Sam. 30, where David, on the merits of the case and against traditional practice, decided that all soldiers—those active in the field and those in the home guard—should receive the spoils of war (vv. 22-5). This case has often attracted attention in so far as it is a virtually unique instance of an Israelite ruler imposing his own law.[28] Indeed, in a culture dominated by divine law and interpretations thereof, the fact that David's ruling became 'law and statute in Israel until this very day' is most striking. Whether this presented a conflict for David himself, or is only problematic for latter-day interpreters of Israel's laws, cannot be determined. What may be observed, however, is that David imposes a substantive decision of his own. There is no contextual reason to suppose that he is either applying or interpreting a divine norm like that in Num. 31:27 ('And you will divide the spoil among the warriors who go to battle *and the congregation*').[29]

The second instance of 'substantive irrationality' in a stress situation is of direct pertinence to inner-biblical legal exegesis. In Judg. 20-1 the tribe of Benjamin was faced with imminent extinction—since a national war of retribution had decimated their males (20:48), and since the other tribes had sworn to forbid their daughters to intermarry with them (21:1, 18). The frightening possibility of the loss of an entire tribal unit (21:2-3, 6) encouraged a legal solution which is actually of an exegetical sort. Since the oath forbidding intermarriage with the Benjaminites could not be rescinded, the pan-Israelite solution was to find women elsewhere; and so they decided to kill the males of Jabesh Gilead (since they did not join the national battle against Benjamin) together with their non-virgin women, and then to take the virgins of Jabesh Gilead to Shilo as wives for the Benjaminites (21:8-12). But despite this stratagem, it is recorded that many males remained with no mate (21:13-14), so that a further instance of 'substantive irrationality'—indeed of popular legal *exegesis*—was employed. For although *formal* marriage procedures were clearly ruled out due to the national oath, it was possible to circumvent the legal force of this by means of a loophole in the interpretation of it. No legal technicality prevented the men of Benjamin from catching the maidens of Shilo at the popular harvest festivities and taking them to their patrimony (vv. 19-21). The grievance of the fathers and brothers of these maidens was not so much assuaged as ignored.[30]

[27] Ibid. 91-2.

[28] See e.g. U. Cassutto, *Book of Exodus*, 260.

[29] Quite possibly the reverse is true: namely, that the phrase 'and the congregation' has been added to harmonize the Pentateuchal law with David's decision.

[30] This case, and the preceding one, which show rational–exegetical solutions

A distinct parallel to this situation can be found in the early monarchic period. For although David swore to Shimei that he would not kill him (2 Sam. 19: 24), on his deathbed he charged his son Solomon with bringing about a situation which would eliminate his old enemy (1 Kgs. 2: 8). Superficially, David is merely acting arbitrarily, after the manner of a despotic potentate. However, it is clear upon closer examination that David has honoured his oath in the breach by a formalistic interpretation of it. He first tells Solomon that he swore to Shimei that 'I shall not kill you by the sword', and then goes on to tell Solomon to be clever enough to eliminate any possible malefactor such as this one upon his accession to the throne. Hence David relies on a literal interpretation of his oath, fully knowing that 'there would have been a non-formalistic . . . natural alternative' which could get him off the hook of his oath and achieve his real desire.[31] As in the foregoing case of the circumvention of the national oath for the benefit of the Benjaminite tribe, so also in this instance the literal and formalistic meaning of an oath has been retained but exegetically circumvented on the basis of a loophole.

A final example of 'substantive irrationality' may also provide a transition to the next legal type, which deals with the legal corpora, among other matters. In an earlier discussion[32] it was pointed out that in the original formulation of the rule regarding the theft of persons in Exod. 21: 16 ('whosoever steals a person and sells him — and he is found [or 'seized'] with him (וְנִמְצָא בְיָדוֹ)—shall be put to death') the phrase and he is found (or 'seized') with him' was absent—it being a legal interpolation which supplements the original rule with a new evidentiary test. In the older legal *traditum* it would appear that one was liable for the theft of another person only if the latter had been sold. Later, mere possession of the *corpus delicti* served as a sufficient evidentiary test. A similar procedure seems to have prevailed in the area of property theft. Comparable to Exod. 21: 16, Exod. 21: 37 deals with a case where a person *steals* an animal, and either slaughters it or *sells* it. In such circumstances, the felon is liable to compensate the owner according to a graded scale of penalties. In this rule the mere possession of the *corpus delicti* does not appear to have constituted a crime. However, by contrast, Exod. 22: 3 states that a person is liable for theft if the *corpus delicti* 'be found in his possession (הִמָּצֵא תִמָּצֵא בְיָדוֹ)'. According to Daube, this latter rule is a development from the earlier legal level

in stress (war) circumstances, support Weber's remark (op. cit. 91) that '[a]mong the most important factors which secularized the thinking about what should be valid as a norm and especially its emancipation from magically guaranteed traditions, were war and its uprooting effects'.

[31] Daube, *VT* 11 (1961), 251-2.
[32] Above, pp. 188 f.

(Exod. 21:37) and parallels the legal levels found in Exod. 21:16 (in substance and terminology).[33] The difference between the two is merely that whereas the new evidentiary test in Exod. 21:16 was incorporated into the formulated *traditum*, the new evidentiary test in Exod. 22:3 has been appended to vv. 1-2 as a *clausula finalis*.[34] As noted earlier, this latter is a method of legal amendment whereby a draftsman may add a supplement to a particular rule at the conclusion of the paragraph of which it is a part—as against interpolating it into the rule itself. In his reconsideration of the matter of Exod. 21:37 + 22:3, B. Jackson has accepted Daube's view regarding the drafting procedure involved, such that Exod. 22:1-2 now interrupts one legal unit, but doubts 'that the earlier stage was as completely exclusive' of the notion that mere possession of the *corpus delicti* was an evidentiary test 'as Daube supposes'.[35] Jackson has speculated that even if at 'the earlier stage, the commonest mode of proof was by evidence of sale or slaughter . . . this does not necessarily mean that evidence of the possession of the *corpus delicti* was entirely excluded as a means of proof'. Rather, 'Exod. 22:3 may represent . . . a process whereby the less common rules of law were made explicit'.[36]

Jackson's viewpoint has some bearing on the present consideration of 'substantive irrationality': for it would appear that the mere possession of the *corpus delicti* was an evidentiary test within the legal reality which underlies the narrative about Joseph and his brothers, in Gen. 44. There, in v. 9, after the brothers are accused of stealing Joseph's divining cup, they say: 'with whomever of your servants it be found (יִמָּצֵא) let him die, and we shall become servants of our lord'. Here, as in the final version of Exod. 22:3, the technical term מצא is used, but the penalty for possession of the *corpus delicti* is death—not compensation. By contrast with the brothers' proposal, the steward of Joseph changes the penalty to servitude for the possessor of the object, and acquittal for the others (v. 10). All this is prior to the search, however. When this is conducted, and the perpetrator found, Judah proposes that all the brothers, 'including him in whose possession the divining cup was found (נמצא . . . בידו)' become servants of the owner of the stolen object (v. 16). Joseph, in his final decision, follows the steward's ruling.

Joseph's decision is a clear instance of 'substantive irrationality'. He decides according to his own lights, though in the context of some previous penalty proposals.[37] Moreover, like the brothers and the

[33] *Studies in Biblical Law*, 90-5.

[34] Thus, Exod. 22:1-2 are not an interpolation, as commonly argued. See e.g. Paton, 'The Original Form of the Book of the Covenant', *JBL* 12 (1893), 82.

[35] *Theft*, 47.

[36] Ibid.

[37] Cf. above, n. 26.

steward, he clearly assumes that mere possession of the *corpus delicti* was a crime; though, unlike the brothers, he attributes no guilt by association. Only the perpetrator of the crime shall become a servant, whatever the possible collusion or involvement of the brothers. This striking diversity in possible penalties suggests that while there was an established tradition that possession of the *corpus delicti* was an evidentiary test, the penalty had not been fixed in all quarters, and remained subject to the adjudicator involved. In this light, Exod. 22: 3 appears as an explicit formulation of the rule regarding possession of the *corpus delicti*, with a fixed penalty of compensation in silver. Indeed, Exod. 22: 3 appears comparatively as a particular formulation and normalization of the type of case in question – one which presumably coexisted alongside such legal traditions as are found in Gen. 44, or even followed them. That some relationship among all these traditions may be posited is clear, given the common use of the technical expression נמצא בידו to indicate possession of the *corpus delicti*. However, it is doubtful whether Exod. 22: 3 preceded the legal traditions in Gen. 44 in fact; for if this were so, it would be difficult to explain the divergence in the Pentateuchal narratives from that found in the Pentateuchal ruling. Perhaps the difference between Exod. 22: 3 and the legal traditions in Gen. 44 is simply that between public formulations of a rule and private traditions or local practice. In any event, the establishment in Exod. 22: 3 of the fixed penalty of double the value of the *corpus delicti* in silver not only undercuts the vagaries of 'substantive irrationality' in the establishment of penalties, but also suggests· that Exod. 22: 3 is a more liberal rule overall. For even if Joseph and his steward do not accept the brothers' various proposals of death or communal guilt, it is nevertheless obvious that a fixed penalty of compensation in silver for possession of a *corpus delicti* is more liberal than a penalty which allows the owner of a stolen object to take the perpetrator of the delict as his servant (Joseph's conclusion). Indeed, the latter legal possibility even suggests that persons could serve as vicarious compensation for objects – a matter quite striking in biblical law.[38] Of course, in so comparing the penalties of Exod. 22: 3 and Gen. 44: 9-10, 16-17, it is assumed that the formulation of the former, which lists only animals in respect of a *corpus delicti*, was meant to be paradigmatic for all possessions. If, however, the animals referred to were not intended by the draftsman as representative examples but as exclusive exemplifications, the differences in penalties in the two texts

---

[38] Such matters are overlooked in M. Greenberg's 'Some Postulates of Biblical Criminal Law', *Y. Kaufmann Jubilee Volume* (Jerusalem: The Magnes Press, 1960), 5-28. The very principle of Greenberg's thesis has been subjected to critical analysis by B. Jackson, 'Reflections on Biblical Criminal Law', in *Studies*, 25-63.

should not be correlated: the penalty of double the value of the *corpus delicti* would hold for animals, while other options were possible for inanimate objects In any event, the coexistence in Exod. 22: 3 and Gen. 44: 9-10, 16-17 of a legal tradition which regarded mere possession of a *corpus delicti* as an evidentiary test would not be gainsaid.

3. *Lawmaking and law-finding which are 'substantively rational'.* Such a modality, according to Weber, occurs when legal decisions or interpretations are principally influenced by the concrete factors of particular cases as rationally evaluated in accordance with utilitarian and experiential rules, ethical imperatives, political maxims, and the like.[39] Hereby, the legal decisions and interpretations, together with the traditions upon which they may be based, are no longer completely in the hands of tribal chieftains or kings, but are increasingly consolidated into collections of rules or norms where they may be inspected, analysed, or enacted. Comparatively viewed, the new stage of legal rationality represented by the systematization and collection of rules or customs is often highly correlatable with periods of national and administrative consolidation in a given society; so that the rational systematization of legal collections parallels the rational systematization of bureaucratic and economic services, and may actually be stimulated by the exigencies and possibilities of the latter.[40] Thus, from the ancient Israelite side, the speculation of many modern biblicists that the collection of rules and customs in the Covenant Code largely reflects the accomplishments and imperatives of the new monarchy under Solomon, during whose reign a vast restructuring of the older administrative and economic orders was undertaken as well, has a self-evident appeal. Similarly, whatever the precise background of the diverse legal traditions which comprise Deut. 12-26, the publication of the deuteronomic legal corpora in the aftermath of Assyrian suzerainty over Judaea, and concomitant with the re-emergence of Judaean religious and political independence, would appear to confirm Weber's perspective.

Indeed, the legal corpus in the Book of Deuteronomy shows, in its own right, many new tendencies in the increasing rationalization of the juridical process. Among these one may note the consolidation of the judiciary into municipal and provincial courts which are hierarchically related (Deut. 17: 8-12),[41] and technical references to judicial inquiry (e.g. 19: 15, 17: 4, 9, 19: 17-18) and witnesses (19: 15-19). Even more

[39] *Law in Economy*, 63-4.
[40] Cf. ibid. 266-9; also 250-1.
[41] Cf. above, pp. 164 f. It may further be contended that the references to 'judges' and 'officers' in Deut. 16: 18-20, 17: 8-13, 19: 15-21, 20: 1-9, and 25: 1-3 reflect a social-juridical stratum superimposed over a stratum which spoke of 'elders', as in 19: 11-13, 21: 1-4, 6-9, 18-21, 22: 13-21, 25: 5-10.

striking in this regard is the deuteronomic reworking of Exod. 18 which, as noted, itself presents a judicial hierarchy in which local magistrates administer justice of a more routine sort, with the difficult cases reserved for Moses and his divine consultations. In Deut. 1:13 the judges are called 'wise, intelligent, and knowledgeable men', and not 'god-fearers' or 'upright men', as in Exod. 18:21. Moreover, in Deut. 1:17 Moses is made to say to his appointees: 'any case which is too difficult for you, *bring to me and I shall hear it.*' No mention whatever is made of God or an oracular request. Similarly, whereas the verb דרש refers to oracular inquiry in Exod. 18:15, it is used as a term of rational legal investigation in Deut. 13:15, 17:4, 9, and 19:18. This particular semantic shift parallels and even precedes the similar one, pointed out earlier, in Ezra 7:10. For whereas the expression 'to inquire (לדרש) of YHWH' occurs in a mantic context of prophetic inquiry in 1 Kgs. 22:8, for example, and the expression 'to inquire of Elohim' occurs in a mantic context of legal inquiry in Exod. 18:15, the expression used in Ezra 7:10 is significantly 'to inquire (לדרש) of *the Torah of YHWH*'. Here the text of divine words serves, as it were, as an *oraculum* for rational-exegetical inquiry. In a comparable manner, the verb פרש * is first found in connection with the oracular inquiries of Lev. 24:12 and Num. 15:34, but is used in post-exilic sources as an entirely rational mode of explanation or exposition of the Torah of Moses (Neh. 8:8).[42]

Despite the fact, then, that the systematization of rules of law and processes of judicial inquiry provides the conditions in ancient Israel for the functioning of the modality of 'substantive rationality' in the application of rules and ethical imperatives in lawmaking and law-finding, precious little evidence of this latter can be found in biblical sources. Just how the rules and imperatives of the legal *traditum* — whether incorporated into the legal corpora or not — actually served as precedents can only be surmised. One fairly clear example seems to be provided by the case résumé found in Jer. 26, which reports how the prophet Jeremiah was accused, arraigned, and tried for false prophecy. Undoubtedly, even here, the historical reality has been filtered through a thick and somewhat garbled narrative historiography, one that is, moreover, highly influenced by deuteronomic values and traditions.[43] But despite the facts that Jer. 26 is a narrative synopsis, and that the deuteronomic historiographer is often concerned to legitimate Jeremiah's prophetic actions by means of deuteronomic criteria,[44] there is reason to suppose

[42] See above, pp. 108 f. Relatedly, also compare Num. 27:18 with Deut. 34:9.

[43] See the recent analyses, with earlier bibliography, of F. Hossfeld and I. Meyer, 'Der Prophet vor dem Tribunal: Neuer Auslegungsversuch von Jer 26', *ZAW* 86 (1974), 30–50. Cf. also A. Rofé, 'Studies in the Composition of the Book of Jeremiah', *Tarbiz*, 44 (1975), 15–19 [Heb.].

[44] Compare e.g. Jer. 1:8; 28:9,15–17 and Deut. 18:18,22. Cf. 1 Kgs. 22:27–8.

that the complex judicial process reflected in Jer. 26 is not a narrative conceit but an accurate reflex of actual historical procedures and modes of legal rationality. In the first place, the procedures are too formalized and routinized to be merely a matter of artifice; and related to this is that fact that the account purports to be a historical report directed to contemporary readers. The historian's authority would hardly benefit from easily perceived distortions in the presentation of legal due process. Accordingly, if Jer. 26 is not historical in the fullest sense, it is at least history-like: a narrative reflex of historical actuality.

At the beginning of the account, following a summary of Jeremiah's doom oracle against the people and Temple of Jerusalem (26: 2-6; cf. 7: 3-15), Jeremiah is seized and threatened with death for preaching the destruction of the Temple (vv. 8-9). In the court scene which follows, the priests, Levites, and princes speak as plaintiffs to members of the nation and formally repeat the charges (v. 11). Then Jeremiah contends that he has been sent by YHWH and is innocent of the charges made (vv. 12-15). On the basis of Jeremiah's defence, it is clear that the plaintiffs cannot believe that the doom oracle is from YHWH, and so apply the rule found in Deut. 18: 20 to the case: '. . . the prophet who dares to speak an oracle in my [YHWH's] name, that which I have not commanded him to speak, . . . that prophet shall die.' Hence, by so following due process, and by so dealing with the case in accordance with rules and standards, the priests and Levites are guided by 'substantive rationality' in their legal judgement. So, too, are the princes; for they respond after Jeremiah's defence with what appears to be a decision in support of the prophet's arguments: they cite as precedent a case when another prophet spoke ill of the Temple and Jerusalem but was believed to have been divinely commissioned and so not put to death (vv. 16-19). These princes thus appear to accept the rational criterion of Deut. 18: 20 without, however, accepting its applicability in the present case. Despite this support of Jeremiah's defence, a counter-precedent is brought forth — presumably by the priests and Levites — in which another prophet who spoke an oracle of doom against Jerusalem was hounded and finally killed (vv. 20-3). This latter opinion apparently carried the day, for v. 24 reports that one Aḥikam ben Shaphan intervened on Jeremiah's behalf, and sequestered him so that he would not be killed by the mob. Such a popular challenge to the verdict of the 'law-finders', and intervention into formal judicial processes, has a notable parallel in 1 Sam. 14: 36-45, where the people refuse to kill Jonathan for his breach of military regulations even after he was condemned by the divine oracle. Comparable instances can be found in early Greek law as well.[45]

---

[45] See H. J. Wolff, 'The Origin of Judicial Litigation among the Greeks', *Traditio*, 4 (1946), 34-9. For comparable matters in old Germanic practice (the *Urteilsschelte*), cf. Weber, op. cit. 90-1.

Apart from Jer. 26, direct or indirect testimonies of 'substantive rationality' in judicial processes are few and far between in ancient Israelite sources. It is thus that the evidence of inner-biblical legal exegesis is of great historical value. For whether any particular instance of such legal exegesis arises from theoretical or practical considerations, they all variously attest to rational deliberations of the law and attempts to deal with the *traditum* as substantively given and formulated.[46] Accordingly, the study of inner-biblical exegesis produces a valuable and untapped source for estimating modes of legal reasoning in ancient Israel. And, in so far as it is not unreasonable to assume a broad transferability between the modes of legal reasoning in legal exegesis and those instances in ancient Israelite jurisprudence whereby 'substantive rationality' was employed to make decisions or adjudicate cases on the basis of rules of law, an inquiry into the modes of rationality found in inner-biblical legal exegesis may have a double historical value. A review of the materials with this end in mind suggests the following classification:

(i) *Analogical exegesis.* In any attempt to disclose the modalities of legal reasoning preserved in inner-biblical exegesis, the analogical mode must be ranked of paramount importance, both in terms of the range of examples preserved and the basic logical operations performed. Several sub-types may be discerned. First, there is 'analogy by simple extension'. In such cases one rule would be compared to another in order to determine or specify certain characteristics which were ambiguous or potentially problematic in nature. The case in Exod. 21: 31, wherein a vicious ox gores minors, is such an instance; for it is compared with the preceding case, wherein such an ox gores an adult, in order to assert that the penalties are similar in both eventualities, and that no variation is permitted. A more common variety of 'analogy by simple extension' involves those cases where the examples of an original rule are extended by means of examples which are 'like' them in order to make the original rule more comprehensive or explicit. For example, the reference to lost oxen and sheep in Deut. 22: 1 is supplemented in v. 3 with the addition of references to asses, garments, and even the more general category of 'any loss'. As there is no intention in the supplement to introduce a new legal category, but rather to extend the reference to losses from animate to inanimate chattels, the new examples given in v. 3 have a simple analogical relation to those found in v. 1. Similarly, the extension of the sabbatical regulations regarding cultivated fields in Exod. 23:10 to vineyards and olive groves in v. 11b is also of a simple analogical sort; although, as noted, the extension may have had the further purpose of foreclosing any

---

[46] More generally, cf. Weber, ibid. 205, 230.

assumption that the rules of the sabbatical year of rest applied only to crops grown on arable land.

Where an original rule or sequence of examples is expanded by a new topic, so that a shift of legal categories or principles is involved, the analogy is of a different type, one which may be termed 'analogy by complex extension'. In Exod. 22: 8, for example, an original rule which deals with the need to have recourse to an adjudicating divine oracle in certain contestations over bailment (v. 7) is extended to include 'every case of contestation' over personal property, and even 'any kind of loss'. The relationship between these cases may be disputed. On the one hand, it may be contended that the only analogical connection between the allegations of misappropriation of property in the course of bailment and the loss of another's property is the required recourse to divine adjudication in all cases.[47] However, as argued earlier, it is more reasonable to suppose that the situations introduced in v. 8 were meant to extend the issue of bailment as outlined in vv. 6–7. First there was added an extended legal clause which required a bailee to come before God in every case where a depositor charged him with misappropriating the bailment, on account of the depositor's claim of identifying the missing item in the bailee's possession. At some subsequent point the phrase referring to 'any kind of loss' was joined to this clause. Three analogies are involved: (1) there is an analogical extension of items concerning which the depositor may charge the bailee with misappropriation (hereby animate objects are added to inanimate ones, and the common denominator is deposits which are missing); (2) there is an analogical extension of deposited items which are missing due to some premeditated action—be it *force majeur* (by an external thief) or stealth (by the bailee)—to deposited items which are missing due to inattention—be it irresponsibility or negligence (hereby unintentional losses are added to losses where intent is involved); (3) there is an analogical extension of the legal category of thievery from the initial case involving an external thief (v. 6) to those cases involving deliberate misappropriation or negligent loss by the bailee, since in the latter two cases a convicted bailee must (like an apprehended thief; v. 6b) pay double the value of the deposited item (see v. 8b; hereby all losses are analogized irrespective of the bailee's intent, and a lost item is considered as one illegally gained if a bailee avers that he has not appropriated it but it is, nevertheless, found in his possession). In the present mini-series on bailment all three analogical levels are complexly interrelated.

A more transformative type in the Hebrew Bible is 'analogy by substantive extension'. In this third sub-type one is faced with a veritable

---

[47] Because the charges may be convincingly contested in the absence of witnesses.

transformation of the meaning and intent of the original rule. Thus, in the reworking or appropriation of Num. 9: 9-14 in 2 Chron. 30, the original rule, which permits persons who have either come in contact with a corpse or who are away on a journey at the time of the paschal-sacrifice to defer their celebration of it for one month, is so extended that people who have become defiled by contact with pagan cult-objects and are far from the central shrine in Jerusalem are permitted to defer their celebration of the paschal-sacrifice for one month. The analogical transformations are substantive and remarkable: first, miasmic defilement is analogized to defilement through contact with idols; and second, distance from the holy land and one's clan is analogized to distance from the one legitimate shrine. The first analogy rests on the premiss that defilements disqualify one from ritual performances; the second analogy appears to rest on more restricted linguistic data. As noted earlier, the phrase דרך רחקה in Num. 9: 10 was probably read in the light of comparable phrases in Deut. 12: 21 and 14: 24 where the reference is to distance from the chosen cultic site.[48] In any event, it will not suffice simply to say that the analogies work by virtue of common premisses or terms. The analogical reasoning involved is also structural and hence more significant.[49] For the legal mind which perceived the analogical transformation in 2 Chron. 30 was able to look past the concrete facts of the case in Num. 9: 9-14 and perceive its abstract relationship to the social-ritual situation at hand. Certainly such mental operations would be of great importance in the normal course of ancient Israelite jurisprudence.

A final sub-type of analogical exegesis may be termed 'analogy of concrete cases', and is pointedly illustrated by Deut. 22: 25-7. In v. 26, an analogy to the basic case dealing with a woman who has been forcibly raped in the field is interpolated from the rules of accidental homicide in Deut. 19: 4-6. The force of the analogy is to correlate features of the two cases so as more fully to perceive their common structure and dynamics. Like the victim of homicide who is forcibly overcome in a premeditated hostile act, a woman raped in the field is also a victim of force and premeditated hostility. Such a victim cannot,

---

[48] Above, p. 157. Lexical analogies were called *gĕzērāh šāwāh* by the ancient Rabbis (for Tannaitic examples, cf. *M. Beṣa* i. 6; *M. Soṭa* vi. 3; *M. Nazir* ix. 5). See the remarks of Liebermann, *Hellenism*, 58-62; also the observations of G. Bregman, 'What is the *gĕzērāh šāwāh*?', *Sinai*, 71 (1972), 132-9 [Heb.]. For early examples in the Qumran scrolls, see E. Slomovic, 'Toward an Understanding of the Exegesis of the Dead Sea Scrolls', *RQ* 7 (1969-71), 5-9.

[49] Such formal analogies were called *heqēš* (for Tannaitic examples, cf. *M. Šeb.* i. 4; *M. Yebam.* iii. 6; *M. Mak.* i. 7; *M. Menaḥ.* vii. 6). For full discussions of *heqēš* and *gĕzērāh šāwāh*, see *Enṣiqlopedia Talmudit*, gen. ed. R. S. Zevin (Jerusalem: Talmudic Encyclopedia Pub. Ltd., 1947-), s.vv. *gĕzērāh šāwāh* (v. 546-64), *heqēš* (x. 357-75).

therefore, be considered a consenting party to the act. Presumably, the introduction of the analogy of homicide in connection with rape in the field is not a mere attempt to develop a theoretical line of legal reasoning, but serves to explain why the woman was not liable in such circumstances. The perception of a structural relationship between the cases thus appears to be the product of legists or jurists engaged in deliberations on the rule of law for quite practical ends. In this respect, it provides a formal link between the structural legal reasoning underlying 2 Chron. 30 and the structural analogies which undoubtedly obtained in actual moments of ancient Israelite jurisprudence.

Perhaps one further link in this chain may be forged, and that on the basis of the legal material underlying the narrative in Josh. 22. In that historical report, members of the trans-Jordanian tribes of Israel are accused by the high priest and representatives of the other tribes of religious malfeasance—in that the tribes of Reuben, Gad, and the half-tribe of Manasseh built an altar in their territory. In the context of their accusation (vv. 13-20), the priest and representatives evoke two broad historical analogies, and therewith show that what they believed to be at stake was an outbreak of divine wrath against the entire people of Israel. The accusation thus uses the case of Achan, and his violation of the חרם, as a precedent (v. 20; cf. Josh. 6-7). They argue that just as he alone engaged in an act of malfeasance but others died with him, so the actions of the trans-Jordanian tribes are not simply a private affair but will affect all Israel besides. The legal argument is *a fortiori*,[50] and uses the historical example for the purpose of a structural analogy. But this expression of 'substantive rationality' was successfully parried by the trans-Jordanian tribes (vv. 21-9), and the accusation of malfeasance was dropped (vv. 30-1).

(ii) *Synthetic exegesis*. A mode of legal reasoning closely related to the analogical, but which produces different results, is what is here called synthetic, and which operates on the basis of textual comparisons or associations of different sorts. One sub-type may be termed 'synthesis by comparative supplementation'. Examples include Lev. 5:15-16, Num. 15:24, and 2 Chron. 7:8-10. In the first of these, the formulation of penalties in the rule regarding accidental desecration of sancta is supplemented by a reference to Lev. 27:25, where the monetary standard which is assumed to apply in Lev. 5:15-16 is explicitly stated. By

---

[50] More formally, this type of argument was the hermeneutical principle *qal wāḥōmer*, which inferred *a minori ad maius*. It is the first of Hillel's principles, found, for example, in *Tos. Sanh.* vii. 11. The argument in Josh. 22 conforms to the 'simple' type of *a minori* argument as set forth by L. Jacobs, *Studies in Talmudic Logic and Methodology* (London: Vallentine and Mitchell, 1961), ch. I, 'The Aristotelean Syllogism and the Qal Wa-Homer', 3-8.

incorporating the reference to Lev. 27: 25 into the formulation of Lev. 5: 15-16, the legal exegete-draftsman has not only interpreted one text in the light of another, and integrated them, but has actually transformed the plain sense of the original rule: the penalty is now shifted from sacrifices to be made in accordance with the value of the desecrated object, as set by the currency exchange in the Temple, to a penalty payable in monetary terms alone. Hence the comparison of different passages for the purpose of bringing to bear on one normative rule the rate of exchange presumed to be normative for it has resulted — intentionally or not—in a more complicated and problematic rule than existed in the first place.

Such was not the result, however, of the synthetic exegesis which produced Num. 15: 24 and 2 Chron. 7: 8-10. In both these cases the reading of one rule or account (Lev. 4: 14 and 1 Kgs. 8: 65-7, respectively) in the light of more normative or predominant procedures resulted in the rewriting of the problematic rule in such a way as to efface the contradictions. Underlying synthetic exegeses of this type is the assumption that certain diversities or contradictions in the biblical record are merely apparent, not real, as well as the assumption that it is one of the tasks of exegesis to indicate how the divergences might coexist. In the two cases under review, the procedure was to assume that the problematic version was merely an elliptical but not inherently contradictory version of the normative or predominant version. In other instances, such as those found in Neh. 10: 32 and 2 Chron. 35: 12-13, other exegetical tactics were necessary. Among these, Neh. 10: 32 is the least barbarous; for since the sabbatical prescriptions found in Exod. 23: 11 and Deut. 15: 2 could easily be regarded as complementary—the one agricultural, the other financial—all that was required was to combine them in one ruling. Where, however, the rules were blatantly contradictory, as is the case with the prescriptions surrounding the paschal-sacrifice in Exod. 12: 9 and Deut. 16: 7, no such solution was possible, as the desperate illogicality of the textual blend in 2 Chron. 35: 13 makes quite clear.

A quite different method employed in inner-biblical exegesis, whereby differences in legal rules could be synthesized, was to redefine the intent or scope of the problematical rule, hence, it may be termed 'synthesis by secondary circumscription'. One example discussed earlier is that found in Deut. 20: 10-18. In so far as the rules of military conquest differed in vv. 10-14 from the normative rule prescribed in Deut. 7: 1-2, and even cited in 20: 17, the legal exegete reaffirmed the norm by redefining the applicability and scope of vv. 10-14. Such a mode of casuistic exegesis shows the availability of forms of 'substantive rationality' in ancient Israel whereby two rules which contradicted each other could be resolved by a third version which mediated between the two.[51] The way certain of the rules of cultic centralization were synthesized preserves a more forceful exemplification of this procedure. Thus, it is explicitly stated in Exod. 20: 24, prior to the whole Covenant Code (Exod. 21-3), that one may build an altar and slaughter upon it 'in any site where I [God] shall pronounce my name'. As is well known, this provision is explicitly rejected in Deut. 12: 5-6—at the outset of the whole Deuteronomic Code (Deut. 12-26)—where it is stated that one may build an altar and slaughter 'only at the site which YHWH, your God, shall choose from among all your tribes, to place his name'. This principle and its implications were so basic to deuteronomic cultic praxis that it is repeated elsewhere in the chapter. In the process, slight variations are introduced which reflect ongoing reflections on the rule. For example, the version beginning in vv. 8-9 states that the profusion of slaughter sites is valid *only* up to complete settlement in the land. The alert reader will at once sense that this latter is a valiant attempt exegetically to resolve the blatant contradiction between Exod. 20: 24 and Deut. 12: 5-6. The rule in Exod. 20: 24 was therefore understood to be of limited historical duration—despite any explicit biblical comment to that end. Accordingly, it may be furthermore supposed that the inherent ambiguity in the phrase 'in any site where I shall pronounce my name' was exegetically exploited to achieve a harmonizing solution. Since 'in any site' may be understood distributively (i.e. 'in any of the sites') or specifically (i.e. 'in whatever particular site'), the exegete of Deut. 12: 8-9 may have felt that he was not so much rejecting the rule in Exod. 20: 20 as specifying its underlying intent.

(iii) *Qualifying exegesis.* A final general category of legal reasoning to be found in inner-biblical exegesis may broadly be termed 'qualifying' in nature. Two distinct sub-types may be discerned within this rubric. The first may be designated 'qualification by cautelary procedure'. By this is meant the anticipation by the legal mind of loopholes or ambiguities in a rule of law, and the legistic or juridical practice of closing it off by a strict or lenient construction of its formulation. Such procedures are well known in the area of Roman jurisprudence, for example, and have been so designated by F. Schultz in his standard treatment of the subject.[52] They also aptly characterize the incremental

---

[51] Also cf. Deut. 12: 21-8 and the resolution noted above, p. 228 n. 131. More formally, this type of casuistic argument was canonized as the thirteenth of R. Ishmael's hermeneutical principles. The text of the 'Beraita d'R. Ishmael' is found in the introductory chapter to *Sifra*. For examples, cf. *Sifre* to Num. 7: 89 and *Sifra* to Lev. 16: 1.

[52] See his *History of Roman Legal Science* (Oxford: Clarendon Press, 1946), 19-22, 49-52, 111. Weber, op. cit. 72, also speaks of *Kautelarjuristen*; and M. Rheinstein says (n. 18) that cautélary jurists are 'lawyers who . . . [use] their skill

introduction of new restrictions now found in Exod. 23:11b and Jer. 17:21-2, for example. As we have had occasion to note, the formulation of the rule for sabbatical rest in Exod. 23:10-11a, and the general prohibitions regarding work on the Sabbath day in Exod. 20:10 and underlying Jer. 17:21-2, inevitably raised certain questions. For example, did the rules for the sabbatical year apply to vineyards and olive groves, and did the prohibition of work on the Sabbath day pertain only to actual buying and selling but not to other manual activities (related or unrelated to commercial interests)? To foreclose the possibility of any misunderstanding, the two rules are supplemented by additional rules and prohibitions.

But the logical operation just described, which reads a rule from the perspective of its maximal implications, and decides whether it has to be qualified in order to make its full force explicit, can work in the opposite direction. Then one may regard the maximal implications of a rule as restrictive, and move to qualify it, or pry open gaps in its formulation, in order to make this as viable or utilitarian as seems necessary. This sub-type of exegetical rationality may be designated as 'qualification by casuistic circumscription', and is exemplified by such cases as Exod. 12:16, Lev. 7:23, and Lev. 25:21-2, among others. In the first two of these instances, general prohibitions — regarding work on the first and seventh days of the feast of unleavened bread, and regarding the prohibition from eating the fat of animals whose flesh was permitted — were qualified. In Exod. 12:16, work was delimited to exclude the preparation of food; in Lev. 7:23-4, the fat of animals whose flesh one was not permitted to eat was permitted for utilitarian use. Natural exigencies obviously underlie the formal distinctions introduced into these two cases, as they also do in Lev. 25:21-2, where the severity of the prohibitions which would obtain when a sabbatical year was followed by a jubilee year needed modification. The legal casuistry involved in this case was much more subtle than in the cases of Exod. 12:16 and Lev. 7:24. The procedure involved went beyond delimiting a general norm, but, as noted, modified the prohibitions of both the sabbatical and the jubilee years in such a way that the substance of the rules was maintained *though in a functional manner*. There is, of course, no reason to assume that the mental operations in evidence in these cases were either formal or routine applications of canons of exegesis and exegetical logic. All that need be asserted is that the exigencies of a living legal *traditio* provided the conditions in which such interpretations of the *traditum* were possible. The degrees of skill and flexibility in such interpretations were undoubtedly further affected

in . . . inventing new clauses for the purpose of safeguarding their clients' interests and of preventing future litigation'.

by the occasions presented by practical jurisprudence. And, no doubt, the influence was mutual.

4. *Lawmaking and law-finding which are 'formally rational'.* Such a modality, according to Weber, represents the apogee of legal rationality. In this modality one moves beyond 'substantive rationality' where decisions are made simply in respect of the concrete case at hand, and not in the light of principles or concepts. Lawmaking and law-finding which are 'formally rational' attempt to disclose 'the legally relevant characteristics of the facts . . . [either by an adherence to the perceptible characteristics of the facts or by a process whereby the legist procedes by a] logical analysis of meaning and where, accordingly, definite fixed legal concepts in the form of highly abstract rules are formulated and applied'.[53] Such a modality develops with the further diversification of social structures and institutions, and, according to Weber, flourishes when the law and its interpretation become increasingly part of closed lawyerly traditions: studied, defined, and refined in law schools.[54]

Classical Roman and Jewish jurisprudence and hermeneutics are replete with legal abstractions and conceptualizations, and with the formalization of rules of analysis and/or styles of formulation. Ancient Israelite legal exegesis cannot be defined or characterized by such elements. Nevertheless, it would be equally incorrect to ignore the uncertain tracings which later helped constitute this trajectory. First, there are many official hermeneutical terms to be found in the Hebrew Bible, such as those evidenced in Neh. 8:8 in connection with official cadres of trained legal exegetes who 'instructed the people' (v. 9). Then, too, there are the many technical formulae which appear in all three legal corpora of the Hebrew Bible, and which provide a clear witness to the formalization of exegetical training and analysis in ancient Israel. And, finally, the types of legal reasoning examined in preceding paragraphs as species of 'substantive rationality' bear out the sense that a distinct habit of mind was being fostered by legal tradents who were presented with a legal *traditum* of frequent incomprehensibility and incomprehensiveness. Many exegeses reflect the clear awareness of such legal categories as evidence or possession; moreover, on occasion, as in 2 Chron. 30, quite abstract and structural interpretations of the *traditum* can even be discerned. Nevertheless, it should be stressed that these latter are neither framed in abstract terms nor refer to abstract norms.[55] Accordingly, in order to perceive the incipient use and

[53] Weber, op. cit. 63.
[54] Ibid. 97, 202–5, 271.
[55] To the end, it would appear, biblical legal exegesis and law-finding are 'empirical'; that is, the process 'always moves from the particular to the particular but never tries to move from the particular to general propositions in order to be

development of categories of some generality one must analyse the lists which were added to rules in order to make them more comprehensive. There, the formula frequently heralds the use of broad legal categories; as, for example, in 'כל every type of contestation' or 'כל every loss' in Exod. 22: 8, or in the phrase 'מכל of everything concerning which one may swear falsely', in Lev. 5: 24. As has been noted, the secondary nature of these types of expansions can regularly be discerned from a close internal examination of the passages involved. However—rarely—the modern interpreter may be aided by a comparison of parallel passages. Thus, a comparison of Lev. 3: 16b-17 and 17: 6 shows that while they share common legislation regarding the use of animal fats for incense during sacrifices, the *traditio* of the former has seen fit to add a comprehensive prohibition against eating 'כל all fat and כל all blood'.

Two final types of generalization may be indicated here. Formally speaking, both are of historical importance in the post-biblical developments of religious and civil law. The first type concerns the development of concepts in the civil law. For in addition to terms like 'every kind of contestation', or 'every loss', the legal corpora preserve instances where abstract nouns appear to function as incipient types of legal categories. Examples include Lev. 5: 21-2 where, under the general species of property offences, the draftsman refers to instances of 'deposit, or misappropriation, or robbery . . . or . . . loss'. A comparison of the similar issues mentioned in Exod. 22: 6-8 is instructive for many reasons; and not least of these is the fact that the formulation in Exod. 22: 6-8 is verbal, whereas that in Lev. 5: 21-2 is largely nominative and hence more abstract. We thus have a possible trace of the emergence of concepts of civil jurisprudence.

The second type of generalization, found in the phrase 'כל־המצות any of the commandments' (Num. 15: 22) is of greater overall significance. As is clear, the use of כל in this case does not have the character of a broad generalization; it rather has a more distributory force, and so means 'any of all' the commandments. However, through this formulation, a generalization of singular import does emerge: for each and every one of the commandments are perceived as of equivalent religio-juridical status.[56] To transgress any one of these commandments by accident requires one standard form of sacrificial atonement; and to transgress any one of these commandments wilfully is to invoke the penalty of כרת (cf. vv. 27-9 + 30-1). No hierarchy among the

able subsequently to deduce from them the norms for new particular cases'. Thus Weber, op. cit. 202, on what would today be called the method of common law reasoning.

[56] It will be recalled that this is the remarkable reworking of Lev. 4: 13, 'any one of the commandments of YHWH which are prohibitory' (lit. 'which you shall not do'); cf. above, pp. 192 f.

commandments is envisaged or provided for, since each is 'the word of YHWH'. To paraphrase a later rabbinic dictum, which here finds its remarkable dogmatic anticipation: a person may not discriminate as to the relative importance of the commandments (that they seem 'light' or 'severe' in the actions or punishments prescribed)—for each one is part of the divine revelation. No formal distinction is made between theft, perjury, or ritual transgression, for example, so that a concept of the divine commandments, as a definable legal–religious category, is here given its preliminary, yet fateful, first expression.

C. The preceding review of types of inner-biblical legal exegesis, and the modes of rationality involved, may be checked against a more immanent biblical dynamic—the relationship between revelation and tradition—and against a more immanent biblical mode of rationality—the nature of authority and its legitimacy. As against a purely social-scientific perspective, which views the growth of legal rationality in relationship to its own increasing degrees of systematization, logic, and abstraction, and in its relationship to the types of organizational and bureaucratic structures to be found in the social and economic orders, a more immanent perspective proceeds with different questions in mind. It is concerned to ask, How does the older legal *traditum* retain or lose its authority in the face of a legal *traditio* which transforms and revises it? Or, furthermore, How does a legal *traditio* attain or assert its author-ity, and to what degree does it emerge as a *datum* in its own right? To the extent that social-scientific and biblical theological perspectives meet or correlate, one may hope that a fuller purchase on the truth will have been achieved.

1. A classification of the dynamics between revelation and tradition with respect to inner-biblical legal exegesis must begin with the *mantic oracles*. In this type, as we have seen, an older revelation is supplemented by a newer one which modifies and reinterprets it for later circum-stances. The procedures are formal and concrete, and, to the extent that the human mediator of the legal oracle speaks, the *responsum* is succinct and *ad hoc* (cf. Lev. 24:14; Num. 15:35, 27:10). Biblical tradition has kept this latter distinct from the more stylized, casuistic rephrasing of the adjudication which generally follows it, wherein the voice of later draftsmen and the deposits of other legal customs and practices have been incorporated (cf. Lev. 24:15-16 + 17-21; Num. 9:10-14, 27:8-11). Nevertheless, each of these stylistic transformations of the *ad hoc* oracles is legitimated as the word of YHWH to Moses. The voice of the human legal *traditio* has been thoroughly subordinated to the divine *traditio*; for which reason alone it has attained the status of an authoritative *traditum*—to be transmitted and studied. The total literary tradition in which the mantic oracles have been preserved thus

preserves two distinct and unmistakable historical layers: the divine oracle, in which the voice of the human *traditio* has been absolutely nullified; and the stylized divine repetition of the oracle in casuistic terms, in which the voice of legists and tradents has been functionally nullified.

Related to the mantic oracle type in the sphere of biblical prophecy are *intuitive oracles*. By this type is not meant the human 'intuitive' derivation of laws, but, as against the foregoing situation where the divine teaching is mediated through technical procedures, here the divine word is communicated directly to the mind of the prophet. Moreover, in such cases as Isa. 56: 4-8, Jer. 17: 21-2, and Ezek. 44: 9-16, the new legal teaching is not the explicit result of legal *quaestiones* posed for a divine *responsum*, but is rather legitimated as immediate divine responses--via the prophets--to concrete historical issues. In the cases just noted, and studied earlier, there are striking exegetical extensions and revisions of the received legal *traditum*. The new divine directive stands out sharply against the past in each case, although it is notable that the legitimation does not rest on divine authority alone: for in each case a rationalization is included. In Isa. 56: 4-8, the eunuchs are incorporated into the community because 'they observe my Sabbaths . . . and hold fast to my covenant'; in Jer. 17: 21-2, the extension of the laws of the Sabbath is presented as that which 'I swore to your forefathers'; and in Ezek. 44: 9-16, the transfer of priestly service to the Zadokites is justified as due to the laxity of the pre-exilic clerics. In all this, there thus appears to be some concession to human reason, as well as a belief, in some circles at least, that the old covenantal laws were neither fixed nor final in any necessary way, but that new legal revelations were possible and fully to be trusted. The revolutionary implications of this belief are self-evident. If new and revisionary divine revelations of law were always possible, the status of any *traditum* would be subtly undermined; the social order based on these *tradita* would be put in jeopardy; and the competition among different groups claiming revelatory legitimacy for innovative (and even self-serving) legislation would be increased in precarious ways. That these are not idle speculations will be justified below.

At this point, however, we must return to the dialectic between revelation and tradition here under review, and note the solution predominant in legistic circles. In the Pentateuchal legal corpora, the prevailing technique may be termed *pseudepigraphic exegesis*.[57] The

---

[57] The discussion of M. Smith, 'Pseudepigraphy in the Israelite Literary Tradition', *Pseudepigrapha*, i, ed. K. von Fritz (Entretiens de la Fondation Hardt, 18; Geneva: Fondation Hardt, 1972), 191-215, is of much value in clarifying pseudepigraphic dimensions in ancient Israel; my attribution of features of inner-biblical legal exegesis to this genre is designed to extend his insights.

incorporation of legal interpretations into the corpora, with and without technical formulae, does not simply mean the subordination of the ongoing human *traditio* to the established and authoritative legal *traditum*. It is, by the same process, a dignification and elevation of human exegesis to the status of divine revelation. For the voice of the human teacher is reauthorized through the voice of Moses, who speaks or repeats the divine revelations given to him. A triple process is thus at work: first, each element of the human legal *traditio* is legitimated by its transformation into a part of the authoritative divine *traditum* given to Moses; second, Moses is thereby transformed from the mediator of specific revelations to the mediator of whatever was spoken in his name, or taught as part of his teachings;[58] and third, the word of YHWH becomes as comprehensive as the *traditum* itself, there being nothing of cultural-religious authority which is not part of the divine revelation.[59] Every legal *traditum*, and every legal *traditio*, thus becomes part of 'the word of YHWH to Moses'. In the narrative historiographies, in fact, where exegetical traditions were not incorporated into any corpora, new human teachings and exegetical blends were authorized as 'according to the word of YHWH through Moses' (cf. 2 Chron. 35: 6), or 'written in the Book of Moses' (cf. 2 Chron. 35: 12).

The development of this process of authorizing or reauthorizing legal traditions by pseudepigraphically ascribing them to Moses from YHWH can be traced, of course, to non-exegetical legal tradition. This can be most clearly recognized in those cases where the body of the law of instruction refers to YHWH in the third person, even though the introit

[58] Cf. the superscriptions to the various instructions in the priestly materials especially; and see the following discussion.

[59] Cf. at the end of the Holiness Code, Lev. 26: 46, the comprehensive attribution of all the stated 'statutes, rules and teachings' to YHWH, through Moses *on Mt. Sinai* – though this is clearly after the original legal revelation; and note the repetition of this comprehensive attribution in Lev. 27: 34, after vv. 1–33. As v. 34 speaks only of 'commandments', it may not so much be an editorial resumption of 26: 46 after an addendum as an attempt to incorporate the teachings of Lev. 27: 1–33 into the Sinaitic corpus. Cf. also the concluding comprehensive attribution of rules and commandments to the plains of Moab in Num. 36:13 (thus including the material from ch. 27; *per* 26:3 this notice involves only the laws in Num. 26–36 – and note the intervening notices in 26: 63, 30: 1, 30: 17, and 34: 29). By contrast, the individual legal superscriptions are dropped in the Book of Deuteronomy, since it purports to be a repetition of earlier laws. Moses is presented as the teacher of all the laws in the comprehensive notice in 1: 5 – though here the word 'Torah' does not refer to individual 'instructions', but rather designates the entire legal *and* historical *traditum*. Of comparative interest is Num 28: 6, where a glossator inserted the notice (within a formulaic cultic description, vv. 5, 7) that the holocaust-offering there described was (like) the kind offered at Mt. Sinai. Possibly this interpolation was designed to serve as a cross-reference to Exod. 24: 5; practically, it served to legitimate (later) ritual praxes as Sinaitic.

presents the material as divinely addressed to Moses (alone, or with Aaron), such that one would expect the divine references to be self-references in the first person.[60] Thus, in Lev. 15, the introduction (v. 1) is followed by divine references in the third person (vv. 14 and 30), and only in the concluding exhortation (v. 31), which stands formally outside the law itself, is there a divine reference in the first person. The materials in Lev. 16: 2 + 3-34, 24: 1 + 2-9, 27: 1 + 2-33, Num. 19: 1 + 2-22, and 20: 2 + 3-16, show a comparable pattern.[61] In all these cases, and probably in many others where the teaching begins with a divine introit, originally anonymous materials have been reauthorized and personalized.[62] Were the materials originally preserved as first-person narrations, one can hardly imagine that this authority would have been effaced for the sake of the preceding pattern — especially when one considers the fact that the authority of the legal teachings rests on their personified, divine character, and especially, too, when one notes cases like Lev. 7: 1 and 11 where the routine pattern of divine ascriptions has not been as carefully followed (cf. Lev. 6: 1-2a + 2b, 12 + 13, and 17-18a + 18b). A particularly striking attempt to refocus old teachings and give them a personified authority occurs in the revelation of the Decalogue, Exod. 20: 2-17. Not only is there an introductory ascription of the material to God in v. 1, which would be redundant were the first-person voice in v. 2 original, but there is the striking shift to YHWH in the third person in vv. 7, 9, 11, and 12. Such a depersonalization of the teaching is unlikely — whether as part of the original rhetoric, or as reflective of a historical development. Much more likely is that an older, anonymous version has been personified by the tradents.[63] This possibility is reinforced by the comparative developments outlined above.

Returning to the priestly materials, the transformation of customary or anonymous materials into those with divine authority even goes as far as the attribution of materials to YHWH through Moses which are never recorded as such in the received legal *traditum* (cf. Num. 31: 21 + 22-4).[64] The same tendency can be observed in the historiographical

---

[60] *Apud* Smith, loc. cit. 201-2.

[61] Cf. the motivational exhortation in Lev. 11: 44-5, after the list of technical instructions (vv. 2-42) and before the subscript (vv. 46-47). The exhortation in Lev. 15: 31 also precedes the subscript (vv. 32-3).

[62] The first-person reference in Lev. 16: 2bβ is part of an explanatory phrase and probably secondary, given the third-person references to YHWH in vv. 7-10, 12-13, 30, 34.

[63] Smith, loc. cit. 200.

[64] This is a very striking case, since Eleazar the priest attributes his recital of the previously given law (vv. 19-20) to YHWH through Moses (v. 21), *even though* (i) v. 15 only indicates that Moses spoke on his own authority; (ii) v. 20 mentions nothing about the purification of metals by fire (cf. vv. 22-3); and (iii) v. 20 mentions nothing about the use of the sacred waters, the *mê niddāh* (cf.

materials where, as noted, innovative cultic practices are explicitly legitimated by ascription to divine authority (cf. 2 Chron. 35: 11 + 12), or where the legitimation is more implicit by virtue of incorporating the custom into authoritative contexts (cf. 2 Chron. 29: 34, 35:14). At any rate, despite the fact that the mode of authorizing materials as part of the revealed *traditum* is more conservative in these priestly and historiographical contexts than in Isa. 56: 4-8, Jer. 17: 21-2, or Ezek. 44: 9-16—where a new divine revelation is openly espoused—the revolutionary theological potential of such attribution procedures, and the potential religious-social conflicts which could develop, are as self-evident for the priestly sources as for the prophetical ones. In fact, reactions to the unrestricted attribution of divine authority to new or customary legal practices can be detected at various points in the Pentateuch, as we shall see.

Pseudepigraphic exegesis thus has its parallels in pseudepigraphic attributions within the legal *traditum* which cannot be considered exegetical by any means. As remarked, they bear witness to the increased tendency to authorize all traditions—be they anonymous laws or the exegetical *traditio*—by divine ascription or attribution. And yet a counter-tendency can be detected, one which may be perceived as a function of the development of rationality among the legal tradents who collected the laws, recombined them, and, of course, commented upon them. This current takes shape within the larger stream of divine authority; and yet there are unmistakable indications of the independent authority of the legists and legal exegetes. Certainly, Num. 15: 22-31 is transitional in this regard. It will be recalled that this material is a legal discourse which takes up, and at once normalizes and develops, the laws regarding ritual errors and their atonements found in Lev. 4. However, in the process of this new teaching, the preacher clearly shifts to his own voice. He says, 'And if you commit an error and do not do . . . all that which YHWH commanded you through Moses' (vv. 22-3). Clearly Moses is not speaking; for even if one were to start with this assumption on the basis of the fact that the preceding paragraph,

v. 23), for metals (non-flammable) and flammable objects (the phrase, *'ak bĕmê niddāh yithattā'* in v. 23aβ is probably a secondary harmonization, requiring use of the sacred waters for the purification of metals as of other materials). Even if Eleazar is referring to the divine command in Num. 19: 1, 14-19, where vessels (vv. 15, 18) and *mê niddāh* (vv. 13, 20-1) are referred to, it would still have to be conceded that in 31: 15-20 Moses is less precise than Eleazar or the 'original' divine ruling (Num. 19); that Eleazar innovates procedures for inflammable objects; and that Moses never indicates his divine authority—which is most singular in these priestly sources. The Samar. version resolves the aforementioned difficulties by introducing after v. 20 a divine command to Moses which establishes the cultic procedures subsequently referred to (vv. 21-4).

beginning in v. 18, presents Moses as speaking, so that the conjunctive 'and' in v. 22 might be assumed to provide a transitional link, the fact that both v. 22 and v. 23 refer to Moses in the third person is sufficient to indicate that Moses is not the speaker. Rather, a legal preacher is the speaker: one who teaches and interprets the divine law. That this *traditio* is now incorporated into the established legal *traditum* not only authorizes and legitimates the new teaching for all time, but indicates that the *traditio* of the exegetical teacher was formally and functionally subordinate to the divine revelation. And, what is more, it means that the teacher does not stand forth alone, on his own authority.

The present consideration that Num. 15: 22-31 is a transitional type, charting the move from divine or divinely legitimated legal exegesis towards independent, *human* exegesis, is of course a purely conceptual, formalistic determination. It should not be taken to imply that Num. 15: 22-31 is *in fact* historically earlier than the independent, human exegesis abundantly found in the post-exilic historiographical texts—for example, the exegetical activities of Ezra and his colleagues in Ezra 9-10, the exegetical innovations of Hezekiah and his councillors in 2 Chron. 30: 2-3, or even the formal legal-exegetical code promulgated by Nehemiah in Neh. 10. To be sure, considerations of genre and the type of circles entrusted with transmitting the tradition undoubtedly played a strong part in the shaping and presentation of these materials. How priestly tradents would transmit their materials, and provide for their authority, would inevitably be different from the way historiographers would transmit the legal-cultic *traditio* of the priests. Nevertheless, given the fact that the dominant resolution of the revelation-tradition dialectic in the Hebrew Bible—the late historiographies included—is to emphasize divine authority and to obscure individual authority, any biblical indications of human exegetical authority are striking and innovative. And since such a development as this last, which becomes most easily observable in the post-exilic period, cannot be assumed to have occurred by a quantum leap, Num. 15: 22-31 may thus serve formally as a mediational type between 'pure' pseudepigraphic exegesis and thoroughly independent human exegesis.

2. It is not necessary to review Weber's entire argument to perceive an overall concordance between his social-scientific perspective of the development of legal rationality and the theological perspective just reviewed. This holds equally for his typological and historical arguments. If any additional comment is necessary it may be the suggestion that Weber's typological factor is of slightly more pertinence for interpreting the biblical data than the historical. Admittedly, Weber regarded his 'types' as pure, rational constructs which enabled him to classify his data and perceive their interrelationship under varying

auspices. Thus, no particular culture had to manifest all of the types (in their own impure ways), or do so in a fixed sequence, for the overall schemata to be valid (for example, cases of 'pure' pseudepigraphic exegesis could coexist with, or follow, mixed types like Num. 15: 22–31, or instances of 'pure' human exegesis like Ezra 9: 1–3). Indeed, Weber's historical sequence is, itself, a formal construction, even though it is abstracted from many historical examples. As a result, no simple correlation between the pure relationship of his types one to the other and their biblical manifestations should be expected. And this turns out to be the case, in fact. For, from the available historical data, one is drawn to the conclusion that biblical religion had the capacity to sustain several types of rationality and diverse modal relationships between revelation and tradition simultaneously. Thus, if mantic oracles and priestly lots are relatively early modes of lawmaking and law-finding in the biblical record, this may indicate early patterns of priestly dominance, but should not be taken to mean that the mantic oracles or the sacral lots were suppressed by other modes. First, there is no information to this end; and second, the occurrence of prophetic legal oracles in the late pre-exilic and early post-exilic record, long after legal codas were collected into corpora, and long after legists and legal exegetes had developed more rational methods for changing, adapting, and reinterpreting older rules of law, is strong testimony for the historical coexistence of different types of legal rationality in ancient Israel. Evidently, different circles of authority were not constrained to relinquish ancient prerogatives; and, most likely, different patterns of accommodation were worked out.

Nevertheless, the possibility that priests, legists, and prophets concerned with the development and continued authority of the legal *traditum* might clash was suggested earlier precisely because each group had its own patterns of legitimating new laws, exegetical innovations, or older customs and rules. Thus, the priests show a particular tendency to preserve the traditions of Moses' desert *responsa*, and to incorporate older legal materials into their corpora by means of patterns of divine reauthorization. The legists, on the other hand, show a preferred tendency to incorporate their materials into the *traditum* itself. They, too, utilize a pseudepigraphic fiction in so far as their exegeses and innovations appear within the overall context of divinely authorized material. Hence these legal exegetes do not introduce their comments with special introits, as do the priests—and prophets. These latter— or the prophetical school traditions which have formulated the teachings of Isa. 56: 4–8, Jer. 17: 21–2, and Ezek. 44: 9–16—introduce their often radical remarks with a legitimation formula, announcing their teaching as a 'word of YHWH'. They thus claim absolute divine authority for the legal content proclaimed.

Given these different legitimation patterns among the different schools, each group could endlessly authorize exegetical innovations, or vaunt their interests, by appeal to the same divine authority as their cogeners. How, then, could such tendencies to expand the authoritative *traditum* be controlled? And how could the tendency to proliferate new and self-serving materials be restrained? Without some mutually agreed limitations, priests could go on adding rules as suited their needs and interests; legists could go on transforming the *traditum* by incorporating their exegetical *traditio* into it; and prophets could announce new legal teachings whenever they felt divinely compelled to, or whenever the attribution of divine authority served their religious or ideological interest (cf. Isa. 56: 1-8 and Ezek. 44: 9-16). Unfortunately, the historical evidence regarding such limitations is sparse; but it js of inestimable value nevertheless. Into this category must go the remark in Deut. 5: 19, where, after the proclamation of the Decalogue (vv. 6-18), reportedly by Moses (v. 5), the text continues with the comment: 'YHWH spoke these words to your entire congregation on the Mount . . . [with] a mighty voice: *and he did not add thereto*; and he wrote them upon the two stone tablets and gave them to me.' Of even more far-reaching significance is the statement found in Deut. 13: 1, 'Everything which I command you, you must take heed to perform: *do not add to it* and do not subtract from it.' Following Deut. 12, which is a radical cultic revision of the rules of altar-building found in the Covenant Code (Exod. 20: 24), and just as much a radical trans- formation of the rules of slaughter found in the Holiness Code (Lev. 17), such a remark is certainly as tendentious as it is programmatic. Moreover, because of the temporal generality of the verb 'which I command' used in this verse, the restriction on innovations and deletions has a broader horizon, and points to the entire deuteronomic corpus of law which follows. Finally, since this deuteronomic corpus is also presented as a repetition of all the past rules and regulations of YHWH to Moses, the restriction on innovations has almost a com- prehensive, dogmatic character—extending to *all* the legal materials of the Pentateuch.

But perhaps the greatest evidence for the eventual resolution of the conflicts which inevitably arose over different modes of legitimating and expanding the legal *traditum*, and for the historical emergence of exegetical rationality as a dominant type, is the historical fact of exile and the very existence of the Pentateuch. As the historical record indicates, the sacred lots were either lost or no longer usable after the exile (Ezra 2: 62~Neh. 7: 65). This, in itself, would have promoted new modes of decision-making among the priesthood. But this is not all. The confluence in the exile of many different priests, each with regional texts and practices, would have been of far greater overall significance.

First, in their meeting in the exile, the diverse priestly and lay traditions which had now become a *public* heritage raised inescapable questions.[65] How could all the different and even conflicting traditions be part of the same Torah of Moses, or derive from the same divine source? And further, how could they be resolved—given the possibility that this could be done, and given the necessity of working out a new national consensus which gave legitimacy to all the teachings of all the peoples who came together in the exile? Inevitably, therefore, new rational modes of exegesis were developed to harmonize and correlate the different legal corpora.[66] Some of these resolutions were incorporated into the Pentateuchal *traditum*, as in Deut. 12: 8-10;[67] others were recorded by historiographers, as the resolution of ritual differences in 2 Chron. 35: 11-12; and still other harmonizations were made part of new covenantal ceremonies and codas, as in the synthesis of sabbatical rules in Neh. 10: 32. But the fact is that most of the resolutions are not recorded in the Hebrew Bible, and thus remained oral—to surface centuries later in early Jewish exegesis among the Pharisees, Dead Sea Covenanters, Sadducees, and Samaritans, or not at all. Still, *the very fact* of the Pentateuch is precious witness to the political, social, and especially exegetical controversies that arose.[68] At the very least, the Pentateuch, with its diverse legal corpora, reflects a great historical compromise among competing religious groups regarding which no record has been preserved.[69] The coexistence within one document of such diverse and contradictory materials is thus a *de facto* indication that an exegetical *modus vivendi* was worked out; that, to use a later rabbinic formula, all the Pentateuchal teachings, both 'these' and 'those' (their origins and redacted nature notwithstanding) are the words of God.[70]

In the volatile furnace in which these diverse and contradictory teachings were smelted, two other factors cannot be overlooked. The

[65] On the public nature of the texts, see the discussions of H. L. Ginsberg, *New Trends in the Study of the Bible* (Essays in Judaism, 4; New York: Jewish Theological Seminary, n.d.), 23, and C. Cohn, 'Was the P Document Secret?', *JANESCU* 1 (1969), 39-45.

[66] Possibly in the exilic synagogues; cf. W. Bacher, *Hastings Dictionary of the Bible*, iv. 535ff. (see above, p. 113 n. 23). Such a *Sitz im Leben* (among others is the precondition for Neh. 8. See above, p. 113. In a much later period, the rabbis still recalled that certain exegeses have 'come to us from the exile'; cf. *Gen. Rab.* xlii. 3.

[67] See above, p. 252.

[68] Cf. M. Smith, *Parties*, 173f., 'Pseudepigripha', 225.

[69] See the pertinent remarks of S. Smith in *The Cambridge Ancient History*, vi (1927), cited above, p. 113 n. 24); also M. Smith, *Parties*, 227.

[70] See *b. Ḥag.* 3a–b, where the issue arose over the multitude of *exegetical* traditions.

first is the issuance of the Persian firman to Ezra. Because of its authoritative character, requiring the returning Judaeans to restore their native traditions, the decree provided a built-in social and political imperative stimulating the teachers and interpreters of the Return to supplement the received *traditum* of the exile—with all its diversity and limitations —and to produce a national consensus of written and oral traditions. This brings us to the second factor. From the time of the exile, and into the post-exilic period, there was a breakdown of older hierarchies of lineage and social status. This can be deduced from (among other things) the intense concern in post-exilic sources with family purity and pedigree lists, and also from the new priestly family patterns and ritual innovations that are advocated and contested. For present purposes, a decisive factor in this breakdown was the fact that the cultic tradition was not practised in the exile. Under such conditions priests could not retain their authority as cult officiants but principally as teachers of the old *traditum*. Group survival without a national cult thus evoked unprecedented challenges, and very much depended, at least in part, upon a sustained consciousness of the ancient *traditum* such as the priests would have been able to provide in gatherings of different sorts. The significant fact that Ezra is initially presented as a teacher of Torah to the post-exilic assemblage in Neh. 8 shows that such practices were not innovated *de novo* upon the Return. However, just this public recitation of the Torah that emphasized lay comprehension further contributed to an atmosphere in which the priests and Levites no longer had a monopoly on the ancient legal *traditum*. Even the most esoteric cultic texts were made public through ritual lections and teachings.[71] This led to a new social fact and a rehierarchizing of religious leadership. From the time of the exile, a new democratic base was prepared in which authority over the *traditum* was an exegetical authority, one which could be wielded by any layman of sufficient training and knowledge. From within the diverse democratic base thus established in the exilic and post-exilic periods there would have been further incentive to co-ordinate the myriad traditions of ancient Israel into one viable whole. The Pentateuch—with its Covenant Code, priestly rules, Holiness Code, and deuteronomic legal corpora—is the synthetic result of such proceedings. The growing consensus among the people on how to correlate the written legal *traditum* would thus have been as much a factor as any other in the eventual limitations put on its growth. It would, therefore, not be mere hyperbole to say that the Pentateuch is the great achievement of early post-exilic legal rationality, or that it is the inner-biblical expression of synthetic legal exegesis *par excellence*.

---

[71] Cf. n. 65, above.

D. A form-critical assessment of inner-biblical legal exegesis is a direct outgrowth of the stylistic, developmental, and contextual issues discussed in previous paragraphs. In the course of that discussion, the great diversity of literary materials in which such exegesis can be found —in mantic oracles, prophetic oracles, legal corpora, legal discourses (e.g. Num. 15: 22-31), mini-corpora (Neh. 10), and in historical narratives—was suggested. However, despite this diversity of literary contexts and genres, *none of these genres are themselves exegetical*, so that the exegeses in them are subordinate to the piece in question. In fact, it appears that there is no distinct exegetical literature or genre to be found in the Hebrew Bible. What is rather to be found is the adjustment of the exegetical component to other literatures and genres. This is, of course, significant in itself: for the incorporation of exegetical materials into other genres gives simultaneous witness to the diverse subordination of inner-biblical legal exegesis to its received *traditum*, and to the literary or scholarly circles within which this exegesis circulated or came to expression. However, as we have seen, the fact that biblical Israel did not develop an independent exegetical literature does not mean that a host of distinct exegetical patterns did not develop. In fact, it has been the particular burden of the preceding chapters to isolate these patterns, and to show just how legal exegesis works in each case.

1. Since the intent of the earlier classification of the various legal exegetical patterns to be found in the Hebrew Bible was primarily to isolate them as historical data, and to enable their techniques and content to be analysed, several comments must be added here of a distinctly stylistic sort. For even if inner-biblical legal exegesis does not constitute a distinct literary form or forms, so that a traditional form-critical inquiry is largely precluded, some form-critical observations can still be made. Principally, I have in mind the fact that *inner-biblical legal exegesis is broadly lemmatic in nature*. By this is meant that in various ways the exegeses are related to an authoritative *traditum*. Such lemmatic exegeses may be further characterized as 'bound', and are manifested in several stylistic forms. One of these may be termed *formal lemmatic exegesis*, and is exemplified by the lectionary-plus-interpretative mode reflected in Neh. 8: 13-16. First the text is read; and then a portion of it is explained, as is necessary. The interpretation is thus not an explanation or reinterpretation of the entire passage, but only of that section of it requiring exegetical comment. There is thus an atomization of its content. Such atomistic exegesis can more clearly be seen in a second stylistic form, one which may be termed *informal lemmatic exegesis*. Here there is no formal break between the textual lemma and the comment, such as occurs in Neh. 8: 13-16, but rather the comment is embedded in the lemma. The interpolations and additions of legal exegeses into the legal corpora are examples of such informal exegesis. For even where technical formulae clearly distinguish between a *traditum* and its *traditio*, there is an attempt to obscure the difference. Admittedly, the legal corpora are literary deposits, and so one must not preclude the high possibility that in legistic study or court sessions teachers first cited a rule, or a portion thereof, and then added its commentary. But it is interesting to note that in Num. 15: 22-31, an oral discourse, the lemmata from Lev. 4 are also not formally distinguished from the interleaving and supplementary remarks.[72] Indeed, by not formally distinguishing between the two, the preacher or legist is able to achieve singular authority for his additions and innovations. Perhaps Lev. 25: 20-2 may be considered a mediating type between the formal and informal modes just mentioned. There the rhetor clearly interrupts his teaching with an interpretation of the preceding rules on the sabbatical and jubilee years—so that there is a somewhat formal break between the lemmata and the exegesis; but he also presents the interpretation in the course of a rhetorical question—so that there is the distinct implication that the reinterpretation was in the teacher's mind all along, and no break between lemmata and exegesis is to be presumed.

A third stylistic form of inner-biblical legal exegesis may be termed *implied lemmatic exegesis*. This occurs in 'bound' and 'free' varieties. In the first category mention should be made of Ezra 9: 1-3, 11-12. In the polemical speech of the princes to Ezra, vv. 1-3, an old Pentateuchal prescription from Deut. 7: 1-3 was reused, by implication, and several other nations were interpolated into that older list. The force of the exegetical polemic is thus bound to a Pentateuchal lemma, and the innovation is made contextual with it. Of a similar sort is Ezra's response. As noted earlier, his remarks are bound to phrases from Lev. 18 and Deut. 23. The force of his exegetical response is therefore not dependent upon any atomization and direct reinterpretation of the lemmata implied; it rather carries weight by virtue of the contextual juxtaposition of the citations. There is thus a cumulative rhetorical force to the passages linked; and a new *exegetical* meaning arises from their interrelationship. In this boundedness to lemmata, the exegeses of Ezra 9: 1-3, 11-12 must be distinguished from the prophetic oratory of Isa. 56: 4-8 and Ezek. 44: 9-16. While it is the case that both of these oratories have an implied lemmatic base in Num. 18, as argued earlier, the fact that these sermons occur outside the legal corpora and are presented as a *new* word of God gives them—form-critically

---

[72] And cf. the homiletical expansion of the lemma *lō 'tō 'kĕlennû* in Deut. 12: 25 —cited from v. 25. No elaboration occurs after the parallel formulation in Deut. 12: 16. The expansionary form of Deut. 12: 23 f. may also be noted by comparison with the concise formulation in v. 16.

speaking—a 'free' character. Their exegetical force is not bound to implied lemmata, but is formally free of them, being bound only to the independent word of God. The implied lemmata provide, as it were, the base metals which are refined in the fire of a new legal revelation; they even provide the ore of the older *traditum* which is being mined in a new era: but they are not formally necessary. The new teaching would still have authoritative force without them.

2. The absence of distinct legal exegetical genres in the Hebrew Bible, and our historical dependence upon survivals of stylistic patterns within other genres, put severe constraints on the second stage of a form-critical inquiry: the assessment of the *Sitz im Leben*, or life-context, to which the literary record bears witness and from which it arises. Among the data, the evidence from the Books of Ezra and Nehemiah is most conducive to a full analysis. Here a full spectrum of exegetical activities are described with some social–historical precision. In Ezra 9: 1–3, 11–12, Ezra and his princes engage in religious polemics against the peoples of the land; and in Ezra 10: 2–4 an exegetical adjudication is offered. The counter-exegesis of the opposite group is naturally not recorded in these historical documents which preserve and promote the vested religious interests of Ezra's party. But such exegetical rebuttals must have existed for this occasion, and for those reflected in Neh. 13: 1–3, 25–6. The polemical exegesis in Isa. 56: 4–8 and Ezek. 44: 9–16 are undoubtedly related to the problems of purity of lineage and cult praxis reflected in Ezra–Nehemiah; but whether we have the right to see here the toe-to-toe repartee of exegetical claim and counter-claim in one historical moment is less certain.[73]

As one moves away from this evidence, the assessment of a *Sitz im Leben* for any given piece becomes more and more suppositious. At one level, for example, the mantic oracles preserved in the Books of Leviticus and Numbers by priestly traditions manifest a clear life-setting: there is a legal crisis and a subsequent recourse to a divine oracle. But whether the literary account accurately preserves a record of events that actually took place is another matter. They may just as easily be narrative paradigms of types of mantic inquiries which could have taken place in the desert in principle, since they undoubtedly took place in ancient Israelite history in fact. Hence, no conclusive answer can be offered. On the other hand, there is the case of Num. 15: 22–31, where the life-setting of a legal discourse breathes throughout the piece, and yet it is impossible even to guess when or where it may have occurred.

---

[73] Rather than attempt to see all these texts as direct responses or counter-responses of contesting groups, it may be best to see them as typical of the competing exegeses in post-exilic Judaea.

The same problem attaches to other cases where the presence of a rhetor is felt, like Exod. 34: 21 and Lev. 25: 20-2.

With materials like the Pentateuchal legal corpora, one is in an even less fortunate position. The existence of legal exegeses within this literary genre provides merely the illusion of knowing their *Sitz* in any meaningful sense. For the exegeses resist historical contextualization. Numerous questions beg solution. Are the various exegeses of the corpora to be regarded as practical solutions, or as the reflex of theoretical deliberations? Are they the product of draftsmen, legistic scholars, or even jurists? Do they reflect the way the rules of law were commonly handled in the oral legal tradition, or are they the prescriptions of an élite few? And, if these questions are irresolvable with respect to the legal corpora, what must be said of the legal exegeses found in the historiographies? Does 2 Chron. 30: 2-3 reflect historical reality or is it mere narrative? Did Hezekiah and his councillors actually reach the exegetical resolution propounded, or is it a solution attributed to them by the historiographer? Does the blend in 2 Chron. 35: 12-13 reflect the historian's personal solution to the contradictory traditions regarding performance of the paschal-offering, or does he merely bring an oral tradition of scholars to literary articulation? Such a catena of questions brings one up sharply before the inherent limitations of the preserved sources, in so far as all assertions regarding the social-historical *Sitz im Leben* of legal exegeses in the Pentateuchal legal corpora and the post-exilic historiographies are concerned.

But the legal historian need not bow out due to total lack of information; for the negative results of the preceding paragraphs only serve to sharpen what can be asserted about the 'setting' of inner-biblical legal exegesis. For no matter how much or how often instances of inner-biblical legal exegesis arose from concrete cases and real-life issues, there would always be occasions where the mere fact of a written *traditum* provided the life-context of interpretation. More precisely, such a life-context was a *textual context*. In such circumstances, tradents, legists, and jurists studied the *traditum* which came to hand. Its verbal and semantic character, in a word, its *textual* character, provided the setting for new exegeses.[74] Legists would study the text, recognize ambiguities or loopholes, and supplement the text with new

---

[74] Comparative anthropologists, focusing on the role and impact of writing in society, have pointed to a paradox of some pertinence to the present discussion: namely, that while written traditions are conservative and resistent to change, writing provides the occasion for a comparison of alternative systems, and for seeing alternative contexts for information or contradictions. This may lead to changes. See J. Goody, *The Domestication of the Savage Mind* (Cambridge: Cambridge University Press 1977), 11, 43. Of course, one could substitute 'fixed' for 'written' traditions and perceive the same dynamic.

materials; historians would study the text, or learn about its ambiguities from legists; and polemicists would study the text, or comb it for allusions, in order to justify their cause or promote their interests. Certainly the involvement of ancient Israelite literati with the closed 'world' of a textual *traditum* and its formulations was not to the exclusion of the many conjunctions and disjunctions possible between texts and ongoing life. But it does help sharpen the focus on another 'setting' which must be recognized: the *mental matrix* of the interpreter. Exegesis is not simply an event in the social world, or one which arises out of texts. It is also one which presupposes certain mental attitudes.[75] Among these, the recognition of an authoritative *traditum* and the concomitant requirement to live within its constraints is one; another is the predisposition to study the textual *traditum*, to be sensitive to its ambiguities, conflicts, and contradictions, and to know how to resolve them. In brief, the fact that all textual exegesis—legal exegesis included —takes shape in a distinct mode of consciousness that regards texts as a basic *datum* of existence, and which is particularly activated by correlations within texts and between them and life, means that the mental standpoint of the interpreter is a most decisive variable.

If we wished, then, to characterize the issue of *Sitz im Leben* as it pertains to inner-biblical legal exegesis, it would be necessary to say that its life-settings are layered and interrelated—consisting of mental, textual, and social-historical modes. This triadic structure was always in interplay, though with different patterns of emphasis in different circumstances. Because of the nature of our textual information, the third of these three modes—the social-historical—is not always in evidence. But it must always be presumed, even as the mental and textual aspects of legal exegesis must never be factored out of any analysis, however skimpy the factual evidence. In time, moreover, with the onset of classical Jewish legal exegesis in all its historical congeries, the mental and textual modes became increasingly predominant; so that, ultimately, it might be possible to say that social and historical circumstances became matrices for legal exegesis precisely because the mental and textual character of biblical exegesis had become a pre-eminent cultural value.

3. Reflections on the triadic structure of the 'life-setting' of inner-biblical legal exegesis are to be supplemented by a complementary triadic structure, which gives some further precision to the various

---

[75] Here I am particularly indebted to A. Jolles's discussion of the relationship between 'elementary genres' (*einfache Formen*) and their literary counterparts, and the underlying 'occupation of mind' (*Geistesbeschäftigung*)—its preoccupations and orientations. See his *Einfache Formen*[2] (Darmstadt: Wissenschaftliche Buchgesellschaft, 1958).

stimuli which occasioned ancient Israelite legal exegesis. Thus, it will be noted that the common denominator underlying the social-historical, textual, and mental settings of legal exegesis is *conflict*. In the social-historical arena this may take at least two forms. First and foremost one must consider conflicts between different interest-groups or exegetes over the true or applied meaning of a text. In the early post-exilic period there were clearly several groups which expressed rival claims to the *traditum*, its interpretation, and its practice. That this great crisis arose from the conditions of the exile is entirely understandable. As noted earlier, the Pentateuch is the silent witness to this conflict and its resolution; even as the events recorded in the Books of Ezra-Nehemiah, and in various oracles in the late portions of the Books of Isaiah and Ezekiel, provide their vocal counterpart.

A second mode wherein social-historical conflict could result in new legal exegesis is where life-circumstances were perceived to be discordant with the *traditum*. These required resolutions of one sort or another, and actually provide a transition to conflicts of a purely textual nature which elicited exegetical solutions. For the dissonance between life and text points up the insufficiency of texts in relationship to life-requirements. It is therefore part of an analytical continuum wherein insufficiencies, conflicts, and contradictions within any one formulation of the legal *traditum*, or between several, are recognized. This perception of textual and inter-textual conflicts of various orders is, of course, a function of the mental matrix of the legist who studies and analyses the legal *traditum* in its full variety. Resolution of this type of conflict is exegesis itself. However, in contradistinction to the triadic structure of life-setting, where all three modes—the social-historical, the textual, and the mental—were simultaneously present in each case of exegesis, *even though different modes might predominate at any one time*, there is no inevitable simultaneity when it comes to conflicts related to texts and their resolution. Most naturally, conflicts in the social-historical arena over texts or claims to texts involve all three modes. But the pure study of legal materials by legists and historians as a textual 'event' in its own right will be independent—resolutely or for theoretical reasons—of social conflicts. And many other mediating positions can be imagined.

E. A form-critical consequence of the generally lemmatic nature of inner-biblical legal exegesis and the fact that its patterns are embedded in other genres, is that these latter have been transformed into *Mischgattungen*, or 'mixed genres'. The Pentateuchal legal corpora are mixed with many instances of exegetical *traditio*; the legal discourse in Num. 15: 22–31 is supplemented by expansionary comments and additions; the narrative histories are replete with exegetical corrections, harmonizations, and innovations of earlier legal materials and practices; most of the mantic oracles in the Pentateuch have been transmitted together with casuistic legal prescriptions, and these often bear the mark of interpolations (cf. Lev. 24:10-12 + 13-16 + 17-21 + 22-3); and finally, even the citations in polemical orations are mixed with interpolations (Ezra 9:1b), or mixed by virtue of their recontextualization and associational juxtaposition.

1. The existence of *Mischgattungen* has several broad implications pertinent to the nature of inner-biblical legal exegesis. First, their presence helps to underscore the basic exegetical reality that the closed form of a *traditum* is opened up and sustained by an exegetical *traditio*. Whether that *traditum* is part of the divine legal revelation or is part of a historiographical account of practices, it attains new life in the ongoing community of faith which reinterprets it in the course of its transmission. Naturally, the theological implications are more radical in the first case than in the second. For the insertion of a human teaching and correcting voice into the context of a divine teaching and prescribing voice serves to highlight the fact that the divine *traditum* survives only in so far as it is transmitted, only in so far as its meanings are understood, and often only to the extent that its meanings are altered or transformed. The embeddedness of the human *traditio* in the *traditum* thus camouflages the dependence of the divine word upon its human transmission and interpretation as well as the very insufficiencies of the divine word which require interpretation and supplementation in the first place. It camouflages the fact that once the divine legal *traditum* is given over to human receivers, it enters on a new and altered course.

These reflections lead to a second implication: the authority of the legal exegesis propounded lies in its relationship to the *traditum*. The *Mischgattung* requires one to recognize that the human exegetical voice, the voice of *traditio*, is a subordinate voice. The divine *traditum* precedes each *traditio*, sets its course, and guarantees it religious-social authority. Thus, just as the legal exegeses in the Hebrew Bible are dominated by the genres in which they are found, the *traditum* has a hierarchical pre-eminence over each and every *traditio*. Indeed, the *traditio* does not exist for its own sake, but solely for the sake of the *traditum* to which it is attached.

A third implication of the existence of *Mischgattungen* is that it shows the attempt by literary tradents to accommodate older genres to the lemmatic reality of inner-biblical legal exegesis. And thus it furthermore heralds the emergence of new, autonomous exegetical genres in later Jewish exegesis. The significance of this implication can fully be appreciated when one recalls that the very designation *Mischgattung* has been a term of opprobrium among practitioners of form criticism.

These have tended to regard *Gattungen* as pure forms, and so regard the interaction between genres, or the impact of one upon the other, as a contamination of sorts – as the devolution of a literary genre historically viewed. But such a historical perspective is tendentious and somewhat misprizes the inner development of literature. For if one does not look from a 'pure' *Gattung* downward, but in the opposite direction, and allows the transformation of literary genres a positive role, it is not a literary devolution which is perceived *but an evolution in fact*. Viewed with an eye to the exegetical genres which were yet to unfold in ancient Jewish legal exegesis, the biblical *Mischgattungen* are a sign of growth and inner life. They do not so much reflect a somewhat desperate attempt of literary tradents to accommodate inner-biblical legal exegesis to pure genres, as their desire and concern to give value to the ongoing *traditio* while not relinquishing the deposits of *traditum* which helped bring it into being. Very much depends, therefore, on whether the latter-day historian chooses to emphasize the foreground – the *traditio* – or the background – the *traditum* – of the *Mischgattung*. The truth lies, no doubt, somewhere in the middle.

2. The historical coexistence of various *Mischgattungen* bearing exegetical content in the post-exilic period is itself a fact of cultural and literary significance. As far as its cultural significance is concerned, the diversity of genres in which legal exegeses may be found says something about the overall *Sitz im Leben* of legal exegesis; namely, that in the post-exilic period there was a remarkable flowering of exegesis which developed in various contexts and was sponsored by a variety of circles of tradition and study. The renewed study of the legal *traditum* occasioned by the exile and its aftermath sought many literary avenues of expression. There was apparently no monopoly on the right to derive new meanings from the old *traditum*, or to clarify and extend its content. The coexistence of legal exegesis in priestly materials, legistic corpora, prophetic discourses, historical narratives, and records preserving synagogal paraphrases and polemical *obiter dicta* is clear proof of that.

This leads to the second point, bearing on literary history. There is no reason to suppose that the various genres preserving legal exegesis in the Hebrew Bible reflect some historical sequence of the ways exegetical comments were preserved. One can surely not say, for example, that when the Pentateuchal legal corpora reached some saturation point in their capacity to absorb exegeses these latter were recorded in the historiographies. First, the materials preserved in the corpora are different from those in the historiographies, by and large; second, the Septuagint and Samaritan Pentateuchs show just how much more exegesis these legal corpora could absorb; and third, there is no historical reason to come to any such conclusion or variation thereof. Indeed, an unbiased view would simply show that the different genres show their own modes of absorption and reflection of legal exegesis—and this in a simultaneous variety. Moreover, an even closer look at this historical simultaneity of genres in which legal exegesis found expression shows that it is paralleled by other simultaneous clusters in other formative periods of early Jewish legal exegesis. For example, corresponding to the legal exegeses interpolated into the Pentateuchal legal corpora in ancient Israel there are the diverse comments woven into the Pentateuch laws in the Temple Scroll from Qumran and in the Samaritan version of the Pentateuch; corresponding to legal exegeses incorporated within historical narratives, like the Books of Chronicles, there is the evidence embedded in the Damascus Document from Qumran and the Book of Jubilees; corresponding to the publication of a topical series of rules regarding lay support of the Temple in Neh. 10, wherein the new rules are not always exegetically derived or justified, there are the diverse topical collections of rules in the Damascus Document from Qumran, and the old topical collections now preserved in the Mishnah but which once had an independent existence (cf. the list in *M. Soṭa* viii. 1-2);[76] and finally, corresponding to the legal discourse in Num. 15: 22-31 there are the assorted fragmentary discourses to be found among the Qumran scrolls and in the transcripts of early sermons preserved both in the classical Jewish collections of Midrash and in the aggadic portions of the Babylonian Talmud.

One upshot of the striking parallelisms just noted is that early Jewish literature was not quick to transform the genres it inherited from ancient Israel. This is particularly noteworthy given the fact that these genres had *already* been mixed with exegetical content in ancient Israel. Early Judaism in some ways, then, perceived the exegetical *Mischgattungen* of the Hebrew Bible as *Gattungen* in their own right, and built on them for their own purposes. A second upshot of the parallelisms goes a step further in adjusting or qualifying the modern perspective on the development of legal exegetical genres in ancient Israel. For one of the most recurrent and energetic debates in traditional and modern Jewish scholarship concerns the historical relationship of legal Midrash to Mishnah, that is, between a genre which is lemmatic and one which is

---

[76] Thus, based on the list in *M. Soṭa* vii. 1-2, we may infer the existence of earlier mini-series on such topics as 'the unfaithful woman' (cf. *M. Soṭa* i-vi), 'the confession of tithes' (cf. *M. Maʿaś. Š.* v. 10-15), 'the lection over the first fruits' (cf. *M. Bik.* iii. 1-8; also *M. Pesaḥ.* x. 4), 'the unshoeing' (cf. *M. Yebam.* xii. 6), 'the king' (cf. *M. Sanh.* ii. 4; also 11Q *Torah* lvi. 16), 'the expiation for unsolved murder' (cf. *M. Soṭa* ix. 1-8), and 'the proclamation before battle' (cf. *M. Soṭa* viii. 1-7). For another mini-series, cf. the 'Order of the Day of Atonement' (*M. Yoma* i. 3 ff.).

hardly ever explicitly, and very rarely implicitly, so. Among other arguments, proponents of the relative priority of Midrash claim that new laws were first derived exegetically from Scripture, which gave them legitimacy, and only subsequently, whether because of the overflow of these lemmatic derivations or simply in the interests of stylistic economy, were the laws published as a Mishnah without the exegetical support being given.[77] Proponents of the opposite viewpoint contend, in the main, that the source of the Halakha is in pure oral tradition, not exegetical tradition; and that this latter is merely a Tannaitic adjunct and interpretation after the fact.[78]

In recent times, moderating and modifying positions of the Midrash-Mishnah controversy have been offered, developing or emphasizing one point or another,[79] and still other innovative reconstructions have been put forth.[80] Their elaboration cannot serve our purpose here, which is, in fact, at distinct cross-purposes with the entire attempt to focus on the relative priority of the genres. For when one goes behind the Tannaitic sources of the Pharisees there is some reason to suspect that lemmatic and non-lemmatic legal exegeses are best regarded as different genres which reflect different styles of presentation, and which coexisted from earliest times. This, at any rate, would be the most reasonable conclusion to be drawn from the simultaneous presence at Qumran of the Temple Scroll, with its extensive lemmatic exegetical supplementations and reworkings of many Pentateuchal laws (from Exodus, Leviticus, Numbers, and Deuteronomy), and the Damascus Document, with its essentially non-lemmatic lists of halakhic prescriptions. Moreover, while the evidence is far more tenuous, the same conclusion would appear to be rooted in the even earlier, biblical material—as represented by the coexistence of texts like Num. 15: 22-31, with its proto-lemmatic exposition of Lev. 4, and Neh. 10, with its essentially non-lemmatic presentation of official rules. In fact, the coexistence within Neh. 10 of normative prescriptions both exegetically and non-exegetically derived (or justified) further indicates that such a 'mixture' of types could even be found *in one and the same text*. The most remarkable proof of this stylistic coexistence is, of course, the Temple

---

[77] J. Lauterbach, 'Midrash and Mishnah', in *Rabbinic Essays*, 163-256.

[78] Y. Halevi, *Dorot ha-Ri'šonim* (Frankfurt-on-Main: J. Goklau, 1906; repr. Jerusalem, 1967), iii/1. 292ff., v. 467ff.

[79] Cf. C. Albeck, 'The Halakha and the Legal Sermons', *Alexander Marx Jubilee Volume* (New York: Jewish Theological Seminary, 1950), *1-8 [Heb. section], and J. N. Epstein, *Mebo'ot le-Siphrut ha-Tanna'im* (Jerusalem and Tel Aviv: The Magnes Press and The Devir Co. Ltd., 1957), 501ff.

[80] Cf. the proposal of E. E. Urbach, 'The Exegetical Sermon', and also the contentions of J. Neusner, 'The Meaning of *Torah Shebe'al Peh* with special Reference to *Kelim* and *Ohalot*', *AJS Review*, 1 (1976), 151-70.

Scroll itself. There, normative prescriptions with exegetical supplements exist side by side with others, collected in lists of rules in topical order. To speak of the Temple Scroll as a *Mischgattung* would be no more apposite than to characterize the Book of Deuteronomy by the same terms. Indeed, such labelling ignores the very anthological nature of ancient biblical and Jewish literary sources, and the coexistence in them of different 'types' of traditional materials.

F. It has been the particular burden of this entire part to suggest an answer to the general question posed in the Introduction: namely, how did a tradition endowed with religious dignity come to be formed? Discussion was limited to the phenomenon of legal exegesis, and the diverse social, historical, and ideological factors which comprise it. In this final section these several lines of argument will not be resummarized. I shall rather limit myself to one theological consideration, and to one historical-theological implication related to it.

From a theological point of view, the historical development of the idea of a legal-exegetical tradition endowed with religious dignity is a direct consequence of the growth of the human legal *traditio* under the auspices of the legal *traditum* believed to be of divine origin. 'Under the auspices' is, to be sure, a wide-winged designation; but it does span several factors which may be recalled here: first, that the *traditio* developed in tandem with the *traditum* and in relation to its formulations, constraints, and possibilities; and second, that the *traditio* is preserved in the main within a legal *traditum*, or is justified by relationship to it (for example, that it *is* part of the 'Torah of Moses'). Thus, it is the scope, the insufficiency, or the very existence of the *traditum* which provide the occasions for and place of the exegetical *traditio* in the literary culture; it is the study of the *traditum* which provides the historical legitimation for the *traditio* which responds to it; and it is the theological and literary character of the *traditum* which dignifies the *traditio* incorporated within it, and which ultimately transforms that *traditio* into a part of the authoritative legal *traditum*.

This leads us, finally, to the second point. The representation of the legal *traditio* as part of the legal *traditum* has the effect of transforming, for the legal tradents at least, the closed sense of the *traditum*. For those who participated in this process, the legal *traditum* would inevitably appear as a historical *datum* which sponsors and incorporates new and often transformative exegetical meanings. Correspondingly, the legal *traditio* would appear as that which explores and even reveals the full potential of the legal *traditum* to deal with new historical circumstances. In a word, an exegetical *traditio* faithful to the determinants of the *traditum* would be preserved and acknowledged as its true historical ally — not as an alien factor. Indeed, one may suspect that the tradents and draftsmen of ancient Israel, who preserved the *traditio* as part of the *traditum*, may even have perceived the *traditio* as having some divine status from its very onset – if only in the sense that the *traditio* was understood as part of the full potential of the original legal revelation. For to the extent that the *traditum* was believed to make sense, and its formulations were considered valid, these had to make sense and be valid in all ways. Hence, obscurities in the *traditum* had to be clarified; its (real or apparent) implications drawn out; its incomprehensiveness supplemented; and its contradictions shown to be more apparent than real. From this perspective, the exegetical *traditio* is a task with sacred responsibilities, since it partakes of the power and authority of the divine *traditum* itself. There would thus develop, over many generations and with different rationales, the notion that the original written legal *traditum* may be – and often must be – supplemented by a legal exegetical *traditio* which is inspired by it, and that the continuous inspiration of the *traditum* upon its faithful exegetes is nothing other than the continuous revelation of God through that *traditum*.

In later generations, the Pharisees did, in fact, reach such a conclusion. As the latter-day tradents of biblical materials, there is no reason to deny that they have preserved an earlier ancient Israelite tradition. Moreover, may it not also be validly supposed that the authoritative status which the Pharisees eventually gave their oral legal exegesis – such that this *traditio* was accepted as a virtual second Torah supplementing the primary written *traditum* – may also in part derive from an older tradition which remembered that the final legal *traditum* of the Hebrew Bible is itself a blend of human *traditio* and divine *traditum*? To come to this conclusion is not to bypass the complex historical and social reasons which induced the early Pharisees to promulgate their notion of an open oral Torah, separate from the closed written Torah, with particular vigour. It is merely to propose that underlying the Pharisaic doctrine of two Torahs may be an older inner-biblical tradition which had long since endowed species of the legal-exegetical *traditio* with an authoritative, even divine, status.

PART THREE

AGGADIC EXEGESIS

10. Introduction. Preliminary Considerations

1. Although a historically laden term, *aggadah* may nevertheless serve aptly to denote that category and range of inner-biblical exegesis which is strictly speaking neither scribal nor legal, on the one hand, nor concerned with prophecies or futuristic oracles, on the other. For the ancient rabbis, who first used this term, *aggadah* was similarly comprehensive in scope, and applied to moral and theological homilies, didactic expositions of historical and folk motifs, expositions and reinterpretations of ethical dicta and religious *theologoumena*, and much more.[1] In brief, the *aggadah* of the ancient rabbis encompasses 'all scriptural interpretation which is non-halakhic in character'.[2] At times, this aggadic exegesis is intimately related to fixed Scriptural lemmata, as in the homilies and expositions on the Pentateuch preserved, for example, in the great Midrash collections of late antiquity; at other times, florilegia, or anthological text-tapestries, are woven from older texts in order to produce a teaching which, in fact, is quite independent of the teachings which comprise its warp and woof. As distinct from the process of halakhic exegesis, which is concerned with developing and expounding the law, aggadic exegesis was at once theological and reflective, moral and practical. It was a mode of textual interpretation thoroughly charged with the religious ethos of Judaism. And further, for all its apparent naïvety and topical freedom, the ancient rabbinic *aggadah* was the product of sophisticated rhetors and teachers, and was replete with its own established hermeneutical canon of procedure and style.[3] To be sure, the inner-biblical precursor of this great exegetical tradition obviously did not benefit from centuries of hermeneutical

---

[1] See W. Bacher, 'The Origin of the Word Haggada (Agada)', *JQR* OS 4 (1892), 406–29, and the literature and texts discussed. This piece was expanded and revised in his *Die Agada der Tannaiten* (Strasburg: K. Trübner, 1903), i. 451–75 (and cf. 475–89).

[2] H. L. Strack, *Introduction to the Talmud and Midrash* (Philadelphia and New York: Jewish Publication Society and Meridian, 1959), 7.

[3] For the 'Thirty-two Hermeneutical Principles of R. Eliezer ben Jose Ha-gelili', see the text in H. G. Enelow, ed., *The Mishna of R. Eliezer* (New York: Bloch, 1933). For discussions of the rules, see Strack, op. cit., 95–8; Lieberman, *Hellenism*, 68–22. For the dating of this collection to the Geonic period, see M. Zucker, 'Towards the Solution of the Problem of the 32 Middot and "The Mishnat R. Eliezer"', *PAAJR* 23 (1952–4), 1–39 [Heb.].

refinement in the synagogue and study-house. Nevertheless, it will be seen that the range of inner-biblical aggadic exegesis is as broad as its rabbinic inheritor, and considerably refined in its techniques and canons of exposition.

In order further to clarify the sphere of aggadic exegesis as it pertains to inner-biblical materials, a comparison of it with legal exegesis may prove helpful. Indeed, such a comparison will serve to isolate pertinent differences of scope and concern between legal and aggadic exegesis, and thus help delineate that area within which inner-biblical aggadic exegesis operates. It will be recalled that, in terms of its scope, inner-biblical legal exegesis is singularly concerned with the reinterpretation (or extension or reapplication) of pre-existing legal texts. By contrast, aggadic exegesis utilizes pre-existing legal materials, but it also makes broad and detailed use of moral dicta, official or popular *theologoumena*, themes, motifs, and historical facts. In a word, aggadic exegesis ranges over the entire spectrum of ideas, genres, and texts of ancient Israel. It is these which form the basis of its textual transformations, reapplications, and reinterpretations.

This leads to the second point of difference between legal and aggadic exegesis, their concerns. Inner-biblical legal exegesis, as explored earlier, is distinctively concerned with making pre-existent laws applicable or viable in new contexts. Moreover, as part of a prescriptive corpus of rules regulating covenantal behaviour, legal exegesis is concerned—both theoretically and practically—with actions based on the received *traditum* or its revised *traditio*. By contrast, aggadic exegesis is primarily concerned with utilizing the full range of the inherited *traditum* for the sake of new theological insights, attitudes, and speculations. Action may, to be sure, be a result (or even intent) of a creative theological reworking of the *traditum* when rhetorically addressed to the covenantal community; but action, or its prescription, is not a necessary characteristic of aggadic exegesis.

2. A comparison of legal and aggadic exegesis suggests at least one further significant difference, the exigencies which occasion exegesis. Earlier, both the relative incomprehensiveness of the legal *traditum* with respect to the topoi collected in the legal corpora and the frequent incomprehensibility (or indeterminacy) of its articulations were emphasized as inherent reasons for the production of biblical legal exegesis. Slightly reformulated, it may be said that the existence or perception of some *lack* in the *traditum* is a significant condition for the rise of legal exegesis. Indeed, such a reformulation also helps to focus on an allusive dimension of aggadic exegesis, since, in contrast to legal exegesis, *fullness* is a significant condition for its emergence. That is: it is precisely because certain features of the received *traditum* are comprehensible,

and predominate in the imagination or memory of its tradents – or, at any rate, it is precisely because certain features of the *traditum* are actively present in the mind of those tradents entrusted with its preservation and reformulation – that they are reused in aggadic exegesis.

Aggadic exegesis is thus not content to supplement gaps in the *traditum*, but characteristically draws forth latent and unsuspected meanings from it. In this way, aggadic exegesis utilizes the potential fullness of received formulations and makes this potential actual. For if inner-biblical legal exegesis particularly serves to fill a felt lack in the *traditum*, and to clarify for all practical or theoretical purposes the plain sense of a Scriptural dictum, inner-biblical aggadic exegesis, by contrast, gives particular emphasis to its *sensus plenior*, its fullness of potential meanings and applications. Legal exegesis and aggadic exegesis thus illumine different facets of a text's inherent possibilities: the one, legal exegesis, shows how a particular law can be clarified and reinterpreted *qua* law; while the other, aggadic exegesis, characteristically shows how a particular law (or topos, or *theologoumenon*) can transcend its original focus, and become the basis of a new configuration of meaning.

3. Self-evidently, an analysis of the strategic reuses of prior *tradita* in aggadic exegesis presupposes a careful methodological distinction between the sponsoring *traditum* and the creative *traditio* of it. But because of the various ways that prior *tradita* were taken over – sometimes through creative recombination of earlier words or topoi, at other times through complex transformations of them – and also because of the imprecise or indirect ways that the aggadic rhetors and tradents revitalized the inherited stream of traditions, this task is not without its difficulties, as is apparent from the pitfalls which have trapped previous researchers.

Earlier, in the Introduction, it was argued that even the discernible variations in such parallel scenarios as the 'Matriarch of Israel in Danger' may not be *exegetically* interrelated – so that Gen. 26 is not a reworking of Gen. 20, and it, in turn, a moralistic revision of Gen. 12: 10-20, as contended by Koch and Sandmel. For it may rather be the case that a core tradition pre-existed or underlies these diverse narratives. If this be the true nature of things, each of the scenarios would then be a separate development of a common type-scene, and the notable variations between them would indicate different versions of this type-scene in different cultural circles: none would be a specific exegetical comment on the other. Certainly this cautionary argument, like other methodological considerations which may be applied to putative cases of aggadic exegesis, is tricky, and may, on occasion, dismiss viable examples. Nevertheless, given the loose and incautious way the notion of reinterpretation has been used in some discussions, it may be the better part of wisdom to err on the side of extreme caution.[4] This is all the more vital since the occurrence of introductory citation formulae in inner-biblical aggadic exegesis is all but absent. One of the rare instances of an explicit citation formula followed by an exegetical revision occurs in Ezek. 18. This text, as we shall have occasion to observe in closer detail below, first introduces an old proverb regarding fathers who eat sour grapes but whose children find their teeth set on edge, with the phrase לאמר 'as follows' (v. 2), and then goes on to reject this proverb (v. 3) by means of an elaborate aggadic reworking (vv. 4-32).[5] Similarly, Ezekiel's contemporary Jeremiah begins 3:1, which contains a passage strikingly similar to the law found in Deut. 24:1-4, with the citation formula לאמר, and then proceeds to reinterpret its contents (vv. 2-5). Or again, the post-exilic prophet Haggai is told to 'question the priests on a matter of Torah, לאמר as follows' (2:11). There follows, in vv. 12-13, a ritual question based on the priestly laws and regulations, together with a prophetic reapplication of it to the post-exilic community (v. 14). In all such cases, neither the objective status of the revised *traditum*, nor its hermeneutical relationship to the *trǎditio* is in doubt. The objectivity of an aggadic revision is also not to be doubted in those few cases, notably in the Book of Jeremiah, where an older *traditum* is referred to prior to its rejection (3:16-17, 16:14-15∼23:7-8, 31:28-9; cf. 31:30-3).[6]

---

[4] A comparison of Exod. 17:1-7 and Num. 20:1-13 is particularly instructive in this respect, for these two texts present comparable traditions of miraculous acts in the desert, when Moses smote a rock and water gushed forth. Apparently independently, both J. Koenig, in 'Sourciers, thaumaturges et scribes', *RHR* 164 (1963), 17-38, 165-80, and A. Rofé, in 'Classes in the prophetical stories: Didactic legenda, and parable', *SVT* 26 (1974), 152, have argued that the second of these texts is less 'magical' in character than the first, and also a 'spiritualizing' interpretation of it. However, it should be noted that even this so-called non-magical revision retains the core motif of Moses' staff-smiting, and the vital shift of emphasis lies in the fact that Moses is rebuked for insufficient trust in the exclusive effectiveness of the divine word (cf. Rashi *ad* Num. 10:12 and S. Loewenstamm, 'The Death of Moses', *Tarbiz*, 27 (1958), 145-46 [Heb.]; Ps. 106:32-2 further sharpens the nature of Moses' lack of faith on the basis of Num. 20:10b). Moreover, although the assumption that Num. 20:1-13 is a revision of Exod. 17:1-7 is suggestive, due caution is warranted, particularly because the JE traditions in Exodus and the P traditions in Numbers reflect several parallel motifs (e.g. desert stone-smiting, providential desert food, appointment of leaders (Exod. 16:18 and Num. 11), and wandering among such sites as Meribah and Qadesh) whose factual details and theological evaluations differ considerably. Accordingly, the relationship between Exod. 17:1-7 and Num. 20:1-13 may be that of two *independent developments* of a common topos, rather than a dependent exegetical reinterpretation of JE by P.

[5] Cf. Ezek. 12:22 + 23-4 — also a cited proverb and its reapplication.

[6] For the formulary involved, and a discussion of the passages, see M. Weinfeld, 'Jeremiah and the Spiritual Metamorphosis of Israel', *ZAW* 88 (1976), 17-19.

Aside from these few instances of *explicit* citation or referral, the vast majority of cases of aggadic exegesis in the Hebrew Bible involve *implicit* or virtual citations. In these cases, it is not by virtue of objective criteria that one may identify aggadic exegesis, but rather by a close comparison of the language of a given text with other, earlier Scriptural dicta or topoi. Where such a text (the putative *traditio*) is dominated by these dicta or topoi (the putative *traditum*), and uses them in new and transformed ways, the likelihood of aggadic exegesis is strong. In other words, the identification of aggadic exegesis where external objective criteria are lacking is proportionally increased to the extent that multiple and sustained lexical linkages between two texts can be recognized, and where the second text (the putative *traditio*) uses a segment of the first (the putative *traditum*) in a lexically reorganized and topically rethematized way. For example, as has been generally recognized, the passage in Ps. 8: 5-7, 'What (מה) is man (אנוש) that (כי) you are mindful of him, and the son of man that you take him into account (תפקדנו)? . . . You have established him by the work of your hands, and placed (שַׁתָּה) everything under his dominion', has been taken over and transformed in the Book of Job. There, in his contestation with his friends, Job questions: 'What (מה) is man (אנוש) that (כי) you raise him up, and that you put (תשית) your mind on him? You take account of him (תפקדנו) every morning, and test him continuously' (7: 17-18).

The exegetical revision of Ps. 8: 5-7 by Job 7: 17-18 is sharp and clear. Whereas the psalmist exalts the human species to near-divine status, and regards this exaltation as a sign of divine favour, Job inverts the liturgical teaching and mocks it; for he implies that God's providence is less than beneficial for humankind. In fact, he uses the psalm's language to state that God is attentive to humans in order to exact an account of them for their actions. This scrupulous divine presence is a burden, Job suggests, and inappropriate—for, indeed, just what is humankind after all, is it really so exalted? Thus, Job has hooked his argument on the latent ambiguity in the question 'What is man?', and transformed it from a remark which marvels how mere humankind could be so exalted by divinity into a sarcastic, contentious sneer. The older question is thus inverted: What, after all, is mankind that you, God, exact such a toll? Indeed, it is precisely because this rebuttal by Job is not composed of neutral terms, but rather utilizes the vocabulary of a paean of praise, that his words are charged with theological irony.

The hermeneutical tension between the positive liturgy of the psalmist and the caustic diatribe of Job marks the space between their two religious attitudes, and delineates the abyss out of which the *traditum* is stripped of its piety and unexamined pretence. By playing on the inherent ambiguity of the psalmist's question, Job has disclosed the dark side of the liturgical paean—a dark side corresponding to the obliqueness of his religious spirit. Indeed, so poignant is the inversion, and so strident, that later Eliphaz, in a perceptible allusion to it, asks: 'What (מה) is man (אנוש) that (כי) he could be innocent,[7] or the off-spring of woman that he should be righteous? (Job 15:14). And he answers: 'For, truly, [God] has no trust in his angels, and [even] the [host of] heaven are impure in his eyes' (v. 15). With this remark, Eliphaz has completed the aggadic inversion of Job who, as noted, first sensed the ambiguity latent in the question 'What is man?' Indeed, he both sensed it and allowed it to be the springboard of his accusation of divine oppression. Eliphaz further plays upon the ambiguity of the question, though he, in turn, redirects the argument against Job. Just who does Job think himself to be, asks this interlocutor, that he should account himself innocent? Is he not but a man? So how should he imagine himself just before God? With this stroke Eliphaz has deflated Job's contention, inverted it, and even, in some measure, ironically re-established the original *traditum*.[8] For his argument indirectly answers the question of the psalm and exalts God who, though mankind be an imperfect being, nevertheless raises this species to glory and honour.

The skein of argument and counter-argument that binds Ps. 8: 5-7, Job 7:17-18 and 15:14-15 is thus achieved through virtual citations of one Scriptural dictum. Perception of this linguistic bedrock discloses both the hermeneutical tensions between the *traditum* and its *traditio* and the transformative power of aggadic exegesis. On balance, then, it would appear quite contrived to presume that these three texts are not exegetically correlated, and that they are simply independent versions of a rhetorical topos. Indeed, the proximity of the two Joban passages, and their taut lexical connection to the liturgical segment from the Book of Psalms, would seem to preclude such a view. Nevertheless, on the basis of far less lexical evidence, it has been repeatedly contended by A. Robert and his followers that a style defined as *procédé anthologique* 're-employs, literally or equivalently, words or formulas of earlier Scriptures',[9] that is, that the earlier biblical texts are exegetically reused, or 'reactualized', in new contexts. In some cases 'the author preserves the literal meaning of his predecessor [texts]

---

[7] Given the several lexical linkages, it is likely that his verb, 'be innocent (*yizkeh*)', is a play on Ps. 8: 5 'are mindful of him (*tizkĕrennû*)'.

[8] In fact, in 15:14-15 Eliphaz actually refers to his earlier argument in 4: 12-18, especially vv. 17-18: 'Can a man (*'ĕnôš*) be righteous (*yiṣdaq*) before God? . . . Behold, he has no trust (*lō' ya'ămîn*) in his [angelic] servants.' Cf. *yiṣdaq* and *lō' ya'ămîn* in 15:14-15. Job appears to allude to this point also in 9: 2 (cf. *yiṣdaq; 'ĕnôš*); and, similarly, see the language and argument of Elihu in 33:12 and 26.   [9] A. Robert, *DBS* v (1957), 410-11, s.v. 'Littéraires (genres)'.

but applies it to another object';[10] in other instances, older terms are extended, transposed, or otherwise given new significance.[11] It is for this reason that Robert calls the texts created through *procédé anthologique*: '*écrits midrashiques*', and defines 'midrash' in a manner fairly concordant with what has here been called aggadic exegesis. He says, 'One may call *midrash* every study of the sense of Scriptures . . . with the aim of actualizing the import of the biblical texts . . . Midrash [may be found] there where the sacred text puts us in the presence of meditations on the divine word, with a concern for practical applications.'[12]

In principle, a controlled comparison of biblical sources is the methodological ideal of this approach. Indeed, one of Robert's programmatic remarks explicitly states that 'the only significant references are those in which identical or synonymous terms contextually treat an identical or positively analogous thought'.[13] However, the achievements and contentions of this school are subject to different evaluations. Thus, for example, Robert claimed that the wisdom teacher of Prov. 1-9 used words and phrases from Deuteronomy, Isaiah, and Jeremiah as the basis of his theological speculations;[14] Delcor argued that Deutero-Zecharia similarly re-employed linguistic fragments of Isaiah, Jeremiah, and Ezekiel for his own apocalyptic purposes;[15] and Diessler proposed that Ps. 119 reutilized material mainly from the Pentateuch, especially the Book of Deuteronomy, and occasionally from such prophets as Jeremiah.[16] But these proposed instances of *écrits midrashiques* are not so much citations of biblical texts as disjointed textual fragments, schematizations, or résumés.[17] Indeed, the textual references which are supposed to derive from earlier sources are generally so vague and disconnected, with virtually no clusters of parallel terms or analogous contexts, that little is gained by calling them exegetical or 'midrashic'.[18]

[10] M. Delcor, 'Les Sources du Deutéro-Zacharie et ses procédés d'emprunt', *RB* 59 (1952), 407.

[11] Cf. A. Robert, 'Les Attaches littéraires bibliques de Prov i-ix', *RB* 44 (1935), 345-50; A. Diessler, *Psalm 119 (118) und seine Theologie: Ein Beitrag zur Erforschung der anthologischen Stilgattung im Alten Testament* (Münchener Theologische Studien, 11; Munich: K. Zink Verlag, 1955), 277-8; Delcor, loc. cit., 407-11.

[12] In the summary of a conference given by Robert on 'midrash biblique', in *Ephemerides Theologicae Lovenienses*, 30 (1954), 283.   [13] *DBS* v. 410.

[14] 'Les Attaches', *RB* 43 (1934), 42-68, 172-204, 374-84; 44 (1935), 344-65, 502-25.   [15] Loc cit. 385-411.

[16] Loc. cit., *passim*.   [17] Cf. Delcor, 'Les Sources', p. 387.

[18] The same criticisms apply to the work of A. Feuillet, 'Les Sources du Livre de Jonas', *RB* 54 (1974), 161-86, to that of B. Renaud, *Structure et attaches littéraires de Michée IV-V* (Paris: J. Gabalda, 1964), and to an earlier example of this methodological procedure by M. Löhr, 'Der Sprachgebrauch des Buches der Klagelieder', *ZAW* 14 (1894), (pt. iv), 41-50.

These critical reflections must serve, in the absence of objective criteria, as internal controls against incautious or fallacious methodological procedures. Other heuristic cautions may be added. For example, comparable to the situation noted earlier, wherein similar narratives with strategic differences may not so much be exegetically as typologically related, there are instances where apparent verbal echoes of early texts in late sources may not constitute a *traditum-traditio* dynamic but rather point to a shared stream of linguistic tradition. In such cases, a common *Wortfeld* provides a thesaurus of terms and images shared and differently employed by distinct – though occasionally allied – literary circles. Thus, in consideration of Robert's own proposition that Prov. 1-9 reflects reutilizations of material in the Book of Deuteronomy, it may be contended that 'wisdom' terms are simultaneously used, altogether independently, by the sage-aphorists who produced the Book of Proverbs, the sage-scribes who, at one point, helped produce the Book of Deuteronomy, and sundry prophets, like Isaiah of Jerusalem.[19] This theoretical possibility does not, of course, invalidate any specific instance of aggadic exegesis in principle, though it does serve as a strict methodological hedge against uncritical assumptions of literary *exegetical* interdependence.[20] It is thus one thing to say that a notable similarity exists between the language of Jeremiah and Deutero-Isaiah,[21]

[19] Cf. the observations of J. Crenshaw, 'Method in Determining Wisdom Influence Upon "Historical" Literature', *JBL* 88 (1969), 132-3.

[20] As regards the exegetical interrelationship between Deuteronomy and Proverbs, each argument must be assessed separately. Thus, there is ground for Robert's contention that Prov. 6: 20-2 is based on Deut. 6: 4-9 (*RB* 42 (1934), 44), as shown by F. Delitzsch, *Biblical Commentary on Proverbs of Solomon*, trans. M. Easton (Edinburgh: T. and T. Clark, 1884), i. 34, and G. Buchanan, 'Midrashim Prétannaïtes, à propos de Prov. I-IX', *RB* 72 (1965), 232. Relatedly, Prov. 6: 20-35 is dependent upon Deut. 5: 6-6: 9; cf. M. Fishbane, 'Torah and Tradition', in *Theology and Tradition in the Old Testament*, ed. D. Knight (Philadelphia: Fortress Press, 1977), 284. However, there are also many counterinstances of deuteronomic dependence on 'wisdom'; cf. M. Weinfeld, *Deuteronomy and the Deuteronomic School*, 260-81, 313-16. It may be further observed, in this regard, that Robert's arguments frequently involve a *petitio principii* (cf. *RB* 43 (1934), 41-7, 50-1, 181, 204, 375). For, as against his assumptions, it bears emphasizing that there are only a few passages in the Book of Proverbs where the word *Torah* may have a covenantal sense (e.g. Prov. 28: 4-5, 9, 19: 18). This situation strikingly contrasts with the wisdom of Ben Sira, where proverbs of the Hebrew Bible have undergone a systematic revision and have been harmonized with the Torah of Moses. On this see E. Bauckmann, 'Die Proverbien und die Sprüche der Jesus Sirach', *ZAW* 72 (1960), 33-63.

[21] Cf. A. Kaminka, *Mehkarim* (Tel Aviv: Debir, 1938), 57-62, and, apparently independently, S. Paul, 'Literary and Ideological Echoes of Jeremiah in Deutero-Isaiah', in *Proceedings of the IVth World Congress of Jewish Studies* (Jerusalem, 1969), i. 102-20. Notably, Kaminka and Paul reach different historical conclusions regarding the parallels adduced.

and it is quite another to assert that this similarity does not so much reflect a direct borrowing or adaptation of a received *traditum* as a common linguistic stream preserved by a particular prophetic school. For the reasons just advanced, the position that Trito-Isaiah (chs. 56-66; particularly Isa. 57: 14-63: 7) cites and transforms the words of Deutero-Isaiah, as advocated by W. Zimmerli, should be questioned.[22] According to Zimmerli, these transformations are variously more abstract, more expansive, or more spiritual than their original source in Deutero-Isaiah. However, as Zimmerli himself concedes, there is no fixed way in which Trito-Isaiah reused his putative *traditum*, which raises the possibility that the snippets of so-called literal and free 'citations' are merely the shared phraseology of a school tradition. Moreover, even if Trito-Isaiah studied Deutero-Isaiah's language, and built upon it, the transformations of usage in the later sources need not derive from any deliberate exegetical intent. Rather, a learned vocabulary may simply have been reapplied by later prophetic tradents in accordance with new tastes and circumstances; so that nothing would be proved with respect to the existence of deliberate *exegetical* revision in the cases in question.[23] Thus, one may, in principle, agree with S. Mowinckel that, since the words of a prophet were living words, 'they were again and again reactualized in new, analogous situations by men who showed themselves to be authorized, inspired transmitters and perpetuators of the heritage';[24] but each particular instance of aggadic exegesis must be established and justified on its own terms.[25]

---

[22] 'Zur Sprache Tritojesajas', in *Gottes Offenbarung. Gesammelte Aufsätze zum AT* (TBü 19; Munich: Chr. Kaiser, 1963), 217-33.

[23] Upon examination, in fact, there is no reason to conclude that, for example, Isa. 58: 8b is more general than 52: 12b; that Isa. 62: 11 is less concrete than 40: 10; that Isa. 57: 14 is more spiritual than 40: 3; or that Isa. 62: 6 is more expansive than 49: 16. Even where there is a series of lexical parallels between Isa. 49 and Isa. 60, the similarities may rather reflect the common language of Isaianic Zion songs rather than species of deliberate exegesis.

[24] From 'Opkomsten av Profetlitteraturen', *NNT* 43 (1942), 83 (following the translation by D. Knight, *Rediscovering the Traditions*, 255). Cf. Mowinckel's *Prophecy and Tradition. The Prophetic Books in the Light of the Study of the Growth and History of the Tradition* (ANVAO 2, Hist.-Filos. Kl. 3; Oslo: Dybwad, 1946), 77.

[25] Frequently questionable is the suggestion that certain phrases in the Psalter are interpolations – evincing hopes, theological and cultural criticisms, and so forth – arising from a *rélecture* of earlier psalmodic texts in the community of faith. Cf., for example, the essays by A. Gelin, 'La Question des "rélectures" bibliques à l'intérieur d'une tradition vivante', *Sacra Pagina*, 1 (1959), 303-15, and H. Cazelles, 'Une Rélecture du Psaume XXXIX?', in *A la rencontre de Dieu. Mémorial Albert Gelin* (Bibliothèque de la Faculté Catholique de Théologie de Lyon, 8; Le Puy: Éditions X. Mappus, 1961), 119-28. Thus, Gelin's assertion (loc. cit. 365-8) that Ps. 47: 8b-9a is a secondary, eschatologizing rereading of the

4. For the sake of typological brevity, the preceding paragraphs have delineated two polar points on the spectrum of aggadic exegesis: those few cases where the textual lemmata are distinguishable from their exegeses by means of clear citation formulary; and those many cases where the lemmatic core of a *traditio* is woven into the new exegesis. In the first series of instances, the question of aggadic exegesis is not in doubt; whereas in the second, where the lemma is part of the very text which reinterprets it, or rather, where it is thought to be part of it, the need for methodological precision is essential. Complex variations of each 'type' will be treated in the ensuing discussions. Before this, however, a third mediating 'type' may be noted. Thus, between the differentiated juxtaposition of *traditum* and *traditio* in one group of texts, and their complex interpenetration in another, are those instances where a *traditum* and its *traditio* occur separately in two parallel texts. The parallel historiographies provide the best evidence for such instances. As was the case in scribal and legal exegesis, aggadic exegeses can often be discerned and controlled by comparing the historiographical account in the Books of Samuel-Kings, say, with the comparable version in the Books of Chronicles. While the value and nature of such comparison should be clear on the basis of earlier discussions, and their worth appreciated, a remark on the difference between historiography in the broad sense, and historiographical exegesis in the more narrow one, may be added. As regards the first, it need hardly be overemphasized that biblical historiography is selective and tendentious in character. It is selective, for example, with respect to the facts deemed worthy of treatment. Thus, the Book of Kings repeatedly refers to the annals of the kings of Judah or Israel, from which material has been abstracted. This species of biblical historiography is mostly concerned with religious obedience, apostasy, cultic centralization, and so on; and, as is well known, the reader is told that, should more information about building projects, wars, and other enterprises be desired, the official royal archives may be consulted. By contrast, the Book of Chronicles has its own agenda, and its own *Tendenz*: it deletes matters pertaining to the north and its apostasies, for example, and it is particularly interested in the cult and city of Jerusalem, the prestige of David, and prophetic sermons. Naturally, such topical differences and emphases do not, in themselves, constitute exegesis. In the broad sense, of course, the selective treatment of

psalm is doubtful because there is no clear reason why one should distinguish between so-called historical (v. 4) and messianic (v. 8a) levels. Indeed, the general fluidity between future and messianic expectations in the Book of Psalms, or their coexistence (cf. de Vaux, *RB* 65 (1958), 106), strongly argues against Gelin's claims. In addition, the contention that Ps. 78: 9 is an anti-Samaritan polemic (pp. 311–12) is not determined by the context.

available facts, in order to impress upon the reader a certain attitude towards history and its meaning, is interpretative, and it is entirely appropriate for a writer like Y. Kaufmann to introduce a term like 'historiosophy' to underscore the tendentious and often programmatic component in biblical historical compositions.[26] But this is not exegesis in the more narrow sense to be used here. Historiographical exegesis, that is, aggadic exegesis in the historical writings, may be defined as occurring where a *specific version of an event* in one historical source has been reinterpreted in another. Hence the concern is not with the emphases or biases of this or that historical source, but with the reinterpretation by the Chronicler of the specific *traditum* which he received from the author(s) of the Book of Kings. In these cases the lemma, or *traditum*, can be compared and juxtaposed with the new *traditio*, even though these two occur in distinct literary sources. It is thus that this 'type' stands, theoretically and practically, between the other two, and presents its own methodological problems and requirements.

To conclude, a brief schema of three broad methodological considerations may be noted for the analysis of aggadic exegesis. These considerations closely parallel those delineated earlier for the analysis of scribal and legal exegesis:

1. The easiest and most explicit means of recognizing aggadic exegesis is where it is formally indicated through technical formulae. By means of explicit citations or text referrals the *traditum* is set off from the *traditio* which reapplies or reinterprets it.

2. Aggadic exegesis may also be noted and isolated by comparing parallel texts *within* the MT, or *between* the MT and its principal versions.

3. A third means of isolating aggadic exegesis depends on a more subjective text-critical judgement. In these cases a *traditum* is incorporated into a *traditio* — which transforms it or re-employs it. Of particular aid and importance in this judgement is the dense occurrence in one text of terms, often thoroughly reorganized and transposed, found elsewhere in a natural, uncomplicated form. This is not an absolute requirement, though it is a heuristic — even essential — methodological guideline.

[26] Cf. his *Toledot*, iv-v, *passim* (see index).

11. Aggadic Exegesis of Legal Traditions in the Prophetic Literature

A. THE LAW AND THE PROPHETS

ANY discussion which purports to consider the relationship between the prophets and the legal materials of the Pentateuch must inevitably come up against the conundrum as to their relative priority. For modern critical scholarship, this issue was particularly well sharpened by Wellhausen, who concluded that the prophets precede the laws.[1] A primary factor in Wellhausen's multi-levelled argument was that if in fact the law came first, one would hardly expect the occurrence of prophecy at all. The basis for this insistence lies in Wellhausen's own estimation of the religious phenomenon of prophecy and its historical transformations. To him, because prophecy lays claim to an independent, direct access to God, whereas the law is concerned with the *received* will of God, one could certainly envisage that a non-mediated relationship with God could harden into law, but one would hardly expect the reverse. As the law could thus not be the basis of new revelations, Wellhausen went on to say: 'It is a vain imagination to suppose that the prophets expanded and applied the law.'[2]

A full reconsideration of this position would naturally entail a critique of Wellhausen's prejudices on the history of religious phenomena, and an attempt to evaluate the antiquity of the biblical legal traditions on an independent basis. A vital first step in this latter process was achieved by W. Zimmerli's broadly based counter-argument that the covenant idea (and so its content) was of considerable antiquity in biblical Israel.[3] Earlier, Y. Kaufmann had contended against the Wellhausian position on the basis of his observation that the Pentateuchal laws never refer to the prophets.[4] This argument and, indirectly,

---

[1] See his *Prolegomenon to the History of Ancient Israel* (Cleveland and New York: Meridian Books, 1965; 1st edn., 1878), 392–410, 422–5.

[2] Ibid. 399.

[3] *The Law and the Prophets* (Oxford: Basil Blackwell, 1965). Despite recent arguments to the contrary, this is also the considered opinion of J. Barr, 'Some Semantic Notes on the Covenant', in *Beiträge zur Alttestamentlichen Theologie. Festschrift W. Zimmerli* (Göttingen: Vandenhoeck and Ruprecht, 1977), esp. 37f.

[4] Cf. *Toledot*, i. 23–47.

that of Zimmerli, can be strengthened on the basis of a complementary consideration *grounded in the prophetic literature itself*. For this latter makes considerable, and even exegetical, reuse of diverse Pentateuchal laws and stylistic patterns.

1. There are a considerable number of instances where a prophet makes *explicit reference* to earlier laws, but without aggadic trans-formations. For example, in Ezek. 22:10-11 the prophet accuses the people of various types of sexual offences, which include degrees of incest, adultery, and cohabitation with a woman in her menses. These various legal references are formulated in the third person singular, and thus follow, lexically and grammatically, the cluster of laws found in Lev. 20:10-18.[5] However, a particularly striking facet of this diatribe is that while the prophet basically follows the legal sequence found in Lev. 20:10-18, he omits any reference to vv. 19-21, which deal with similar content. A close internal analysis of Lev. 20:10-21 clarifies this omission, however, for it reveals that vv. 19-21—which are not integrated with the other incest prohibitions, and are distinct in the gender and number used in the legistic formulation—comprise a late legal addendum to the whole piece.[6] One may therefore conclude that Ezek. 22:10-11 was formulated prior to this particular addendum to the Holiness Code.

As regards the continuity of Ezekiel's condemnation in vv. 12-13, which moves from sexual offences to civil abuses such as bribery, usury, and extortion, it is striking to note the comparable topical sequence recorded in Deut. 27:20-5,[7] and the literal parallels found in Deut. 23:20-1 and 24:14-15—this latter derived from Exod. 22:24 and 23:8. Such links between Ezekiel and the Covenant Code, via the deuteronomic laws, are not limited to the foregoing instance. For example, when this prophet, in Ezek. 18:1-32, revises the older doctrines of collective responsibility, and contends that responsibility for offences is solely limited to the offending party, he lists a sequence of delicts which follows those in Exod. 22:10, 24-6 and their reworking in Deut. 24:10-18, where the emphasis on *individual* responsibility is particularly marked (v. 16). A later post-exilic confrere of Ezekiel, the prophet Malachi, also makes an explicit reference to this list of delicts in the

---

[5] For the internal structure of this unit, and the judgement that vv. 17-18 are an appendix, see Daube, *Studies*, 78-80. While various parallels between Lev. 20 and Lev. 18 exist (cf. 18:7, 9, 15, 19), the latter is formulated in the second person singular, not the third. Thus, Lev. 20:19 may have been 'concocted . . . from 18:12 and 13'; so Daube, op. cit. 81.

[6] Daube, ibid. 80 (vv. 19-21 are thus a second *clausula finalis*; see n. 5 above).

[7] Cf. the consecution of sexual offences (27:20-3) followed by civil abuses (vv. 24-5).

Covenant Code. In Mal. 3:5 the condemnations of witches and false oaths, and of the abuse of widows, orphans, and strangers, all find their distinct echoes in Exod. 22:17, 19-21 (cf. 23:6,9).

There are other examples in the Book of Ezekiel where the prophet makes explicit reference to Pentateuchal cultic laws without any aggadic reinterpretation or reuse of them. Among these one may number the passage in Ezek. 33:25-6 and in 44:21-5, 31. In the first of these, the prophet contends with the self-confidence of those Israelites who dwelt among the ruins of the land by citing their pride in being heirs of Abraham (33:24), and thereupon asking them a series of rhetorical questions. If they eat meat with its blood, worship false gods, and pour blood,[8] and if they commit abominations such as adultery, becoming impure thereby, do they yet imagine that they shall inherit the land (vv. 25-6)? The answer to these rhetorical questions was assumed to be self-evident; for a series of divine punishments follows forthwith (vv. 27-9). In fact, the language of these punishments echoes the punishments for covenantal malfeasance listed in Lev. 26:19, 25, 30-3, and thus underscores the fact that the delicts noted in Ezek. 33:25 refer to acts of covenantal malfeasance found in Lev. 17-18. There, the people are explicitly told not to pour blood (17:4), worship chthonic gods (17:7),[9] or eat sacrificial meat with its blood (17:10-12), and there, too, the people are told not to commit adultery (18:20); for by such abominations (vv. 26-30) the land will become impure (18:25, 27-8, 30) and the nation will be disinherited from it.

In Ezek. 44 the prophet also makes explicit use of an ensemble of cultic laws. Earlier, in connection with legal exegesis, it was pointed out that Ezek. 44:9-16 is a polemical reinterpretation of features found in Num. 18, in connection with the prophet's intention to give exclusive priestly rights to the Zadokite line. Following this, various priestly regulations are stated which derive from earlier Pentateuchal sources: priests may not shave their hair or let it hang loose (44:20), as *per* Lev. 10:6 and 21:5,9; they may not drink fermented beverages (44:21), as *per* Lev. 10:9; they may not marry Israelite widows or divorcees, but they may marry Israelite virgins (44:22), as *per* Lev. 21:13-14;[10] they

---

[8] In libations to chthonic deities; cf. the ensuing parallels to Lev. 17:4, 7 noted below, and n. 9.

[9] The pouring of blood and the chthonic worship are clearly related, and rejected by the author of Lev. 17 in his new prescriptions of sacrificial blood. See J. M. Grintz, 'Do Not Eat on the Blood', *ASTI* 8 (1970-1), 78-105. The deuteronomist goes much further in his desacralization of ritual blood; cf. Deut. 12:15-16, 22-3, which are based on the language of Lev. 17:4, 10-14.

[10] But here the reuse is not quite symmetrical with the Pentateuchal material, because Ezek. 44:22 refers to *all* priests while Lev. 21:13-14 refers to the high priest *only*. Also, Ezek. 44:22 permits the priests to marry widows of priests, on which the Pentateuchal text is silent. As regards common priests, Lev. 21:7

must instruct the people regarding the differences between the sacred and profane, and the pure and impure (44: 24-5), as *per* Lev. 10: 10-11; they may not come into contact with corpses, save those of their immediate family (44: 25), as *per* Lev. 21: 1-4;[11] they are not to receive a landed inheritance, but may make up for it through sacrificial emoluments and perquisites (44: 28-30), as *per* Num. 18: 8-20); and they may not eat animal or bird flesh which has died on its own accord in the field or been ripped by predators (44: 31), as *per* Lev. 22: 8. This remarkable cultic anthology draws principally from such legal clusters as Lev. 10: 9-12, 21: 1-5, 9, 13-14, and Num. 18: 8-20. No aggadic adaptation is added.[12]

2. In addition to explicit prophetic references to Pentateuchal laws, there are many other cases where the relationship is *implicit* and much less precise. Typical of such Pentateuchal allusions are the doom proclamations of the prophet Amos, from the eighth century BCE, studied by E. Würthwein[13] and R. Bach.[14] According to their researches, Amos's critique of oppression in 4: 1 and 8: 4 recalls Deut. 24: 14 (cf. Exod. 22: 20-1; Lev. 19: 13); his critique of extortion through liens and loans recalls Deut. 23: 20 (cf. Exod. 22: 24); his critique of the perversions of justice and the taking of bribes in 2: 7 and 5: 7, 10, 12 recalls Deut. 16: 19 (cf. Exod. 23: 1-3); his critique of manipulating weights and measures in 8: 5 recalls Deut. 25: 13-14; his critique of the misuse of security deposits in 2: 8 recalls Deut. 24: 17; and there are others. In the preceding cases, the references to Pentateuchal laws are oblique and indirect; and only the parallel between Amos 2: 8 and Deut. 24: 17 (concerning security deposits) has a firm lexical basis. But even this lack of explicit references is not sufficient to gainsay the strong impression made by the sources that Amos was aware of ancient Israelite legal traditions, and that he made use of them in the course of his diatribes and forecasts of doom.

Bach, however, in his reworking of Würthwein's argument, seeks to

impliedly permits all virgins, and explicitly prohibits divorcees; nothing is stated about widows of priests.

[11] Since Lev. 21: 11 notes this too, concerning high priests, and also mentions the prohibition of loose hair (v. 10), as in Ezek. 44: 20, one may surmise that here, too, Ezek. 44 has applied the rules of Aaronid high priests to all Zadokite priests.

[12] For another Ezekelian example see Ezek. 34: 4, which clearly derives from Deut. 22: 1. Among non-Ezekelian examples, cf. Isa. 30: 22, which H. L. Ginsberg considers derived from Lev. 15: 33 (in the late Persian period); see *The Book of Isaiah* (Philadelphia: Jewish Publication Society, 1973), 15.

[13] 'Amos-Studien', *ZAW* 62 (1950), 44-7.

[14] 'Gottesrecht und weltliches Recht in der Verkündigung des Propheten Amos', *Festschrift für Gunther Dehn*, ed. W. Schneemelcher (Neukirchen: Kreis Moers, 1957), 23-34.

go beyond a catalogue of parallels and ambitiously draws form-critical implications from the data. Accepting the well-known distinction made by Alt, that ancient Israelite law may be divided between casuistic legal formulations deriving from the ancient Near East and apodictic legal formulations deriving from Israel's native resources, Bach determined to inquire which of these two formulations (and conceptions) of law underlies the legal allusions or references in the Book of Amos. His striking conclusion is that Amos drew solely upon the apodictic formulations. If correct, this observation would certainly tend to confirm the antiquity of apodictic formulations of law in ancient Israel, and also give further support to the case that the prophet made considerable use of ancient Israelite legal traditions. But one must be determinedly cautious here. For, to prove his point, Bach chose from among the possible parallels to Amos in the Covenant Code and the Book of Deuteronomy precisely those apodictic cases found in the deuteronomic collection. Thus, Deut. 23: 20 (apodictic) is preferred to the parallel in Exod. 22: 24 (casuistic); and Deut. 24: 17 is preferred to Exod. 22: 25. But there is no necessary reason to argue in this vein. Given the generally allusive nature of the legal references in the preachings of Amos, one will more readily grant Bach's more substantial point, and Würthwein's before him: that Amos was both aware of an older Israelite legal stratum—be this official or local, ethnic or civic, oral or written—and utilized it in the course of his diatribes.[15] Recent studies of the preaching of Micah tend to confirm this more general point as well.[16]

B. THE EXEGESIS OF CULTIC LAWS
WITH FORMULAE OF CITATION AND COMPARISON

Haggai 2:11-14 and Rules of Cultic Contamination

In the early decades of the post-exilic period, the prophet Haggai was instructed by YHWH to put two questions to the priests: (i) if a person were to carry consecrated meat in his garment, and this latter then touched bread or lentils, wine or oil (i.e. dry or liquid goods), would such foods become consecrated? And, (ii) if a person defiled by a

[15] Cf. Würthwein, 'Amos-Studien', 48, and Bach, 'Gottesrecht', 29. H. W. Wolff, *Amos The Prophet* (Philadelphia: Fortress Press, 1973), 4, also observed that 'verbal dependence' of Amos upon received ancient Israelite legal prescriptions 'can in no way be proven'.

[16] Cf. W. Beyerlin's *Die Kulttradition Israels in der Verkündigung des Propheten Micha* (Göttingen: Vandenhoeck and Ruprecht, 1959), 50–64, though he, like Bach, wishes to stress Micha's particular use of apodictic law. For a recent evaluation of the entire issue, see R. Berger, *The Prophets and the Law* (Monographs of the Hebrew Union College, 4; Cincinnati and New York: Hebrew Union College and Jewish Institute of Religion, 1974).

corpse were to touch any of these latter, would they become unclean or not? The answer to the first question is no, to the second, yes (vv. 11-13).

The reasons for the priests' responses are not given. Since the questions are divinely inspired, and since the prophet is told to 'ask the priests Torah לֵאמֹר *as follows*', it is likely that the questions are based on lemmata derived from priestly sources.[17] And this is, in fact, the case. Underlying the first question is a regulation like that found in Lev. 6: 20 which, in similar terms, states that if a person touches meat that is consecrated through proper sacrifice, he is thereby consecrated too; i.e., he is put in a comparable ritual state. On this basis, one may reconstruct the legal reasoning of the priestly *responsum*. It would seem that, while *direct* contact with consecrated meat does consecrate (renders קָדֵשׁ) whatever touches it, contact with an intermediary substance diminished the holiness of the consecrated object. Hence ritual meat will *not* affect the ritual status of bread, lentils, and the like, *if* these latter do not come into *direct* contact with the consecrated object. The ruling of the priests thus presupposes a form of reasoning common in the later second Temple period.[18] All the while something is holy in the first degree (here, sacrificial meat), what comes into contact with it is consecrated in a lower degree (here, the garment); but this latter is no longer an active miasmic agent, and hence cannot affect other objects (here, the foodstuff *in* the garment). However — and here we turn to the second question — direct contact with a corpse (having primary or first-degree impurity) renders a person who touches it into a prime carrier of the miasma, so that while he is an intermediate agent his contact with another object contaminates it as well (cf. Lev. 7: 19; Num. 19: 22).

In effect, the prophet is only really concerned with the second of these two questions. He depends on a negative reply to the first question in order to set up a positive answer to the second — which he then uses rhetorically to establish an analogy between the hypothetical ritual case and the actual situation of Israelites. Thus, after the questions and their *responsa*, Haggai notes, in v. 14: 'so it is (כֵּן) with this people,

---

[17] The pertinent antecedent is thus 'Torah', not 'ask'; and it would seem that such 'Torah' here indicates some priestly 'instruction', as is common in the P source and in post-exilic prophetic texts when unqualified (cf. Mal. 2: 17 vs. *tôrat mōšeh*, 3: 22). Wellhausen, *Die kleinen propheten*[4], (Berlin: W. de Gruyter, 1963) 175, is of the opinion that 'Die Thora lebt noch und geht weit hinaus über das Buch der Thora.'

[18] Concern with degrees of purity and impurity, and the related issues of contagion or miasma, was a primary topic of debate in early Judaism. See the text-analyses and interpretations of J. Neusner, *A History of the Mishnaic Laws of Purities* (SJLA 6; Leiden: E. J. Brill, 1974-7), vols. i-xxii, and the works cited above, p. 128 n. 58.

and so it is (וכן) with this nation before me . . . , and so is it (וכן) with respect to their deeds; thus, whatever they sacrifice . . . is impure.' The analogy constructed by the prophet is clearly linked to the second question. For reasons not stated, the people, like those touching a corpse, are impure in the first degree; so that whatever they do or sacrifice is thereby defiled.

Now it is quite obvious that this analogical transfer of the state of corpse defilement to the entire people of Israel cannot be literally true. What the prophet has therefore done is to identify the nation with a particular ritual state so as to heighten rhetorically the force of his castigation. Presumably, because the Temple had not as yet been rebuilt (cf. 2:1-9), the prophet wished to suggest that the people were in a defiled state. From this perspective, Haggai implied that without the proper rituals of atonement and purification the people were impure; and whatever they touched became the same. His repeated, explicit use of the analogical term כֵּן keeps the hermeneutical tension between the Torahistic references in the lemmata and their aggadic application rhetorically alive and dynamic. Indeed, by a series of analogies that move successively from the general to the particular, the prophetic rhetor is able to present his rebuke on several simultaneous levels, and to force the people addressed to reconsider their life-situation and generate a new attitude towards it. In a word, the people are forced to recognize their own impurity and the impurity of their deeds without the Temple – and are thereby provoked to rectify matters.[19] The truth value of Haggai's exegetical analogy does not, therefore, solely depend on the technical applicability of priestly minutiae to the people's ritual status; it is also a function of the capacity of these concrete ritual regulations to serve as action-begetting metaphors of the nation's own hazardous spiritual condition. Such an instance of aggadic exegesis thus arises from the analogical conjunction of Scripture with the behaviour of an ideally Scripturally guided people.

Hosea 9: 4 and the Food of Mourners

Hag. 2:11-14 has provided an example of the use of formulae of citation (לאמר) and comparison (כן) in an aggadic reinterpretation of cultic regulations. The prophet Hosea develops his aggadic exegesis solely by the use of a formula of comparison (כ). Thus, following his condemnation of apostate fertility practices, the prophet announces that for such behaviour Israel will be sent into exile and there eat unclean foods (טמא יאכלו, 9:1-3). He then goes on to say that while in

---

[19] This proposal concerning the *Sitz im Leben* of Hag. 2:10-14 is presumptive, though strongly suggested by the context, 2:1-9, 20-3, and especially the sequel in vv. 15-19.

exile the people 'will neither pour wine libations to YHWH nor bring him their meat-offerings; [these will rather be] like mourners' food (כְּלֶחֶם אוֹנִים) for them, [so that] whoever will eat of it will be defiled (כָּל־אֹכְלָיו יִטַּמָּאוּ); [indeed] their food will be theirs alone,[20] and will not enter the Temple of YHWH' (v. 4). The point of Hosea's aggadic analogy is clear. Because (כִּי, v. 1) the people have defiled the holy places with their practices, they will be bereft of shrines, and will be condemned to a thoroughly desanctified and impure life. By comparing the exiles' food to mourners' food, the prophet rhetorically suggests that, in exile, the people will contract defilement from their meat slaughtered there.

The ideological background of Hos. 9: 4 may be approximately stated on the basis of known Pentateuchal sources and ideas. Thus, in connection with an old law preserved in Deut. 26: 14, a celebrant, upon bringing his tithe to the shrine, declares that he has neither eaten of it when in mourning (בְאֹנִי), nor disposed of it while impure, nor donated it to the dead: for such would have defiled the new grain.[21] In this regard, one may recall that in the Holiness Code priests are prohibited the use of sancta (which include tithes) when they are in a state of defilement (Lev. 22: 3-16); and, comparably, Num. 19: 11, 14-16 indicates that everything in an Israelite mourner's tent is impure, as well as anyone who comes into it. As particularly stressed in Hag. 2: 13, there are, then, gradations of defilement which existed in ancient Israelite cultic law due to miasmic contamination with the dead. Evidently, Hosea has utilized these old legal notions aggadically — although just how, and in what state, these were known to him is uncertain. The force of his analogical argument, and his use of the technical term אוֹנִים, suggests that the people will be defiled by the food that they will eat in exile. In a word, because of their ritual aberrations, the existence of the people of Ephraim in Egypt and Assyria will be comparable to that of contaminated mourners.

In this manner, the prophet Hosea has exegetically reinterpreted

---

[20] Cf. the view of R. Eliezer of Beaugency ad loc., in *Kommentar zu Ezechiel und den XII Kleinen Propheten* (Schriften des Vereins Mekize Nirdamin³, 5, Lieferung 2; Warsaw, 1910), 130. For the view that *napšām* refers to the dead, see J. Halévy, 'Recherches bibliques', *REJ* 12 (1886); 28.

[21] The antiquity of this confession is clear not in its reference to the possible defilement of new grain but in its unique biblical reference to votary donations to the dead — here rejected. Presumably, these grains were believed to 'sustain' the dead and encourage them, or their ruling spirits, to be gracious in fertilizing the new harvest. Presumably, too, the custom of leaving sheaves of grain in the field (Lev. 23: 22a) — while not part of a funerary cult — was a comparable votary offering to the chthonic spirits, in the hope of their beneficence at harvest time. Later tradition demythologized this practice, and reinterpreted it in social-moral terms (v. 22b).

Israel's life in exile in terms of mourners' food. The textual transformation is aggadic. For Hosea has not in any way reinterpreted the particular laws of mourners' food. Nor was that the intent. As in Hag. 2:11-14, the aggadic rhetoric in Hos. 9:4 does not exist *for the sake of the priestly law*, that is, for the sake of its *legal* exegesis. Rather, the aggadic exegesis exists solely for its own rhetorical sake, and the law functions as the particular *occasion for* the rhetorical-exegetical enterprise which results, not more.

C. THE EXEGESIS OF CULTIC LAWS
WITHOUT FORMULAE OF CITATION AND COMPARISON

Jeremiah 2:3 and Cultic Donations

After the commission to prophecy (Jer. 1:5-7, 9-10) and the divine promise of protection (vv. 8, 17-19), Jeremiah begins his prophetic proclamations with the statement that YHWH has remembered Israel's faithfulness in bygone days, at the time of her covenant espousals, when she followed the Lord through the unsown steppe (2:2). This emphasis on ancient faithfulness in the desert is particularly striking in the light of the dominant Pentateuchal tradition which emphasizes Israel's rebelliousness during this time (cf. Exod. 32; Num. 11-16), and also in the light of the tradition of repeated faithlessness in the desert enunciated by Jeremiah's contemporary, Ezekiel (20:13, 21). At any rate, following this recollection of ancient faith in the divine first person (e.g. 'I remember', 'when you followed after me'), Israel is declared consecrated to YHWH, the first fruits of his produce; hence Israel is declared the beneficiary of divine protection against all enemies (v. 3). It will, of course, be observed that v. 3 shifts to the third person, and does not maintain the initial first-person address. This grammatical shift, which appears to reflect a switch from the divine to the prophetic voice, is not the only arresting feature of this passage. For the syntactic relationship between v. 2 and v. 3 is also not clear. On the one hand, it is possible that v. 3 is entirely resultative: because of Israel's desert faithfulness she has been consecrated to YHWH and will be protected. On the other hand, it is quite possible that Israel's ancient faithfulness and consecrated status are simply statements of fact, and only the promise of divine protection in v. 3b is resultative. Because of the grammatical shift, the first of the two possibilities seems the most likely, so that v. 3 would be best regarded, in its entirety, as an explication of the rewards for faithful service.

On a purely rhetorical level, the transition from the reference to Israel's faithfulness in an unsown region to its consecrated status as 'first fruits' has some inner logic. Indeed, later, in the preamble to his controversy with the people (2: 4-8), Jeremiah pointedly notes the great example of divine beneficence when Israel was led through the desert wastes to the fruitful land-inheritance (נחלה) of the Lord (vv. 6-7). Viewed from this angle, the difference between 2: 6-7 and 2: 2-3 is that whereas the former regards the land as God's fruitful possession given to Israel, the latter treats Israel metaphorically: Israel *is* the very fruitful produce of the land. Nor in itself is this variation altogether unusual. Elsewhere in the Hebrew Bible, in fact, particularly in those deuteronomic circles which influenced Jeremiah, there is a frequent oscillation in regarding the land and the people as YHWH's נחלה (cf. Deut. 4: 20-1). And since in another oracle Jeremiah also refers to the people of Israel as the 'land-inheritance' of YHWH (10: 16~51: 19), there is no reason to be surprised that also in 2: 3 Israel is described as the possession of the Lord.

But these observations only refer to the inner logic of the rhetorical transition in Jer. 2: 2-3. They explain nothing concerning the inner-logical and rhetorical background of v. 3 itself. For that, the angle of vision must be extended somewhat; and what we earlier noted to be a shift in v. 3 from a divine voice to its prophetic explication can now be examined for what it is: an aggadic exegesis of an old priestly law. A comparison of the passages will make this clear:[22]

Lev. 22: 14-16	*Jer. 2: 3*
And if a man[23] eats a consecrated (קדש) donation by accident, he must add one-fifth to its value and give the consecrated item to the priest. And they [the priests] shall not allow the consecrated donations of the Israelites to be desecrated . . . and thereby cause them [the Israelites] to bear [their] iniquity[24] of guilt (אשמה)[25] when they [the Israelites] eat (באכלם) their [own] consecrated donations . . .	Israel is consecrated (קדש) to YHWH, the first fruits of his produce; whoever destroys him (אכליו) will be judged guilty (יאשמו), and evil will befall them: oracle of YHWH.

---

[22] I initially discussed this connection in lectures on the Book of Jeremiah at the Hebrew University of Jerusalem, 1974-5. It has since been observed, independently, by J. Milgrom, *Cult and Conscience. The Asham and the Priestly Doctrine of Repentance* (SJLA 18; Leiden: E. J. Brill, 1976), 70f.

[23] This rendition, and the ritual logic involved, basically follow Milgrom, op. cit. 63 f.; significant variations will be noted.

[24] Or 'bear the responsibility/penalty'; cf. W. Zimmerli's analysis of the idiom *nś' 'wn* in 'Die Eigenart der prophetischen Reden des Ezechiel', *ZAW* 66 (1954), 8-12; see Milgrom, op. cit. 64.

[25] Or 'reparation'; so Milgrom, ibid. 64, 66. Thus *'šmh*, like *'šm*, is used in a

As is evident, the preceding priestly regulation deals with the accidental
desacralization by the laity of consecrated offerings donated to the
Lord for the priests. The priests are to be vigilant in this—not for their
own self-interest, since they nevertheless receive the perquisite plus a
penalty surcharge in case of its desecration, but for the laity's sake, for
through such inadvertence they cause the people to incur guilt.[26] And
because the priestly regulation in Lev. 22:14-16 refers to a concrete
cultic behaviour, the terms used have a concrete, literal force: the
'consecrated' donations refer specifically to those animals and products
—of which first fruits are included—mentioned in Num. 18:11-19,
25-9, especially v. 12; the 'eating' thereof means just that; and the
'guilt' incurred involves a fixed reparation. Not so Jer. 2:3, which
reassembles all these technical terms, but reuses them in an idiosyncratic, exegetical manner. Indeed, in Jeremiah's rhetoric the various
terms take on a figurative, even metaphorical, aspect. Israel, the
covenant-espoused people, is not only 'consecrated' to the Lord but
his own 'first fruits'; the 'eating' thereof is semantically extended to
connote destruction;[27] and the 'guilt' involved is not a cultic fault
requiring reparation but a matter of historical accountability.

The metaphorical transformations of this piece of aggadic exegesis
thus conceal a series of analogies with the old ritual rule: Israel is the
consecrated donation of YHWH just as the cultic offerings are the
consecrated donation of lay Israelites; and Israel's destruction by
enemies involves retaliatory punishments just as the accidental
desecration of donations requires retributive reparation. Of course, the
analogies are not all symmetrical. Thus, the priestly law is concerned
with ritual accidents, while Jeremiah's homily implies aggressive intent;
the ritual accident in Lev. 22:14-16 is committed by the donor, while
the destruction of Israel in Jer. 2:3 is by a third party; and the reparation for the ritual accident in the Pentateuchal regulation is paid by
the donor to the donee, whereas in Jeremiah's version the possessor of
the produce (YHWH) punishes those who 'desecrate' it. Even so, these
various points of tension between Lev. 22:14-16 and Jer. 2:3 do not

consequential sense, in addition to the more general idea of legal 'guilt'. For this
sense see the detailed comments of Milgrom, pp. 3-12, and the earlier literature
there cited, pp. 3-4, nn. 7, 14-15.

[26] See n. 24, above. The priestly idiom *nōśē' 'āwôn* is the basis of a rhetorical
play in the cultic critique found in Hos. 4:8.

[27] For the metaphor of eating used to denote military destruction, cf. also
Jer. 30:16, where *'ōkēlayik* 'your consumers' is used together with *ṣārayik* 'your
oppressors', *šō'sayik* 'your plunderers', and *bōzēzayik* 'your despoilers'. The metaphor of eating/consuming is also used with destructive fire, cf. Amos 1:4, 7, 10,
12, 14, 2:2. Comparatively, Akk. *akālu* also has literal and figurative senses.
See *CAD*, A. pt, 1, pp. 253 f. Among other kinds of related metaphors for physical destruction, the imagery of 'consuming/swallowing' is also poignant; cf. Isa.
49:19 (*mĕballĕ'āyik*).

subvert the rhetorical force and analogical power of the aggadic application. Since Lev. 22: 14-16 serves Jeremiah's oration, the several asymmetries are obscured and transcended by the more forceful hermeneutical analogies at play.

But just what, after all, permits Jeremiah's metaphorical transfer of a priestly notion, dealing with a concrete ritual donation, to the corporate body of Israel in the first place? Presumably, the basis for this transfer lies in the older deuteronomic notion, taken over from Exod. 19: 4-6, that Israel is a 'holy' or 'consecrated' nation to YHWH 'עם קדוש לה' (Deut. 7: 6; cf. 'Israel is consecrated to YHWH קדש ישראל לה'' in Jer. 2: 3). As discussed earlier,[28] this consecrated status of Israel is corporate and unconditional, and was an ideology passed on to future generations in conjunction with the Isaianic reference to the survivors of an early exile or destruction as a זרע קדש ('holy seed', 6: 13). Thus, in their post-exilic reworking of Deut. 7: 1-3, Ezra's colleagues remark that the survivors of the Babylonian exile have intermarried and so 'mixed זרע הקדש the holy seed [of Israel] with the peoples of the land' (9: 2b). This latter reference is an obvious allusion to the older deuteronomic prohibitions, since both the deuteronomist and Ezra's colleagues refer to Israel as 'holy' *after* references to the prohibition of intermarriage (Deut. 7: 3; Ezra 9: 2a). Jeremiah's reuse of this ideology is not for the purpose of stressing Israel's ethnic purity, however, and does not derive from any attempt to dissociate Israel from foreign elements. In Jeremiah, the deuteronomic notion has rather more free play than it does in its readaptation to post-exilic polemics.

As noted, the lemmata from Lev. 22: 14-16 are absorbed into Jeremiah's reinterpretation of it without any technical formulae. The analogical relationship between the Pentateuchal and prophetic materials is therefore not that of a simile – as in Hag. 2: 11-14 and Hos. 9: 4 – but rather of a metaphor: Israel *is* the consecrated donation of YHWH, in fact. Thus, the use of a metaphorical trope to portray the unconditional, consecrated status of Israel for YHWH is markedly appropriate. The alternative use of a simile would have considerably undermined the latter notion, and suggested that Israel is only *like* a consecrated donation. The rhetorical difference in these two alternatives can be seen by comparing Jer. 2: 3 with Hos. 9: 10. In the latter passage the prophet states (for YHWH): 'Like grapes in the desert steppe I found Israel; and like the first fruit of figs in their first season I regarded your ancestors . . .' Here, as in the Jeremianic oratory, God's relationship to Israel is comparable to first fruits, though Hosea is particularly intent on emphasizing the joy and delight of this relationship. Thus, the simile

---

[28] Above, pp. 121-3. Milgrom, op. cit. 72, also considers the deuteronomic ideology as a basic component in Jeremiah's aggadic exegesis.

serves to outline an attitude and a relationship: the desert encounter between Israel and her God is comparable to the previous moment when the wayfarer in the steppe land finds ripe grapes and figs. But nothing is implied about Israel's status or condition. By contrast, just this last constitutes the force of the metaphorical figure 'Israel is consecrated to YHWH' in Jer. 2: 3: for this trope makes use of a ritual formula (קדֹש . . . לה׳) designating the sacred status of certain objects in order to underscore Israel's transformed and permanent status as a sanctum of the Lord.[29] Israel is not simply *like* the first fruits of the desert; it *is* 'first fruit' in fact, and is therefore inviolable.

Isaiah 58: 1–12 and Ritual Asceticism

The prophetic critique of national behaviour and attitudes in Isa. 58: 1–12 unfolds in a coherent and increasingly virulent fashion.[30] At the outset (v. 1) the prophet is told by God to raise his voice like a trumpet (כשופר), and tell the people their transgressions (פשעם) and sins (חטאתם). For they come to seek (ידרשון) God (v. 2), and ask: 'Why have we fasted and you do not attend, why have we tormented ourselves in fasting (עינינו נפשנו) and you do not acknowledge [it]?' (v. 3a). In reply, the prophet delivers a searing attack on the people's religious life. They pursue business (חפץ) on their fast day; indeed, their fasting only results in contention and social oppression (vv. 3b–4). By contrast, a true fast, when one would torment himself (נפשו . . . ענות)and find divine favour, would be a day of service to the oppressed and poor (עניים) (vv. 5–8). YHWH will only answer (ענה, v. 9) those supplicants who cease from interpersonal iniquities, and who satisfy the tormented in body and spirit (נפש נענה, v. 10).

In this fiercely ironical rebuke, the Israelites are told that they cannot force divine favour by fasting, but that they can elicit it by feeding the hungry. True fasting, the prophet emphasizes, is a spiritual, not just cultic-physical, asceticism. It consists in providing services and sustenance to those who hunger *against their will*. One cannot seek (stem: חפץ, v. 2*bis*) God by a formal fasting, by pursuing business (חפץ, v. 3),[31] and by continuing social oppressions at the same time.

---

[29] The act of doing or dedicating something *la YHWH* 'to YHWH' is a technical cultic expression; see, for example, Lev. 27: 2, 26, 28; Num. 6: 2, 30: 3; Jer. 4: 4 (cf. Exod. 4: 25b, where *ly* is probably an abbreviation for *lYHWH*).

[30] I agree with H. Kosmala's analysis of the 'Form and Structure of Isaiah 58', *ASTI* 5 (1966–7), 69–81, though his assumptions of phraseological dislocations are less convincing.

[31] This stem is repeated twice in v. 13, which, together with v. 4, is an appendix to the rebuke in vv. 1–12. The precise sense of the expression *mĕṣô' ḥēpeṣ*, as 'do business', may be established by the parallel expression *'ăśôt derek* 'to make a

Through the repetition of such verbal stems as חפץ and ענה (vv. 3, 5, 8, 9, 10),[32] and through the use of such particles as הֵן (vv. 3, 4), הֲ (vv. 5, 6, 7), and אִם (vv. 8, 9), in positive and negative assertions, the texture of the prophet's rebuke is thickened and its theological paradoxes underscored.

But Isa. 58: 1-12 is more than a religious-social critique in passionate, but ultimately self-referential, terms. There is, in fact, an unmistakable external reference to the language used by the prophet: specifically, Isaiah makes explicit use of terms found in Lev. 16 and 23: 24-32 — two biblical texts which deal with fasting and cultic-ascetic practices. In these documents it is recorded that a trumpet blast was sounded on the Day of Atonement (Lev. 23: 24) and the people were required to afflict themselves (וְעִנִּיתֶם אֶת־נַפְשֹׁתֵיכֶם, 16: 31 and 23: 27, 32; cf. 16: 29, 23: 28) — so as to be purified of their sins (16: 30) — and to cease totally from work on that day (16: 29, 23: 28, 31). Moreover, during this day Aaron officially confessed all the people's sins and transgressions (כָּל־פִּשְׁעֵיהֶם לְכָל־חַטֹּאתָם, 16: 21).

Given the compact congruence between the imagery and linguistic forms found in Isa. 58: 1-12 and Lev. 16 and 23: 24-32, and the shift in focus and concern, it may be concluded that the former is a deliberate piece of homiletical–aggadic exegesis. The Pentateuchal legal materials dealing with the rules and regulations of the Day of Atonement thus serve as the linguistic and ideological matrix for their inversion and reapplication in Isaiah's discourse. The powerful spiritual redefinition of fasting undertaken by the prophet so balances the old cult practices on the edge of rhetorical hyperbole that the hermeneutical tension between the two is taut and unyielding. However, it must be stressed that Isa. 58: 1-12 is not antinomian: it neither attempts to weaken nor to reject the Pentateuchal law. In fact, the text specifically condemns work on the fast day (v. 3). Accordingly, what the prophet ultimately seeks to effect is a social-spiritual extension of an authoritative religious practice. To be sure, the aggadic reinterpretation in Isa. 58: 1-12 is of such fundamental religious weight that the inherent value of the cultic act of fasting is perceptively undermined — and this by a new divine revelation. Nevertheless, since the *fact* of fasting is not spiritualized,

journey [for business]' and their exact Akkadian cognates ṣibûtam kašādu and ḫarranam epēšu, respectively — both used in mercantile contexts. See M. Weinfeld, 'King-People Relationship in the Light of 1 Kngs. 12: 7', Leš. 36 (1971-2), 9 n. 43 [Heb.], and J. C. Greenfield, 'Studies in the Legal Terminology of the Nabatean Funerary Inscriptions', Seper Zikaron le-Zeker H. Yalon, edd. Y. Kutscher, S. Liebermann, and M. Kaddari (Jerusalem: Kiryat Sepher, 1974), 67 n. 20 [Heb.].

[32] Also, cf. the strategic repetitions of the stem rā'āh (vv. 3, 7), or the pun maṣṣāh tāṣûmû (v. 4).

but it is rather only the *idea* of it that is transposed in terms of social action, the original divine command to fast on the Day of Atonement remains. Isa. 58:1-12 is thus an *aggadic* exposition of a legal *traditum*; it is not a legal exegesis of it.

Jer. 7: 21-3 provides an interesting aggadic parallel to the situation just described. Like the pre-exilic Isaiah, who rejects the value of sacrifices performed by iniquitous celebrants (1: 11-17), and even more like the prophet Amos, still earlier, who emphasizes the practice of morality over the performance of sacrifices, because the Israelites were not required to present meat- and meal-offerings to YHWH during the forty years of their desert wanderings (5: 25), Jeremiah states:

> Thus says YHWH of hosts, the god of Israel: 'Add your holocaust-offerings to your meat-offerings, and eat [their] flesh! – for I neither spoke nor commanded your ancestors concerning holocaust- and meat-offerings when I took them out of Egypt. But this is rather what I commanded them: "Hearken to My voice, that I be your god and you be my people . . ."'

It would appear from these references that both Amos and Jeremiah were heirs to a tradition which taught that the sacrificial cult derived from the post-Sinaitic period. But Jeremiah is far more radical in his remarks than Amos – and it is in this that his diatribe is comparable to Isa. 58:1-12. Amos simply gives a primary religious–theological emphasis to the practice of morality; he does not advocate antinomian acts, as does Jer. 7: 21-3, when the people are told 'Add your holocaust-offerings to your meat-offerings, and eat [their] flesh!' For whether one sees here a reference to the required public offerings of the official cult, or a reference to the individual voluntary offerings brought by the people,[33] the fact is that in no case is the holocaust-offering eaten: it is always totally consumed on the altar. Hence, when Jeremiah tells the people to eat the flesh of their offerings, he is telling them to violate a fixed cultic *traditum* – one that was established and authoritative in his time. If, in this, the prophet is referring to the public offerings of the Temple, then the violation would be twofold; for, unlike the voluntary meat-offering of individuals, the flesh of the required meat-offering was prohibited to the laity and given to the clerics as a divinely ordained perquisite.

Admittedly, Jeremiah's remarks are rhetorical and hyperbolic, and are primarily aimed at underscoring the worthlessness of holocaust- and meat-offerings performed by those who violate the covenant. But in

---

[33] M. Weinfeld, 'Jeremiah and the Spiritual Metamorphosis of Israel', *ZAW* 88 (1976), 52f., considers the reference to be to the official cult; J. Milgrom, 'Concerning Jeremiah's Repudiation of Sacrifice', *ZAW* 89 (1977), 273-5 has argued against this, and for the individual voluntary offerings.

choosing to tell the people – in YHWH's name – that it is all the same if they eat proscribed sacrificial flesh or not, the divinely authorized sacrificial regulations are contradicted. In this, the *traditio* of Jeremiah is more daring – for all its rhetorical flourish – than Isa. 58: 1-12. For even if Jeremiah does not teach new sacrificial regulations, or even, for that matter, controvert the essential authority of the old ones, the fact that anti-cultic behaviour is divinely articulated in order dialectically to emphasize the primary importance of covenantal fealty ('I neither spoke nor commanded . . . but this is rather what I commanded') is altogether remarkable. In Isa. 58: 1-12, as noted, the aggadic *traditio* delineates the true, social-spiritual meaning of the cultic act of fasting. But this latter is not to be violated – however secondary or preparatory it is to other 'social-cultic' behaviour – even temporarily, even didactically.

D. THE EXEGESIS OF CIVIL LAWS
WITH FORMULAE OF CITATION AND COMPARISON

Jeremiah 3: 1-5 and Repentance

In the ritual question posed by Haggai to the priests (2:12) a precise sequence is followed. First a hypothetical situation is presented (introduced by הֵן 'if'); then a complicating second factor is added (introduced by וְ 'and'); and finally, an adjudication is requested (introduced by the interrogative particle הֲ). In Hag. 2: 13 the prophet asks a second ritual question, and only slightly modifies this formulation.[34] As noted, both questions derive from Scriptural lemmata which are introduced by the citation formula לֵאמֹר. In terms of the history of ancient rhetorical patterns, it is particularly noteworthy that both of the aforementioned elements – the citation formula and the question-and-answer schema – are attested in the Book of Jeremiah from the preceding century. Thus, in Jer. 3: 1, following the citation formula לֵאמֹר, the prophet asks: 'If (הֵן) a man divorces his wife, and (וְ) she leaves him and belongs to another, may (הֲ) he return to her?' (v. 1a). As in Hag. 2: 12-13, the Jeremian sequence is initial condition + secondary complication + ritual question. And, finally, like Haggai's queries, Jeremiah's legal question is also followed by an answer, in v. 1b.

The linguistic and topical similarity of the hypothetical legal scenario brought by Jeremiah has often been compared with the rules of palingamy found in Deut. 24: 1-4. This regulation states that if a man divorces his wife, and she marries another, he may not remarry her (if she is subsequently divorced or widowed), and that such behaviour is

---

[34] The hypothetical situation is carried over from v. 12, and hence unrepeated; and the new complicating factor is introduced by the particle *'im*.

adjudged reprehensible and able to pollute the land. While some minor divergences can be observed between the terms used in MT Jer. 3:1a and MT Deut. 24:4b with respect to the pollution to be brought upon the land by the delict,[35] and also between the MT and LXX versions of Jer. 3:1,[36] these variations may be accounted for either by rhetorical licence, or by such slight fluidity as can be expected where the phrasing of a legal topos was not fixed in a final, unalterable version.[37] At any rate, it is notable that the lexical variations between the Pentateuchal and prophetic passages of the MT occur in the hortatory-paraenetic conclusion, not in the technical and operative sections of the legal topos, as the following synoptic comparison shows:

Deut. 24:1-4	*Jer. 3:1*
If a man (אִישׁ) marries a woman (אשה). . . and divorces her (וְשִׁלְּחָהּ) . . . and she goes and belongs to another (והלכה והיתה לאיש־אחר) . . . [and subsequently her second husband divorces her or dies], her first husband, who divorced her, may not 'return' (לֹא יָשׁוּב). . . to remarry her . . . that you not pollute (תחטיא) the land (הארץ) . . .	If a man divorce his wife (אשתו) (ישלח איש את) and she goes (הלכה) from him and belongs to another (והיתה לאיש־אחר), will he return to her (הישוב אליה) again? — will not that land (הארץ) become defiled (תחנף)? But you have whored with many males; thus will you return to me (ושוב אלי)?!

If one may validly conclude from the foregoing that the lexical and topical components of Deut. 24:1-4 provided the substantive matrix for Jeremiah's speech,[38] it is none the less the aggadic variations of this latter which constitute its uniqueness. Thus, whereas the old law is formulated as a civil *Rechtspraxis* for the individual Israelite, Jeremiah has recast it twofold, in national and in spiritual terms. The national application, for its part, makes use of the theological metaphor that

[35] See the citations below. The verbal variation is not decisive, cf. Num. 35:33-4.

[36] In the question, the LXX has 'will *she* return to *him*?', and in the answer '*she* shall return to me'. But this variation is not necessarily a tendentious correction designed to accommodate the overall rhetorical issue of Israel's repentance to YHWH. Hos. 2:9 also speaks of the woman (Israel) returning. If this is not simply an initiative without legal consequence, and depended on the husband's ultimate decision to remarry his former wife (see v. 11), then it is possible that different rules or customs coexisted in ancient Israel. Formally, *lāšûb* in Deut. 24:4 denotes repetition, since it is coordinated with the following verb (cf. Gesenius-Kautsch-Cowley §120 *d*). A literal translation has been used here to anticipate Jeremiah's hermeneutical work.

[37] Thus, I see no reason to posit an original form of the law of which Deut. 24:1-4 and Jer. 3:1 are independent variations, as does Hobbs, 'Jeremiah 3:5 and Deuteronomy 24:1-4', *ZAW* 86 (1974), 23f.

[38] A view shared by J. Bright, *Jeremiah* (AB; Garden City, NY: Doubleday, 1965), 23, and W. Rudolph, *Jeremia*[3] (HAT; Tübingen: Mohrs, 1968), 24.

Israel's relationship to YHWH is that of a bride to her husband (cf. 2: 2; also 3: 8), and specifies the people's religious apostasy as its participation in Canaanite fertility practices. By so using the sexual dimensions of Israel's apostasy as metonymic for her covenantal infidelity, Jeremiah is able to effect a striking link between YHWH's rejection of Israel and the civil law, which allowed the husband grounds for divorce if his wife engaged in acts of sexual misbehaviour. For, though the precise legal contours of the operative clause ערות דבר in Deut. 24: 1 is a famous interpretative crux, there is little doubt that it carries a clear sexual component.[39] Hence its meaning is stronger than 'shameful thing', and comes closer to a 'matter of sexuality'.[40] Accordingly, Jeremiah has applied a *Rechtspraxis* which counts sexual misdemeanours as a condition for divorce to Israel's legal-religious situation.

But it is here that a precise homology between Deut. 24: 1-4 and Jer. 3: 1-5 breaks down for the sake of the aggadic *traditio*. Whereas Deut. 24: 4 stresses that a husband may not legally *'return'* (לשוב) and remarry his first wife under the conditions stated, Jeremiah's aggadic reinterpretation of the law gives this clause an entirely unexpected spiritual dimension. Under the impact of the overall metaphorical and national reclassification of the *Rechtspraxis* in Jer. 3: 1-5, the operative legal term 'return' or 'repeat' undergoes a semantic transformation, and refers to *religious return* – or repentance – not palingamy.[41] A serious question remains, however. For while the spiritual reinterpretation of

---

[39] For a full discussion of *'erwat dābār*, see A. Toeg, 'Does Deuteronomy xxiv, 1-4 Incorporate a General Law on Divorce?', *Dine Israel*, 2 (1970), pp. v-xxiv. Toeg considers this phrase as qualifying the more vague words 'not find favour'; but see R. P. Merendino, *Das deuteronomische Gesetz*, 297, who considers both phrases to be secondary. In Tannaitic discussions, *'erwat dābār* was given a sexual interpretation in *M. Giṭ.* ix. 10, where the two Pentateuchal motivations for divorce are mentioned. Shammai accepted sexual indecency as grounds for divorce; Hillel permitted any reason. Matt. 5: 31f. parallels the first view, *Antiq.* iv. 253 the second. For the later rabbinic controversy on the relationship between the clauses, see *b. Giṭ.* 90a.

[40] The Hebrew form is an inversed *status constructus* – like *maśśa't mĕ'ûmāh* in Deut. 24: 10. On this feature in biblical Hebrew, see A. Schulz, 'Der Status constructus in der Geschichte der Exegese', *ZAW* 54 (1936), 270-7. *'erwat dābār* is thus equivalent to *dĕbār 'erwāh*; and *'erwāh* means, basically, 'nakedness', possibly even 'pudenda'. Cf. Lev. 18, *passim*; and 1 Sam. 20: 30, Ezek. 23: 10, Hos. 2: 11, Mic. 1: 11, and Nah. 3: 5.

[41] R. Yaron, 'The Restoration of Marriage', *JJS* 17 (1966), 1-11, argued that the prohibition of palingamy in Deut. 24: 1-4 was to prevent incest (p. 8) and thus protect the stability of the second marriage. But Carmichael, *The Laws of Deuteronomy* (Ithaca: Cornell University, 1974), 203-7, has rightly objected that incest pertains to the family group, and the law is too obscure if its concern is to protect the second marriage; for the husband can divorce his second wife at will (see *ûśĕnē'āh* 'and he hate her', 24: 3). The position of Yaron has subsequently been strengthened by G. Wenham, 'The Restoration of Marriage Reconsidered', *JJS* 30 (1979), 36-40.

Jeremiah's exegesis is clear enough, the meaning of the phrase 'thus shall you return to me?!' is thoroughly ambiguous. There are no contextual reasons to prefer one to construe it as a question rather than a declaration. Each seems equally apropos. Thus, if one were to understand the phrase as a question, with God as the speaker (viz., 'will you, therefore, return to me?'), it would appear that the point is rhetorical, and that the prophet wishes to indicate that Israel's infidelity has prevented her religious restoration. However, if the phrase is construed as an affirmative declaration ('nevertheless, return to me!'),[42] one may conclude that its intent is to suggest that *if* Israel (the subject) repents then YHWH will break his own law and take her back.

Despite such ambiguity, it may nevertheless be proposed that this semantic knot need not be severed, and that it is around this twisted cord that the legal–religious paradox of Jeremiah's aggadic rhetoric is spun. For while, on the one hand, it would appear that both interpretative possibilities are made superfluous by the Pentateuchal legal analogy, which prohibits the return of a wife who has married another man, the law has its source in the same god who repeatedly advocates the repentance of Israel elsewhere in the Book of Jeremiah (and it is conceptually unlikely that the opportunity of repentance would be foreclosed at the beginning of Jeremiah's ministry when it is allowed thereafter). It is this tension between the legal impossibility of return and the religious possibility of repentance and divine remission that is captured in the ambiguous phrase 'thus shall you return to me'. Jeremiah, it would seem, pulls both cords at once: he invokes the authoritative legal *traditum* in order to introduce a theological exegesis of it. Israel cannot legally expect a restoration with her god, but divine grace can provide hope where it is least to be expected.

Such allowance for a suspension of the law if the people repent causes a further rent in the homology between the Pentateuchal rule and the prophetic *traditio*. For in the civil law return is prohibited, whereas in its aggadic reinterpretation this is a theological possibility. Moreover, in both the civil law and its recitation in Jeremiah, the husband is the active agent. In Deut. 24: 4 it is stated that 'he may not return to remarry her'; and in Jer. 3: 1a it is similarly asked, 'Will he return to her?' By contrast, in Jer. 3: 1b the option of repentance, or return, is given to Judah, the 'wife'. Through such structural dislocations, the innovative quality of Jeremiah's aggadic interpretation is underscored, as well as the fact that, in the Hebrew Bible, aggadic exegesis often bends the *traditum* to its particular rhetorical goals.

As considered, the aggadic exegesis of Jer. 3: 1–5 is both allegorical

[42] *b. Yoma* 86b.

and didactic. To be sure, the deuteronomic law (or its near congener) which serves as the matrix for the prophetic interpretation is not changed or modified. Jeremiah's exegesis thus has no legal force with respect to civil procedures. Indeed, it is just because the meaning and force of the civil *Rechtspraxis* is not in doubt that the prophet is able to achieve such a striking theological tension and reversal. And yet it may be argued that Jeremiah is not at all innovative in implying a double standard of justice here – one civil, for humans, the other theological, for YHWH – but that he is merely giving a theological reflex to a common social-legal practice. Support for this contention would appear to lie in other biblical strata, where it is indicated that, in some locales and periods, an Israelite husband had the prerogative to reconcile himself to his wife even after proven sexual indecency. An allusion to such behaviour is reflected in Prov. 6: 32-4, and also in Hos. 2: 4-15 – where theological and national overtones are present as well.[43] But even if the possibility of matrimonial reconciliation after adultery or promiscuity existed in ancient Israel, it is still the case that the unique rhetorical and theological force of Jer. 3: 1-5 presupposes and uses the language and topos of a *Rechtspraxis* like that found in Deut. 24: 1-4, which does *not* ostensibly permit reconciliation.

Granting this, it may nevertheless be the case that Jeremiah was influenced here, as so frequently elsewhere, by the prophet Hosea.[44] Firstly, in 2: 4-15 Hosea also speaks of a sexually promiscuous wife who follows (אלכה) other lovers and is divorced, but who subsequently decides to return (ואשובה) to her first husband (אישי הראשון; cf. איש . . . הראשון, Deut. 24:1, 4) who then decides himself to return to her (אשוב) and to be reconciled in remarriage.[45] In addition, this legal theme is allegorized both in Jeremiah's discourse and in Hos. 2: 4-15 in terms of God's relationship to apostate Israel who follows the Canaanite gods, and in both texts marriage and sexual promiscuity are metonyms for the covenantal bond and infidelity. Finally, Hos. 2: 16-17 and Jer. 2: 2 both refer to God's espousal of Israel in the 'steppe land', on the way out of Egypt, in the time of her 'youth'. Accordingly, while there is no necessary reason to suppose that, in this marriage-remarriage topos, Hosea has based himself specifically on the deuteronomic

---

[43] Cf. LH 130. Prov. 6: 32-4 is striking because it indicates that even in cases of provable adultery death was not the only option (in some locales or periods). Cf. S. Loewenstamm, *Beth Miqra*, 7 (1961-2), 55ff. [Heb.].

[44] See the still valuable study by K. Gross, 'Hoseas Einfluss auf Jeremias Anschauungen', *Neue kirchliche Zeitschrift*, 42 (1931), 241-56, 327-43.

[45] Cf. n. 36 above. The legal scenario just described (together with similar terms) also appears in Judg. 19: 2-3, as correctly observed by Y. Zakovitch, 'The Woman's Rights in the Biblical Law of Divorce', *The Jewish Law Annual*, 4 (1981), 38f.

tradition, despite the likelihood of the latter's original northern provenance, it seems suggestive, nevertheless, that Jeremiah was *inspired to introduce* the theme of reconciliation into his aggadic reinterpretation of Deut. 24:1-4 precisely because he derived the metaphor of a covenantal marriage from Hosea, who based himself on an older, legal tradition which permitted matrimonial reconciliation after a divorce due to sexual misbehaviour.[46]

The Analogy of the Seized Thief in Jeremiah 2: 26, 34

Jeremiah's predilection for Pentateuchal case laws as the lexical and topical matrix for his aggadic exegesis shows up again in his reuse of Exod. 22:1-2a:

Exod. 22:1-2a	Jer. 2: 26, 34
If a burglar (גנב) is caught (יִמָּצֵא) while in a clandestine act/tunnelling (במחתרת)[47] and struck dead, [then] he [the property-owner] has no blood-guilt (דמים); but if it [the crime] was done in broad daylight, [then] he [the owner] shall be liable (דמים), and shall pay reparations.	As a burglar (גנב) is ashamed when caught (יִמָּצֵא), so is all Israel ashamed . . . truly the life-blood (דם) of the innocent poor has been found (נמצאו) on the hem of your garment; you did not catch them (מצאתים)[48] while tunnelling/secretly (במחתרת), but right out in the open.[49]

It is generally acknowledged that the rule in Exod. 22:1-2a interrupts the legal sequence of Exod. 21:37 and Exod. 22:2b-3, which deals with theft and the thief's potential insolvency.[50] Set within this

---

[46] This view of the matter would accord with R. Yaron's reconstruction of the legal stages of ancient Israelite divorce; see his 'On Divorce in Old Testament Times', *RIDA*[3] 4 (1957), 124-8.

[47] The comparative evidence of LH 21, which uses the Akk. verb *palāšu* 'to pierce' in a case dealing with the burglary of a house, as well as the use of the verb *ḥātar* in Ezek. 8: 8, 12: 5, 12 (with a wall) and in Job 24:16 (with a house), suggest that 'tunnelling' or even 'housebreaking' is the best translation. Such a view, which presupposes some fortification, argues against the burglary of a cattle-pen (cf. Finkelstein, 'The Ox That Gored', p. 38 n. 32). However, whatever its original focus, the present contextualization of the rule before Exod. 22: 2b (see below, and n. 50) – which can only refer to the thief in 21: 37 – allows one to construe this case in relationship to the burglary of cattle-pens (cf. Jackson, *Theft in Early Jewish Law*, 49).

[48] Viz. the innocent poor.

[49] The translation 'right out in the open' (or 'everywhere') is a free rendition of the perplexing *'al-kol-'ēllê* based on the legal logic of the passage (by analogy with Exod. 22:1-2a). A. Ehrlich came to a similar conclusion on the basis of stylistic considerations. See his *Mikrâ ki-Pheschutô* (Berlin 1901; New York: KTAV reprint, 1969), iii. 176.

[50] Cf. already Paton, 'The Original Form of the Book of the Covenant', *JBL* 12

sequence, Exod. 22:1-2a outlines a paradigmatic situation of burglary which restricts self-help to cases of surreptitious breaking and entering, but requires reparation where the property-owner could reasonably estimate the malice or intent of the alleged intruder. The case is formulated in casuistical style, with two protases and two apodoses, and it uses the extreme situation of manslaughter as the legal model. Presumably, if a property-owner is judged innocent of manslaughter when the intrusion is במחתרת, he would also be acquitted of liability for any lesser bodily assault. The implicit legal logic underlying this paradigm is thus *a fortiori*.

In the course of his legal arraignment of the people (cf. 2:9), Jeremiah is manifestly dependent upon the content and terminology of this Pentateuchal rule. But as his concern is with an exegetical reuse of it, he selected from the details of Exod. 22:1-2a, altered its style, and allegorized its subject-matter. The aggadic transposition is apparent from the outset. First, Jeremiah transforms the casuistical format of Exod. 22:1-2a into an analogical construction with technical formulae (כ . . . כן 'as . . . so', 2:26). The effect is to shift the legal mode from a hypothetical case (אם 'if . . . [then]') to an applied situation. Moreover, by means of this analogy, the subject of the case is shifted from the specific acts of a burglar to the delicts of all Israel. Significantly, this reapplication is achieved through a free transformation of the focus of the original rule concerning breaking and entering. At the outset, in v. 26, Jeremiah suggests that God has caught Israel *in flagrante delicto* – on the analogy of the property-owner and the burglar – in the overt course of her covenantal infractions. This feature of the aggadic piece parallels the focus of the case in Exod. 22:1-2a. When, however, the thread of the legal topos is resumed in v. 34, the situation is more complicated. Like the original rule which continues by focusing on the blood-guilt or exculpation of the property-owner who slays an intruder, Jeremiah also invokes the theme of blood-guilt and exculpation for murder – though with the significant difference that Israel is no longer presented as the intruder (as in v. 26) but as the perpetrator of a delict. The reason for this alteration is obvious: the prophet wishes to sustain his focus on the guilt of Israel. Accordingly, he portrays Israel as a burglar in v. 26 and a manslayer in v. 34. In the latter instance particularly, Jeremiah's rhetoric is marked by his free adaptation of the

(1893), 82, J. Hogg, 'Exod 22:23 [*sic*] ("Nocturnal Thief" and "Restitution")', *AJSL* 44 (1927), 58–61, and many moderns, who propose that Exod. 22:1-2a is a secondary interpolation. Alternatively, it has been argued by Daube, *Studies*, 93, that 22:2b–3 is rather a *clausula finalis* – a view endorsed and given 'linguistic support' by Jackson, *Theft*, 139. Either way, 22:1-2a now interrupts the consecution of the case of insolvency. For a comparable legal-literary interruption, cf. *Tos. Sanh.* x.3, which disrupts the sequence of x.1-2, 4.

technical terminology of Exod. 22:1-2a to his purposes. In this way,
Israel is charged with flagrant guilt; indeed, their stain of blood-guilt
is incontrovertible since those slain were not burglars caught while
tunnelling but innocent people assaulted out in the open. Whatever the
concrete nature of Israel's crimes, therefore (and one can hardly doubt
that Jeremiah's charge of widespread murder is tinged with hyperbole),
it is nevertheless clear that the aggadically transformed legal topos in
Jer. 2: 26, 34 serves the prophetic rhetor as a prism for presenting the
malfeasances of the people, and as a means of arraigning and judging
them (v. 35) according to the principles of God's own covenantal law.

E. THE EXEGESIS OF CIVIL LAWS
WITHOUT FORMULAE OF CITATION AND COMPARISON

Jeremiah 5: 21-24 and Images of Rebellion

Another instance of inner-biblical aggadic exegesis may be seen in
the way Jeremiah transforms the deuteronomic law about the wayward
son. In fact, the levels of intersection between Deut. 21:18-21 and the
prophetic rhetoric derived from it are subtle and variegated. Through a
remarkable reallocation of the terms of the old law, and a series of
allusions and alliterations, the Jeremian diatribe achieves its singular
rhetorical force:

(21) Hear now (שמעו), you foolish and thoughtless (אין־לב) people
— who have eyes but see (יראו) not; who have ears but hear
(ישמעו) not.

(22) Will you not fear (תיראו) me? — oracle of YHWH; will you not
trouble before me, who has set the sand as a boundary to the sea:
a fixed law (חק) which it will not transgress . . .?

(23) But this people has a rebellious and contentious mind (לב סורר
ומורה) they have turned aside (סרו) and departed [from YHWH].

(24) They have not thought in their mind (בלבבם): 'Let us fear
(נירא) YHWH, our God, who provides the former (יורה) and
latter rains in due season, [and who] guarantees for us the weeks
fixed (חקות) for harvest.'

The structure of this condemnation is balanced and integrated, so
that while each of the verses provides a distinct image, a clear line of
development carries the separate images forward cumulatively. The
nation is first charged with folly, and addressed in terms used to
describe blind and dumb idols (cf. Pss. 115: 5-6, 135:16-17). Indeed,
this initial jibe sets the course of the pathetic and biting tone which
dominates the entire speech: for the prophet opens his rebuke with an
appeal to those who have *not* heard to hear and to attend. The positive
call to 'hear' in v. 21a is thus set against its negative corollary in v. 21b,

a negativity which is the reason for the call itself. However, since the people do not ever listen or see, the appeal by the prophet for attentiveness is not so much an appeal for the sake of repentance as an appeal for the sake of an arraignment. The diatribe is thus ironic from the outset.

The foregoing introductory impression of an address which does not truly invite a response is rhetorically deepened at v. 22, which contains a series of rhetorical questions. These also do not invite a direct response; for they are immediately followed by a detailed condemnation of the people for their disregard of the creator, who sets the boundary to the sea, and who fixes its laws. In their rebellion, the people give no mind to the fact that it is YHWH who provides the rain and who sets the seasons and their harvest on their eternal and trustworthy course. The opening address to a thoughtless people thus moves swiftly to a glorification of the god who is so disregarded, and punctuates the arraignment with a series of repeated words and alliterations. Thus, the thoughtless (אֵין־לֵב) people of v. 21 are described as those who never think (בלבבם) of the fear of the Lord (v. 24); and the people who have eyes that do not see (יִראוּ, v. 21) are the same as those who never think to fear (stem: ירא) YHWH (vv. 22, 24), who sets a fixed law (חק) for the sea (v. 22) and fixed weeks (חקות) for the harvest (v. 24).

In addition to these co-ordinating terms and images, and set between the opening and closing sections of the orations, which stress the thoughtlessness of the people who do not attend to YHWH's power, is v. 23. This verse, with its lexical link (by the word לב) to the surrounding context, is much more than a transitional point in a prophetic rebuke. For through its allusion to Deut. 21:18-21, whose language and legal topos form the nuclear matrix of Jer. 5:21-4, v. 23 serves as the pith of the prophet's oratory, and the generative power of his exegetical rhetoric. Deut. 21:18-21 reads as follows:

If a man has a rebellious and contentious (סורר ומורה) son, who does not listen (שמע) to his father or mother, and they reproved (וְיִסְּרוּ) him but he [still] does not listen (ישמע) to them, then his father and mother shall seize him and take him to the elders of his city, to the gate of his locale, and shall say to the elders of his city: 'This son of ours is rebellious and contentious (סורר ומורה) . . . [And the punishment shall be carried out] that all Israel may hear (ישמעו) and fear (ויראו).

Comparing this citation from Deut. 21:18-21 with Jer. 5:21-4, the strategic role of the deuteronomic rule in Jeremiah's rhetoric can easily be appreciated. On the one hand, the opening call by Jeremiah to the 'rebellious and contentious' people to 'hear', and the charge that they do 'not hear לא ישמעו', are comparable to the claim made by the parents of a 'rebellious and contentious' son before the elders of their city that he 'does not listen לא שמע' to them. Similarly, this 'rebellious

'סורר' son, who was duly 'reproved ויסרו' by his parents before the
execution of justice by the townsfolk, is strictly comparable to the
'rebellious סורר' Israelites who 'turned aside סרו' from YHWH and are
warned by the prophet before the execution of divine wrath. And
finally, just as the 'contentious מורה' son is punished that all may learn
and 'fear ייראו' from his example, so the 'contentious מורה' Israelite
people do not 'see ייראו' that YHWH brings the 'former rains יורה', and
thus neither 'fear ניראa' him nor follow in his ways. Taken altogether,
the dense texture of lexical and paranomastic cross-references between
the two pieces, comprising different alignments of meaning and irony,
co-ordinates the force of Jeremiah's diatribe as a legal arraignment on
behalf of God. By his superimposition of Pentateuchal terms upon his
critique of the people's behaviour, the prophet has succeeded in giving
particular gravity to his remarks: for as the civil case led to sure and
swift punishment, so the faults of Israel, metaphorically assimilated to
it, will result in divine punishment if the people do not heed this
arraignment. The complex series of thematic and verbal relations with
Deut. 21:18-21 thus give Jeremiah's speech a pointed legistic—and not
just rhetorical—force.

As with the preceding case of aggadic exegesis in the Book of
Jeremiah, discussed earlier, Jer. 5:21-4 nationalizes the original Pentateuchal rule and gives it a covenantal dimension. Hence it is not a
particular son who is accused, but the people; it is not the father or
mother who accuse, but the divine law-giver; and it is not a case of
parental authority which is called into question, but one of divine
authority and fealty to the covenant. The 'crime' depicted in Jer.
5:21-4 is therefore not an isolated act of familial—and so social—
insurrection, but rather a matter of theological apostasy and rebellion
by the entire nation.

It is particularly because the people's acts of religious rebellion
imply a disregard for the covenant and its rules that the prophet has
used one particular instance from these as a synecdoche for the whole.
One should not, therefore, see in Jeremiah's particular use of Deut. 21:
18-21 a studied piece of rhetorical exposition. His oration is rather the
product of a fertile religious imagination—one which brings forth a new
divine word from the free interplay between the religious life of the
nation and a case from the authoritative covenantal law that strikes him
as singularly apropos. Just because Jeremiah so strongly believed that
divine punishment was the consequence of infidelity to the covenant,
the imagery of that law—here in the form of one specific case—activated
his spiritual awareness. For him, Deut. 21:18-21 gave singular expression
to what he perceived to be the stubbornness .and infidelity of his
people. And since Jeremiah's aggadic exegesis is an imaginative—not
scholastic—application of one covenantal law to Israel's social-religious

life, the vitality of his discourse must be judged solely by its capacity to address the religious consciousness of its hearers, not to reinterpret the civil case from which it is derived. Jeremiah's task is not to reveal a new law or to interpret the older one; it is rather to renew the nation's allegiance to the covenant and the God who is the divine source of its prescriptions. The prophet thus alludes to the 'reproved' son who does not 'listen' in order that the entire community of Israel may be warned of misdeeds, and advised to amend them.

12. Aggadic Transformations of Non-legal Pentateuchal Traditions

A. NARRATIVES

Genesis 9: 1-7 and the Image of Man

The detailed reuse in Gen. 9: 1-7 of language from the creation narrative in Gen. 1: 26-9 — regarding the creation of man, his blessedness, his fertility, and his dominion over other earthly creatures — is well known. Indeed, the overall linguistic recapitulation is so precise as to leave little doubt that the post-diluvian restoration of life is modelled on the very creation of life,[1] and that Noah is an Adam *redivivus*.[2] This intertextual stylistic dependence is also strikingly evident precisely where variations between the two texts are most blatant. Thus, while it is obvious from Gen. 9: 3 that mankind is permitted to eat animal and reptilian life, whereas earlier, in Gen. 1: 29, only vegetation and its products were permitted, the particular *way* this change is introduced into the narrative is of exegetical interest. For when Gen. 9: 3 states that *'every living and moving thing* may be food for you; I have given you everything: *just as* [I once gave you] the green vegetation', it takes over the phrases 'may be food for you' and 'I have given you every' from Gen. 1: 29, and substitutes 'every living and moving thing' for 'every vegetation'. After the flood, all life-forms — and not just all greens — are permitted. The fact that the narrative *traditio* has indicated that the new edibles are a divine allowance, 'like' those permitted in the older *traditum*, shows a deliberate attempt to relate the new dispensation to the original source and its authority. Thus, the older *traditum* is not revised, but only supplemented; for while Gen. 9: 3 is a new divine revelation on edibles, its purpose is to extend the legal scope of Gen. 1: 28.[3]

---

[1] Such lexical variations as the different terms used for mankind's domination over creatures in Gen. 1: 26b, 28b, and 9: 2b are inconsequential from this regard, and certainly not contradictory.

[2] Cf. my remarks in *Text and Texture* (New York: Schocken, 1979), 33 f.

[3] Whether or not the narrator presupposes such cultic differentiations among edible creatures as are noted in Gen. 7: 2, or more carefully delineated in Lev. 11, the divine dispensation in Gen. 9: 3 is notably vague (note *kol remeś* 'every creature that lives').

The variations between the two texts extend to arrangement of its basic clauses. In Gen. 1 the sequence is (*a*) man created in the image of God; (*b*) human dominion over creaturely life; (*c*) divine blessing of mankind and the injunction to multiply; and (*d*) the reference to permissible greens. This consecution is altered in Gen. 9: 1-5 to (*c*), (*b*), (*d*), and (*a*). Such a variation is, to some extent, controlled by the exigencies of the new circumstances. Since the nucleus of mankind survived the deluge, attention is first given to a reversal of its estate, from punishment to blessing and regeneration, and thence to the various other matters, like earthly dominion and permissible edibles. The unit concludes in v. 7 with a stylistic repetition of the opening line which commanded regeneration and propagation of the human species – thus underscoring a basic concern of the text.[4]

However, while the core components in Gen. 9: 1-7 are comparable to those in 1: 26-8, and indeed, have been formed under its influence, the impact of the second piece is totally different from its forerunner. Beyond the textual and stylistic modifications referred to above, whereby permission to eat the flesh of animals has been granted, a major aggadic reorientation is brought about by the inclusion of vv. 4-6a in the reiteration of the creation-pericope. Following the permission to eat flesh (v. 3), these verses state:

(4)   However (אַךְ), flesh with its life-force – its blood – you may not eat.

(5)   Similarly, I shall demand recompense[5] for your lifeblood: of every beast I shall demand it; of man (also) shall I demand recompense for human life – of everyone for that of his fellow.[6]

(6a)   Whoever sheds a man's blood, his blood will be shed by a man . . .

This material is clearly a legal qualification of the permission to eat animal flesh found in v. 3. By use of the technical legal formula אַךְ,[7] v. 4 first prohibits the consumption of blood – thereby bringing this rule into some alignment with those later priestly norms which prohibit the eating of blood (cf. Lev. 17: 10-12).[8] The next clause (v. 5a), which also opens with the formula אַךְ, is parallel to v. 4 in language, though it is not simply a prelude to v. 5b. For the central concern of v. 5a is not

---

[4] The following pericope on the rainbow (Gen. 9: 8-17) is also framed by an *inclusio* (vv. 9 and 17).

[5] Or 'demand satisfaction' (NEB). Being more direct, such a translation is preferable here to RSV and NJPS 'require a reckoning'. Cf. Jackson, *Essays in Jewish and Comparative Legal History* (SJLA 10; Leiden: E. J. Brill, 1975), 116f.

[6] Cf. U. Cassuto, *A Commentary on the Book of Genesis* (Jerusalem: Magnes Press, 1964), ii. 126, 'of every man, of every man's brother' (i.e., especially if it is his brother).

[7] Cf. Num. 18: 15b, discussed above, pp. 184f.

[8] And cf. the further desacralization of blood in Deut. 12: 16, 23.

merely that God announces that he will demand recompense for human
blood shed by beasts (v. 5a) and humans (v. 5b), but is apparently also
a conditional divine promise related directly to v. 4.[9] If man will not
misuse or appropriate animal blood, God promises to protect human
blood from animals, and to secure its proper restitution to the clan if
spilt by them.[10] The latter clause is balanced by the further divine
promise to punish manslaughter, life for life (vv. 5b-6a). Following
this notice the pericope returns to the language of Gen. 1, and adds the
phrase 'for man was created in the image of God' (v. 6b).

It is thus obvious that vv. 4-6a have been incorporated into this
reworking of Gen. 1: 26-8. Of vv. 4-6a, it would appear that vv. 4-5 are
part of the basic reworking, and that v. 6a is a secondary element, both
because v. 5b continues the topic broached in v. 5a, in the same style
and language (and also emphasizes divine action), and because v. 6a
introduces the new topic of an injunction against manslaughter in
distinct stylistic terms (and formulates the legal recompense in a neutral
lapidary way). However this may be, the inclusion of these several
matters into the overall reworking of Gen. 1: 26-8 affects the function
of v. 6b – that man was created in the image of God – such that v. 6b
becomes the pivot of a unique piece of biblical aggadic exegesis. First, it
will be noted that whereas the reference in Gen. 1: 26-7 to man being
created in the image of God refers to mankind's special dominion over
the creatures of the earth, the same issue in Gen. 9: 6b has been transformed. For since vv. 4-5 provide a divine guarantee to mankind that
if they not misuse animal blood their own blood will be divinely
safeguarded ('I shall demand', v. 5 *bis*), the clause 'for he created man in
the image of God' *now* explains the reason for the divine action. With
the introduction of the further issue regarding manslaughter, yielding
the text as we now have it, the motivation clause in v. 6b assumes an
entirely different force. It functions not solely to explain why God will
restore human blood (to a clan) when humans have been killed by
animals, *but also to explain the prohibition of manslaughter and the
inevitable legal retribution*. Whoever kills another person will be killed,
states the text, *because* mankind has been created in the image of God.[11]

Among the various issues which underlie Gen. 9: 4-6, one of them
is clearly some attempt to understand why animals may be killed and
eaten – the new dispensation – whereas the killing of persons by animals
and persons is subject to human and divine retribution. With the
inclusion of the phrase that man was created in the image of God an
explanation may be found. Indeed, in the light of the received text, one

[9] As proposed by B. Jackson, op. cit. (n. 5 above), 117.

[10] On this matter, see Daube, *Studies*, 121-4.

[11] Cf. Cassuto, op. cit. ii. 127; von Rad, *Genesis* (OTL; Philadelphia: The
Westminster Press, 1961), 132.

may reasonably conclude that the aggadic interpretation in v. 6b constitutes a deliberate and seminal part of the overall teaching. For it will be observed that whereas the divine voice speaks directly from v. 1b on, and particularly in v. 5, the motivation clause in v. 6b is in the third person. It is thus the voice of the narrator and *his* aggadic *traditio*. The narrator of 9: 1a has thus betrayed his aggadic activity by grammatically reverting in 9: 6b to the oblique perfect (from 'I shall demand' to 'he created man in the image of God').[12] The motivational 'for' in v. 6b is thus pivotal to the aggadic exegesis. With it, the narrator has not only taken over language from Gen. 1: 26-8, but has substantially transformed its original function.

Genesis 1 and Moses' Oration in Deuteronomy 4

In addition to a host of diverse reflexes of creation imagery in the Hebrew Bible, many of which bear the imprint of ancient Near Eastern topoi of theomachy,[13] there are also a variety of instances where Gen. 1 serves as the literary model for the speaker or writer. For example, the rhetoric of Jer. 4: 23-6 underscores the anticipated destruction of the created world by referring to a known creation account, and the disintegration of Job's inner world is dramatized in 3: 1-13 via a reversal of an image of the created world as found in Gen. 1. But the latter are not—strictly speaking—aggadic reinterpretations. Rather, Gen. 1 has been freely reused for new stylistic and rhetorical purposes.[14]

Another identifiable group of texts which reuse Gen. 1 in a marked aggadic exegetical way can be exemplified by Deut. 4: 16b-19a.[15] Here there is an explicit aggadic adaptation of Gen. 1 for the purposes of an exhortation against idolatry. Indeed, in the context of a long and integrated sermon which forms the basis of Deut. 4,[16] Deut. 4: 16b-19a reuses the very language and sequence of its prototype to indicate the typical instances of prohibited idolatry.[17] Moses warns the people that

[12] Cassuto's explanation, op. cit. ii. 128, that v. 6b is to be understood as 'impersonal' (i.e. 'man was made', not 'he made man') is apologetic and skirts the issue. The LXX removed the difficulty by using a first-person form.

[13] Cf. my *Text and Texture*, 13-15, 126-8, 135-8.

[14] On these texts, particularly the second, see my 'Jer. 4: 23-26 and Job 3: 1-13: A Recovered Use of the Creation Pattern', *VT* 21 (1971), 151-67.

[15] Cf. *ZAW* 84 (1972), 349. For the aggadic reuse of Gen. 1. 1-2: 4 in Exod. 39-40, see *Text and Texture*, 12, and references.

[16] On the stylistic unity of Deut. 4, see G. Braulik, *Die Mittel deuteronomischer Rhetorik* (*An. Bib.* 68; Rome: Biblical Institute Press, 1978), 91-100; N. Lohfink, 'Auslegung deuteronomischer Texte, IV', *Bibel und Leben*, 4 (1964), 252f, has attempted to demonstrate its topical coherence.

[17] Deut. 4: 16b-19b is the kernel of the unit usually isolated as vv. 15-22. It will be noted that vv. 15-20 shift between the second person singular and plural.

neither human nor animal images, nor those of birds, reptiles, or fish, nor, indeed, even the heavenly bodies themselves, are permitted for worship, for no image was seen at the divine revelation on Sinai, only a voice was heard (Deut. 4:12-14). Quite clearly, the pattern of imagery found in Gen. 1:14-27 has been followed in Moses' discourse – though in reversed order, now moving upward from the earthly realm of human and animal forms to the heavenly domain of the sun, moon, and stars. The result of this aggadic adaptation, moreover, is to establish a distinct rhetorical nexus between the themes of creation and idolatry. While such a conjunction is not entirely unique in the Hebrew Bible, as an examination of the patterning (whether original or redactional) of several post-exilic prophetic orations attests,[18] their particular inter-relationship in Deut. 4:14-19 is stylistically unique and theologically notable. For, like these prophetic orations, but in a form intensified by its aggadic invocation of an authoritative *traditum*, Moses' discourse powerfully reinforces the Israelite *theologoumenon* that idolatry is a sin against the creator and his transcendence.[19]

Genesis 1:1-2:4a and Demythologizing Trends in Deutero-Isaiah

The reuse and reinterpretation of creation accounts or cosmogonies

---

The variation is rhetorical, and has nothing to do with sources here. Although G. M. de Tillesse, 'Sections "tu" et sections "vous" dans le Deutéronome', *VT* 12 (1962), 29-87, did not treat Deut. 4, H. Cazelles did, in 'Passages in the Singular within Discourse in the Plural of Dt. 1-4', *CBQ* 29 (1967), 213. His arguments have been countered by J. Levenson, 'Who Inserted the Book of the Torah?', *HTR* 68 (1975), 204-7. For a treatment of the change of address in Deuteronomy along stylistic lines, see N. Lohfink, *Das Hauptgebot. Eine Untersuchung literar-ischer Einleitungsfragen zu Dt. 5-11* (*An. Bib.* 20; Rome: Pontifical Biblical Institute, 1963), 30-1, 239-58.

[18] Cf. Isa. 40:12-26, 44:6-20, 45:18-21, 46:5-11.

[19] The recurrence of anti-idolatry diatribes in exilic prophecy (cf. n. 18) is one of several reasons commonly adduced for an exilic dating of Deut. 4; cf. A. D. H. Mayes, 'Deuteronomy 4 and the Literary Criticism of Deuteronomy', *JBL* 100 (1981), 48-51. This factor also bears on the dating of the prohibition of images in the Decalogue, in Deut. 5: 7 for example. Thus the manifest similarity between Deut. 4:16b-19 and Deut. 4: 7, where a prohibition of images and creation language are also conjoined, plus the occurrence in Deut. 6:10-15 of a sermon on divine sovereignty which cites the Decalogue (Deut. 5: 6-7, 10) *but omits the prohibition against images*, raises the possibility that the prohibition against idolatry in the decalogic prohibition is also quite late – if not exilic. On these matters, see the remarks of W. Moran, 'The Ancient Near Eastern Background of the Love of God in Deuteronomy', *CBQ* 25 (1963), 85-7, and 'The Conclusion of the Decalogue (Ex 20, 17; Dt 5, 21)', ibid. 29 (1967), 553f. That the prohi-bition against images is, in any case, a secondary element in the Decalogue is strongly indicated by W. Zimmerli's fundamental form-critical observation that the phrase 'do not bow down to them' in Deut. 5: 9 continues the issue against 'other gods' in v. 7. See his 'Das zweite Gebot', in *Festschrift A. Bertholet*, edd. W. Baumgartner *et al.* (Tübingen: J. C. B. Mohr, 1959), 550-60.

is not uncommon in other ancient Near Eastern civilizations. Here, too, different forms are expressed, even though a dominant motivation in this regard is the replacement of older divine heroes by newer ones, or the transfer of certain gods to a more central role – all in accordance with changing hierarchies in the pantheon in different historical circumstances. As is well known, the older kernels of *Enuma elish* gave central positions variously to the gods Ea and Enlil, long before Marduk came to pre-eminence through his city, Babylon;[20] and when the same creation account was adapted to the Assyrian milieu, the god Aššur was then given the role of chief divine protagonist.[21]

A tendency towards exegetical explication and even spiritualization can also be noted in several Egyptian texts. An extract from the seventeenth chapter of the *Book of the Dead* may serve as an example of exegetical explication. The text is a speech of the god Atum, with glosses. The following is representative:

'I am Atum when I was alone in Nun; I am Re in his [first] appearances, when he began to rule that which he had made.' Who is he? This 'Re, when he began to rule that which he had made' means that Re began to appear as king . . .
'I am the great god who came into being by himself.' Who is he? 'The great god who came into being by himself' is water; he is Nun, the father of the gods. Another version: He is Re.[22]

The text goes on in this way, alternating lemma and commentary, thereby contemporizing the meaning of the text and expanding its theological reference. Atum was the ancient god of Heliopolis, and a reference to his primal creativity is included in this text. A more specific, and earlier, text dealing with Atum's creation is also known. This text portrays a physical creation, but is not very precise.[23] Indeed, one key line simply refers to the 'Great Ennead which is in Heliopolis . . . whom Atum begot'. The latter point is, however, particularly significant when we take note of an even earlier text from Memphis. There the god Ptah was proclaimed as creator-god. The significant point for present purposes is not solely that his creation is presented as a verbal

---

[20] See T. Jacobsen, in *Before Philosophy*, ed. H. Frankfort (Baltimore: Penguin, 1963), 155f.

[21] See A. Heidel, *The Babylonian Genesis* (Chicago: University of Chicago Press, 1963), 1. Also cf. R. Kutscher, *Oh Angry Sea* (a-ab-ba hu-lah-ha). *The History of a Sumerian Lament* (Yale Near Eastern Researches, 6; New Haven: Yale University Press, 1975), 7, 20, 72, where the reference to the devastation of Nippur is redactionally replaced by a reference to the city of Babylon; and Samar. Deut. 27: 4, where Mt. Gerizim replaces Mt. Ebal of the MT.

[22] This translation is from J. Pritchard, *ANET* 3f.; cf. the translation and edition of H. Grapow, *Religiöse Urkunden, Ausgewählte Texte des Totenbuchs* (Leipzig, 1915), 4 ff. For other examples of lemmatic commentary in Egyptian literature, see my 'Qumran Pesher', 101 and nn. 21-2.   [23] See *ANET* 3.

not physical—achievement, but that, building upon an old version of Atum's physical creation, an exegetical adaptation and spiritualization of this myth of creation is produced. Thus

> His Ennead is before him in [the form of] teeth and lips. That is [the equivalent of] the semen and hands of Atum. Whereas the Ennead of Atum came into being by his semen and his fingers, the Ennead [of Ptah], however, is the teeth and lips in this mouth, which pronounced the name of everything. . . . Thus all the gods . . . all the divine order really came into being through what the heart thought and the tongue commanded.[24]

Among the striking facets of this document is the polemical substratum which lies behind the theological exegesis and spiritualizing appropriation of an older—and, in some sense, quite definitely authoritative—tradition of divine creation. Since the older discourse about Atum's creation could neither be simply taken over, nor totally disregarded, the theological adaptation of it had to provide a mode of transfer from the one view to the other. Towards this end, an exegetical construction proved the most productive process whereby all necessities were achieved. The felt hermeneutical tension between the old and new theologies, which is so explicitly dramatized by lemma-plus-commentary schema, gives profound witness to the underlying cultural and cognitive processes involved.

To be sure, ideological clashes need not result in exegetical adaptations, and may be denied or suppressed. While such polemical postures are well known in the history of religion, the opposite process is the more intriguing for present purposes. A series of texts in Deutero-Isaiah provide a striking comparative instance of this process from biblical sources, for they show how certain creation formulations found in Gen. 1:1–2:4a were exegetically reinterpreted due to a new theological temperament and a new historical situation.

Deutero-Isaiah's extraordinary concern with the theme of creation has long been of recognized interest to scholars—particularly the link between creation and redemption. Within that framework of concern, some commentators have recognized in Deutero-Isaiah a preponderance of creation terms and verbs reminiscent of those found in Gen. 1.[25] A. Kapelrud, who has justly stressed this point, has even suggested that Isa. 42: 5 and 45: 18 are actually phraseological allusions to Gen. 1.[26] One can hardly doubt the merits of this observation and, indeed, an earlier generation of commentators had also referred to linguistic or

---

[24] Ibid. 5.
[25] Cf. B. Anderson, *Creation and Chaos* (New York: Association Press, 1967), 124–6.
[26] 'The Date of the Priestly Code (P)', *ASTI* 3 (1964), 58–64.

stylistic similarities between these two literary sources – but were stymied in the relative dating of them by their presumption that P unilaterally postdated Deutero-Isaiah.

More recently, M. Weinfeld has offered a seminal suggestion with respect to such allusions, proposing that Deutero-Isaiah provides a spiritualizing polemic against a variety of notions embedded in the creation account of Gen. 1:1-2:4.[27] Examples culled from several categories of his argument will exemplify this point:

1. Gen. 1:2 simply refers to the pre-existence of such hylic materials as תהו ובהו 'waste and void' and חשך 'darkness'. What, one might ask, is their ontological status? Are they rival powers of the creator god; and did YHWH, in fact, 'create' chaos? Such questions have bothered modern interpreters and were, quite likely, very prevalent in the Jewish exilic community of ancient Iran, where such issues as cosmological dualism were undoubtedly discussed.[28] Such texts as Isa. 45:7, 'He forms light and create חשך darkness... I YHWH make all these things', and Isa. 45:18, 'He who בורא creates the heavens, he is God; he who forms the earth and makes it, he establishes it; לא־תהו בְרָאָהּ he did not create it as chaos, but formed it for a dwelling: I am YHWH, there is no other [God]', counter these notions. The God of Israel is, the prophet argues in language targeted towards Gen. 1, the only god; and primal matter was utilized in a structured form: it never had the status of a restive or unformed chaos.

2. In Gen. 1:26 it is stated that God consulted with his pantheon and created man in his own דמות 'likeness'. The basilomorphic and anthropomorphic notions embedded here have long raised various theological issues for modern scholars. Is the divine court a projection of an earthly royal court with its councillors, and is man truly in the physical likeness of God? These notions were no doubt difficult for some people in antiquity as well. It is against this background that we can appreciate the remarks in Isa. 40:18, 25 and Isa. 46:5, where the question is asked – rhetorically and ironically – whether, indeed, an appropriate דמות 'likeness' of God can be found.[29] Similarly, when Deutero-Isaiah emphasizes that God was alone at the time of his creation (cf. 44:24), and did not consult with anyone (40:13-14), it would

[27] 'The Creator God in Genesis 1 and the Prophecies of Deutero-Isaiah', *Tarbiz*, 37 (1968), esp. 120-6 [Heb.]. In the first part of this essay, Weinfeld decisively shows that Gen. 1-2:4 is less 'spiritual' and more anthropomorphic than usually contended.

[28] Cf. Nyberg, *Religionen des alten Iran* (reprint of 1938 edn.; Osnabrück: Zeller, 1966), 347f.

[29] On the relationship between Gen. 1:26 and Isa. 40:18, cf. already B. Duhm, *Das Buch Jesaia*[5] (HKAT[3], 1914; Göttingen: Vandenhoek and Ruprecht, 1968), ad loc.

appear that he also voices a spiritualizing polemic against 'let *us* make man', and the theological conceptions or implications which underlie it.

3. The preceding examples of anti-anthropomorphism set the context of an anti-anthropopathic comment in Deutero-Isaiah. For though there is hardly any doubt that Gen. 2: 2-3 portrays God as physically resting after the labour of creation—a perspective more graphically underscored in other P or P-influenced documents (cf. Exod. 31:17; also Exod. 20:11)—the implications of this viewpoint are categorically countered in Isa. 40: 28. Hereby a remarkable transformation occurs, for the prophetic text reads and stresses: 'He who creates the ends of the earth shall be neither weary nor tired; there is no limit to his wisdom.' One senses here a stern rejection of any physical impact of the creative act upon God; as well as a remarkable, incipient intellectualization of the means of creation (i.e., creation through divine wisdom).

In conclusion, though the various issues noted by Deutero-Isaiah appear seriatim in his discourses, it must be stressed that we have much more than a scattered prophetic polemic. Indeed, while the texts are isolated, the content and language of Deutero-Isaiah's remarks are unquestionably keyed to Gen. 1:1-2:4a. And just because this is so, there is an explicit *exegetical core* to the polemical challenge presented. The prophet has not chosen his language indiscriminately. By alluding to Gen. 1:1-2: 4a in his spiritualization of it, a hermeneutical tension is posed. Deutero-Isaiah could not accept the received creation account in Gen. 1:1-2: 4a as it was—in the light of his theological attitudes and the challenge of the Persian ideological milieu. Particularly sensitized by the latter, one may presume, he *exegetically reappropriated* Gen. 1:1-2: 4a and transposed it into a new theological key.[30] The underlying cognitive concern was not so much to undermine Gen. 1:1-2: 4a as to maintain it in a newly understood way. As seen, this could not be completely achieved, for notions like a divine likeness in man or divine rest were not spiritualized but completely rejected. Despite this, the exegetical character of Deutero-Isaiah's ideological achievement is in no way diminished, and remains a remarkable instance of the aggadic transformation of a creation tradition in the Hebrew Bible.

The Manna Tradition and its Aggadic Transformations

According to the old JE tradition, the congregation of Israel complained to Moses and Aaron that they would have preferred death in Egypt, where there was 'לחם food for satiety', to their present famine

---

[30] The implications for relative dating should not be ignored. Self-evidently, Gen. 1:1-2: 4a *preceded* Deut. 4:16b-19 and the polemic of Deutero-Isaiah.

in the desert (Exod. 16: 3). In response, 'YHWH said to Moses: "Behold, I shall rain down for you לחם food from heaven; and the nation will go gather it daily, so that I may test it concerning obedience to My Torah"' (v. 4). The events took place as predicted, and Israel was tested regarding the manna and its collection on the Sabbath day – and found wanting.

A reflex of this tradition is incorporated into a historiographical psalm, Ps. 78, amidst a catena of instances where Israel disregarded the manifest goodness of God towards Israel (cf. vv. 9, 17-18, 32, 41). While the composer of this psalm may have known the manna and quail tradition of Num. 11 (and possibly even a different sequence of the desert traditions from that found in its received Pentateuchal form),[31] the explicit reference in Ps. 78: 24 to the manna raining from heaven, and the description of the manna in Ps. 78: 24-5 as a heavenly good, strongly suggest that its composer was in some manner dependent upon the formulation preserved in Exod. 16. An inverted witness to this dependency is the transformation of the original act of divine testing (cf. Exod. 16: 4) into one whereby Israel tested and rebelled against YHWH (cf. Ps. 78: 18). No testing tradition is referred to in Num. 11.

In Deut. 8 an altogether novel aggadic reuse of the earlier manna tradition occurs. In an exhortation within Moses' peroration on the plains of Moab, the people are told to observe every God-given commandment when they enter 'the land which YHWH had promised' the ancestors (v. 1), and to remember the desert sojourn, when YHWH 'humbled you to test you', whether you would be obedient and observe the commandments (v. 2). He humbled them by famine, and then provided the manna 'to make you aware that no one lives by לחם food alone, but that one lives by every utterance of the mouth of YHWH' (v. 3).

In this reworking, with its allusion to the testing tradition of Exod. 16: 4, there is no reference to Israel's complaints in the desert. The testing is rather a sovereign – not responsive – act by God, designed to see whether Israel would obey his commandments and recognize him as the source of all sustenance. The people are thus tested in the desert with respect to their observance of all the commandments – not just the Torah-instruction concerning the manna (as in Exod. 16: 4). In the aggadic reworking of Deut. 8, the specific testing associated with the giving of manna (after a prior – providentially determined! – famine) was designed to bring Israel to recognize that 'the creative will of God, in whatever way it may, upon occasion, specifically exert itself, is also a sustaining power, on which man may find himself obliged to rely'.[32]

---

[31] For example, the tradition of 'desire' (*ta'ǎwāh*) follows the manna tradition in Ps 78: 29f.; in Num. 11: 4 it precedes it. The matter does not appear in Exod. 16.
[32] S. R. Driver, *Deuteronomy* (ICC; Edinburgh: T. and T. Clarke, 1895), 197.

Moreover, as 'food from heaven' (Exod. 16: 4), the manna is interpreted in Deut. 8: 3 as 'that which comes from the mouth of YHWH'—just like his teachings.[33] The two are thus exegetically correlated.

But the aggadic transformation of Exod. 16 is not limited to this reuse alone; for it is clear that the manna tradition has also been ironically reused as an exhortation to the children of the desert generation not to forget their dependence upon God when they come to the bounteous land and enjoy its boon (Deut. 8: 7-14). The danger forecast by the preacher is that of misplaced pride (cf. vv. 14, 17-18). The paraenesis thus recalls the divine giving of the manna in order to teach a new generation proper humility and acknowledgement before YHWH— now singularly expressed through adherence to the commandments (vv. 6, 11). As the Lord was the sovereign source of succour in the desert, so he remains; and as an earlier generation was brought to this vital religious consciousness, before Sinai, so is the present post-Sinaitic generation bidden to do as well. It is not famine which now threatens the nation, but the dangers of plenty and creaturely pride. For this reason, events in the lives of the fathers are set forth as examples for their sons.[34] In the process the old manna tradition is remarkably reinterpreted in terms of Israel's ultimate dependency on YHWH, and therewith applied to a new generation in totally new circumstances. 'Everything that comes from the mouth of YHWH' is, for this new generation, the entirety of commandments, laws, and ordinances which the Lord set before them (cf. v. 11), *and* the bounteous land which he promised to the patriarchs (vv. 1, 18).

The striking oratorical structure of Deut. 8: 1-18, within which the foregoing teachings are taught, deserves a brief concluding comment. For the paraenesis is arranged in a chiastic pattern, so that its argument is reinforced through a systematic recapitulation of its contents. Thus, the piece opens (A, v. 1) and closes (A', v. 16) with references to the promises sworn to the patriarchs. Within this framework is a second ballast pair: vv. 2-3 (B), which refer to the divine guidance through the desert and the giving of the manna; and the corresponding unit, in vv. 15-16 (B'), which does the same. Within these two concentric frames lies the centrepiece: a paean of praise for the bounty of 'the favourable land'. Notably, this matrix is also chiastically structured: it opens (C, v. 6) and closes (C', v. 11) with admonitions to heed the command-ments, and it continues with references to the favourable land (D, v. 7a; D', v. 10b). The middle unit of the centre-piece, vv. 7b-9 (E), is a series of phrases in descriptive praise of 'the favourable land'—blessed

---

[33] See D. Flusser, 'Society and Religion in the Second Temple Period', in *The World History of the Jewish People*, ed. M. Avi-Yonah and Z. Baras (Jerusalem: Massada, 1977), viii. 14.

[34] Ibid. For a later typological reuse of the manna tradition, see Matt. 4: 1-4.

as it is with surface water and wells, by grains and fruits, and by natural fertility and natural resources. It is this anticipated bounty which rhetorically binds the admonitions which follow (vv. 12-14) to the historical reflections which introduce it.

B. LITURGICAL AND THEOLOGICAL FORMULAE

The Priestly Blessing and its Aggadic Reuse

The great priestly blessing in Num. 6: 23-7 concludes a cycle of priestly instructions to the people of Israel. It opens with an instruction to the Aaronids delivered by Moses, 'In this manner shall you bless (תברכו) the Israelites', and then proceeds with the blessing itself:

(24)	May YHWH bless you	יברכך ה'
	and protect you;	וישמרך
(25)	May YHWH brighten	יאר ה'
	his countenance	פניו
	towards you	אליך
	and show you favour;	ויחנך
(26)	May YHWH raise his	ישא ה'
	countenance towards	פניו אליך
	you and give you peace.	וישם לך שלום

At the conclusion of this blessing, there is a final instruction: 'And when they shall put (ושמו) my name (שמי) over the Israelites, I shall bless them (אברכם)' (v. 27).[35] In this way, the narrative instruction in v. 27 balances, in both form and content, the instruction found in v. 23; and it furthermore provides a stylistic envelope to the encased poetic blessing.[36]

In addition to this formal presentation, there are hints elsewhere in Scripture that the Priestly Blessing was enunciated by the priests on

---

[35] The Samar. reading is *wśymw*, probably a plural imperative in order to balance the command/instruction in v. 23. Comparably, the LXX transposes v. 27 to the end of v. 23, and thereby tightens the nexus between the verses. However, v. 27 is resultative, and so no verse transposition is necessary; see also below for comments on the formal symmetry of the MT, which reinforces this point. In any event, the precise meaning of v. 27, and its relationship to the previous prayer, is an old crux. See the most recent review by P. A. H. de Boer, 'Numbers 6: 27', *VT* 32 (1982), 1-13, though his reconstruction, which claims that *'al* 'over' is a misreading of an original divine epithet 'The Most High of the Israelites' is problematic and gratuitous: it is problematic because it leaves the verb without an object; and it is gratuitous because it is the divine name YHWH which recurs in the blessing itself.

[36] The narrative framework is also textually linked to the blessing; cf. the stem *bārēk* in vv. 23-4 and the stem *śîm* in vv. 26-7. For other stylistic aspects, and a critique of certain reconstructions based on 'symmetry', see my 'Form and Reformulation of the Biblical Priestly Blessing', *JAOS* 103 (1983), 115 and n. 3.

various occasions. In what appears to be a deliberate reference to Num. 6: 24-6 in Lev. 9: 22, it is said that Aaron, after the appointment of the priests, raised his arms and 'blessed' the people (cf. Num. 6: 23); and, similarly, it is stated in Deut. 10: 8 and 21: 5 that the levitical priests constitute a special class, one designated to serve YHWH ' and to bless (ולברך) in his name' (cf. Num. 6: 27). In addition to these circumspect allusions, and the frequently repeated requests in the Psalter for divine blessing, for the manifestation of the radiant divine countenance (cf. the refrain in Ps. 80: 4, 8, 20), or for grace and favour (cf. Pss. 25: 16, 86: 16) – piecemeal expressions which may derive from common metaphorical usage – the clustered technical terminology in Ps. 67: 2 leaves no reasonable doubt that its source is Num. 6: 24-6. In this instance, the psalmist opens his prayer with the invocation, 'May Elohim show us favour (יחננו) and bless us (ויברכנו); may he brighten his countenance יאר פניו among us – selah.' Not only have the priestly liturgists - or their lay imitators – been decisively inspired by the language and imagery of the Priestly Blessing, but, as is evident, they have reused it creatively. The verbs have been selectively chosen and regrouped innovatively, and there is a use of verbs from both halves of each of the cola.

Ps. 4 contributes another example of the impact of the Priestly Blessing on the liturgical life of ancient Israel, as reflected in the Psalter. It is particularly significant since it provides a literary form manifestly different from that found in Ps. 67. In the latter, Num. 6: 24-6 is first (partially) cited and only then applied (cf. v. 3). By contrast, in Ps. 4 the key terms of the Priestly Blessing are spread throughout the piece, serving simultaneously as its theological touchstone and its ideological matrix. The psalmist first calls upon YHWH to ' חנני favour me' and hear his prayer (v. 2); then, after citing those disbelievers 'who say: "Who will show us (יראנו) good?"', the psalmist calls upon YHWH to 'raise over us (נסה־עלינו) the light of your presence (אור פניך)' (v. 7).[37] The psalmist concludes with a reference to שלום, peace or well-being (v. 9).[38]

These and other references to the Priestly Blessing in the Psalter and, particularly, the recurrence of similar language in the Psalter and many biblical genres, suggest that such imagery as 'shining the face' in favour,

---

[37] In this context *yar'ēnî* is a pun on PB *yā'ēr*; and *něsāh* is a play on *yiśśā* (if it is not simply an orthographic error). I find no basis for the emendation of M. Dahood, *Psalms*, i (AB; Garden City: Doubleday, 1966), 26, which introduces new problems.

[38] Heb. *šālôm* appears to combine Akk. *šulmu/šalmu* 'be well, unimpaired, at peace' and *salīmu/sulīmu* 'be favourable, gracious'; cf. M. Weinfeld, 'Covenant Terminology in the Ancient Near East and its Influence on the West', *JAOS* 93 (1973), 191f. and n. 31, and the references cited.

or 'raising the face' in beneficence, were widely diffused throughout the culture. Indeed, one may turn to the abundant use of such imagery in ancient Near Eastern literature, where it recurs in a wide range of genres, as the source for the diffusion of this imagery.[39] In addition, several Mesopotamian documents actually indicate a remarkable linguistic and stylistic similarity to the biblical Priestly Blessing.[40] But these parallels do not constitute instances of aggadic transformation any more than, from the strictly biblical side, Pss. 4 and 67 are aggadic transformations of Num. 6: 24-6. These psalms merely reuse its liturgical prototype, sometimes creatively; that is all.

The strong claim made by L. Liebreich, over a generation ago, that the entire ensemble referred to as the 'Songs of Ascent' (Pss. 120-30) reuses the key language of the Priestly Blessing, falls into this general category.[41] For although a number of key terms recur in Pss. 120-30 and, arguably, give the ensemble its coherence, the contention that all this reflects reapplication of the old Priestly Blessing for the post-exilic community ('the earliest interpretation of the Priestly Blessing, an interpretation that may be considered to be the precursor of the homilies on the Priestly Blessing in Midrashic literature') is doubtful.[42] Given the commonplace nature of the words and verbs emphasized and, especially, given the fact that these words and verbs do not occur in clusters which either dominate or transform the meaning of the psalms in question, it is possible to observe that certain liturgical terms were used in the 'Songs of Ascent' in order to convey the sense of blessing and peace so much hoped for by the post-exilic community. But it is quite another matter to assume, on the basis of these references to blessing and protection, that any one of the psalms—let alone the ensemble—is an interpretative reuse of the Priestly Blessing.[43]

[39] For Ugaritic literature, cf. UT 1126: 6; and for Akkadian literature, see the examples collected and discussed by E. Dhorme, 'L'Emploi métaphorique de parties du corps en hébru et en akkadien', *RB* 30 (1921), 383ff., and A. L. Oppenheim, 'Idiomatic Accadian', *JAOS* 61 (1941), 256-8, 'Studies in Accadian Lexicography, I', *Orientalia*, NS 11 (1942), 123f. Also cf. next note.

[40] See the texts published by L. W. King, *Babylonian Boundary-Stones and Memorial-Tablets in the British Museum* (London, 1912), No. 36, and by H. Lewy, 'The Babylonian Background of the Kay Kaus Legend', *An. Or.* 17/2 (1949), 51f. On the latter see my remarks in 'Form and Reformulation', and the fundamental observations of Y. Muffs, *Studies in the Aramaic Legal Papyri from Elephantine* (Studia et Documenta ad Iura Orientis Antiqui Pertinentia, 8; Leiden: E. J. Brill, 1969), 130-4.

[41] 'The Songs of Ascent and the Priestly Blessing', *JBL* 74 (1955), 33-6.

[42] Ibid. 36.

[43] O. Loretz, in 'Altorientalischer Hintergrund sowie inner- und nachbibliche Entwicklung des Aaronitischen Segens (Num 6: 24-26)', *UF* 10 (1978), 118, has claimed that the Priestly Blessing already contains exegetical expansions. But (1) his 'exegetical expansions' are not exegetical in any meaningful sense; and

These methodological qualifications may serve to highlight the case of Mal. 1: 6–2: 9, a remarkable post-exilic example of the aggadic exegesis of Num. 6: 23–7. Indeed, Malachi's outspoken and vitriolic critique of cultic and priestly behaviour is, at once, a systematic utilization of the language of the Priestly Blessing and a thorough exegetical transformation of it. With great ironic force, the prophet turns to the priests and says:

Where is your fear of Me (מוראי), says YHWH of hosts, to you, priests who despise my name (בוזי שמי) . . . You offer polluted meat upon my altar . . . [and] bring it to your governor. Will he accept you, or will he be gracious to you (הישא פניך) . . .? So, now, beseech the countenance of God (חלו־נא פני־אל) that he may show us favour (ויחננו) ; . . . will he be gracious to you (הישא מכם פנים)? Would that there was one among you to close the door [of the Temple] that you do not kindle (תאירו) my altar in vain (חנם) . . . I will not accept your meal-offerings . . . [for] my name (שמי) is awesome (נורא) among the nations (1: 6–14)

After this condemnation, Malachi levels a harsh statement of ensuing divine doom at the priests:

If you do not hearken . . . and give glory to my name (שמי), says YHWH of hosts, I shall send a curse (המארה) among you and curse (וארותי) your blessings (ברכותיכם) . . . Behold, I shall . . . scatter dung upon your faces (פניכם) . . . and raise you (ונשא אתכם) to it (אליו).[44] For you know that I have sent you this covenant, that my covenant was with the Levites . . . and my covenant was with them for life and peace (השלום); and I gave them fear that they might fear me (מורא וייראני) and . . . my name (שמי). A true Torah was in their mouth; . . . but you have turned from the path . . . and so I shall make you contemptible . . . for you do not guard (שמרים) my ways; but [you rather] show partiality/favour (נשאים פנים) in [the administration and teaching of] the Torah. (2: 2–9)

The foregoing indicates, boldly and decisively, that all the key terms of the Priestly Blessing are alluded to, or played upon, in the prophet's diatribe. On the one hand, the dense clustering of these terms makes it clear that Mal. 1: 6–2: 9 has more than casual, terminological similarities with Num. 6: 23–7. Indeed, the transformed reapplications of these terms indicate that Malachi's oration is *exegetical* in nature. The prophet has taken the contents of the Priestly Blessing—delivered by the priests,

(2) the whole enterprise rests on his reconstruction of the text's strata, which is dubious. For he isolates the 'original' components from later accretions on the basis of metric criteria (cf. p. 116), though he has, thereby, introduced new asymmetries, since the *waw*-clause is retained only for the first blessing.

[44] The LXX reads something like *ûněśā'tîkem* 'and I bore you'. A. Ehrlich, *Mikrâ ki Pheschutô*, iii. 192 [Heb.], has posited the Niphal form *wěniśśā'tem* 'und ihr werdet darauf angewiesen sein'.

and with its emphasis on blessing, the sanctity of the divine Name, and such benefactions as protection, favourable countenance, and peace — *and inverted them.* The priests, the prophet contends, have despised the divine name and service; and this has led to a threatened suspension of the divine blessing. Even the governor will not give his gracious acknowledgement of the offerings.[45] The only hope lies in YHWH's favour and beneficence. The gift, articulated in Num. 6: 24-6, of a brightened divine countenance which leads to divine favour (יאר ה' פניו), (ישא ה' פניו אליך ויחנך and the raising of the divine countenance אליך) which leads to שלום, peace or well-being, are punningly countered by the prophet's wish that the priests will no longer ignite (תאירו) the alter in vain (חנם), and by the anticipated divine curse (המארה וארותי). Indeed, the priests' perversion of their sacred office is such that they who asked YHWH to raise his counterance (ישא ה' פניו) for the good of the people now 'raise the countenance' (theirs and others') in overt partiality and misuse of the Torah and its laws (נשאים פנים בתורה). In truth, says the prophet, the priests have spurned the divine gift, entrusted to them, of שלום; so that what will be 'raised' for them, or against their 'faces' (על־פניכם ... ונשא אתכם אליו) will be the polluted refuse of their offerings, nothing more. Those who neglect their office, and do not guard (שמרים) YHWH's ways, can hardly be permitted, implies the prophet, to invoke the Lord's blessing of protection (cf. וישמרך) upon the people of Israel.

A more violent condemnation of the priests can hardly be imagined. Nor does the ironic texture of the diatribe stop with the preceding lexical and conceptual cross-reference between Mal. 1: 6-2: 9 and the Priestly Blessing. On closer inspection, one will further note that the prophet's speech is replete with interlocking puns that condemn the priests 'measure for measure'. Note, for example, the initial ironic appeal to 'beseech' (חלו) God, which is countered by the reference to the priests' desecrations (מחללים),[46] or the initial reference to the 'governor' (פחה), which is echoed in the punishment of utter blasting and ruination by God (הפחתם),[47] or the failure of the priests to fear YHWH's awesome (נורא) presence, which leads to the extinguishing of the altar lights (תאירו) and the onset of divine curses (המארה וארותי),[48] or the priestly contempt of the divine name (בוזי שמי), which leads to the contempt (נבזה) of the priestly offering and the priests themselves (נבזים).[49]

The ironic reversal of the priests' language, actions, and hopes is thus textured through a series of reworkings and plays on the liturgical

---

[45] Ehrlich, ibid., suggested that the subject of Mal. 1: 9 ('will he be gracious to you') is God, not the governor, and compared Num. 6: 25.

[46] Mal. 1: 9, 12.   [47] Mal. 1: 8, 13.

[48] Mal. 1: 10, 14, 2: 2.   [49] Mal. 1: 6, 12, 2: 9.

language of Num. 6: 23-7. In this way, the priests' cultic language is desacralized and their actions cursed. By unfolding the negative semantic range of most of the key terms used positively in the Priestly Blessing, the rotten core and consequences of the language and behaviour of the priests is echoed throughout the diatribe. And further, in so far as the prophetic speech of Malachi is presented as a divine word, Malachi's speech is revealed to be no less than a divine exegesis of the Priestly Blessing, and a divine mockery of the priests who presume to bless in his name. The sacerdotal language of the Priestly Blessing is thus, by further irony, systematically desecrated and inverted by YHWH himself. The priests, bearers of the cultic Blessing, and sensitive to its language, could not have missed the exegetical irony and sarcastic nuance of the prophet's speech.

The relationship between form and content in Mal. 1: 6–2: 9 supports and illumines the foregoing reflections. As against the fairly balanced and symmetrical style of Num. 6: 23-7, the reuse of it in Mal. 1: 6–2: 9 is unbalanced and asymmetrical. If the formalized style of the positive blessing in the old Priestly Blessing is the objective literary correlative of the hopes for protection, well-being, favour, and sustenance expressed therein, then the disorder of Malachi's condemnation – its narrative effusiveness, its redundancies, and its disjointed and scattered allusions to Num. 6: 23-7 – is the literary correlative of the fracture and disruption of harmony forecast in the threats and curses. The transformation of the sacerdotal blessing into a curse is thus expressed both on the manifest level of content and on the deeper levels of structure and form. The deep ironical core of Malachi's speech inheres in its destabilizing liturgical mockery, a mockery which curses the forms and language of order, cosmos, and blessing as entrusted to the priesthood. The *Mischgattung* created by this interweaving of liturgical language with prophetical discourse thoroughly transforms the positive assurances of the former into the negative forecasts of the latter. It may, finally, be wondered whether Malachi's diatribe does not have its very *Sitz im Leben* in an antiphonal outcry in the gates of the Temple. Viewed thus, the mounting crescendo of exegetical cacophony in the prophet's speech served as an anti-blessing, a veritable contrapuntal inversion of the sound and sense of the official Priestly Blessing simultaneously performed in the shrine.[50]

[50] For the possibility that Ps. 119: 135 is a reinterpretation of Num. 6: 25, and a reapplication of it to wisdom and Torahistic piety, see M. Gertner, 'Midrashim in the New Testament', *JSS* 7 (1962), 276. As I noted in 'Form and Formulation', 120, it is striking that all eight verses of this acrostic Psalm beginning with the letter *pe*, of which Ps. 119: 135 is one, have some terminological link to the Priestly Blessing. Cf. especially vv. 130, 132, and 134 (plus v. 135). The wisdom-Torahistic exegesis in Ps. 119: 135 thus precedes the extended exegesis of the same type in 1Q *S.* ii. 2-9.

The Divine Attributes and their Exegetical Transformations

Modern critical scholarship has provided a considerable range of speculation regarding the form and language of the divine attribute formulary in the Hebrew Bible, and has attempted to provide a relative literary-historical dating of the various occurrences.[51] The methodological criteria and procedures used in such investigation vary widely, and constitute a distinct subunit of biblical form-critical studies. Such complex matters shall perforce remain subordinate here to aggadic issues, that is, to a perspective that focuses on the diverse biblical exempla of the attribute formulary, and sees in its theological-ideological variations deliberate exegetical modifications. Since partial occurrences of the attribute formulary recur throughout the Hebrew Bible, it is initially necessary to locate a formulation of relative antiquity and completeness which could have served as an authoritative model for the exegetical reuses of it. It is generally agreed that the version of the divine attributes found in Exod. 34: 6-7 fulfills both of these conditions: [52]

Then YHWH passed before him, and YHWH called: 'YHWH a god (אל) gracious and compassionate (רחום וחנון), long forbearing (ארך אפים), and abundant in faithful love (חסד ואמת); who keeps (נצר) kindness to the thousandth [generation] ; who forgives iniquity (נשׂא עון), transgression, and sin (ופשע וחטאה). But he will not acquit (ונקה לא ינקה) [guilt forever; but will] requite (פקד) the iniquity (עון) of fathers (אבות)¹ on their children and grandchildren, to the third and fourth generation thereof.'

The speaker of the formulary in this text is ambiguous. For it is uncertain whether God passed before Moses, who called 'YHWH, YHWH', or – as rendered above – whether YHWH himself said 'YHWH' as part of the introduction to the attributes which follow. The latter alternative has been followed here in the light of the re-citation of this text by Moses in Num. 14: 18, where the formulary is introduced by Moses' petition: 'And now, let the Lord's might be shown in its greatness, *as you spoke, saying*' (v. 17). From this it is clear that Moses recites the formulary to YHWH as a reminder to him of the divine attributes revealed after the people's apostasy through worship of the golden calf. It must be kept in mind, however, that Num. 14: 17 may actually reflect an interpretation of Exod. 34: 6a – an exegetical *traditio* -not the original sense of the *traditum*.

[51] Cf. especially J. Scharbert, 'Formgeschichte und Exegese von Ex. 34, 6f und seiner Parallelen', *Bib.* 38 (1957), 130-50; M. Weiss, 'Studies in the Biblical Doctrine of Retribution', *Tarbiz*, 31 (1961-2), 236-63, ibid. 32 (1962-3), 1-18 [Heb.]; and the articles cited there and below.

[52] I agree with Scharbert, loc. cit. 131, that Exod. 34: 6-7 is the oldest 'Textgestalt', and that the formulation in the Decalogues is later.

In any event, the divine attributes of forgiveness and compassion in Exod. 34: 6 are set against those of retributive punishment in v. 7 – although the result is not symmetrical, since it is stated that the merit of a father can extend divine forgiveness vicariously to the thousandth generation of his descendants, whereas a father's iniquity may be requited only to the third or fourth generation that follow him. This reference to vicarious punishment clearly refers to divine punishments, as against the penal sanctions of human jurisprudence.[53] Indeed, it has been frequently observed that the biblical law corpora are decidedly opposed to vicarious punishment, and that many rules reflect the attempt to provide practical limits upon such practices (cf. Exod. 21: 31).[54] From this point of view, it may be concluded that a double standard of justice was prevalent in ancient Israel from early times – a theological standard, applicable to God alone, which envisaged trans-generational effects for actions committed, and a human standard, applicable in human jurisprudence, which held the transgressor to be culpable and punished for his own delict.

Attractive as this possibility is, caution is in order. First, it is clear that some of the early rules against vicarious punishments (like Exod. 21: 31, examined earlier) are the product of deliberate exegetical revision; and, secondly, the fact that the late deuteronomic corpus must state apodictically that 'Fathers shall not be put to death instead of their sons, nor shall sons be put to death instead of their fathers; [but] everyone shall be put to death for his sin' (Deut. 24: 16) shows a considerable concern to curb this practice. Additionally, vicarious or deferred guilt undoubtedly continued within the civil sphere in those regions or circumstances where customary practices of self-help obtained,[55] or where the guilty party went unpunished. Significant in this regard are two cases preserved in the old historiography, the civil transgressions of David and Ahab, whose punishments were applied to their descendants (cf. 2 Sam. 12: 11-14; 1 Kgs. 21: 19-29). The case of David may of course reflect the extenuating circumstances applied to royalty, though the case of Ahab seems to reflect the popular attitude that transgressions which went unpunished in the civil sphere were eventually requited. Of course, repentance is involved in both instances, and this too may have been considered a mitigating factor.[56] In any event,

---

[53] Cf. P. J. Verdam, ' "On ne fera point mourir lès enfants pour lès pères" en droit biblique', *RIDA* 3 (1949), 405f., 412; M. Greenberg, 'Some Postulates of Biblical Criminal Law', *Y. Kaufmann Jubilee Volume*, ed. M. Haran (Jerusalem: Magnes Press, 1960), 20-7.

[54] Cf. Greenberg, ibid.   [55] Cf. the discussion of Gen. 44 above, pp. 242-4.

[56] For the opinion that the deferral of punishment was often positively regarded in ancient Israel, and considered a manifestation of divine mercy, see the remarks of Y. Muffs, 'Reflections on Prophetic Prayer in the Bible', in *Eretz Israel*, 14, ed.

the available evidence requires one to draw the qualified conclusion that while the legal corpora tend to reject vicarious punishment, this latter notion probably coexisted with other ones.[57] In this there is a distinct parallel to the coexistence of individual and extended family punishments in connection with delicts in the sacerdotal sphere.[58]

1. The considerable weight of the notion of vicarious punishment, *as a theological factor*, is powerfully reflected in the contestations of the matter in the late prophecies of Jeremiah and Ezekiel. In them decisive attempts were made to qualify ambiguities and injustices which were felt to obtain in the juridical notion of transgenerational or deferred punishment – ambiguities and injustices latent in the formulation of Exod. 34: 6-7 as well. Indeed, in the context of exile, the matter became one of pressing concern: for there was little motivation for the sons to practise proper behaviour, or to take responsibility for their actions, if they believed themselves subject to the delayed or extended punishments due to their fathers. Thus, it is entirely likely that Jeremiah's rejection of the notion of vicarious responsibility *for the New Age*, in Jer. 31: 28-9, is a deliberate response to such concerns. On the basis of a divine revelation to him (v. 26), Jeremiah rejects the older *traditum* of vicarious guilt by citing and rejecting the old proverb that spoke of fathers who ate sour grapes but whose sons' teeth were set on edge thereby. In a near-citation of Deut. 24: 16, he states that *'everyone shall be put to death for his own iniquity*:[59] whoever eats sour grapes will have his own teeth set on edge'. As he himself remarks, this new teaching was a teaching of hope for the post-exilic period, and is thus to be joined with his other teachings that the new life of Israel in her land will be established upon a new or renewed basis (cf. 31: 31-3). But it also reflects a sharp rejection of the older *traditum*, epitomized in the proverb; and this is its main aggadic thrust.

That the problematics inherent in the doctrine of vicarious or deferred responsibility were, in fact, discussed in the exile is more evident in the prophecies of Ezekiel, where it is precisely these queries and issues which form the basis of his new teaching *for the exilic community*. Like Jeremiah, Ezekiel, on the basis of a divine revelation, cites the old proverb of sour grapes (18: 1), and then rejects it categorically (v. 2), saying, in yet another variation of Deut. 24: 16, '. . . *the soul that sins shall be put to death*' (v. 4b).[60] And like Jeremiah, Ezekiel's

---

M. Haran (Jerusalem: Israel Exploration Society and Jewish Theological Seminary of America, 1978), 50-2 [Heb.], and the discussion below.

[57] Cf. Verdam, loc. cit. 405f., 412.

[58] e.g. Josh. 7: 24; and cf. Deut. 13: 13-18.

[59] *'awônô* 'his iniquity' vs. Deut. 24: 16, *ḥeṭ'ô* 'his sin'.

[60] *nepeš* 'soul' vs. *'îš* in Deut. 24: 16.

citation of Deut. 24:16 in connection with the proverb on 'sour grapes' serves to undermine and counter the older doctrine of transgenerational responsibility. But Ezekiel's teaching goes further. First, it is clear from the continuity of his discourse that he understands Deut. 24:16 in an expansive sense. For if Deut. 24:16 prohibits vicarious punishment of fathers/sons but makes no explicit comment on civil cases, the legal instances which Ezekiel cites to support his argument derive from the Pentateuchal civil jurisprudence. For example, the cases referred to in 18:7-8 (cf. vv. 12-13, 16-17) are derived from such cases-types as Exod. 22:20, 24b-26, Lev. 25:36-7, Deut. 23:20-1, 24:6,10-15,17. These juridical allusions are all the more striking since none of the Pentateuchal formulations articulates a penalty; they are rather addressed to the moral will of the person. In Ezekiel, by contrast, such cases as the misuse of loans or interest are cited *with punishments*, capital punishments to boot (cf. vv. 14, 18, vs. acquittal as 'life' in vv. 9, 19). Since such penalties are unthinkable in actual biblical law, one may conclude that Ezekiel's hyperbolic rhetoric was designed to rebut thoroughly the prevailing notions of vicarious guilt, and to emphasize the unilateral application of the standard of individual responsibility.

Ezekiel thus goes further than Jeremiah, and shows his thoughtful reconsideration of the juridical problematic involved in matters of vicarious punishment. He stresses that if a transgressor repents, or a righteous person transgresses, such a one will be judged by his final act (cf. 18:18-32, 33:12-20). There is a double reason for this. On the one hand, the prophet is concerned to counteract despair and loss of hope induced by the presumption that if one has transgressed he is forever guilty, or if one is righteous he may act with impunity; on the other, he is concerned to inspire the courage for repentance and thus show the exiles a way of religious renewal.[61] By narrowing the scope of individual responsibility to each and every separate action, so that repentance for a past transgression can lead to divine acceptance, the prophet has sharpened the issue of individual responsibility in order to spur the Israelites to the realization that they need not wallow (or hide) in notions of inherited guilt. Each person is responsible for his legal-religious life. Undoubtedly, the necessity for such strong rhetorical measures was due to the intransigence of his audience, who protested with the question, 'Why does the son not bear the guilt of the father? (18:19), and with the criticism, 'The Lord acts without principle לֹא יִתָּכֵן דֶּרֶךְ אֲדֹנָי' (18:25, 29, 33:17, 20).[62] By this they contended that the old proverb of 'sour grapes' was more just, for it guaranteed

---

[61] Cf. B. Lindars, 'Ezekiel and Individual Responsibility', *VT* 15 (1965), 464f.

[62] So NEB. I thus understand the verb *yittākēn* as derived from the stem *tākēn* 'to measure', with S. D. Luzzatto, *Perushei Shadal 'al Yirmiyah, Yeḥezqe'l, Mishlei we-'Iyyob* (Lemberg: A. I. Menkes, 1876), *ad* Ezek. 18:25. Cf. Prov. 16:2.

punishment for sins.[63] It was Ezekiel's goal and burden to contradict this attitude. By juxtaposing Deut. 24:16 and cases from the civil law with his rejection of the proverb, he implies an exegetical analogy: all cases, theological and civil, are alike. There is thus no double standard of justice, individual responsibility being the juridical fact for all transgressions. In speaking thus, Ezekiel does not speak in his own voice alone, but uses the authority of a divine revelation. The older *traditum*, like that articulated by YHWH in Exod. 34:6-7, is rejected, and a new transformative *traditio* is introduced — a new teaching by the ancient covenantal god.

The sources of Ezekiel's exegetical imagination are, of course, difficult to determine, particularly in an example like the preceding. Nevertheless, there are some reasons to suppose that the prophet's citation of Deut. 24:16 in order to contradict the old proverb on vicarious punishments is a valuable clue. For, on the one hand, this deuteronomic source apparently provided the matrix for the prophet's stock of examples in his aggadic discourse; and, on the other, the prophet may well have chosen this apodictic rejection of vicarious punishment precisely because he knew that it is itself an aggadic revision of an earlier *traditum* on divine capital punishment. As to the first matter, an examination of Ezekiel's language in 18:7-8,13,16, and 18 shows that many of the cases which he cites as examples of civil delicts are in fact drawn from a series of cases found in close association in Deut. 23:20-1, 24:6, 10-15, 17. This correlation assumes greater significance in the light of the prophet's repeated citation of or allusion to the prohibition of vicarious punishment as formulated in Deut. 24:16 (cf. 18:4, 20); for it suggests that Ezekiel was drawn to cite these deuteronomic cases precisely because they were *already* associated in his *traditum* and were found in close proximity to a legal principle which rejected vicarious punishments. But what, it must be asked, is this latter principle doing in this particular series of cases, especially since Deut. 24:16 prohibits the vicarious punishment of death, while the surrounding material simply presents a number of severe socio-economic delicts without any penalty appended? Presuming the intelligence of the legal draftsman, one might hazard the speculation that the principle of rejecting vicarious punishment was incorporated into this legal unit in order to counter tendencies to exact vicarious retributions in cases of economic collapse. In such cases, it is implied, fathers may neither be dunned nor killed (in compensation) for the debts of their

---

[63] The issue therefore is the 'injustice' of repentance, whereby evil deeds can be nullified without legal–religious consequences. Cf. the view of R. Eliezer of Beaugency, *Kommentar zu Ezechiel*, 29 (fo. 147[a-b]). The people clearly wanted a more 'measurable' accountability for injustice — even if this worked itself out over several generations.

sons, nor vice versa: each person is rather to be regarded as a self-contained economic unit.

Naturally, one can easily imagine that severe economic sanctions were exacted by local lenders and professional loan-sharks in ancient Israel; and the very fact that the deuteronomic draftsman has appended his rules of slavery to rules about loans near the sabbatical year and exhortations enjoining generosity to the Israelite poor (Deut. 15: 1-6+ 7-11+ 12-18; cf. Lev. 25: 1-22 + 23-55), shows that the legal authorities were fully conscious of the dangers of voluntary or enforced servitude for non-payment of debts. Indeed, in the light of the deuteronomic principle prohibiting vicarious punishment it may not be irrelevant that the slavery rules in Deut. 15: 12-18 say nothing about children born to a debtor-slave during servitude—thus suggesting that the deuteronomic draftsman rejected the possibility of lifelong servitude ('death') for sons on account of the deeds of their fathers, a situation which the corresponding legal pericope in Exod. 21: 2-6 certainly countenances. But, however this may be, one may nevertheless ask why—if our hypothesis about the contextual meaning of Deut. 24: 16 is correct—the deuteronomic draftsman invoked a rule prohibiting vicarious death if his concern was with limiting economic liability. The answer lies in the restrictions which a received *traditum* imposed upon the deuteronomic draftsman and in his capacity to exploit it for the sake of his moral–legal values.

An examination of the deuteronomic pericope which inspired Ezekiel indicates that it is actually derived from the cluster of apodictic injunctions dealing with economic justice found in Exod. 22: 20-23: 12. Indeed, a juxtaposition of the sources reveals the following correspondences: (1) Deut. 24: 10-11~Exod. 22: 24; (2) Deut. 24: 12-13, 17b~Exod. 22: 25-6; (3) Deut. 24: 14-15~Exod. 22: 20-1; (4) Deut. 24: 17a~Exod. 23: 6; (5) Deut. 24: 19-21~Exod. 23: 11-12; (6) Deut. 25: 1~Exod. 23: 7. This concordance of cases is, in itself, of legal–historical interest; but in the present context it is unit (3) which must be the focus of attention. Thus, after the exhortation not to oppress the weak in Exod. 22: 20-1 the legal draftsman-teacher has included this divine sanction: 'For if you do in fact oppress him [viz., the weak], I shall truly heed his cry if he appeals to me; and my anger will be aroused and I shall kill you by the sword, so that your wives shall become widows and your sons orphans.' In context, this dire warning prophesies dreadful divine sanctions for economic oppression of widows and orphans. Possibly, this danger of exploiting the legally disadvantaged (cf. 1 Kgs. 4:1) is the clue to the particular formulae found in Deut. 24: 16, which also follows an apodictic injunction not to oppress the weak 'that he not call to YHWH against you' (vv. 14-15). Given his *traditum*, the deuteronomic draftsman could not avoid the divine warning in Exod.

22: 23 of death for economic oppressions; but given his sensibilities, he could not simply recopy his source. In addition, he received the legal *topos* of economic exploitation and oppression but thoroughly revised its concern and application. Whereas in Exod. 22: 23 God is portrayed as protector of the economically oppressed, who promises to exact capital punishment upon the oppressor of widows and orphans, the text in Deut. 24: 14-16 eliminates this horrific divine punishment —reducing the oppressor's punishment to a 'sin' before God—and extends the *topos* of oppression into one of transgenerational economic exploitation, something that presumably lay within the power of a lender but which is categorically proscribed.

If, then, Deut. 24: 16 is at once a triumph for legal rationality, replacing the fear of divine retribution with an exhortatory. dictum that appeals to the moral sensibility as a constraint against transgenerational oppression, it is also a triumph for the aggadic imagination, replacing a *theologoumenon* about divine retribution with one that focuses on human *cultic* transgression (oppression is a 'sin', not just indecency). Withal, it is clear that the draftsman's aggadic-legal revision of his *traditum* resulted in a formulation that is contextually disruptive, since Deut. 24: 16 prohibits vicarious death while the surrounding cases deal with socio-economic oppression without appending penalties. Most probably, the original formulation of Deut. 24: 16 was solely concerned to prohibit vicarious substitutions in capital cases, or their gross extension to blood relatives; and, indeed, this *traditum* was construed in just such a manner in 2 Kgs. 14: 5-6. Nevertheless, Deut. 24: 16 is not an isolated legal *topos* within Deut. 24. Accordingly, if the draftsman— under the broad constraints of his exegetical *traditio* —was not completely unaware of the anomalous character of Deut. 24: 16 in context, we may presume that he intended Deut. 24: 16 to be *contextually construed* as a hyperbolic legal exhortation stressing that a lender may not seek vicarious satisfaction of any kind for defaulted debts. Conceivably, Ezekiel, who was concerned to emphasize individual responsibility for theological as for civil transgressions, was aware that Deut. 24: 16, his key text, was itself an exhortation rejecting earlier notions of vicarious punishment for economic crimes. If not, he remarkably arrived at a similar aggadic application of it by other means.

2. The wording of the divine attribute formulary as known from Exod. 34: 6-7 is not found in the contestations of Jer. 31: 28-9 and Ezek. 18. A reflex does occur, however, in Jer. 32: 18-19, and with a striking exegetical twist. In v. 18 Jeremiah refers to the standard version of retributive justice by YHWH, though with some distinctive terms ('who does kindness unto the thousandth [generation], and repays the iniquities of the fathers upon their sons after them'). This

verse contradicts, of course, the eschatological prophecy of Jeremiah that just such a procedure would end with the return from exile. It is therefore quite possible that this phrase reflects the older stereotypic attitude of Jeremiah before his revision of it in 31:28-9. But in the light of the latter such a reference to vicarious punishment was embarrassing – particularly in a prayer which was responding to Israel's future restoration in the land.[64] For this reason, apparently, the sequence of 32:18-20 was interrupted with the exegetical revision which states that YHWH's greatness (cf. v. 18b) actually lies in the fact that 'He deals with each person according to his ways and according to the fruit of his actions' (v. 19b).[65] In this way the two theological attitudes were harmonized.

While the main force of the preceding contestations is to revise the doctrine of vicarious punishment it should not go unnoticed that this emphasis on immediate divine justice was at the expense of divine mercy. Indeed, as Y. Muffs has plausibly argued, the attribute formulary in Exod. 34:6-7, coming as it does *after* the episode of divine apostasy in Exod. 32:1-6, and after Moses' request that YHWH forgive the people's sin (אם־תשא חטאתם, 32:32a; cf. חטאה . . . נשא, 34:6) and YHWH's concession and decision to requite the sin in the future (ביום פקדי ופקדתי, 32:34b; cf. פקד, 34:7), is actually an expression of divine חסד, or gracious mercy.[66] From this perspective, the entire attribute formulary stresses YHWH's attribute of mercy and forgiveness, for he is a god who can and will *defer* punishment.[67] That such a divine action was considered positively is strikingly confirmed from the encounter between Isaiah and King Hezekiah in 2 Kgs. 20; for there, although Hezekiah sinned, Isaiah announces in YHWH's name that the punishment will be deferred to the sons of Hezekiah, and the latter responds: 'The oracle of YHWH which you have proclaimed is *good*' (vv. 12-19).[68] To later generations, like that of Jeremiah and Ezekiel, such vicarious punishment was *not* good, and they chose to stress immediate divine punishment. When Jer. 32:19b contradicts and revises v. 18a, which recites the attribute formulary from Exod. 34:7,

---

[64] W. Rudolph, *Jeremia* (HAT 12; Tübingen: J. C. B. Mohr, 1958), 193, and J. Bright, *Jeremiah* (AB 21; Garden City: Doubleday, 1965), 294, regard vv. 17b–23 as a later insertion into the prayer.

[65] It appears that this entire verse is exegetically keyed to v. 18. Thus, YHWH's greatness in v. 18b is understood as 'great in counsel', in v. 19a, and his might understood as 'might of *'ălîliyyāh'* – not as a historical 'deed' (cf. Ps. 78:7) but as divine recompense to each person for *ma'ălālâw* 'his deeds'.

[66] Loc. cit. (above, n. 56), 52.

[67] Ibid.

[68] Ibid., and also Muffs' convincing explanation of the petition in Num. 14: 13-19, where Moses refers to God's deferred requital of guilt in the context of a request for mercy (pp. 52f.).

the point that is made, therefore, is that the true expression of divine mercy and kindness lies in his immediate punishment of the actual perpetrators of the delict.

The same point is even more forcefully made in Pentateuchal sources, from Deut. 7: 9-10, which may derive from a pre-exilic stratum. Set within the context of a larger oration, Moses refers to the fact that YHWH delivered the Israelites from Egypt (v. 8), and stresses that he is a faithful god,

who preserves (שֹׁמֵר) covenant-loyalty (חֶסֶד) for those who love him (לְאֹהֲבָיו) and observe his commandments (וּלְשֹׁמְרֵי מִצְוֹתוֹ), even to the thousandth generation; but who repays [the iniquity] of those who hate him (לְשֹׂנְאָיו), destroying him directly: he will not postpone with one who hates him (לְשֹׂנְאוֹ); but will repay him directly. (vv. 9b-10)

As is evident, this teaching is an aggadic revision of the version of the attribution formulary found in the Decalogue. Moses first refers to the exodus (cf. Deut. 5: 6), then to the observance of the commandments (cf. שֹׁמְרֵי מִצְוֹתָו, Deut. 5: 10), and finally to the faithful as 'lovers' and the disobedient as 'haters' (cf. לְשֹׂנְאַי and לְאֹהֲבַי in Deut. 5: 9-10).[69] The latter terms appear only in the version of the attribute formulary found in the Decalogue; they are absent from Exod. 34: 6-7. Accordingly, Moses took over the *theologoumena* of extended grace and punishment *and revised them*. Dissatisfied with the notion that divine mercy was expressed through deferred punishment, he deleted references to this idea and announced that YHWH enacts swift and individual justice for covenantal delicts. In this teaching, Moses' *traditio* is an outright contradiction and rejection of a divinely proclaimed *traditum*. And, in so far as Moses' aggadic revision also purports to be a reteaching of earlier divine utterances, the theological daring is doubly remarkable. With one stroke, later tradition thoroughly controverted an earlier revelation, and *authenticated its novel viewpoint by means of a presumptive misquote*.

This aggadic reuse of the attribute formulary in the Decalogue deserves somewhat closer inspection, for Deut. 7: 9-10 has reread a version of the attribute formulary which is distinct in character and also has an aggadic component. First, it will be observed that in Deut. 5: 9-10 (~ Exod. 20: 5-6) the punishment clause precedes that of beneficence, while just the reverse is found in Exod. 34: 6-7. Undoubtedly, this is due to the distinct rhetorical dimensions of both pieces: Exod. 34: 6-7 is, as noted above, a divine self-revelation of merciful attributes (even v. 7!) after the apostasy of the calf; whereas Deut. 5: 9-10 follows

---

[69] The notion of 'loving' YHWH has a precise covenantal sense, derived from technical Near Eastern treaty language, as first observed by W. Moran, 'The Near Eastern Background' (above, n. 19), 77-87.

directly upon the prohibition of worshipping other gods, and so first emphasizes the punishment for such malfeasance before adding the beneficences for proper behaviour.[70] Moreover, whereas Exod. 34: 6-7 is a *theologoumenon* which stands on its own, Deut. 5: 9-10 is rhetorically linked with what precedes it by the motivation formula כי 'because'. The punishment motif is thus a hortatory motivation not to worship other gods, and may in fact have been originally intended to indicate that vicarious punishments or benefits were related to just such 'commandments'—and not to the whole range of covenantal stipulations, though this was clearly how the passage was read and contested by later tradition.

Observation of the motivational dimension of Deut. 5: 9-10 links it to the other motivation clauses of the Decalogue which also form part of its paraenetic reworking (cf. vv. 11b and 15a, which also begin with כי; and vv. 14b and 16b, which use למען). In particular, attention should be drawn to v. 11b. This clause follows the prohibition of oaths which misuse the divine name (v. 11a), and states that YHWH 'will not acquit (ינקה) anyone who swears (ישא) falsely in his name'. At first glance this motivation simply avers unconditionally that false oaths shall not be forgiven. But this initial assessment is transformed with the observation that the verb נקה is precisely the verb normally used in the attribute formulary as the bridge between divine forgiveness and the deferral of punishment (cf. Exod. 34: 6-7), *but which is missing* in the version of the attributes found in the Decalogue. The omission of the phrase 'נקה לא ינקה he will not acquit' from the punishment motif in Deut. 5: 9 was undoubtedly due to the fact that the latter now precedes the motif of divine beneficence rather than follows it (as in Exod. 34: 6-7). The result is a different theological assertion from that found in Exod. 34: 6-7; for now the emphasis is on vicarious punishment and not its merciful deferral. At the same time, the לא ינקה clause was transferred to v. 11b where it serves as the motivation for the prohibition of false oaths. That vv. 9-10 and 11b together constitute the attribute formulary of Exod. 34: 6-7 suggests that this latter served as the source for aggadic reuse of the aforementioned motivation clauses.[71] Perhaps a further stimulus for the attachment of לא ינקה to v. 11a was that this command begins with the verbal stem נשא, just like Exod. 34: 6. But whereas the latter states generally that YHWH 'נשא forgives' but ultimately will 'לא ינקה not acquit', the motivation clause in the Decalogue just says that YHWH 'לא ינקה will not acquit' anyone who 'ישא swears'

---

[70] For an explanation along these lines, with differences, see M. Weiss, 'Studies in the Biblical Doctrine of Retribution', *Tarbiz*, 32 (1962-3), 4 [Heb.].

[71] The disjointed and motivational use of the attribute formulary is one reason to consider the Decalogue a secondary reuse of Exod. 34: 6-7; another is the covenantal reuse via the notions of love and hate (cf. n. 70). See next note.

falsely in YHWH's name. There thus emerges an unexpected theological parallelism between the two motivation clauses. Just as the first subordinates the issue of mercy and deferral of punishment to an emphasis on retributive justice across generations, the second motivation clause states categorically that in the matter of oaths which misuse the divine name there is no acquittal. Again, mercy is subordinate to justice; and again aggadic exegesis has reinterpreted and reapplied an old and venerable *traditum.*[72]

3. The rejection of the punishment clause of the attribute formulary in Deut. 7:10 took the form of revision. In other cases the matter was dropped entirely. The prophecies of Joel and Jonah provide cases in point. In the first instance, an invasion of locusts brings the prophet to exhort the people to repent (שֻׁבוּ) through acts of fasting and wailing and keening (2:12); 'for' YHWH 'is gracious and compassionate . . .; long-forbearing and abundant in kindness, וְנִחָם עַל־הָרָעָה and relents of the evil [planned]' (v. 13). 'Who knows,' continues the prophet, 'He may turn and relent (וְנִחָם) . . .' (v. 14). Forthwith the people engage in repentant practices in the manner advised, and call upon YHWH to have mercy (חוּסָה) upon his nation (v. 17). In the light of the actual circumstances involved, it appears that this account in the Book of Joel reflects a liturgical tradition and reuse of the attribute formulary; and that the Book of Jonah, where all the above phrases recur in a pseudo-historical prophetic meditation on such themes as prophecy, repentance, and divine mercy, is a derived adaptation.[73] In the Book of Jonah, for example, the prophet eventually announces the doomsday of Nineveh, but the king advises his subjects to repent (וַיָּשֻׁבוּ) with rites of supplication and petition (3:8); 'for who knows,' he goes on, 'perhaps the god will return and relent (וְנִחָם)' (v. 9). And the god does so (v. 10). In response to this the prophet Jonah then

---

[72] If the *lāmed* of *lĕśōnĕ'āy* and *lĕ'ōhăbāy* in the Decalogue is indicative or explicative, and means something like 'who are' or 'with respect to', then the sense of Deut. 5:9-10 would be that God checks or inspects the behaviour of the sons to see if they act wrongly, or like their fathers, and if so punishes them. From this angle, Deut. 5:9-10 would *already* contain the notion of individual responsibility. This general line of argumentation is found in J. Scharbert, 'Das Verbum PQD in der Theologie des Alten Testaments', *BZ* 4 (1960), 209-26, and it is also the position taken by the ancient rabbis (e.g. *b. Ber.* 7a; *b. Sanh.* 27b; *b. Šeb.* 39), *Tg. Onq.*, and the medieval commentators (cf. Rashi, Rashbam, Ibn Ezra, Seforno, and Ramban).

[73] On the relative priority of Joel, cf. A. Lods, *Histoire de la littérature hébraïque et juive* (Paris: Payot, 1950), 587; W. Rudolph, *Joel, Amos, Obadja, Jona* (HAT 13. 2; Gütersloh: G. Mohn, 1971), 360; H. Wolff, *Joel and Amos* (Hermeneia; Philadelphia: Fortress Press, 1977), 49. For the priority of Jonah to Joel, cf. A. van Hoonacker, *Les Douze Petits Prophètes* (Paris: Gabalda, 1908), 314, and G. Cohn, *Das Buch Jona* (Assen: Van Gorcum, 1969), 99, n. 2.

turns to YHWH and says 'That is why I initially fled to Tarshish; for I knew that you are a righteous and compassionate god, long forbearing and abundant in kindness, ונחם על־הרעה and who relents of the evil [planned]' (4:2). Ignoring the substance of this remark, YHWH then educates Jonah by means of the parable of the gourd, and tells him that as he – Jonah – had mercy (חַסְתָּ) for the gourd so does he – YHWH – have mercy (אָחוּס) for Nineveh and its inhabitants (4:10-11).[74]

Jonah is taught that YHWH can act as he will, and that no doom oracle is final: for all depends upon human repentance and divine mercy—although, the prophet is advised, the two are not mechanically related. By taking up revisions of the attribute formulary which arose in liturgical settings, as well as other phrases in the Book of Joel which may also derive from the cult, the writer of the Book of Jonah is able to achieve an aggadic exposition on the problem of repentance and divine mercy. His exposition is all the more striking since it contains a theological deepening of the notion that YHWH 'relents of the evil'— which is itself an aggadic transformation of the punishment motif of the attribute formulary. The expositor of the Book of Jonah may have been inspired in his reflections by another inner-biblical reference which, like the situation described in the Book of Joel, thoroughly contrasts with the initial attitude of Jonah which is eventually rebutted. For it will be observed that interpolated into Jeremiah's famous parable of the potter (18:1-6, 11-12) is a divine dictum,[75] which proclaims that if a nation repents (וְשָׁב) of its evil ways 'then I shall relent (וְנִחַמְתִּי) of the evil (עַל־הָרָעָה) which I planned to do'; whereas if a nation subsequently turns to evil, then, reciprocally, YHWH will 'relent (וְנִחַמְתִּי)' and bring disaster (vv. 7-11).[76] Just such divine behaviour was known to Jonah, as he says; and his rejection of the conditionality of a divine oracle led him to try to escape his prophetic burden. But escape it he could not, the author teaches; for oracles of doom are not magical words which must achieve their end irrespective of the human response to them. The prophet learns that although YHWH 'relents' he does so for his own reasons.[77] Thus, like oracles, the words and acts of repentance are also not magical: YHWH does not relent *because* of

---

[74] E. Bickerman, *Four Strange Books of the Bible* (New York: Schocken, 1967), 44, has seen in this reuse of *hûs* yet another indication that the writer of Jonah is indebted to the language and issues in the book of Joel (cf. his comments, p. 41).

[75] Verse 11 clearly resumes the theme and language of v. 6, and begins with *wĕʿattāh*, which draws the hortatory and prophetic implication. On this term, see H. A. Brongers, 'Bemerken zum Gebrauch des adverbialen *wĕʿattāh* im Alten Testament', *VT* 15 (1965), 289-99.

[76] The thematic and lexical link between this passage and Jonah has been observed, and the problems acutely addressed, by Bickerman, op. cit. 29-45.

[77] Ibid. 45-8.

them. The prophet Joel knew this (2:14), and so did the king of Nineveh (3:9). Jonah, for his part, only comes to realize this; and that is the 'burden' of the book.

4. It would be wrong to conclude from the foregoing that the only revisions and adaptations of the old attribute formulary were to emphasize divine mercy or forgiveness. Such is not the case, as an examination of Nahum 1:2-3 clearly shows.[78] In that context, the prophet fulminates against the Assyrian army and envisages the imminence of divine vengeance portrayed through a series of vengefully reapplied references and allusions to Exod. 34:6-7.[79] The older *traditum* is thus transformed by a *traditio* which preaches wrath and doom, with no trace of mitigating divine mercy. However, this piece is, to a degree, an exception; for it is the theme of divine mercy that is generally stressed in inner-biblical reuses of the divine attribute formulary, particularly liturgical petitions—be these from the Pentateuch (like Num. 14:17-19) or from the Psalter. Indeed, the key terms of the attribute formulary recur as the organizing principle in a host of psalms (cf. 40:11-13, 18, 78:38, 79:5-6, 8-10, 21, 85:3-4, 6, 8, 11, 86:2-3, 5-6, 11, 16, 99:8, 111:1, 4-5, 7, 145:7-10), among other liturgical recitations.[80]

As elaborate liturgical developments built around the attribute formulary, in contexts of petition for divine aid, these psalms are, in a real sense, aggadic embellishments. Two additional examples may be isolated for special comment, for they exemplify the way that the attributes of vengeance or forgiveness served as the organizing principle of an extended petition. They also show how primary and secondary exegetical features are utilized, or function as aggregates within a larger theological focus.

Ps. 109 may serve as an example of the ways a psalmist might focus his attention on the attributes of retribution. In vv. 3-4 the speaker begins from a self-referential perspective, saying that his enemies have requited his kindness with ill. Therefore, he requests God to appoint (הפקד) a wicked person against his enemy (v. 6), and prays that his enemies' goods (פקדיו) be seized from him and his sons be orphaned (vv. 8-9). The psalmist continues his vindictive appeal with a request to God to deny all grace (חסד) and compassion (חונן) to his enemy, to hound his future generations (vv. 12-13), and so make his enemies'

---

[78] See my remarks in 'Torah and Tradition', in *Tradition and Theology in the Old Testament*, ed. D. Knight (Philadelphia: Fortress Press, 1977), 280f.

[79] In this setting *nôṭēr* 'rage', in v. 2 is a dialectical pun on *nōṣēr* in the attribute formulary.

[80] Cf. the clustered terminology in Prov. 16:4-7 and 19:9, 11, 16-17. For similar language in the prayer inscription found at Khirbet Beit Lei, Inscription B, see P. D. Miller, jun., 'Psalms and Inscriptions', *SVT* (1981), 328-31.

* children bear the iniquities of their fathers (עון אבתיו, v. 14). In this way the psalmist hopes for a personal vindication and salvation.

As is evident from the terms, allusions, and legal topoi, this prayer was thematically inspired and organized around a traditional *theologoumenon* as formulated in the attribute formulary, that YHWH could enact vengeance even to successive generations. This *theologoumenon* of divine justice gave the psalmist the trust that his petition would not be in vain. And it shows how, on the popular religious level at least, the hope in the eventual divine punishment of malevolents or their descendants was not only a form of theodicy, but gave vibrancy to notions of deferred and vicarious punishment as well.

Ps. 103 produces an opposite emphasis. It is a sustained appeal for divine compassion, addressed to a forgiving God who is addressed as 'gracious and compassionate . . . long forbearing and of abundant kindness' (v. 8). Such a God, the psalmist continues, 'will not contend forever, nor rage without end' (v. 9). This surprising continuation of the formulary recalls comparable phraseology in Jer. 3: 5, 12, and is a rejection of the attributes of retribution in favour of those of compassion.[81] For YHWH, avers the psalmist, does not requite sins and iniquities (עונתינו . . . חטאינו, v. 10), but is rather a god of transcendent grace and compassion (חסדו), who removes all transgressions (פשעינו) from those who truly fear him (vv. 11-13).[82] In this glorification, the speaker provides an aggadic embellishment of the formulary cited earlier (v. 8); and, in a continuation of this theme, stresses that YHWH's חסד is without beginning or end, and that his righteousness is given to succeeding generations (v. 17), to those who obey his covenant and keep his commands (פקדיו, v. 18). With these final remarks, the psalmist clearly applies the old attribute formulary to observance of the covenant, as did the paraenetic embellishment of the Decalogue quite independently.

There are other exegetical features discernible in this psalm. One of these occurs in v. 14—a transitional phrase which stands between the remarks that God does not necessarily requite sins with punishment because of his חסד (vv. 10-13), and the paean in praise of YHWH's everlasting חסד (v. 17). In fact, v. 14 functions as an explanation of the gracious divine activities outlined in vv. 10-13, and states כי־הוא ידע יצרנו זכור כי־עפר אנחנו. Given the parallelism, one is tempted to translate 'For he [YHWH] knows our created nature;[83] [for] it is

---

[81] Also noted by Muffs, loc. cit. 53 f., who stresses the exegetical dimension.

[82] As Muffs, ibid., emphasizes, this psalm underscores the divine attributes of grace and forgiveness: in it there is no deferral or suspension of judgement to later generations.

[83] Cf. RSV, 'frame'; M. Dahood, *Psalms 101-50* (AB; Garden City: Doubleday, 1970), 28, 'form'. Muffs, loc. cit., glosses *ṭibʿēnû*, presumably man's psychical nature.

known [to him] that we are but dust.' But the parallelism is doubly intriguing. For in so far as the stem appears to relate to mankind's creaturehood, as 'formed' from the earth, it may be suggested that v. 14 is also an aggadic adaptation of Gen. 2: 7 'And YHWH Elohim formed (יצר) the man from the dust (עפר) of the earth.' Human mortality, indeed, mankind's created nature, is thus invoked in Ps. 103:14 as a factor which should limit God's vindictive designs. And this leads to a third, and final, aggadic dimension which may be concealed in v. 14. For it will be recalled that, after the flood, YHWH forswore a future destruction of the earth with the explanation 'because the will (יצר) of man is evil from his youth' (Gen. 8: 21). Taken altogether, one may venture to propose that Ps. 103:14 is an exegetical reuse of Gen. 2: 7 while simultaneously punning on 8: 21, so as to deepen the exegetical thrust. The psalmist thus appeals to YHWH to refrain from requiting sin with punishment, both because he knows man's mortal nature and also because of mankind's all-too-human will.

The petititonary use of the attribute formulary in the preceding psalms finds its complement in another, liturgical-aggadic reflex of this language. But Mic. 7: 18-20, far from being a request, is an expression of gratitude which concludes a larger liturgical structure of lament, confession, and assurance of divine grace.[84] The celebrant rejoices:

(18) Who is a God (אל) like you, forgiving iniquity (נשא עון) and passing over the transgression (פשע) of the remnant of his inheritance?! [Who] has not remained angry (אפו) forever; for he delights in kindness (חסד).

(19) May he again have compassion over us (ירחמנו), cleanse our iniquities (עונתינו), and cast all our sins (חטאתנו)[85] into the sea.

(20) Give steadfastness to Jacob, (and) gracious love (חסד) to Abraham – as you swore to our ancestors in days gone by.

There can be little doubt that in vv. 18-19 the prophet Micah has readapted the language of Exod. 34: 6-7 into a catena of hope and thanksgiving.[86] The aggadic reapplication of an old guarantee, that YHWH would be compassionate and forgiving thus provides a new warrant of hope in a later time. Following this recitation of divine

[84] On the ensemble Mic. 7: 7-20, see H. Gunkel, 'The Close of Micah: A Prophetical Liturgy', in *What Remains of The Old Testament, and Other Essays* (New York: Macmillan, 1928), 115-40 (from *Zeitschrift für Semitistik*, 2 (1924), 145-78), and B. Reicke, 'Liturgical Traditons in Mic. 7', *HTR* 60 (1967), 349-67.

[85] Read thus, vs. MT *ḥaṭṭōʾtām*. For examples of this scribal error, see the study of R. Weiss, 'On Ligatures in the Hebrew Bible' (loc. cit., p. 38, n. 55 above).

[86] For a post-biblical reuse of Exod. 34: 6-7 in 4 Ezra 7: 132-40, cf. D. Simonsen, 'Ein Midrasch im IV. Buch Esra', in *Festschrift I. Lewy*, edd. M. Brann and J. Elbogen (Breslau: M. and H. Marcus, 1911), 270-8.

mercies, the prophet then concludes with an appeal to YHWH to act
on behalf of the descendants of Abraham and Isaac, as had been
promised to earlier generations. It would appear that the individual
names of Abraham and Jacob serve here as metonyms for the contemporary people of Israel.[87] Such a phenomenon is of a marked aggadic
character, and invites a fuller examination.

C. TYPOLOGIES

As is well known, the term 'typology' and the hermeneutical aspect
with which it is associated, which sees in persons, events, or places the
prototype, pattern, or figure of historical persons, events, or places that
follow it in time, are particularly associated with classical Christian
exegesis,[88] although significant and diverse examples are known already
from ancient Near Eastern sources,[89] from the New Testament,[90] from
the writings of Josephus,[91] and even from the literature of the Qumran
scrolls.[92] This style of thought was commonly employed by the ancient
rabbis as well, and the formulation of Immanuel of Rome (thirteenth/
fourteenth century), 'All that happened to the fathers was a sign for
their sons', became justly famous and widespread in Jewish literature.[93]

Taking all this into account, it would seem to be both anachronistic
and methodologically problematic to use a term like typology in
connection with inner-biblical exegesis. After all, the term is not
indigenous to the Hebrew Bible, the literary-historical scope and significance of the phenomenon is clearly post-biblical, and the term and its
uses have been subject to a vast array of usages and applications. From

[87] The comment of W. Rudolph, loc. cit. (n. 73) 136, that the reference is to
the individuals Abraham and Jacob because Abraham is nowhere used typologically, is doubly problematic. First, if Mic. 7: 20 refers to the 'grace of Abraham'
etc., the sentence is without an object; and second, typological allusions to
Abraham can be found in Gen. 15: 7, Isa. 51: 2, and Ezek. 33: 24. On these texts,
see the discussions below.

[88] For bibliography, see S. Bercovitch (ed.), *Typology and Early American
Literature* (Amherst: University of Massachusetts Press, 1972), 250-337.

[89] See below, nn. 106 and 109.

[90] Cf. Acts 7: 43-4; Rom. 5: 14, 6: 17; Heb. 9: 24, Philem. 3: 17; 1 Pet. 3: 20f.
On the effect of typology on an entire Gospel, cf. J. Enz, 'The Book of Exodus as
a Literary Type for the Gospel of John', *JBL* 76 (1957), 208-15.

[91] Cf. D. Daube, 'Typology in Josephus', *JJS* 31 (1980), 18-36.

[92] See the study of D. Flusser, 'Pharisees, Sadducees and Essenes in Pesher
Nahum', in *Meḥqarim be-Toledot Yisrael ube-Lašon ha-Ivrit*, edd. M. Dorman,
S. Safrai, M. Stern (Tel Aviv: ha-Kibbutz ha-Me'uḥad, 1970), 133-68 [Heb.].

[93] For the phenomenon of typology in ancient rabbinic texts, see I. Heinemann, *Darkhei ha-Aggadah* (Jerusalem: The Magnes Press, 1950), 32-4. Immanuel's
adage is quoted in I. Davidson, ed. *Otzar ha-Meshalim weha-Pitgamim* (Jerusalem:
* Mosad Harav Kook, 1957), 2, with earlier authorities cited (pp. 2f. n. 40).

this perspective it would seem best to employ a neutral terminology for the biblical phenomena to be considered, and to avoid obfuscation and anachronism. However, it is of decisive importance that the term typology is a concrete historical designation, and that its various usages easily fall within marked parameters. This being so, the post-biblical phenomena at once help to identify the inner-biblical phenomena related to them comparatively, and further, since the post-biblical phenomena are not restricted to one definition or characterization, the unique character of the inner-biblical examples is not forced to fit alien models. One final benefit may be added to this comparative approach, and serves further to justify calling both the biblical and the post-biblical phenomena typologies. This is that, by aligning the phenomena, a historical–literary spectrum is established and the inner-biblical phenomena are firmly located within the long and diverse history of this form of biblical exegesis.

Based on these reflections, an initial characterization of inner-biblical typologies may be offered at this point, a characterization which may also serve as an operational definition of the examples to be studied. In the light of its post-biblical congeners, it may be observed that inner-biblical typologies constitute a literary–historical phenomenon which isolates perceived correlations between specific events, persons, or places early in time with their later correspondents.[94] Since the latter occur either in the present or in the immediate or envisaged future, there is an implied emphasis on the linear and historical aspects of the correlations. And this is vital for another reason as well. For in so far as the 'later correspondents' occur in history and time, they will never be precisely identical with their prototype, but inevitably stand in a *hermeneutical* relationship with them. The reasons for this are twofold. On the one hand, while it is in the nature of typologies to emphasize the homological 'likeness' of any two events, the concrete historicity of the correlated data means that no new event is ever merely a 'type' of another, but always retains its historically unique character.[95] Moreover, and this is the second factor, nexuses between distinct temporal data are never something simply given; they are rather something which must always be exegetically established. Indeed, in the Hebrew Bible

[94] G. W. H. Lampe, in G. W. H. Lampe and K. J. Woollcombe, *Essays in Typology* (Naperville, Illinois: A. R. Altenson, 1957), 29 f., has put his finger on this point when he says that historical typology 'consists in a recognition of historical correspondences and deals in terms of past and future'. Typologies within the Hebrew Bible are broader than the mere 'historical', as will be developed below.

[95] For such reasons I think it misleading to subsume biblical typologies within the framework of cultic reactualizations of historical events, as does H. Hummel, 'The Old Testament Basis of Typological Interpretation', *Biblical Research*, 9 (1964), 47-9.

such nexuses are the product of a specific mode of theological–historical speculation – one which seeks to adapt, interpret, or otherwise illuminate a present experience (or hope, or expectation) *by means of* an older datum.

Typological exegesis thus celebrates new historical events in so far as they can be correlated with older ones. By this means it also reveals unexpected unity in historical experience and providential continuity in its new patterns and shapes. Accordingly, the perception of typologies is not solely an exegetical activity, it is, at the same time, a religious activity of the first magnitude. For if legal and other aggadic exegeses emphasize the verbal aspects of ongoing divine revelation, typological exegesis reveals its historical concreteness. Typological exegesis is thus not a disclosure of the *sensus plenior* of the text, in the manner of other forms of inner-biblical exegesis. It is rather a disclosure of the plenitude and mysterious workings of divine activity in history.

A direct approach to the typologies found in the Hebrew Bible is facilitated by the occasional use of terminology which indicates the correlated data. In some instances, fixed rhetorical terms are used; in others, fixed rhetorical expressions are reused if newly adapted to the circumstances; and in still other cases, non-technical expressions are used in prophetic discourses which serve as deictic elements that indicate the typological correlations proposed. In the first category, that of fixed rhetorical terms, the clause כאשר . . . כן 'just as . . . so' and its variants are particularly frequent. With it, a past historical event may be cited *before* a present or future event with which it is correlated. Thus, for example, YHWH says to Joshua that he will exalt him during the crossing of the Jordan, and 'כאשר as I was with Moses [so] shall I be with you' (Josh. 3: 7). Correlatively, the same clause may *follow* the occurrence of the new event (cf. Josh. 4: 14 and 23), or its projected occurrence (cf. Isa. 11: 16). Now and then כאשר is replaced by כ־ and variants (cf. Hos. 2: 17).[96]

The 'just as . . . so' clause is not unique to typological exegesis, however, being found in legal exegetical comparisons (cf. Deut. 22: 26), and elsewhere more rhetorically.[97] By contrast, juxtaposition of such terms as ראשנות and קדמניות, which indicate 'first' or 'former' things, over against חדשות or אחרנות, which indicate 'new' or 'latter' things, recurs exclusively in Deutero- and Trito-Isaiah in various contexts (cf. Isa. 43: 18-19, 65: 16-17). Clearly, such terminological contrasts

---

[96] In Isa. 54: 9 *kĕ-* and *'ăšēr* are separated for rhetorical effect. Thus, read *kĕmê*, not *kîmê* or *kî-mê*.

[97] e.g. Exod. 27: 8, 39: 43; Num. 2: 17, 14: 28; 2 Sam. 3: 9, 16: 19, Isa. 55: 10-11, 65: 8, Jer. 5: 19, 31: 27; Ezek. 12: 11; Zech. 7: 13; Prov. 24: 29. Cf. *ka'ăšēr* + *kākāh* in Eccles. 11: 5. Typology and rhetoric are combined in 1 Sam. 6: 7.

constitute a fixed rhetorical expression which emerged and circulated in a distinct prophetic school tradition. In a similar way, the prophet Jeremiah juxtaposes old and new events with a fixed rhetorical style, as can be seen by a comparison of his statement in 31: 30-2 that the new covenant will 'not be like' (. . . כ לֹא) the older one 'but rather' (כי זאת) of a different type, with the rhetoric found in 3: 17, 31: 28-9, and 31: 33. Indeed, it appears that the latter rhetorical phraseology circulated more broadly among prophets who were contemporary to him, and who were equally concerned to juxtapose the bad times with the good ones to come (cf. Ezek. 34: 22, 28-9, 36: 14-15; cf. Isa. 54: 4).

Apart from these instances, there is another broad category wherein the typologies are indicated by non-technical idiosyncratic usages, employed by the speaker for the situation at hand. A good example of this technique may be found in Isa. 11: 11, where YHWH states that 'he will continue יוסיף' to redeem Israel in the future, a 'second time שנית', just like the first. The language used here marks the typological correlation very well, and explicitly indicates its two vital features, the new moment *and* its reiteration. But such language is used only by Isaiah and is not repeated elswhere in the Hebrew Bible. In addition, there are many other cases of inner-biblical typology which are not signalled by technical terms at all. To recognize the typologies at hand, the latter-day investigator must be alert to lexical co-ordinates that appear to correlate apparently disparate texts (as in the Adam-Noah typology to be discussed below, or to various forms of paratactic juxtaposition. Sometimes, moreover, motifs are juxtaposed, sometimes pericopae, and sometimes recurrent scenarios.[98]

All these techniques recur in the Hebrew Bible, but do not, in themselves, provide the basis for a flexible and comprehensive categorization of the variety of typologies to be identified. For this it is necessary to look beyond form and technique to the contents of the typologies. It is here that a methodologically viable categorization may be discerned—one that will be at once of heuristic benefit for the analysis of the biblical data and for its correlation with comparable non-biblical and post-biblical evidence. Accordingly, the following morphology of inner-biblical typologies will be established: (1) cosmological–historical correlations; (2) historical correlations; (3) spatial correlations; and (4) biographical correlations. Within each category, moreover, it will be possible to discern literal, allegorizing, spiritualizing, and moralizing typological applications of an earlier *traditum*. The applications employed depend, necessarily, on the situation at hand and the concern of the particular speaker or narrator.

---

[98] For examples, see below.

Typologies of a Cosmological-Historical Nature

The most singular trait of this category is the use of a cosmological event as the prototype or warrant for a historical redemption to come. The structure is, therefore, eschatological; for basic to it is either the hope or the promise that a primordial cosmological configuration will be renewed in historical time.[99] The most blatant indication that the anticipated or forecast transfiguration of history will have cosmological proportions is Isa. 65:17, where God promises '. . . behold, I shall create a new heaven and new earth; the ראשנות former things will no longer be mentioned, nor will they again be recalled'. The prophecy then goes on to announce the exact nature of these new things. In addition to a restored Jerusalem, the prophet promises human longevity, a peaceful and productive earthly habitat, and a peaceful and transformed world of nature (vv. 18-25). In this way, Deutero-Isaiah promises a re-created world, almost Eden-like, where longevity and pacific behaviour will be the norm even among rapacious animals, and where labour will evermore be bountiful and productive. The vision reflects a primordial nostalgia for the restitution of lost harmony on earth, a yearning for a *restitutio in integrum*, a hope that the imminent end will be *like* the beginning, when once, before history, harmony reigned supreme in the human-natural world. But, it should be added, this envisaged new creation is not part of an apocalyptic scenario which outlines a cosmological renewal *after* the cosmos's dissolution. Rather, here, the new heaven and new earth which YHWH will create is continuous with the older ones. For Deutero-Isaiah envisages a divine reparation in the very heart of creation—a reparation, however, of such spiritual magnitude that the old world will be forgotten, the torments of physical existence will be assuaged, and Jerusalem will be brightened by everlasting joy.

In other instances where eschatological hope is enlivened by memories of creation, it is strikingly the *process* of primordial beginnings that is stressed—when *ab origine* YHWH destroyed the monsters of chaos in theomachian strife. For to the ancients, like Deutero-Isaiah, this event constituted a fundamental expression of divine power, one which was, moreover, re-expressed in historical forms, as at the time of the exodus. Indeed, it was the perceived typology between the constitutive power of primordial victory and its salvific reflex in history that established the basis for hope in a redemptive remanifestation of that same power. Thus, in his well-known oracle-prayer, Deutero-Isaiah first invokes the divine arm to arise, as it did in the archaic past (ימי קדם), when it

---

[99] For a succinct discussion of the relationship between cosmogony and eschatology in the history of religions generally, see M. Eliade, *Myth and Reality* (New York: Harper and Row, 1963), ch. 4.

'split Rahab, pierced Tanin' before the creation, and as it did later on at the exodus, when it 'shrivelled Yam, the waters of mighty Tehom' in order to safeguard the redemption of the Israelites. Then, these momentous events recalled, the prophet adds his hope that YHWH will again manifest his power for the sake of the Judaeans in exile. As is obvious, the archaic combat with the sea-monsters and the later historical victory at the sea form the typological prologue to the heart of the piece, which is a prayer for a remanifestation of this ancient primordial power by the prophet. Perceiving the past in typological terms, he is able to perceive in the present the conditions for an extension of the typology; indeed, it is the prophet's *exegetical correlation* between a primordial theomachy and the exodus that is returned to YHWH in prayer and request. For in Isa. 51: 9-11 YHWH is requested to renew a typology which man has perceived through historical reflection and need.

But this modality of historical consciousness, which correlated primordial and historical events for the sake of contemporary hope, has deep Israelite roots. For if it only comes to explicit expression in the words of Deutero-Isaiah in the Babylonian exile, its tracings can be discerned much earlier. For example, when, after the exile of the northern tribes, Isaiah of Jerusalem announced that YHWH would redeem his people 'a second time', 'just as it was for Israel when it came up from the land of Egypt' (Isa. 11: 16b), the event is envisaged as a time when YHWH

will raise his hand against the Nile; [and by the blast of] his wind he will cleave the sea;[100] and will smite it into seven streams, and [lead the people through] dry-shod. (Isa. 11: 15)

Clearly, the imagery of a mighty wind that splits the sea recalled the exodus;[101] but with the image of the shrivelling and sundering of the sea into seven streams it is clear that an older mythic battle is indicated, much like the reference in Isa. 51: 9 and elsewhere (cf. Pss. 74: 12-14, 78: 13, 89: 11). In fact, in a well-known dramatic episode in Ugaritic literature, Ba'al destroyed his arch-enemy 'Sir Sea', the 'seven-headed monster', with his magical staff.[102] Moreover, in so far as this particular scenario was broadly distributed throughout the ancient Near East, as in Mesopotamia, where the hero Marduk killed and clove the sea-monster

---

[100] As suggested in *Text and Texture*, 126, *ba'yām* is a corruption of *bāqa'yām*. This correction, which assumes the accidental elimination of the letter *q*, finds support in Exod. 14: 21, Ps. 78: 13, and Isa. 63: 12.

[101] Ibn Ezra further suggested that the stems *hāram* and *nākāh* also refer to the splitting of the sea.

[102] On this topos, see C. H. Gordon, 'Leviathan: Symbol of Evil', *Biblical Motifs; Origins and Transformations*, ed. A. Altmann (Brandeis Texts and Studies; Cambridge, Mass.: Harvard University Press, 1966), 1-9.

Tiamat in theomachian strife with his lance and blasts of wind, it may be reasonably concluded that the battle imagery and reference to 'seven streams' in Isa. 11:15 are rooted in the typological perception that the new victory will reiterate a primordial prototype from the time of the creation. And further, if Isa. 11:15-16 reflects a triadic typological scenario which correlates creation-exodus and future redemption (new exodus), and is therefore a covert version of the explicit correlations found in Isa. 51:9-11, then both help disclose the deep structural core of the imagery in Exod. 14-15. For there, in that Pentateuchal passage, Moses cleaves the sea with his magical staff through divine aid (Exod. 14:16) and YHWH, a 'warrior', smashes his enemy with his mighty 'arm' and cleaves the depths (תהמות) with mighty winds (Exod. 15:3, 6, 8).[103] Quite evidently, the use of this topos and language in Exod. 14-15 suggests that it is a narrative historicization of an older mythic motif of primordial combat—a historicization which either already embodies a typological insight or, as is more likely, gave rise to such an insight.

Texts like the foregoing, and many others which reflect a typological parallelism between primordial acts at the beginning and future ones at the end of time,[104] between the *Urzeit* of origins and the *Endzeit* of hope (be this latter at the full end of time or in the immediate future, within the process of time), are valuable indices of some aspects of ancient Israelite historical consciousness. First, it is important to observe that, from the perspective of typology, key events in Israelite history are perceived as the reiteration of foundational cosmic patterns from a *pre*historical period. Thus, the mythic configuration of divine combat and victory provides the symbolic prism for disclosing the primordial dynamics latent in certain historical events (like the exodus), and so generates the hope for their imminent recurrence. Indeed, a deeper unity of history is perceived by means of the typological correlation of separate events, and the requested or promised redemption is grounded in its unity and continuity with the past. The mythic prototype thus provides a dual service: it enables the historical imagination to assess the significance of certain past or present events; and, correlatively, it projects a configuration upon future events by which they are anticipated and identified.

A second consideration pertinent to ancient Israelite typological thinking is that the reiteration of cosmic prototypes in historical time results in the historicization of myth, a development of major import.

[103] Cf. the name of the Mesopotamian mythic personification of the sea, Tiamat; and cf. the masculine form *těhôm* in Gen. 1:2. For other instances, see Ps. 77:17, which is co-ordinated with 'ancient wonders', vv. 12-13.
[104] e.g. Isa. 27:1; Hab. 3:8-15.

For with the typological reactualization of prehistorical events in later history, older mythic structures and their central actors are variously transformed (as, for example, in the identification of the demonic and restive forces of precreation chaos with the historical enemies of Israel, or in the fact that the sea is not considered a personified dragon but a historical-geographical entity).[105] In these and other ways archaic mythic elements, known and absorbed in the Israelite cultural stream, are demythologized. But here, too, it is important to recognize a counter-movement that affects this demythologization process, and actually serves to remythicize the contents of history in a unique way. For to the degree that the routing of the enemies and evil ones of Israel's history is typologically presented as a reactualization of a primordial cosmic event, historical redemption becomes a species of world restoration and the dynamics of history reiterate creative acts of divine power. Inevitably, the status of the historical is profoundly affected. This is not to imply that the events in question lose their concrete historical facticity. It is rather to emphasize that for Israel's typological consciousness a new dimension is added to historical events with their correlation with foundational prototypes of divine activity.

In the light of the above – and this is the third point – it will be readily granted that the phenomenon of typological exegesis requires a modification and reconsideration of the common view that the Israelite apprehension of history is linear only and never cyclical. Clearly, such a dichotomy is forced and artificial, for the issue cannot be easily polarized into a juxtaposition of a 'mythic ahistorical paradigm', in which fundamental patterns recur cyclically, and a 'biblical historical paradigm', in which new and unique events unfold linearly. Rather, the phenomenon of typological exegesis makes clear that (new) salvific moments in Israelite history may partake of prototypical patterns, and are, in this respect, reiterations of them. To the degree that this happens, the presentation of the unique is, simultaneously, a representation of the fundamental, the prototypical. Thus, where the latter is an ahistorical mythic event, it paradoxically bestows on the former a metahistorical dimension. History is thus transformed just where it utilizes non-historical models, just where temporal events are correlated with pretemporal ones – typologically.[106]

---

[105] Cf. Ezek. 29: 1-12.

[106] These dynamics of typology are also found in ancient Mesopotamia and Egypt. For example, a first-millennium Assyrian text reinterprets the New Year Festival in Babylon in the light of a historical rivalry between the gods Ashur (of Assyria) and Marduk (of Babylon). See T. Jacobsen, 'Religious Drama in Ancient Mesopotamia', in *Unity and Diversity; Essays in the History, Literature and Religion of the Ancient Near East*, edd. H. Goedicke and J. J. M. Roberts (Baltimore and London: Johns Hopkins University Press, 1975), 76, 'Meslamtea is

Typologies of a Historical Nature

In contradistinction to the foregoing, where the typological construction was grounded in a mythic prototype, there is another pattern where a strictly historical paradigm is used. This type also has wide currency in the Hebrew Bible and, as with the first, the interpreter is faced with a bimodal structure. On the one hand, the typological prototype provides the terms or configuration for the way a later event is presented; on the other hand, the prototype provides the terms or configuration for the way a future hope is formulated. Of the two modes, the use of typology in the first is generally implicit and part of the covert narrative structure — as in the case of Exod. 14-15 or Isa. 11: 15 discussed earlier — whereas, in the second mode, the typology is generally explicit and overt — as in Isa. 11: 16 or 51: 9-11. Since, in the first mode, the prototype is discerned retrospectively, the form of typology may be called *retrojective*; and since, in the second mode, the prototype is the basis for a prospective hope, its form of typology may be called *projective*.

Josh. 3-5 is an excellent example of the retrojective mode of typology, where one historical event serves as the prototype for the descriptive shaping of another. Indeed, in Josh. 3: 7 the reader is made to anticipate a correlation between the past exodus and the present conquest from the outset. There, prior to the crossing of the Jordan river, YHWH tells Joshua that 'I will be with you כאשר as I was with Moses'. Joshua is thereupon told to inform the priests that when they enter the Jordan its waters will split and stand upright like a column (נד, 3: 13; cf. Exod. 15: 8); and this is just what happened. With the ark at the vanguard, the priests, followed by all Israel, entered the sundered water and passed through on dry land (חרבה; cf. Exod. 14: 21). Thus, it came about that the people feared Joshua as (כאשר) they had Moses of old (4: 14). To commemorate this memorable event, stelae were erected, so that future Israelites might see these stones and be told that 'the Jordan was יבשה dry land when Israel crossed over, and YHWH, your God, dried

Marduk who goes down to the Netherworld. He goes down because Anshar [i.e. Ashur] pursued him to the hole and he closed the door.' For a transliteration of *KAR* 307 *rev.* 7-8, see ibid. 97. What distinguishes this ritual commentary from others is that an authoritative mythic–ritual scenario serves as the pattern by which later mythic and (not so dimly disguised) *historical* antagonisms are portrayed.

From the Egyptian sphere comes an interesting example in which the traumatic Hyksos invasion of historical antiquity was assimilated to the mythic antagonism of Horus and Seth, whose end was the expulsion of the latter. In the words of J. G. Griffiths, 'The Interpretation of the Horus-Myth at Edfu', *JEA* 44 (1958), 85, the 'Horus-myth of Edfu, in so far as it reflects a historical–political rather than a cult-feud, probably mirrors the ejection of the Hyksos'. For other ancient typologies, see n. 109 below.

up the waters of the Jordan in front of you until you had gone across, כאשר just as YHWH, your God, did at the Red Sea, which he dried up for us until we had crossed' (4: 22-4).

No more explicit correlation between the conquest and the exodus could be expected: the old exodus imagery of the sea-crossing is strategically used and emphasized, and Joshua is portrayed, in parallel circumstances, as a new Moses. Other indicators further reinforce these two typological factors. First, the time of the passage is similar in both instances. Like the prototypical event of the exodus, the crossing of the Jordan takes place at the Passover season, on the tenth day of the first month (cf. Exod. 12: 6); and, immediately upon entering the new land at Gilgal, they celebrated the paschal-offering and the subsequent first-grain rituals (Josh. 5: 10-11). Second, immediately prior to his siege of Jericho, Joshua is addressed by a divine messenger who tells him to 'remove your sandal from your foot, for the place upon which you stand is sacred' (5: 13-15). Here, too, there is a distinct parallel with an event in Moses' life. Indeed, the foregoing citation is a virtual reiteration of Exod. 3: 5, when Moses was addressed by YHWH, who appeared in the midst of a burning bush at the foothills of Mount Horeb. Significantly, both numinous events were at the onset of a task of divinely guided liberation.

In his correlation of the exodus and the conquest events, the historiographer of Josh. 3-5 may have been aware of early liturgical reflexes of this same typology. Thus, in a concise fusing of the two events, the liturgist in Ps. 114 first refers (vv. 1-2) to the exodus and chosenness of Israel in language which echoes Exod. 19: 1, 6,[107] and then proclaims: 'The sea looked and fled; the Jordan turned round about' (v. 3). Since the parallelism of sea to Jordan is not required by sense or context, it makes sense only in the light of a typological identification by the author of two historical events separate in time but comparable in the religious-historical imagination. In this, Ps. 114: 3 is similar to the ancient liturgy in Exod. 15, where, as is generally recognized, the first part (vv. 1-11) deals with one historical circumstance—the Pharaoh, the Egyptian enemy, the 'walling up' of the waters, and the death of the Egyptians in the sea—whereas the second part (vv. 12-18) deals with quite another—the might of YHWH against the peoples of Philistia, Moab, Edom, and Canaan, and their rout in conjunction with Israel's advance into the land.[108] Evidently, the first part of the liturgy deals

---

[107] Noted by M. Weiss, *The Bible and Modern Literary Theory* (Jerusalem: The Bialik Institute, 1967), 181 [Heb.].

[108] For the scholarly discussion, see B. Childs, *The Book of Exodus* (OTL; Philadelphia: The Westminster Press, 1974), ch. 10. Childs correctly emphasizes that the nexus between the exodus and the conquest may be organic (not artificial); see pp. 251 f.

with the theme of the exodus, while the second is concerned with the period of the conquest. But for the ancient liturgist these two historical moments were not thoroughly disparate events, as their juxtaposition and lexical co-ordination make clear beyond doubt. Rather, for the liturgist, the two events layered in this literary setting disclose their prior and profound layering in the ancient Israelite historical imagination — a typological layering comparable to that found in Josh. 3-5. For like his liturgical conterparts, the historiographer of Josh. 3-5 was not at all concerned with historical reportage *as such*, 'wie es eigentlich gewesen'. To him, what 'really happened' at the crossing of the Jordan, as a prelude to the conquest, was a remanifestation of divine redemptive power. The typological description of the 'events' is thus, at once, a reordering of the facts at hand and an aggadic reinterpretation of them.

In this form of typological construction, moreover, the new event is elevated into the history of divine promises and acts of redemption; for the event takes on new meaning precisely by virtue of its correlation with, and depiction in terms of, the great originating event of Israelite redemption, the exodus. Under the aegis of typological exegesis, then, the historiographer allows the latter-day reader to share his observation that the particular significance of certain historical actions — like the crossing of the Jordan — lies in its reiteration of certain foundational patterns. For him, certain events have both a manifest and a latent dimension, a topical sequence and a deeper religious signification. Typologies serve, therefore, as the means whereby the deeper dimensions perceived to be latent in historical events are rendered manifest and explicit to the cultural imagination. For this reason, the fact that a particular event is not rendered solely in its own terms, but is rather reimagined in terms of another — a prototype — is not due to its paucity of religious significance but rather to its abundance. By means of retrojective typologies, events are removed from the 'neutral cascade of historical occurrences and embellished as modalities of foundational moments in Israelite history.[109]

As noted earlier, in addition to the retrojective redescription of past

---

[109] The typological reconstruction of history iš also evidenced in the ancient Near East. For example, from Mesopotamia comes the striking instance in which the Guti invasion of *c.* 2500 BCE — reflected in the Sumerian lament over Ur (from *c.* 2100 BCE) — serves as the pattern used to describe the Seleucid invasion of Babylon and its despoliation, in a text dated from 287 BCE. See T. Pinches, 'Assyriological Gleanings – II', *PSBA* 23/175 (1901), 196-9. In Egypt, the Hyksos invasion served as a typological paradigm in historiography down to Hellenistic times, when it even surfaces in connection with anti-Jewish sentiments. See R. Weill, *La Fin du moyen empire égyptien* (Paris: Imprimerie Nationale, 1918), esp. 22-68, 76-83, 605-23, and J. Yoyette, 'L'Egypte ancienne et les origines de l'anti-Judaïsme', *RHR* 163 (1963), 133-43.

events in terms of certain prototypes, typologies can also provide the linguistic and ideologic prism for projective forecasts of future redemption. This may occur in a variety of forms, as a comparison of two eighth-century BCE prophets, Hosea and Micah, indicates. Speaking in a figurative context, in which the relationship between YHWH and Israel is presented as that between a husband and his wife, Hosea first admonishes Israel and then promises her a divinely guided spiritual restoration. As a bride, Israel will be led to the steppe land where their covenantal-nuptual alliance will be reconsecrated, 'as in the days of her youth, and כיום as the time of her going up from Egypt' (2: 16-17).

Israel's spiritual renewal is thus projected as a new exodus and a new covenant (cf. 2: 18-21). More than that, the typology is extended to embrace the conquest as well; for the sign of Israel's restored relationship with God is announced as the renewal of her vineyards (כרמיה) and the transfiguration of the Valley of Achor into the Entrance of Hope (v. 17). In this forecast, one can hardly miss an allusion to the place where Israel first sinned upon entering the land. In Josh. 7: 1, 18, Achan (called Achor in the LXX and 1 Chron. 2: 7), the son of Carmi (כרמי), misappropriated the spoils of Jericho, with the result that the initial venture into the land was desecrated. At that time, Joshua led him and his possessions to the Valley of Achor (עכור, 7: 24), and said: 'For what reason have you עכרתנו brought woe upon us? [In recompense] YHWH יעכרך will make you woebegone' (v. 25). Thereupon, Achan and his entire family were stoned, burned, and buried in that place, which, ever after, was called the Valley of Achor (v. 26). Ever after, that is, until the new moment of restoration projected by Hosea, when this ancient and formative scenario would be repaired and the valley of 'woe' would become the passageway to new hope.[110] In sum, the religious reconciliation between YHWH and Israel was envisaged by the prophet Hosea typologically, with the result that the original spatial topography of Josh. 7 served as both prism and outline for a more interior journey that would restore Israel, and guide her towards a renewed covenantal fidelity with YHWH.

Over against the spiritual dislocation depicted in Hos. 2, Micah, a later contemporary, is faced with the reality of Israel's physical dislocation. The northern tribes have been scattered in exile and, in prophecy, Micah projects their restoration to Canaan as a new exodus. Responding to an appeal, YHWH says that 'I will show forth wonders as when you (כימי) left Egypt' (7:14). In these words, in the framework

---

[110] In Hos. 2: 17 the positive counterpoint to the Valley of Achor is *petah tiqwāh* 'Gateway of Hope'. Notably, this typology of a new conquest survived into post-exilic oracles, where it is linked to the return from the exile. Thus, in Isa. 65: 10 the prophet envisaged that the Valley of Achor would become a *rēbeṣ bāqār*, a 'pasture for cattle'.

of a typological analogy, hope is forecast and finds its warrant. The new exodus will conform to the old one in its wondrous and transformative power; and it will be a renewal of this awesome divine might—though not necessarily a supersession of it. This latter point, remarkable as it may sound, is, in fact, the bold assertion made by Jeremiah a century later, when he announced that future oaths of confidence will not refer to the exodus as the exemplary basis for trusting in divine might, as formerly, but will be replaced by an oath 'by the life of YHWH who has restored the Israelites from the northern land and all the lands to which they had been banished . . .' (16:14-15; cf. 23: 7-8).

The projected supersession of the old exodus by the new in Jeremiah adds a new dimension to this enquiry into inner-biblical typologies, and leads one to ask, What is the *status* of the correlation projected in the typologies? And further, What is the nature of the analogies involved? Are they analogies of equivalence, or proportion, of similarity of circumstance, or something else? Given the imprecise character of the biblical evidence, any answer must be provisional. Nevertheless, one may cautiously propose that the typologies considered thus far instantiate *analogical relationships of structural similitude and of proportion.*[111] That is, events are correlated in terms of the similar redemptive topoi involved (e.g. divine power over antagonistic forces) and in terms of their similar structural dynamics (e.g. restoration from a state of physical or spiritual servitude, or relocation to the national homeland after a period of dislocation). Biblical typologies, therefore, do not assert a precise conformity between discrete historical circumstances. On the lexical level, this is clearly implied by the recurrent use of such terms as כאשר or כ־ to *correlate* the different events. And, at a more fundamental level, it must be stressed that an inherent disproportion between the ballasts of a typology lies in the fact that the *traditio* (the *new* exodus or conquest) derives significance from a foundational *traditum*. In this respect, the latter is proportionally more dominant than its typological correlate. However, as just seen in the case of Jer. 16:14-15, the balance may be dramatically reversed. Then the paradoxical result is that the *traditio* virtually annihilates the *traditum* which gives it initial significance.

Comparable to the sources just considered, the typologies of a new exodus and conquest in texts—reflecting post-exilic circumstances—are retrojective and projective in nature, and are found in both historiographic and prophetic materials. With respect to the retrojective and historiographical side, it has been suggested, with some basis, that the

---

[111] Though rooted in a very different frame of discourse, I have found the reflections of J. F. Anderson, *The Bond of Being, An Essay on Analogy and Existence* (St. Louis: B. Herder Book Co., 1949), very helpful.

histories in Ezra-Nehemiah and Chronicles have been partially shaped by typological considerations. Thus, K. Koch has argued that 'Ezra's march from Babylonia to Jerusalem was a cultic procession which Ezra understood as a second Exodus . . .'[112] More specifically, he calls attention to the facts that the date of the departure from Babylonia occurs during the first month, just when the exodus occurred (*per* 'P'; cf. Exod. 12: 2; Num. 33: 3), and that the 'delay at the river Ahawa because no Levite had arrived, seems . . . conceivable only against the background of the order of the march through the desert after the original Exodus'.[113] To continue his contention, it may be added that when the returnees 'went up' from captivity they took with them silver and gold, wherewith to rebuild the Temple (Ezra 1: 4-6), a topos that recalls the original exodus, when the Israelites despoiled their captors of silver and gold upon their departure from Egypt (Exod. 12: 35). Moreover, just as the exodus generation and its descendants were warned not to intermarry with the Canaanites and to preserve their holy status (cf. Exod. 34: 15-16; Deut. 7: 1-6; cf. Judg. 3: 3-6), so was the post-exilic concern with intermarriage defined in the light of these prohibitions, and articulated with respect to the original, autochthonous Canaanites (Ezra 9: 1-2). The resettlement was then, typologically, a new conquest.

However, it is to the projective typologies in prophetic sources that one must turn to see the extent to which post-exilic prophecies are saturated with the exodus and conquest. In particular, these matters dominate the prophetic consciousness of Deutero-Isaiah.[114] Indeed, his sense that the events transpiring in his day were 'new things' (חדשות) in contrast to earlier, 'former things' (ראשנות) of the pre-exilic period, establishes a dichotomous typological vision that pervades his speeches. On some occasions this contrast between new and former things refers to prophecies of hope which had accompanied earlier oracles of doom (cf. Isa. 41: 22, 42: 9); on others, as in Isa. 65: 16-18, the contrast is between former earthly woes and the establishment of 'a new heaven and a new earth' with the new dawn of salvation.

But it is in connection with the exodus event that the juxtaposition of 'former things' and 'new things'—the post-exilic salvation-restoration of the exiles to Judaea—assumes a particularly subtle and variegated expression. For example, in Isa. 43: 16-21, the prophet opens his oracle

112 'Ezra and the Origins of Judaism', *JSS* 19 (1974), 184 (italics deleted).
113 Ibid. 186 f.
114 For earlier treatments, see J. Fischer, 'Das Problem des Neuen Exodus in Isaias c. 40-55', *Theologische Quartalschrift*, 110 (1929), 111-30, B. Anderson, 'The Exodus Typology in Second Isaiah', in *Israel's Prophetic Heritage*, edd. B. Anderson and W. Harrelson (New York: Harper and Row, 1962), 177-95, and my remarks in *Text and Texture*, 133-8.

of promise in the name of YHWH, 'who made a path in the sea, and a way through the mighty waters; who led forth [to doom][115] horse and chariot, hero and troop . . .'. Continuing to speak in the divine name, Isaiah admonishes the people: 'Do not recall the former things . . . behold! I shall do a new thing'; and he goes on to state: 'I shall make a path in the sea, and streams in the barren waste . . .' Quite clearly, the original exodus event is not only a prototype for what will soon transpire but a warrant for it as well—though in a quite different manner from that of Isa. 51: 9-11, where precedents of divine power were humanly invoked by the prophet in prayer.[116] Here, YHWH himself reinforces the validity of his present promise by reference to earlier, constitutive acts of his own doing.

The typological allusion in Isa. 43:16-21 to the exodus *traditum*, as presented in Exod. 14-15, with its references to destruction and salvation in the sea, is underscored by the concluding reference: 'the nation which (עַם־זוּ) I have created will recount my praise' (v. 21). For in this phrase there is a direct allusion to the particular circumlocution and designation of Israel in the Song of the Sea as 'the nation which עַם־זוּ I have created/redeemed' (Exod. 15:13, 16). Moreover, just as Exod. 17: 3-6 follows the exodus account with a description of divine beneficence in the desert, when streams of water were brought forth from rocks, the same point is made in Isa. 43: 20, and again in 48: 20-1, where an even more literal Pentateuchal allusion to this matter can be found (cf. 49: 9-11).

But however much the prophet was concerned to recall the first redemption and thus anticipate a renewal,[117] he was aware of discontinuities which, in some measure, affect the proportional weight of the *traditio* with respect to its *traditum*. Thus, in his projection of it, the new exodus will have a distinct *novum*. For in contrast to the original exodus, which occurred in an atmosphere of anxiety and haste (בְּחִפָּזוֹן, cf. Exod. 12:11; Deut. 16:3), the people are now told 'לֹא בְחִפָּזוֹן not in haste will you leave, nor will you go in flight' (Isa. 52:11-12). By this explicit reversal, the prophet avers that in the new exodus disquietude will be replaced by calm. The new exodus will therefore not simply be a remanifestation of an older prototype, but will have qualitative distinctions of its own.

The innovative dimensions of the new exodus in Isa. 52:11-12, which, as in Jer. 16:14-15, set it apart from the old exodus *traditum*,

---

[115] Instead of this elliptical formulation, NJPS *Isaiah* (1973), 126 translates 'Who destroyed' on the assumption that '*Hoṣi* is here equivalent to Aramaic *sheṣi*'. Cf. Ezra 6:15 for the latter form.

[116] Cf. above, pp. 354 f; and Ps. 77: 11-21; Isa. 63: 7-17.

[117] For a discussion of Isa. 50: 2-3 and 63: 7-19, see *Text and Texture*, 136-40. Also cf. the exodus imagery in Hag. 2: 22.

have other reflexes in prophetic literature at once more profound theologically and more extensive literarily. One of these reflexes can be found in Ezek. 20, a text dark and obscure in its point of origin but remarkably explicit with respect to the typologies portrayed. The initial obscurity lies in the particular content of the question which the people address to the prophet at the outset (v. 1) and which he rejects in fury (vv. 2-4, 31).[118] Since the text repeatedly refers to acts of apostasy throughout Israelite history, and it culminates with references to the proper place of sacrifices, upon the people's restoration from exile (vv. 39-44), the surmise that the request which infuriates the prophet concerns the innovation of sacrifices of some sort in Babylon seems likely.[119] But such desecrations will never happen, says YHWH; for before this occurs he will take Israel out of exile in wrath, with 'a mighty hand, an outstretched arm, and fuming fury' (v. 33).[120] In this way he will save Israel from further idolatry and apostasy, as he did earlier, in Egypt, when the Israelite slaves were engaged in idolatrous practices but were nevertheless delivered from there in wrath and not destroyed (cf. vv. 6-8).

The conjunction of the motifs of wrath and exodus is not, in itself, the unique element here; for this conjunction occurs in other prophetic contexts, like Jer. 21: 2, 5-6, and Joel 3: 3, where it serves to express a threatened divine fury. What is thoroughly unique in Ezek. 20 is the depiction of the Israelites as idolators in Egypt, who were, moreover, warned to give up this practice and had to be forcefully saved from it by an exodus of wrath. Nothing to this effect is known from other biblical traditions. In the old *traditum*, the promise to the patriarchs served as the warrant for the exodus when the Israelites were oppressed in bondage (Exod. 6: 4-9), and as an argument by Moses to assuage divine wrath *after* the apostasy of the golden calf (Exod. 32: 11-14). For Ezekiel, by contrast, the promise to the patriarchs is recited in conjunction with a reference to apostasy in Egypt (vv. 5-6 + 7-8),[121] whereas the motivation for a suppression of divine wrath after further

[118] The verb used here is *dāraš*, which suggests an oracular inquiry via the prophet; it is repeated punningly, in a positive way, in v. 40.

[119] See the related argument in M. Greenberg, 'Ezekiel 20 and the Spiritual Exile', in *'Oz le-David, Festschrift* for David Ben Gurion (Jerusalem: Qiryat Sepher, 1964), 440 [Heb.], with earlier literature cited. Greenberg has now retracted this view, *Ezekiel 1-20* (AB 22; Garden City, New York: Doubleday, 1983), 387f., stressing that since there is no divine response to the elders' request it is not justified to look for a response in the sequel.

[120] Verses 33-42 aggadically adapt the technical forms of liberation used in Exod. 6: 6-8, as well as references to the patriarchal promises. See *Text and Texture*, 132.

[121] Ezek. 20: 5-6 aggadically adapts the central terms and topoi of Exod. 6: 1, 7-8. Cf. *Text and Texture*, loc. cit.

acts of rebellion by fathers *and* sons in the desert is clarified by the dual
divine concern to act for the sake of his name and not to be desecrated
'before the nations' (vv. 13-14, 21-22; cf. Exod. 32:12!). Indeed, on
the first of these occasions of desert apostasy YHWH swore that he
would not bring the people to the land, but relented entirely, while on
the second occasion he relented but decided to punish the people *with
exile* (v. 23). Thus, quite remarkably, Ezekiel has used the Pentateuchal
topos of apostasy in the desert in order to *explain* Israel's exile in
Babylon as a punishment deflected from the original perpetrators and
transferred to a later generation.

Perhaps, among other traditions, this notion was common in Babylon.
But the more intriguing issue is the basis for such an argument. While
this explanation may simply be a desperate search for a theodicy, and
without textual basis, there is ground for proposing that Ezek. 20:33
is, in fact, a piece of aggadic exegesis. For it will be recalled that when
Moses interceded for the sins of Israel after their apostasy with the calf
(Exod. 32:30-2), YHWH told him that he would punish those who
sinned (v. 33)—*but only when* he decided to; 'but at the time of my
visitation (וביום פקדי) I shall requite (ופקדתי) them for their sins'
(v. 34).[122] Here, already, is a precise textual comment announcing
YHWH's decision to defer punishment for the apostasy of the calf[123]
—one that could have inspired or supported Ezekiel's announcement
that the exile was in fact the divine punishment for sins committed
generations earlier.[124]

The new exodus and new covenant in the desert concerning which
Ezekiel speaks in 20:33-8 thus provide a theological reconciliation
and historical closure of the most profound sort. For, in the context
of a new act of wrath, a cycle of wrath which had cast its pall over the
entirety of Israel's history hitherto would be assuaged and brought to
closure. Thus, in addition to the negative typology of an exodus of
wrath, there is a reversal of the desert apostasy scenario upon Israel's
return from exile. As earlier (v. 10), the people of Israel will again be
brought to a desert (v. 35) and be judged there 'face to face'; for
כאשר just as I entered into judgement with your ancestors in the
desert of the land of Egypt, כן so shall I enter into judgement with
you—says the Lord YHWH' (v. 36). The past judgement referred to is

---

[122] This interpretation of Exod. 32:34 follows Muffs, loc. cit. (n. 56), 52.

[123] Following this announcement, the attribute formulary in Exod. 34:6-7
now reinforces its theological presuppositions—and with the same verb *pāqad*.
Presumably, Exod. 32:24 is actually an aggadic application of the 'attribute'
traditum.

[124] This argument contrasts remarkably with Ezek. 18, where the prophet
rebuts at length the old proverb about 'sour grapes'—i.e., about vicarious punishment.

presumably the arraignment for apostasies in the desert and the forecast of the people's exile. Now, however, the judgement has *positive* overtones: the people will be reconnected to the ancient covenant (ברית) and the rebellious transgressors will be cleansed (ברותי) from their midst (vv. 37-8). In this way, the second typology in Ezek. 20, concerning divine judgement in the desert, undergoes a transformation: the *traditio* of restoration transforms the older *traditum* and does not simply parallel it.

As striking as is Ezekiel's transmutation of the exodus and desert tradition into new typological terms, it somewhat pales before the theological reversal found in Isa. 19: 19-25.[125] For in that eschatological oracle what is most astonishing is its audacious inversion and transfer of a national tradition of redemption to the very people—the Egyptians— who were its original enslaver. This transformation is brought about by a deliberate and extended play on the language of the exodus cycle, particularly such segments of the Pentateuchal account as are found in Exod. 3: 7-9 and 8: 16-24. In these passages we learn that YHWH sees the torment of 'my people' (עמי), hears their cry (צעקתם), sees the Egyptians oppressing (לחצים) them, and sends (stem: שלח) Moses as a deliverer to bring them out and save (והצלתי) them. When he sends signs (eg. אות) that the Egyptians might know (stem: ידע) his power, Pharaoh relents and offers to let the Israelites sacrifice (stem: זבח) in Egypt. But Moses refuses on the grounds that worship of YHWH could take place only outside Egypt. Pharaoh also begs Moses to pray (stem: עתר) for him. However, in the end, Pharaoh's non-compliance with Moses' demands led to divinely sent plagues (note the stem נגף, in Exod. 7: 27, 12: 23, and Josh. 24: 5).

With sustained exegetical counterpoint, the oracle in Isa..19: 19-25 touches on all the foregoing terminological features and topoi of the exodus tradition and radically transforms them. Now it is the Egyptians who have oppressors (לחצים) and who cry (יצעקו) to YHWH; and now, remarkably, an altar to YHWH will be built *in* Egypt as a sign (אות) that he will send them (stem: שלח) a deliverer to save them (והצילם) Through these acts of deliverance, moreover, YHWH will be known (stem: ידע) to the Egyptians, who will sacrifice to him (stem: זבח). Though YHWH will plague (ונגף) the Egyptians, he will in the end respond to their prayers (stem: עתר) and heal them.

Through such a metamorphosis, it would seem that the phenomenon of biblical historical typologies is brought to its conceivable limit. For hereby the subject-matter has been inverted to such an extent that just that redemptive event which constituted Israel's particular destiny has become the prototype by which a more universal, messianic

---

[125] Cf. 'Revelation and Tradition', 354.

reconciliation is envisaged. Egypt, the first oppressor, will one day have
its share in an exodus-type event; indeed, teaches the prophet, the true
new exodus will be nothing less than the redemption of the original
enemy in a manner typologically similar to the foundational redemption
of YHWH's chosen people. In fact, the typological daring on this point
is so complete that even the older notion of Israelite chosenness is
qualified: for in v. 25 Isaiah projects a time when Egypt, like Israel,
will also be called 'my people' (עמי) by YHWH (cf. Exod. 3: 10). That
such a *traditio* delivers the *coup de grâce* to the original exodus *traditum*
was particularly felt by later tradents who attempted to thwart this
blow to national pride. Thus, in the rendition of Isa. 19: 25 in the
LXX and Targum, Isaiah's typological reversal is actually reversed.
Assertively at variance with this divinely authorized prophetic *traditum*,
these versions reverse the universalism of the MT and state that *only*
Israel was the people of YHWH. This tendentious change bears witness
to the transformative and innovative capacities of typology in ancient
Israelite literature, as well as to its theological power and spiritual daring.

Typologies of a Spatial Nature

Another aspect of the typological imagination in ancient Israel is the
tendency to identify diverse *loci* of sacred geography. In line with the
phenomenon widely known from the history of religions, foundational
events and institutions are located at a 'sacred centre'—an *axis mundi*
where the powers of heaven and earth conjoin—which provides the
prototype for later events and institutions.[126] What is particularly
unique about these typologies is that the correlations emphasize spatial
elements or attributes. Sometimes this is achieved by the juxtaposition
of the *loci* in question, as in 2 Chron. 3: 1, were it is stated—against all
historical–geographical likelihood—that Solomon built 'the Temple of
YHWH in Jerusalem, *on Mount Moriah*', the mountain of Abraham's
near-sacrifice of Isaac (Gen. 22: 2, 14). In other instances, the correlation is achieved by the wholesale transfer of spatial imagery from one
narrative topos to another. Particularly notable in this regard is the
typological reapplication in different biblical genres ·of the archaic
imagery of Eden to Canaan, Zion, and the Temple in Jerusalem.

    Among the archetypal expressions of sacred geography in the Hebrew
Bible, the imagery of Eden is particularly dominant.[127] Located in the

---

[126] See M. Eliade, *Patterns in Comparative Religion* (New York: Meridian
Books, 1963), 374-9, and A. Wensinsk, *The Ideas of the Western Semites Concerning the Navel of the Earth* (Amsterdam: J. Müller, 1916). W. Gärte has dealt
with preliterary manifestations in his 'Kosmische Vorstellungen im Bilde prä-
historischer Zeit . . .', *Anthropos*, 9 (1915), 956-79.

[127] Cf. *Text and Texture*, 17-19, 111-20, for an earlier treatment. M. Eliade,
in his 'Psychologie et histoire des religions – A propos du symbolisme du "centre"',

primordial past, Eden is set on a mountain from which four streams flow to the quadrants of the earth. Like an umbilical cord, it is the font of all sustenance and blessing: jewels and riches enrich the garden, together with two semimagical trees planted in its midst, the repositories of the secret powers of life and knowledge. The garden of Eden thus symbolizes primordial harmony and order in space, a channel of divine blessing and beneficence which was ruptured with the primordial human transgression of the divine interdiction. In consequence of this delict, mankind was cast bodily from Eden, barred from its blessings, and condemned to the dislocations and curses of historical existence. The garden is thus a literary residue of an archetypal memory of spatial harmony and divine bounty, and as such, it is the basis for a profound inner-biblical nostalgia for spatial harmony that attaches itself –repeatedly in history–to certain spatial institutions or *loci* which were felt to embody this longing. Where the institution or *locus* is perceived through the imagery of Eden, then retrojective typologies can be identified; and where future hope is envisaged with this imagery, projective typologies occur.[128]

Reflexes of retrojective spatial typologies recur in the paeans to Zion in the psalms of the cult. In them, this ancient mythographic imagery serves to deepen profoundly the status of the holy city of Jerusalem. As the font of order and blessing for the Judaean kingdom, Jerusalem was a 'historical Eden'; and as located on the 'mountain of YHWH' set over the cosmic deep (Ps. 48: 3), it was a city from whose centre flowed 'rejoicing' waters (Ps. 46: 5; cf. 48: 2-4, 12-14). And here, too, at Zion, was the 'foundation stone' of origins–an ancient symbol of sacred geography, grounding, as it were, certain places as *loci* of order and harmony (cf. Isa. 28: 16).[129]

But it was not until the woe and dislocation of the exile, and with it the destruction of the land and Temple, that the symbolism of Eden emerges with singular emphasis. In the mouths of the post-exilic prophets, this imagery serves as the organizing prism for striking visions

Eranos-Jahrbuch, 19 (1950), 247–82, has provided seminal reflections on the symbol of the sacred centre and the need for a special methodology.

[128] On tracing 'Eden' as a motif with transformations, the remark of P. Berger, in 'The Sociological Study of Sectarianism', *Social Research*, 21 (1954), 477, is particularly pertinent. He notes that '[t]he concept of a religious motif . . . refers to a specific pattern or gestalt of religious experience, that can be traced in a historical development'. The whole issue is, of course, set within the broad framework of tradition–history. Cf. the exploration of H. Gross, 'Motivtransposition als Überlieferungsgeschichtliches Prinzip im Alten Testament', *Sagra Pagina*, 1 (1958), 324–34.

[129] On this symbol, see M. Eliade, op. cit. (n. 126), 231–3. On some comparable rabbinic traditions, see R. Patai, (*Man and Temple* London: Nelson and Sons, 1947), 53–9, 85.

of spatial renewal. Thus, on the one hand, the restored homeland is explicitly projected as a new Eden (cf. Isa. 51: 3; Ezek. 36: 35). Longing for order and spatial restoration, the prophets imagined the ancient national centre as an old-new Eden from which the people were evicted. But, quite unlike the old Adam, this new national counterpart will return to Edenic bliss—this being the return to Zion and to national dignity in the land. Perhaps for this reason, Ezekiel (or his redactor) juxtaposed the oracle of hope that the old Eden would be restored (36: 35) with the parable of dry bones, whereby he envisages the re-creation of the corporate body of Israel—much like a new Adam—with a new flesh and a new spirit (37: 4-9). By this coupling of Edenic and Adamic imagery, national nostalgia and primordial fantasies are blended.[130] For the typological mind, the restoration to Zion was nothing less than a profound *restoratio in integrum*.

However, the typological reuse of Edenic mythography in post-exilic prophecy is nowhere more forcefully evident than in connection with the new Temple. Ezekiel, for example, places his envisaged future Temple at the cosmic centre of Zion. From this axial point, streams flow from the door of the Temple, and provide healing sustenance to the fish and flora which teem around it (47: 1-12).[131] Thus, the new Temple, like the old, will be a font of blessing for Israel, a 'mountain of god', linking the highest heaven to the nethermost earth.[132] Here the old ruptures will be repaired, and the new will be like the old. Indeed,

---

[130] Cf. M. Eliade's suggestive essay. 'Nostalgia for Paradise in the Primitive Traditions', *Myths, Dreams, and Mysteries* (New York: Harper Torchbooks, 1967), 59–71. For the transformation of this longing into Utopian fantasy and energy, particularly in Western thought, see F. and F. Manuel, 'Sketch for a Natural History of Paradise', *Daedalus* (Winter 1972), 83–128.

[131] Ezek. 47: 12 includes the imagery of health-giving trees. The theme of the 'tree of life' is also found in the Book of Proverbs (3: 17-18, 11: 30, 13: 12, 15: 4). See R. Marcus, 'The Tree of Life in the Book of Proverbs', *JBL* 62 (1943), 117–20. Especially interesting is the association of true wisdom with the 'tree of life' in Prov. 3: 17-18—a blending of a thematics of the two mythical trees referred to in Gen. 2: 9, and without the penalty of death. The themes of wisdom and life are more assertively identified and nomicized in *M. 'Abot* vi. 7. The thematic of 'desire' found in Prov. 13: 13 is reminiscent of Gen. 3: 6.

[132] It is striking that Ezekiel describes the base platform of the altar of the envisaged Temple as *ḥēq hā'āreṣ* 'bosom of the earth' (43: 14) and its summit, with four horns, as *har'ēl* 'mountain of God' (43: 15). The latter term is probably a popular etymology for Akk. *arallu* 'mountain of the gods' and 'underworld'; see W. F. Albright, *Archeology and the Religion of Israel*[5] (New York: Anchor Books, 1965), 146 f. Cf. consonantal *'ry'l* in Isa. 29: 1 and Ezek. 43: 15-16. The former term, *ḥēq hā'āreṣ*, is the precise Hebrew equivalent of Akk. *irat erṣitti/ kigalle* 'Bosom of the earth/underworld', found in contemporary neo-Babylonian inscriptions. Cf. S. Langdon, *Neubabylonische Königsinschriften* (Leipzig: J. Hinrichs, 1911), i. 1. 36 (Nabopolassar); and i. 2. 31, vi. 2. 1-2, xii. 2. 23 (Nebuchadnezzar).

by infusing Temple imagery with Edenic symbolism, Ezekiel, like other prophets after him, projected an ancient nostalgia for spatial harmony and blessing into the future and thus reveals the depth of the Israelite yearning for restoration and the axial significance of the Temple.[133] In all this, Ezekiel was not alone. His visions are reinforced by other post-exilic prophets. Thus, Joel likened the promised land to a garden of Eden (2: 3) and envisaged its restoration in terms of a fountain of sustenance flowing from the Temple of YHWH (cf. 4: 18, 20-1), and Zechariah spoke of a day when 'living waters will come out of Jerusalem' and fructify the earth (14: 8-11).

These typological alignments have deep exegetical dimensions, in so far as they 'read' one historical moment in terms of another, and thereby project the powerful associations of the past into future images of longing and hope. But it must be noted that not all such typological alignments reflect a free religious tendency to identify fundamental spatial events and images. At times, by contrast, certain spatial identifications are decidedly political in motivation. In this category belongs the transfer of Sinai images to Zion in Ps. 68: 16-18 and Isa. 2: 1-4. In the first text, which reflects the period of the fall of Samaria and the transfer of all legitimacy to Judaea and the Davidic line, YHWH is portrayed as leaving Sinai and taking up residence in Zion, his chosen city.[134] One may therefore suspect this relocation motif to be a political apologia by Davidic court liturgists concerned to enhance the glory of Zion, and to legitimate its succession of other royal cities—with the fall of Samaria, its ancient rival. The same political background seems to apply to the second text as well. Here Isaiah, the prophet of Jerusalem and the spokesman of its special sanctity in the age of the fall of Samaria, typologically projects a future time when Sinai will be replaced by Zion as the ἱερὸς τόπος of Israel, a time when 'Torah will come forth from Zion and the word of YHWH from Jerusalem'.[135] In this way

---

[133] In gauging the religious power of these visions it must be recalled that just like the old Tabernacle, which was a *typos* of the heavenly shrine (cf. Exod. 25: 9, 40, 26: 30, 27: 8), the blueprint of the new Temple is envisaged by Ezekiel in a heavenly vision. In this respect, Ezekiel is a new Moses and the new Temple again follows a heavenly prototype. For the notion of a correspondence between heavenly and earthly shrines in the history of religions generally, see M. Eliade, 'Centre du Monde, Temple, Maison', in *Le Symbolisme cosmique des monuments religieux*, ed. E. Orienta (Série Orientale Roma, 14; Rome: Instituto Italiano per il Medio ed Estremo Oriente, 1957), 57-82. For this theme in classical rabbinic sources, see V. Aptowitzer, 'The Cosmic Temple according to Rabbinic Sources', *Tarbiz*, 31 (1930-1), 137-52, 257-87 [Heb.].

[134] Reading *b' msyny* 'come from Sinai' for Massoretic *bm syny*, with many scholars.

[135] Cf. also Isa. 4: 5, where it is envisaged that the cloud, smoke, and fire of the Sinai theophany (Exod. 19: 16, 18, 20: 18, and Deut. 5: 4, 20-3; Deut. 5: 5 is a harmonistic interpolation), which later rested on the desert Tabernacle and

Isaiah gives importance to the new centrality of Jerusalem, and buttresses new hope with the accumulated force of sacred memories.

Typologies of a Biographical Nature

The typological alignment in the Hebrew Bible of persons, and the correlation or interfusing of their personal traits and personal behaviours, provide yet another dimension to our discussion. Here the focus is on the *character of an individual life*, rather than on the character of a particular historical event or spatial topos. A variety of forms and modes can be distinguished.

In one set of instances, typologies of a biographical nature can serve to structure historical sequences and schemata. As noted earlier, Noah is a new Adam who, in Gen. 9:1-9, presides over a restored world, a renewal of creation depicted in the terms and imagery of Gen. 1: 26-31. In addition, Noah appears in the tenth generation after Adam and, as aggadically indicated by an ancient redactor of the old genealogies, he was the one expected to comfort human beings 'from the travail (עצבון) of our hands [on] the earth (אדמה) which YHWH had cursed (אררה)' (Gen. 5: 29). The allusion here is to the divine curse directed against Adam in Gen. 3:17, when YHWH Elohim said to Adam that 'the earth (האדמה) will be cursed (ארורה) on your account; [for] you will eat in travail (עצבון) all the days of your life'. These verbal features, which establish a typological link between Adam and Noah, and guide the reader to that perception, provide an added ironic undertone to the divine remarks found in Gen. 6: 6. There, the old hope that Noah would provide comfort (ינחמנו) from the earthly travail (עצבון) of labour (ממעשנו) is punned upon when the hope and comfort come to naught,[136] when 'YHWH regretted (וינחם) that he made (עשה) mankind on earth, and it grieved (ויתעצב) him greatly'.[137] But the flood came, and after that the restoration, until ten generations later — typologically comparable to the span between Adam and Noah — Abram received from YHWH the gifts of land, seed, and earthly blessing (12: 1-3). In this typological context, it cannot fail to strike one that these three

protected Israel in the desert (cf. Exod. 40: 35-8; also Neh. 9:12, 19), would be recreated in Zion (note the verb *bārā'*).

136 Cf. RSV, 'Out of the ground which the Lord has cursed this one shall bring us relief . . .' It is rather from the toilsome cultivation of things 'from' the earth that Noah brings comfort.

137 Cf. *Text and Texture*, 21. A further reflex of all these terms with respect to a promise of post-exilic restoration can be found in Isa. 14: 1, 3 – possibly an aggadic allusion to Noah and the folk etymology on his name in Gen. 5: 29.

blessings are, in fact, a typological reversal of the primordial curses in Eden: directed against the earth, human generativity, and human labour.

Typology may, furthermore, hold the key to the repetition of scenarios and narrative structures in the patriarchal narratives as well. Thus, the repetition of certain themes like the problematic birth of the heir through the favourite wife (who is barren, and whose pregnancy is announced by a divine oracle), the motifs of fraternal strife and hierarchical supersession of a younger sibling over elders, and the descent of a patriarch to a foreign land because of drought (together with the motif of the patriarch's duplicity regarding his wife's status), may be a deliberate attempt of the narrative tradition to present the 'fathers' as figures of each other, as typologically interrelated.[138] Indeed, it is just in this regard that the rabbinic dictum cited earlier, which observed that 'All that happened to the fathers was a sign for the sons', is most appropriate.

Notably, however, this father-son typological nexus is not restricted to physical paternity. It is also applied to spiritual parallels or relationships of different sorts. Thus, on the basis of a general similarity of spatial topoi and appellatives, some moderns have concluded that later Davidic court circles perceived a typological link between Abraham and David, and modelled or adapted their royal histories to the older patriarchal narratives to make this explicit.[139] In particular, it may be that the promise to Abraham, which announced that 'kings will issue from you' (Gen. 17: 6), is an anachronistic retrojection by these circles concerned to correlate Abraham and David, and to see in David the fulfilment of a promise addressed to his prototype, Abraham. Such an example is an implied typology, designed to emphasize spiritual-historical continuities. Similar to it are the parallel motifs pointed out earlier which correlate Joshua to Moses, or the typological portrayals of Elijah or Ezekiel as a new Moses.[140]

In all this there is the double motivation to legitimate the successor of an earlier leader, and to show a deep homology that unifies the spiritual leaders of the past. This double concern is reflected in the

---

[138] Recognition of the patterning of patriarchal narratives was an old rabbinic tradition. For example, citing an unknown source, the *Midrash ha-Gadol*, ed. M. Margulies (Jerusalem: Mosad Harav Kook, 1967), *Genesis*, 446, noted that Abraham and Isaac both experienced famine, went into exile, used their wives as a pretext, were subject to Philistine jealousy, and sired sons in their old age— among other parallels.

[139] Cf. R. Clements, *Abraham and David; Genesis XV and its Meaning for Israelite Tradition* (London: SCM Press, 1967), 55-60.

[140] Regarding Elijah and Moses, see R. Carlson, 'Elie à l'Horeb', *VT* 19 (1969), 413-39. For a typological link between Ezekiel and Moses, cf. n. 133 above.

presentation of the classical prophets as well. Not only does the deuteronomist emphasize that all true prophets are 'like' Moses (see Deut. 18: 15), but the revisors of prophetic traditions were concerned to make the same point. Seen thus, the commission scene of Jeremiah is not just a deuteronomic stylization of an old tradition, but a deliberate attempt to legitimate the mission of this prophet who receives God's words into his mouth as required by the old prototype (דברי בפיך, Jer. 1: 9; cf. Deut. 18: 18). This motif of preparing the mouth of the prophet for his new spiritual role recurs in the commission scenes of Isaiah and Ezekiel, and so serves to validate their task as well. The first occurrence of the motif is found in connection with Moses, the prototype of all prophets (Exod. 3: 12, 4: 10-16); its last is found in a late post-exilic prophecy, where it is forecast that upon the redemption of Zion and the spiritual renewal of Israel the entire people will have the divine teachings placed in their mouth (דברי . . . בפיך, Isa. 59: 21). By this typological link, the old prophetic motif is both nationalized and normalized: beginning with the new age, all Israel will speak as prophets 'forever'. This hope is echoed in Joel 3: 1-2, and may derive from Num. 11: 29.

Deutero-Isaiah also draws biographical correlations into his vast typological net. In one instance he refers to Noah in a most striking way. After referring to the desolations of the exile caused by divine wrath (Isa. 54: 7-8), the prophet adds: 'כי־מי this is like the waters[140b] of Noah to me; אשר just as I swore that the waters of Noah would never again inundate the earth, כן so do I forswear future anger and wrath against you. For though the mountains may move and the hills be displaced, my graciousness will not depart from you, nor shall my covenant of peace be disrupted—says YHWH, your consoler' (vv. 9-10). What is expressed here is a typological association between the primordial flood and the late Judaean exile. Just as the former was an expression of wrath, but ended with a divine promise of permanence in the natural order (Gen. 8: 21-2, 9: 15-17), so now the wrath of exile will give way to an era of eternal divine grace. In this way the ancient covenant with Noah and his descendants will be recapitulated in the post-exilic period. For just as the post-diluvian world involved a divine renewal of the primordial creation, and a divine promise that such destruction would 'never again' be repeated (cf. עוד . . . לא, Gen. 8: 21), so now Deutero- and Trito-Isaiah repeatedly emphasize the theme of YHWH as creator (e.g. 40: 12-31, 42: 5, 44: 24, 45: 9-13, 18, 47: 13, 51: 13, 16)—even of a new heaven and new earth (65: 17)—and emphasize that the wrath of the past will 'never again' recur (cf. עוד . . . לא, 51: 22, 52: 1, 54: 4, 60: 18-20, 62: 4, 65: 19-20).[141] As elsewhere in the prophecies of Isa.

[140b] This translation follows the LXX and the sense of the MT, with most moderns. Also, note the comment on p. 352 n. 96, above.

[141] This construction recurs repeatedly in the eschatological–restoration prophecies of Jeremiah and Ezekiel and underscores a strong theological-

40-66, one typological model links with others, thereby giving dynamic expression to the totalizing character of the typological imagination in ancient Israel.

However, in the post-exilic period, it is not only the covenantal promise to Noah which provides a typological warrant for new hope but the life of Abraham as well. Responding to the despair of the exiles, the prophet encourages the people to 'recall Abraham your forefather, and Sarah who bore you: for he was one when I called him, but I blessed him and made him numerous' (Isa. 51:2). Here Abraham becomes a 'type' for the favourable response to a command to return to the promised land. The people are asked, in effect, to repeat this patriarchal action. And, just as Abraham was promised a great seed and blessing (Gen. 12:1-3)—a bounty realized in subsequent history—so are the exiles implicitly guaranteed national renewal if they follow his example. Such was the hope, at any rate, a hope based on the *a fortiori* argument that since Abraham was one and multiplied, Israel, his typological heir, could anticipate a great renewal if it would return—however small the nucleus—to the ancestral land. In this argument to the exiles there is a positive counterpoint to a negation of this *a fortiori* contention by the roughly contemporary prophet Ezekiel. For during this period those Judaeans who had not gone into exile, and who 'dwelt among the ruins' of Jerusalem and Israel, said to the prophet: 'Abraham was but one and he inherited the land, and we are many [so how much the more so] is the land given us as an inheritance!' (Ezek. 33:24). In swift response, Ezekiel arraigns these people for their sins and forecasts the final ruination of their land (vv. 25-9).[142] The people's typological identification with Abraham has led, according to Ezekiel, to a false and presumptive confidence. Years later, in the mouth of Deutero-Isaiah the same typological correlation would serve as a proclamation of consolation and exhortation.

Indeed, one might further add that the typological use of Abraham in connection with the 'new exodus' may have its roots in an earlier association made between Abraham and the original exodus. One hint in this direction occurs at the very outset of the Abrahamic traditions when, immediately upon his entrance into the land, the patriarch migrates down to Egypt because of a famine in Canaan and sojourns there. However, after an episode in which he introduced his wife as his sister—thereby setting the stage of Pharaoh's amorous advances—YHWH brings a 'plague' against the Pharoah and his household, the result of which is that the Pharoah sent Abraham out of his land. The

psychological concern of the times. Cf., for example, Jer. 16:14, 23:4, 36. 30:8, 31:11, 28, 33; Ezek. 16:42, 34:10, 22, 28-9, 36:14-15, 30, 37:22-3.

[142] For the Pentateuchal allusions in the condemnation, see above p. 294.

parallelism—topically and lexically—between this event and the exodus from Egypt is self-evident: Abraham was clearly understood as anticipating in his lifetime the destiny of his descendants.[143] Such a typological reshaping of a narrative tradition about Abraham helps explain the use of the verb הוֹצֵאתִיךָ 'I [YHWH] took you out' in Gen. 15: 7, in connection with Abraham's migration from Ur. Since there is no explicit biblical tradition that Abraham was in any peril in his homeland,[144] one may conclude that this particular term was chosen because it was part of the stock of traditional terms used to convey the Exodus (cf. Exod. 6: 6, 20: 2) and the narrator wished to establish a typological nexus between the two events.[145] He was further aided in this by the incorporation into Gen. 15: 13-16 of a divine oracle which vouchsafed to Abraham that his ancestors would sojourn in Egypt as slaves, but in the fullness of time would go out (יָצָאוּ) with great wealth.[146] Thus, in all these various forms Abraham came to serve as the prototype of Israel for later generations. It remained for the later post-exilic prophets —and perhaps, too, the somewhat earlier example of Isa. 29: 22[147]—to make this Scripturally explicit.

The typological reuse of the life and behaviour of the patriarch Jacob also has notable aggadic reflexes in the prophetic literature: For example, in Hos. 12 the sibling rivalry between Jacob and Esau, as well as other instances of Jacob's deceptions and deeds, form the basis of a trenchant diatribe against latter-day Israel. Thus, as a species of typological exegesis, the historical wiles, deceptions, and treacheries of corporate Israel are represented as a national reiteration of the behaviour of their eponymous ancestor, Jacob-Israel. To be sure, it may be contended that the roots of this typological correlation actually lie in the fact that Jacob was the ancestor of all Israel,·and that the Pentateuchal Jacob Cycle *already* reflects national-ethnic consider-

---

[143] Cf. U. Cassutto, *Commentary on Genesis*, ii (Jerusalem: The Magnes Press, 1964), 334 f. Cf. *Gen. Rab.* 40: 8.

[144] According to the midrash in *Gen. Rab.* 38, however, the *'ûr* or Ur of the Chaldees is understood literally —i.e., Abraham was saved from 'the furnace of the Chaldees', some sort of persecution (cf. Dan. 3: 21-3).

[145] J. Weingreen, *'hôśē'tîkā* in Genesis 15: 7, in *Words and Meanings, Essays Presented to D. W. Thomas*, edd. P. Ackroyd and B. Lindars (Cambridge: Cambridge University Press, 1968), 209-15, also notes a concern in Gen. 15: 7 to establish a parallel with the exodus; but his argument that this parallel was adopted because a story that Abraham was saved from peril of some sort, as noted in rabbinic tradition (see preceding note), is unconvincing. More simply, the writer wishes to underscore a typological nexus between two 'exoduses'.

[146] This tradition is reiterated in Neh. 9: 7.

[147] The verb here is *pādāh*, as in the parallel formula uttered by David in 2 Sam. 4: 9.

ations.[148] While accurate to a degree, this argument minimizes two significant factors: first, that Hos. 12 applies events in the individual biography of Jacob to the nation as a whole, and second, that national considerations do not gainsay the fact that the Jacob Cycle is rooted in the life of one person, Jacob son of Isaac. Thus, whether or not Hosea knew a Jacob tradition in precisely the form preserved in Gen. 25: 11-35: 22,[149] one can hardly imagine that any version of the Jacob Cycle was ever anything but an individual history.

Minimally, then, Gen. 25: 11-35: 22 is the story of a person called Jacob, and this story — or a reflex of it — is transformed in Hos. 12. Indeed, in this aggadic version, Jacob serves as the typological prototype for *all* Israel and their various covenantal transgressions. To achieve this, two exegetical transformations occur. The first relies on a rereading of Jacob's actions with particular attention to the deceits and mendacities recorded. In this condemnation, the prophet was preceded in fact by the Pentateuchal narrator, who, though somewhat restrained because of Jacob's patriarchal status, used Isaac, Esau, and Laban as displaced personae for his own voice. Thus, Isaac explicitly calls Jacob's theft of the blessing a deceit (מרמה, Gen. 27: 35); Esau says that Jacob has displaced him twice (יעקבני, v. 36); and Laban rebukes Jacob for his displacement of an elder sibling, and thus echoes the older deceit (29: 25-6).[150] But the prophet seems to go further than this. Just after referring to the fact that Jacob has supplanted (עקב) his brother in the womb, Hosea repeats the Pentateuchal tradition of Jacob's encounter with Elohim (v. 4b) — the divine being at the Jabbok ford (v. 5a). Since these episodes are introduced with references to Jacob-Israel's national misdeeds, for which punishment was due (ישיב, v. 3b), and are followed by a call to repentance (תשוב, v. 6a) and a catalogue of sins, there is every reason to suspect that Jacob's *personal* activities were considered the typological antecedent for Israel's *national* transgressions. Seen

---

[148] For example, in the oracle of Gen. 25: 25, where it is forecast that Esau-Edom will be subjugated to Jacob-Israel. This may be a *vaticinum ex eventu* reflecting Judah's suzerainty over Edom after David conquered it and set up garrisons (2 Sam. 8: 13 f.; 1 Kgs. 11: 15 f.). Similarly, the oracle of Edom's eventual independence in Gen. 27: 40 probably reflects the temporary break in Judah's hegemony near the close of Solomon's reign (1 Kgs. 11: 14-22, 25; cf. LXX). On this oracle as a retrojection, see M. Haran, 'Observations on the Historical Background of Amos 1: 2-2: 6', *IEJ* 18 (1968), 207 and n. 18.

[149] Among the many parallels, cf. Hos. 12: 4a and Gen. 25: 26; Hos. 12: 4b-5a and Gen. 32: 23-33; Hos. 12: 5a and Gen. 32: 27; Hos. 12: 5b and Gen. 28: 13; Hos. 12: 13a and Gen. 28: 5; and Hos. 12: 13b and Gen. 29: 15-30. Clearly, some sequences, like Hos. 12: 13a and b, are quite out of keeping with the old *traditum*, as generally recognized. For a thoughtful textual treatment, see Y. Kaufmann, *Toledot*, iii/1. 134-6.

[150] Cf. *Text and Texture*, 55.

thus, Jacob's contention with Elohim in v. 4b is a foreshadowing of later religious rebellions.

That the prophet fully intended this conclusion is also evident from the way he has exegetically linked Jacob's biography to the later history of 'Jacob' through a series of deft verbal associations and puns. Hosea underscores the negative prototype of Jacob's acts—*including* the encounter with Elohim. Thus, like Isaac's condemnation of Jacob's actions as 'deceit מרמה', Hosea refers to contemporary Jacob as a trader who connives with 'false scales' (מרמה; v. 8),[151] and, just as old Jacob 'strove with Elohim in his manhood (באונו)' (v. 4b; possibly 'with his strength'), so does latter-day Jacob deceitfully find 'wealth' (און) with the hope that his 'iniquity' (עָוֹן) will not be found out (v. 9).[152] Indeed, for these 'bitter provocations' (תמרורים,v. 15), as for other, cultic acts of iniquity (אָוֶן, v. 12), the north will be punished.

In this particular example of typological exegesis, more is involved than recording a series of correlations between events in the past and present. It would appear that for the prophet, in so far as the individual Jacob-Israel is the ancestor of Israel, his behaviour has to some degree *determined* the behaviour of his descendants. Indeed, because of the eponymous link between the person Israel and the nation, the parallelism drawn between the actions is not a mere rhetorical trope, but drives deep into the very 'nature' of Israel. The nation is not just 'like' its ancestor, says Hosea, but *is* its ancestor in fact—in name and in deed. Thus, in this instance, aggadic typology discloses the inner nature of Israel, its rebellious core *ab origine*. For the later Judaean editors, who inherited Hosea's northern preachments, Jacob-Israel's inherent sin must have been seen as a reason for Ephraim's fall. With the southern kingdom still intact, these tradents could not resist the comment—interpolated just after a denunciation of Israel's deceit—that 'Judah *still* follows El, and is faithful with the holy ones' (v. 1b).

One concluding example of the same type may be added. As in so many matters, the prophet Jeremiah echoes many motifs found first with Hosea, who undoubtedly, in some fashion, was his spiritual teacher.[153] And so it is not surprising to find another instance of a strong diatribe against Israel phrased typologically around the old language of the Pentateuchal traditions. Thus, in Jer. 9: 3-5 numerous key terms are adapted from the Jacob Cycle to stress that the new Israel is like the old—filled with mendacity and duplicity in interpersonal relationships. As he says,

Be wary of your neighbour, and do not trust your brother (אח); for

---

151 Cf. *mirmāh* also in v. 1a.
152 *yimṣĕ'û*; cf. *yimṣā'ennû* in v. 5, the prototype.
153 Cf. Gross, loc. cit. (p. 311 n. 44).

every brother (אח) is a deceitful supplanter (עקוב יעקב) . . . They speak no truth but train their tongue in falsehood. . . . Secrecy within secrecy, deceit (מרמה) within deceit (מרמה);[154] they refuse to know me – oracle of YHWH.

In these strong terms the prophet Jeremiah implies that contemporary Israel – like Israel of old – is deceitful and perverts the trust upon which all human intercourse depends. Playing on the terms known from the *traditum*[155] the prophet subtly dehistoricizes the historical Jacob-Israel, and revises him in accordance with the contemporary scene. For him, the misdeeds and deceptions of the past are renewed in the misdeeds of Jacob's descendants. As with the typology in Hos. 12, here too the diatribe nationalizes the old tradition and gives it a covenantal dimensions. No neutral correlation is drawn; rather, Israel, like Jacob, is a deceitful supplanter: his past is their present; their deceptions reiterate ancient patterns. As with other examples of typology, a covert thread within history is made manifest. The new is like the old.

---

[154] This rendering follows the LXX division, which links the consonants *šb* of MT *šbtk* (v. 5a) to v. 4b, and reads *tk* as *tōk*. The nouns *tōk* and *mirmāh* are a hendiadys in Pss. 10: 7, 55: 12.

[155] Also cf. *yĕhātēllû* in Jer. 9: 4 and *hētel* in Gen. 31: 7.

13. Aggadic Exegesis in the Historiographical Literature

A. INTRODUCTION

In the preceding chapters, the phenomenon of aggadic exegesis was traced through a variety of genres: Pentateuchal narratives and sermons; legal teachings; liturgical expressions; prayers and psalms; and prophecy. The one significant genre that was not considered was the historiographical literature—whose aggadic exegesis introduces distinct considerations and features. Some of those considerations, in so far as they bear decisively on the methodological reappropriation of the phenomenon as a species of inner-biblical interpretation, must be noted at the outset.

An important initial distinction that must be drawn in the treatment of aggadic exegesis within historiographical literature is that between historiography *per se* and aggadic exegesis within it. Strictly speaking, this distinction seeks formally to separate the tendentiousness of a historian in his writing—or revision—of history and the exegetical transformation of specific texts or traditions. Indeed, with respect to the first half of this differentiation, it will readily be granted that historiography may reconceive a distinct approach to the past as previously known and understood: certain sources may be selected or emphasized, while others are deleted; certain ideological themes may be highlighted or elaborated, while others are pushed to the background; and certain values may be sponsored or propagated, while others are variously obscured or criticized. Broadly viewed, such historiographical matters are exemplified by the Books of Samuel–Kings and Chronicles —separately and in juxtaposition. For example, as is well known, Samuel–Kings tends to emphasize a fatalistic historical dimension in which negative prophecies are fulfilled and royal sins lead to the punishment of exile. It is also a historiography in which Solomon's role in establishing the Temple is emphasized and due weight is given to events in the northern kingdom. By contrast, the Chronicler is less fatalistic in his conception of historical causality, and frequently introduces examples which dramatize the fact that human repentance could halt a cycle of divine punishments.[1] In addition, the Chronicler gives new

---

[1] On this, see the classic discussion of the Chronicler's narrative of Manasseh's repentance by K. H. Graf, 'Die Gefangenschaft und Bekehrung Manasses 2 Chr. 33', *TSK* 32 (1859), 467, where its inauthenticity is stressed.

weight to David's role in establishing the royal Temple cult, and deletes the examples of northern apostasy which constituted a leitmotif for the writer of Kings. Also, in contrast to the historians of the Books of Samuel-Kings, the Chronicler's work is often expository, didactic, or edifying. But neither these latter matters, nor those previously noted, qualify as aggadic or 'midrashic' features.[2] They are rather the features of historiography, and no more.

On the other hand, aggadic exegesis within historiography is the specific reinterpretation or reworking of specific sources. Accordingly, it is not identifiable with the wider historiographical enterprise noted earlier, but rather constitutes a specific technique within it. The central issue is thus not solely a reconceptualization of the events of the past, or a new narrative style or arrangement. Central to aggadic historiography is rather the rewriting or correcting of *specific* blocks of the received historical *traditum*.[3] Significantly, such aggadic reinterpretation is not an overt narrative element, but is assimilated to the larger historiographical context. Several factors contribute to this result: one is of a distinct formal nature, and involves the historian's concern for narrative uniformity and the normalization of the revisions effected thereby. A second factor, related to the preceding one, is more rhetorical, and involves the historian's concern to present his work as history — not as *aggadah* — as the *traditum* and not as mere *traditio*.

This last point is pivotal, and introduces a second consideration. For it is one thing for modern scholarship to assert that the ancient biblical historian who transformed his received *traditum* — say Samuel-Kings — did so wittingly and with technical expertise, it is quite a different matter to assume that the ancient Israelite reader to whom that historiography was originally addressed was either aware of the earlier historical *traditum* or — in such an unlikely event — kept it in mind, so that the Book of Chronicles was read *in the light of* the exegetical transformations of it. To assume that such a bifocal perspective was the way ancient Israelite readers approached or understood the Book of Chronicles is thus to project upon the ancient reader the compositional procedure of the historian himself — or, even worse, the analytic procedure of the modern scholar. And yet just this obfuscation recurs in modern discussions of the Chronicler's 'exegetical method'. One writer, for example, has stated that the Chronicler's 'style of history-writing, exegesis in the best sense of the word, aims at clarifying the understanding of the source, at illuminating the primary underlying worth in

---

[2] Against W. E. Barnes, 'The Midrashic Element in Chronicles', *Expositor*, 44⁵/4 (1896), 426-33.

[3] P. Ackroyd, 'The Chronicler as Exegete', *JSOT* 2 (1977), 2-32, often blurs this matter: he stresses the 'reuse' of sources but often limits his analysis to the Chronicler's 'selecting and arranging and interpretation of information' (p. 14).

relation to a precise historical-theological point, a *Heilsgeschichte*, at bringing the text of the original to concentrate on this theme, and at clarifying its interconnections'.[4]

As a statement of historiographical procedure the above character-ization is of course very helpful. But it is not designed to clarify this point. The remark is made in the context of the observation that the Book of Chronicles 'cannot be understood' and 'was not intended to be understood' apart from the Books of Samuel-Kings.[5] Such comments assume, moreover, that the ancient Israelite reader knew Samuel-Kings and read the Book of Chronicles in their light, and that the Chronicler hoped to redirect the reader's historical viewpoint.[6] Such an evaluation is of course rife with suppositions. There is, first of all, no evidence to justify the view that ancient Israelite readers knew such historical sources as Samuel-Kings, or that the Chronicler expected or intended a synoptic-comparative reading of his work in relation to them. Moreover, the perspective evidenced by the preceding citations fundamentally confuses the historiographical means with its end-product, the process of *traditio* with the completed result, a *traditum*. In both content and style the Book of Chronicles is not presented as a *traditio* of an earlier, more authoritative piece of historiography. It appears as a final docu-ment; it purports to tell the past 'wie es eigentlich gewesen'.

This last point serves as the basis of a third introductory consider-ation, which concerns the authority of the aggadic exegeses in biblical historiography. Much as the legal exegeses incorporated into the Penta-teuchal legal corpora partake of the authority of the speaking voice—YHWH through Moses—and so present an exegetical *traditio* as part of the original *traditum*, the exegetical revisions of Samuel-Kings within the Books of Chronicles are part of the authoritative speaking voice of the historian overall. That narrative voice is unobtrusive and 'inherent' in the narrative-historical unfolding. Indeed, according to some linguists, such a narrative voice in history-writing communicates to the reader the sense that the events are disclosing themselves neutrally, without any human intervention.[7] As a result, the reader is confronted with *the* account of the past, and not with a version of the events or a polemical rebuttal of other viewpoints. In the language used here, the ancient Israelite reader received a historiographical document not as a historio-graphical event but as a historical finality, as the authoritative *traditum* of how things transpired *in fact*.

---

[4] T. Willi, *Die Chronik als Auslegung* (Göttingen: Vandenhoeck and Ruprecht, 1972), 66.

[5] Ibid.

[6] Cf. Ackroyd, loc. cit. 21.

[7] Cf. E. Benveniste, 'Les Relations de temps dans le verbe français', in his *Problèmes de linguistique générale* (Paris: Gallimard, 1966), 237-50.

In a fundamental sense, the modern reader like his ancient confrères also confronts the historiography of the Book of Chronicles as a *traditum* in its own right, and not as a discursive *traditio* of another 'source' which gives it authority. If, however, the modern critic also uncovers the historiographical *traditum* as a species of *traditio*, he for one is no longer addressed by the inherent power of the Chronicler's stylistic rhetoric, but has substituted his own hermeneutics of suspicion for the controlling voice of the text. But one hastens to add here that, by so doing, the modern interpreter has not simply substituted one historical truth for another, the truth of ancient historiography for those of modern historical inquiry. For paradoxically, the goal of the critical recovery of the *traditio* behind the *traditum* is the reconstruction of the ancient historian's exegetical imagination – and so *his* historical truth.

B. THEOLOGICAL TRANSFORMATIONS

1. The point was repeatedly made in the preceding discussion that one can recover the exegetical concerns of the Chronicler on the basis of a comparison of the Books of Chronicles with those of Samuel-Kings. But before proceeding to this, it is instructive, as a first stage, to recognize that exegetical transformations within historiography can be recovered by a comparison of materials within Samuel-Kings itself. For example, 2 Sam. 15 presents David in despair over the rebellion of Absalom and the sedition of Ahitophel. To counteract these events David first calls upon YHWH to pervert the advice of his erstwhile councillor, Ahitophel (v. 31); and then, in an independent solution towards this end, David counsels his own aide-de-camp, Hushai, to lie to Absalom and thereby help nullify the advice of Ahitophel (v. 34). The motivation for this latter action is manifestly human, for there is no suggestion that it is based on divine inspiration given in response to David's earlier appeal for help. But just this non-divine motivation appears to have bothered latter-day tradents of this material. For after this incident, at the successful conclusion to Hushai's ruse, a summarizing notice reports that the entire course of events – Ahitophel's advice and the ruse – were instigated by YHWH in order to quell Absalom's rebellion (2 Sam. 17:14b). By this means, a strong exegetical motive has been introduced into the narrative. The net result is an entirely different view of historical causation from that advanced earlier. Indeed, the fairly verbatim reuse of 2 Sam. 15:34 in 17:4b makes it clear that while a later interpreter received a *traditum* like that found in 2 Sam. 15, he rejected it – and therewith sought to promote his particular theological design on the whole episode. And just this is the retroactive effect.

2. The process of theological revision demonstrated above can be further illumined by tracing one particular theological topos, the value of Torah and its study, through diverse narrative reflexes. Each instance provides a valuable index of the modes and techniques of aggadic exegesis employed within historiography.

From a host of ancient Near Eastern and biblical sources, it is quite certain that phrases like 'be strong' or 'do not fear' originally served to exhort an individual to take courage in the face of a new and difficult task.[8] In biblical sources such terminology is also used within military orations and exhortations, and is even put in the mouths of non-Israelites. It is thus of no unique rhetorical consequence that Moses, before his death, encourages the Israelites to 'be strong and of good courage' when they invade the land and fight the local population (Deut. 31: 4-6). This exhortation is repeated by Moses to Joshua—his successor and leader of the attack—in vv. 7-8, and he also stresses that YHWH 'will be with you' when Joshua leads the Israelites into the 'promised' land. In fact, Moses' peroration is repeated a second time by YHWH to Joshua at the onset of the conquest (Josh. 1: 5-6, 9). On this second occurrence, however, an entirely new dimension is added: for encased within the old military exhortation formula (in vv. 6, 9) is a piece of aggadic theologizing where Joshua is told to 'be strong and of good courage' *in obeying the Torah*, since only in this manner will he
* succeed in his great adventure (vv. 7-8).

The exegetical import of this intrusion is self-evident. Not only is there a remarkable new emphasis on the value and ideology of Torah, but the intrusion transforms the exhortation to physical prowess and courage into an exhortation to spiritual fortitude. In other military cases, the exhortation formulary is used to emphasize YHWH's unconditional support for an Israelite venture. In Josh. 1: 5-9 *victory is made conditional upon Israel's observance of the law*. With this aggadic transformation, the conquest is transformed from something inevitable and assured—based on ancient promises to the patriarchs (cf. Deut. 31: 7; Josh. 1: 6)—into an event dependent upon faithfulness to the divine covenant. In this way, the deuteronomistic tradents introduced a topic of theological value into the old narratives, and simultaneously transformed the conquest narrative in accordance with their theology of history. The corollary to this teaching, that disobedience to the Torah will result in the failure of the Israelites fully to conquer the land, as promised, is articulated in Josh. 23: 6-13, at the conclusion of the Book of Joshua. Balancing the opening exhortation, this peroration by Joshua before *his* death (like Moses) urges the nation to 'be very

[8] For a summary of the evidence, with discussion, see my 'The "Sign" in the Hebrew Bible', *Shenaton. An Annual of Biblical and Near Eastern Studies*, 1 (1975), 217-19 [Heb.].

strong' and continue to obey the Torah *for the sake of the completed conquest.*[9] Once again, obedience to the Torah is presented as the condition for all historical success; and, again, the unconditional divine promises to the patriarchs—'To your seed I have given this land' (Gen. 15:18b)—and the old military advice given to later leaders—to 'be strong and of good courage'—are radically and thoroughly transformed.

The transformations just considered have a remarkable parallel in the deuteronomistic reworking of 1 Kgs. 2:1-9, wherein David provides Solomon with his last will and testament.[10] In the spirit of *Realpolitik*, father counsels son to 'be strong' and acquit himself valorously and with vengeance against his dynastic enemies, now that he has secured full power. This command is articulated in unconditional military terms in vv. 1-2 and 5-9, which is a sequence unified by both subject-matter and style. From this perspective, one is thoroughly struck by vv. 3-4, an exhortation to be faithful to the Torah as the very condition for David's success in this particular venture and, indeed, for the mainten- ance of his dynasty. Given the fact that both v. 3 (success in his attempt to secure his rule) and v. 4 (success in preserving his dynasty) have motivation clauses (לְמַעַן), the text may be doubly composite. What- ever the case, the content of the second addition is particularly notable as an exegetical transformation. For if v. 4 cites 'Scripture' to prove the conditional nature of the dynastic promise, the fact is that this citation is based upon 2 Sam. 7:12-16, where it is explicitly unconditional. Thus, not only is David's purely military advice to Solomon reinterpreted in terms of Torah piety, but the older divine promise of unconditional *grace* to the Davidic line is transformed as well. David now tells his son —via a redactor's tendentious misquote—that he should 'be strong' and obey the covenantal prescriptions: for in that way 'no heir will be cut off for you from the throne of Israel' (v. 4b; cf. 2 Sam. 7:15-16). As in Josh. 1:5-9, military prowess has its centre in spiritual fortitude and faithfulness.

3. The Books of Chronicles provide an interesting series of parallels and variations on the foregoing aggadic transformations. Of one type are those instances where those kings who are favourably assessed in the Book of Kings are redescribed by the Chronicler in terms of having fostered or promoted Torah observance. Indeed, these new descriptions are incorporated into the historical *traditum* which clearly derives from the Books of Kings. For example, the report found in 1 Kgs. 15:11-13, referring to Asa's campaigns against cultic abominations, was taken over

---

[9] In Josh. 23:12-13 there is reference to the language and themes of Exod. 23:24-33, 24:11-16, and Deut. 7:3-5, 16, 20-2 discussed earlier.

[10] Cf. the observations of Weinfeld, *Deuteronomy and the Deuteronomic School*, 11.

by the Chronicler in 2 Chron. 14: 1-2, 4, and supplemented by the notice that Asa beseeched YHWH 'and obeyed the Torah and commandments' (v. 3). Similarly, the reform and new covenant enacted by Yehoiada in 2 Kgs. 11: 17-20 was taken over in 2 Chron. 23: 16-17, 20-1. To the latter account, however, was added the observation that Yehoiada restored the cultic administration to the priests and Levites so that sacrifices were performed 'as written in the Torah of Moses' (v. 18). And finally, into the older reference in 2 Kgs. 23: 28, which notes the achievements of Josiah as recorded in the royal annals, the Chronicler added 'and his righteous deeds, as written in the Torah of Moses' (2 Chron. 35: 26b).[11]

These various interpolated references to Torah, particularly Asa's and Josiah's observance of it, have a strong aggadic component; for they represent bygone pre-exilic kings 'who did the good in YHWH's eyes' as ones who were particularly righteous with respect to the Torah and its observance. Such transformations serve to highlight the post-exilic ideal of Israelite piety, an ideal which repeatedly promoted that type of religious person who is ceaselessly concerned with the Torah, its study and its observance. Indeed, it is in the light of these changes that one may best appreciate the transformation made by Solomon, in his Temple dedication prayer, to the old promise of YHWH to David in 2 Sam. 7: 15-16. As in the earlier reworking of the latter passage in 1 Kgs. 2: 3-4, Solomon introduces a conditional-covenantal reinterpretation of the original unconditional divine promise to the dynasty of David, and has YHWH say that 'no one who will sit on the throne of Israel will be cut off from me *if* your sons heed their ways, to go before me as you went before me' (1 Kgs. 8: 25). In the parallel account of this dedication prayer in 2 Chron. 6: 16 even this revision is aggadically revised. Not content to state that future kings must 'go before me', the Chronicler rewrote the passage in the light of his values, and produced the line 'to go *in my Torah* as you went before me'. In this way, the mediating position of the Torah as the condition of dynastic continuity is significantly and radically underscored.

But if the foregoing substitution of 'my Torah' for 'before me' is particularly striking, there are other near-corollaries in the exegetical work of the Chronicler. One example is of special interest. It appears at the conclusion of a deuteronomic prayer put into the mouth of Jehoshaphat, who appeals for divine aid in the face of a severe military threat (2 Chron. 20: 1-13).[12] The divine response is not long in coming

---

[11] On the word 'Torah' and its uses and transformations in the Hebrew Bible, see my discussion in *Enc. Miq.* viii. 469-83, s.v. 'Torah' [Heb.].

[12] Jehoshaphat's prayer is based upon, and alludes to, Solomon's prayer in 1 Kgs. 8: 22-52, especially in its reference to prayer in times of military threat. Among the variations, one will observe that whereas Solomon refers to himself as

–and actually comes through the ecstatic voice of a prophet, who cites the old military exhortation formulary when he tells the king 'do not fear and do not be afraid before this great multitude for the war is not yours but Elohim's . . . [so] fall into ranks, stand up and see the salvation of YHWH for you . . . do not fear and be not afraid; go out tomorrow against them and YHWH will be with you' (vv. 15, 17).[13] Elated, the king summons his troops and tells the citizenry of Judaea and Jerusalem הַאֲמִינוּ trust in YHWH, your God, וְתֵאָמֵנוּ and you will endure; הַאֲמִינוּ trust *in his prophets* and succeed!' (v. 20). In this last remark the Chronicler has inserted into the mouth of the king a transformation of an older oracle delivered by Isaiah, centuries earlier, at the time of the Syro-Ephraimite aggression. Then, too, the prophet told Ahaz 'do not fear and let your heart not grow weak' (Isa. 7: 4), for YHWH would not allow the invasion to occur (v. 7). But truly, he adds, 'if you do not תַאֲמִינוּ have trust you will not תֵאָמֵנוּ endure' (v. 9b).[14]   *

In his reuse of the formulary found in Isa. 7: 4, 7, the Chronicler has subtly adapted his *traditum* to later concerns. Like that earlier source, the Chronicler was concerned to emphasize trust in YHWH and his oracles of confidence; but he does so by strongly emphasizing the central role of the prophets, by whose divinely inspired words Israel will find success. In this he gives new shape to a theme which characterizes his style and exegetical method. For not only has the Chronicler sought to highlight the importance of the prophets by interpolating references to them in references to the royal annals cited from the Book of Kings (cf. 2 Chron. 32: 32, 33: 18), but he has them appear repeatedly as exegetical orators or advocates of repentance in contexts where the Book of Kings preserves no oratory and no prophetic interventions.[15] Instances of this will appear in many of the examples to follow, where, moreover, it appears that a post-exilic reality is addressed via these prophetic personae of the Chronicler. Against this background one may equally surmise that the recitation of Isaiah's old words of

the Temple-builder (cf. 1 Kgs. 8: 13, 27, 43), Jehoshaphat reflects the Chronicler's all-Israel interest and refers to the Temple as having been built by the people (cf. 2 Chron. 20: 8).

[13] On the parallels in Exod. 14: 13 and 1 Sam. 17: 47, cf. G. von Rad, 'The Levitical Sermon in *I* and *II Chronicles*', in *The Problem of the Hexateuch*, 273; and on other reflexes of the holy war ideology in this passage, see von Rad's *Der heilige Krieg im alten Israel* (Göttingen: Vandenhoeck and Ruprecht, 1969), 9.

[14] For an analysis of the integration of Isa. 7 around the military–exhortation formula, see my 'The "Sign" ', 220–2.

[15] On the subject of prophecy and prophetic speeches in Chronicles, see A. Welch, *The Work of the Chronicler* (London: Oxford University Press, 1939), 42–54; C. Westermann, 'Excursus: Prophetic Speeches in the Book of Chronicles', in *Basic Forms of Prophetic Speech* (Philadelphia: Westminster, 1967), 163–8; T. Willi, *Die Chronik*, 215–44; and below, n. 24.

trust by the Chronicler cannot be dismissed as mere scholasticism, but seeks to address his contemporary audience with the importance of trust in YHWH and his spokesmen.

4. In a novel episode found in 2 Chron. 15:1-7, it is reported that another prophet, Azzariah ben Oded, was inspired with the 'spirit of Elohim' and said to Asa, king of Judaea and all Judaea and Benjamin:

(2) YHWH will be with you when you are with him: for if you seek him (ותדרשהו), he will be present (יִמָּצֵא) to you, but if you abandon him, he will abandon you.

(3) Now for a long time Israel was without a true God, an instructing priest or Torah.

(4) But when in distress (בצר) [Israel] turned (וישב) to YHWH, God of Israel, and sought him (ויבקשהו), he was present (וַיִּמָּצֵא) to them.

(5) In those times there was no peace whatever for those who went out or came in, but tremendous disturbances assailed the inhabitants of the lands;

(6) and nations and cities smashed each other to bits: for God confounded them with every distress.

(7) But you, now: be strong and let your hands not slacken; for there is recompense for your deeds.

This prophetic discourse, and even the prophet in whose name it is spoken, are unknown to other biblical sources, and appear to reflect the handiwork of the Chronicler who has woven together several strands of tradition in order to confront his contemporary readership with a matter of 'prophetic' concern to him. The oratory opens with language which echoes the exhortation formulae known from early sources, and concludes in the same wise: 'YHWH will be with you', he says, and 'be strong' (vv. 22, 7), just like the exhortation in 2 Chron. 20:17, or earlier in Josh. 1:9. To this opening confrontation are added the clarifications that YHWH will be present to those who seek him, and will recompense those who follow in his ways. Thus, from the outset we again see the transformation of an old military exhortation formulary through its juxtaposition with spiritual-covenantal concerns. As in Josh. 1:7-9, the notion of strength and courage is transfigured and reinterpreted as strength for spiritual endeavours. But the precise force of the request by the prophet to seek YHWH that they be rewarded, and its background, can only be appreciated from the subordinate passage in vv. 3-6, which is a strategic aggadic anthology of several Scriptural sources.

At first glance, vv. 3-6 appear to exemplify v. 2, by describing a time when Israel had abandoned YHWH, who thereupon abandoned them to their dismay, until—and only until—they sought him, whereupon he was again present to them. In addition this historical vignette seems also to provide motivational force for the concluding exhortation to the people to 'be strong', that is, to beseech YHWH as did their forebears in the example cited in order that they reap reward and not doom, 'for there is recompense for your deeds'. But this historical analogy is much more than a vague rhetorical conceit. Closer analysis of its language reveals that it refers to an event just past, the exile. Indeed, a striking reflex of the terms used in 2 Chron. 15: 4 is found in Deut. 4: 29-30, a passage also of post-exilic origin in which the Israelites are told in precisely similar terms that if they beseech (בקשתם) and seek (תדרשנו) YHWH, and repent (ושבת, i.e. turn) in distress (בצר), he will be present (ימצאוך) to them.[16] To portray the physical and spiritual horrors of exile, the Chronicler further surrounds this line (v. 4) with other passages derived from earlier oracles of doom and exile. Thus, in v. 5b for example, the Chronicler's reference to 'tremendous disturbances', using the rare expression מהומות רבות, is literally based on Amos 3: 9.[17] And the earlier verse, 'for a long time Israel was without a true God, and instructing priest or Torah' (v. 3), is an exegetical revision of Hos. 3: 4, which refers to the northern exile with the words 'for many days the Israelites dwelt without a king . . . or slaughter[18] . . . or image (אפוד) or household gods (תרפים)'. Like this passage, the Chronicler has Azzariah refer to 'many days' in exile 'without a king' and without means of divine instruction. But instead of referring to old cultic traditions, which were known in Hosea's day (cf. Judg. 8: 27), the later Chronicler is concerned to emphasize instruction via priests—though, of course, he may also allude to the loss of the tradition of priestly mantic practice during the exile (cf. Ezra 2: 63). In any event, a clear indication of the Chronicler's aggadic transformation of this earlier *traditum* is certain from his reference to 'Torah'—a matter unnoted by Hos. 3: 4, but of recurrent concern in his historiography.[19] Significantly, the Chronicler concludes this list of losses with his reference to a

---

[16] On the dating of this editorial layer of Deuteronomy, cf. A. Mayes, loc. cit. (p. 322 n. 19). 50f. Even if the passage is late pre-exilic, it refers to an exilic dispersion and restoration for 'seeking' YHWH (Deut. 4: 27-30)—two points of importance to the Chronicler who adapted it; see below. The deuteronomistic editor of the Book of Jeremiah also used this text in connection with the exile; cf. Jer. 29: 13-14.

[17] The verb *hûm* and the noun *měhûmāh* are 'holy war' terms; cf. Deut. 7: 23; 1 Sam. 4: 5, 5: 9, 11; Isa. 22: 5; Zech. 14: 13. The verb *hāmam* also recurs in 'holy war' traditions. See Exod. 14: 24, 23: 27; Deut. 2: 5; Josh. 10: 10; Judg. 4: 5; 1 Sam. 7: 10; 2 Sam. 22: 15; Ps. 18: 15.

[18] Possibly read *mizbēaḥ* for *zebaḥ*. The resulting parallelism *mizbēaḥ* ~ *maṣṣēbāh* is repeated in Hos. 10: 1-2. The LXX to 3: 4 seems to have read *mizbēaḥ* for *maṣṣēbāh*; but this may be a theological softening (cf. Hos. 8: 11).

[19] Cf. above, p. 386 and n. 11.

seeking out of YHWH and to repentance (15: 4). The prophet Hosea, whose words were clearly in the latter-day historian's mind, similarly follows his list of losses with the comment 'After that the Israelites will turn (יָשֻׁבוּ) and seek (וּבִקְשׁוּ) YHWH . . . and fear [him] . . .' (v. 5).

Azzariah's prophetic discourse, it now appears, is an aggadic blend of several passages—from the Pentateuch and from old prophecies—which refer to the discomforts and punishments of exile and to the repentance of those in historical straits. Like the deuteronomic passage, the Chronicler states that those who seek YHWH and repent will be restored to him, for he will be present to them.[20] But despite this manifest dependence on older traditions, the contemporary aim of the Chronicler is less clear. If he is using the prophet Azzariah as a narrative persona in order to address Israelites still in exile, and to encourage them to return to YHWH, then Azzariah functions like Ezekiel who earlier encouraged the exiles to return to YHWH, promising them an immediate and individual 'recompense' for this act. If, however, the Chronicler is addressing those Israelites who have returned to their land but are again involved in sin, then the historian uses Azzariah to utter a direct prophetic challenge: seek YHWH that evil not befall you as it did your forefathers, for, as with them, there is 'recompense' for one's 'deeds'.[21]

The prophetic voice of Azzariah is immediately responded to by Asa, who thus provides a contemporary model for proper piety. In response to Azzariah's command to 'be strong', which we saw was reused in this context to refer to spiritual fortitude and rectitude, the king 'strengthened himself' and got rid of the accumulated abominable practices in Judaea, Benjamin, and the recently conquered hills of Ephraim (v. 8). In these actions many natives and strangers joined in, seeing that 'YHWH . . . was with him' (v. 9)—as promised by Azzariah (cf. v. 2)—and 'entered the covenant to seek (לִדְרשׁ) YHWH' (v. 12). Through such seeking (בִקְשֻׁהוּ) YHWH was again present to the people (וַיִּמָּצֵא) and gave them rest from their enemies round about (v. 15).[22] The course of Asa's paradigmatic piety was thus such as to inspire a religious return to YHWH, and YHWH's return to the people—even as the prophet Azzariah had foretold.

Through prophetic personae and pious examples, the Chronicler was

---

[20] The Chronicler's dependence upon Deut. 4 is also evident in his use of the verb *yirpû* 'slacken' in 2 Chron. 15: 7a (cf. *yarpĕkā* 'fail you' in Deut. 4: 31), and in his use of the expression *bĕkol lĕbābām* 'with all their heart' in 15: 15, together with 'seeking' YHWH that he be 'present' (cf. *bĕkol lĕbābĕkā* in Deut. 4: 29, in the context of 'seeking' YHWH that he be 'present').

[21] For the late expression *śākār lip'ûllatĕkem*, cf. Jer. 31: 5; also cf. Isa. 40: 10, 62: 11.

[22] Rest from surrounding enemies is a fixed deuteronomic expression: cf. Josh. 21: 42, 23: 1; Judg. 2: 14, 8: 34; 1 Sam. 12: 11.

thus able to teach his contemporaries about the restorative power of repentance and the rewards for piety.[23] Indeed, so important were these thematics for the Chronicler that they dominate his entire 'history' of King Asa and give further insight into the varieties of his exegetical procedure. In this instance, one can observe how the Chronicler filled in and transformed the old historical *traditum* derived from the Book of Kings, where Asa gets very brief mention—even though he is among the few kings to be referred to favourably. 1 Kgs. 11:11-12 states that Asa 'did good and right in the eyes of YHWH' and removed features of false worship; v. 13 refers to his eradication of the abominations of Maacah; v. 14 then notes that despite these actions the high places remained; and v. 15 refers to his restoration of sancta to the Temple. The narrative then continues with a reference to Asa's wars with Baasha. By contrast, the Chronicler cites 1 Kgs. 11:11-12 at the outset of his report on Asa, in 2 Chron. 14:1-2, but does not pick up the thread of his source until 2 Chron. 15:16-18, when he refers to the abominations of Maacah, to the remaining high places, and to the restoration of the sancta to the Temple. In between, the Chronicler speaks glowingly of how Asa urged Judaea 'to seek (לדרוש) YHWH ... and observe the Torah and the commandments' (2 Chron. 14:3), and of how he got rid of cultic abominations, thereby bringing peace to his kingdom (vv. 4-5, 6) and victory against Israel's enemies (vv. 10-14). As in the episode found in 2 Chron. 15:1-19, discussed earlier, Asa is presented as a pious king who reaped the rewards of that piety. Indeed, to underscore his point, the Chronicler gives a slight aggadic shift to the report in 1 Kgs. 11:16 which refers to Asa's wars with Baasha. Having emphasized Asa's exemplary piety, and concerned to display its consequences to his readership, he changed 'And war reigned between Asa and Baasha all their days' to 'And *there was no war until* the thirty-fifth year of the reign of Asa' (2 Chron. 15:19).

Strains of the Chronicler's aggadic strategy of teaching and exemplification, commented upon in connection with 2 Chron. 15, are thus more fully disclosed by the extended perspective provided by 2 Chron. 14-15. First, the historian has adapted his sources to his chief concerns —the primacy of Torah, its observance and its rewards—by focusing attention on an exemplary individual like Asa, through whom the consequences of piety and repentance are dramatized. In addition, as in other cases like the episode of King Jehoshaphat (2 Chron. 20:1-20), the Chronicler does not merely use his narrative voice—the authoritative

---

[23] I. L. Seeligmann, in 'Die Auffassung von der Prophetie in der deuteronomistischen und chronistischen Geschichtsschreibung', *SVT* 29 (1978), 254-84, has sought to determine the Chronicler's position on repentance among the other ideological positions at that time.

voice of impersonal history—but employs the confrontative, exhort-
ative, and instructive voice of prophetic personae as well. In the course
of the historical exposition, moreover, both voices—refracted through
the stylistic forms of reported speech and reported events—reinforce
each other. The prophetic oratories serve to set the course of the
narrative reports and to exemplify them, while the narrative reports
reciprocally comment upon these speeches and teach through them.
The addressees of the Book of Chronicles are thus confronted with two
literary dimensions which are hortatory in complementary ways. For,
variously viewed, the speeches provide background to the narratives or
serve as their foreground. This continuous oscillation is, in its effect,
part of the expository power of the Chronicler. Added to it is his
aggadic ability to teach *through the traditions*. That the addressees may
not have been aware of the hermeneutical transformations involved
does not of course diminish the Chronicler's didactic impact. In a way,
it rather magnifies it. For in so far as the addressees of the Book of
Chronicles did not regard its reports and teachings as the aggadic
traditio of an older *traditum*, this content confronted them as a *traditum*, as *the* authoritative version of the ancient *traditio* made present
as witness and as challenge. No less than his prophetic personae, then,
the Chronicler's narrative addressed his generation, in the twilight of
classical prophecy, with a 'prophetic' voice.

C. NEW THEOLOGICAL EXPLANATIONS

1. As his account of Asa's compliance with the divine oracle makes
clear, the Chronicler was at pains to vivify through concrete historical
examples certain dimensions of his view of divine providence and
historical causality. This exemplification is a basic part of the communication which he addresses to his audience, the exegetical transformation
and elaboration of earlier sources being an aggadic means towards this
end. As an example of this broad concern to teach old values in a new
way, and to address his readership in the light of the *traditum* as it
was known in his day, the Chronicler's reworking and updating of the
old traditions reporting the transfer of the Ark of the Covenant to
Jerusalem are of particular interest. According to the account of this
event preserved in 2 Sam. 6, David, together with his militia and other
members of the Judaean confraternity, 'loaded the Ark of Elohim on a
new cart and transported it (וַיִּשָּׂאֻהוּ)' from the homestead of Abinadab
in Gibeah towards Jerusalem, with Uzzah, one of the sons of Abinadab
among the leaders (v. 3; cf. v. 4).[24] However, during the course of this

---

[24] Verses 3-4 apparently contain a dittograph, from the second *ḥădāšāh* in
v. 3 through *baggib'āh* in v. 4. See Weiss, 'Studies', 48.

conveyance, the oxen tottered and Uzzah 'cast forth וישלח' his hand to stay the Ark (v. 6). At this deed, YHWH became infuriated at Uzzah and 'smote him ויכהו' on the spot (v. 7). Then 'David became infuriated because YHWH burst forth (פרץ) a bursting against Uzzah, and he called that place Peretz Uzzah' and decided to leave the Ark for a time at the homestead of Obed Edom (vv. 8-10). It was only after a period of three months that the transport resumed its pilgrimage, when the signs seemed propitious (vv. 11-12).[25] At that time, the 'transporters of the Ark of YHWH' bore the holy object up to Jerusalem to the constant accompaniment of sacrifices and regaling (vv. 13-15).

In reporting this event in his own day, the Chronicler kept one eye on his source and another on the theological problems involved. Since, for him, history was a didactic communication of the *traditum* to new generations, ancient theological features in 2 Sam. 6 had to be updated, impieties explained, and the unity of the tradition established. Reflecting his concern for national unity in the post-exilic period,[26] the Chronicler first stresses that David convened the leaders of all *Israel* and requested their advice about bringing the Ark to Jerusalem, urging that all the priests and Levites be gathered for the event as well (1 Chron. 13:1-6). The Chronicler then follows his source more closely, reporting the episode of Uzzah and its sequel much as it was known to him from his sources (vv. 9-14). One divergence, however, deserves mention, viz., the absence of reference to the transport of the Ark, although the fact that the cart was 'loaded' is expressly noted. This deletion may be judged more deliberate than would appear on first glance. As heir to the priestly traditions, the Chronicler knew the divine prohibitions which barred lay persons from the sacred precincts where the Ark and other holy objects were kept, and from any share in its transport (cf. Num. 3: 5-10, 38). Later, in order to prevent any possible inference that non-cultic personnel had transported the Ark in 2 Sam. 6: 13, the Chronicler has David say that 'only the Levites may carry (לשאת) the Ark of Elohim, because YHWH has chosen them to carry (לשאת) the Ark of Elohim, and to serve him, forever' (1 Chron. 15: 2). This dictum is an explicit reference to Num. 3: 5-10, wherein it is announced that only the Levites could 'serve' with the Aaronids and be allowed 'to carry' the Ark about (Num. 4: 15). Indeed, in the desert wanderings, only the levitical clan of Kehath had this 'holy task' of bearing the holy object on 'המוט staves' (Num. 4: 10), upon their shoulders (בכתף יִשָּׂאוּ, Num. 7: 9). In the Chronicler's estimation, then, the verb נשא was theologically 'loaded'; for this reason he chose to avoid its use in 1 Chron. 13: 7. The divine wrath which burst

---

[25] i.e., when divine 'blessing' was evident.

[26] On this, see H. Williamson, *Israel in the Book of Chronicles* (Cambridge: Cambridge University Press, 1977), 87-140.

forth against Uzzah may also be understood in the light of these priestly rules. For Uzzah was a layman, forbidden to encroach upon cultic sancta; in doing so, he was punished by divine wrath. Even here, in fact, the Chronicler betrays his ritual sensibility: for it will be noted that in 2 Sam. 6: 6 Uzzah actually touches the Ark, whereas in 1 Chron. 13: 9 the verb is so modified as to suggest intent but *not* actual contact.[28b]

The Chronicler's work is thus not simply an anachronistic harmonization of his early sources with the priestly law as it was literally known to him. Indeed, he is not so much concerned with harmonizing his historical *traditum* as using his cultic *traditum* to *explain* an ancient episode in normative terms. This, in fact, is the exegetical component of his treatment. The Chronicler has taken over the 'facts' of his sources and presented them in the light of the normative piety he wished to stress and foster through David – now a teacher of Torah and no mere brigand or warrior. Indeed, in contrast to his source, David prepares for the proper transfer of the Ark to Jerusalem even while it is at the homestead of Obed Edom (1 Chron. 15: 1,3), and tells the heads of the levitical clans to 'purify' themselves and take the Ark to its appointed place (v. 12); 'for on the first occasion you did not [carry the Ark, and] YHWH, our God, burst (פרץ) against us:[27] for we did not seek Him (דרשנהו)[28] according to the [established] norm' (v. 13). Forthwith, the purification took place 'and the Levites carried (וישאו) the Ark of Elohim, just as Moses had commanded by the word of YHWH: on their shoulders (בכתפם) with staves (במטות) upon them' (v. 15). On this occasion, then, the porterage was thoroughly in conformance with the divine norm, explicitly cited from Num. 4: 10 and 7: 9. Whether in all this the Chronicler is also indirectly admonishing his own generation to take diligent care in their own reinstallation of the Ark in Jerusalem,. and to be certain that the Levites perform the 'Scriptural' prerequisites in this regard, can only be surmised.

2. Not in all instances, however, does the Chronicler reinterpret his sources by means of the Pentateuchal cultic *traditum*. Elsewhere, there is a perceptible struggle to understand the historical *traditum* on its own terms and in the light of certain moral considerations. The *traditio* which treated David's desire to build a temple in Jerusalem, and its transformation in the hands of the Chronicler, provide an instructive

---

[27] The Chronicler uses the old term *pāraṣ* for the divine 'outburst' in 1 Chron. 13: 11 – following his source. Also like his source, the Chronicler uses this verb as a connecting link with battle reports of engagement with Philistine forces (cf. 2 Sam. 5: 20 ~ 1 Chron. 14: 11) – although in the old *traditum* this report does not follow the Uzzah episode but precedes it. The theme-word *pāraṣ* is also used positively by the Chronicler in 1 Chron. 13: 2.

[28] Compare David's use of this expression at the auspicious outset, 1 Chron. 13:2.　　[28b] This shift was brought to my attention by Mr Bernard Levinson.

perspective on this aggadic process. According to the historical *traditum* which follows the account of the transfer of the Ark to Jerusalem (2 Sam. 6), David decided to build a temple after 'YHWH had given him rest from all his surrounding enemies' and he himself enjoyed a permanent royal dwelling (2 Sam. 7:1-2). Of these two recorded motivations, the first is from the hand of the deuteronomic editor, for whom there was an established tradition that religious-cultic anarchy would cease and a centralized shrine be established when YHWH would 'give you rest from your surrounding enemies so that you will dwell in security' (Deut. 12:10). At a later time, when Solomon prepared to build the Temple in Jerusalem, this matter is again cited verbatim, and applied by Solomon to his own era (1 Kgs. 5:18). Indeed, as this latter reapplication of the tradition of 'rest' indicates, David was denied permission to build the Temple. And this follows the main outline of the oracle vouchsafed to the prophet Nathan, where the king was denied the building, but promised a lineage (a בַּיִת)—now that 'I have given you rest from all your enemies' (2 Sam. 7:11)—and that an heir would build a temple (a בַּיִת) 'for my name' (v. 13a).

In this shift in 2 Sam. 7 from a denial to David, based on the principle of a non-locative deity with a portable shrine (vv. 6-7), to permission granted his heir (v. 13a), one may detect several strands and accretions. Certainly the kernel of this document lies in its formal legitimation of David and his successors on the throne of Israel. This kernel begins in v. 8—with a special introit[29]—and rises to a climax in vv. 15-16 with the divine affirmation that David's 'dynasty' (בַּיִת) would be firmly established, unlike that of Saul, his predecessor. Such anxiety for continuity and legitimation at the heart of this royal 'apologia' drew to it, in time, accretions which formally guaranteed the perpetuity of the dynasty (vv. 12b, 13b, 16).[30] Added to this core, and verbally entwined with its emphasis on 'rest' and 'dynasty' (בַּיִת), is the strand which deals with the building of the Temple (בַּיִת) since 'rest' from surrounding enemies has been achieved. While the impulse for the building project may, in actual historical fact, derive from David or his immediate courtiers, the *traditum* as received undoubtedly reflects the later period of Solomon; for it was in his day that the Temple was built and a legitimation of the venture was needed. Certainly, at the least, the

[29] Cf. the divine word in vv. 5-7, which rejects David's desire to build a temple, and has its own introduction.

[30] Following I. L. Seeligmann, 'From Historical Reality to an Historiosophical Conception in the Bible', *P'raqim*, ii, ed. E. Rosenthal (Jerusalem: Yearbook of the Schocken Institute for Jewish Research, 1969-71), 301 [Heb.]. This stratification contends with the general view that 2 Sam. 7 was from the first a foundation document of dynastic perpetuity; cf. L. Rost, *Die Überlieferung von der Thronnachfolge Davids* (Stuttgart: W. Kohlhammer, 1926).

reversal of the divine rejection of David's proposal, and its procrastination until the reign of his heir, served Solomonic interests. In this respect H. Gese is undoubtedly correct to observe that Nathan appears more as Solomon's prophet than as David's.[31] Nevertheless, apart from the decisive divine support for a deferred building project in 2 Sam. 7: 13a, there is a glaring absence of any explanation of *why* a temple could be built only a generation after its categoric denunciation.[32]

The tradents who passed on this *traditum* found an interesting aggadic solution to this dilemma. They seized upon the tradition of 'rest' from warfare mentioned in 2 Sam. 7: 8-11 and assumed that David could not build the permanent Temple because 'rest' was not yet achieved in his day and it was necessary to move the Ark about from battle to battle. Proof of this 'reading' of the old *traditum* is provided by 1 Kgs. 5, where Solomon addresses a letter to Hiram of Tyre, his hired architect, and tells him: 'You know that David my father could not build a temple to YHWH his god because of the warfare which surrounded him ...; and now, YHWH my god has given me rest round about ... and so I have determined to build a temple' (vv. 17-19). With these words, Solomon applied the old oracle to himself explicitly (v. 19), and legitimated his project. He states that it was not the construction of a permanent temple that was prohibited, but only its construction in David's time. Thus, Solomon implies that had David achieved 'rest' from his enemies in his lifetime he could have done the job. But as he was 'unable' to do this—being preoccupied by war—the project was postponed. This oblique legitimation of David is complemented by another reference to the old oracle of 2 Sam. 7 put into Solomon's mouth in connection with his words to the assembled populace at the Temple's dedication. In this speech David's desire is, in fact, thoroughly legitimated. 'And my father David wished to build a temple to YHWH, the god of Israel', Solomon announces, but YHWH said to David, his father, 'whereas you considered to build a temple to my name—*you did right to consider it*; nevertheless, you will not build the temple but your son will ...' (1 Kgs. 8: 17-19). This aggadic *traditio* supports the interpretation found in 1 Kgs. 5: 17-19 and overcomes the problematics felt to inhere in 2 Sam. 7: 4-16. In legitimating Solomon's actions, the tradents did not, however, denigrate David, but rather enhanced his image. In fact, David made Solomon's

---

[31] See 'Der Davidsbund und die Zionerwahlung', *ZTK* 61 (1964), 19.

[32] Conceivably, the acceptance, then outright rejection, of David's project— 2 Sam. 7: 3 + 5-7—may reflect social-theological tensions within the young monarchy, between the old nomadic cult tradition and the new institutional pressures. Such a tension, with its compromise, finds a striking parallel in the earlier tension between the old nomadic antimonarchists and those who wanted to be 'like all the nations'—cf. 1 Sam. 8: 4-5 + 6.

achievement possible; though his concern was right, he was preoccupied with battle and simply 'unable' to do the deed. But in this solution the *traditio* dared state what is hardly justified by the original *traditum*.

The Chronicler inherited these traditions, and, for his part, sought to give added glory to David by innovating material unknown from the Book of Kings. In 1 Chron. 22: 2-3 he has David himself make preparations for the Temple; in v. 6 he has David command Solomon to do the job (according to a blueprint which he—like Moses—envisages through the divine spirit; cf. 1 Chron. 28: 11-19); and in 1 Chron. 23-7 he has David establish the priestly and lay courses for service in the Temple. In this broad context embellishing David's stature, it is all the more striking to note how the Chronicler transformed the aggadic *traditio* concerning the denial to David of permission to build the Temple. Since he could have easily reported the fact of David's pre-occupation with warfare, as does 1 Kgs. 5: 17-19, the Chronicler's moral censure of David reveals his own ethical and theological struggle with the ancient *traditum*. Thus, in 1 Chron. 22: 8, the Chronicler has David tell Solomon that the reason YHWH denied him permission to build the Temple was that 'you have spilled much blood and waged many wars' (cf. 28: 3). In flagrant violation of the ancient *traditum* and its various revisions, the Chronicler states that the Temple was promised to David's son because he would be 'a man of rest' for whom YHWH would provide 'rest' from his enemies, and he would, moreover, be called Solomon, שלמה, since in his day there would be 'שלום peace and tranquility' (v. 9). Not bound by any pressing contemporary concern to legitimate the building of the first Temple, the Chronicler introduced his moral values into the *traditum*.[33] His exegetical *traditio* thus speaks to his own generation as a *traditum* with strong moral force; indeed, one may surmise that it was in some sense addressed to the violence and dissension which split the restoration community of his day into several rival factions. The historian reminds the nation—aggadically—that the Temple of Jerusalem was, and is, founded upon 'peace'.

3. As a post-exilic condemnation of violence in connection with cultic matters, the foregoing invites comparison with a contemporary aggadic fragment found in another species of historiography, the historiographical liturgy in Ps. 106. In this psalm many Pentateuchal traditions are referred to and in minor ways transformed. Of particular interest is the reworking of the old *traditum* reporting the apostasy of the Israelites in the desert, recorded in Num. 25: 1-8. According to the old

---

[33] Additionally, like the deuteronomistic editors of Joshua-Kings, the Chronicler has David tell Solomon to 'be strong', not to 'fear', and to observe the Torah. See 1 Chron. 22: 11-13, 28: 20. In the latter contexts, however, courage and obedience will lead to a successful completion of the building project.

narrative, the Israelites became yoked (וַיִּצָּמֶד) to Ba'al Pe'or and ate of the meat sacrificed to the gods of the Moabite women (זִבְחֵי אֱלֹהֵיהֶן), and performed fertility rites with them. At this, divine wrath broke out and Moses was ordered to tell the people to impale all those 'yoked' to this Ba'al. Acting with zeal to quell the plague of death brought on by YHWH against this apostasy, Phineas the priest took a sword and lanced (וַיִּדְקֹר) two transgressors, Zimri ben Salu and Cozbi bath Zur, *in flagrante delicto*, 'וַתֵּעָצַר הַמַּגֵּפָה and the plague was stayed'. For this act of pious zeal Phineas was rewarded with the promise of a permanent priestly lineage (vv. 10-15).

This ritual apostasy was already known in some form to the prophet Hosea, although he reports nothing about Phineas, being concerned to emphasize the blasphemous dimension of the occasion.[34] By contrast, the historiographical liturgist does refer to all salient aspects of the Pentateuchal *traditum* when he says that the Israelites in the desert 'yoked' themselves (וַיִּצָּמְדוּ) to Ba'al Pe'or' and ate the sacrificial meats (זִבְחֵי מֵתִים);[35] so that a plague burst forth and 'Phineas arose (וַיַּעֲמֹד) and intervened (וַיְפַלֵּל)[36] and the plague was stayed (וַתֵּעָצַר הַמַּגֵּפָה)'— an act for which he was well reckoned (vv. 28-30). Given the close topological and lexical link to the Pentateuchal *traditum*, the aggadic *traditio* which substituted the reference to Phineas's lancing of the transgressors with a reference to his intervention is all the more marked. As against the old priestly narrator, who not only reported the violent event but actually used it as an aetiology for Phineas's priestly pre-eminence, the psalmist used a word which was at once faithful to the events—for an act of intervention did occur—but transformed the priest's deed into a non-violent act. For if the old *traditum* cast Phineas in the role of a prototypical enforcer of ritual purity—much like the Levites in Exod. 32: 26-9, who similarly owed their clerical office to a zealous act of retribution against cultic apostates—the new *traditio* gave him a more 'legal', even prophetic, role. Phineas now functions like Moses who, after the early ritual apostasy with the calf, 'stood (עמד) in the breach (בפרץ) before [YHWH] to quell his destructive wrath' (Ps. 106: 23). Indeed, Phineas too rose up (וַיַּעֲמֹד) to quell the wrath which burst (וַתִּפְרֹץ) forth against the people (vv. 29 f.). It was thus for his role as an intercessor that this priest was rewarded and served as a model of piety.[37] In the hands of a later tradent, then, an old tradition

---

[34] Hos. 9: 10b.

[35] This condemnation is more specific than the Pentateuchal variant, though it is uncertain whether the change is sacrifice to 'lifeless gods' (NEB) or offerings to the dead (JB, NJPS).

[36] There is a legal-judicial overtone here. Cf. 1 Sam. 2: 25; also Exod. 21: 22; Deut. 32: 31; Job 31: 11, 28.

[37] This interpretation is indebted to a conversation with Professor Y. Muffs, Dec. 1979. See now his remarks in *Torah Nidreshet* (Tel Aviv: Am Oved, 1984), 78 f.

of violence served as the basis for an aggadic transformation that emphasized the faithful intercessor and the staying of divine wrath. For the psalmist in exile, and for his co-religionists with whom he atoned for past sins and petitioned for divine mercy and deliverance from the dispersion (vv. 4, 6, 46-7), the interventions of Phineas and Moses were exemplars of hope—no matter that for Phineas the old *traditum* was aggadically transformed. For, as elsewhere, the fate of a *traditum* lies in its *traditio*—the new *traditum*.

4. Among the various techniques which mark the aggadic work of the Chronicler is one of particular exegetical interest, for it involves the reworking and reinterpretation of earlier historical traditions by means of a recontextualization of the materials. Sometimes this involves simply an interpretation of the received texts on the basis of the received sequence. In such cases the very contiguity of the passages generates the exegetical *traditio* or interpretation. In other instances, recontextualization is more than the isolation of an existent textual juxtaposition and involves the creation of a new contiguity by means of a regrouping of the passages of the *traditum*, either through the reallocation of their parts or the deletion of certain portions thereof. Such tendentious spotlighting of the received materials, or their recombination, thus involves a revised perspective on the original context and yields new interpretations of the older *traditum*. In fact, this type of exegetical *traditio* resembles the later rabbinic practice of interpreting materials on the basis of the contiguity of isolated words of whole pericopae—a technique enunciated as כל פרשה שהיא סמוכה לחברתה למידה הימנה 'Every pericope which is found near another may be interpreted with respect to it'.[38] It is also concisely referred to as סְמוּכִין, or 'conjunctions'.[39] By this hermeneutical principle, received materials were variously recontextualized and recombined—thus yielding singular exegetical correlations. Given its potential, the old rabbis were justifiably cautious in the use of this exegetical technique, which fits broadly into the category of exegesis by analogy since any one passage was used to illumine another on the basis of certain common elements.

While there is a strong possibility that the exegetical technique of סמוכין explains in some instances the received consecution of pericopae in the legal corpora,[40] the Chronicler's reworking of earlier historio-

---

[38] See the comment of R. Aqiba in *Sifre Num., Balak* (*ad init.*).

[39] See W. Bacher, *Die exegetische Terminologie der jüdischen Traditionsliteratur* (Leipzig: J. C. Hinrichs, 1899-1905), i. 133, ii. 142f.

[40] Thus G. B. Gray, *Numbers* (ICC; Edinburgh: T. and T. Clark, 1912), 182, proposed that the pericope of the person seized *in flagrante* in Num. 15: 32-6 was appended to Num. 15: 22-31, which concludes with warnings of intentional transgressions, on the assumption that it was an actual example of the theoretical

graphical literature establishes a firm comparative basis for this phenomenon in the Hebrew Bible. Indeed, in each of the following two cases,
a comparison of the Book of Chronicles with the parallel accounts of
the earlier *traditum* in the Book of Kings indicates that the Chronicler
recombined his sources in order to promote new—exegetically derived
—insights into the workings of divine providence and historical causality;
and, at the same time, to emphasize the value of Torah and its pious
observance.

(*a*)   In the summary report of the reign of Rehoboam found in
1 Kgs. 14: 22-28 it is recorded that the Judaeans 'did evil' and 'incensed'
the king by their acts of cultic apostasy (vv. 22-4). There follows a
brief account of the invasion of the Egyptian Pharaoh Shishaq in
Rehoboam's fifth regnal year, and the consequential looting of the
Temple treasures (vv. 25-8). What is particularly striking overall is the
emphasis on the *people's* faithlessness, using the formula 'do evil in the
eyes of YHWH' to characterize it. In this condemnation, the king himself is not presented as an apostate, but is rather portrayed as indignant.
Given the terse collocation of elements which marks such summaries in
the Book of Kings, no connection between the report of the people's
'evil' and the account of Shishaq's invasion is expected—and none, for
that matter, is made.

In the Book of Chronicles, however, the formal disjunction between
the two situations is altered decisively. Explicitly based on 1 Kgs. 14:
22-8, the Chronicler begins his account of Rehoboam's reign with a
reference to apostasy (2 Chron. 12:1), and follows this with verbatim
citations of the older *traditum* of Shishaq's invasion in Rehoboam's
fifth year (v. 2a) and the consequent looting of the Temple treasures
(vv. 9-11). Within the skeletal conformity to the older sources which
this review indicates, the Chronicler has introduced several issues of
aggadic import. First, in his report of the apostasy in Rehoboam's
time, the Chronicler omits references to the details found in his *traditum*, and substitutes the fact that Rehoboam 'abandoned the Torah'
together with all Israel. Thus, in this *traditio*, the king is portrayed as
faithless to the Torah and so responsible for the national apostasy.
But this new condemnation of Rehoboam and interpolation of Torah
values by the Chronicler into his materials is overshadowed by another
aggadic element, the remark 'because they rejected YHWH' in v. 2b.
Since this historical-theological judgement *follows* the references to
the abandonment of Torah in v. 1 and the invasion of Shishaq in v. 2a,
it may be assumed that the Chronicler interpreted the invasion as due

norm. On this likelihood, the redactors interpreted Num. 15: 32-6 in the light of
vv. 27-31 and established a formal textual link between them—so that all future
readers would be drawn to this same exegesis.

to covenantal infidelity. He thus took two disjunctive notices from his *traditum* and read them conjunctively — exegesis by סמוכין.

Significantly, the Chronicler did not brazenly rewrite his sources but interpreted their contextualization. He undoubtedly believed that the textual nexus in 1 Kgs. 14: 22-8 was an inherent indictment of Rehoboam and the people, so that his exegetical task was merely to make the implicit causal links explicit.[41] At the same time, one should hasten to add that the Chronicler's very perception of a meaningful relationship between two separate historical notices — apostasy and foreign invasion — is itself an *exegetical* perception. By means of this aggadic exegesis, in fact, he was able to project his own values into his sources and so instruct his generation concerning its past *for the sake of its present*. For his *traditio* became the new and reorienting national *traditum*. In this connection one may recall the comment of the modern historian J. Huizinga, who pointedly observed that history is the means whereby a culture renders account to itself of its past.[42] To this one may add that a historiography based in part on the aggadic reinter-pretation of older historical materials accentuates the contemporary thrust of all such accounting. The transformed reactualization of the past for the sake of its didactic use in the present is thus not the least of the Chronicler's aggadic achievements.[43]

(*b*) A second example of the Chronicler's exegesis by סמוכין may be recognized in 2 Chron. 20: 31-7, a passage clearly derived from the historical *traditum* in 1 Kgs. 22: 42-50. Indeed, at the outset, the Chronicler adhered very closely to his source concerning Jehoshaphat's age upon ascension, his genealogy, and his relationship to the religious activities of his predecessor, Asa (cf. 1 Kgs. 22: 42-4 ~ 2 Chron. 20: 31-3). So close is this adherence, in fact, that one can observe but one divergence — and that of a typical spiritualizing sort. In 2 Chron. 20: 33b the Chronicler changed 'and the people continued to slaughter and burn incense on the high places' to 'and the people *continued not to set their hearts before the God of their fathers*'. The sequence which follows 2 Chron. 20: 31-3, however, is of a more complex exegetical sort, and diverges radically from the *traditum* in the Book of Kings.

---

[41] With Willi, *Die Chronik*, 219 n 14, who also observed the phenomenon of *sĕmûkîn*.

[42] 'A Definition of the Concept of History' in *Philsophy and History, Essays Presented to Ernst Cassirer*, edd. R. Klibansky and H. J. Paton (New York: Harper and Row, 1963), 9.

[43] For the re-presentation of the past in the liturgy, and its theological-didactic dimensions or purposes, see Claus Westermann, 'Vergegenwärtigung der Geschichte in den Psalmen', *Forschung am Alten Testament* (TBü 24; Munich: Chr. Kaiser Verlag, 1964), 306-35.

	1 Kgs. 22	2 Chron. 20
(i)	Verse 45 reports a treaty[44] between Jehoshaphat and Israel.	[*Missing*]
(ii)	Verse 46 gives notice about 'the rest of Jehosphaphat's accomplishments . . .'	Verse 34 gives notice about 'the rest of Jehoshaphat's accomplishments . . .'
(iii)	Verses 47–8 record religious reforms and a historical notice.	[*Missing*]
(iv)	Verses 49–50 state that 'Jehoshaphat made Tarshish-boats to bring gold from Ophir; but he did not go because the boats were broken up in Etzion-Gever. Then Ahaziah . . . said to Jehoshaphat: "Let my stewards go with yours on the boats; but Jehoshaphat was unwilling."'	Verses 35–7 state that 'Afterwards Jehoshaphat . . . allied himself with Ahaziah . . . therewith acting wickedly. And he made an alliance with him to build ships to Tarshish;[45] and they made ships in Etzion-Gever. Whereupon Eliezer . . . prophesied against Jehoshaphat: "Since you allied yourself with Ahaziah, YHWH will destroy your project." Then the ships were broken up and they were unable to go to Tarshish.'

From the preceding schema it may be observed that the sequence of presentation in 1 Kgs. 22 is both logical and clear. After the reference to a treaty between the Judaean and Israelite kings (i), there follows a notice of further exploits (ii), some of which are recorded in (iii)-(iv). Accordingly, it is not necessary to presume that (iv) is simply an afterthought related to (i) so that Ahaziah's statement to Jehoshaphat must be construed in the pluperfect temporal mode.[46] By contrast with this narrative consecution, the parallel sequence in 2 Chron. 20 is quite awkward. For while the absence of reference to a treaty between the kings in (i) is non-problematic, the major historical notice in (iv) is confusing, since it begins with 'afterwards', and there is no precise or even discernible antecedent to this temporal allusion.

---

[44] Heb. *wayyašlēm*. For the biblical use of the verb and its derivatives to refer to treaties and treaty-making, along with the interdialectal evidence from Mesopotamia, see M. Weinfeld, 'Covenant Terminology in the Ancient Near East and its Influence on the West', *JAOS* 93 (1973), 191f. and n. 31.

[45] For the view that Aram. *'ethabbar* (v. 35) and Heb. *wayhabběrēhû* (v. 36) refer to a shipping syndicate, see B. Maissler, 'Canaan and the Canaanites', *BASOR* 102 (1946), 10, and the observations of W. F. Albright, 'The Eastern Mediterranean, About 1060 BC', in *Studies Presented to David M. Robinson*, ed. G. E. Mylonas (St. Louis, Mo.: Washington University Press, 1951), 230.

[46] Willi, op. cit. 219, argued that this was the way the Chronicler understood it (i.e., *'āz 'āmar* in 1 Kgs. 22: 50 means 'at that time PN said'). Even if he did, he deleted the unwillingness of Jehosphaphat; see below.

However, the Chronicler's narrative lapse in 2 Chron. 20: 35a is one thing; his overall aggadic transformation of 2 Kgs. 22: 45-50 – a *traditum* at once confusing and insufficient to him – is another matter entirely. According to this *traditum* in 2 Kgs. 22: 45-50, there was a treaty between Kings Jehoshaphat of Judaea and Ahaziah of Israel, but no maritime alliance – Ahaziah's proposal was rejected by Jehoshaphat; and there was a breakup of Jehoshaphat's southern fleet in Etzion-Geber but no explicit cause for this is given. To account for these two issues the Chronicler performed several aggadic operations on his *traditum*. First, he deleted the reference to the treaty in (i) and referred only to a maritime alliance in (iv) – which, according to his *traditio*, did take place and actually *preceded* the breakup of the fleet; and second, he rearranged his *traditum* so that the reference to the destruction of the boats now *follows* Jehoshaphat's alliance with Ahaziah which – for reasons not stated – is also referred to as a 'wicked action' and deserving of divine punishment according to a prophetic speech by one Eliezer. This new alignment and recontextualization of the components of the received *traditum* thus allowed the Chronicler to explain the ruination of the Judaean shipping fleet as an act of God. Whereas, in fact, 1 Kgs. 22: 49 reported the disaster in quasi-naturalistic terms, the Chronicler provided a supernatural explanation, exegetically and causally correlating two events unassociated in his sources – the maritime alliance and the destruction of the fleet. Accordingly, whether in this case the Chronicler actually believed that his aggadic rewriting merely made the old *traditum* explicit, or whether he regarded it as a deliberate *tour de force*, the fact remains that his perception of the relation between discrete historical events is an *exegetical perception* and formally realized through the technical procedure of סמוכין. The results of this deft recontextualization of the *traditum* is, in the end, no *traditio*, but in fact a new *traditum*. And just this, one may assume, was the historian's intention all along.

5. The Book of Psalms and the historical superscriptions provide a concluding series of examples of aggadic exegesis via the technique of סמוכין. This exegetical subtype of exegesis is not immediately apparent, however, primarily because there seems to be little relationship between those psalm titles with historical references and the content of the psalms which they precede. This initial impression of discordance is furthermore reinforced by a review of the even greater diversity of historical ascriptions provided for these and other psalms in the LXX.[47]

---

[47] For discussions, see W. Staerk, 'Zur Kritik der Psalmüberschriften', *ZAW* 12 (1892), 91-151; B. Jacob, 'Beiträge zu einer Einleitung in die Psalmen', *ZAW* 16 (1896), 288-91.

the Targumim,[48] and the Peshitta versions,[49] and also because of the widespread tendency in early rabbinic midrash to 'historicize the non-historical',[50] that is, to correlate the psalms of the MT with events known from the sacred history—in line with the dictum that 'Everything which David said in his book was said of himself, of all Israel, and of the past and future of Israel'.[51] But any impression of complete discordance and arbitrariness between psalms and their historical titles must be decidedly modified in the light of the perspective introduced by several contemporary scholars. Observing clusters of linguistic affinities and conceptual parallels between various psalms and the historiographical sources to which the psalm titles make reference, B. Childs[52] and E. Slomovic[53] in particular have suggested that the historical notices in the psalm titles of Pss. 3, 7, 18, 34, 51, 52, 56, 57, 59, 60, 63, and 143 among others actually reflect the exegetical perception of a connection between the psalms in question and historical narratives.[54] Viewed thus, the titles provide an exegetical bridge between two textual units—a psalm and a narrative—and thus evidence a type of סמוכין, since two disparate contexts are synoptically brought into association.

As noted, one primary guide to the aggadic correlation of psalm texts and historical narratives lies in the perceived affinities between their words and ideas. For example, in the case of the well-known superscription to Ps. 51, which is ascribed to the time 'when Nathan the prophet came to him [viz. David], after he had gone into Bathsheba', one·will note that the penitent refers to his transgression and says חטאתי 'I have sinned' (Ps. 51: 6), the precise phrase enunciated by David in the old historical account when he was accused by the prophet Nathan for his delict (2 Sam. 12:13a).[55] Or further, like David who prayed that YHWH would be gracious to him (יחנני,v. 22) after he condemned him for doing evil (לעשות הרע בעיניו, v. 9), the psalmist appeals to his God to be gracious to him (חנני, v. 3) in so far as he too has done evilly before him (והרע בעיניך עשיתי, v. 6).[56] And finally, the

---

[48] Cf. H. D. Preuss, 'Die Psalmüberschriften in Targum und Midrasch', *ZAW* 71 (1951), 44–54.

[49] See J. M. Vosta, 'Sur les titres des Psaumes dans la Pešittā, surtout d'après la recension orientale', *Bib.* 25 (1944), 210–35.

[50] For this phrase and examples from rabbinic literature, see N. N. Glatzer, *Untersuchungen zur Geschichtslehre der Tannaiten* (Berlin: Schocken, 1933), 45–61.   [51] *Midrash Tehillim* xvii. 1; cf. xxiv. 3.

[52] 'Psalm Titles and Midrashic Exegesis', *JSS* 16 (1971), 137–50.

[53] 'Toward an Understanding of the Formation of Historical Titles in the Book of Psalms', *ZAW* 91 (1979), 350–80, esp. 365–80.

[54] In addition to these psalms, Slomovic, ibid., includes Pss. 30, 70, 90, 127. On the superscription to Ps. 30, see my comment in 'Torah and Tradition', 287.

[55] Cf. Childs, 'Psalm Titles', 145; Slomovic, loc. cit., 371.

[56] Cf. Slomovic, ibid.

theme of a 'broken spirit' and a 'crushed heart' in Ps. 51:19 is either 'reminiscent of David's mood' after the death of the child born to Bath-Sheba,[57] or of his overall spiritual contrition.[58] Most of the other historical titles show similarly detailed correspondences.

In addition to historical events as such, some psalm titles also refer to individuals, as in the case of the superscription to Ps. 90, 'A prayer of Moses, man of Elohim'. Here, too, while there is no reference to a historical event, one may deduce the exegetical basis of the ascription. In the present instance, the psalmist (a pseudo-Moses) appeals to his God to 'turn back' (שובה, v. 13) from his 'fury' (אפך, v. 11) and 'relent' (והנחם, v. 13) 'for the sake of your servants' (על־עבדיך, v. 13), for truly we are 'destroyed through your fury' (כלינו באפך, v. 7; cf. v. 9). And he closes with an appeal that his Lord manifest his kindness to his servants and their descendants. In a striking parallelism to this penitential topos Moses, after the apostasy of the golden calf, hears YHWH say: 'Leave me be that my fury (אפי) be inflamed against them to that I may destroy them (ואכלם)' (Exod. 32:10). In response, Moses prays to YHWH that his 'fury' (אפך, v. 11) be not inflamed to 'destroy them' (לכלתם, v. 12), and specifically calls upon him to 'turn' (שוב, v. 12) from his 'fury' and 'relent' (והנחם, v. 12) in remembrance of the promise made to the patriarchs his 'servants' (עבדיך, v. 13) for them and for their descendants (v. 13).[59] It was undoubtedly in the light of such a synoptic perception of the concordance between Ps. 90 and this Pentateuchal prayer that an ancient exegete ascribed the psalm to Moses, and the Targum, more expansively, entitled it 'A prayer of Moses the prophet, when the people of Israel sinned in the desert'.

The two preceding cases also provide an indication as to how the tradents of the psalms may have arrived at their aggadic perception in the first place. In the case of Ps. 90 it was undoubtedly of significance that the historical narrative in Exod. 32:11 states that 'Moses supplicated' the Lord. In other cases, like Ps. 51, there is another factor which may explain the basis of the exegetical perception, or retroactively support it. For in a large number of the cases the historical narrative referred to in the psalm title has a פִּסְקָא בְּאֶמְצַע פָּסוּק, or an intersentential lacuna. The Massoretic lists of this phenomenon vary, as do the theories concerning its origin and meaning.[60] Some scholars are

[57] Ibid.   [58] Cf. Childs, loc. cit.

[59] Slomovic, loc. cit. 376, has noted the verbal links of 'turning' and 'relenting'. For another view of this superscription, see A. Kaminka, 'Neueste Literatur zu den Hagiographen', *MGWJ* 71 (1927), 291, and id. in *Encyclopaedia Judaica* (Berlin: Verlag Eschkol AG, 1929), iv. 621, s.v. 'Bibelexegese'.

[60] See P. Sandler, 'Concerning Research on the *pisqā' bĕ'emṣā' happāsûq*', in *D. Neiger Memorial Volume* (Israel Society for Biblical Research, 7; Jerusalem, 1959), 229–49 [Heb.].

persuaded that it often simply serves to mark Massoretic disputes regarding sectional divisions;[61] others are convinced that the פסקא points either to the repression of esoteric teachings,[62] or to the separate existence of sources of a less sacred character.[63] Thus, it has been suggested that such lacunae in the MT 'aim at', 'call attention to', or 'allude to' extratextual matters—whether biblical or non-biblical.[64] The merits of the latter hypothesis are debatable. But even if a פסקא would doubtfully function as a cross-reference indicator, there is every reason to presume that it did stimulate or reinforce exegetical correlations— סמוכין. For it is remarkable that in over 40 per cent of the cases—half a dozen instances—a פסקא occurs in those historical texts referred to by the psalm titles, *and in precisely those contexts where one might expect or presume a prayer.* Thus, (i) in 2 Sam. 12:13 David responded to Nathan's rebuke regarding the Bath-Sheba episode with the remark 'I have sinned before YHWH'—whereupon there follows a פסקא. As described, Ps. 51 echoes the language and content of this episode. (ii) A פסקא also occurs in 2 Sam. 16:13, in the context of David's flight from Absalom to the desert (15:23, 16:2, 17:29) and of the abusive curses of Shimei ben Gera. According to several scholars the superscription to Ps. 3 refers to this flight,[65] and the prayer itself reflects the anguish of a person surrounded by oppressors (cf. the superscription to Ps. 63 and its content). (iii) Another פסקא occurs in 1 Sam. 21:10, in the context of David's flight from Saul and his deceit of Achish, King of Gath (vv. 11-14). These various episodes are referred to in the titles to Pss. 34[66] and 56,[67] and their respective contents portray moods of personal oppression and thanks for divine aid in overcoming the enemy. And finally, (iv) there is a פסקא found in 1 Sam. 23:4, in the context of David's appeal to God in battle and the betrayal of the Ziphites. This episode is referred to in the superscription to Ps. 54, which contains a request for divine aid in a time of trouble.[68]

---

[61] Cf. M. Z. Segal, 'The *pisqā' bĕ'emṣā' pāsûq*', *Tarbiz*, 29 (1960), 203-6 [Heb.].

[62] D. Cahana, *Masoret Seyag la-Miqra* (Vienna, 1882, repr. Jerusalem: Makor, 1970), 114.

[63] Cf. M.A.Chatzkes, 'The Pleasure of Resolving Doubts', *Kenesset ha-Gedolah*, 2 (Warsaw, 1847), 114 [Heb.].

[64] See S. Talmon, 'Pisqa Be'emṣa' Pasuq and 11QPsᵃ', *Textus*, 5 (1966), 18-20.

[65] Cf. Childs, loc. cit. 143, Slomovic, loc. cit. 365f., and Talmon, loc. cit.

[66] Cf. Childs, loc. cit. 144; Slomovic, loc. cit. 369f. The superscription to Ps. 34 has Abimelech. For the variation of the PNs Achish-Abimelech, see Childs, loc. cit. 144f.

[67] On lexical links between the psalm and the narrative established by the stems *ṭa'am* and *hallēl*, see Childs, ibid. Similarities between Pss. 34 and 56 have been noted by F. Delitzsch, *Biblischer Kommentar über die Psalmen* (Leipzig: Dörffling and Franke, 1894), 393.

[68] Cf. the observations of Childs, loc. cit. 145f.

It is not, of course, possible to estimate with any finality the direction in which the intuition of סמוכין worked—whether notice was first drawn to lacunae in the historical sources (in contexts suggesting some prayer or outcry) and thence to the comparable psalms, or whether the historical titles reflect the attentive study of the psalms and their subsequent correlation with comparable narratives. Presumably, the process varied from case to case, though the evidence from the MT and the other versions suggests that it was occasional and non-systematic in nature. There clearly was no thoroughgoing attempt to correlate the content of the psalter with the received historical narratives. This suggests that many of the historical titles are the product of living religious intuition and study, and not merely or simply the result of scholastic activities.

But whatever the direction of hermeneutical movement, and circles of origin, the סמוכין in the psalter are nevertheless primary evidence for the existence—however nascent—of a unifying 'Scriptural' višion. Such a vision may, in fact, be characterized as synoptic in nature, in so far as it envisages disparate texts in one co-ordinated focus, and thereby clarifies or embellishes one *traditum* by another. In this respect, at least, the historical superscriptions reflect a type of aggadic *traditio* which seeks to co-ordinate distinct traditions—not harmonize, transform, or otherwise obscure them. Indeed, such an aggadic adjustment of separate traditions is entirely distinct from another type of adjustment incorporated into various psalms, namely, the ongoing transformation of certain content in response to new theological, historical, or national agendas.[69] If, on balance, the addition of historical superscriptions to certain psalms served dialectically to emphasize their historical character, as the words of the spiritual giants of the past, the ongoing revisions of many psalms served to make the liturgical *traditum* responsive to contemporary issues. It is thus not so much the correlation between one text and another that is here in evidence as the equally powerful hermeneutical correlation of texts with ongoing life.

[69] For such rereadings—which are in effect rewritings—note the cases for a transformative *traditio* in the psalter presented by A. Gelin, 'La Question des 'relectures' bibliques a l'intérieur d'une tradition vivante', *Sacra Pagina*, 1 (1959), 303-15, and H. Cazelles, 'Une Relecture du Psaume XXIX²', in *A la rencontre de Dieu. Memorial Albert Gelin* (Bibliothèque de la Faculté Catholique de Théologie de Lyon, 8; Le Puy: Editions Xavier Mappus, 1961), 119-28. Also cf. the various shifts and adjustments proposed by J. Becker, *Israel deutet seine Psalmen* (Stuttgarter Bibelstudien, 18; Stuttgart: Katholisches Bibelwerk, 1966).

14. Conclusions

A. The range of styles, topics, and hermeneutical techniques associated with inner-biblical aggadic exegesis is considerable. Culled from a broad spectrum of genres, including epic narrative, historiography, oratory, liturgy and prophetic oracles and condemnations, this aggadic exegesis also derives from a broad variety of ancient Israelite traditions. Thus, the received aggadic interpretations utilize legal traditions found in the civil law corpora or the epic narratives (cf. Gen. 9: 1-7; Jer. 2: 26, 34, 3: 1, 5: 21-4), descriptive materials drawn from theological, epic, court, and royal narratives (cf. Deut. 4: 16-19, 8: 3; Josh. 1: 6-9; 1 Chron. 13: 7-14, 15: 1-2, 12: 15; Hos. 12; Jer. 9: 3-5; 2 Chron. 20: 31-6), liturgical traditions derived from the attribute formulary or the priestly benediction (cf. Deut. 7: 7-10; Mic. 7: 18-20; Mal. 1: 6-2: 9), cultic rules and behaviours taken from priestly prescriptions (cf. Jer. 2: 2; Isa. 58: 1-10; Hag. 2: 10-14), as well as prophetic oracles of various sorts (cf. 2 Chron. 15: 3-5, 20: 20). From these and similar examples it is clear that the imaginative life of the aggadic reformulators of the Israelite traditions was nurtured significantly by these ancient teachings. Regarding this dynamic much more must be said. At this point, however, it is first necessary to draw attention to a distinguishing characteristic of aggadic exegesis that is accentuated by the broad spectrum of genres from which such exegesis is derived and into which it is cast. This characteristic may be succinctly identified by the double shift involved in aggadic exegesis, a shift in historical and literary context. Put differently, one may say that the movement from *traditum* to aggadic *traditio* involves both a shift to a new historical setting, such that a given *traditum* is aggadically revised by new teachers in new life-settings, and a shift to a new literary setting, such that an aggadic *traditio* is embodied in new literary milieux and, commonly, in new literary modes as well.

   1. A proper understanding of the historical shift just alluded to does not rest solely upon recognizing the temporal belatedness of a given aggadic *traditio* in relation to the *traditum* from which it is derived, or in the fact that the *traditio* is articulated by teachers or spokesmen who have inherited the various forms of ancient *traditum*. Such factors are, of course, essential, though they are inevitably subordinate to the more vital issue which pertains to the historical exigencies that elicited the literary transformations in the first place. These exigencies can be

grouped into three broad categories, each of which expresses a particular type of crisis or dislocation which affected the continuity of
perception of the inherited *traditum*.[1] These three categories concern
crises with regard to the covenantal tradition as a whole; with regard to
specific covenantal traditions; and with regard to the continuity or
survival of the traditions from one historical epoch to another. Catalys-
ing these categories, moreover, are such dynamic tensions as covenantal
allegiance versus rebellion (or disinterest); cognitive coherence versus
dissonance; and cultural memory and hope versus the irrelevance of the
past and despair. The character and interpenetration of these categories
and dynamics—basic to the historical shifts of aggadic exegesis—may
be briefly described as follows.

First, in connection with those crises which affected the continuity
of the entire covenantal *traditum*, one can observe the important role
of aggadic exegesis in the attempt of teachers to restore covenantal
allegiance in its totality. That is, on occasions of religious rebellion or
simply passive disaffection, when the demands of the covenant are
disavowed in practice, the aggadic rhetors of ancient Israel frequently
reused specific pieces of the *traditum* in order to realign the community
with its entire heritage. The prophet Jeremiah was particularly skilful
in this regard. In his condemnations of contemporary behaviour, he
frequently took specific case laws, like the rule of the person caught
in flagrante while breaking into a house/pen (cf. Jer. 2: 26, 34) or the
case of the contentious and rebellious son (cf. 5: 21-4), and used them
pars pro toto for Israel's covenantal malfeasance. Or, comparably, the
case law of remarriage was aggadically transformed to confront the
populace of Judaea with its infidelity to YHWH and the covenant, and
to indicate the way of possible restoration (cf. 3: 1). In all these cases
there is no concern to teach the civil laws as such. Indeed, the specific
instances of rebellion indicated by the legal examples serve primarily to
concretize the broader problem of covenantal allegiance. For this
reason, the aggadic transformations indicate the content of the laws
only indirectly, their main goal being to reorientate the addressees by
strategic examples towards the covenant *as a whole*.[2]

---

[1] The reflections of L. Bitzer, 'The Rhetorical Situation', in *Rhetoric: A Tradition in Transition*, ed. W. R. Fisher (Ann Arbor: University of Michigan Press, 1974), 252f., are very much to the point. Considering the importance of the historical situation in rhetorical discourse, Bitzer isolates 'exigency' as a basic constituent of this situation, and defines it as 'an imperfection marked by urgency' and capable of 'modification by discourse'.

[2] The importance of audience and its attitudinal changes is, of course, a vital component of rhetorical discourse; cf. Bitzer, ibid. 250, 252, and the definition of C. Perelman and L. Olbrechts-Tyteca, *The New Rhetoric* (Notre Dame and London: University of Notre Dame Press, 1969), 19: 'audience, in rhetoric, is *the ensemble of those whom the speaker wishes to influence by his argumentation*'.

The second broad category of interest here involves the reinterpretation or transformation of a specific element of the *traditum*. Here, as in the preceding category, aggadic exegesis attempts to repair a break or dislocation in the continuity of the *traditum*. But since the focus is not on the tradition as a whole, but rather a specific part of it, the aggadic issue turns on more narrow cognitive concerns—like the meaning and value of deferred or vicarious punishment—which have lost their assent or hold on a latter-day generation. Thus, in Deut. 7: 9-10 Moses misquotes the divinely articulated attribute formulary of Exod. 34: 6-7 in order to bring it into line with contemporary, seventh-century notions of divine equity. In other cases, like Ezek. 18, the new aggadic teaching aggressively manoeuvres to establish a cognitive break with older notions of divine punishment in order to generate a more functional continuity with the older traditions. Indeed (according to Ezekiel's divinely inspired view), simple continuity with the received *traditum* would have resulted in religious and spiritual stultification. Aggadic exegesis, in this and related cases, functions as a strategic intervention by the bearers of the *traditum* for the sake of a more fundamental continuity with the covenantal heritage than would have been achieved without it. In the case of the prophet Jonah, a self-serving emphasis on divine mercy in his recitation of the attribute formulary—itself a strategic dislocation from the more normative formulations—is itself dislocated and theologically transposed by the divine speech which concludes the book and transforms the entire composition into an aggadic revisioning of the prophetic task and its assumptions.

Two further types of cognitive dissonance may be pointed out under this general rubric. The first returns us to many of the modes of aggadic exegesis found in the Book of Chronicles, or in earlier historiography. Hereby, later interpreters and transmitters of the historical *traditum* reread or reworked that *traditum* in the light of prevailing contemporary notions of religious praxis or divine activity. As we observed in connection with the Chronicler's rearticulation of episodes from the time of Kings David, Asa, and Jehoshaphat, a frequent form of aggadic transformation of this sort is the representation of older historical narratives in terms of later views of divine causation, repentance, and the historical process. Thus, for latter-day historiographers, it appears that earlier historical renditions were authoritatively traditional without being theologically normative articulations of the past. Accordingly, where cognitive dissonance was felt to exist between the earlier historiographies and subsequent religio-historical values, the older *tradita* were strategically transformed by aggadic reworkings of them.

Another dimension of this aggadic shift from outmoded, alienating, or even problematic texts to cognitively more appealing versions thereof may be exemplified by the interpolations found in Josh. 1: 6-9 and 1 Kgs. 2: 2-4, where traditions of military might were spiritually transvaluated. In these texts the cognitive validity of the worth of obedience to the commandments of the Torah is asserted for such cases as the conquest of Canaan and the maintenance of royal stability. In the process, older military ideals specified in the original *traditum* were transformed or effaced. In other instances, the spiritual revisioning of earlier traditions goes beyond this, and led later teachers to new—and sometimes transformative—expressions and clarifications. For example, on the level of religious praxis, one may refer to the case of Isa. 58: 1-10, which expresses the people's disgruntled reaction to the failure of austere fasting (presumably on the Day of Atonement) to achieve the desired divine response, and the prophet's inspired response to them that true fasting is not simply a willed abstinence from food but a donation of food to those for whom fasting is an unwilled deprivation. In this instance the people express a dissonance between the realized and expected result of religious performance, and are furthermore confronted with the fact that their very dissonance is a function of their limited spiritual vision and state. Hence, by aggadic rhetoric, the people's attitudes are subverted, and they are put in mind of their own fundamental discordance with the tradition in its 'truest' sense.

Another example, this time on the level of ideas (versus praxis—as above), is Deutero-Isaiah's spiritual critique of the anthropomorphic language of the *traditum* of Gen. 1:1-2:4a. Fundamentally aware of the authority and significance of this text, but not able to affirm its contents without qualification and clarification, the post-exilic prophet mends the cognitive rift which separates him from those notions in Gen. 1: 1-2: 4a which imply the coexistence with YHWH—at the beginning—of 'darkness' and 'void', as well as mankind's resemblance to the divine. Deutero-Isaiah does this by clarifying, in some instances, the (to him) true verbal or semantic import of the theological narrative, and also by denaturalizing the received imagery—as in Isa. 40: 28, where he imputed to the old *traditum* a kind of intellectualization of the creation. One might say that the result of the prophet's teaching is to provide a secondary demythologization of the Bible's opening *traditum* of the creation, in so far as the latter text is itself an intellectual transformation of ancient Near Eastern mythological traditions. The prophet thus attempts to establish the proper cognitive gauge for this ancient *traditum*. Paradoxically, he opens a wedge between older and more contemporary estimates of the meaning of Gen. 1: 1-2: 4a even as he attempts to retrieve this very text in accordance with his latter-day theological sensibilities.

The preceding review of modes of cultural retrieval achieved by aggadic exegesis brings us to the third of the three categories to be isolated at this point, aggadic attempts to bridge the more massive crises and dislocations of the Israelite (northern) and Judaean (southern) exiles. The epochal gap which erupted between past and present caused by these events of monumental spatial dislocation and spiritual disorientation—events which elicited the threat of absolute or, at least, of fundamental cultural discontinuity and loss—was crossed on many fronts by the would-be heirs and survivors of the old *traditum*. From an aggadic perspective, the following three types of 'reformation' are notable: (i) the aggadic emphasis on the radical newness of the *traditio* and the obsolescence of the *traditum*; (ii) the aggadic emphasis on the fundamental continuity between the older *traditum* and the contemporary *traditio*; (iii) and the aggadic emphasis on the retrieval and representation of historical memories. While analytically separable, these three types naturally coincide in reality.

The first type of aggadic reformation, which put its stress on the newness of the *traditio* and the 'pastness' of the *traditum*, envisages new religio-cultural realities in the New (post-exilic) Age. In particular, as noted earlier, the teacher explicitly contrasts the old with the new: this may relate to the non-existence of the Ark, to new modes of divine punishment, or to the internalization or inner knowledge of the Torah's teachings (cf. Jer. 3: 16-17, 31: 28-9, 30-2, 33). By these means, the epochal rift between the past and present is acknowledged and stressed; but while the traditions of the past constitute the orientating memories of the present, they are nevertheless relegated to the cultural-historical background. It is the *new* future that is stressed; and its discontinuity with 'former days' is emphatically highlighted. Aggadic exegesis serves, in such cases, as the hinge between the one and the other, swinging the door which closes on memory and opens towards hope.

By contrast, and far more pervasive and culturally fundamental, is that mode of aggadic reformation which seeks to envisage the future in the light of the past, and thereby affirm continuity between past and present as the sure link between memory and hope.[3] The technique generally employed to achieve this end is that of typology, which, as noted, projects paradigmatic images of the past into the present and future, and sees these as reshapings and renewals of foundational actions, scenarios, or topoi of the ancient past. Notably, for the present inquiry, these images generally emerge in times of crisis. Thus, after the northern exile Micah (7: 15), Isaiah (11: 11-16), and Jeremiah (16: 14f. ∼ 23: 7f.) refer to a new exodus and return; or, comparably, after the southern exile the prophets Deutero-Isaiah (cf. 43: 16-21, 51: 9-11)

---

[3] Cf. the pointed observation of F. Ohly, 'Vom geistigen Sinn des Wortes im Mittelalter', *Schriften zur mittelalterlichen Bedeutungsforschung* (Darmstadt: Wissenschaftliche Buchgesellschaft, 1977), 321: 'Typologie ist ein Prinzip der Ordnung der Geschichte . . .'.

and Ezekiel (ch. 20) project a new exodus in order to bridge the contemporary crisis of historical discontinuity. Similarly, in response to the spatial dislocation of this same southern exile, prophets like Ezekiel (47: 1-12), Joel (4: 18), and Zechariah (14: 7-11) envisage the relocation of a sacred centre in Jerusalem, at the Temple mount. Many other images were employed typologically, ranging from the creation itself to historical personages and their exploits in *illud tempus*, in order to convey or assert the fundamental continuity linking contemporary Israel in crisis with the Israel of sacred memory. Here, as in the preceding paragraph, aggadic exegesis serves to link the past with the present and future, only now the *traditio* is regarded as a reactualization of the *traditum*, and not its replacement; and the *traditum* does not serve as the backdrop and foil for a discontinuous *traditio*, but is rather the screen upon which national hope and renewal is contextualized, even imagined.

The third type of reformation relates to the aggadic retrieval and representation of cultural memories. Indeed, it would be fair to say that this type of aggadic exegesis is actually a reformation of memory itself: for hereby teachers like the Chronicler have taken over older historical traditions and reformulated them in the light of contemporary emphases, values, and ideals—emphases like the Chronicler's concern with divine historical causality, values like obedience to the commandments and repentance, and ideals like the purity of proper cultic worship in the Temple of Jerusalem. In this way the heirs of historical crisis, the post-exilic generation, not only retrieve their past but also reorientate themselves towards the future. Accordingly, for the 'reformers' of memory there is no past 'as such' which must be transmitted; there is only the past *traditum* which has been aggadically transformed by its tradents—the teachers of a new *traditum*, in fact. For, as emphasized earlier, the *traditio* of aggadic historiography is presented as the authentic *traditum*, there being no overt juxtaposition or linkage between past traditions and the present but only a teaching about the past in the present. By reforming the historical *traditum* to make it congruent with contemporary religious practices and ideologies, the *traditio* presents an exemplary version of the past; for it at once exemplifies a certain normative relationship between divine and human actions, and also provides a hortatory example of the consequences of behaviour to a later generation which it hopes to 'reform' to covenant piety. It may be added, without strain, that this type of aggadic reworking of historical memories transforms the historical composition itself into a 'type' of sorts, since the teachers of memory wish to indicate the paradigmatic character of past events for the present, i.e., the continuity into the present of the consequences of covenantal allegiance as demonstrated by past events. Aggadic exegesis thus, here too, arises from cultural and cognitive crisis and strives to restore contact with the ancient *traditum* for the sake of the present and future.

2. In addition to the matter of historical context, it was remarked earlier, aggadic exegesis also involves a shift in the literary context of the received and transformed *traditum*. Naturally, the two shifts are correlated and interrelated, in so far as the movement from a *traditum* to its aggadic *traditio*, effected by new teachers in new life-settings, takes shape in new (i.e. different) literary milieux and modes. A brief retrospective of the genres and styles from which a given *traditum* is derived and into which its *traditio* is reformulated bears out this observation. For example, laws from the Covenant Code, the priestly rules, and the deuteronomic civil corpora reappear in prophetic speeches or exhortations (cf. Isa. 58: 1-10; Jer. 2: 3, 26, 34, 3: 1, 5: 21-4; Hag. 2: 11-14); topics from theological narratives like Gen. 1: 1-2: 4a reappear in prophetic oracles (cf. Isa. 40: 17-18, 25-6, 28-9, 45: 7, 18-19); priestly liturgical formulations like that in Num. 6: 24-6 reappear in prophetic denunciations and curses (Mal. 1: 9-2: 6); *theologoumena* like the attribute formulary reappear in the Decalogue (cf. 20: 5-7), historical narratives (cf. Num. 14: 18-19), prophetic narratives and oracles (cf. Jer. 31: 28-9, 32: 18-19; Ezek. 18: 2-4; Jonah 4: 2; Nah. 1: 2), psalms (cf. Pss. 103, 109), and sermons (cf. Deut. 7: 9-10); epic narratives like the exodus account reappear in prophetic oracles (cf. Isa. 11: 11-16, 19: 19-25, 51: 9-11; Ezek. 20); narratives about the patriarchs reappear in prophetic denunciations (cf. Jer. 9: 3-5; Hos. 12) and oracles (cf. Isa. 51: 2; Ezek. 33: 24-9); sermonic exhortations like the militaristic appeal to vigour and strength reappear in historical narratives dealing with obedience to the Torah (cf. Josh. 1: 6-9) or in new oracular settings (cf. 2 Chron. 15: 2-7); prophetic oracles such as that enunciated by Isaiah in Isa. 7: 9b reappear transformed in the mouth of laymen giving exhortations (cf. 2 Chron. 20: 20b); and so forth.

To be sure, in stressing these generic and stylistic shifts there is no attempt to deny that, in many other cases, the same literary form may be employed, as, for example, the representation of narrative episodes from Samuel-Kings—concerning the lives of Uzzah, Asa, and Jehoshaphat—in the Books of Chronicles, or the recitation of features from 2 Sam. 7 in 1 Kgs. 5: 16-19, 8: 18-19 and 1 Chron. 22: 7-10, 28: 2-7. But even in these cases where the narrative or stylistic form remains the same, or where the speaker is—at least formally—the same (i.e., an historian 'speaks'), the various aggadic innovations make it clear that the *traditum* is no longer in its original context, that it has been recontextualized. Thus, on one end of the spectrum, where aggadic exegesis occurs within the same narrative mode (like narrative history), or even within a subspecies of that mode (as in the repetitions by David or Solomon or the vision reported by Nathan in 2 Sam. 7 – within the context of narrative history), the recontextualization of a *traditum* is evident upon comparing *internal* variations within such a piece with earlier or parallel accounts of it. Yet the fact that the subunits of a narrative history may also be rearranged, as a comparison of 2 Sam. 5: 19-25 + 6: 1-19 with 1 Chron. 13: 6-14 + 14: 10-16 + 15: 1-2 + 26-16: 3 reveals, indicates that the recontextualization of a *traditum* can involve *external* variations as well.

As one moves across the spectrum to the sermons and oracles and liturgies in which the aggadic *traditio* is now found, this latter aspect of recontextualization takes on sharper focus. For it is evident that the *tradita* embedded in the aggadic exegeses of these cases have been decontextualized from their original settings and combined with new material. Thus, parts of a larger literary context – legal corpora, narrative, liturgy – have been isolated and aggadically transformed for a new time and place, and this new literary expression has been itself reinserted into a new literary ensemble, be it a collection of oracles or psalms or teachings. It is at this point in the spectrum, then, that the double nature of the literary shift involved in aggadic exegesis – of an internal shift in the content of the *traditum* and an external shift in its place of occurrence – is most marked and clear. And it is at this point, moreover, that the two metaphors used earlier to express the fact of historical shifts underlying aggadic exegesis – dislocation and relocation – can be reapplied with profit to the literary shifts involved. For, characteristically, traditions are first dislocated (decontextualized) from their received form and then aggadically reworked, a reworking which may, of course, be simultaneous with its initial presentation in oral or literary form. Subsequently, whether gradually or immediately, the reworked traditions are relocated (recontextualized) in new literary ensembles. The two steps of literary dislocation and relocation are equally transformative. But it deserves emphasis that the first phase transforms a *traditum* into a *traditio*, whereas in the second the new aggadic *traditio* becomes a *traditum* in its own right.

In addition to the foregoing, there are two further points which deserve mention in connection with the literary shifts involved in aggadic exegesis. The first of these is the fact that, characteristically, aggadic transformations are not articulated 'for the sake of' the *traditum* from which they are derived. This point can be easily misconstrued, but it is basic enough. To be sure, any given aggadic *traditio* may reinforce the authority of the *traditum* whose language and ideas it reuses, even as some instances of aggadic exegesis can be understood to be 'for the sake of' the covenantal tradition as a whole. This is one thing. Quite another is the fact that aggadic exegeses do not explicitly clarify, resolve, harmonize, or even reauthorize earlier traditions. What they rather do is to serve the *traditio* — and its particular concern — 'by means of' the *traditum*. Even where citation formulae are used to refer to the authoritative *traditum*, as in Jer. 3:1 or Hag. 2:11-14, the content of that *traditum* remains unaffected and unchanged by the *traditio* which uses it for its own ends in the present. Similarly, the spiritual rereading of the ritual of fasting in Isa. 58:1-10 is not designed to undermine the normative regulations of Lev. 16 and 23:26-32, but rather uses that *traditum* skilfully in order to expose a matter of moral concern to the prophet. Finally, even where a given *traditum* is rejected in one way or another, be it in the style of Deut. 7:9-10, Jer. 31:28-9, or Ezek. 18:2-4, the *traditio* presents itself as *the* authoritative tradition on the subject, and serves the ideas with which it is engaged. All this is quite naturally the case where a *traditum* is employed 'for the sake of' the *traditio*, as in the uses made of the attribute formulary in Pss. 103 and 109, or where the *traditio* is quite literally presented as the *traditum*, as in the many modes of aggadic exegesis found in the historiographical narratives.

There is no need to rehearse the entire corpus of inner-biblical aggadic exegesis in order to emphasize this point. The previous examples fully support the generalization that the literary shift from a *traditum* to its aggadic *traditio* is characteristically a shift in the direction of the *traditio* — to its concerns, preoccupations, and values. Again, this does not mean that the larger values of the *traditum* are not served, or that the *traditio* is not congruent with these values; nor does it mean that aspects of the *traditum* may not *in fact* be clarified by the *traditio*. As we have seen, the exegeses in Jer. 2:26, 34, 3:1, or 5:21-4, for example, do have the values and concerns of the tradition as a whole very much in mind; similarly, an analytic-synoptic reading of Samuel-Kings with Chronicles shows many ways whereby the former has been clarified or theologically elucidated by the latter. However, the fact that Jeremiah's aggadic reuse of legal texts is congruent with the religious concerns of the covenant, or that the Chronicler's teachings do, in the end, clarify and reinterpret implicit and explicit features of Samuel-Kings, must not obscure the facts that the prophet does not use covenantal laws to reinterpret the content and meaning of the laws *in their legal context*, and that the Chronicler's clarifications do not refer the reader to any other historical context. It is rather the new 'literary' event which matters in both cases: be it the oratory of the prophet and his message or the historical teachings of the historian — to take just these two instructive types. Indeed, it is the new *traditio* and its content which address the reader or hearer or user of it. And this is altogether appropriate. For the tradents and teachers involved in aggadic exegesis are not concerned to reproduce the *traditum*, but to reactualize it in a new setting and a new way. Their aim is not to present the *traditum*, but rather to represent it — and this is *traditio*.

This leads to a final matter pertaining to aggadic exegesis and the literary shifts involved. Up to this point consideration has been given to the movement from one literary type or form to another, and the movement from one literary context to another. These reflections necessarily gave implicit and explicit emphasis to the relationships between a *traditum* and its *traditio*, but not to the relationships between the speaker (or voice) of a *traditio* and his intended audience. In this later regard, it would be more appropriate to speak of a series of rhetorical shifts — that is, shifts in rhetorical strategy. For it makes a great difference whether, for example, YHWH reveals his attributes to Moses (and Israel) after the apostasy of the calf (Exod. 34: 6-7), or whether Moses recites them to him in a prayer (Num. 14:17-19) or to the people in a sermon (Deut. 7: 9-10); or whether prophets and laymen recite them to YHWH after national or private crises (cf. Mic. 7: 18-20; Pss. 103, 109). Similarly, it is of vital literary and rhetorical consequence whether priestly rules regarding desecration of sancta are taught to priests for their own instruction (Lev. 22:14-16), or are reused by a prophet to emphasize the sacral nature of the people of Israel (Jer. 2: 3); or whether a civil *Rechtspraxis* forbidding palingamy to members of the covenantal community (Deut. 24:1-4) is subsequently reused to encourage religious 'return' to those who have lapsed from that community (Jer. 3: 1). In these and comparable cases, the *traditum* is transformed in relation to the addressee (the audience) and the goal or intent of the address itself. The same holds true, *mutatis mutandis*, where the *traditio* is not a public or expressly verbal event, like a prayer or exhortatory speech, but is *au fond* a narrative event, like the exegeses in the historiographical narratives. Since in the latter cases there is also an intended audience with whom the historian wishes to communicate, and whose values and ideas he hopes to influence or affect, the aggadic transformations are simultaneously literary shifts of a rhetorical nature.

The literary shifts that arise from, and because of, the new historical situation in which the bearers and recipients of the *traditum* find themselves, and which produce transformations of literary style, form, and context, are thus complemented by a series of rhetorical shifts. For, by contrast with its *traditum*, an aggadic *traditio* often proceeds with different goals of communication, with different methods of communication, and with different assumptions about what is in fact communicated. Moreover, these two triadic series — of literary style, form, and context, and of rhetorical goal, method, and assumption — are not static and unrelated elements of an abstract analysis. Indeed, they dynamically interpenetrate with every occurrence of the fundamental formal triad — a *traditum*, its aggadic *traditio*, and the real or intended situation-audience. For what is fixed and received in the *traditum*, and fluid and receptive in the situation-audience, is connected and mediated by the *traditio – which uses literary means for rhetorical effect*. Thus, in the process and event of *traditio* the literary, rhetorical, and historical-situational components of aggadic exegesis come together, and the contents of the literary and rhetorical triads outlined above interfuse. Since these remarks are solely of a general nature, designed to characterize in a summary way some of the chief traits of the phenomenon of literary shifts in aggadic exegesis, it remains to sharpen these observations by focusing attention first on the actual techniques and logic of aggadic exegesis, and then on the rhetorical transformations and strategies involved.

B. By early medieval times, with the remarkable proliferation of aggadic exegesis–in diverse academies under the tutelage of different masters, and in different synagogues, with the performance of lay and professional rhetors–there were many opportunities to reflect upon proper and appropriate techniques and their systematization. One major collection, comprising thirty-two canons of 'aggadic hermeneutics', has been preserved under the name of R. Eliezer ben Jose Ha-gelili.[4] Such a collection, like any systematization of exegetical techniques, naturally brought the processes of *aggadah* to written self-consciousness–though the transformation was certainly preceded by generations of self-conscious teachings of 'techniques' in the oral tradition. Indeed, a simple glance at any page of *aggadah* preserved in the name of Tannaitic sages (after Amoraic accretions–where they exist–have been stripped away) is enough to show how early formal hermeneutical measures were employed by the most ancient Jewish 'masters of midrash', And if, furthermore, one pushes back these Tannaitic traditions to the even earlier (proto-)Pharisaic strata, or to the contemporary aggadic materials preserved in the Qumran scrolls, the existence of noticeably stable exegetical techniques, on the one hand, and their recognizable correlation with techniques 'canonized' in later aggadic sources and manuals–like R. Eliezer's–on the other, is both clear and significant.[5]

[4] See H. L. Strack, *Introduction to the Talmud and Midrash* (Cleveland and New York: Meridian Books, and Philadelphia: The Jewish Publication Society, 1959), 95–8, and *Mishnat Rabbi Eliezer*, ed. H. Enelow (New York: Bloch, 1944), i. 9–41. For the dating of this collection, see above, p. 281 n. 3.

[5] W. Brownlee, 'Biblical Interpretation Among the Sectaries of the Dead Sea Scrolls', *BA* 24 (1951), 54–76, was among the earliest to observe exegetical comparisons between these scrolls and early rabbinic hermeneutics. See also my remarks in 'The Qumran Pesher', 98–100, for the ancient use of techniques found in R. Eliezer's collection. For such techniques at Qumran as *gĕzērāh šāwāh*, *zēker laddābār* and *'asmaktā'*, see E. Slomovic, 'Toward an Understanding of the Exegesis in the Dead Sea Scrolls', *RQ* 7 (1969), 3–15.

In attempting, in the following discussion, to isolate and typify some of the methods and modes of aggadic exposition in the Hebrew Bible, and its attendant (usually immanent) logic, it would hardly be of much methodological or historical value to try to capture the naïve and unsystematized inner-biblical phenomenon in the net of later, more formal, procedures. The reasons are self-evident, and are rooted in the principle that the varieties of inner-biblical aggadic exegesis must be organized on the basis of the biblical evidence itself, and not on arbitrary, limiting, or even far-reaching post-biblical features.[6] At the same time, this strong inhibition against methodological anachronism will not inhibit the occasional heuristic use of later rabbinic insights for discovering or even labelling certain inner-biblical phenomena. Indeed, just because the rabbinic 'masters of midrash' were such good aggadic exegetes — and not because of any a priori assumption of a continuous oral tradition of aggadic methods from biblical to post-biblical times — their ways of interpreting the biblical text will necessarily enlighten the eyes of modern interpreters whose habits and assumptions of reading and interpretation have been affected by two millennia of culture. Ultimately, however, the concrete exegetical value — in any real instance — of the habits of perception retrieved from this sphere, like the hermeneutical canon of סמוכין analysed earlier,[7] must stand analytically on its own.

Aggadic techniques and logic

1. In attempting to organize in a useful and productive manner some of the techniques of inner-biblical aggadic exegesis, one must turn first to the formal procedures and methods which are evidenced. The first such technique to be noted here may be termed *lemmatic deduction or inference*. By this procedure, a particular *traditum* is first cited, summarized, or posited before an addressee, and then a conclusion is either deduced or inferred from the topos as a whole or specific terms contained therein. For example, in Hag. 2:11-14 a series of ritual questions are put to the priests, who answer them, but then find their answers reapplied to (i.e. deduced for) a broader ritual consideration. Specifically, in the pertinent second question, the priests are asked about the ritual status of objects touched by a person defiled by the dead. In this query, nothing is stated about the people as a whole — yet this is the focus of the prophet's remark; and nothing is asked about the entire range of possible contacts (including non-sanctified items) —

---

[6] Cf. the work of A. Wright, *The Literary Genre Midrash* (Staten Island, NY: Alba House, 1967), and the incisive critique by R. Le Déaut, 'Apropos a Definition of Midrash', *Interpretation*, 25 (1971), 259-83.

[7] Above, pp. 399-407.

yet precisely this is the sweep of the prophet's conclusions. Indeed, the prophet has not only imputed a state of impurity comparable to corpse defilement to the people, without evidence, but has furthermore gone on to deduce from it the impurity of all sanctified and also (*a fortiori*) of all non-sanctified obejcts with which the Israelite might come in contact. The key term ('impure'), used in the lemma (v. 13) and its application (v. 14), provides the formal exegetical nexus between the premiss and the deduction.

Parallels to this aggadic technique can be found earlier, in Jer. 3: 1, where again a question-answer scenario is used, with the lemma preceding the application (linked by the key verb שׁוּב). As noted in our discussion of it, the prophet's answer to his own question is paradoxical —an apodictic inference based on the rhetorical-religious intent of the speech, and not on the jurisprudential logic. Among other comparable instances, it will be recalled that Ezek. 33: 24 cited a popular dictum concerning the people's putative claim to settlement in the land. The dictum was formulated as a קַל וָחֹמֶר argument[8] *a minori ad maius* — 'Abraham was one and he inherited the land, and we are many: [certainly] the land is given us for an inheritance'—and so seems to foreclose any further conclusions. What the prophet does, however, as discussed earlier, is first to recite a list of heinous malpractices from the Pentateuch, and then *and on that basis* to invert the lemma via the key verb יָרֵשׁ 'inherit' (cf. vv. 25b and 26b) with a קַל וָחֹמֶר argument of his own. The implied deduction of rights to the land based on the original *a minori* inference was wrong, implies Ezekiel, because the people have not paid attention to the decisive Pentateuchal premisses. Indeed, according to the logic of the case, one must observe that while Abraham was told on divine authority that he would 'inherit' the land defiled by the Amorites (Gen. 15: 7, 16), the previous inhabitants of the land, his descendants were instructed that they would forfeit this inheritance if they 'defiled' the land with just those sins decried by Ezekiel (cf. Ezek. 33: 25-6 and Lev. 18: 20, 26-30). Thus, the people's inference is misguided and ill-informed, since national inheritance of the land presupposed fulfilment of the covenantal stipulations. Or, in *a minori* terms: the people would inherit the land if they would be as faithful to the Torah as Abraham was to the divine promise.[9]

Isa. 58: 1-10 offers a final instance of lemmatic deduction in aggadic

---

[8] For an appreciation of this exegetical–rhetorical form *within* ancient Israelite discourse, see L. Jacobs, 'The *Qal Va-ḥomer* Argument in the Old Testament', *BSOAS* 35 (1972), 221-7.

[9] There are other examples of *qal wāḥōmer* reasoning among Ezekiel's speeches. For two explicit cases, with characteristic technical terms, see Ezek. 14: 15-21 (with the comment of Kimḥi *ad* v. 21), and Ezek. 15: 1-5.

exegesis: for if Jer. 3:1 and Hag. 2:11-14 posit Scriptural lemmata which are exegetically revised, and Ezek. 33:24 presents a popular dictum whose inferential logic is soundly reversed, Trito-Isaiah here creates a blend of the two types. On the one hand, the prophet recites the people's complaint that they have fasted and there is no divine response, and then shows that their query and expectation are a false deduction, for they have not performed the 'proper' fast—this being the performance of deeds of charity and kindness to the needy. In aggadically reversing the popular question, the prophet relies on the very words of the people in v. 3 and, by their exegetical transformation, provides the 'proper' deduction and application of their words. But the force of Isaiah's aggadic speech is, as we earlier noted, far more than a clever reversal of popular language. It is, in fact, a spiritual transformation of language derived from Lev. 16 and 23:26-32, the regulations regarding the Day of Atonement and the required fast. What the prophet says, aggadically, is that the people have falsely inferred the worth and character of their ceremonial fasting, and so their cavilling deduction is false. In truth, they are made to realize that they have hardly begun to fulfill the religious requirement of 'fasting'. Moreover, were they properly to do so, there would in fact be no need for their anguished deductions or expectations, since YHWH would respond immediately to their needs (vv. 7-10).

2. Of a different sort entirely is the broad aggadic technique which establishes exegetical meaning by *correlation*. In fact, these correlations may be of two types, polarity and analogy, and may occur with and without technical terms. Typical of the aggadic polarities, whereby a *traditum* is offset, demoted, or even replaced by a new *traditio*, are those several instances in the Book of Jeremiah where the prophet says 'In those days . . . they will no longer say . . . [rather] in those days' (3:16-18), or 'Behold days are coming . . . and one will no longer say . . . but rather . . .' (16:14-15),[10] or 'In those days they will no longer say . . . but rather . . .' (31:28-9), or 'Behold days are coming . . . not like . . . but this . . .' (31:30-2). In all such cases, the fixed terminological pattern links the polarized topoi and correlates them as part of an integrated historical process. Indeed, it would not be an exaggeration to say that these two dominant elements in 'correlations of polarity'— the progressive displacement of the past topos in relation to the expected reality, and the integration of the discrete events of history—are the leitmotifs of all aggadic correlations, even those of an analogical sort. For even in the many instances of typology where positive correlations are established between events, persons, and spatial topoi, and where

---

10 Cf. Jer. 23:7-8, with plural verbs.

the terminology is not pejorative—and simply correlates 'first' and 'later' things or states that one thing (or person) is (or will be) 'like' another—the new event or topos is to the speaker of relative hierarchical value. In short, while the 'first' event or topos is paradigmatic and essential for the correlation which is aggadically intuited or projected, the 'later' analogue is the moment or figure of exegetical and existential significance—and so it functionally eclipses or absorbs its prototype.[11]

It may furthermore be noted that whether in their analogical or polar forms, aggadic correlations do not generally compare radically dissimilar things. Indeed, there is an observable concordance between one event and another, one person and another, and one spatial topos and another. Thus, the exodus tends to be correlated with the return from the exile, Adam with Noah, Eden with Zion, and so forth. In those instances where, by contrast, the correlations appear less precise and some discordance is felt—as when the Ark as divine throne is correlated with the city of Jerusalem (Jer. 3:16-17), or when an individual patriarch like Jacob is correlated with the people as a whole (e.g. Hos. 12), or where the desert manna is correlated with divine revelation (Deut. 8:3)—closer examination suggests that the aggadic 'performance' actually serves to indicate a deeper continuity between the items juxtaposed. This matter may be confirmed by a second look at the preceding three representative examples:

(*a*) As noted, the correlation between the Ark and the city of Jerusalem in Jer. 3:16-17 is of a polar nature, contrasting a 'type' and its 'antitype'. According to the prophecy, the Ark, erstwhile manifestation of the throne of YHWH in the Temple of Jerusalem, would be displaced ('forgotten', not 'called to mind') by the locus of Jerusalem itself. Not a cultic appurtenance but a royal city would be the new spiritual seat of the Lord: for if the former was a physical and visible symbol of the divine reality, it proved of no spiritual consequence for the people, who nevertheless 'followed . . . the stubbornness of their evil heart'. Accordingly, and by contrast, the new invisible throne would replace its concrete prototype and be a place of divine presence for all peoples. Thus, despite the initial contrast, with its asymmetry of correlated items, a deeper nexus is brought to mind. For the new type is not so much a rejection of the older prototype as its substitution— re-establishing the primary intention of the Ark in the Temple of Jerusalem, viz., to be a focus for the presence of YHWH.

(*b*) A second example of apparent discordance lies in the correlation between the life of an individual and the activities of the nation. Such occurs in Hos. 12, where the life-cycle of the patriarch Jacob-Israel is

---

[11] On some rhetorical dimensions of comparisons and analogies, see Perelman and Olbrechts-Tyteca, *The New Rhetoric*, 242-3, 371-98.

presented as a figure for the activities of latter-day Jacob-Israel. The shock of this correlation is eased somewhat by the realization that the prophet has merely established a latent dimension of Gen. 25: 19-35: 22. For in so far as Jacob was himself the eponymous ancestor of Israel, his very life bore an immanent national aura and character. Indeed, it is this dimension of Jacob's existence which was utilized by Hosea and correlated with the life of the nation. Thus, in this second case as well, a correlation which seems to be marked initially by asymmetry serves in the end to elucidate and focus attention on a fundamental continuity between the original Pentateuchal 'type' and its prophetic reuse.

(*c*) Finally, with respect to the correlation established in Deut. 8: 3 between the manna and the words of divine revelation, the apparent initial discordance between a physical gift and revelatory words is resolved by Moses' pneumatic reinterpretation of the manna as a spiritual gift—'from the mouth of YHWH'—just like the Torah. In this way the paraenesis seeks to redirect the attention of its audience to a deeper continuity of divine sustenance than was immediately apparent, and to the manifold ways that sustenance may be manifested. For far from it being a natural bounty sent by a supernatural agency, Moses teaches the people that the manna is essentially a supernatural gift —a concretization of the gracious divine will, just like the tablets of the law. In this third case too, then, an apparent dissimilarity in the typological correlation is resolved, and a new aggadic or theological appreciation of the initial *traditum* is achieved.

3. In addition to lemmatic deductions, inferences, and correlations, another technique of inner-biblical aggadic exegesis is that of *interpolation and supplementation*. These two ways of introducing aggadic additions to an original *traditum* are complementary: the first inserts the *traditio into* the original *traditum*; the second puts the new *traditio after* the *traditum*, or in conjunction with a revised version of the entire *traditum*. As noted, the purpose of these types of addenda is generally to introduce new meanings, new values, or new coherence into the received tradition—though sometimes this is the unexpected result. Thus, the infusion of the ideal of obedience to the Torah into the context of military exhortation formulary transfigures these speeches and gives them a spiritual, 'Torahistic' quality (cf. Josh. 1: 6-9; 2 Kgs. 2: 2-4; 2 Chron. 15: 2-7). The frequent occurrence of the ideal of Torah observance in the Book of Chronicles which supplements the *traditum* received from Samuel-Kings is a comparable aggadic item. Indeed, in such instances the interpolations introduced serve a conscious aggadic intent and purpose. Quite the reverse is the situation in Gen. 9: 1-7. As noted earlier, this text contains a typological repetition of

Gen. 1: 26-30 as well as several ritual-legal appendages (vv. 4-6a) which follow the new permission to eat meat. However, with this ritual-legal interpolation, the original narrative consecution between the species of edibles which mankind rules and may eat, and the reference to mankind's creation in the divine image (vv. 2-3, 6b)—a consecution integrated, though in a different order, in Gen. 1: 26-30 as well—is radically truncated. The result is that the clause concerning mankind's creation in the divine image does not now explain mankind's dominion over all earthly creatures but provides a remarkable theological explanation of the special status of humans among the creatures of the earth. For while they may kill animals for food, their murder by animals or other persons is a crime which will be divinely requited.

The forms of aggadic supplementation are even more varied, and include a medley of strategic theological or axiological substitutions. We have already noted the infusion of 'Torahistic' values into the Book of Chronicles. Among other types where new information or perspectives are added, one may recall the supernatural explanation provided for 2 Sam. 15: 34 in 17: 14b, the moral explanation of David's failure to build the Temple in 1 Chron. 22: 8 and 28: 3, the exhortation to put one's religious trust in the prophets—alongside YHWH—in 2 Chron. 20: 20b, or the Chronicler's particular formulation of the Uzzah episode and his pietistic concern to delete any hint of a breach of levitical regulations in the transport of the Ark (1 Chron. 13: 7-14, 15: 2, 12-15). With respect to the latter text, moreover, it was pointed out that the Chronicler's revision of 2 Sam. 6: 3 omitted the vital verb נשא—even though he later repeatedly used it to explain the reason for the divine outburst and the proper procedure to be employed (cf. 1 Chron. 15: 2, 12-15)—and that that omission may have been deliberate, i.e., the Chronicler utilized a species of גְּזֵרָה שָׁוָה reasoning,[12] inferring the ritual impropriety involved in lay transport from the use of the verb נשא in 2 Sam. 6: 13 on the basis of its usage in such 'levitical' passages as Num. 7: 9. Realizing the hint of a cultic misdemeanor, he deleted this technical verb in 1 Chron. 13: 7 but cited Num. 7: 9 in 1 Chron. 15: 15, in connection with a depiction of the ritually correct practice.

4. Related to the foregoing instance of aggadic interpolations and supplementations in historiographical narratives is the exegetical technique of סמוכין. As shown earlier, 2 Chron. 12: 1-2 and 20: 34-7 juxtapose pericopae or sentential units not meaningfully related in the historical *traditum* and draw therefrom new conclusions regarding divine causality and the importance of repentance and obedience. Since the original *traditum* in each of these two cases was understandable and

---

[12] On the *gĕzērāh šāwāh* technique, see above, p. 249 n. 48.

coherent on its own terms – the minor obscurities being easily resolvable – the rereadings of the *traditio* are decidedly tendentious in intent and aggadic in nature. However, as pointed out, such aggadic tendentiousness need not imply that the Chronicler actually believed that he was radically departing from the implicit sense of the received traditions. Since in the second case, 2 Chron. 20: 34-7, he performed a minor transposition of the narrative elements (a type of סֵרוּס),[13] in addition to providing a theological commentary to the unit, it could rather be assumed that the Chronicler found himself faced with what appeared to be a somewhat defective text – partly from the viewpoint of its narrative coherence, but mostly with respect to theological aetiology and axiology – and revised it in accordance with his theological-exegetical suppositions and presuppositions. His primary exegetical task may thus have been to make the implicit more explicit. Similar motives may have affected his *traditio* in 2 Chron. 12: 1-2.

Rhetorical transformations and strategies

An overview of the reuses to which the traditions have been put in aggadic exegesis points to the remarkable fact that most instances are the result of a metaphrastic shift, a decisive movement from one genre or style to another in conjunction with the movement from one speaker or teacher to another. Rules and regulations formulated in a casuistic style by a legislator, for example, reappear as metaphors, similes, and descriptions (cf. Jer. 2: 3, 2: 26, 34, 5: 21-4); rules presented apodictically reappear with motivational exhortations (cf. Exod. 20: 5-7); liturgies recited solemnly by priests are caustically recited by prophets (Mal. 1: 9-2: 6); *theologoumena* disclosed by the deity become the basis of prayers of petition and praise (Mic. 7: 18-20; Pss. 103, 109); narratives recited anonymously in one place are recast as personified prophetic critiques or as oracles (Hos. 12; Isa. 19: 19-25); and so forth. What appeared, therefore, as an instruction or a ceremony to one generation is frequently decontextualized in aggadic *traditio* and presented to a later group in a very different form and for very different reasons.

Three types of transformation of the *traditum* are of particular

---

[13] In rabbinic usage, *sērûs* often involved a 'rearrangement' of letters or words, although the related technique *muqdām šehû' mě'ûḥar bā'inyān*, 'something which precedes which is placed later', listed as no. 31 in R. Eliezer's canon, already shows that rearrangements included transpositions of pericopae or smaller units. Cf. the expression *miqrā' měsôrās*, and the discussion in Bacher, *Terminologie*, i. 136, ii. 144. The term *sērûs* may derive from the Alexandrian interpretative method of *anastrophe*. See D. Daube, 'Alexandrian Methods of Interpretation and the Rabbis', *Festschrift H. Lewald* (Basel: Helsing and Lichtenhahn, 1953), 27-34; and cf. the comments of W. S. Towner, *The Rabbinic 'Enumeration of Scriptural Examples'* (Leiden: E. J. Brill, 1973), 49-50, 103-4.

rhetorical moment:

1. The first may be called the *spiritualization of content*. Within this category one can distinguish the following subtypes: (i) the application of a spiritual sense to legal rules or regulations—as in the case of Jer. 2: 3, which identifies the holy status of Israel with priestly sancta, or in the instance of the reinterpretation of remarriage in terms of a covenant renewal in Jer. 3: 1; (ii) the recontextualization of older formulae—as in the transformation of militaristic exhortation into encouragements of spiritual fortitude and obedience in Josh. 1: 6-9 or 2 Chron. 15: 2-7; (iii) the pneumatic revaluation of earlier content—as in the new understanding of the desert manna as deriving 'from the mouth of YHWH' like the commandments of the Torah; and (iv) the polemical or didactic purification of content—as in Deutero-Isaiah's demythologizing of the content of Gen. 1: 1-2: 4a, or in Trito-Isaiah's remarkable transvaluation of the meaning of fasting in Isa. 58: 1-10.

2. A second major category of literary transformation within the framework of the rhetoric of aggadic exegesis is the *nationalization of content*. Here at least two subtypes may be distinguished: (i) the use of one instance of legal-covenantal transgression as a synecdoche for covenant violations generally—as in Jer. 2: 26,34, which uses the figure of a thief caught *in flagrante* to exemplify Israel's covenantal deviance and YHWH's apprehension of the people 'in the act', or the reuse of the law of a wayward and rebellious son to typify national covenantal malfeasance generally in Jer. 5: 21-4; (ii) the rhetorical identification of the activities of the nation with the individual deeds of one person —as in the personification of the perfidy and mendacity of Israel and Judaea in terms of the wiles and ways of the patriarch Jacob, their namesake, in Hos. 12 and Jer. 9: 3-5.

3. A third type of transformation involves the *nomicization and ethicization of content*. Under this rubric several distinctions can be introduced: (i) the interpolation into a *traditum* of 'Torahistic' values, precepts, or regulations—as in Josh. 1: 6-9 and 1 Kgs. 2: 2-4, or frequently in the Book of Chronicles (e.g. 1 Chron. 15: 12-15 or 2 Chron. 12: 1); (ii) the reinterpretation of a *traditum* in terms of a certain moral standard—as in the explanation provided in 1 Chron. 22: 8 and 28: 3 for David's failure to build the Temple; and (iii) the concern to repress a violent or aggressive tradition in favour of a more ethical or noble version of it—as in the case of the aggadic treatment of Num. 25: 1-9 in Ps. 106: 27-30.[14]

In the preceding classification, the stress was placed on the trans-

---

[14] For nomicizing–ethicizing revisions in the LXX at 1 Kgs. 18: 45b, 20: 16, and 21: 27-9, see D. W. Gooding, 'Ahab According to the Septuagint', *ZAW* 76 (1964), 269-80.

formations of content characteristically involved in aggadic exegesis. These transformations, and the new genres and styles involved, are functionally interfused with the rhetorical strategies employed — deliberately or unconsciously. For one of the goals of rhetoric is to address a certain content to an audience (individual or collective) and attempt to transform their attitudes, knowledge, perception, or values.[15] Revision, reorientation, and reversal of the standpoint of the addressee are thus major preoccupations of the rhetor or writer who may use aggadic exegesis and embellishment as his tool; and irony, subversion, co-optation, selective emphasis, or didacticism (lapidary and indirect, or exhortatory and direct) are some of the other rhetorical devices used. Thus, a prophet may involve his addressee in a question-answer scenario in order to establish a certain objective logic of inference or possibility — only to redirect the topic to the subjective condition of the listeners in order to shock them into new realizations and attitudes (cf. Jer. 3: 1; Hag. 2: 11-14);[16] or a certain *obiter dictum* of the people may be similarly subverted in order to reorientate the addressees by strategic disorientation (cf. Isa. 58: 1-10; Ezek. 18: 2-4 and 33: 24-9). Similarly, prospective typologies invariably try to reorientate an addressee mired in inertia or despair towards new hope and possibilities. Hereby, the analogical correlations are rhetorically geared to shift the addressee's attention from the present to the past — and its paradigmatic events, biographies, and spatial topoi — for the sake of a new future and the requisite human actions which may be involved. Contrapuntal correlations (of polarity) are similarly strategic; and they too attempt to generate new attitudes and visions in their intended audience.

As noted, a major component of the rhetorical strategy employed in the foregoing examples was the direct involvement of the addressee. Indeed, through a series of strategic manoeuvres the rhetor invites or directs his audience to a revaluation of previously held views, or he invites or directs them to apprehend them in a new way. In this way, the addressee is rhetorically co-opted and his attitudes are disengaged and rechannelled. By a sometimes subtle and sometimes forceful conjunction between normative interpretations of laws and dicta and their subversion or reinterpretation, the intended audience is led to perceive a significant disjunction in its present reality; and by a confrontation with past prototypes or paradigms a given generation is encouraged to look towards the future for their reiteration or transformation. Indeed, such strategic balancing between audience expectation and surprise plays a vital role in many other species of

---

[15] Cf. Perelman and Olbrechts-Tyteca, *The New Rhetoric*, 27.

[16] Cf. the type of rhetorical procedure called 'deliberative' (Perelman and Olbrechts-Tyteca, ibid.), and its basis in Aristotelian categories.

aggadic exegesis. It is thus the unexpected and forceful conclusion that YHWH 'relents' over evil at the conclusion to Jonah's recital of the attribute formulary that gives the latter its rhetorical punch and swerves the reader towards a new apprehension of the teaching of the book. Similarly, it is the breadth of semantic assumptions normally linked to the priestly blessing that provides the rhetorical pivot for Malachi's thoroughgoing reversal of it; and it is the nationalistic associations intimately tied to the exodus event which Isaiah trades on when he reuses that language to generate—with surprise and irony—a more universal and generous attitude towards Egypt. Finally, it is Jehoshaphat's surprising addition of the exhortation to believe in the prophets, in his recitation of Isaiah's ancient words, that unsettles the listener and challenges set ideas and views.

These reflections on rhetorical strategy in inner-biblical aggadic exegesis would not be complete, however, if two further forms of instruction went unmentioned. The first may be termed lapidary, for whether or not a reader is aware that an older *traditum* has been interpolated or supplemented in a historiographical narrative, the latter simply teaches through its written content. Through it an addressee may be confronted with the importance of Torah or repentance or the divine law; or he may apprehend why David was forbidden to build the Temple and why the Lord chose Solomon; or he may learn the theological implications of the fact that man was created in the divine image. In none of these examples is there any subversion of previous attitudes or challenge to them. Quite different, however, are those instances where one explanation of a historical event is immediately replaced by another (cf. 1 Sam. 15: 34 and 17: 14b), or where the teachings of a text (Gen. 1: 1–2: 4a) are atomistically and polemically reinterpreted by a later teacher (Isa. 40: 17-18, 25-6, 28-31, 45: 7, 18-19). In such cases there is a direct engagement with the audience and an attempt to replace new values or apprehensions with older ones.

In sum, there is in aggadic exegesis an ongoing interchange between a hermeneutics of continuity and a hermeneutics of challenge and innovation. For if, on the one hand, the 'continuity' is the *traditum* which is relied upon directly or indirectly by the tradents, rhetors, and writers, the *traditio* is invariably a matter of 'challenge and innovation'—a challenge to each generation to confront its religious situation and mundane needs, to reform its values and heritage, and to renovate its ideals and history. Indeed, this very balance between the new and the old, and the concomitant use and revision of the cultural imagination and its attitudes, was, from its inception in ancient Israel, the lodestar of aggadic exegesis on its historical course.

C. Were the evidence of aggadic exegesis in the Hebrew Bible more sufficient, ramified, and self-conscious, as it is for example in classical Tannaitic and Amoraic midrash, it would be of decided interest to explore the various literary forms employed and their relationships to different concerns of exegesis and to different life-contexts. In short, it would be of interest to engage in a straightforward form-critical analysis of the data. But, as we have seen, the evidence is meagre, the genres are virtually identical with the genres of non-exegetical materials (e.g. sermons, rebukes, historical narratives, prayers, etc.), and the precise life-context is only rarely indicated in the documents—so that one must resort to inference and assumption based on what appears to be the situation addressed and on which historical period or milieu seems to underlie it. Nevertheless, despite these lacunae, the traditional categories of form criticism—form and context—may still provide a valuable analytical function for the historian of ancient Israelite literature and exegesis if employed more abstractly. And if there is some inevitable overlap in what follows with topics noted or alluded to in earlier discussions, the net value of a form-critical reclassification of the material is ensured by the sharper literary and cultural delineation of aggadic exegesis in ancient Israel which it affords.

1. A reclassification of the techniques and procedures of aggadic exegesis from the viewpoint of its *exegetical form* points to the following three major types and their subtypes:

(*a*) The first of these may be called *lemmatic form*, and involves the overt presentation of a *traditum* followed by its application. As we have seen earlier, this form may cite a Scriptural lemma or problem, as in Jer. 3: 1 and Hag. 2: 11-14, or it may cite a popular dictum, as in Ezek. 18: 2 and 33: 24, or a popular comment, as in Isa. 58: 3. In all these cases the *traditum* commented upon stands apart from the application which picks up a word or words from it. Thus, if there is not exactly what might be called an atomization of the contents of the *traditum* in the application-*traditio*, there is at least an atomizing selection of a key term (or terms) from the *traditum* and an exegetical recontextualization of it.

(*b*) A second type of exegetical form in aggadic interpretations is the *embedded form*, and involves the covert presentation of a *traditum* in connection with its new application-*traditio*. On the one hand, this form may involve an oral discourse, as in the prophetic speeches of Isa. 58: 1-10 and Mal. 1: 9-2: 6, where a radical or ironic reuse of terms from a normative *traditum*—the fasting regulations of the Day of Atonement, or the Priestly Blessing—supplants, inverts, and redirects that *traditum* in unexpected ways. By this means the older sense is the deep structural core of the surface discourse, so that once the latter is recognized as an exegetical *traditio* a vertical hermeneutical tension may be imaginatively recovered. The *traditum* is thus embedded within the surface *traditio* even as this latter is embedded within an oral discourse which utilizes it in order to make its rhetorical point. By contrast, the embedded form of exegesis may also occur in narrative discourse, as, for example, so frequently in the Book of Chronicles. In such cases the new aggadic *traditio* is interweaved alongside the received *traditum*, providing strategic aggadic ligatures, fillers, and supplements. Once the latter may be isolated from the *traditum*, whether through synoptic comparison with other texts or by formal analysis, the horizontal character of this type of embedded exegesis may be recovered and appreciated.

(c) The third type of exegetical form in aggadic interpretations in the Hebrew Bible may be termed *taxemic form*, and involves the creative combination or recombination of elements from the tradition. Several subtypes can be distinguished. (i) First, there is the embellished reuse of a *traditum*, usually in a new genre and with a different sequential pattern of its component parts. Typical of this type of taxemic exegesis are the reuses of the attribute formulary in Mic. 7: 18-20 and Pss. 103, 109. In these lexical cases the various key terms of the divine attributes comprise the lexical grid of the prayers. Related to the latter are those cases where the attribute formulary is apocopated, semantically adjusted, or given selective emphasis in order to sharpen a rhetorical or theological point (cf. Exod. 20: 5b-6; Deut. 7: 9-10; Jer. 32: 18-19; Jonah 4: 2). (ii) A second subtype involves an anthological reuse of components from the *traditum*, as particularly in 2 Chron. 15: 2-7, and also in Ps. 103. Basic here, of course, is the fact that the different units of tradition are substantive in nature and pick up a phrase from the *traditum*. Such creative anthologizing must therefore be clearly distinguished from cases where it is alleged that isolated words derive from specific Scriptural passages, but where they are actually free-floating components from the traditionary lexical stock—the thesaurus of tradition—and where, in any case, the particular terms in question serve no perceptible exegetical function in the new piece.[17] (iii) A final subtype of taxemic exegesis is the explicative reuse of components from the tradition. Here, too, there are different ways taxemes may be combined. In Deut. 4: 16-19, for example, the creation *traditum* from the Book of Genesis is joined to a sermon against idolatry (itself a paraenetic attempt to preclude false inferences from Exod. 19: 16-20 and 20: 18-21, and perhaps even an aggadic sermon stimulated by the סמוכך of Exod. 20: 18-21 + 22-3).[18] In Isa. 45: 18-19 the taxemic

---

[17] This critique applies—grosso modo—to the results of the so-called exegetical *procédé anthologique* of A. Robert and his followers. See above, pp. 286-7.

[18] It seems likely that Jeremiah's juxtaposition of his rhetorical question 'Is

sequence is derived from Gen. 1:1-2:4a. And of an entirely different sort is the linking of explicative superscriptions to various psalms, thus establishing explicit taxemic relationships between items in the historiographical tradition and prayers in the Psalter. Finally, one may point to passages with כִּי or לְמַעַן clauses, like Gen. 9:6a or Exod. 20:5-6b, 7b, 11, 12b, as instances where an older *traditum* takes on new meaning by the taxemic addition of motivational or explicative comments—though it must be noted that in Gen. 9:6b the כִּי clause is part of the *traditum*, whereas the clausal additions to the Decalogue are part of the didactic *traditio*.

2. It should be self-evident that the foregoing is not an exhaustive analysis of aggadic exegetical form in the Hebrew Bible. Nevertheless, it must be equally apparent that even if the exegetical techniques employed are naïve and not based on formal stylistic procedures or types, one can at least apprehend a *movement towards form*. This point gains in cultural-historical significance when we compare the above classification of inner-biblical exegetical forms with those found in early Jewish *aggadah*, and the relationship of these forms to the literary genres employed. When we do, the incipient character of the biblical evidence comes into even sharper focus, together with the fact that, with apparently naïve intuition, most of the imaginative literary possibilities of early and classical Jewish *aggadah* are anticipated by the biblical evidence. Of course, one could productively turn the issue around and note the strong internal continuities between inner-biblical aggadic exegesis and the later Jewish forms. But to approach the issue from this side would be merely to make the same point from a different angle, viz., that Jewish *aggadah* evolved in a marked way from native—if inchoate—cultural forms, and did not depend upon the classical Jewish heritage, and its milieu of Greek or Roman rhetoric, for its genesis.

Without, therefore, attempting to impose a genetic argument upon the data, or positing invariable and direct continuity between inner-biblical and Jewish *aggadah*, it is nevertheless of interest to observe how the exegetical forms and genres in ancient Israel parallel and 'anticipate' their more developed congeners in early Judaism. First to be noted, of course, is the phenomenon of lemmatic exegesis, one of the recurrent hallmarks of rabbinic sermons and expositions. This can be found in such great early collections of aggadic midrash as *Genesis Rabba, Leviticus Rabba* and *Sifre Deuteronomy*, for example, but also *in situ* in many aggadic expositions in the Babylonian Talmud, and in the valedictory citations which at times conclude mishnaic tractates. Moreover,

this Temple a cave of *pārişîm*-trespassers?' (Jer. 7:11) to his citation of the Decalogue (v. 9) is a *sĕmûkîn* derived from the citation of the Decalogue in Hos. 4:2a followed by the verb *pārāşû* in v. 2bα.

among the early evidence of lemmatic expositions one may pay special attention to the so-called *Yelammedenu-Midrashim*, because of the incipit which inaugurates a legal question and its aggadic exposition.[19] It is not at all necessary to see any genetic relationship between these aggadic teachings, Jer. 3:1, and Hag. 2:11-14 in order to be struck by the way in which, from earliest times, legal and ritual questions could serve as the rhetorical basis for aggadic exegeses which involved the addressees in the implications of certain technical details, and then abruptly transformed the exposition and redirected it to new spiritual or moral ends.

Different in exegetical form from the latter cases are embedded interpretations. Here again there are notable parallels between inner-biblical and early Jewish aggadic exegesis, as where the exodus topos serves as the deep structural matrix for a sermonic exposition in the *Wisdom of Solomon*,[20] or where older narrative sequences and traditions are expanded and transformed by aggadic additions, as in the *Book of Jubilees*. For a more creative variety of this phenomenon, where the relationship between historical kernel and aggadic *novum* is reversed in favour of the latter, mention must be made of Chapter 26 of the aggadic collection known as *Pesiqta Rabbati*, wherein the prophet Jeremiah describes and evaluates the Fall of Jerusalem.[21] In the latter works, moreover, as in the comparable biblical historiography (or historiographical psalms), later values and concerns are anachronistically inserted in order to update and normalize the great historical past.

Finally, some mention must be made of what we have here called taxemic exegesis, the creative combination and recombination of elements from the tradition. Indeed, any random glance at a classical aggadic composition is sufficient to convince one that herein lies one of the fundamental expressions of the classical midrashic imagination. Whether one looks to the great proems to rabbinic homilies, or to the homilies themselves, the associative linking of Scriptural units generates meaning, controls rhetoric, and produces theology and instruction.

[19] Thus, many *sĕdārîm* of the so-called *Tanhuma Yelammedenu* collection begin with the distinctive halakhic proem, starting *yĕlammĕdēnû rabbēnû* 'May our master teach us . . .'. For a brief characterization and outline of critical issues, see *Encyclopedia Judaica* xv. 794 f.

[20] See E. Stein, 'Ein jüdisch-hellenistisher Midrasch über den Auszug aus Ägypten', *MGWJ* 78 (1934), 558-75; R. Siebeneck, 'The Midrash of Wisdom 10-19', *CBQ* 22 (1960), 176-82; and A. Wright, 'The Structure of Wisdom 11-19', ibid. 27 (1965), 28-34.

[21] See L. Prijs, *Die Jeremia Homilie, Pesiqta Rabbati Kap. 26* (Studia Delitz-schiana, 10; Stuttgart: W. Kohlhammer, 1966), and the recent discussion by J. Heinemann, 'A Homily on Jeremiah and the Fall of Jerusalem', in *The Biblical Mosaic*, edd. R. Polzin and E. Rothman (Philadelphia: Fortress Press, 1982), 27-41.

The prophetic sermon in 2 Chron. 15: 2-7 preserves an early and valuable foreshadowing of this phenomenon.

In this development from the relatively naïve biblical phenomena to the more sophisticated and systematic rabbinic data, and from the *ad hoc* inspiration of prophets and lucubrations of historians to the studied practice of the sages and their disciples, the mediating position −at least formally−of the expositions in the Qumran scrolls must not be overlooked. In these documents one can isolate a wealth of aggadic exegeses, including lemmatic exegetical sermons or instructions,[22] historiographical narratives with embedded and lemmatic embellishments,[23] and different examples of taxemic exegesis.[24] From their relative lack of clear technique and form, and the chance collection of examples preserved, they bear strong resemblance to the biblical data which we have attempted to analyse. On one point, however, these Qumran scrolls strike a forceful pose away from their biblical patrimony and towards the rabbinic world, and that is in the notable variety and recurrence of citation formulary linking their aggadic exegesis with passages from the 'Torah of Moses'.[25] Clearly, where a *traditum* was for a biblical exegete the traditionary basis of his aggadic *traditio*, for a later interpreter like the Teacher of Righteousness this *traditum* was Scripture−and that is a shift of major significance.

3. In addition to the foregoing reclassification of aggadic exegesis from the perspective of exegetical form, attention must be paid to its complementary form-critical feature, *exegetical context*−that is, the particular setting or matrix in which inner-biblical *aggadah* may be located. Analysis of the preserved data suggests three major 'contexts':

(*a*) The first of these is the *socio-historical*, which indicates the real life-setting of the aggadic discourse at a particular time and place.[26] This setting is, of course, basic to all exegesis which is historically conditioned. But as our received biblical sources do not always indicate the precise occasion involved, it is necessary to infer this from the content. For example, from Jer. 2: 26, 34, 3: 1, and 5: 21-4, one can infer a general occasion of covenantal malfeasance, but hardly much more concerning when such malfeasance took place or by what groups. Similarly, the rebuke of laymen and priests in Hag. 2: 11-14 and Mal.

---

[22] e.g. 1Q *S.* ii. 2-9.

[23] e.g. CDC iv. 3 f., 13-v. 1.

[24] e.g. 4Q pIsa.*c* i. 7-14, ii. 3-19; 4Q *Flor*; 4Q Testim.; 4Q Tanḥumim i. 1-11.

[25] For a classification, see J. Fitzmyer, 'The Use of Explicit Old Testament Quotations in Qumran Literature and in the New Testament', *NTS* 7 (1960-1), 297-33.

[26] This, of course, correponds to Bitzer's historical situation of rhetorical discourse; cf. n. 1 above.

1: 9–2: 6 indicates clear and strong concerns with cultic purity in the post-exilic period (a matter corroborated by other contemporary data), but many obscurities remain for a thorough historical understanding. And finally, if it is clear that Deutero-Isaiah's typological prophecies and exhortations are rooted in post-exilic realities, the precise conditioning factors which elicited these outbursts of hope and encouragement —the invasion and conquest of Babylon by Cyrus, or Cyrus's decree, or later developments under Darius—often remain obscure.

(b) These various considerations serve to underscore the fact that it is often analytically more fruitful to focus on the *textual-narrative context*. In the framework of this, it is the literary setting of the aggadic exegesis *as it now stands* that must be considered, as well as the socio-historical settings which are ascribed to the text by historical notices and general context. Thus, whatever the historical background of Gen. 9: 1-7, Deut. 4: 16-19, 7: 9-10, and 8: 1-18, or the speeches of David and Solomon or assorted prophets in the Book of Chronicles, or the theological and legal interpolations and explanations in sundry historiographical contexts—all these must be approached as narrative events, recording their own historical setting and linked to a received literary milieu. Considerations of a literary-narrative context are also concerned with how a type of specific aggadic exegesis functions within a specific argument, with how it functions as a component of a wider, unified argument, and with how it relates to other related pericopae or oracles (for example, the catena of speeches in Deuteronomy or Chronicles, the various typologies in Deutero-Isaiah, the several qualifications of Gen. 1: 1-2: 4a in Isa. 40 and 45, and the סמוכין in the Psalter and the Book of Chronicles). By this token, the very fictive-narrative context of the Book of Jonah must provide the dominant setting for understanding and evaluating the aggadic transformation of the attribute formulary therein.

(c) Finally, we come to the third of the major contexts of inner-biblical aggadic exegesis, that of its *mental matrix*. Through this rubric a number of significant considerations may be broached and accounted for. First among these is the fact that aggadic exegesis involves a mode of perception of the historical *traditum*—whether this means a revisioning (literally) of the way discrete texts do or may hang together, or the metaphorical or spiritual possibilities of certain literal laws, or how axiological or theological lacunae in received documents may be supplemented, or how *theologoumena* may be updated or personalized, or how events or figures from the past may serve as models or paradigms for the present and future. In some of these cases the revisioning of the given *traditum* may involve revisionistic concerns (for example, by restoring allegiance to the covenant, or by emphasizing covenantal values); in other instances they may be purely visionary (as in the typological prophecies and exhortations or in the polar correlations of the evanescent past versus the imminent new age); and in still other circumstances the aggadic exegeses are downright revisionary and radical (as in the rejection of deferred punishment in Deut. 7: 9-10 or in Trito-Isaiah's analysis of the 'true' meaning of fasting).

Related to the foregoing is the fact that aggadic exegesis presupposes for its practitioners some consciousness of being heirs to a distinct historical *traditum*. Thus, the aggadic exegete presumably knows himself to be a latecomer on the stage of Israelite culture — for he is the recipient of tradition before he is the maker or transmitter of it. Being such a latecomer means, first of all, that one's creative freedom is conditioned, since it is a freedom to live within the ideologies of the theological *traditum* and its literary fund, to shape it and to redirect it, to utilize it and to grow with it. From this point, confirmed by the biblical evidence, it is justified to observe that the purveyors and creators of aggadic exegesis appear to live with 'texts-in-the-mind' — that is, with texts (or traditions) which provide the imaginative matrix for evaluating the present, for conceiving of the future, for organizing reality (the inchoate, the negative, the possible), and even for providing the shared symbols and language of communication. With aggadic *traditio* the world of Israelite culture is thus one which talks and thinks, which imagines and reflects, and which builds and rejects, *through* the traditions. Recalling the classic observation of T. S. Eliot, that every significant addition to a literary corpus repositions all the components of that corpus,[27] we may add that each event of aggadic *traditio* in ancient Israel simultaneously serves to reconstellate a given *traditum* in relationship to those in the culture who perform or apprehend the exegesis, and to reorder the hierarchy of teachings within the cultural palimpsest thus formed — so that the occurrence of a teaching in time does not invariably correspond to its relative significance.

D. The preceding consideration of the form-critical dynamics of *traditum* and *traditio* — in life-settings, literary contexts, and the mind of the interpreter — brings us to a final matter, the roles and expressions of authority, revelation, and tradition in inner-biblical aggadic exegesis. Here special note may be taken of the continuities and discontinuities that exist between the voice of an original *traditum* and the ongoing voice(s) of its *traditio*. Of prime significance; of course, is the *divine voice* which both initiates a tradition and reuses it for one aggadic purpose or another. Thus, for example, the attribute formulary in Exod. 34: 6-7 is a divine self-revelation, and its motivational recitation

---

[27] 'Tradition and the Individual Talent', *Selected Essays* (new edn.; New York: Harcourt, Brace, and Co., 1950), 5.

in the Decalogue is also presented as a divine communication. Similarly, the rules of the legal corpora are presented as the teachings of the divine legislator, and just these rules are reused by various prophets in divine communications of aggadic proportions (cf. Jer. 2: 26, 34, 3: 1, 5: 21-4). In other instances, where the *traditum* is derived from a human exhortation (Deut. 31: 7-8), a popular adage (Ezek. 18: 2), or an omniscient human narrator (Gen. 1: 1-2: 4a), the *traditio* may still be presented as a divine revelation (see Josh. 1: 2-9, Ezek. 18: 3-4, Isa. 40: 18-19, 25, 28-9, 31, 45: 7, 18-19). Such various divine reuses of inherited traditions thus vigorously underscore an ongoing divine involvement in the life of ancient Israel, authorize (literally and figuratively) the new teachings—whether these spiritualize, polemicize, ethicize, or simply interpret the *traditum* involved—and, finally, reveal new semantic and theological levels of meaning in the old revelations.

Of a distinct type are those instances of aggadic exegesis where the *Mosaic voice* is of primary importance in the *traditio*. In fact, this voice —pseudepigraphic in the Book of Deuteronomy—is a composite of many teaching voices, deriving from the many teachers of the deuteronomic tradition. Thus, Deut. 7: 9-10 purports to cite and represent the divinely revealed attribute formulary, but is rather a tendentious sermon by 'Moses' which is concerned to nullify the divine teachings of deferred punishment. Of a less radical character is Deut. 4: 16-19 and 8: 3—the latter being part of a 'Mosaic' sermon utilizing the narrative tradition of Exod. 16, the former a speech against idolatry which is, most likely, a post-exilic composition incorporating the creation tradition from the Book of Genesis for new aggadic ends. In each of these three cases, the authority of the new teaching is derived from the fact that it reports or cites an authoritative text, tradition, or speech from the past. Moses' traditional authority as guardian and teacher of the traditions is thus capitalized upon. The fact that these instances of *traditio* are from his mouth—together with the significant fact that he purports to report divine words from the past which he himself had mediated—helps, furthermore, to cast a strong authoritative aura over his 'deuteronomic' words, an aura which a pseudepigraphic author could boldly and productively utilize.[28]

The next two categories display a more observable shift—formally speaking—to a human voice in the aggadic *traditio*. In the first of these,

[28] This intrusion of reported speech with authorial retort and commentary has the strategic effect of obliterating the boundaries between the reported words of YHWH and the reporting words of Moses. As a formal literary issue, see V. N. Vološinov, 'Reported Speech', in *Readings in Russian Poetics*, edd. L. Metejka and K. Pomorska (Michigan Slavic Contributions, 8; Ann Abor, 1978), 155. R. Polzin has effectively exploited this element in his *Moses and the Deuteronomist* (New York: Seabury, 1980), 43-69.

there is found an *uninspired prophetic or lay voice*. Thus, for example, the radical revision of the exodus *traditum* in Isa. 19:19-25 is without any formal divine authority, and Micah's aggadic utilization of the attribute formulary in 7:18-20 also appears as a human construction (cf. Pss. 103, 109). This shift to a human reportage of a divine speech — with aggadic transformations — is much more marked in David's and Solomon's accounts of the divine vision to Nathan in 1 Chron. 22:2-10, 28:3-10, where these two kings present similar explanations of David's failure to build the Temple of Jerusalem. Similarly, Jehoshaphat's response to an inspired oracle is a recitation of the divinely inspired words of Isaiah without ever reporting them as such (2 Chron. 20:20b). Presumably, like the attribute formulary, the prophet's words had simply become part of the tradition — established with authority — and available for free aggadic reuse.[29] Isaiah's utilization of the exodus traditions would presumably also fall into this category. Nevertheless, one cannot fail to observe that with these human dicta dimensions of the old words and acts of YHWH are newly 'revealed'. Human exegesis may thus faithfully plumb the depths of revelations and prolong their divine import in new and often revolutionary ways.

Quite different is the *narrative voice* of the historiographer. In these cases the authority for the *traditio* is indistinguishable formally from the authority of a historical *traditum*. For whether the aggadic tradition involved is a supplement, an interpolation, or an aggadic rewriting *in toto*, there is no shift of voice: the narrative constitutes a continuous human, though *impersonal*, teaching.[30] Thus, it is the human narrator who utilizes Gen. 3:17-19 in 5:29, and the latter in 6:6, or who reinterprets 2 Sam. 15:34 in 17:14b, or who reworks the episodes of Uzzah, Asa, or Jehoshaphat from Samuel-Kings in the Book of Chronicles. Indeed, as we emphasized earlier, one upshot of this particular historiographical feature is that every version of the traditions presents itself as the *traditum* — even when it is actually a revision of an earlier *traditum*.

And yet, having underscored with all due force the non-revelatory character of exegetical *aggadah* within biblical narrative historiography, as well as the complete absence of rubrics of divine authority from such texts (the Chronicler's pseudepigraphic prophetic speeches being, of course, an exception), it may nevertheless be contended that this

---

[29] Cf. the observation of G. von Rad, 'The Levitical Sermon in *I* and *II Chronicles*', in *The Problem of the Hexateuch and Other Essays* (New York: McGraw-Hill, 1966), 279, that in his sermonizing the Chronicler 'falls back on the old established stock of written material'.

[30] Cf. the observations of Vološinov, loc. cit. 154, 157, on the relationship between the depersonalization of reported speech and the authoritarian dogmatism of the discourse.

material *does* have a revelatory 'intention'. That is to say, while the aggadic supplements and revisions in the historiographical *aggadah* are not revelations in any traditional sense, they do disclose faithful attempts to discern the divine revelations *within* historical events and to teach this to new generations. The notion of revelatory 'intention' must thus be understood in two basically complementary senses—as the divine intention and activity within the historical process (divine revelation through historical acts), and as the human intention to perceive and teach that divine involvement (the human communication of such divine non-verbal revelations). Indeed, it is through the latter processes that historiography 'reveals' the divine revelations of past history, and thus becomes a rhetorical mode for that revelation.

To bring these reflections to sharper focus a brief side-glance at the work of von Rad will prove instructive. Indeed, in reflecting upon the formation of the Hexateuch and the Genesis traditions in particular, von Rad suggested that the latter are the product of an extensive 'linear historical span' during which the materials were formed, fused, and arranged. As part of this process, and basic to it, he further observed that the various tradition-complexes took shape under the growing impact (on the arrangers) of the 'kerygmatic intention' of the material —that is, the redactors' own perception of the divine plan (intention) for history and their concern to communicate it.[31] Accordingly, even where the old narrative complexes do not present direct revelations through oracles or other interventions, a more indirect revelatory character may be attributed to them, in so far as they reveal—through the vision of the historian-compiler-theologian—the divine intentions for and works within history.

Returning to the historiographical narratives, it may consequently be said that they reflect different perceptions of how the divine is revealed in history. Thus, though the Book of Kings does not purport to be a revelation *per se*, it *does* have a revelatory intention in so far as it reveals divine revelations through the historical process. Even later historiography, like the Book of Chronicles, takes this *traditum* and, under the impress of new events, values, and interests, perceives in the (actual or imagined) formulations and lacunae of this *traditum* traces of the divine intention for Israelite history. The aggadic exegesis of this historiography thus consists in various attempts to explain YHWH's workings in history (for example, that YHWH is attentive to repentance and Torah observance, that ritual and moral faults do not go unpunished, and that divine providence is continuous and gracious). By properly gauging divine activity in history, and by showing (via aggadic revisions) the 'true' nature of divine–human interactions, aggadic historiography is

---

[31] See his essay 'The Form-Critical Problem of the Hexateuch', op cit. 63–73.

not only a mode which reveals how and where history is a non-verbal revelation of divinity (guided by the principles of the verbal revelation at Sinai), it is also revelatory in a more 'prophetic' sense in that it counsels covenantal behaviour in the light of the past. In an age, therefore, which begins to show the abatement of the forms and concerns of pre-exilic classical prophecy, the historiography of the Book of Chronicles, through pseudepigraphic prophetic speeches and aggadic revisions, donned the mantle of prophecy and instructed a new generation.

The fact that a teacher of *traditio* is always in a strategic and privileged position in relationship to his audience and the *traditum* itself may serve to underscore the salience—even predominance—of instruction as *the* literary trope of aggadic exegesis. Recurrently, the divine voice teaches the *traditum* through a *traditio* of it; so do Moses, laymen, or uninspired prophetic types; and, of course, so do the ancient historiographers. Indeed, one may even say that part of the rhetorical force of the citations of the attribute formulary in Mic. 7: 18-20 or Pss. 103, 109 is that they purport to instruct the divinity regarding a particular temporal situation by obliquely reminding him of his own nature. Such a mode of strategic instruction is most noticeable, it will be recalled, in Isa. 51: 9-11, where the prophet Deutero-Isaiah first refers to the creation and then the exodus—two archetypal salvific acts, in primordial and historical time—before turning to the subject of his immediate concern, an appeal for salvation from the Babylonian exile. This typology thus includes an 'instructive' retrospective of former *magnalia dei*.

Furthermore, the position of the teacher in aggadic exegesis is not solely privileged with respect to the sources of the tradition, but equally so with respect to their modes of presentation. The teacher selects and arranges, modifies and adapts, connects and separates, even transfigures and contradicts the ancient *traditum*. The 'instructing' character of such *aggadah* may thus move from attempts to restore allegiance to the tradition—to motivate compliance, to jar complacency and disloyalty, even to admonish and exhort—towards the goal of basic instruction. It may utilize pieces of the tradition, through the short or moderately long speeches of prophets, or it may attempt to communicate—as do the historiographers—the basic version of the traditions. The figure of Moses is thus pivotal in any reflection on the trope of instruction in aggadic exegesis. This is so not merely because he revises and exhorts and reports traditions in the Book of Deuteronomy, and not solely because he is the paradigmatic type of all prophets, whose instructing words are continued through the mouth of many others. Moses is markedly pivotal because, through the very shape and scope of the Book of Deuteronomy, we are reminded that the taxemic and strategic reuses of the traditions are not restricted to short paraenetic remarks about them, but extend to their very arrangement and presentation. In this respect, the Book of Moses, the Book of Deuteronomy, is paradigmatic as well. For—historical and literary-critical matters aside—the very fact that the traditions are represented on the Plains of Moab to the post-exodus generation is emblematic of the fundamental trope of instruction basic to aggadic exegesis—that the traditions have to be retaught and revised in each generation. Indeed, since enough has been said in previous chapters about the scribal, legal, and aggadic revisions of this book as to leave its exegetical character beyond doubt, it will suffice here to emphasize that the new instruction in Deuteronomy is not simply a *traditio*—if that is restricted to mean its unvaried transmission—but *the traditum* for the receptors. It is *the* Torah, which, for Deut. 1:5 as for Ps. 78:5 (in a historiographical psalm), means *the entirety of the traditions*—the historical, the hortatory, and the legal.[32]

The dominant trope of instruction in aggadic exegesis thus suggests that every teaching which somehow transforms the received traditions in the process of their representation has its place within the immense structure of inner-biblical *aggadah*, a structure which includes the paraenetic-revisionary sermons of 'Moses', the teachings of the desert and Sinaitic traditions in the Book of Deuteronomy, and the revisionary or supplemental teachings embedded in the conquest and post-conquest historiographies, particularly the Book of Chronicles. Moreover, if we are guided by the very anthological character of the received Hebrew Bible—which includes the Book of Deuteronomy alongside Exodus-Numbers, despite notable differences, and which preserves the Book of Chronicles in the same corpus as Samuel-Kings—one may furthermore observe that the very fact of such an ensemble of traditions is aggadically instructive. For it requires one to recognize, with the final tradent-teachers, that the Hebrew Bible is a variety of teachings and responses which each generation has added to its *traditum*, and that each successive layering of *traditio* is, inevitably, a reordering of the relative authority of the received traditions. In this sense, the received cánon of Scripture, as a form of instruction, is quintessentially an aggadic trope.

---

[32] On the idea of tradition in Ps. 78:5, see Westermann, 'Vergegenwärtigung', 328.

PART FOUR

MANTOLOGICAL EXEGESIS

15. Introduction. The Shape and Nature of Mantological Material as Factors for Exegesis

A FINAL major category to which ancient Israelite scholars and tradents devoted a considerable amount of exegetical energy may be broadly termed mantology, by which is meant the study of material which is ominous or oracular in scope and content. Thus, though we have had the occasion to indicate the scribal elucidation of various prophetic oracles (i.e. their lexical, semantic, and referential clarification) or their aggadic transformations (by simile, metaphor, typology, and ironic reversal), there has not been any discussion of these oracles as a subject of exegesis in their own right, nor any consideration of the exegesis of dreams, visions, and omens, the other genres of mantological exegesis. This substantive lacuna must now be filled, together with an estimation and analysis of the various techniques, styles, and cultural or theological implications involved.

For introductory purposes and preliminary consideration, the various mantological genres may be subdivided into two basic types: dreams, visions, and omens – visual phenomena – on the one hand; and oracles – auditory phenomena – on the other. A further phenomenological assessment of them will serve to indicate the correlations between each type and its characteristic modes of exegesis, and to bring these correlations into sharpest relief. Thus, with respect to dreams, visions, and omens, it may be observed that we are dealing with an inherently covert mantological type. For whether the images presented to view occur internally, as in dreams, or in external hallucinations or observations, as in visions and omens, they are esoteric and require decoding. In brief, the representational status of what is 'seen' must be clarified. In some instances, as we shall see, the image (of a dream or omen) is interpreted by a wise man (though often with divine inspiration ascribed)[1] after the initial recipient of the image is perplexed in its interpretation; while in other circumstances the image (of a vision) is divinely interpreted – directly or through a mediator figure – after the initial recipient is unable to decode the figures or words. Basic to all this, therefore, is the fact that the hermeneutical role of the interpreter

---

[1] Cf. Gen. 41: 25, 32-3; Dan. 2: 28, 4: 5-6, 5: 11-12, 14.

is to *open* the text to comprehension, to enlighten what is dark and obscure. Accordingly, whether the interpreter is a human oneiromancer, like Joseph or Daniel, or a divine voice, as occurs in the visions of Amos or Zechariah, the concern is to provide a meaningful correlation between what is seen in the present and unseen in the future – the obscurity of the images being, therefore, an objective correlative for the difficulty of perceiving the shape and meaning of future events. And since, moreover, the interpreter is requested – by a dreamer or those befuddled by 'ominous' configurations – to perform an interpretation, or the divine being directly provides a solution to a vision presented to the visionary, the *traditum* – the deposit of images awaiting explication – and its interpretation appear together. Indeed, characteristic of this mantic type is the fact that the lemmata and their solutions form one stylistic ensemble. There is, therefore, no *traditio* to speak of, if that means the reinterpretation of the lemmata at another point in time; there is only the careful transmission of the *traditum* with its interpretations.

At this point, we may profitably contrast the foregoing with a parallel phenomenological characterization of prophetic oracles. Of most immediate comparative consequence is the fact that the latter are of an inherently overt type – presented by a divinely inspired person to challenge, warn, or exhort an audience. Indeed, precisely because the content of the oracles is exoteric in nature, the essential hermeneutical issue for their exegesis does not arise on the level of manifest content *even where the precise occasion for the actualization of the forecast is unstated or obscure*. Thus, the prophetic spokesman of divine words may present an embellished version of an oracle known from another context, or even be at pains to specify the reference to his remarks; but he does not, in this, function as an interpreter of a *traditum* (those few instances where the embellishments or specifications belong to a later exegetical *traditio* are another matter, of course). The essential hermeneutical issue rather arises for this *traditum* when later prophets regard its manifest content as having failed, and so as being in need of revision; or as having referred all along to the period in which they now flourish. In such circumstances, the latter-day prophet presents an exegetical *traditio* of an older oracular *traditum*. Thus, only in so far as key elements from that *traditum* are referred to, in the course of its application to contemporary events, may one say that the *traditum* and its exegetical *traditio* occur together – though, it is essential to emphasize, *not* necessarily as a set stylistic form of lemma-plus-reinterpretation. Fundamentally, then, the *traditum* of an oracle is prospective and not in need of immediate exegesis – *contra* the prospective imagery of dreams, visions, and omens – whereas its exegetical *traditio* is a later, retrospective phenomenon. This is the case, moreover, even in those instances where an oracular content is transmuted into a symbolic omen, or where later tradents transmute non-oracles into oracles, and vice versa.

These preliminary phenomenological contrasts will be fully substantiated in the ensuing discussions. For the present, they may usefully be sharpened further. Taken together, then, it may be observed that both types arise from cognitive dissonance, with breakdowns or conflicts of meaning or sense. In the first case, that of dreams, visions, and oracles, the cognitive crisis arises immediately, on the level of manifest content, in so far as the envisaged words or images appear as opaque symbols to be decoded. In the second case, that of oracles, the cognitive crisis does not characteristically arise on the level of plain sense; for, as indicated, the words and images are not assumed to be symbols but semantically self-evident content. Certainly, as we shall demonstrate, the original spokesmen (or later tradents) were very much concerned to make sure that their oracles were understandable, and that their various references were clearly identifiable. But this is not the characteristic element of the mantological exegesis of oracles *per se*. For the latter, the cognitive crises arises when valued oracles have not been actualized, when their manifest meaning is cast in doubt, or when events seem to refute them.[2] Paradoxically, then, the hermeneutical problem *becomes* a problem of their manifest content—though now at the level of truth. Thus, the real cognitive crises for oracular exegesis is disclosed as theological in nature, and the abiding and underlying critical question is: Will the divine word, on which so much is based, be fulfilled? For this reason, the essential hermeneutical role of oracular exegesis is twofold: to reopen or prolong confidence in an oracle's content; and, more importantly, to establish its *closure*, i.e., to show how the oracle has been, or will soon be, actualized.

The permutations of the latter issues will be taken up below, for they bear on the very core of oracular exegesis and its particular forms of rationality. For the present, however, and as an initial task, we must return to the mantological exegesis of dreams, visions, and omens, and do so for three essential reasons: first, the occasions which give rise to such exegesis are textually noted and analytically straightforward (these being the perplexity of individuals in decoding the symbolism of received images); second, the methodological procedures involved in their investigation are directly apprehensible and analytically straightforward (since the content to be interpreted is given, and given conjointly

[2] Most recently, R. Carroll, *When Prophecy Failed* (New York: Seabury, 1979), has also observed the phenomenon of cognitive dissonance and related it to biblical prophecy. He provides a succinct summary of the psychological literature on pp. 86–110, and weighs its value for prophetic traditions, pp. 111–28. His examples should be consulted, though there is little overlap with our ensuing discussion.

with interpretations); and finally, the techniques of such interpretation
are overt and stable (in all three genres, in both form and language).
By contrast, investigation of the exegesis of oracles will prove far more
problematical on all counts.[3]

[3] The visions of Ezekiel require special comment; for, unlike other biblical
visions whose explication is part of its primary form, Ezekiel's visions are marked
by clarifications and cross-references which appear to have been added to the
traditum–whether by prophetic tradents or by the prophet himself. The reason
for the special character of these vision-reports lies in the fact that the event
preserved in Ezek. 1 was not originally a literary composition meant for publication, but was a private religious experience whose 'meaning' lay in the overwhelm-
ing manifestation of the divine majesty and in the message which it introduced–
not in an elucidation of the envisaged details. Only later, when Ezek. 1 served as a
public *traditum* that authenticated the prophet's dire predictions (and commission), and was circulated in prophetic schools in other times and places (where it
was studied first as the master's experience and, relatedly and soon independently,
as a disclosure of divine mysteries), was the meaning of the content a primary con-
* cern. Similar considerations obtain, *mutatis mutandis*, for the vision in Ezek. 10.
There are strong internal indications of an exegetical *traditio* within Ezek. 1.
Thus, *mittôk hā'ēš* in 1: 4 appears to be a gloss explaining the preceding *ûmittôkāh*,
after which (v. 5a) the description resumes following a repetition of the explicated
term (in the *Wiederaufnahme* fashion, on which cf. p. 85 above). Similarly, it
seems that *haḥayyôt* in 1: 13b is linked to *wĕhaḥayyôt* in v. 14a following a paraphrastic elaboration of the 'fire'. The copula was presumably added in v. 14a in
order to resolve the syntactical confusion produced when the resumptive technique
was no longer understood and the word *haḥayyôt* there was read a second time
(rather than simply serving as a dittograph marking the closure of the gloss). As
regards Ezek. 10, the exegetical issue is more complicated and goes beyond the
mere regularization of grammatical problems in Ezek. 1 (cf. Zimmerli, *Ezechiel*,
I, 28 f., 239); for whether or not one accepts the entire argument of D. J. Halperin
(in 'The Exegetical Character of Ezek. x 9–17', *VT* 26 (1976), 129–41), who
seeks to demonstrate a parallel structure between 1: 15–18 and 10: 9–12, 16–17
with paraphrastic additions in the latter (including an 'angelological' conception
of the 'wheels'), there is little doubt that 10: 13, 15 contain intrusive clarifications
and cross-references (note the deictic *hî'* in v. 15; cf. v. 20) with Ezek. 1. The self-
referential aspect of these comments amid the descriptions suggests that here, at
least, the prophet has annotated his experience as he reports or transcribes it. By
the same token, the scholarly exegeses in 10: 9–12, 16–17 need not inauthenticate
the event as a whole (even allowing for the 'influence' of Ezek. 1 upon it), even as
they strongly suggest that such 'commentary' has its origin in prophetical-mystical
conventicles of the late biblical period.

16. The Mantological Exegesis of Dreams, Visions, and Omens

A. THE TYPES AND THEIR TERMS

A REMARKABLY consistent and common set of structural and terminological components are found with the interpretation of dreams, visions, and (visualized) omens.[1] Most salient is the recurrent citation and atomization of the mantological content in the course of its decoding-explication. There is thus, characteristically, first a presentation of the entire content, and then a selected repetition of its lemmata with interpretation. In Gen. 40, for example, the entire dreams of the butler and baker are first reported to Joseph, whereupon their pertinent subunits are repeated together with their interpretation (cf. vv. 10-11, 12-13; v. 17 and vv. 18-19).[2] Similarly, after the presentation of Pharaoh's dream-work in Gen. 41, the content is atomistically cited and explained in vv. 26-7. The hermeneutical form is characteristically: 'the x [the lemma cited] is/are (הוא/הם) y.' Corresponding structural features appear in the interpretations of the dreams of Nebuchadnezzar in Dan. 2 and 4. In the latter cases, the lemmata cited from the dream-report are introduced by such phrases as ודי חזיתה 'and whereas you saw' (2: 41, 43; cf. 2: 45, 4: 17, 20) and ודי אמרו 'and whereas they commanded' (4: 23).

In Dan. 7 the oneiromancer Daniel himself has a dream, which is first reported and subsequently interpreted by a divine being (vv. 2-14 + 17-27). Once again the successive atomizing citations of the dream-content are introduced by various distinctive phrases and particles, like ועל, אלין, and ו. However, what deserves particular note in this dream report, and strongly emphasizes its ominous nature, is the fact that the dream-report is based on a *written* text: באדין חלמא כתב 'then he wrote the dream' (v. 1). Indeed, the written nature of this dream links it to Dan. 5 (also purportedly from the reign of Belshazzar), which is a report and interpretation of an omen inscribed (די רשים) on a wall

---

[1] Cf. my earlier comparative discussion in 'The Qumran Pesher', 105-10.

[2] When the baker says that Joseph had *ṭôb pātār*, it means that he had interpreted the dream 'favourably'. Compare the Akkadian expression *šunāte damqāte* 'favourable dreams'; and see further A. L. Oppenheim, *The Interpretation of Dreams in the Ancient Near East* (*TAPS* 46; Philadelphia: The American Philosophical Society, 1956), 229f.

(v. 25). Significantly, this written omen is also interpreted by an atomizing recitation of the lemmata (vv. 26-8).

An exegetical structure parallel to that of the foregoing dreams—
often called 'visions' in Daniel—and omens can be found in the early
post-exilic stratum of the Book of Zechariah, specifically the dream and
visions recorded in 1: 8-10, 2: 1-2, 3-4, 4: 1-6a, 10b-14, 5: 1-9, 6: 1-7.
Among the most notable of these features for the present inquiry is the
fact that a ubiquitous מלאך הדבר בי, an attending *angelus interpres*,
communicates the meanings of the dream or vision imagery to the
prophet (1: 9, 2: 2, 4: 5, 5: 5, 6: 4).[3] In some cases, the prophet first
sees the imagery and then asks מה־אלה 'What are these?' (1: 9, 2: 2, 4,
6: 4) or מה־היא 'What is it?' (5: 6). The angelic being then decodes the
symbolism for him. In other cases, the attending *angelus* directs the
attention of the prophet to a certain image, and asks מה אתה ראה
'What do you see?' (4: 2, 5: 2). At this point the prophet describes the
phenomenon and it is explained (though the question of its meaning
may also be put, as in 4: 4).

Despite these minor variations in structure, it is clear that the dream
and visions in Zech. 1-6 share a common exegetical tradition. This also
extends to the terminology used by the divine being to introduce his
atomized interpretations. One may thus note the constancy of such
terms as אלה or זאת (i.e. 'these are/mean' or 'it is/means')—with and
without specific reference to the lemma (cf. 1: 10, 2: 2, 4: 10, 14, 5: 3,
6-8, 6: 5)—in all six mantological settings. Unfortunately, the explanations of the symbolism have been occasionally mixed together with
other materials in the course of transmission or redaction. Thus, whereas
in Zech. 2: 2 the interpretation answers the question posed, this same
interpretation reappears intrusively and awkwardly in v. 4b, between a
different question (v. 4a)—related to a different vision (v. 3)—and its
explanation (v. 4c).

A second instance of conflation occurs in Zech. 4, where oracles
have been interpolated into the *traditum*. Indeed, the two oracles in
vv. 6b-7 and 8-10a are easily distinguishable from the surrounding
visions regarding the temple furniture (vv. 1-6a, 10b-14) on the basis
of stylistic form and content.[4] To be sure, the received Massoretic
punctuation has obscured this insertion; but the original textual consecution (of the visions) can be re-established on the basis of the
exegetical form which we have been analysing. Thus, vv. 1-3 present
the vision of seven lamps and two olive-trees, and this is followed in
vv. 4-5 by the prophet's question מה אלה. The beginning of the divine

---

[3] The *angelus* is presumably the speaker in 2: 4a as well.
[4] This division has been generally accepted. Cf. the discussion and review in
A. Petitjean, *Les Oracles du Proto-Zacharie* (Paris: J. Gabalda, 1969), 215-67.

being's answer appears in v. 6a ('And he answered and said to me') and clearly continues in v. 10b, where the number of lamps is referred to and explained ('These "seven" are the eyes of YHWH'). Thereupon the same pattern as in vv. 6a + 10b recurs. First the prophet asks about the symbolic meaning of the olive-trees (vv. 11-12) and then receives an interpretation (v. 14). Thus, the pattern of lemmatic citation followed by an explanation appears identically for both features of the vision-content.

Of great importance for the reconstruction of a continuous ancient Israelite exegetical tradition for dreams and visions is the fact that markedly earlier traces of this literary form can be detected in the ominous visions shown to Amos in 7: 1-9 and 8: 1-3, and to Jeremiah in 1: 11-14 and 24: 1-10. A series of features links these two text-clusters. First, in Amos 7: 1 and 8: 1 the episodes are introduced by the phrase כה הראני אדני ה' והנה 'thus the Lord YHWH showed me, and behold'.[5] This introit is paralleled by הראני ה' והנה in Jer. 24: 1. Second, after each 'vision' YHWH first says to the prophet מה־אתה ראה 'What do you see?' (cf. Amos 7: 8, 8: 2; Jer. 1: 11, 13, 24: 3), and then the vision-content is recited followed by its interpretation. Clearly, strong similarities of form and language link these mantic scenarios with those found in the Book of Zechariah, discussed above. But while a clear exegetical-stylistic tradition is evident, there are two other common elements in the visions of Amos and Jeremiah that distinguish them from their post-exilic congeners. The first of these is that none of the pre-exilic texts has a trance- or dreamlike quality; the second is that none of these interpretations is communicated by an angelic being.[6]

In consideration of the trancelike element in the post-exilic visions of Zechariah, a final example may conclude the present picture, the hallucinatory vision of the prophet Ezekiel in Ezek. 37. In his account of it, the prophet states that he was ecstatically transported ('by the spirit of YHWH') to a valley of dry bones (vv. 1-2), and instructed there by the Lord YHWH to prophesy regarding their resuscitation and transformation into living breath and flesh (vv. 3-10). After all this came to pass before his 'vision', the meaning of the symbolism was forthwith explained to him in lemma-like fashion. Thus, referring to the visionary content, YHWH tells Ezekiel that אלה 'these bones are the

---

[5] Cf. also Amos 7: 1, 4; but these are without the subsequent divine question and explanation.

[6] B. Uffenheimer has provided a helpful commentary on the Zecharian material; and though he does not focus on structural features, he does make a phenomenological distinction between the nature of early visions and their late apocalyptic mode in Zechariah. See his *Ḥazonot Zekaryah* (Jerusalem: Qiryat Sepher, 1961), 139-45.

entire house of Israel' (v. 11). This explication is then further developed
in terms of a comprehensive national application (vv. 12-14). One can
hardly doubt, therefore, that at least as regards the stylization of this
vision with interpretation, Ezek. 37 is a clear link in a long exegetical
chain.

B. THE MEANS AND MODES OF EXEGESIS

Despite the marked uniformity of style and content, the hermeneutical
techniques whereby the lemmata of dreams, oracles, and visions are
interpreted vary considerably. Most frequent among these techniques
is the *numerological*, whereby a number or numerical pattern in the
content is taken up in the interpretation. Thus, for example, Joseph
focuses on the *three* clusters of grapes seen by the butler in his dream,
and the *three* loaves of bread seen by the baker, and interprets accordingly (Gen. 40: 10, 12, 16, 18). Similarly there are *seven* fat and *seven*
lean cows, and *seven* good and *seven* blasted ears of corn which are
interpreted in Gen. 41: 26-7; a *seven*-branched candelabrum and *two*
olive-trees envisaged in Zech. 4: 2-3; and *four* chariots and *four* metals
which are 'seen' and explicated in Zech. 6: 1-7 and Dan. 2, respectively.
At the same time, however, there is no self-evident sense for the particular interpretation and application involved (i.e., the three grape
clusters could just as well refer to three days rather than years, etc.)
or, for that matter, for the decoding of the images in symbolic terms
(i.e., there is no necessary correlation between winds and chariots, or
between metals and kingdoms). Apart from the inspirational considerations that are recurrently adduced to justify the oneiromancy, one can
nevertheless observe various contextual considerations that support the
interpretations arrived at. For example, the positive interpretation given
to the butler's dream, and the negative one given to the baker's, are less
dependent on the inherent symbolism of wine or bread—both being
positive—than on the dream-context itself, since the butler squeezes the
grapes into the Pharaoh's goblet, whereas the baker's bread is pecked by
birds. Similarly, there is a fairly obvious correlation between the good
cows and corn and the good years forecast, and vice versa. In other
cases, one may note the importance of images drawn from the socio-
historical context for the interpretation of dreams of visions. Thus, the
interpretation in Zech. 4: 10-14 of the seven-branched candelabrum as
'the eyes of YHWH' that 'range over the entire earth' and of the two
olive-trees as 'the two consecrated with oil who attend the Lord of the
earth' derives from contemporary Persian policing techniques, on the
one hand,[7] and the pressure for a dyarchy in the post-exilic community,

---

[7] According to Xenophon, *Cyr.* viii. 6. 16, the chief Persian spy was called
βασιλέως ὀφθαλμός 'the eye of the king', a phrase remarkably parallel to *'ênê*

on the other. Correspondingly, in Dan. 2 the explication of the four metals which comprise the royal statue in terms of four successive historical monarchies is based on widespread contemporary symbolism. Links between physical metals and metaphysical ages are known from early Greek and contemporary Persian sources.[8]

In addition to the foregoing numerological considerations, *paranomastic* associations and elaborations often provide the key to many other interpretations of dreams, visions, and oracles. Among many examples, one may point to the play on שֶׁבַע in Gen. 41: 29 to link the dream lemma 'seven' with its meaning of שָׂבָע 'satiety'; to the pun on קַיִץ in the vision in Amos 8: 1-3 to relate the basket of 'summer' figs with Israel's threatened קֵץ 'end'; or to the pseudo-linguistic parsing of the wall-oracle in Dan. 5: 26-8 in order to forecast doom (cf. מְנָא and מְנֵה in v. 26). Notable in all these cases, and others,[9] is that the lemmata interpreted are based on visions of the eye or on night visions. The hallucinatory content of Ezek. 37 thus stands somewhat apart and deserves independent comment. For in this case the lemma interpreted is not solely based on the vision of vv. 4-10 but equally on a popular adage cited in v. 11: יָבְשׁוּ עַצְמוֹתֵינוּ 'our bones have dried up; our hope is lost: we are thoroughly doomed.' Indeed, the adage and the despondency reflected therein actually appear to be the very basis of the vision — despite the fact that it appears textually after the vision.[10] For one thing, the adage self-evidently preceded the vision in time; and for another, the adage is cited immediately after the visionary content is explicated, and is thus preparatory to the more forceful repetition of the meaning of the vision in vv. 12-14.

The dramatic and pivotal position of the adage with its explication in v. 11 may be further appreciated from a broader structural perspective,

YHWH 'the eyes of YHWH:, which 'roam throughout the earth' in Zech. 4: 10. For the same verb concerning Satan's function as a cosmic inspector-general, see Job 1: 7, 2: 3. The imagery and language of Zech. 4: 10 is reused in the prophetic sermon of 2 Chron. 16: 9, where YHWH inspects the earth and manifests his might to the blameless.

[8] See Hesiod, *Work and Days*, 106-201, and the first chapter of the Zand-i Vohuman Yasn. In this last, Zarathustra has a dream-vision of a tree with four branches (one of gold, one of silver, one of steel, and one of mixed iron). Ahura Mazda interprets the dream in terms of four kingdoms. See E. Meyer, *Ursprung und Anfänge des Christentums* (Stuttgart and Berlin: J. G. Cotta, 1921), ii. 189-99.

[9] For example, in Jer. 1: 11-12 the interpretation of *maqqēl šāqēd* 'almond branch' is *šōqēd* 'be diligent'; the interpretation of *sîr nāpûaḥ* 'boiling cauldron' in Jer. 1: 13-14 is *tinnāpah* or *tāpûah* 'will blast' (*pace* LXX ἐκκαυθήσεται vs. MT *tippātaḥ*), and in Dan. 9: 24 the interpretation of *šibʿîm* 'seventy' is *šābūʿîm* (!) 'weeks'. For examples of paranomasia in the interpretation of oracles and omens in ancient Egypt and Mesopotamia, and at Qumran, see 'The Qumran Pesher', 99, 103.

[10] Note Ezekiel's use of adages in 12: 22-5 and 18: 2-4.

which reveals a chiastic arrangement of the materials. First (A) the text opens with a reference to Ezekiel's inspiration by means of the divine spirit (רוח) and his relocation (ויניחני) in a death valley (vv. 1–2), and it concludes (A′) with references to Israel's resuscitation through YHWH's spirit-breath (רוח) and its relocation (והנחתי) in its ancestral homeland (v. 14). Between these two units there is the divine instruction (B) to Ezekiel to 'prophesy' over the dead bones that they revive, which is accomplished (vv. 3–10), and the divine explication (B′) regarding the national meaning of this miraculous resurrection (vv. 12–13). At the very centre of the two concentric units is v. 11, divisible into two parts. The first half, v. 11a, interprets the preceding vision and anticipates the following interpretation, while the second half, v. 11b, anticipates the following explication ('behold . . . therefore') and gives an idiomatic focus to the preceding vision. Once the national import of the vision is set, moreover, through the national interpretation and the citation of the popular adage, a deeper theological reversal within the stylistic form is disclosed. For if Ezekiel, an individual, was initially inspired and relocated in the exile, in the valley of dead bones, the entire unit closes with the divine assertion that YHWH will inspire the entire nation (i.e., revive them to new life) and relocate them upon their land. The linguistic–chiastic affinities of vv. 1–2, 14 thus harbour a more profound theological transformation, one, which the prophet symbolically embodies from the very outset.

C. COMPARISONS AND CONTINUITIES

As well as the stability and continuity in structure, language, and technique among the dreams, visions, and omens of ancient Israel reviewed to this point, it is also noteworthy — and this has broad inter-cultural implications — that corresponding structures, language, and techniques are recurrently found in contemporary ancient Near Eastern documents[11] and in subsequent post-biblical literature.[12]

1. The technique of citation and atomized exegesis may be found in Egyptian sources as early as *The Book of the Dead* (Speech XVII),[13] and is frequently found in Demotic materials, both literary and mantic. Thus, in the commentary copy of Pap. Carlsberg I, a mythological piece is cited and the comments are introduced by *dd* 'it means'.[14] The same

[11] Cf. 'The Qumran Pesher', 98–105, and immediately below.

[12] See ibid. 97f.

[13] See the translation and edition of H. Grapow, *Religiöse Urkunden. Ausgewählte Texte des Totenbuches* (Leipzig: J. C. Hinrichs, 1915).

[14] Cited in F. Daumas, 'Littérature prophétique et exégétique en Egypte', in *A la rencontre de dieu. Mémorial Albert Gelin* (Bibliothèque de la Faculté Catholique de Théologie de Lyon, 8; Le Puy: Xavier Mappus, 1961), 212f.

term recurs in the so-called Demotic Chronicle from the Ptolemaic period,[15] in which numerous cryptic oracles are cited and ominously interpreted. The interpretations in these and related texts regularly utilize a keyword in the lemma and frequently pun on it.[16]

Similar exegetical structures and techniques are attested in a wide variety of Mesopotamian commentaries. Earlier, in connection with our discussion of inner-biblical lexical exegesis, reference was made to two broad types of such cuneiform commentaries: the *ṣâtu*, or lexical type, and the *mukallimtu*, or exegetical type.[17] In both cases the comment is frequently preceded by a full citation of the pertinent textual lemma. In other examples from Mesopotamian commentaries, the word and its explanation are juxtaposed, and connective relative pronouns (like *ša* and *aššu*) are found. In the commentary to the so-called 'Address by Marduk to the Demons' the exegetical form employed is (1) a lemmatic citation followed by (2) an indented interpretation on the next line.[18] To further establish the exegetical structure, these interpretations are introduced by such terms as *ma ana, ana, ma, aššum*, and *ša*; and they are regularly concluded by a form of the verb *qabû* (e.g. *iqabbi, iqtabi*). Characteristically, then, the commentator of the 'Address by Marduk' introduces his remark with the phrase 'concerning *x* it [the lemma] speaks'. Similar terms and structures appear in a commentary on the incantation series *Maqlû* i. 24, 42,[19] on the Babylonian creation epic *Enuma elish* iv. 135[20], and in neo-Assyrian oracles.[21]

The technique of lemma-plus-comment is most clearly attested in the dream-reports of Gudea and Dumuzi.[22] In the former instance,

[15] The text was published by W. Spiegelberg, 'Die sogenannte demotische Chronik des Pap. 215 der Bibliothèque Nationale zu Paris', *Demotische Studien*, 7 (1914), 30ff. Cf. also F. Daumas, loc. cit., and the historical discussions of E. Meyer, *Kleine Schriften* (Halle: M. Niemeyer, 1924), ii, ch. 1, and N. Reich, 'The Codification of Egyptian Laws by Darius and the Origin of the "Demotic Chronicle" ', *Mizraim*, 1 (1933), 178-85.

[16] Cf. iii. 17-iv. 2. In addition to *dd* other deictic terms are used; cf. v. 1, 6f., 17.

[17] Above, p. 39.

[18] See the edition of W. Lambert *AfO* 17 (1954-6), 310-21. The commentary was published earlier by G. Meier, 'Ein Kommentar zu einer Selbstprädikation des Marduk aus Assur', *ZA* NF 13 (1942), 241-6.

[19] Cf. the use of *ma, ša*, and *qabû* to introduce comments in *KAR* 94. 16-24.

[20] In *KAR* 307. 1-2 the interpretation is placed before the expansion on the lemma. Cf. R. Labat, *Le Poème babylonien de la création* (Paris: Adrien-Maisonneuve, 1935), *ad* iv. 135.

[21] For the neo-Assyrian example of *KAR* 883. 17-19, see S. A. Strong, 'On Some Oracles to Esarhaddon and Ašurbanipal', *Beiträge zur Assyriologie*, 2 (1894), 645; *ANET* 450f,; and *CAD*, Ḫ, 43, s.v. *ḫallalatti*.

[22] See A. L. Oppenheim, *The Interpretation of Dreams*, 245f. (trans. T. Jacobsen).

whole dream-units are first repeated and then interpreted; in the latter case, each separate feature is taken up and juxtaposed with a comment. These exegetical features recur most notably in the double dream of Gilgamesh (I v. 27–vi. 23). Here, the dreams are first reported and then the various subunits are cited and commented upon. The following example in I. vi. 18 is representative:[23]

[*ḫa-aṣ-ṣi-n*]*u ša ta-mu-ru amēlu*

(concerning) [the ax]e which you have seen: (it is) a man.

2. The international and diachronic character of the preceding exegetical procedures becomes even more evident when we return to the Palestinian *Umwelt*, and to the post-biblical exegetical structure of lemma-plus-comment in the *pesher*-literature from Qumran. In this last, a lemma is variously linked to its interpretation by assorted constructions based on the noun פשר 'interpretation', with and without pronouns and relative clauses, or simply by demonstrative pronouns or relative clauses, e.g. ואשר אמר, פשרו אשר/על, פשר הדבר (על), פשרו, המה הוא, זה . Thus, reminiscent of the Akkadian 'Address to the Demons', the commentator of biblical prophecies at Qumran began his remarks with such phrases as 'its interpretation is' or 'regarding what was said', or simply 'concerning', when a certain lemma is recited more than once, or when successive comments are given.[24] Also of comparative interest are the facts that an indented space regularly separates a lemma from one of the above-mentioned clauses announcing its פשר; and that diverse paranomastic techniques and typological symbols are employed.[25] Significantly, many of these techniques and structures—used at Qumran to elucidate prophetic oracles—reappear in later midrashic[26] and talmudic literature,[27] in the pseudepigraphic book of

---

[23] Cf. the text of R. Campbell Thompson, *The Epic of Gilgamish* (Oxford: The Clarendon Press, 1930), 16.

[24] For example, in pHab. ii. 1–10 three distinct interpretations are given for *bôgĕdîm*, being introduced by *pišrô*, *wĕ'al*, *wĕkēn*, and *pēšer haddābār 'al* (the third case has an additional explication). In the 'Address to Marduk', multiple interpretations are preceded by *šaniš* and *šalšiš*, 'secondly' and 'thirdly', respectively (in Meier's edition, *obv.* 4, 12; *rev.* 6–7, 11). For the same in a *ṣâtu*-commentary, cf. R. Labat, *Commentaires assyro-babyloniens sur les présages* (Bordeaux: Imprimerie de l'Université, 1933), 17 and v. 5. For multiple interpretations in ancient Egypt, cf. the expression *ki t'et* X *pu* 'otherwise said, X *it is*', in the Papyrus of Ani. See E. A. Budge, *The Book of the Dead, The Papyrus of Ani* (reprint of 1895 edn.; New York: Dover, 1967), Pl. VII, pp. 27ff.

[25] For puns, cf. pHab. i. 5f., v. 1–6, vi. 2–5, xi, 2ff.; and for typological symbols, cf. pHab. ii. 10–12, xii. 3f., 7; pNah. i. 3, ii. 2—all discussed in 'The Qumran Pesher', 99f.   [26] *Gen. Rab.* 9: 73.

[27] *b. Ta'an.* 23a, on Job 22: 28–30; noted by D. Flusser, *Scrolls from the Judean Desert* (Jerusalem: The Aqadamon Press, 1968), 59 [Heb.].

IV Ezra,[28] in the Targumim,[29] the New Testament,[30] and even in non-Jewish gnostic literature.[31] Indeed, a whole midrashic genre, the so-called *Petirah Midrashim*, can be related to this interpretative structure and its technical terminology.[32]

Within this remarkable stream of tradition from Mesopotamia to Qumran, and beyond, one briefly noted lexical item deserves independent notice, the technical term for 'interpretation'. As we have seen, the term used in the *pesher*-literature is פשר. It may now be added that this term is the latter-day inheritor of a rich patrimony. On the one hand, it is related to the Akkadian verb *pašāru* 'to solve, interpret', used in magical and divinatory contexts as well as in dream interpretations, such as that found in the Gilgamesh epic (I. vi. 6).[33] On the other hand, the verb, derived from the Semitic stem *ptr*, recurs in the Hebrew and Aramaic phrases זה פתרנו and פשרה . . . דנה 'this is its interpretation', found in the introit to Joseph's (Gen. 40: 12, 18) and Daniel's (Dan. 2: 36, 4: 15) dream interpretations, respectively. Moreover, just as variations on this expression are found in the Hebrew Bible in connection with written omens, as when Belshazzar appeals to anyone to deal with 'this writing and its interpretation' (Dan. 5: 7), or when Daniel states דנה פשר מלתא 'this is the interpretation of the word/ oracle' (v. 26),[34] so is its Akkadian parallel *ki anni pišišru* 'indeed, this is its interpretation' used at the conclusion of a wide variety of tetralogical and astrological omen reports from Mesopotamia.[35]

The international character and style of our biblical exegetical materials were undoubtedly due, in large part, to the residency of local experts in mantology in different royal courts, where they both learned new techniques and shared professional information. Indeed, some verification for this hypothesis can be seen in the great formal impact

---

[28] 10: 10, 16, 18, 22, 26, 35f.

[29] *Tg. Jer. I and II* to Gen. 15: 12.

[30] e.g. Acts 4: 24-8 (on Ps. 2), see Flusser, op. cit., 59f.; Rom. 10: 6-8, see J. Bonsirvan, *Exégèse rabbinique et exégèse paulinienne* (Paris: Beauchesne, 1939), 42ff.; Eph. 4: 9, see M. McNamara, *The New Testament and the Targum to the Pentateuch* (Analecta Biblica, 27; Rome: Pontifical Biblical Institute, 1966), 72.

[31] Cf. J. Carmignac, 'Le Genre littéraire du "pesher" dans "Pistis Sophia"', *RQ* 4 (1964), 497-522.

[32] See the remarks of L. Silberman, 'Unriddling the Riddle', *RQ* 3 (1961), 224-35. Basic structural work on this form was done by P. Bloch, 'Studien zur Aggadah', *MGWJ* 34 (1884), 264-9, 385-92.

[33] See Oppenheim, *The Interpretation of Dreams*, 217-20.

[34] For rabbinic uses of *miltā'* with a mantic sense, see *b. Hull.* 7b.

[35] Cf. Oppenheim, op. cit. 220, for references; add W. Harper, *ABL*, No. 1134, and R. Thompson, *The Reports of the Magicians and Astrologers of Nineveh and Babylon* London: Luzacs, 1900), Nos. 89, 176, 256A. For the verb in other omen contexts, see Harper, Nos. 335, 1118, and Thompson, Nos. 83, 170.

which Mesopotamian oneiromancy had upon Egyptian practices,[36] and in the recorded presence of an Egyptian dream interpreter (*ḥr tp*) in the Mesopotamian court (called *ḥardibi*) from the seventh century.[37] Moreover, it should not be overlooked that both Joseph and Daniel performed their oneiromantic services in foreign courts,[38] where they grew up, having been transported to Egypt and Mesopotamia respectively during periods of mass population migrations (drought and exile). No matter how idealized and stylized these texts, a comparative perspective shows that their techniques were definitely 'at home' in those two courts.

3. Given the *official mise-en-scène* of many of the biblical interpretations of dreams and omens which have structural and verbal parallels in Mesopotamian sources, it is fitting to conclude these comparative descriptions with a long-misunderstood instance of shared nomenclature in a *popular* setting.

In the context of his battles with Midian, the Israelite warrior-hero Gideon is told by YHWH to go to the Midianite camp, if he is faint-hearted and needs confirmation for his task, and there listen to what is being said (Judg. 7: 10–13). Technically, it may be added, the decision to regard chance remarks or sounds as an omen is a form of divination known as kledonomancy, and is found throughout the ancient Near East.[39] To be sure, the chance nature of the omen's advent is mitigated in this case by the divine prognosis, just as elsewhere (cf. 1 Sam. 5: 23–4). Be this as it may, when Gideon goes to the camp he overhears a Midianite dream-report and its interpretation (regarding his imminent victory). Referring to this dream, the narrator notes that Gideon heard

מספר החלום ואת־שִׁבְרוֹ

the dream-report and its interpretation. (v. 15)

In order to understand this phrase, and the use of שברו to mean 'interpretation', a brief side-glance at a Mesopotamian dream-report of a priest of Ishtar is necessary.[40] In this document it is stated that the priest tells a supplicant *tabrīt mūši ša Ištar ušabrûšu*, 'the vision which Ishtar had revealed'. Remarkably, the expression *tabrīt mūši* 'night-vision' is similar to the Aramaic expression חזוא די־ליליא found in

---

[36] See the view of Oppenheim, op. cit. 245.

[37] Ibid. 238 and references there.

[38] Notably, Joseph vied with the *ḥarṭummê miṣrayîm* 'dream interpreters of Egypt' (Gen. 41: 8); and Daniel competed with *ḥarṭummîm* in the neo-Babylonian court (2: 2; also note *rab ḥarṭummin* in 5: 11).

[39] Cf. Oppenheim, op. cit. 210f. For the parallel phenomenon of *bat qôl* in rabbinic literature, see Lieberman, *Hellenism*, 194–9, and D. Sperling, 'Akkadian *egerrû* and Hebrew *bt qwl*', *JANESCU* 4 (1972), 63–74.

[40] See A.C. Piepkorn, *Historical Prism Inscriptions of Assurbanipal*, i (AS 5; Chicago: The University of Chicago Press, 1933), 66 f. (ll. 50 f.).

Daniel's dream-reports (Dan. 2:19; cf. 7:7, 13).[41] Furthermore, the other clause, *ušabrûšu* 'revealed (to him)', also has a biblical parallel in the Hebrew הראני '(God) showed me', which recurs in connection with the visions of Amos (7:1, 4, 7, 8:1) and Jeremiah (24:1). Given these stylistic similarities, it is of particular interest to compare *ušabrûšu* and שברו in Judg. 7:15.

The first point to note is that the Akkadian verb is derived from the *š*-causative *šubrû*, meaning 'to show', or 'reveal (in a dream or vision)'. This derivation is significant for comparative purposes not solely because many of the related forms of *šubrû* are widespread in exegetical and mantological contexts,[42] but also because the Hebrew stem שבר ('to break') is not at all pertinent in Judg. 7:15. Accordingly, it is likely that שברו is based on a pseudo-triconsonantal root * שבר, and must be construed as a *š*-causative nominal form like שלהבת (cf. Ezek. 21:3; Job. 15:30) plus pronominal suffix. Given this likelihood, שברו presumably goes back to the biconsonantal stem * בר in the shaphel, and is thus comparable to *šubru* < *barû* (which is not a regular triconsonantal). Having forgotten its derivation and pronunciation, later Massoretes therefore pointed שִׁבְרוֹ as a *qal*-nominal form based on the common triconsonantal שבר— and thus inadvertently produced an incorrect pseudo-form. Alternatively, given the rarity of *š*-forms in Hebrew, it is just as likely that שברו in Judg. 7:15 was simply taken over from Akkadian *šubrû* (this being an established technical verb) and subsequently nominalized.[43] In any event, both contextual usage and morphological form strongly indicate that שברו is cognate with Akkadian *šubrû* in its oneiromantic usage—once again underscoring the international character of mantological forms and vocabulary in the ancient Near East.

---

[41] Cf. Dan. 7:2.

[42] Cf. *CAD*, B, pp. 116–18, s.v. *barû* A (1c′, 2a, 5b).

[43] A related instance occurs in the mantic context of Isa. 47:13b, where, in an anti-Babylonian diatribe, *hōbĕrê* (Q) 'of the heavens' is parallel to, and seemingly qualified by, 'the star-gazers who foretell your future month by month'. *Hōbĕrê* is clearly related to Akk. *bārû* 'diviner', though the form is difficult. One possibility is that it had rendered a form with an *š*-causative into a pseudo-Hiphil form. The *qal* form *lābûr* in Ecc. 9:1 is another biblical variant of **br*; the parallelism *lĕbārām* ~*lir'ōt* in Ecc. 3:18 is a wonderful pun.

17. The Mantological Exegesis of Oracles

By contrast with the interpretation of dreams, visions, or omens, all of which have some ocular or visual quality, the exegesis of oracles is concerned with a mantological type which is characteristically aural and oral in nature: a prophet 'hears' a divine voice and communicates it. Sometimes, to be sure, the aural aspect is of minor or little significance, as in those instances, marked in the earliest strata particularly, where the prophetic type is inspired to 'see' or perceive a future event, but even here it is essential to point out that the mantic product is spoken, and any related or subsequent interpretations of it start from its (real or affected) verbal and oral content.

Naturally enough, as has been thoroughly recognized by students of biblical prophecy, the received oracles are the product of long and faithful processes of transmission. The very survival—whatever the motivation—of such a variegated bulk of ancient oracles into the post-exilic period is in itself proof of this assertion. In some cases, as is well known, oracles were preserved by faithful disciples and students of the great prophets (cf. Isa. 8:1-2, 16-18). In other instances, amanuenses like Baruch ben Neriah copied versions of older oracles for posterity (cf. Jer. 36:32). Added to this, of course, is the fact that prophetic circles and schools reworked whole collections of prophetic materials and added to them—as various generations of deuteronomistic tradents did to the older oracles of Jeremiah[1]—or found in the prophecies or phraseology of earlier prophets elements appropriate and seemingly applicable to their times.[2]

---

[1] This has been recently well argued by A. Rofé, 'Studies in the Composition of the Book of Jeremiah', 1-29 [Heb.]. The complex additions to the Book of Isaiah are well known, and the speculative procedures—not doubting, however, the existence of textual difficulties—lead to inconclusive results. Characteristic is J. Blenkinsopp, 'Fragments of Ancient Exegesis in an Isaian Poem (Jes 2: 6-22)', ZAW 93 (1981), 51-61. Methodologically speaking, one is on safest ground where inner-textual indications can be used, as in the case of Isa. 1: 27-8. Clearly these verses are separate from vv. 21-6, a unit lexically circumscribed by similar words in vv. 21 and 27. Apparently responding to the lament ('*ēkāh*) over Zion in v. 21, and associating it with the scroll of lamentations over Zion after the fall (cf. '*ēkāh*, Lam. 1: 1), a pious post-exilic tradent juxtaposed words of hope with the old *traditum*—stressing its key terms.

[2] See below.

Obviously, in any of these processes, small and large changes could and did creep into the older *traditum* inadvertently, and often enough quite deliberately. Sometimes, to be sure, the changes in the *traditio* appear entirely inconsequential – as when the legal citation of Mic. 3: 12 ('Therefore . . . Zion will be ploughed over; Jerusalem will be a waste-land עִיִּין; and the Temple mount a forested ridge') in Jer. 26.18bβ changes the northern form עִיִּין to עִיִּים, its Judaean dialectical equivalent.[3] But even in such instances one must constantly be alert to other, more transformative processes. Thus, to remain with the previous oracular text, it appears that Micah's anti-Temple and anti-Jerusalem forecast should be related to the passage in 1 Kgs. 9 where Solomon is told that if the covenant is not followed 'this Temple will be exalted (עֶלְיוֹן): every passer-by will be aghast and hiss' (v. 8a). Clearly, the two stichoi (be exalted ~ be aghast) are contradictory, and one is prompted to assume that עֶלְיוֹן is a pious correction for something like לְעִיִּין 'as a wasteland'. Indeed, even if this putative reconstruction of 1 Kgs. 9: 8a is not the source of Micah's oracle, then it is its formal prototype, and remarkably shows how the very same theological sensitivity which led to Jeremiah's arraignment for forecasting doom against the Temple and Jerusalem (cf. Jer. 7: 14, 26: 6) produced a תִּיקוּן סוֹפְרִים in the book of Kings.[5] This latter change, however, clearly preceded the Chronicler, who struggled to make the best of a perplexing textual situation and exegetically recast the older passage to read 'and as for this Temple, *which was once* exalted: every passer-by will be aghast' (2 Chron. 7: 21a).

For the historian of ancient inner-biblical mantology the task thus arises of searching the received oracles, and of culling from them all traces of exegetical *traditio*. Because of the cultural importance of such exegetical features, and not least because of the methodological difficulties involved, it is vitally important not to assume that every textual confusion or contradiction is the product of later exegetical and exegetical–editorial hands. Thus, here, as earlier, interpretative and

---

[3] Since the inter-vocalic *hê* was elided in the northern dialect, perhaps 'forested ridge', *lĕbāmôt yā'ar*, is equivalent to Judean *libĕhēmôt yā'ar* 'for wild beasts of the forest'.

[4] See N. Tur-Sinai, *Peshuto shel Miqra'* (Jerusalem: Qiryat Sepher, 1965), ii. 231. For another change involving *'elyôn* (if it is not a scribal error), see Ps. 106: 7 (compare Ps. 78: 17), observed by Z. H. Chajes, *Sepher Tehillim*, ed. A. Cahana (Zitomer, 1903, repr. Jerusalem: Makor, 1970), ad loc.

[5] Dialectically problematic; one may prefer *lĕ'iyyîm* to *lĕ'iyyin* in 1 Kgs. 9: 8a – not solely on the basis of Jer. 26:18bβ, but also in the light of Ps. 79:1, which shows that this topos of desolation occurs in different settings. Other suggestions are, of course, feasible (e.g. *lišĕmāmāh*); but the fact that some word for waste or destruction underlies 1 Kgs. 9: 8a seems beyond doubt, and gains further support from the Syr. version and *Tg. Jon.*

explicative traditions will be isolated on the basis of (1) introductory or deictic technical phrases; (2) comparison of inner-biblical repetitions and variations, or comparison of the MT *traditum* with variants in the LXX and other versions; and (3) inner-stylistic criteria which provide analytical grounds for assuming that a given oracular *traditum* has been supplemented in one way or another.[6] In what follows, the material will be separated into two formal categories: those instances of exegesis which are *non-transformative* in nature, that is, where the interpretations of the oracular *traditum* do not change the content of the oracle, and may even be part of its presentation; and those instances which are essentially *transformative* in nature, that is, where the *traditio* readapts, reapplies, or otherwise revises an older oracular *traditum*. The examples chosen will outline the morphologies and types of these categories.

A. NON-TRANSFORMATIVE EXEGESIS:
EXPLICATIONS, CLARIFICATIONS, AND SECRET CODES

1. One of the inevitable features of the imagery used in prophetic oracles, and a part of their secret strength, is the frequently indeterminate or ambiguous nature of the predictions. Indeed, because of this, the open-ended nature of many oracles could be maintained, and it was hard to invalidate a given prediction if the wording was vague enough to be easily reconstrued. Historical records from the ancient world—one thinks particularly of the age of Alexander—sufficiently attest to the fact that many oracle-mongers owed their fame and their very life to the success of their forecasts, a success frequently dependent on the inherent ambiguity of the oracular articulation. A biblical version of the latter phenomenon will be discussed below. At this juncture it may suffice to point to a different aspect of the indeterminacy and vagueness of oracles in ancient Israel, one which elicited a corresponding exegetical dimension.

In some instances, as in Isa. 9:13, a prophet may formulate his oracle in vivid though imprecise terms. Turning to the Israelites, Isaiah states: 'Thus YHWH will cut off from Israel head and tail, palm branch and rush—in a single day.' From the context it is, of course, clear that the imagery of head and tail, palm branch and rush, refers to elements in Israelite society. But these are not specified. In fact, such imagery was apparently a common prophetic topos, for elsewhere, in an oracle against Egypt, precisely the same imagery is used: 'Egypt will be left without anything possible to do, which a head or tail, palm branch or rush, might do' (Isa. 19:15). Here again, the larger context—which refers to Pharaonic counsellors and sages, even princes and fools (vv. 11-14)—makes it clear that the concluding imagery refers to various

---

[6] Cf. the example in Isa. 1: 27-8, cited in n. 1 above.

personages of the realm. In Isa. 9:13, however, such summary vagueness was not sufficient, and the prophet himself – or a latter-day tradent – added:

The elder and haughty one: הוא (this) is (the meaning of) the 'heads'; and the prophet [and] false teacher[7]: הוא (this) is (the meaning of) the 'tail'.

(v. 14)

While the foregoing explications are not complete – for there is no corresponding application of the palm branch or rush to other societal elements – the style of the comments, and the use of technical deictic pronouns corresponding to those found in scribal glosses and other mantological exegesis, suggest that we are faced with an exegetical convention of sorts. First, the entire lemma is presented, and then elements from the lemma are atomistically explicated, after a transitional technical term. Although this example is informative, however, it also indicates how difficult it is to determine whether such a phenomenon is an original feature of the prophet's rhetoric – and thus an *ad hoc* explicatory convention – or one of scribal or scholastic musings (cf. Ezek. 31:18b). The life-setting of this exegesis is thus very much in doubt.

2. A corresponding type of oracular exegesis, in which the language of a given oracular *traditum* is developed in a *traditio* of it, involves the homiletical elaboration of a set rhetorical form. It is of particular interest, when compared with the foregoing, chiefly because the elaborations are rhetorically integrated into the old pattern and not added by some later tradent. As an example of such exegetical-homiletical embellishment, we may turn to a prophetic form noted earlier, in which denunciations are levelled at various social strata and leaders, such as priests, prophets and wise men. In some instances, this form may simply list these strata, as in Ezek. 7:26; in other cases the groups are mentioned seriatim with various derogatory or explanatory comments appended, as in Mic. 3:1-8, 9-11. Here, *in nuce*, we see a rhetorical elaboration of a set form, though without true exegetical components. To see the latter, it is sufficient to compare Zeph. 3:1-4 – itself a good example of the listing of social elements together with elaborating castigations – and Ezek. 22:24-8. As D. H. Müller long ago noted, the latter text is based upon the Zephanian prototype – paralleling its various elements and topoi, but also expanding upon them.[8] A comparison of

[7] *Pace* the parallelism; alternatively, 'the prophets who gave false instruction' (NJPS) – presumably assuming the haplography of final *mêm* of MT *wnby'* – or 'the prophet, the false teacher'.

[8] See his 'Der Prophet Ezechiel entlehnt eine Stelle des Propheten Zephanja und glossiert sie', in *Komposition und Strophenbau* (Vienna: A. Hölder, 1907), 30-6. Cf. the comment, apparently independent, of Y. N. Simchoni, 'The Prophet Ezekiel', *He'atid*, 4 (1912), 220: 'The particular sins listed Ezek 22:25ff. remind us of the words of Zeph. 3:1-4' [Heb.].

these two texts, in fact, succinctly shows the degree to which Ezekiel's rhetoric is actually a species of exegetical embellishment. In what follows, the Ezekielian material has been slightly rearranged to correspond to its Zephanian prototype, and the exegetical elaborations have been italicized.

Zeph. 3: 3–4	*Ezek. 22: 25–8*
(3a) Her princes in her midst are roaring lions;	(25) Her princes[9] amongst her are like a roaring lion, tearing prey; *they have devoured life, seized treasure and wealth, that widows multiply therein.*
(3b) her judges are evening wolves, that do not store for the morning;	(27) Her officers[10] in her midst are like wolves tearing prey, *shedding blood and destroying human life to get ill-gotten gain.*
(4a) her prophets are impetuous and deceitful;	(28) Her prophets smeared whitewash; *their visions are false, their divinations a lie; they say, 'Thus says the Lord YHWH', and YHWH has not spoken.*
(4b) her priests have desecrated holy things and done violence to the Torah.	(26) Her priests did violence to my Torah and desecrated my sacred things; *they do not distinguish between sacred and profane, do not inform concerning the pure and impure, and have disregarded my sabbaths – that I be profaned amongst them.*

The strong similarity of the lists of officials mentioned in the two preceding texts, and the near-identity of castigations presented, show that a common rhetorical structure is involved. In fact, this common structure extends to the conclusions of the two pieces as well. Thus, the judgement with which Zephaniah's diatribe culminates ends with the divine promise that he will 'pour upon them my wrath, the full blast of my fury' (3: 8b)—a passage which parallels YHWH's comment through Ezekiel that 'I shall pour upon them my wrath, and shall

---

[9] Reading *nĕśi'ēhāh* for MT *nĕbî'ēhāh*, on the basis of the LXX, the parallel schemata with *nĕbî'ēhāh* in Ezek. 22: 28 and Zeph. 3: 4a, and the exact imagery in Ezek. 19: 3, 6 used – as in Zeph. 3: 3a – with princes (cf. *nĕśî'ê yiśrā'ēl*, 19: 1).

[10] Reading *śōpĕṭêhāh* for *śārêhāh* with Müller. See his justification, op. cit. 32 n. 1, and the imagery in the schematic parallel, Zeph. 3: 3b.

destroy them with the fire of my anger' (22: 31a).[11] But beyond these close links, the diatribe in Ezekiel manifests clear homiletical embellishments designed to clarify and specify the imagery and general condemnations. Indeed, in these various aggadic expansions one hears the unique contribution of the prophet Ezekiel, who variously used fixed priestly phrases as well as his own. For example, (i) the condemnation of the chiefs in v. 25a is supplemented by remarks strikingly similar to another Ezekielian critique of chiefs in 19: 3, 6; (ii) the reference to the desecrations of the priests in v. 26a is developed by phrases which recall the priestly prescriptions found in Lev. 10: 10 and Ezek. 44: 23-4; (iii) the elaboration of the violence done by the judges, reported in v. 27a, utilizes imagery also found in 19: 3, 6, 22: 3-4, 6, 9, 12-13, 33: 31, and (iv) the indication of the falsity of the prophets in v. 28a is expanded with phrases which literally echo the prophet's denunciations in 13: 6-9, 10-11, 14-15. This reuse of language from chapter 13 in Ezek. 22 is further underscored by the fact that the former, like the latter, includes references to a 'breach' in the cultural walls and the absence of anyone who might prevent national ruin (cf. 13: 5 and 22: 20).[12]

In the present context, of course, there is no reference to the fact that Ezekiel's denunciation is basically derived from inherited doom rhetoric, nor any suggestion that the homiletical elaborations derive from the prophet. The doom prophecy and the expansions are rather presented as one seamless whole—the revealed words of YHWH to Ezekiel. Nevertheless, our comparison of the Ezekielian developments with their Zephanian prototype is instructive regarding aspects of the relationship between tradition and innovation in biblical prophecy. For in this case, reacting to the iniquity of his time, the inspired prophet drew upon a fixed form and phraseology—learned and studied in the schools—and added to them older and idiosyncratic verbal elements which seemed to suit the situation and more exactly specify the general imagery used. By this exegetical *traditio*, an older *traditum* derived from Zephaniah's prophecies became a new *traditum* in Ezekiel's hands. And by virtue of this *traditio* which wove into Zeph. 3: 3-4 various authoritative phrases from legal and prophetic sources, the denunciations in Ezek. 22: 25-8 acquire a double force. Not only does the prophet back up his critique with specific charges, having established covenantal-legal ramifications, but his speech is nothing short of a catena of traditions, which bring their whole forceful weight to bear on the present.

[11] Also note the attempt by Müller, op. cit. 35, to see in Ezekiel's opening, 22: 24, a paraphrastic commentary of Zephaniah's 'Überschrift' in 3: 1a.

[12] For a full discussion of Ezek. 13, see M. Fishbane and S. Talmon, 'The Structuring of Biblical Books', 131-8.

3. A final type of exegetical feature in biblical oracles which does not change the original meaning of the words is cryptography. By this means a reference in an oracle is encoded by one esoteric technique or another, so that it must first be exegetically decoded in order for it to make any sense. Most notable among inner-biblical cryptographic techniques is the deliberate permutation of letters to produce cryptic ciphers of the *'atbash'* type. This technique, known particularly from later Jewish sources, exchanges the first letter of the alphabet with the last, the second with the penultimate, and so forth (thus: א״ת ב״ש). Guided by this code, the meaningless ששך in Jer. 25: 26 and 51: 41 can be deduced to 'stand for' בבל (Babylon). Similarly, an application of *'atbash'* permutations to לב קמי in Jer. 51: 1 yields כשדים (Chaldaeans), as was first correctly deciphered in the ancient Targum – though its sense is also disclosed by the parallelism and in Jer. 51: 1. Presumably, tenuous or dangerous political situations encouraged the obscuring of revolutionary oracular contents.[13] It may be added that cryptograms are also found in cuneiform sources. Sometimes these are merely playful *jeux de mots*; but, just as commonly, there is a concern to guard esoteric knowledge. Among the techniques used are permutations of syllabic arrangements with obscure and symbolic puns,[14] secret and obscure readings of signs,[15] and numerological ciphers.[16] The continuity and similarity of these cuneiform cryptographic techniques with similar procedures in biblical sources once again emphasizes the variegated and

[13] Two other proposals, if correct, suggest comparable 'studious codings' of texts. One, suggested by A. Bertholet, *Das Buch Ezekiel erklärt* (Kurzer Hand-Commentar zum Alten Testament; Freiburg: Mohr, 1897), 26, is that the number 390 at Ezek. 4: 5, 9 in the MT, Aqila, and Symmachus is a substitution for 190 in the LXX, in order to agree with the computation of the numerical value of the consonants, *ymy mṣr* (cf. *ymy hmṣwr* in MT 5: 2). Regarding this procedure, cf. the rabbinic hermeneutical technique known as *gematria* (i.e. γεωμετρία) and the contemporary Greek ἰσόψηφα (an important feature of the *onirocritica*; see Lieberman, *Hellenism*, 69, 72 f.). Another possible example of textual 'coding' in the Hebrew Bible is the apparent acrostic *šm'n* in Ps. 110. Since the latter is a royal psalm, it is posible that we have here a coded propaganda text on behalf of the Hasmonean priest-king Simeon. See the comments of Flusser, loc. cit. (above, p. 454 n. 27).

[14] Cf. Lambert's remarks in 'Address by Marduk', 320 n. 8, and his comments on text F. 6; the hermeneutic of Marduk's fifty names in *Enuma Elish*, vii, discussed by Labat, *Le Poème*, a.l.; and features of the so-called Chedarlaomer texts, analysed by M. Astour, 'Political and Cosmic Symbolism in Genesis 14 and its Babylonian Sources', in *Biblical Motifs*, ed. A. Altmann (Brandeis Texts and Studies, 3; Cambridge: Harvard University Press, 1966), esp. 100ff.

[15] Cf. the treatment of signs and ideograms in C. J. Gadd and R. Campbell Thompson, 'A Middle-Babylonian Chemical Text', *Iraq*, 3 (1936), 87-96.

[16] See the four examples in Leichty, 'The Colophon', 152 f., and the famous statement by Sargon II that he made the circumference of the city 16,263 *qānu* and 2 *ammatu*, the *nibīt šumija* 'the number of my name'. See F. Peiser, 'Ein Beitrag zum Bauwesen der Assyrer', *MVAG* 5 (1900), 50 f.

well-established tradition of mantological exegesis in the ancient Near East—a tradition which found ancient Israel a productive and innovative tradent.

B. TRANSFORMATIVE EXEGESIS:
ADAPTATION, APPLICATIONS, AND REVISIONS

The transformations of oracular content through exegesis are a recurrent element in biblical literature, and notably diverse in both nature and technique. In the present context we shall not consider the more radical of these transformations, whereby oracles may be actually transposed into a different genre, but focus on those instances where a received oracle-format or its language is retained though its meaning is transformed by virtue of additions, specifications, or applications. Even here it will be helpful to distinguish between two broad oracular types: those where the forecast is vague or open-ended, and those where the prognostication is precise and clear. Naturally enough, the exegetical techniques vary accordingly. In the first type, we shall note a general tendency to supply or specify the missing or unspecific oracular content, sometimes by redrafting the text, or by quoting it in a revised form, or even by anachronistic adjustments of the original oracle. In the second type, a variety of alternative processes may be discerned which attempt to deal with the real or apparent failure of specific prophecies, or which seek to show that certain precise oracles really apply to the time in which the new spokesman flourishes. By the latter process there is an attempt to make apparently specific prophecies even more specific, and so rob them of their original specificity. Many unexpected twists thus take place when closed, failed, or unspecified predictions are reopened, revitalized, and respecified; and many unexpected streams of prophetic tradition are disclosed as the later prophetic teachers and (especially) tradents search the prophetic 'Scriptures' for divine words awaiting fulfilment in the present. Indeed, as indicated earlier, in Chapter 15, nothing so much characterizes the hermeneutical issue of biblical oracles as the concern to *close* divine predictions which have remained open, i.e. unfulfilled. The techniques and tactics of oracular closure are, therefore, among the primary features of the transformative exegesis of biblical oracles. It is to a typological sampling of these that we now turn.

Vague or Imprecise Predictions Specified

As we discussed earlier, the oracular promise to David of a son who would succeed him and build a Temple to YHWH is repeatedly mentioned in 2 Sam. 7:11-13a, 14-15. But if a son is promised, he is neither mentioned nor specified. Historically, this indeterminacy is due to the fact that the original oracle was concerned primarily to ensure dynastic succession, and this—in a formal divine promise—did not require mention of the heir apparent. Be this as it may, there can be little doubt that the very ambiguity of this oracle helped ensure its realization, and that just this ambiguity provoked the subsequent rivalries and claims to heirship which broke out in the royal court (cf. 2 Sam. 12- 1 Kgs. 1-2). Indeed, so authoritative was the indeterminacy of the divine promise, that even the eventual victor among the claimants did not dare tamper with its original wording when he cited this oracle to Hiram, King of Tyre, in connection with procuring provisions for building the Temple (1 Kgs. 5: 19). The same restraint holds true for Solomon's recitation of this promise *at the time of its fulfilment*, at his dedicatory prayer made upon completing the building of the Temple (1 Kgs. 8: 19-20).

The first time this ambiguous oracle is specified with respect to Solomon is, in fact, in 1 Chron. 28, where David explains his inability to build the shrine (v. 3) and says that 'from among all my sons—for YHWH granted me many sons—he [YHWH] chose Solomon my son to sit on the throne of the kingship of YHWH over Israel. And he said to me: "Solomon, your son, will build my Temple . . ."' (vv. 5-6a). Such an oration, attributed to David, is clearly a *vaticinium ex eventu*, a proclamation after the fact designed to adjust the old promise to the historical reality. The specification at once clarifies the original ambiguity of the oracle while it retroactively legitimates the historical victor (Solomon) as the divinely approved *and intended* heir.

The promise of 1 Chron. 28 is also characterized by a reinterpretation of the unconditional dynastic promise of 2 Sam. 7 in terms of the conditional covenantal law (v. 8)—a matter reflected in 1 Kgs. 2: 4 and 8: 25, as we have seen.[17] There need be little doubt, moreover, that this transformation of an unconditional promise into a conditional one preceded the post-exilic historiographies of Kings and Chronicles. In fact, both elements are integrated into Ps. 89 (cf. vv. 4-5, 30). This psalm, as N. Sarna has thoroughly established, is built upon a detailed citation and reuse of 2 Sam. 7 by a Judaean king who, faced with the possible destruction of his (Davidic) dynasty, prays for the continued viability of his throne, as was divinely promised to David of old.[18]

[17] Since Ps. 132: 11- 12 clearly refers to 2 Sam. 7: 12-16, *with a nomistic revision*, there is added support for the suggestion of von Rad, 'The Levitical Sermon', 275f., that 1 Chron. 28: 2 'has been borrowed' from Ps. 132: 7 (cf. also vv. 8, 14)—since this is the only other place where the ark is called a footstool. This point follows J. W. Rothstein, *Kommentar zum ersten Buch der Chronik* (KAT 18/2; Leipzig: Deichert, 1927), ad loc.

[18] 'Psalm 89: A Study in Inner Biblical Exegesis', in *Biblical and Other Studies*, ed. A. Altmann (Brandeis Texts and Studies; Cambridge: Harvard University Press, 1963), 29-46.

Indeed, in order to reapply this old royal oracle our psalmist-exegete introduced several strategic changes:[19] (i) the key reference to the Temple project in 2 Sam. 7:10-13 was ignored, thereby giving full emphasis to the present dynastic crisis; (ii) the promise in 2 Sam. 7:10 of respite from national enemies is changed in Ps. 89:23-4 and restricted to King David alone, thereby, again, highlighting the contemporary threat to the royal line; and (iii) whereas the father-son relationship mentioned in 2 Sam. 7:14 referred to the relationship between YHWH and David's son, it is presented in Ps. 89:27-8 as applying to David—the divinely graced founder of a royal line. In this way, (iv) the psalmist-exegete began an inner-textual process of reinterpreting David as a dynastic symbol—a process completed in v. 31, where the threatened punishment for sin is transferred from the son of David (as in 2 Sam. 7:14) *to the entire Davidic line*.

By these exegetical transformations, the old royal document of 2 Sam. 7—designed to ensure an older historical issue—was clearly reapplied to a new historical situation, and its ambiguities and original foci were reshaped accordingly. What is particularly important here is the degree to which Ps. 89 reflects a reality in which divine oracles were believed to be vital, 'event-begetting' potencies,[20] and the fact that their theological credibility was both so basic and indeed so important that subtle adjustments were necessary to ensure oracular validity. So powerful was this cognitive-theological motivation, in fact, that our psalmist does not turn from actually misquoting YHWH's own oracular words back to him (cf. also the introit to the citation: 'Then you spoke/prophesied in a dream-vision to your faithful ones(!), and said', v. 20),[21] and even reinforces the old oracle with another exegetical change. Finally, Ps. 89:4, 35-6, 40, 50 strikingly refers to the prophecy in covenant-legal terms. No such reference is found in the prose version of the dynastic oracle in 2 Sam. 7.[22]

Precise or Particular Predictions Reused and Revised

Naturally, the more specific and important the oracle, the more of a burden was placed on latter-day exegetes faced with its real or apparent failure to materialize; but also, we should hasten to add, the greater the likelihood of their tendentious manipulation or reformation of such older material. At stake, of course, and at the root of these hermeneutical

[19] See Sarna, ibid. 37-9.

[20] Cf. the description of the prophetic word as 'an active force begetting future events', by I. L. Seeligmann, 'Aetiological Elements in Biblical Historiography', *Zion*, 26 (1961), 167 [Heb.].

[21] In this additional change, the vision is addressed to the *entire Davidic dynasty*!

[22] See Sarna, loc. cit.

machinations, was a basic theological–ideological concern of biblical
oracles, the necessary fulfilment of prophetic predictions, truly sponsored by YHWH. While this issue gained notoriety in deuteronomic
circles through the unambiguous criterion 'If the prophet prophesies in
the name of YHWH and the oracle does not come to pass and does not
come true, that oracle was not spoken by YHWH' (Deut. 18: 22a),
a review of various strata of biblical literature reinforces the wide
currency of this concern in the most basic way; for it is possible to
isolate an established cluster of technical terms which gave direct
expression to a belief in the inherent and dynamistic power of YHWH's
דָּבָר, or prophetic word (oracle), delivered by his messengers. It is said,
for example, that this word 'comes' (stem: בוא) to fulfilment (cf. Deut.
18: 22a; Josh. 21: 43, 23: 14; Judg. 13: 12, 17; 1 Sam. 9: 6; Jer. 15: 15;
Hab. 2: 3),[23] 'comes to pass' (stem: היה; cf. Deut. 18: 22a), is 'done'
(stem: עשה; cf. Num. 23: 19), or is 'fulfilled' (stem: מלא; cf. 2 Chron.
36: 21) by YHWH. Among other terms found, it is frequently reported
that the divine oracles do not fail or 'fall' (stem: נפל) to the ground
(cf. Josh. 21: 43; 1 Sam. 3: 19; 1 Kgs. 8: 56; 2 Kgs. 10: 10), but are
rather 'established' (stem: קום) or brought to realization (cf. Deut. 9: 5;
2 Sam. 7: 25; 1 Kgs. 8: 20, 12: 15; Isa. 44: 26; Jer. 28: 6, 33: 14; Dan.
9: 12; Neh. 9: 8; 2 Chron. 10: 15). In other contexts it is said that the
powerful prophetic oracle 'will not return' unrealized (לא ישוב, Isa.
45: 23; 55: 11) to its divine source. The pagan prophet Balaam sums up
the whole matter in technical form when he says to Balak (Num. 23:
19–20): 'Would he [YHWH] speak and not act (יעשה), promise and
not fulfil (דבר ולא יקימנה)? Truly, my message was to bless: and when
he blesses I cannot reverse it (ולא אשיבנה).' The emphasis in these last
cases of powerful oracles which do not return or cannot be reversed is
reminiscent of the imprecations found in a variety of Mesopotamian
incantations, which express the wish that the nefarious words of
sorcerers 'return' unfulfilled to the mouth of their speakers.[24]

This ideology of the fulfilment of divine oracles could bring in
its wake a number of interesting consequences. For example, the
occurrence of certain historical events which appeared to be of particular significance could be anachronistically interpolated into older
oracles. In this way, realized events are given prestige, after the fact, as
ancient divine predictions, and the overall character and future validity
of divine prognostications is underscored. Such is the case with the
sixty-five-year oracle found in Isa. 7: 8b. As is generally agreed, this
oddly specific prediction is best understood as a *vaticinium ex eventu*,

[23] The same term is used of oracular signs; cf. 1 Sam. 2: 34.
[24] Cf. *Maqlû* i. 28, v. 5–6; and in general, see L. Dürr, *Die Wertung des gött-
lichen Wortes im Alten Testament und im antiken Orient* (Leipzig: J. C. Hinrichs,
1938).

from after the fall of Ephraim.[25] Comparably, the ideology of the fulfilment of oracles even led to entirely specious references to realized prophecy *even though no such oracle is known or ever referred to* (cf. 2 Kgs. 14:25-7). In another, equally remarkable, instance, the Chronicler has the pagan Pharaoh Necho receive a divine oracle *unknown in the received Book of Kings* and recite it to a disbelieving Josiah (2 Chron. 35:21-2). In this way, the historian was able to justify retroactively the death of the pious Judaean monarch: for the oracle forecasting Josiah's death if he continued his impetuous military intervention was forthwith fulfilled (vv. 23-4). And, finally, knowledge of an oracle also provided persons in power with the means to authenticate devious behaviour—as in the case of Jehu, who used his knowledge of Elijah's oracle to Ahab, regarding the death of the latter's sons, in order to establish credibility and warrant for his acts of aggression. He repeatedly claimed that his acts fulfilled Elijah's old anti-dynastic oracle (see 2 Kgs. 9:25-6, 36a-37; 10:9-10a).

As these examples suggest, and many more confirm, the pattern of promise and fulfilment of divine oracles is particularly dominant in the Book of Kings.[26] Indeed, the prevalence of this scheme in this post-exilic corpus seems to be part of an intense preoccupation with the power of prophecy at this time. On the one hand, the many instances of a promise–fulfilment nexus reinforced the framework of providential causality inherent in the predictions of an Israelite and Judaean exile (2 Kgs. 17:13, 21:10-16, respectively), which came to pass (2 Kgs. 17:23, 24:2-3);[27] while on the other hand, the very fulfilment of these doom-oracles reinforced the hope that the past and present prophecies of consolation and restoration would have equal validity. Accordingly, prophets like Deutero-Isaiah polemically stressed the realization of past oracles of doom as the condition *and basis* for the realization of old and new oracles of hope (see Isa. 41:21-9, 42:5-9; 43:1-10, 11-13, 44:6-23, 24-8, 45:18-25, 46:5-11, 48:1-11, 12-16).

1. Preoccupation with oracular fulfilments stimulated a variety of exegetical innovations on the part of the deuteronomic historians, particularly their transposition of individual predictions of doom into

---

[25] The date of this *ex eventu* gloss apparently refers to the settlement by Esarhaddon of foreign rulers in Samaria in 671; see O. Kaiser, *Isaiah 1-12* (OTL; Philadelphia: Westminster, 1972), 92, and the literature cited. The gloss in v. 8b has long been noted; among others, cf. B. Duhm, *Das Buch Jesaia*[5] (Göttingen: Vandenhoeck and Ruprecht, 1968; orig. edn., 1892), 73f.

[26] This fundamental feature was first duly emphasized by G. von Rad, 'The Deuteronomistic Theology of History in the Books of Kings', in *Studies in Deuteronomy* (SBT 9; London: SCM Press, 1953), 74-84.

[27] Note esp. Zech. 1:4-6.

ones of national import. A typical instance of this can be noted with respect to the oracle of Ahiyah the Shilonite in 1 Kgs. 14. According to the old narrative, Jeroboam's wife went to the prophet in disguise in order to inquire about the fate of her sick child. The prophet discerned her identity and predicted the death of the child upon her return home, and this came to pass. This sequence of events is preserved in vv. 1-6, 12, 17 in a uniform style. The prediction is directly related to the personal concern of the enquirer ('What will be the fate of the child?', v. 3); and, as A. Caquot has intriguingly suggested, the particular negative forecast may even reflect an act of revenge on the part of Ahiyah, who had presumably supported Jeroboam in the hope that the latter's secession from Jerusalem would bode favourably for his own shrine of Shiloh, but was annoyed when Jeroboam subsequently favoured Dan and Beth-el instead (1 Kgs. 12: 29-32).[28]

Interpolated into this coherent scenario, however, is a later deuteronomistic layer, stereotypically threatening the downfall of Jeroboam's dynasty and the subsequent exile of the northern tribes beyond the Euphrates (vv. 7-11, 14-16).[29] This anti-dynastic oracle undoubtedly arose from later theological perceptions. Its intrusion into the prophetic story at this point exegetically transforms the entire character of the narrative. It is now an *ex eventu* prediction which reinforces the principle of divine control over history, and the aetiology—actually, the theodicy—of the northern exile in terms of cultic sins performed by the kings of Israel. Retroactively incorporated into an old popular setting, a decisive exegetical transformation occurs which gives a unitive prophetic character to the course of biblical history. On formal grounds, such *ex eventu* historiography may be compared to the ancient Mesopotamian technique of incorporating historical scenarios into omens taken prior to a military or other venture. When the old oracles were first consulted, they simply contained a protasis—referring to some anatomical or terrestrial configuration—and a neutral apodosis, predicting success or failure. After the venture, the apodosis was supplemented —*ex eventu*—with detailed historical information. The end-product, therefore, was that the apodosis appeared as a specific and accurate prediction of future events.[30]

[28] 'Ahiyya de Silo et Jeroboam Ier', *Semitica*, 11 (1961), 17-27.

[29] See the discussions of M. Sebass, 'Die Verwerfung Jerobeams I. und Salomos durch die Prophetie des Ahia von Silo', *Welt des Orients*, 4 (1968), 166-9, and M. Weinfeld, *Deuteronomy and the Deuteronomic School*, 16-18.

[30] See the discussion of J. J. Finkelstein, 'Mesopotamian Historiography', in *Cuneiform Studies and the History of Civilization* (*TAPS* 107; Philadelphia: The American Philosophical Society, 1963), 461-72, and the important earlier literature cited in n. 5.

2. Predictions of exile also made their way into other strata of the deuteronomistic corpus, like Josh. 23: 3, 16, and late sections of the Book of Deuteronomy itself (cf. 28: 63-5). A particularly striking instance of this exegetical reapplication of older oracular material can be observed by a comparison of Deut. 8: 19 and 4: 26. The first of these texts predicts 'I [YHWH] bring heaven and earth to testify against you that you will surely be destroyed (אבד תאבדון)' if you worship other gods. Now, significantly, the nature of this destruction is not specified,[31] and one is inclined here to follow W. Zimmerli's observation that, in retributive contexts, Deuteronomy and biblical wisdom literature use identical terminology (save for the deuteronomic preference for the verb אבד instead of מות to designate 'death': Deut. 7: 20, 28: 20, 22; but cf. Prov. 11: 10, 28: 28).[32]

As noted earlier,[33] Deut. 4: 25-31 is commonly regarded as part of a post-exilic passage. Within it, vv. 26-7 show a late exegetical transformation of the formulary found in 8: 19. The Israelites are warned that if they worship idols (v. 25) 'I [YHWH] bring heaven and earth to testify against you that you will surely be destroyed (אבד תאבדון) *from off this land . . . and YHWH will scatter*(הפיץ) *you among the nations . . .*' (v. 27). In the present context, the verb אבד, qualified by הפיץ,[34] now indicates exilic dispersion and not simply national death or destruction.[35] The addendum thus exegetically converts an older wisdom warning to the later exilic situation.

3. A comparison of texts within the Book of Jeremiah suggests another instance of the exegetical transformation of an earlier prophecy under the impact of the exile. The two texts in question are Jer. 23: 5-6 and 33: 14-16.

Jer. 23: 5-6	*Jer. 33: 14-16*
Behold days are coming – oracle	Behold days are coming – oracle

---

[31] Note the qualifications/specifications in Josh. 23: 13, 16, cited earlier.

[32] 'Zur Struktur der alttestamentlichen Weisheit', *ZAW* 51 (1933), 195.

[33] Above, p. 322 n. 19.

[34] The verb *hēpîṣ* also indicates exilic dispersion in Deut. 28: 64, and Ezek. 20: 23bα. Possibly emend the verb *lĕhāpîl* in Ps. 106: 27 to *lĕhāpîṣ*, since the ideology is exile for desert sins, as in Ezek. 20, and the parallel verb is *lĕzārôtām* (*bā'ărāṣôt*), which is also used in Ezek. 20: 23bβ (cf. *lĕzārôt 'ôtām bā'ărāṣôt*). The occurrence of *lĕhāpîl* in Ps. 106: 27 is probably influenced by the same verb earlier, in v. 26. Neh. 1: 8 seems to allude to a text like Deut. 28: 64, though it uses the noun *mā'al*, found in the curse-predictions of exile in Lev. 26: 38-40.

[35] According to G. M. de Tillesse, 'Sections "Tu" et sections "Vous" dans le Deutéronome', *VT* 12 (1962), 52-5, the plural use of *'ābad* is post-exilic and not part of the earliest deuteronomic strata. Nevertheless, it is obvious that Deut. 4: 27 has further qualified the doomsday language in v. 26 with the more precise allusions in v. 27.

of YHWH – when I shall establish (וַהֲקִמֹתִי) for David a righteous shoot . . . who will do justice and right in the land. In his day Judaea will be saved and Jerusalem will dwell in safety; and this is the name which one will call him: YHWH is our Righteousness.

of YHWH – when I shall establish (וַהֲקִמֹתִי) *the good word which I proclaimed to the House of Judaea and Israel. In those days and at that time I shall cause to sprout* for David a righteous shoot, who will do justice and right in the land. In those days Judaea will be saved and Jerusalem will dwell in safety; and this is what she shall be called: YHWH is our Righteousness.

The oracle in 23: 5-6 predicts the establishment of a scion of David, a 'righteous shoot'.[36] The redactional context sets this piece after an oracle of doom against evil kings who caused the exile of the people (vv. 1-2), and after an oracle predicting that this people will be divinely restored to its land and led by favourable kings (vv. 3-4). Accordingly, the royal prediction in vv. 5-6 is presented as an intensification of the royal prediction in v. 4. Indeed, the two pieces are linked by the *Stichwort* והקמתי. By the same token, the oracle of a new exodus and restoration of Israelite exiles to their homeland in vv. 7-8 may be taken as a specific intensification of the promise of national in-gathering forecast in v. 3. And indeed, these two pieces are also linked by *Stichwörter* (cf. הדחתי . . . מכל הארצות in v. 3 and הארצות . . . הדחתים in v. 8), so that the oracular intensifications in vv. 5-6 and 7-8 are chiastically related to the general predictions (i.e., v. 3 : v. 4 :: vv; 5-6 : vv. 7-8, or ABBA). The occasion for this oracle was undoubtedly the exile of 597 BCE and the subsequent enthronement of Zedekiah (צדקיה), for his name is alluded to in the designation of the future Davidic line, 'YHWH is our Righteousness צדקנו'.

Comparison suggests that Jer. 33: 14-16 is a later exegetical reflex of the oracle in 23: 5-6. First, 33: 14-16 (and vv. 17-26) are absent in the LXX, and so apparently reflect a later redactional phase of the book. And second, the particular language used in 33: 14-16 indicates a situation in which the original prediction has not yet come to pass. Indeed,

---

[36] The royal title *ṣemaḥ ṣedeq* 'righteous shoot' appears in North-west Semitic inscriptions; see *KAI* 43. 10f. It recurs elsewhere in the form *'abdi ṣemaḥ* 'my servant the shoot' (Zech. 3: 8), or simply one whose 'name is Shoot', *ṣemaḥ* (Zech. 6: 12). The combination of tree imagery and a king who does righteousness is also found in Isa. 11: 1, 4-5, 10. The language *hôṭer miggeza' yišāy wĕnēṣer miššārāsáw*, 'a branch from the stock of Jesse and a shoot from his roots' (Isa. 11: 1) finds a precise contemporary parallel in the description of Esarhaddon as *pir'u Baltil šūquru . . . kisitti sâti* 'a precious branch of Baltil . . . an enduring shoot' (Borger, *Asarhaddon*, § 20. 17).

it even appears that a reference to the original prediction has been interpolated into the old oracle. The prophetic exegete-redactor achieved this result by taking the verb והקמתי, which in 23:5 indicates the firm establishment of Davidic rule, and applying it to 'the good word which I proclaimed . . .'[37] Following this phrase and its sequel in 33:14b-15a, both of which are not found in 23:5-6, 33:15b again picks up the language of its prototype and refers to a king who does righteous acts. Presumably, then, the new prediction which refers to an earlier oracle of restoration is of a later date than Jer. 23:5-6, and comes after the fundamental break in Davidic rule which occurred at the exile.

The transformative character of this piece, and further support for its exilic ambience, are indicated by the shift of emphasis in 33:15-16 —a shift away from the future Davidic line ('in his days' becomes 'in those days') and towards the spatial topoi of Judaea and Jerusalem. Instead of the announcement 'and this is the name which one shall call him', followed by an allusion to Zedekiah, we now read 'and this is what *she* shall be called'. The reference of this phrase is, most likely, Jerusalem, which shall now be called 'YHWH is our Righteousness'. If this is so, then an older royal designation has been exegetically reused as an honorific for the future city of peace. This too reflects the post-exilic mood and hope, for a characteristic of the late Isaianic strata is that they joyfully predict and announce new names for the rebuilt Jerusalem (cf. Isa. 62:2,4,12).[38]

But even if Jer. 33:14-16 reflects an exegetical reuse of 23:5-6, there is still no exegetical closure to the prophecy. The theological tension remains, and is actually accentuated. On the one hand, the reference to 'the good word which I proclaimed' sharpens the pole of expectation, and to the degree that YHWH's word promoted confidence, also recharges the hopes of the addressees. On the other hand, however, the reference to 'in those days' makes the expected fulfilment of the oracle less immediate, and prolongs the confident waiting. This

---

[37] Cf. the parallel expression in Jer. 29:10, in connection with the fulfilment of the seventy-year oracle. In other contexts, *haddābār haṭṭôb*, 'the good word', has a more legal-contractual sense and is thus comparable to similar terms and phrases elsewhere in the Hebrew Bible, in the Aramaic Sefire inscriptions, and in various Akkadian sources. See the discussions and examples of W. Moran, 'A Note on the Treaty Terminology of the Sefire Stelas', *JNES* 22 (1963), 173-6; and M. Weinfeld, loc. cit. (above, p. 470 n. 29), 10-12. The legal-contractual (covenantal) and predictive aspects of the expression are found together in 2 Sam. 7:28 (cf. the verbs denoting oracular fulfilment in v. 25).

[38] Here Trito-Isaiah picks up an earlier Isaianic tradition, as comparison of 62:2, 4, 12 with 1:26 suggests. Of striking import in connection with the name in Jer. 33:16 is that Isa. 1:26 foresees calling Zion *'îr haṣṣedeq* 'the city of righteousness'.

is less an exegetical manœuvre than an attempt to save the authority of the prediction by opening it further towards the future. Implicitly, the tension is shifted away from the authority of the oracle and towards the spiritual state of the addressee. The prediction will come to pass, but one must wait for it. This passive mode of dealing with 'future fulfilments' is explicitly articulated in a number of other prophetic passages, like Isa. 10: 25 and Hab. 2: 3,[39] and in the popular proverb found in Ezek. 12: 22, which the prophet twice rebuts with new divine words (vv. 23-5, 26-8).[40] Another, more active mode is the attempt to 'compute the end' of an unfulfilled prediction, or to reinterpret the temporal application of prophecies which have apparently 'fallen to the ground empty'. It is to these that we now turn.

The Scholarly Study and Respecification of Prophecies

As background—even contemporary background—of the biblical materials to be discussed here, it is of considerable interest to observe the scholarly-exegetical transformation and reuse of oracles in ancient Near Eastern sources. Indeed, there are several examples of prophetic predictions used for propagandistic purposes. From Egypt, for example, there is a hieratic text dated to 1991 BCE and presented as a prophecy of one Neferti, before King Snefru of the Fourth Dynasty.[41] It describes the ascendancy of a king who will overcome all manner of evils— rebellions, foreign invasions, and the like. As G. Posner has convincingly argued, however, this prophecy is in reality a *vaticinium ex eventu* composed in support of the royal legitimacy of Ammenemes I, of the Twelfth Dynasty.[42] Another, later example of a prophecy used for the purpose of political propaganda is the so-called 'Demotic Chronicle'.[43] After the Battle of Raphia, there were, for a long time, uprisings against Ptolemaic rule by various native 'rebels'. In order to support the claims of one of these contenders, and the restoration of native rule his

[39] For an analysis, see R. Carroll, 'Eschatological Delay in the Prophetic Tradition', *ZAW* 94 (1982), 47-58.

[40] The proverb and the divine responses are replete with technical terminology which had a wide distribution in prophetic circles. Thus, for the proverbial statement in v. 22 that 'the days have been prolonged (*ya'ărĕkû*) and every vision comes to nought (*'ābad*)' there are parallels in Jer. 29: 28 and 18: 18, respectively; for the divine response which says that the 'time is near (*qārĕbû*, v. 23)' and the fulfilment 'will not be prolonged (*lō' yimmāšēk*, vv. 25, 28)' there are technical parallels in Isa. 5: 12 and 13: 22, respectively; and for the idea that an oracle 'will be done/accomplished (*yē'āśeh*, vv. 27-8)' there is a precise parallel in Num. 23: 19.

[41] For a translation, see Pritchard, *ANET*[2], 444-6.

[42] *Littérature et politique dans l'Egypte de la XIIe dynastie* (Paris: Librairie ancienne Honoré Champion, 1956), 21-60, 145-57.

[43] See the references cited above, p. 453 n. 15.

dynasty would achieve, the 'Chronicle' cites oracles which refer to acts performed by Egyptian kings that parallel acts accomplished by the rebel supported by the author of the 'Chronicle', and even mentions specific dates referring to the precise beginning of his rebellion and coronation. Clearly, these oracles were composed after the fact, and retroactively serve to support the new king's claims to rule and present him as one of the saviour-kings traditionally expected to save the Egyptians from foreign domination.

Ancient Mesopotamia, for its part, offers several examples of *ex eventu* prophecies serving political goals.[44] One particularly notable case is the description of an evil ruler who removed sancta from the shrine of Uruk, and the prediction of a 'king [who] will arise' and restore them. On the basis of royal inscriptions, the former king has been identified with the eighth-century Babylonian, Eriba-Marduk, and the latter with Nebuchadnezzar II.[45] The credibility of the oracle, written *after the fact*, is dramatically demonstrated; and its major concern to buttress the authority of the ensuing prediction about Nebuchadnezzar's son (the neo-Babylonian king Amel-Marduk)—and so gain support for his reign—is contextually established.[46]

In addition to these instances of *vaticinia ex eventu*, the reinterpretation and 'updating' of old predictions is also very much in evidence in ancient Near Eastern sources. Perhaps the most intriguing instance is the so-called 'Potter's Oracle', whose text-tradition and successive reworkings have been studied by L. Koenen, and appear to derive from the prototype known from Neferti's prophecy noted earlier.[47] The original oracle was supposedly made by a potter in the reign of Pharaoh Amenhotep in response to the smashing of his pottery by zealots who considered his actions on the island of Helios to be sacrilegious. The

[44] See the so-called Text A, among others, published by A. K. Grayson and W. G. Lambert, 'Akkadian Apocalypses', *JCS* 18 (1964), 7–23, and the discussion of it by W. W. Hallo, 'Akkadian Apocalypses', *IEJ* 16 (1966), 231–42.

[45] The text was published by H. Hunger, 'Die Tontafeln der XXVII. Kampagne', *Vorläufiger Bericht über die . . . Ausgrabungen in Uruk-Warka*, 26 (1972), 87, and translated and discussed by H. Hunger and S. A. Kaufman, 'A New Akkadian Prophecy Text', *JAOS* 95 (1975), 371–5; S. A. Kaufman, 'Prediction, Prophecy, and Apocalypse in the Light of New Akkadian Texts', in *Proceedings of VIth World Congress of Jewish Studies* (Jerusalem: Academic Press, 1977), i. 223–5.

[46] For the underlying political struggles of the period, see V. A. Beljauski, 'Der politische Kampf in Babylon in den Jahren 562–556 v. Chr.', *Beiträge zu Geschichte, Kultur und Religion des alten Orients*, in memory of Eckhard Unger, ed. M. Lurker (Baden-Baden: V. Koerner, 1971), 197–215.

[47] For the text, see his 'Die Prophezeiungen des "Töpfers"', *Zeitschrift für Papyrologie und Epigraphik*, 2 (1968), 178–209; for Koenen's analysis, followed here, see 'The Prophecies of the Potter: A Prophecy of World Renewal Becomes an Apocalypse', in *Proceedings of the Twelfth International Congress of Papyrology*, ed. D. H. Samuels (Toronto: A. M. Hakkert, 1970), 249–54.

potter predicted the destruction of Egypt and its eventual restoration under a saviour-king. According to Koenen, this event most likely reflects the revolt of Harsiesis (*c.* 130 BCE) and predicts the restoration of native rule from the Greeks.

But this predicted overthrow of Greek hegemony did not occur, with the result that significant interpolations were inserted into the old oracle, as is evidenced by the version of it preserved in P. Oxyrhynchus 2332 (third century CE). The original prediction assigned a reign of fifty-seven years to the saviour-king; a later gloss reversed this, and added it to an older prediction by 'Bokcharis the Lamb' of the period of evil to be brought on by the advent of the Greeks (P. Oxyrhynchus 2332, lines 31-4).[48] If one subtracts this time-period from the end originally predicted by Bokcharis, one comes to 137 CE for the end of the period of evil. This period would have been just prior to the onset of the next Sothis cycle (139 CE); and so, argued Koenen, the old prophecy was transformed into an apocalypse which would have its onset at the beginning of a new world-cycle.[49] A similar notion of an apocalyptic restoration of native rule from Greek hegemony, also formulated as the climax to a divine cycle, recurs in the contemporary Dan. 10-12, to be examined below. And, as we shall also suggest with respect to this biblical prediction, one cannot but suspect that such prophecies as the 'Potter's Oracle' actually helped foment and authorize native rebellions.

1. There are numerous indications of unfulfilled or failed prophecies in the Hebrew Bible, and of subsequent attempts to reinterpret them. Fortunately for our historical reconstruction, the failure with reinterpretation is often specifically indicated. Thus, in Isa. 16:13 the prophet refers to the previous oracle against Moab and acknowledges its failure: 'this is the prophetic word (זה הדבר) which YHWH spoke to Moab *formerly* (מאז).' He then continues, in v. 14a, to correct this oracle and to predict '*But now* (ועתה) YHWH has spoken as follows, "In [but] three years . . . the glory of Moab shall be disgraced — for all its vast horde."' Another indication of the revision of old predictions occurs in Ezek. 29. Basing himself on his older oracles against Tyre and Sidon (26:1-28:24, esp. 26:7-14), the prophet notes, at the end of a series of doom-prophecies against Egypt, that Nebuchadnezzar did not destroy Tyre, and that 'he had no recompense for himself or his troops . . . for the siege-labour which he made against it' (vv. 17-18). Following

---

[48] See J. Krall, 'Vom König Bokchoris', *Festgaben zu Ehren Max Budingers* (Innsbruck: Wagner, 1892), 3 ff., and Koenen, 'Die Prophezeiungen', 189, n. 22, 'The Prophecies', 252.

[49] The cycle prophesied by 'the Lamb' is 900 years. See Koenen, 'The Prophecies', 252f., for an explanation of its symbolic meaning.

this, Ezekiel adds a new prophetic word which predicts that Egypt will be given to the Babylonian king as 'recompense for his troops . . . as the wages for his service' (vv. 19-20). The juxtaposition of the two oracles, and the recitation of the unfulfilled prediction in the new one (v. 18b and vv. 19-20a), make clear that this Ezekielian passage is reinterpreting an old prophecy. As in the Isaianic forecast, the prophet is dependent upon a new word of God because the original one has gone unfulfilled.

A much stronger and more precise reference to an unfulfilled prophecy and its imminent realization can be found in Ezek. 38:17. In that passage, after two extended oracles referring to Gog and the apocalyptic destruction which that country would wreak on Judaea, the prophet rhetorically inquires, 'are you [Gog] not the one of whom I [YHWH] spoke (בימים קדמונים) aforetimes by means of my servants, the prophets of Israel, who prophesied then for years concerning your advent?' Clearly the prophet saw the advancing devastation as the fulfilment of ancient prophecies. One may presume, given that Gog is addressed in vv. 15-16 as one who will 'come from the recesses of the north, and . . . will arise against my people Israel as a cloud . . .', that the prophecies alluded to in v. 17 are those of Jeremiah, who predicted that YHWH would 'bring' evil 'from the north' and would 'arise like clouds' (4:6, 13; cf. 1:14-15, 6:22). This impression of Jeremian influence is further reinforced by the fact that, in his earlier references to Gog's advent, Ezekiel referred to this enemy as one that would 'arise as a cloud' (38:9).[50] While other prophecies also appear to be cited by Ezekiel,[51] it is his expectation of devastation 'from the recesses of the north' that seems uppermost in his mind. This is most striking, for, in the citation of Jer. 1:15 in Jer. 25:9, it is clear that a later deuteronomistic glossator understood the advent of Nebuchadnezzar of Babylon in 605 BCE as the fulfilment of the old oracle of destruction 'from the north'. Presumably, Ezekiel (or a pseudo-Ezekiel) believed the advent of Gog to be the true fulfilment of this ancient prediction. In the process, a national oracle has been expanded and has assumed apocalyptic significance.

2. In addition to these circumstantial and often precise references to the fact that new—contemporary—oracles are the fulfilments of older ones, it is possible to point to at least two instances where the formula כי פי ה׳ דבר 'for so YHWH has prophesied/said' serves the same

---

[50] The use of these Jeremian texts by the author of Ezek. 38 was set forth by G. Hölscher, *Hesekiel – der Dichter und das Buch. Eine literärkritische Untersuchung* (BZAW 39; Giessen: A. Töpelman, 1924), 177-84.

[51] e.g. Isa. 10:3 at Ezek. 38:9.

end.[52] Both texts are part of late post-exilic prophecies. The first occurs
at Obad. 17-18. There, in the context of a prophecy against Edom, the
people of Jacob-Israel are told that they 'shall dispossess those that
dispossessed them '(וירשו . . . את מורישיהם). Then shall the house of
Jacob be fire . . . and the house of Esau chaff . . . and the house of Esau
shall have no survivor (שריד); for so YHWH has prophesied.' One can
hardly doubt that this prophecy was intended to fulfill the ancient
prophetic words of Balaam, who predicted the stellar rise of Jacob in
Num. 24:17, and announced in v. 18 that 'Edom shall be his [con-
quered] possession (יְרֵשָׁה); Seir, his enemy, shall be his [conquered]
possession (יְרֵשָׁה) . . . Jacob shall trample them down, and destroy
every survivor (שריד) of Ir.' But at what historical moment, and for
what precise reason, the ancient words of a foreign prophet took on
urgency for Obadiah, is hard to say. Evidently, some nationalist revival
is anticipated. In this connection it is striking to note that the royalist
imagery in Num. 24:17 is loudly echoed in Obad. 20-1 — which eagerly
anticipates the eschatological dominion of YHWH overall.

The second example of the formulary 'for so YHWH has prophesied'
comes from Isa. 58:14, where Trito-Isaiah tells the Israelites that if they
would strictly obey the Sabbath, and refrain from all manner of work,
'then you will rejoice with YHWH; and I shall lead you (והרכבתיך)
over the highlands (על־במותי (K) ארץ) and sustain (והאכלתיך) you
with the inheritance of Jacob (נחלת יעקב), your father'. In this promise
with exhortation, the prophet is clearly invoking Moses' song at Deut.
32:9, 13. There the people are told that 'Jacob is the portion of his
inheritance (נחלתו) ' and that YHWH 'led him over the highlands
(ארץ (K) ירכבהו על־במותי), and sustained [him] (ויאכל) ' with bounty.
Several subtle changes have thus crept into the reuse of the old song. In
the first place, this last is a warning and an inspired premonition of
future Israelite behaviour, but it is non-revelatory, versus the oracle in
Isa. 58:14 which makes use of it. We thus have YHWH citing a human
traditum, though a close examination of the shifts in voice involved (cf.
'then you will rejoice *with YHWH*' followed by '*I* sustained you' and
'*for so YHWH* has prophesied') shows the individual prophet struggling
to suppress his own authority. Furthermore, it will be noted that the
selection from the song is descriptive of past benefactions, not prescriptive of future ones — and does not even hint of such. The reinterpretation is thus a *tour de force*. And finally it should be added that
Isa. 58:14 refers to the land as the inheritance of the people, not the
people as YHWH's inheritance. Such a transformation fully accords

---

52 A. Kaminka, 'Expressions of Moses and the Psalms in Isaiah', *Leš.* 1 (1928-
* 9), 40f. [Heb.], deserves credit for identifying this phenomenon. In addition to
the two cases developed below, he mentions several others which I consider
dubious. His understanding of *kî* has been followed here.

with the pervasive post-exilic concern with return to the land, with the added factor that true Sabbath observance is the key to sustained tenure there. In this matter, too, Trito-Isaiah echoes the contemporary ideology of the axial position of the Sabbath – an ideology which, as shown earlier,[53] saw in the desecration of the Sabbath the principal reason for Judaea's destruction, and, correspondingly, believed its reconsecration to be vital.[54]

3. The foregoing are isolated instances of reapplied prophecies. In the following we shall turn to one continuous tradition of oracular reinterpretation, the diverse applications made of Jer. 25: 9-12. This oracle predicts that 'This whole land shall become a ruin and a waste and these people shall be subjugated to the king of Babylon for seventy years', after which there would be a reversal of fates, and Israel's oppressor, Babylon, would be devastated.

The first of the various inner-biblical reapplications of this oracle is, significantly, found in interpolations added to the Massoretic version of this prophecy. Thus, in MT Jer. 25: 9, 11-12 the northern enemy is specifically identified with Babylon and her king. These secondary identifications are noticeably missing in the Septuagint account which, accordingly, attests to an older textual stratum before the northern enemy was identified. This identification of the 'north' with Babylon was already in place, however, in the first formal allusion to the oracle in Jer. 29: 10.[55] Here the hopeful conclusion of the original prophecy – regarding the eventual suppression of the enemy – was taken up and reworked in a letter sent by Jeremiah to the Judaean exiles. The older

---

[53] Cf. Neh. 13:15-18, and the central position of the Sabbath in Ezek. 20.

[54] Other examples of oracular reference to earlier oracles include (1) Joel 3: 5, which uses the phrase *ka'ăšer 'āmar YHWH* 'as YHWH had said/predicted' after an apparent allusion to Isa. 4: 2; and (2) Hab. 2: 13a, which uses the phrase *mē'ēt YHWH* 'from YHWH' before a citation of Isa. 11: 9b.

[55] The reinterpretation in Jer. 29: 10 opens the sub-unit of vv. 10-15, which comprise the logical and rhetorical pivot of Jeremiah's letter to the Judaean exiles (vv. 4-28). Here the prophet delivers an oracular rebuttal to the contestations of the 'false' prophets (referred to in vv. 8-9, 21). Jer. 29: 10-15 also stands at the literary centre point of the letter and its editorial framework – particularly if vv. 16-20 are a later interpolation, as suggested thematically and by the absence of these verses from the LXX (cf. the occurrence of vv. 16-20 *between* vv. 14 and 15 in the Lucian version). Note the symmetry of topic and language in vv. 1-3 (A) and v. 29 (A'); vv. 4-7 (B) and v. 28 (B'); and vv. 8-9 (C) and vv. 21-7 (C') – which chiastically surround vv. 10-15 (D). Besides these stylized elements, the original epistle has been embedded in a narrative history and has substituted prophetic for epistolary formulae, as already observed by D. Pardee, 'An Overview of Ancient Hebrew Epistolography', *JBL* 97 (1978), 330f. and n. 47. Deuteronomistic phrases and topoi are especially noticeable in vv. 11 (cf. Jer. 18: 7), 12-13 (cf. Deut. 4: 26-30, 30: 1-5), 18 (Deut. 28: 25; Jer. 34: 17) and 19 (Jer. 7: 13, 25, 11: 7).

(pre-exilic) emphasis in Jer. 25:12, which predicted that YHWH would 'visit' (אפקד) punishment upon the oppressor of Israel, was deftly reformulated in 29:10 to express a more conciliatory (post-exilic) concern. YHWH would 'remember' (אפקד) his exiled people in seventy years' time, would establish his 'good' prophetic oracle (cf. Jer. 33: 14b), and would restore the exiled people of Israel to their homeland. Accordingly, the prophecy which had been formulated originally to forecast doom on the native land and the subjugation of its inhabitants in exile for a period of seventy years, was subsequently reinterpreted as a prophecy of hope for the diasporic community.

Just how the prophet Jeremiah came to predict a period of seventy years' subjugation is not certain. On the one hand, it is clear from both inner-biblical prophecies (Isa. 23:15-17, against Tyre) and contemporary Assyrian texts (an inscription of Esarhaddon)[56] that a seventy-year period of destruction or subjugation was an established typological motif in the ancient Near East. What complicates the matter is that there is a clearly witnessed position in our biblical sources that some Judaeans in Babylon regarded Cyrus' decree of national restoration (538 BCE) as a sign that the old forecast of doom was over. This fact might, of course, suggest that the period of nearly seventy years of Babylon's rule over Palestine (sixty-six to sixty-five years) was itself the basis for an *ex eventu* prophecy attributed to Jeremiah.[57] But if this is so, three problems remain: first, *ex eventu* prophecies tend to be – and can afford to be – precise, like the sixty-five-year prediction in Isa. 7: 8; second, as just noted, the period of seventy years was evidently a typological number well established in the contemporary eighth-seventh-century Near Eastern *Umwelt*; and third, the Jeremian prophecy in 25:9-12 only mentions the destruction of the land and only refers the period of seventy years to Israel's subjugation to Babylon in Babylon – there being no reference either to the fact that the *land* would lie waste for seventy years or to the destruction of the Temple,[58] two issues which one would expect to be mentioned *if* Jer. 25: 9-12 was an *ex eventu* prophecy, and which are actually taken up in the later prophetic reinterpretations themselves.

For example, in the earliest preserved non-Jeremian reinterpretation, made by the Chronicler in 2 Chron. 36: 18-21, it is clear that it is precisely the destruction of the Temple and Jerusalem, and the exile of the remnant population to Babylon, which was considered to be the

---

[56] R. Borger, *Asarhaddon*, p. 15, Episode 10, Fassung A. 2b-9 and B. 19-20. Cf. the earlier observations of D. D. Luckenbill, 'The Black Stone of Esarhaddon', *AJSL* 41 (1925), 167.

[57] See the argument of A. Orr, 'The Seventy Years of Babylon', *VT* 6 (1956), 304-6.

[58] A point also made by Orr, ibid., though with an opposite conclusion to that drawn here.

fulfilment for Jeremiah's prophecy of seventy years' destruction of the homeland. Quite certainly, this in itself is an exegetical revision of significant interest. But the Chronicler introduced an even more novel element when he incorporated into his citation of Jeremiah's oracle an excerpt from Lev. 26: 34-5. Compare the parallel passages:

Lev. 26: 34-5	*2 Chron. 36:19-21*
Then shall *the land make up for its sabbaths*; for *all the time that it lies desolate* shall the land *rest and make up for its sabbaths.*	And they [the Chaldeans] burnt the house of God, and broke down the walls of Jerusalem . . . to fulfil the word of YHWH by the mouth of Jeremiah, until *the land had made up for its sabbaths; for all the time that it lay desolate it rested* to fulfil 70 years.

Viewed synoptically, one may surmise that even as the Chronicler's general priestly penchant drew him to this passage, it was Lev. 26: 34-5 which shaped his interpretation that the seventy years of doom in the Jeremian oracle were recompense *to the land*. Moreover, since Lev. 26: 34-5 is itself set within a prophetic context—a prediction and warning for potential acts of covenantal malfeasance—one may assume that the Chronicler also considered Jer. 25: 9-12 to be a prophecy *based* upon that covenant warning which also included a forecast of exile and restoration (cf. vv. 41-5).

The seventy-year oracle is also referred to twice in the prophecies of Zechariah. Once in 1:12 (datable to 520/19; cf. 1:7), when an angel challenged YHWH and asks 'How long will you withhold compassion from Jerusalem and the cities of Judaea with whom you have been angry *these seventy years*?'; and again in 7: 5 (datable to 518/17; cf. 7:1), when YHWH refers to a series of fast-days which many Israelites observed '*these seventy years*' in remembrance of the destruction of Judaea. As the prophet also spoke of the rebuilding of the Temple during this period (note 1: 16, which continues the sequence of v. 12 + vv. 13-15),[59] and as it was completed soon thereafter (in 516/15; cf. Ezra 6: 15), it is conceivable that the anticipated fulfilment of a seventy-year oracle believed to have been effective from the second Judaean exile (in 587/6) may have actually fuelled national energies towards the restoration of the Temple (in 516/15). In any event, both the Chronicler and Zechariah attempted to apply the Jeremian oracle of wrath and reconstruction quite literally: seventy years meant seventy years—the alternative attempts to date the onset of the oracle notwithstanding. However, if for the Chronicler—despite his strong interest in a revitalized Temple elsewhere—the 'realized eschatology' of the Jeremian oracle focused on a restoration of the land, and the people's return to it, the

[59] See also 4: 9 and Ezra 6: 14.

prophet Zechariah added his own touch. For him, apparently, the realization of the seventy-year period meant that the Temple – formerly destroyed and subjected to foreign rule – could be restored. In this he anticipates Daniel, as we shall see.

These several reinterpretations of the old Jeremian prophecy, like the reapplication of divine oracles generally, imply two religious postures – on the one hand, trust in the basic accuracy of predictive revelations; on the other, its corollary, an acute sense of divine involvement in Israel's historical destiny. The result is a paradox: the very tensions elicited by oracular expectations – particularly when intensified by dissonance between prediction and reality – were transcended by the inherent authority of the oracles themselves. As these were believed to be of divine authority, and so testified to YHWH's involvement in history, failed expectations were not abandoned, *but rather reinterpreted*. However, where the gap between promise and fulfilment widened, the paradox of God's historical concern was increasingly resolved on a more mysterious plane. Once the direct nexus between the words of an oracle and their apparent historical reference was broken through successive reapplications, it was not long before their true signification seemed totally inaccessible to plain human understanding. Then, only God could divine the real meaning of his words; then, living, spoken prophetic oracles gave way to revealed interpretations of them as fixed, studied texts. All this broached a profound change in the nature of biblical prophecy.[60]

The processes just noted are exemplified by Dan. 9. This text begins with the wise Daniel inquiring into prophetic books in the hope of discerning the correct application of Jeremiah's seventy-year oracle concerning the period of Jerusalem's desolation (v. 2). To be sure, the historical fiction of the book is that Daniel was a Judaean exiled to Babylon following Nebuchadnezzar's siege of Judaea, in the third year of King Jehoiakim (*c.* 606/5; see 1: 1-6) – so that the Jeremian oracle would, once again, appear to apply literally to the immediate exilic situation. But such is not the case. It is clear from Dan. 9: 24-7 that the oracle was interpreted to embrace a much longer historical period, seventy sabbatical cycles, or ten jubilees. This interpretation was presumably stimulated by 2 Chron. 36: 21 which, owing to its reuse of Lev. 26: 34-5, seems to have understood the seventy years of Jeremiah's oracle as ten sabbatical cycles. Another influence on Dan. 9: 24-7 was undoubtedly the jubilee computation of Lev. 25: 1-55 as a whole, wherein it is taught that a jubilee cycle of forty-nine years marked both

[60] Cf. J. J. Collins, *The Apocalyptic Vision of the Book of Daniel* (Harvard Semitic Monographs, 16; Missoula: Scholars Press, 1977), 85-7; also, in general, R. North, 'Prophecy to Apocalyptic via Zechariah', *SVT* 22 (1972), 47-71.

the maximal period of indentured servitude and the maximal period wherein land may be alienated – due to economic distraints – from its ancestral heirs.[61] It is quite striking that Dan. 9: 25 apportions one entire jubilee cycle to the period from the assumed effective onset of the Jeremiah oracle to the end of the exile and Cyrus' decree (the years 587-38). This period thus marks the first of ten jubilees, and so the first stage of release from foreign hegemony. In short, the initial period of Jerusalem's servitude was interpreted to be of forty-nine years' duration, so that its subsequent restoration to Israelite ownership would constitute a דרור, or the return of ancestral patrimony to its rightful heir (cf. Lev. 25: 10).[62] It is intriguing to suppose that the references in Isa. 61: 1 to the post-exilic restoration as a release of prisoners may reflect an even earlier exegetical application of Lev. 25: 1-55.[63]

The span of 490 years, or 70 sabbatical cycles, is an attempt to represent the span of ancient Israelite history from the destruction of the first Temple in Jerusalem (in 587 BCE) to the expected destruction of the abominations polluting the rebuilt Temple in the days of the Seleucid Antiochus IV Epiphanes (175-64 BCE). It thus marks the middle period of Israelite history: a time of servitude and desolation, after an era of ancient cultic-national glory and prior to its future advent and renewal. But, it must be stressed, the 70 sabbatical cycles essentially constitute a *schematic* span of time based on multiples of 7 and 70 – a factor which helped give the ancient Jeremian oracle renewed credence – and not much more: for after the first jubilee period (7 sabbaticals; Dan. 9: 24) there yet remains a total of 63 sabbatical 'weeks' or 441 years (divided into two segments: 62 'weeks' and 1 'week'; cf. vv. 25, 27) until the final *kairos*, whose date was thus well beyond the imminent and meaningful historical horizon of our apocalyptic writer. Of undoubtedly more concrete significance to him, then, was the overall symbolic scheme, in the first instance, and the final sabbatical 'week', in which time he believed himself to be living.

[61] Cf. P. Grelot, 'Soixante-dix semaines d'années', *Bib.* 50 (1969), 178-81.

[62] B. Z. Wacholder, 'Chronomessianism: The Timing of Messianic Movements and the Calendar of Sabbatical Cycles', *HUCA* 46 (1975), 205f., incorporates the first jubilee cycle within the initial sixty-two-week period, thereby requiring a third stage of another forty-nine years *after* the restoration of the Temple. It seems simpler and neater to interpret Dan. 7: 25 to mean that the first jubilee cycle was distinct from the next nine – so that Cyrus' decree would conclude the first stage of redemption, and the restoration of Jerusalem (v. 27) would conclude the Jeremiah oracle.

[63] It is striking that Isa. 61: 1, and possibly also Dan. 9: 24f., are cited in the apocalyptic speculations in 11Q *Melch*. 3. ii. 3-9 (18-19²). For this *pešer* fragment, see J. T. Milik, 'Milki-sedek et Milki-resaʻ dans les ancient écrits juifs et chrétiens', *JJS* 23 (1972), 97-9.

This last time-frame, apportioned into two equal parts (vv. 26f.), included a succession of cultic sacrileges and collusions between the Seleucid dynasty and an extreme wing of Hellenizing Jews. Its onset is quite assuredly marked from the year 171 BCE, or shortly thereafter, when the high priest Onias III was murdered and the pro-Hellenizers gained new power (Dan. 9: 26; 2 Macc. 4: 1-38; cf. Dan. 11: 22). For it will be observed that somewhat over three years after this event, on 15 Kislev 167, the Temple was plundered and desecrated by Epiphanes (1 Macc. 29-35, 54-9; 2 Macc. 5: 22-6; 6: 1-2), and that these events plus other anti-Jewish persecutions led in due course to the Maccabean revolt that climaxed in the victorious rededication of the Temple three years thereafter, on 25 Kislev 164.

In short, the period 171-164 BCE was clearly a crucial sabbatical 'week' divided into two parts, just as Daniel had predicted. But even if this is so, one will note that the dating of each half ('for half a week', Dan. 9: 27) is not as precise as one would expect from a *vaticinium ex eventu* – unless, of course, the two halves represent an intentional schematic periodization of the final 'week'. It may therefore be supposed that the author of Dan. 9: 24-7 spoke some time after the year 171 BCE and offered a genuine prediction of the course of events. This prediction may even have served as a type of 'calculated' messianic propaganda in support of the great anti-Seleucid uprising. Regrettably, a final determination of these matters is not forthcoming from our sources, although we do know that this application of the old Jeremian oracle was itself neither determinative nor final: for when new events forced even further adjustments to the older expectations and computations, the same oracle was repeatedly revised (cf. Dan. 12: 7, 11-12).[64] Such a phenomenon suggests a sense of being at the brink of a providential moment. It furthermore attests to the fact that the exoteric dimension of earlier prophecy has been decisively altered and has entered a new phase. Prophetic words are no longer predominantly living speech, but rather inscribed and inscrutable data whose true meanings are an esoteric mystery revealed by God to a special adept and his pious circle (cf. Dan. 9: 22-3, 10: 14-21, 11: 33-5, 12: 9-13).[65]

---

[64] The fact that the phrase *šiqqûṣ měšōmēm* in Dan. 9: 27 (and 11: 31, 12: 11) is also found in 1 Macc. 1: 54, with reference to the Temple desecration, further points to the period of Antiochus IV for the interpreted oracle. E. Nestle long ago suggested that this phrase is a euphemistic correction for *ba'al šāmēm*; cf. 'Zu Daniel', *ZAW* 4 (1883), 284. On Josephus' use of this imagery, the seventy-year oracle and some of Daniel's dream images, and its bearing on ancient Jewish expectations, resistence, and revolt in the Roman period, see F. F. Bruce, 'Josephus and Daniel', *ASTI* 4 (1965), 148-62. For another contemporary usage, in the so-called Marcan apocalypse, see C. H. Dodd, 'The Fall of Jerusalem and the "Abomination of Desolation"', *Journal of Roman Studies*, 37 (1947), 47-54.

[65] The appearance in Dan. 9 of a revelation based on an ancient text, together

It may be added that such reworking of oracles, and their supplementation by divine exegesis, complement tendencies observable in biblical laws. With oracles as with law, the meanings of original revelations were dependent upon, and mediated by, exegesis. However, the reinterpretation of prophecy produces a sharper hermeneutical-religious tension than legal exegesis. The reason lies in the separate structures of the two phenomena. Whereas legal traditions may be perceived as special applications of, or supplements to, an already realized revelation, unfulfilled prophecies raise the more unsettling question of the very realizability of predictive revelations. Even the projection of these oracles into a far-off eschatological moment, and their transformation into codes to be deciphered by God, could not diminish this fundamental tension. On the contrary, such a tension served to open an abyss in the religious imagination whose ultimate expression was apocalyptic consciousness. With this development, the face of prophetic predictions has turned fatefully heavenward, leaving the individual powerless to envisage their meaning without divine intervention. This trust that a God-given solution will come to pass is the hope of hopelessness as elicited by unfulfilled prophecies.[66]

4. As indicated, Dan. 9 envisages the culmination of Jeremiah's seventy-year oracle in the time of Antiochus (Epiphanes) IV, during which time the Seleucid oppression and the Maccabean religio-nationalistic rebellion occurred. This oppression and rebellion have, in fact, left their stamp on the structure and contents of the entire book. For whatever the traditionary background of the motifs of Daniel in the lion's den (ch. 3), or in the pit of fire (ch. 6), and despite their occurrence in Babylon and not in Palestine (Coele Syria), it is quite certain that they present images of religious persecution, steadfast faith, and miraculous divine intervention which could not but have been of solace to the Maccabean editor(s) who lived in a fearsome time of religious testing, and whose apocalyptic texts counselled steadfast faith and hope in divine vindication during the times of trial (esp. Dan. 11: 30-6, 12: 1-3, 9-13). Moreover, these two martyrdom motifs are symmetrically arranged in the opening seven-chapter unit (note the subscript in 7: 28,

with those based on dreams and omens, reflects what A. M. J. Festugière called the 'literary fictions' of revelations in the Hellenistic world. See *La Révélation d'Hermès Trismégiste*, i. *L'Astrologie et les sciences occultes* (Paris: Gabalda, 1950), 312-27.

[66] The importance of the fulfilment of older prophecies in the development of apocalyptic eschatology was given detailed early emphasis by J. Wellhausen, 'Zur apokalyptischen Literatur', *Skizzen und Vorarbeiten*, 6 (1899), 225-34. He uses the felicitous phrase 'elasticity of hope' to characterize the mode of consciousness involved.

'here concludes the piece') with two other chapters envisaging historical cycles of four kingdoms (chs. 2, 7).[67] This fourfold sequence (Babylonia, Media, Persia, Greece) affects both the climactic chronology of the opening chapters, which thus anticipate the onset of Greek hegemony (cf. 1: 1-5: 29, 5: 30-6: 27, 6: 28), and the climactic chronology of the final apocalyptic visions in Dan. 9-12. The latter culminate in visions of angelic and earthly battles consequent upon the rise of the final Seleucid era (Dan. 10-11), and preceding the victory forecast for the Jewish faithful (Dan. 12). As recent studies of common schemata in Persian, Greek, and Roman oracle-collections have now conclusively shown, such a climactic tetralogy served as a form of native protest, reflecting the nationalistic aspirations of conquered peoples whose kingship and religious ceremonies were variously curtailed under Hellenistic overlords.[68] Finally, it may be added that the 'Potter's Oracle' referred to earlier is a contemporary parallel from Ptolemaic Egypt to this phenomenon of oracles apocalyptically predicting the end of a world-cycle and the restoration of a native cult and kingship. The temporal span referred to in the 'Bokcharian' interpolations lasts 900 years, a period of symbolic and cosmic significance.[69]

Dan. 9 fits into this overall picture: it is dated to the period of the Medes (i.e. Cyrus); it describes foreign hegemony and the Temple desecrations of Antiochus IV (167 BCE); and it anticipates the restoration of a native religious order at the conclusion of a 'divine' span of ten jubilee cycles (vv. 24-7). Moreover, as suggested, the shift in this text to an angelic interpreter is a notable development in the very nature of prophecy. Indeed, such a trajectory away from living prophetic words and towards the scholarly study and reinterpretation of earlier ones—paralleled by the existence of 'scholarly' oracles and oracular interpolations in the surrounding cultures[70]—forms the culmination of

[67] On such structural aspects of Dan. 2-7, cf. A. Lenglet, 'La Structure littéraire de Daniel 2-7', *Bib.* 53 (1972), 169-90.

[68] See the seminal observations of J. Swain, 'The Theory of the Four Monarchies—Opposition History Under the Roman Empire', *Classical Philology*, 35 (1940), 1-21.

[69] Cf. Koenen's remarks, loc. cit. (above, n. 47). Regarding the combination of cycles and apocalyptic speculations, also cf. 6Q 12 and 11Q *Melch.* 3 ii.

[70] In addition to the 'Demotic Chronicle' and the 'Potter's Oracle', one may mention, for example, the tendentious reinterpretation of a liver omen in support of the revolt of Molon of Media against Antiochus III. Regarding this document, see A. T. Olmstead, 'Intertestamental Studies', *JAOS* 56 (1936), 245, and F. Thureau-Dangin, *Tablettes d'Uruk* (Musée du Louvre, Textes Cunéiformes, 6; Paris: P. Guethner 1922), No. 6, Pls. XVI-XVII. Of related interest are the pseudo-predictions of the so-called 'Dynastic Prophecy', composed in the Seleucid period and published by A. K. Grayson, *Babylonian Historical-Literary Texts* (Toronto Semitic Texts and Studies, 3; Toronto: University of Toronto Press, 1975), ch. 3.

a process noticeable from the end of the pre-exilic period. As observed, the reinterpretations of the seventy-year oracle by the Chronicler, Zechariah, and Daniel show an increasing epigonal interest in ancient oracles.[71] Such study of prophetic 'Scriptures' and their anthological reuse is further attested to in Dan. 9: 24-7. Study of this passage will provide an introduction to the more complex and pervasive epigonal reuse of older prophecies in Dan. 11-12.

(*a*) *Daniel's prayer in Dan. 9: 4-20.* This prayer—found after the *mise-en-scène* concerning Daniel's studious encounter with the old Jeremian oracle (v. 2) and before the appearance of the angelic interpreter of that oracle (v. 21)—has had its detractors and supporters.[72] Most notable in the debate over its authenticity is the fact that the content of the prayer is one of supplication and confession, whereas one might have contextually expected a prayer for illumination.[73] Additionally, the language of the prayer is formulated in the traditional deuteronomistic manner, reflects a deuteronomistic theology of history (emphasizing rewards or punishments for covenantal allegiance or malfeasance), and witnesses to a rare use of the tetragram YHWH in the Book of Daniel.[74] But such considerations do not go sufficiently to the heart of the matter. For although an old liturgical pattern has been used, it has been stylistically adapted to its context; and further, the apparent theological inconsistency of a confession reflecting divine punishment in a context where one might have expected a request for illumination (in decoding an old oracle of hope) is no inconsistency at all, once it is properly understood.

First, the stylistic integration of the prayer (vv. 4-20) with its context (vv. 2, 21-7) is quite explicit and ramified. For example, it is said that Daniel 'searched' (בִּינֹתִי) the old books and found the old

---

[71] One may add, as well, the studied reuse of old oracles found in 2 Chron. 15: 2-7, discussed earlier. Such tendencies even precede the exile, as is suggested by reworkings of Isaiah in Zephania. Cf. H. L. Ginsberg, 'Gleanings in First Isaiah', *Mordecai Kaplan Jubilee Volume* (New York: Jewish Theological Seminary of America, 1953), English Section, 258f.

[72] Among negative appraisals, cf. J. Marti, *Das Buch Daniel* (KHAT 18; Tübingen: J. C. Mohr, 1926), 64f.; J. A. Montgomery, *Daniel* (ICC; Edinburgh: T. and T. Clark, 1927), 362; H. L. Ginsberg, *Studies in Daniel* (New York: Jewish Theological Seminary of America, 1948), 33, 41. For positive assessments, cf. N. Porteous, *Daniel* (OTL; Philadelphia: Westminster, 1965), 136 (originally appeared in German, ATD 1962); O. Plöger, *Das Buch Daniel* (KAT; Gütersloh: G. Mohn, 1965), 135; and the forceful review by B. Jones, 'The Prayer in Daniel IX', *VT* 18 (1968), 488-93.

[73] Cf. R. H. Charles, *A Critical and Exegetical Commentary on the Book of Daniel* (Oxford: Clarendon Press, 1929), 226.

[74] See already E. Bayer, *Danielstudien* (Alttest. Abhandlungen, 3/5; Münster: Aschendorff, 1912), 49.

oracle (v. 2) whose comprehension eluded him. Responding to Daniel's ensuing prayer, and echoing these phrases, the angelic being tells Daniel that he has come forth to make him understand (יצאתי להשכילך בינה) the fate of Israel (v. 22; cf. v. 25), in marked contrast to Israel's ancient historical inability—noted in the prayer—to understand (להשכיל) the truth of God's ways and repent of their evil actions (v. 13). Further, Israel's intransigence repeatedly led to the fact that the Lord 'poured out (וַתִּתַּךְ) . . . the curses and oaths written (כתובה) in the Torah of Moses' (v. 11). This language anticipates—literally and punningly—the situation at the end of the period of abominations when, according to the *angelus interpres*, the doom which 'has been decreed' will be 'poured out' (תִּתַּךְ, v. 27). And finally, with a clear eye on the present context of this piece, as distinct from other deuteronomistic versions of this liturgical type, the prayer requests divine compassion for the shrine which is 'desolate' (השמם,v. 17), and for the desolation (שממתינו, v. 18) of the people. For indeed, as the angel Gabriel says, the time of 'desolations' (שממות,v. 26) has been set, so that the shrine's desolation (משמם, v. 27bα)—now so evident—is near the final end when 'the final destruction will be poured out on the desolate thing (שומם) (viz., the shrine; v. 27bβ).[75]

If one follows these significant verbal echoes one reverberation further, the 'exegetical' basis of the appearance of just this type of prayer at just the present point—between Dan. 9: 2 and 9: 21—becomes clear, Daniel avers the justice of divine wrath in recompense for the covenantal disloyalty (במעלם אשר מעלו־בך, v. 7)[76] of the Israelites, in consequence of which both the shrine and the people have been made desolate (stem: שמם, vv. 17-18). Speaking for himself and the nation, Daniel confesses (מתודה, v. 20) his sins and appeals to divine mercy. Now just this cluster of elements recurs in Lev. 26, in the context of its prediction of a period of divine wrath measured in sabbatical cycles—a prediction of which Daniel was perfectly aware (cf. vv. 24-7). Lev. 26 forewarns the people that their covenantal disloyalty (במעלם אשר מעלו־בי, v. 40) will result in the desolation (stem: שמם, vv. 31-5) of the shrine and the native land for the aforementioned period (vv. 34-5). And then comes the most pertinent part. The people are told that if in exile they confess (התודו) their sins (עונם, v. 40), the Lord will remit their sins and remember the promised land—now desolate (vv. 41-2).[77]

It was suggested earlier that when the Chronicler blended Jer. 25:

---

[75] Many of these stylistic links and echoes have also been noted by Jones, loc. cit. 491.

[76] Following the interpretation of *māʿal* in J. Milgrom, *Cult and Conscience*, *passim*.

[77] Also note Lev. 26: 44 *lĕkallōtām* and Dan. 9: 27 *kālāh*.

9-12 with Lev. 26: 32-5 in 2 Chron. 36: 21-3 he wished thereby to suggest that the old promise of doom for covenantal disobedience was being fulfilled. It may now be added that the key purpose of Daniel's prayer was not solely to suggest that old curses had been fulfilled. It was also to emphasize the more hopeful side of Lev. 26, which announced that repentance could terminate the severe decree.

The compiler of Dan. 9 thus produced a skilful exegetical ensemble. He had Daniel turn from the oracle of Jer. 25: 9-12 to a confessional prayer – that is, to precisely that type of prayer required by Lev. 26: 40 for the remission of sins and the termination of the sabbatical cycles of doom and desolation for the land. Gabriel's favourable response to the prayer intimates that the confession was accepted and the end (hitherto esoterically concealed) could now be publicly revealed. The whole of Lev. 26: 27-45 has thus been exegetically reworked through a *recontextualization* of its contents, and cast as a prophecy of doom and hope for which Dan. 9 is the fulfilment and antidote. Moreover, the inherent contradiction between the fact that Jeremiah's oracle had a clearly determined end, and the fact that the termination of the cycle of sabbaticals of wrath in Lev. 26 was conditional upon human confession and divine grace, was resolved in the process: Daniel's confession led to a revelation of the timetable of divine historical activity, consoling the repentant one by declaring that the culmination of doom and the onset of restoration were equally nigh. That Jer. 25: 9-12 had long been cut loose from its original textual moorings, and associated with Lev. 26: 32-5, undoubtedly contributed to the 'exegetical redaction' of Dan. 9. The added lexical fact that Jer. 25: 12 spoke of an utter desolation (שממות עולם) for Israelite sins (עוֹנם) – using terms identical with those found in Lev. 26: 32-5, 38-40 – conceivably explains the Jeremiah-Leviticus connection first utilized by the Chronicler.

(*b*) *Other inner-prophetic allusions.* Several significant details may be added to the foregoing analysis of Dan. 9 as an epigonal reworking of older sources. First, in addition to the generative Jeremianic reference in v. 2, the prayer itself provides a Jeremianic allusion in v. 14 – thereby linking v. 2 to its subsequent interpretation. Just before the vindication of divine wrath, Daniel states 'and YHWH was attentive (וישקד) to the evil'. This choice of terminology is an undoubted verbal allusion to a unique Jeremianic expression repeatedly used to indicate divine attentiveness to his prophet's word (1: 12, 5: 6; 31: 27; 44: 27). In addition, there is at the end of Dan. 9 another cited reference to a pre-exilic prophecy, Isa. 10: 22-3.

As an inheritor of this Isaianic fragment in the times of Seleucid oppression, the author of Dan. 9: 26-7 would certainly have been sensitive to its opening exhortation to rely on the Lord alone (Isa. 10:

20), and particularly encouraged by the forecast that a remnant would remain of the people and the time of 'destruction decreed' (כלה נחרצה, Isa. 10: 23a and Dan. 9: 27bβ; cf. Isa. 10: 22aα). Moreover, the very ambivalence of that Isaianic passage would have suited his sensibilities most admirably. For in it was forecast not only the destruction of all the enemies of YHWH (v. 23), but apparently also of the faithless in Israel as well (v. 22). Here, then, was an old oracle for the times—uniquely prescribed, one might say, for the desolate days of Antiochus IV. By quoting the Isaianic oracle from the age of Assyrian domination, the author of Dan. 9: 26-7 meant to suggest that the old prophetic text was spoken for his day, when Israel still anticipated the decreed destruction and revival in glory. In the process, moreover, he made a typological identification: the contemporary Seleucids were like the Assyrians of old, and Daniel's circle of intimates were the 'remnant' that would 'return', be restored.

This particular cluster of Isaianic phraseology had earlier caught the eye of Nahum in his exultation of the fall of Nineveh, Assyria's mighty bastion (see 1: 6-9).[78] It clearly caught our apocalyptic author's imagination as well. For it is significant that the terminology of Isa. 10: 22-3 is not only cited in Dan. 9: 26-7, but, as often noted, its language dominates Dan. 11, which describes the historical phases of the Seleucid empire leading towards the final hour.[79] But since the language of that Isaianic unit is echoed in Isa. 28:15-22, which also deals with the Assyrian advance, one cannot exclude the possibility that this latter was the immediate source of the language in Dan. 11. Thus, the verb שטף found in Isa. 10: 22 and 28:15, 17-18 (also Dan. 9: 26), and suggestive of the 'rush' of military onslaught, dominates the political and military panorama unfurled in Dan. 11 (vv. 10, 22, 26, 40). Further, the old phraseology of destruction, כלה ונחרצה, found in Isa. 10: 23 and 28: 22 (cf. 19: 22, 25), also recurs in Dan. 11: 36, where it is blended with a citation from Isa. 10: 25 which speaks of an imminent end to divine זעם, or 'wrath' (the overlapping verb כלה, found in Isa. 10: 23 and 25, was decisive in this nexus). The latter term would have been associated in Daniel's mind with the immediately preceding designation of Assyria as the rod of divine זעם (cf. Isa. 10: 5). And finally, it is notable that Isa. 28: 15, 17 refer to כזב, 'perfidy' or 'false trust', and v. 19 to the שמועה, or 'sound' of the enemy's advance. Both terms strategically recur—though with quite different subjects—in Dan.

---

[78] The imagery is part of an acrostic hymn in Nahum 1: 2-8 (minus vv. 2b-3a, a disruptive interpolation of the attribute formulary). On the acrostic, see H. Gunkel, 'Nahum 1', *ZAW* 13 (1893), 233-44.

[79] Cf. the remarks of H. L. Ginsberg, 'The Oldest Interpretation of the Suffering Servant', *VT* 3 (1955), 401, and the earlier observations of I. L. Seeligmann, *The Septuagint Version*, 82.

11: 27 and 44, respectively,[80]

Through these learned citations, associations, and lexical links, it is clear that the author of the apocalyptic scenario in Dan. 11 saw in Syria the fulfilment of old doom prophecies spoken concerning Assyria. If it was the geographical proximity of these two historical states which helped foster his exegetical association, this could hardly have been the decisive factor. More significant, one may presume, was the fact that the great Isaianic oracles against Assyria had *not yet* been fulfilled. Indeed, the very fact that the latter prophecies had been sealed up (חתום) among Isaiah's disciples (Isa. 8: 16b) while the prophet himself 'awaited (וחכיתי) YHWH who has hidden his face' (v. 17a) may have had special relevance for our apocalyptic author – who also sealed up a set of prophecies (cf. חתמים, 12: 9; also v. 4) for a future time, and praised those faithful ones who would 'await' (המחכה, 12: 12) their fulfilment amid the purifying tribulations of their suffering (12: 10 cf. 11: 35).[81]

(*c*) In addition to the foregoing, there are two other studied applications of older prophecies in Dan. 11 which deserve special note. The first is a citation from the concluding oracle of Balaam, which forecast that 'ships from Kittim צים מכתים [shall come against him] and he shall be humiliated'[82] (Num. 24: 24). This passage, cited in Dan. 11: 30 ('Kittim ships ציים כתים will sail against him and rebuff him'), was understood in the Daniel apocalypse as an allusion to the humiliation of Antiochus IV (in 168 BCE), when the Roman legate Populius Laenas came by ship to Alexandria and instructed him to evacuate immediately.[83] This precise (*ex eventu*?) correlation of events in his own day with Balaam's old oracular prophecy thus served contextually to establish the credibility of the other apocalyptic predictions which follow – and this may indeed have been the original intent of this scholarly allusion.[84]

---

[80] Regarding *kāzāb*, see further below; and also note the use of *šĕmû'āh* (regarding the retreat of the Assyrians) in Isa. 37: 7.

[81] Like these topoi, Nahum 1: 7 (set among references to *za'am*, *šeṭep*, and *kālāh*, vv. 6, 8-9) *also* refers to patient trust in YHWH.

[82] I follow Ginsberg's reading of *ṣîm mikkitîm* for the MT *ṣîm miyyad kittîm*, plus his restoration; presumably the omission is due to haplography. See loc. cit. 401. This passage in Dan. 11: 30 supports this restoration, and may actually reflect the older Balaam text. Seeligmann, *The Septuagint Version*, 82, also noted Daniel's reuse of Num. 24: 24.

[83] *Pace* F. F. Bruce, 'The Earliest Old Testament Interpretation', *OTS* 17 (1972), 42. The old Greek version paraphrase of Dan. 11: 30 substituted 'Romans' for 'Kittim'; and cf. *Tg. Onq. ad* Num. 24: 24.

[84] The propagandistic function of such precise *ex eventu* notices for enhancing the prestige of claims and predictions has been repeatedly emphasized. See Collins, *The Apocalyptic Vision*, ch. 7, and the broad considerations of E. Osswald, 'Zum Problem der *Vaticinia ex Eventu*', *ZAW* 75 (1963), 27-44. Dan.

The other learned reference in Dan. 11 of particular interest is the striking allusion there to the divine response to Habakkuk's protest against apparent divine inattention to the evils which have befallen his people. The prophet is told (2: 2-3a) to write the 'vision' (חזון) for the people, 'for there is yet a vision for the appointed time כי עוד חזון למועד and a witness for the final time ויפח לקץ; and it will not lie לא יכזב'. Given the context of oppression by an invader, the citation of these words of Habakkuk in Dan. 11: 27 is remarkably apposite, and allows the reader to reason that the חזון of Habakkuk will be fulfilled in the חזון of Daniel (cf. 9: 21). Thus, the Daniel apocalypse announces: 'And the . . . kings will speak treachery (כזב),[85] but it will not succeed; for an end remains for the appointed time (כי-עוד קץ למועד).'[86] On several further occasions the author of the Daniel apocalypse again refers to this oracle, so that one can hardly doubt its function as a 'scholarly'—divinely warranted—source of consolation and assurance. One may also note references to a 'time of the end' or 'an appointed time' in Dan. 11: 35, 40, 45, and in 12: 4, 9. Finally, it may have been under the impact of Habakkuk's oracle that the Aramaic phrase עדן ועדנין ופלג עדן ('a time, times, and half a time'), from the timetable in 7: 25, recurs in 12: 7 in the form מועד מועדים וחצי.

As a vision of hope, then, Hab. 2: 3a was of profound importance to the author of Dan. 11: 12. But it was not simply as an oracle of hope in a time of foreign oppression that Hab. 2: 3a attained its authoritative force. The admonition of v. 3b, 'if it tarry wait (חכה) for it; for it will surely come and not be too long off', was also undoubtedly of great solace to the people enjoined to wait (המחכה) for the fulfilment whose advent was periodically postponed (Dan. 12:12). Indeed, as YHWH had earlier counselled Habakkuk (3: 4), 'the vindicated one [or, righteous person; צדיק] will survive through his confidence *in it*' (viz.,

---

11: 14 has often been considered an *ex eventu* prophecy, but the precise allusions of its terms have been debated since the days of Porphyry and Jerome. See the analysis and proposal of E. Täubler, 'Jerusalem 201 to 199 BCE. On the History of a Messianic Movement', *JQR* 37 (1946-7), 1-30, 125-37, 249-64; note esp. 16-30.

[85] The use of *kāzāb* in Isa. 28: 15, 17 amid terms also found in Isa. 10: 22-3, 25 may have provided the association with the Habakkuk passage and/or support of it; but the cluster of terms makes it clear that Habakkuk is the source. See my 'The Qumran Pesher', 114. The impact of Hab. 2: 3 on Dan. 11: 27 was also noted by Seeligmann, op. cit. 82.

[86] Significantly, the adverb *'ôd* in Hab. 2: 2, which should be amended to *'ēd* 'witness' on the basis of the common parallelism *'d ~ yph* in Ugaritic and biblical literature—a point conclusively established by S. Loewenstamm in *Leš.* 26 (1961-2), 205-8 [Heb.]—*is also mistakenly repeated* in the citation in Dan. 11: 27. Even earlier, pHab. ii. 5-8 reinterpreted the Habakkuk passage to mean *'ēd*.

this oracle).[87] And it was just such a confident trust in the divine plan, supported by their knowledge of the future secrets, that the Hellenistic-Jewish conventicle of מַשְׂכִּילִים 'wise ones' possessed (Dan. 12:10), sure that it would teach the many who might attend (11:33) and that it would enable them – through teachings and martyrdom – to be called 'vindicators (מַצְדִּיקֵי) of the many' (12:3).

As repeatedly observed, the preceding references to מַשְׂכִּילִים, to 'vindication', and to 'the many' allude to and even reinterpret the great 'servant' passage of Isa. 52:13-53:12.[88] It is said there of this righteous (צַדִּיק) servant that he 'will prosper (יַשְׂכִּיל)' (52:13) and 'will vindicate (יַצְדִּיק) . . . the many (לָרַבִּים)' (53:11). Quite certainly, the author of Dan. 11-12 wished to stress that his group was heir to the mantle of the suffering servant of YHWH. As that servant suffered, so do they; as he was later glorified (cf. Isa. 53:12), so will they be resurrected to eternal life; and in so far as this group read the 'servant song' as a description of the historical tribulations of the nation of Israel, the מַשְׂכִּילִים believed themselves to be the true Israel, the righteous remnant. To reinforce the hope of these 'wise ones' in resurrection, a strategic exegetical reference is made in Dan. 12:2 to Isa. 26:19 and its promise of resurrection; and in order to intone a corresponding doom (דֵּרָאוֹן) upon the wicked, a citation from Isa. 66:24 is juxtaposed to it. Through this interweaving of prophetic sources, the apocalyptic author hoped to reinforce confidence in divine vindication at the final end, whose fulfilment was forecast of old, and now believed to be an imminent reality.

5. The epigonal character of Dan. 9-12, particularly of chapters 11-12, thus presents an imposing concatenation of prophetic authorities used by the author of our apocalypse. Simply on the basis of the texts referred to above, citations have been identified for Dan. 11:10, 22, 26-7, 30-1, 33, 35-6, 40, 45, 12:1-4, 7, 9-10, 12 – and this excludes conflated citations in single verses. Certainly, a proclivity to compose such a prophetic patchwork attests both to a scholarly attentiveness to authoritative sources received in the prophetic *traditum* and to a sense of apocalyptic immediacy. And, surely, just this is the desired impact of the concatenation upon the reader. By strategically and cumulatively assembling numerous prophetic pronouncements the author leads us into the mental world of wise believers, Daniel's מַשְׂכִּילִים, and the tangle of authoritative texts which encoded their universe and provided

[87] For a thoughtful reassessment of this famous verse, see now J. G. Janzen, 'Habakkuk 2: 2-4 in the Light of Recent Philological Advances', *HTR* 73 (1980), 53-78.

[88] Cf. Montgomery, *Daniel*, 422; Charles, *Daniel*, 331; and Ginsberg, 'The Oldest Interpretation', 402f.

an atmosphere of confidence in the inevitability of the apocalyptic forecast.

Among several additional prophetic citations which may be identified (e.g. Isa. 17:12 in Dan. 11:10; Isa. 7:7 in Dan. 11:17;[89] or Jer. 30:7 in Dan. 12:1) there is one final reference in Dan. 11–12 whose pertinence to the shrinal desecrations of Antiochus IV can hardly be doubted. In Dan. 11:31 it is stated that enemies 'shall profane (וחללו) the mighty Temple (המקדש המעוז); [90] shall remove the continual burnt offering; and shall set up an abomination that makes desolate (משמם השקוץ). The desecration of the Temple is referred to in similar terms in Dan. 9:27 (cf. 12:11) and in extra-biblical sources (cf. 1 Macc. 1:44ff.), and the epithet of desolation is itself a punning opprobrium referring to the status of Baʿal Shamem (שמם) set up in the Temple, as Nestle noted nearly a century ago.[91] But however much the ʿcontemporary Hellenistic realia may have given the latter divine epithet a 'modern' connotation, there can be little doubt that it and the entire description derive from Ezek. 7 and its denunciations.

In Ezek. 7 the Israelites stand condemned for having set up their idolatrous abominations (שקוציהם, v. 20), and so profaned (חללוה) the sacred shrine (v. 22). In consequence, the oracle is given in v. 24 that YHWH will bring on enemies who will destroy 'the pride of the strong (גאון עזים)',[92] and inherit their sanctuaries (מקדשיהם). This forecast, itself possibly influenced by the predictive curse formulary in Lev. 26:19a ('then I shall destroy the גאון עזכם pride of your strength'), was clearly in the mind of the author of Dan. 11.[93] Studiously aware of this forecast, he sensed that its words were fulfilled in his day. One need not, therefore, regard this prophetic allusion as an *ex eventu* prophecy in order to realize the effect it would have on those apocalyptic circles for whom the combined fulfilment of old prophecies forged a chain of verified expectations and proof positive that they lived in a time of 'realized eschatology'. Dan. 11 is thus at once a testimony of faith within the conventicle of wise believers and a manifesto of vindication to 'the many'. Indeed, for the conventicle the times were pregnant with prophetic sense. Guided by their pneumatic leaders, this community

---

[89] For *tāʿămôd* as a translation of *yāqûm*, see Ginsberg, *Studies in Daniel*, 57.

[90] Cf. *NJPS*, 'the Temple, the fortress'. The noun *māʿôz* and its derivatives dominate Dan. 11; cf. vv. 7, 10, 12, 31, 38.

[91] Loc. cit. (above, n. 64).

[92] Or *ʿuzzām, pace* LXX; and cf. Ezek. 24:21, 25. Rashi already identified the Temple with the word *ʿōz*. See further Kaufmann, *Toledot*, iii/2. 541.

[93] There are other textual indications supporting the reuse of Ezek. 7 in Dan. 11, like Ezekiel's use of *qēṣ* 'end' (v. 6, reused from Amos 8:1–2; cf. Dan. 11:6 etc.), *ḥāzôn* (v. 26; cf. Dan. 11:14); *ṣĕbî* 'splendour' (v. 20; cf. Dan. 11:16, 41, 11:31), and *tibbāhalnāh* (v. 27; cf. Dan. 11:44).

—like the Qumran covenanteers who were also instructed in the true meaning of ancient prophetic statements—transformed old predictions into omens. One searched the times with one hand, and the prophetic 'Scriptures' with the other: for the secret of the final days was inscribed in the entrails of older exoteric prophecies. The wise man could divine this future by correlating the signs of the texts with the signs of the times. The 'clear' fulfilment of many predictions—assiduously gathered and powerfully anthologized in texts like Dan. 11-12—inevitably provided the religious illuminati in Daniel's circle with external confirmation of their inner belief, justifying their inner reality despite all indications to the contrary. Partial realization of the anticipated *eschaton*, and lists of 'proofs' like Dan. 11, help to explain, in part, why the failed timetables projected on the basis of divine illumination were repeatedly revised in the social support system of the faithful (cf. Dan. 8:14, 12:11, 12) and not rejected entirely.[94] Indeed, once the very delays in the fulfilment of the divine word were linked to mysterious obstructions and a mystagogy anent of suffering and faithfulness, failures were easily rationalized as a testing of the purity of the faithful.[95] Maintenance of this cognitive structure was, it appears, the antidote to any cognitive dissonance inherent in unfulfilled prophetic timetables.

6. Intense preoccupation with earlier prophecy also marks the post-exilic content of the Book of Isaiah (the so-called Deutero- and Trito-Isaiah). We earlier had occasion to refer to Deutero-Isaiah's emphasis on the fulfilment of older prophecies, the 'former things', and noted that his rhetoric was polemical in intent. Its avowed goal was to underscore the realization of YHWH's doom oracles in order to elicit trust in his present oracles of consolation. This interest in old prophecies is more highly specified in the reuse of older oracular formulations in the last parts of the Isaianic corpus. On the one hand, O. Eissfeldt has succinctly demonstrated that Isa. 55:1-5 is a nationalization of the promises to David as formulated in Ps. 89.[96] On the other, W. Zimmerli and others have argued that many phrases in Trito-Isaiah are reworkings and adaptations of Deutero-Isaiah's language.[97]

---

[94] For a comparative perspective on the fact that the proliferation of eschatological texts at particular periods is often an index to eschatological pressures, see P. Alexander, 'Medieval Apocalypses as Historical Sources', *The American Historical Review*, 83 (1968), 1002.

[95] Cf. Dan. 11: 35, 12:10.

[96] 'The Promises of Graces to David in Isaiah 55:1-5', in *Israel's Prophetic Heritage*, edd. B. Anderson and W. Harrelson (New York: Harper and Row, 1962), 196-207.

[97] See above, p. 289 and nn. 22-3 for sources and evaluations. Cf. also the cogent case offered by A. Rofé, 'The Question of the Realization of the Prophecies

It is the inner Isaianic revisions that interest us specifically at this point. For whether these reformulations by Trito-Isaiah of the earlier content of Isa. 40-55 are the product of an established school of prophetic study, or merely the latter-day perceptions of a post-exilic prophet that earlier Isaianic prophecies parallel his own theological agenda, the close ties thus established between the separate prophetic units could easily lead to the redactional juxtaposition of one prophetic corpus with another. The existence of common factors between Isa. 40-55 and 55-66 thus helps explain their unification in a prophetic anthology. Similarly, the theological concordance between the highly distinct Zech. 1-8 and 9-14 helps explain their redactional anthologization.[98]

As regards the Book of Isaiah as a whole, D. Jones has suggested that the very arrangement of Isaiah's early oracles (especially chs. 1-4) reflects a redactional rereading of them in the exilic period, when a penitent acknowledgement of doom and the assertion of hope were crucial.[99] Following R. North, Jones further asserted that it is precisely these doom oracles, as well as those which allude to the fall of Babylon at the hands of Media (13: 17-22), which were believed by post-exilic tradents to be the prophecies sealed up for a future time (8: 16-18; 30: 8) and referred to in Isa. 41: 22-3, 42: 9, and 48: 3 as the 'former things which have come to pass' (42: 9).[100] Such an assertion goes a long way towards explaining the eventual redactional unification of Isa. 1-39 with 40-66, such that the entire structure of the Book of Isaiah conforms to the prophecy-fulfilment pattern which so preoccupied post-exilic theology in general and Deutero-Isaiah in particular. Indeed, as an old medieval tradition recognized, the nexus between prophecy and fulfilment is sharpened at precisely the point where the eighth- and sixth-century prophecies were joined.[101] Isa. 39 forecasts the invasion of Babylon, the sacking of the Temple, and the transformation

in Isaiah 55: 6-11 and the Problem of Trito-Isaiah', in *Proceedings of the VIth World Congress of Jewish Studies* (Jerusalem, 1977), i, 213-21 [Heb.].

[98] See the comparative thematic observations of R. Mason, 'The Relation of Zech. 9-14 to Proto-Zechariah', *ZAW* 88 (1976), 227-39, and his lexical–stylistic notes in *The Books of Haggai, Zecharia and Malachi* (CB; Cambridge: Cambridge University Press, 1977), 85, 89, 90-3, 99, 106, 116, 124.

[99] 'The Traditio of the Oracles of Isaiah of Jerusalem', *ZAW* 67 (1955), 226-46.

[100] Ibid. 245. See C. R. North, 'The "Former Things" and the "New Things" in Deutero-Isaiah', in *Studies in Old Testament Prophecy*, ed. H. Rowley (New York: Scribners, 1950), 124.

[101] See the introductory comments of Ibn Ezra to Isa. 40. According to R. Moses Ha-Kohen, who is cited, the comforting promises refer to the restoration of the Temple by Zerubbabel; however, Ibn Ezra interpreted these words messianically, such that the prophecies concerning the Babylonian exile served merely as contemporary examples of the final redemption.

of Davidic kings into stewards of the Babylonian kings – all of which
came to pass (cf. 2 Kgs. 25: 7, 12-17, 27-30; 2 Chron. 36: 18-20). By
contrast, Isa. 40 opens with a call of consolation, announcing the end
of servitude and the return from the Babylonian exile.

Focus on the 'new things' and 'comfort' underscores the emphasis
on hope in the post-exilic chapters of Isaiah. Indeed, it is hard to miss
the vital theological echo which reverberates through the emphatic
use of the verb נחמו in Isa. 40: 1 (and elsewhere; cf. 66: 13)[102] and
transforms the old elegiac emphasis in the Book of Lamentation that
Zion is 'without any consoler' (מנחם, 1: 2, 17, 21; cf. 2: 13). Within
this context of hope, bolstered by the formal structure of prophecy-
fulfilment in Deutero-Isaiah (and other post-exilic texts), the reapplication of old Isaianic prophecies in the post-exilic period finds its
proper ideological matrix.

There are many striking reapplications of the prophetic words of
Isaiah of Jerusalem in the later 'Isaianic' tradition. All bear on the
presentiment that the words forecast by Isaiah of old are now near
fulfilment, or are about to be reversed. With respect to the latter, Isa.
62: 4 recalls the old threat in 1: 7 that 'your land (ארצכם) will be
desolate (שממה)', and reinvigorates it with the hope born of new
beginnings: '. . . your land (ארצך) will *no longer* be called desolate
(שממה) but . . . your land [will be called] "owned".' The continuity
of this prophecy by Trito-Isaiah also has earlier allusions. In 11: 10 the
prophet speaks of the Davidic line when he says that '. . . the root of
Jesse will be . . . as a standard for nations (לנס עמים), which peoples
will beseech (ידרשו)'. In 62: 10-12, on the other hand, this cluster
of elements recurs but to different effect: now a call goes out to the
faithful to 'raise a standard for the nations (נס על־עמים)' to announce
the onset of salvation and call Zion 'beseeched דרושה'. Thus, old
Isaianic references come to mind for our latter-day prophet as the
advent of Israel's restoration is at hand. The several recitational allusions
collectively serve to invigorate present expectations with the power of
older hopes.

Along the same lines, one may note the recitation in Isa. 65: 25 of
the oracle about the future transformation of natural aggression found
in 11: 6, 9. While the hope is not portrayed as fully realized, the effect
of recontextualization is that fulfilment is imminent. A similar expression of imminence seems to underlie the use made of 9: 1, 3 in 60: 1-2,
17-19. The older text forecasts that 'the people who walked in darkness
(ההלכים בחשך) have seen a great light (ראו אור גדול); light has burst

---

[102] Isa. 40: 1 and 66: 13 are part of a complex *inclusio* linking Isa. 40 and 60.
See L. Liebreich, 'Compilation of the Book of Isaiah', *JQR* 46 (1955-6), 276f.

(אוֹר נָגַהּ) upon them'. Never again will this people feel the rod of the 'taskmaster נֹגֵשׂ' upon them (v. 3). The realization of this promise is referred to and joyfully proclaimed in Isa. 60:1, 3. There the people are exhorted: 'Arise, be bright, for your light (אוֹרֵךְ) has dawned; for behold! darkness (חֹשֶׁךְ) covers the earth . . . but YHWH has shined over you. Nations will go by your light (אוֹרֵךְ), and kings by the glow (נֹגַהּ) of your splendour . . .'. In those days, Israel's oppressors (נֹגְשַׂיִךְ) will cease and justice and light will prevail evermore (vv. 17-19).

A more ironic use of this old Isaianic piece (9:1) may be found in 50:10-11. It is there said that the people do not hearken to the divine servant, 'who has walked in darkness (הָלַךְ חֲשֵׁכִים) without illumination (אֵין נֹגַהּ)'. These people put their trust in lights which they themselves ignite, and so are told to 'go (לְכוּ) by the light (בְּאוּר) of your burnings!' —for in this 'they will surely collapse in despair'. Part of the power of this passage, it would seem, lies precisely in the inversion and thwarting of older hopes ironically recalled through the linguistic allusions generated by the new divine word.

A final example shows another skilful interweaving of a cluster of old Isaianic oracles into a new, post-exilic proclamation. One recalls the great oracle of universal reunion in 2:1-4, followed by an exhortation humbly to follow God, forsaking pride and idolatry (vv. 5-22). It is there stated that 'all peoples (כָּל־הַגּוֹיִם) will swarm (וְנָהֲרוּ) to Zion'; and Jacob is both exhorted to 'go (לְכוּ) . . . in the light (בְּאוֹר) of YHWH' and reminded of its past apostasy, when silver and gold (וְזָהָב כֶּסֶף) filled the land, and when the haughtiness of men was brought low (וְשַׁח). The prophecy in Isa. 60:3, 5, 14, 17 picks up all these themes, when it states that with Zion's renewal 'peoples will go by your light (וְהָלְכוּ גוֹיִם לְאוֹרֵךְ) . . . and you [Israel] will swarm (וְנָהַרְתְּ) . . . . to bring . . . their silver and gold (זָהָב . . . כֶּסֶף) . . . [when] your oppressors come to you bent low (שְׁחוֹחַ)'.

The dense concordance ɔf details linking this—and other—late Isaianic passages with the earliesᵗ strata of the Book cannot be dismissed as a chance, occasional, or casᵘᵃl pʰᵊnomenon. Rather, this phenomenon is clearly the result of the serious scʳᵘᵗiny of the words of Isaiah of Jerusalem by late prophets, or their circles. Many more links could be added to reinforce this point; but enough evidence has been assembled to indicate that a learned preoccupation with older prophetic language is characteristic of late biblical prophecy, which saw itself in the shadow of the great exilic prophets, especially Isaiah.[103] At the same time, one cannot presume that these epigonic allusions, or their full impact, were directly meaningful to the post-exilic Judaean community

---

[103] Compare, for example, Isa. 1:21, 24, 27 with 59:4-5, 17; 7:7 with 46:10; 10:5, 22 with 66:12, 14; 11:12 with 56:8; and 12:6 with 60:14.

without supplementary clarification—any more than one can presume this for such a learned piece of prophecy as Dan. 9-12. What can be safely presumed, however, is the meaningfulness of these old allusions to the latter-day prophetic formulators themselves. It was they who studied the old oracular words—perhaps especially in times of apparent divine silence—and sought thereby to find their place in the ancient divine scheme of things, as revealed in the pre-exilic period when, so it seemed, YHWH spoke 'ceaselessly' to his people Israel.

18. Generic Transformations

A. FROM NON-ORACLES INTO ORACLES

IN the preceding chapters, we explored various exegetical dimensions of related genres of biblical mantology, viz., omens, dreams, and oracles. In all instances, the particular elucidation, reinterpretation, or reutilization involved was directly related to the genre at hand. In what follows, the focus shifts to the phenomenon of generic transformation. Here, non-oracular texts are reinterpreted as or reworked into living oracles, and vice versa. One example of this phenomenon was discussed earlier, namely the transformation of the descriptive historical words of Moses' peroration in Deut. 32: 9, 13 into the prescriptive promise found in Isa. 58: 14.[1] Beside this example, several other instances will be considered from such genres as curse and hymnic blessing.

Curses into Oracles

1. At the conclusion of the pericope describing the Israelite sack and destruction of Jericho, and subsequent to the rescue of Rahab from the rubble, the military leader 'Joshua swore . . . as follows: "Cursed before YHWH is the one who will arise and build this city—Jericho; the laying of its foundations shall cost him his first-born (בבכרו ייסדנה), (and) the erecting of its gates shall cost him his youngest (יציב דלתיה בצעירו)!' At a later point, the deuteronomic historian reports that this awesome curse in Josh. 6: 26 was fulfilled, centuries later, in the days of Ahab, by one Ḥiel of the Elid clan. The historian goes on to report that this Ḥiel laid its foundations (יסדה) with Abiram his first-born (בכרו) and erected its gates (הציב דלתיה) with Segib his youngest son (צעירו)—according to the word which YHWH spoke through Joshua bin Nun' (1 Kgs. 16: 34).

In this report, the old curse is literally cited and referred to—not as a human curse, which it manifestly is, but rather as a divine word, which it manifestly is not. In conjunction with this shift goes the misreading of the curse as a prophecy. Presumably Ḥiel—and others—understood the predictive 'the laying/raising . . . shall cost him' in the curse as a subjunctive condition (something like 'would needs cost him'). Whereas the original phrasing of Joshua's imprecation simply specifies that the curse will befall the infractor of the asseveration, the infractor construed the specified actions as just those conditions required for the rebuilding of

[1] Above, p. 478.

the city. That is, the imprecation was understood as two separate clauses: (i) one would be cursed if he rebuilt Jericho, (ii) *unless* he built it over the graves of his first-born and youngest sons. Whether because of the potential syntactical ambiguity of the oath, or because of ambitious greed, Ḥiel fulfilled the curse—and the historian reports it as an instance of fulfilled prophecy.[2]

2. Of less awesome proportions is the reuse of Deut. 28: 28 in Zech. 12: 4. The old deuteronomic language—itself literally derived from ancient prototypes—threatens disobedience of the covenant with the curse that 'YHWH will smite you with madness, blindness, and confusion'. To be sure, such a conditional curse has an oracular element, but its distance from a pure prophetic forecast is clear from the transformation of it in Zech. 12: 4. In the context of a prediction of a massive siege of Jerusalem (vv. 1-3), the prophet states: 'On that day—oracle of YHWH—*I will smite* every horse *with confusion* and its horseman *with madness*; I will set my favourable glance upon Judaea, but I will *smite with blindness* every horse of the nations.' While the language of Deut. 28: 28 is literally employed here, the curse is re-employed. It is now a prophecy of doom against the nations which contend against Israel. The ancient curse of woe has thus become an eschatological prophecy of Israelite salvation—a transformation of its original burden.

Blessings into Oracles

1. The farewell blessing of Jacob to his sons in Gen. 49 serves as the basis for two transformations. In vv. 10-11 Judah is told that 'the staff of Judah will not depart . . . until he comes (עַד כִּי־יָבֹא) to Shilo . . .' and that 'he will hitch (אֹסְרִי) his ass (עִירֹה) to the vine, and the progeny of his she-ass (בְּנִי אֲתֹנוֹ) to the bramble . . .'. The latter passage is apparently part of a traditional benefaction. This promise of exalted royalty for Judah has a clear political overtone, and hints that the blessing is really a *post factum* legitimation of the early Judaean hegemony.

For all its obscurity, the famous promise of rulership 'until he comes to Shilo'[3] was understood in messianic terms from early post-biblical times, that is, as a royal expectation projected in terms of a future Davidic line.[4] It is therefore of particular interest to note the considerably earlier royalist-messianic reflex of this passage in Zech. 9: 9:

[2] See the exegetical reuse of Josh. 6: 26 in 4Q *Testim.* 11. 21-7. MT 1 Kgs. 16: 34 is missing from LXX[BL].

[3] For a review of older views, and an ingenious proposal, see N. H. Tur Sinai, *Tarbiz*, 13 (1941-2) 213-17 [Heb.]; also the review and suggestion of W. Moran, 'Gen 49, 10 and its Use in Ez 21, 32', *Bib.* 39 (1958), 405-16.

[4] Cf. A. Poznanski, *Schiloh. Ein Beitrag zur Geschichte der Messiaslehre*, i. *Die Auslegung von Genesis 49, 10 im Altertume bis zu Ende des Mittelalters* (Leipzig: J. C. Hinrichs, 1904).

'Behold your king (יָבוֹא לָךְ) will come unto you, triumphant, his victory won, humble, riding on an ass, the foal of a she-ass (בֶּן־אֲתֹנוֹת).'[5] The eschatological character of this forecast continues in v. 10, which takes over language from the royal hymn of Ps. 72: 8 and expands it. The associative attraction to this psalm may have been stimulated by its references to this king as a righteous judge of the humble, and as a saviour.[6] Be this as it may, Zech. 9: 11 returns to the language of Gen. 49: 11 when the prophet proclaims that YHWH 'will send forth your prisoners (אֲסִירַיִךְ) from the waterless pit (מִבּוֹר אֵין מַיִם בּוֹ)', and to the old patriarchal narratives of Joseph, who was first cast into a 'waterless pit' by his brothers (וְהַבּוֹר רֵיק אֵין בּוֹ מַיִם, Gen. 37: 24), and later became an אָסִיר in the Pharaoh's dungeons (Gen. 39: 20-2).

One may safely presume that Zechariah's predilection for Gen. 49: 10-11 stems in part from the manifestly prophetic character of the blessing—which announces 'what will occur in the future' (v. 1). Within this framework, the obscure temporal expression '*until* . . . comes' was adapted by him to post-exilic, royalist-messianic hopes. Inspired by the old prediction, then, Zechariah gave it a new exegetical twist for his contemporaries. The old clan blessing-promise became a positive national oracle for his time.

2. But Zechariah was not the first to adapt Gen. 49 to a new prophetic context. As several scholars have argued, Ezekiel's dirge in chapter 19 is richly inspired by Jacob's blessing.[7] The remarkable concordance of terms and images between the two leaves little doubt on this point. But the allusions are not reused in a positive sense; for, as W. Moran has reasoned, the dirge is actually a forecast of the imminent reversal of the old hopes of Judaea as inspired by Gen. 49. The lioness which once lived on prey (Ezek. 19: 1-3; Gen. 49: 8-9) will be caught and exiled (Ezek. 19: 5-7); the vine which provided the staff of rulers (Ezek. 19: 10-11; cf. Gen. 49: 10a) will be cast down and burnt; 'and there will be no strong branch in her, no staff to rule'.[8]

Even bleaker than this prophetic reversal of Gen. 49 is the reuse of the old phrase 'until . . . comes' in Ezek. 21: 32. The old suspicion that these two passages are related is now fully confirmed by the analysis of Moran. Once more the old blessing-promise undergoes a thorough

---

[5] Interpreting 9: 9bβ as a parallel stichos to v. 9bα. On the imagery involved, see S. Feigen, '"Humble and Riding on an Ass" and its Babylonian Parallels', *Qobeṣ Mada'i le-Zeker M. Schorr*, edd. L. Ginzberg and A. Weiss (New York, 1944), 227-40 [Heb.].

[6] Note *ṣaddîk*, *nôšā'*, and *'ānî* in 9: 9 and the comparable terminology in Ps. 72: 1-3, 7; vv. 4, 13; and vv. 2, 4, 12, respectively.

[7] Cf. A. Bertholet, *Hezekiel*, 103; G. Fohrer, *Ezechiel* (HAT 13; Tübingen: J. C. Mohr, 1955), 126. Cf. Moran, loc. cit. 417, for a summary.

[8] Ibid. 423 f.

reversal in a new oracle. Set in the time of Zedekiah, with the onset of the Babylonian invasion (21: 23-8), the divine oracle announces that Israel will be fully confounded for her infidelity (v. 31). She will be repeatedly brought to depair 'until the one comes (עד־בּא) to whom is given the judgement' (v. 32). Only then, when the appointed historical agent comes, will the punishment be fully effected and the nation handed over to its enemies. By so harking back to the old phrase עד כי־יבא, Ezekiel at once historically reapplies and grammatically explicates the old blessing-promise.[9] In one oracular stroke, then, old confidences have become predictions of despair. The ancient *traditum*, and the presumptions based on it, are thus ironically and utterly transformed.

B. FROM ORACLES INTO NON-ORACLES

In the preceding, examples of the transformation of non-oracles into oracles were considered. In what follows, a converse transformation will be explored, the reuse of ancient oracles in the formulation of a new law.

It is reported at the close of the Book of Esther (9: 29-31) that Queen Esther gave full authority to Mordecai to send all the Jews letters of 'שלום ואמת peace and truth', and instruct them 'to make the observance of these days of Purim at their appointed times binding, as Mordecai the Jew and Esther the Queen had prescribed, and as they had made the regulations of the fasts (הצומות) and their lamentations binding upon themselves and their descendants'.[10] These letters constituted a 'second letter about Purim' (v. 29). The first historical allusion in v. 31 ('as Mordecai . . . had prescribed'), and the phrase referring to the celebration of Purim 'at their appointed times', hark back literally to the reference to the first series of letters in 9: 21. The significant difference between the two letters is that the first was a spontaneous expression of popular piety, while the second was sealed with royal authority.

The second historical allusion in v. 31 ('as they had made the regulation of the fasts . . .') and the earlier reference to words of 'peace and truth' actually rework language from Zech. 8: 19: 'The fast (צום) of the fourth, fifth, seventh, and tenth months shall become festivals

---

[9] Ibid. 417-23.

[10] Interestingly for the exegetical interpretation to be offered below, vv. 29-32 may be part of a secondary addition to Esther 9; for vv. 28-32 are lacking in the Greek 'A-Text' (the so-called Lucianic recension of Esther), vv. 30-2 are lacking in the Old Latin. Cf. also the variants in the LXX. For a text-critical analysis, see S: Loewenstamm, 'Esther 9: 29-32: The Genesis of a Late Addition', *HUCA* 42 (1971), 117-24. His approach to the 'fasts' referred to in v. 31 differs from that suggested below.

of joy and gladness　(לששון ולשמחה ולמועדים טובים)　for the house of
Judah. Just love truth and peace (האמת והשלום).' Indeed, this allusion
to Zech. 9:19 in Esther 9:30-1 has been recognized since medieval
times.[11] According to H. L. Ginsberg, 'The reference to this verse
implies the following midrashic interpretation of it: Having adopted
those fasts, the House of Judah is bound—as a matter of honesty and
equity!—to adopt new holidays as well.'[12] But Ginsberg's observation
does not explain the analogy, why it was chosen, or its very authority
to bind new behaviour. To explain these points a closer examination
of the citation from the Book of Zechariah is required.

First, the language of Zech. 8:9, just cited, states that the four
fast-days—commemorating the dates of the downfall of Judaea[13]—
will become לששון ולשמחה ולמועדים טובים. Significantly, this very
reference to joy and festivals appears in Esther 8:16-17 to describe the
happiness of the Jews when they were informed to the king's new decree
allowing them to defend themselves. 'For the Jews there was light and
gladness (שמחה), joy (וששון) and honour. In every province and city
reached by the royal command and decree there was gladness and joy
(שמחה וששון) for the Jews, feasting and festival (יום טוב)'. The combined effect of the learned reuse of Zech. 8:19 in Esther 8:16-17 and
9:30-1 is to suggest an understanding of the old Zecharian prophecy
in the light of contemporary events, i.e., the old divine promise that the
four fast-days would become a time of joy and festivity was considered
to be fulfilled in the days of Esther. In applying the prophecy, the
exhortation to 'love truth and peace' has been slightly transformed.
It now serves as the signet of Mordecai's decrees, called 'words of
peace and truth'.

But these several correlations and reworkings hardly explain the
very choice of the citation. What drew the attention of our late author
to Zech. 8:19 in the first place? To answer this question, one simply
has to observe the depiction of the events following Ahasuarus' initial
decree. First, it is reported in Esther 4:3 that 'wheresoever the command of the king reached there was great mourning (אבל) among the

[11] See Ibn Ezra *ad* Zech. 8:19. The citation in Esther reverses the original
lemma, as is the general rule for intra-biblical citations, established by M. Zeidl,
'Parallels between Isaiah and Psalms', *Sinai*, 38 (1955-6), 149-72, 229-40, 272-
80, 333-55 [Heb.].

[12] *The Five Megilloth and Jonah; A New Translation* (Philadelphia: Jewish
Publication Society of American, 1969), 88.

[13] The four fast-days commemorate (1) the siege of Jerusalem, on the tenth
of Tebeth (cf. 2 Kgs. 25:1-2; Jer. 52:4-7); (2) the breaching of the walls of
Jerusalem, traditionally on the seventeenth of Tammuz (cf. Jer. 39:2, where the
date is the ninth); (3) the destruction of the Temple and Jerusalem, traditionally
on the ninth of Ab (cf. 2 Kgs. 25:8, where the date is the seventh; also Jer. 52:
12-13, where the date is the tenth); (4) the day of the murder of Gedaliah,
traditionally on the third of Tishri (cf. 2 Kgs. 25:25; Jer. 41:1-2).

Jews, fasting (צום), wailing, and keening; sackcloth and ash were donned by many.' And second, after Esther decided to importune the king on her people's behalf, we learn that she and all the Jews of Shushan fasted (4: 16).

It is undoubtedly to this אבל that 9: 22 refers when it says that with the defeat of the enemy the month of Adar 'turned for them from [a time of] woe to gladness (לשמחה) ; [and] from mourning (אבל) to festival (יום טוב)'. This reversal of fortune, from fasting to celebration, thus furnished the immediate link for the author of Esther 9 to the prophetic topos in Zech. 8: 19. It is noteworthy that the original letters of Mordecai are not phrased with allusions to Zechariah. For this reason, one may suspect that a later reviser of the Book of Esther saw in this promise a prophecy for his time. So applied, the festival legislation now appears to the discerning eye as the *result* of a fulfilled prophecy. In this way, the older oracle has been used to legitimate — subtly and scholastically — a human legislative innovation.

Given the learned nature of this citation from Zech. 8: 19, it is not unlikely that the exegete responsible for it was also aware, on the basis of Zech. 7: 1-5, which refers to these fasts in the same breath as a reference to the seventy-year oracle of Jeremiah, that the expectation of the end of the four fast-days commemorating the fall of Jerusalem signalled the fulfilment of the Jeremian prophecy. If this is so, the author of Esther 9 wished to foster two implications, the first being that the new festival of Purim reversed the fasts of exile, and the second that the old Jeremian forecast of the end of exilic oppression was realized. While there is no explicit indication of this, there is nevertheless an indirect hint in that the historical fiction of the novella places it immediately after the Judaean exile in 597 BCE (Esther 2: 6), a timeframe within which the ancient Jeremian oracle was still operative.

Whatever the plausibility of this suggestion, there can be little doubt that the composer of Esther 9: 29-31 was a subtle savant who utilized an old oracle of Zechariah to provide theological support for a humanly inspired festival (9: 21).[14] This legitimation may be compared to the later Maccabean festival of Hanukkah, which celebrated the rededication of the Temple after the Seleucid desecrations of it. While the latter festival was also instituted without divine authority, biblical legitimation was subsequently derived for it through a clever analogy with the ancient festival of Tabernacles.[15]

[14] The author also deepened his novella with a shrewd typological touch, linking the genealogy of Mordechai to Saul (2: 6) and the genealogy of Haman to Agag the Amalekite (3: 1); thus the scenario alluded to the events of 1 Sam. 15 on the one hand, and Deut. 25: 17-19 on the other.
[15] See M. Liber, 'Hanoucca et Souccot', *REJ* (1912), 20-9; but cf. the alternative construction of S. Zeitlin, *The First Book of Maccabees, Introduction and Commentary* (New York: Harper and Bros., 1950), 53f.

19. Conclusions

A. The foregoing analysis of mantology in ancient Israel was subdivided into two categories: the interpretation of dreams, omens, and visions, on the one hand; and the interpretation and reinterpretation of oracles, on the other. Significantly, both of these categories showed a remarkable degree of formal and procedural coherence—internally, with respect to the biblical materials themselves, and externally, with respect to the broader Near Eastern *Tradentenkreis* and its forms and technical procedures.

Among the most salient features of the biblical mantology of dreams, omens, and visions is their symbolic and esoteric character. Accordingly, the variously envisaged phenomena required decoding for their ominous meaning to become clear. This was achieved in several ways. On the one hand, particularly with respect to dreams and omens, the mediating interpreter was a wise man, like Joseph and Daniel, who was brought to the receiver of the imagery and then provided the solution. But even within this type there is an expressed acknowledgement by the interpreter, or his clientele, that the solution benefited from divine inspiration (cf. Gen. 41: 25, 32-3; Dan. 2: 28, 4: 5-6, 5: 11-12, 14). Human wisdom is thus not solely a characteristic achieved through experience and insight, but a divine gift as well. In these cases the wise man does not receive the divine revelation directly, but once contácted he knows what to make of it.[1]

The pivotal position of a mediating interpreter is also to be found in connection with the mantology of visions—although here a clear distinction can be observed between the pre-exilic and post-exilic data. In the former, as exemplified by shared patterns in the Books of Amos and Jeremiah, the prophet-receiver of the vision or imagery is directly informed of its meaning by the addressing divine voice. Here, then,

---

[1] In the case of Gideon, a charismatic warrior, YHWH reveals in advance the portentous significance of a dream-report to be overheard in the Midianite camp (Judg. 7: 9-15). The episode thus blends foreign oneiromancy with Israelite kledonomancy—within the overall framework of a divine exhortation of confidence before battle. The Midianite dream interpretation appears dependent on contextual symbolism (cf. above, p. 450). However, in this Hebrew report of it, a pun is presumably involved: for *leḥem śĕ'ōrîm* 'barley bread' in Judg. 6: 13 may play on the military expression *leḥem šĕ'ārîm* 'war in the gates'—a soldierly phrase found in Judg. 5: 8. The noun *ṣĕlîl* may also be a *double entendre*, evoking the sense of 'cake' (cf. *Tg. Jon.*) and 'rustling' or 'rushing sound' (so Kimḥi; and cf. Isa. 19: 1; Hab. 3: 16).

the interpretation is immediate in the sense that the giver of the signs and omens is also their decoder; but it is also mediated, in so far as the receiver is not able to discern the plain sense of the imagery unaided. In the post-exilic period, by contrast, as exemplified by shared patterns in the Books of Zechariah and Daniel, an *angelus interpres* communicates the meaning of the imagery to the visionary. Here, the giver of the omens is distinctly removed from their interpretation and decoding; and the receiver of the envisaged content does not turn to a human wise man, but is rather addressed by a divine messenger who unlocks the configurations. Corresponding to this pre-exilic–post-exilic development is a parallel shift from normal terrestrial observations to hallucinations and extraterrestrial visions. In the post-exilic era, the eye of the visionary moves increasingly away from the earth as the envisaged content becomes increasingly esoteric; and the mediating interpreter becomes the bearer of a special divine gnosis, of a secret wisdom which is thoroughly beyond the ken of even the wisest of the earthly wise men, like Daniel (cf. Dan. 8: 13-27, 9: 21-5).[2]

Over against the foregoing, analysis of biblical oracles and their reinterpretation presented another configuration—one at once distinct from the mantology of dreams, omens, and visions, and yet correlatable with it at significant junctures. Thus, on the one hand, oracles are initially both non-symbolic and non-esoteric. Indeed, the very evocative and communicative force of these oracles depends on their comprehensibility, on the exoteric plain sense of the language employed. The prophetic receiver of such revelations thus transmits these divine communications to an audience—which does not summon him—with the full expectation that they will be understood. The problem of meaning or validity does not therefore arise at the outset, either at the time of the original hearing of the divine words or their communication to the public realm, but is an issue which arises with time, due to complicating historical exigencies and the human expectation that divine words are accurate and must be fulfilled. This does not mean, of course, that prophets did not embellish or clarify their materials in the course of their presentation of them—especially if the materials were felt to be vague, in need of non-ambiguous modifiers, or requiring specifications regarding the particular social reality to which they were directed (cf. Isa. 9: 13-14; Ezek. 22: 25-8). Nor does this mean that perfectly clear oracles could not also be accompanied by obscure visions which required decoding. Indeed, it is precisely this interpenetration

[2] This element is sharpened by a strong use of terms denoting comprehension, wisdom, and understanding (cf. Dan. 8: 19, 27, 9: 22-3, 25, 10: 1) of sealed truths known only to the angels (cf. Dan. 10: 21, 12: 9). In consequence, the apocalyptic conventicles are called 'illuminati' (Dan. 11: 33, 35)—true servants of YHWH (cf. Isa. 52: 13)—and will illumine–inform others (Dan. 11: 33; cf. Isa. 52: 15).

of vision and oracle which characterizes the material dealt with in Amos
(cf. 7: 1-9, 8: 1-3), Jeremiah (cf. 1: 11-16, 24: 1-10), and Zechariah
(cf. 1: 8-17, 2: 1-6, 5: 1-11, 6: 1-8). Nevertheless, the oracular component is assumed to be clear and distinct in all these cases.

Of special interest in this context is the particular relationship
between vision and oracle found in Dan. 9; for the divine communication which Daniel receives in 9: 21-7 is the reinterpretation of an older
divine oracle, now become an omen to be decoded by a mediator of
divine secrets. In this example, then, the visual dimension of visions has
thoroughly superseded the aural one of ancient oracles—for the old
Jeremian prophecy is seen in a book and Gabriel, the *angelus interpres*,
is seen by Daniel—and the immediate, terrestrial quality of ancient
prophecy is replaced by a mediating extraterrestrial being who reveals
secret wisdom.[3] Spoken prophecies have become envisaged omens to be
decoded, and the prophet has become a wise man graced with special
divine understanding. Nowhere, perhaps, is this contrast more starkly
demonstrated than the reuse in Dan. 10: 15-19 of the *mise-en-scène* of
divine initiation found in Ezek. 2-3.[4] In the latter, the prophet is directly
overcome by YHWH and initiated into his mediating role as a communicator of the divine word; while in the Daniel passage the sage is similarly
overcome, though now initiated into a divine gnosis regarding the true
meaning of an ancient prophetic word by a divine intermediary. Daniel's
position is thus doubly removed from divinity: what he receives is
wisdom from an angel, not the spirit of prophecy directly from YHWH.

B. The initial esoteric nature of dreams, omens, and visions on the
one hand, and the initial exoteric nature of prophetic oracles on the
other, raise the question of cognitive dissonance and consonance.
With respect to the former group, one may say that the dissonance of
the material envisaged is its cognitive opacity—that is, its seeming inscrutable strangeness in relation to normal meaning. Now this confusion

---

[3] Significantly related to this shift is the nature of the disclosure which, in
apocalyptic, is strictly speaking neither reproving nor exhortatory, but rather
informative in nature. Cf. J. C. H. Lebram, 'Apokalyptic und Hellenismus im
Buche Daniel', *VT* 20 (1970), 516-22.

[4] See my remarks in 'The "Sign"', 224f. n. 28, where this reuse is set out
schematically and in detail. To this add Dan. 10: 15~Ezek. 3: 26. What is particularly striking is that beyond the recurrence of isolated words—noted by such
earlier commentators as J. Montgomery, *Daniel* (ICC; Edinburgh: T. and T.
Clark, 1927), 408, 414—Dan. 10: 15-19 recapitulates the prophetic commission
scenario and its technical vocabulary found in Exod. 3-4, Isa. 6, Jer. 1: 4-9, and
Ezek. 2-3. The pattern is now transposed to serve an initiation into secret wisdom,
not active prophecy. Note especially the uses of the verbal stem *nāgaʿ* in Isa. 6: 7,
Jer. 1: 9, and Dan. 10: 16-17 (cf. 9: 21); or the function of the *sēper*-scroll in
Ezek. 2: 9-10, 3: 1-3, and Dan. 9: 2, 10: 21, 12: 4, 9.

is initially in the foreground, while the predictive aspects of the mantic images stand in the background. As the material is decoded, however, this relationship shifts; then the predictive elements become dominant and the initial dissonance is dispelled and relegated to the background. This shift is, in fact, the basic goal of this branch of biblical mantology. For what the receiver of the imagery wants above all is a solution to the obscurity (and often anxiety-provoking character) of the symbolic divine communication. Accordingly, the scenarios are not solely concerned with whether the dream interpretations of Joseph or Daniel came true, or whether and how the interpretations of the mediating angels were accurate. Of vital importance is the fact that the oneiromancer or interpreter has relieved the recipient of the assorted imagery of his initial anxiety by providing a coherent rational explanation, long before any verification of the interpretation could be had.[5]

By contrast, prophetic oracles demonstrate a different relationship between dissonance-consonance than the one just observed. Initially, because oracles are clear, exoteric communications, the matter of dissonance lies in the background while the predictive element is correspondingly in the foreground. However, since oracles provoke the promise of an ending, the issue of cognitive dissonance arises with the passage of time and the absence of the promised closure. In those circles where the predictive quality of divine forecasts remained strong, and verification of the original divine word was at stake, unfulfilled oracular promises were dealt with in a variety of ways. In some cases, as noted, prophets stressed that fulfilment of the oracle was temporarily delayed or soon to be realized (cf. Isa. 10: 25; Hab. 2: 3); in others, the failure of the original oracle was acknowledged and a revised prediction added (cf. Isa. 16: 13-14; Ezek. 38: 17);[6] finally, in yet another group, the anthology of prophecies found in Dan. 9-12, the delay is overcome by a revelation announcing that the old predictions were always really intended for the contemporary era in which this secret knowledge is now disclosed. In this latter type, the solution is remarkably similar to that found among the nearly contemporary Qumran texts, where it is expressly stated that the divine words originally spoken through such prophets as Habakkuk were never intended for their day – a fact to

---

[5] For the acknowledgement that Joseph 'interpreted favourably' (*ṭôb pātār*) before verification of his oneiromancy, see Gen. 40: 16, 22; and cf. Gen. 41: 33, 54. For acknowledgements of Daniel's interpretative skill without subsequent verifications, cf. Dan. 2: 46-7, 5: 29.

[6] Cf. also the adjustment to new historical events in Ezek. 17: 17, discussed by Greenberg, *Ezekiel*, 315. In other instances, new realities encourage new readings of old oracles – as, for example, the blindness of Zedekiah, which led to a re-reading of parts of Ezek. 12. See Greenberg, ibid. 215, and his intriguing proposal that a prototype of the later *'al tiqrê* device underlies the transformation.

which the Israelite prophets were oblivious, not being graced by a special dispensation of the spirit, as was the Teacher of Righteousness.[7]

Basic to this overall issue of cognitive dissonance in the fulfilment of divine oracles, and its resolution through reinterpretation and reapplication, is the fact that the oracles establish divine frameworks of temporal meaning. Each prediction establishes an interval between promise and fulfilment within which the recipient waits. Thus, just as the onset of the prediction is divinely established, so is its closure. The recipient stands between these two poles, taken out of the random accumulation of events and thrust expectantly into a divinely ordered chronicity. Predictions thus project a rational order on to the apparent disorder of events and give clear guidelines for divine providence and involvement in history. When these orders broke down or failed to materialize, cognitive crises could surface—these being the price for such rationalizations of the temporal order. Accordingly, the exegetical redirection of lapsed or unfulfilled oracles functioned to re-establish cognitive consonance and to realign the predictive hope with empirical reality. The concomitant result was to reframe units of future time into new patterns of divinely ordered meaning.

Put slightly differently, the rational frameworks established by predictive oracles allow for a transcendence of the terrors and irrationality of history through an assertion and expectation of divine control over it. This latter operates even at the most minimal level, where the predictions are often vague or incomplete, and seemingly focused on immediate contemporary realities. It also operates on more maximal levels, where the temporal framework is more extensive or precise—like the seventy years or ten sabbatical cycles predicted in the Jeremian oracle in its successive variations, or the periodization of time into one jubilee period (cf. Isa. 27: 30-2, 61: 1) or even multiple jubilee periods (Dan. 9: 25-7). The temporal cycle of four monarchies culminating in a fifth—its ultimate successor—shows yet another pattern which was used to order time and elicit hope within history. As these frameworks extended their temporal scope, and gradually shifted from being structures which ordered units of time into structures which ordered and correlated historical time in an increasingly comprehensive scope, the burdens of cognitive dissonance became more acute. The receiver of these predictions depended more and more on them for his whole perception of historical order. Such, at any rate, is the shift that may be perceived in the post-exilic period where, for example, the earlier vague predictions of an enemy from the north are reinterpreted by the author of Ezek. 38-9 into a vision of world significance; or where the repeatedly reinterpreted Jeremian oracle is combined with patterns of

[7] See pHab. vii. 1-4. On prophetic mysteries, see also 1Q *S.* i. 3, viii. 15-16.

four monarchical cycles in the Book of Daniel to produce a temporal framework spanning hundreds of years and many nations.

Thus, if most pre-exilic predictive oracles focused the orientation of their receivers on limited promises and defined historical units, these promises and units became, in time, an increasingly comprehensive — indeed, *the* comprehensive — way of perceiving historical time and its processes.[8] With this development, dissonance did not merely threaten more restricted promises or hopes — like the threatened non-confirmation of divine promises to the Davidic dynasty (cf. Ps. 89), or the prediction that Ahab or his line would be punished for his heinous crime (1 Kgs. 21: 20b-26). With the gradual expansion of the parameters of promise and hope, and the interlocking of all other meaning-structures with them, what was jeopardized was nothing less than the entire framework within which a believer lived and through which he might transcend persecution, oppression, and the large-scale repression of native symbols of meaning. For this reason, the readjustment of predictive timetables in the course of Hellenistic domination as found in Dan. 11-12 was a radical cognitive necessity, and no mere theological apologetic or solution.[9] The paradox of this whole mode of resolving cognitive dissonance which arises from unfulfilled prophecies is thus as follows: while the very transformation of older exoteric oracles into esoteric codes initially solves the problem of their unrealized nature by protecting them from outright disconfirmation (for only the masters of their secrets know their true applicability), the risk that is inevitably taken by disclosing the secret intent of these oracles is far more than their simple empirical failure. What is ultimately put at stake is the very rational order which gives cognitive coherence to time and its terrors. Under these circumstances, the pivotal power of mantological exegesis is self-evident.

C. Another axis along which the two categories of mantological exegesis may be compared is the form-critical one. Here, such matters as literary or oral form, the styles and techniques of exegesis, and the relationship of the latter to various contexts and matrices — socio-historical, literary, and mental — must be considered.

---

[8] According to K. Koch, 'Spätisraelitisches Geschichtsdenken am Beispiel des Buches Daniel', *Historische Zeitschrift*, 193 (1961), 1-32, one of the characteristics of apocalypticism is the expansion of the temporal horizon to include world history.

[9] This, to my mind, puts the matter more sharply and more accurately than the opinion of L. Hartmann, who almost factors out the pathos of the revised calculations by his resort to the notion of redundancy in information theory as an explanation. See his 'The Function of Some So-called Apocalyptic Timetables', *NTS* 22 (1975-6), 1-14.

1. The dream-reports with their interpretations in Gen. 40-1 and Dan. 2, 4, and 7 (cf. Gen. 37), like the vision-reports with their interpretations in Zech. 1-6 and Dan. 9-12 (cf. Amos 7: 1-9, 8: 1-3; Jer. 1: 11-15, 24: 3-10) and the omens with interpretation in Dan. 5 (cf. Judg. 7: 9-15), constitute a fairly separate genre of mantology. The exegeses are characteristically atomistic and lemmatic, and follow the presentation of the initiating image(s); and these exegeses are preceded by recurrent deictic pronouns that link the esoteric content with its explication. In addition, the *mise-en-scène* of the dream-scenes – where the dreamer is alarmed, confused, and initially unable to seek satisfactory answers from a professional coterie of diviners – is a stable element; so too are the invocatory questions which are addressed to the receiver of the terrestrial or extraterrestrial visions. From all this one is driven to the conclusion that biblical tradents were heir to a coherent scholarly tradition of mantology. Indeed, the professional nature of this tradition of interpretation, and the careful form of its transmission, are confirmed, as we have observed, from a broader Near Eastern perspective, where precisely the same forms, terms, exegetical structures, and even exegetical techniques (cf. the contextual numerological, paranomastic, and permutational techniques discussed earlier) recur.[10] Evidently, then, we have in the Hebrew Bible the ancient Israelite reflex of widespread and shared patterns. Indeed, given that Egyptian oneiromancers are attested at the Mesopotamian court, the fact that both Joseph and Daniel are presented as Israelite natives performing at foreign courts where just these forms and procedures are fully evidenced must not go unmarked .as valuable historical–cultural evidence. For whatever conclusions one might draw regarding the historicity of the situations portrayed, or regarding the dating of their final literary stylization, the inevitable form-critical conclusion is that the conventions of oneiromancy preserved in the Hebrew Bible originated in such professional and royal settings as are documented in ancient Egyptian and Mesopotamian sources.[11] With respect to the biblical evidence, a final point may be noted. The similarity of visions to dreams suggests the influence of oneiromancy upon the former, although the generation of a parallel inner-prophetic tradition for the elucidation of divine visions should

---

[10] This even pertains to the narrative reuse of conventional Near Eastern dream scenes and terms. On the incubation scene in 1 Sam. 3 and the language in v. 9, cf. the Mesopotamian analogues noted by Oppenheim, *The Interpretation of Dreams*, 188–90, 199–201. For a literary analysis, see my '1 Samuel 3: Historical Narrative and Narrative Poetics', in *Literary Interpretations of Biblical Narratives*, ii, ed. K. R. R. Gros Louis (Nashville: Abingdon, 1982), 191–203.

[11] J. J. Collins, *The Apocalyptic Vision*, 55, even goes so far as to suggest that the provenance of Dan. 1–6 was perhaps 'Jews in the Diaspora, especially those who functioned or aspired to function at a gentile court'.

not be discounted. In such an event, the continuity of form, language, and technique in the latter would indicate that such a tradition was the ward of prophetic schools and their professionalized curriculum of rhetorical and literary conventions.

By contrast with dreams, visions, and omens, the biblical mantology of oracles evidences no comparable unity of genre, language, or technique. Indeed, the occurrence of exegetical elements is variously integrated into the different genres where an oracular *traditum* or its *traditio* is reported. Thus, for example, the embellishment of Zeph. 3: 3-4 in Ezek. 22: 25-8 is integrated into that oracular context; the divine dynastic promise in 2 Sam. 7 is found exegetically adapted in the prayer of Ps. 89 and the speech reported in 1 Chron. 28; the Jeremian seventy-year oracle is found differently reinterpreted and stylized in an oracular setting (Jer. 29: 10), a historiographical narrative (2 Chron. 36: 21-2), a vision (Zech. 1: 12), and an angelic revelation (Dan. 9: 24-7); and the oracles of Zech. 7: 4-7, 8: 18-19 are transformed in Esther 9: 30-1. The reasons for this variety of genres and exegetical techniques lie in the fact, stressed earlier, that oracles—being exoteric in nature—did not initially require their exegetical reinterpretation or reapplication. Accordingly, the exegetical *traditio* is, in the main, an *ad hoc* matter—something secondarily related to the original oracular *traditum*. The two most notable exceptions are Isa. 9: 13-14 and Ezek. 22: 25-8, though here, too, the matter may not go unqualified. On the one hand, it is clear that the lemma in Isa. 9: 13 is explicated atomistically in v. 14, with the use of deictic pronouns. However, given the notably vague nature of the oracular pronouncement and others like it, the possibility remains that both v. 13 and v. 14 constitute a unified oracular utterance—the utterance of the *traditum* without secondary exegetical elaborations. Similarly, there need be little doubt that Ezek. 22: 25-8 also constitutes a primary, unified saying. However, when this text is compared synoptically to the oracle in Zeph. 3: 3-4 it is also clear that Ezek. 22: 25-8 is a theological-moral embellishment of an older set piece—that it is a *traditio* and not solely a *traditum* in its own right. Thus, the mode of integrating an exegetical addendum to a received oracular *traditum* in Ezek. 22: 25-8 is but one stylistic mode among many others.

Within the variety of forms in which an exegetical *traditio* may occur, the resolution of the tension between a *traditum* and its *traditio* —the accommodation of one to the other, or the authentication of one through the other—varies considerably. In fact, several types may be isolated along a spectrum where one pole clearly distinguishes between an oracular *traditum* and its *traditio* and the other variously blurs that distinction. Starting at the first pole, one must mention such texts as Isa. 9: 13-14, where the lemma is explicated by a series of exegetical comments introduced by deictic pronouns, or Isa. 16: 13-14, where the failure of a past prophecy is acknowledged and the updated version is technically marked and acknowledged ('this is the oracle . . . *formerly*; *and now*. . .'). A similar cross-reference between a *traditio* and its earlier *traditum* is marked at Ezek. 38: 17 ('Are you not the one of whom I spoke . . . *aforetimes* . . .?'). On other occasions the exegetical *traditio* may refer to key phrases of the *traditum* (cf. Jer. 29: 10; 2 Chron. 36: 21-2 — referring to the 'fulfilment' formula and the seventy years);[12] or it may refer to the *traditum* as 'my/the good oracle' (cf. Jer. 29: 10, referring to 25: 10-11; Jer. 33: 14, referring to 23: 5-6; or it may use the formula '*for so* YHWH has prophesied/said' (cf. Isa. 58: 14b; Obad. 17-18).

Moving to the other pole, where the precise content of the *traditum* is obscured in various ways, we may actually start with the just-mentioned examples from Jer. 29: 10 and 33: 14. As remarked earlier, these texts manifestly misrepresent the earlier oracle in so far as the *traditio* deals with a content different from the *traditum* which is purportedly cited. Comparable to this phenomenon is the strategic misquote of the divine dynastic promise of 2 Sam. 7 in Ps. 89. Here, though the psalmist begins his appeal with the words '*then* you spoke in a vision to your faithful ones, and said' (v. 20), the presentation of the divine words which follows contains a striking variety of exegetical revampings which accommodate the older oracle to the later conditions. Thus, although the citation purports to be a venerable, divinely sponsored *traditum*, it is actually a transformed *traditio*. Here, as in Jer. 29: 10 and 33: 14-16, the exegetical innovation of the *traditio* has been strategically obscured. A further example of this phenomenon appears in the Chronicler's report of David's speech to all Israel in 1 Chron. 28. As in Ps. 89, the dynastic oracle is purportedly cited ('And Elohim said to me . . .', v. 3), but now with an *ex eventu* legitimation of Solomon interpolated along the way (vv. 5-6). The innovative quality of the *traditio* is thus effectively and authoritatively blurred.

Another cluster of texts shows additional procedures employed to obscure the innovative force of a *traditio*. As distinct from the foregoing examples, where the new text referred back to a *traditum* and sought to conceal its exegetical *traditio* by presenting itself as a citation of the older oracle, there is here a contextual integration of the one with the other. Among the possible examples, one will recall that the phrase 'Oracle of YHWH; and to Nebuchadrezzar, king of Babylon, my servant' is missing in the LXX version of Jer. 25: 9. Its occurrence in

---

[12] The Hebrew verb *mālē'* 'fulfilled' is used technically in biblical oracle contexts; cf. also 1 Kgs. 2: 27 and 2 Chron. 36: 21 (*ap.* Jer. 25: 12). The Akkadian interdialectal cognate *malû* is similarly used; cf. R. Borger, *Asarhaddon*, p. 15, Episode 10, Fassung B. 19-20, and the editor's commentary ad loc.

the MT thus clearly serves to specify the vague enemy from the north referred to just before. As it now stands, then, the MT is syntactically redundant — with the interpolated phrase disrupting the set deuteronomic phraseology of the verse ('families of the north . . . and I will have them brought'; cf. 1: 15, 'families . . . of the north . . . and they shall come') and preceded by the formula *nĕ'ûm YHWH*, which often marks an addition to earlier textual strata in the Book of Jeremiah.[13] But these complications aside, the new exegetical *traditio* is now contextually blended with the older oracular *traditum*. The result is the transformation of a *traditio* into a *traditum* and, thereby, its reauthorization. The exegetical commentator to MT Jer. 25: 9 thus clearly wished to obscure his voice. The same holds true for the author of the second letter about Purim, referred to in Esther 9: 30-1. Here, however, the matter is more complex, since the writer sought to advocate the on-going celebration of festivities in the month of Adar through a precise reformulation of the oracular *traditum* in Zech. 8: 18-19. Because of this, he could hardly have failed to regard his *traditio* as the long-anticipated closure to the oracular pronouncement of the prophetic *traditum*. If, nevertheless, no explicit reference was made to that *traditum*, one can only assume that this scholar-legist did not feel authorized to legitimate his innovation through reference to divine authority — pseudepigraphically or otherwise — and rested content with the *tour de force* of his covert exegesis, the achievement of one scholar-exegete for his scholarly fellows.

One final form-critical dimension bearing on the relationship between *traditum* and *traditio* in oracular mantology may now be considered, and that is the anthologizing of old prophetic pronouncements in Dan. 9-12. Several factors give this clustering its particular cultural and exegetical value. First, Dan. 9-12 does not simply contain the *ad hoc* explication, reapplication, or (re)specification of the then ancient Jeremian oracle (Jer. 25: 9-12), but is a coherent formulation of an apocalyptic programme out of many earlier prophetic pronouncements. The document is thus one literary whole, a composite piece that elucidates the timetable of one dominant oracle — the fulfilment of Jeremiah's ancient forecast — while alluding to many other prophecies as well. Indeed, one may add that, given the strategic importance of the *angelus interpres* in disclosing the secret meanings found in Dan. 9: 24-7 and Dan. 11, the reuse of linguistic fragments from the ancient prophecies of Balaam, Isaiah, and Habakkuk is more than an epigonic

---

[13] For some text-critical implications and functions of this formula, see R. Rendtorff, 'Zum Gebrauch der Formel *ne'ûm jahwe* in Jeremiabuch', *ZAW* 66 (1954), 27-37. In other instances, like Ezek. 21: 33-7, new material is incorporated by means of a *Wiederaufnahme*. See B. Lang, 'A Neglected Method in Ezekiel Research', *VT* 29 (1979), 39-44.

curiosity or archaizing stylistic feature.[14] It is this and more. In the context of Gabriel's disclosure of secret prophetic information these prophetic allusions attain renewed and independent significance. Indeed, the secret interpretation of Jer. 25: 9-12 – the central text of this apocalypse – is the prism through which these fragments are recontextualized and their true historical import brought to light.

A related literary point is that Dan. 10: 1-12: 10,[15] with its revealed secrets, prophetic allusions, and angelic figures, abrupt consummation of history, grand temporal schemes, and references to the vindication and resurrection of righteous believers, is the virtual prototype of all the early Jewish apocalyptic texts which appear in the next few centuries.[16] Seen generically, Dan. 10: 1-12: 10 is the report by a chosen adept of the true explication and application of an ancient prophetic oracle and a catena of prophetic fragments which both bear on the calculation of the end (revealed by an angelic interpreter) and provide consolation to the community of the faithful. The propagandistic dimension of this literary genre must not, therefore, go unremarked. For, as a published vision-report, Dan. 10: 1-12: 10 is not solely the private disclosure to one wise man about the final timetable of the end but a public document disclosed to the apocalyptic community – giving them the secret gnosis through which they may take heart.[17] Three attendant modes of transcendence may therefore be discerned. First, the crisis community waiting steadfastly for the end is given the means to withstand the terrors of time through knowledge of its true course and final stages; second, they can also transcend the persecution

---

[14] Cf. the epigonic legal collection in Ezek. 44: 9-31 and the archaizing stylistics in 2 Chron. 15: 1-7, discussed above.

[15] Dan. 12: 11-13 are a series of addenda, revising the earlier apocalyptic schedule. Thus, apocalyptic secrets are mentioned in Dan. 12: 4 and 9-10, which form an *inclusio* summing up the apocalyptic document. After this, the technical term '*ēt* 'time') – used twice in the *inclusio* – is again mentioned in v. 11 to introduce a *new* timetable. Yet a third schedule follows in v. 12 (with apparent allusion to Isa. 8: 16 f and Hab. 2: 2, where 'sealed' scrolls and the counsel to 'wait' for the divinely appointed 'end' occur). Seen thus, Dan. 12: 13 is an editorial *Wiederaufnahme* literally recapitulating v. 9 f *before* the apocalyptic addenda.

[16] For a convenient summary of features and patterns of early Jewish apocalyptic, see D. S. Russell, *The Method and Message of Jewish Apocalyptic* (Philadelphia: Westminster, 1964), ch. 4. I tend to accept I. Gruenwald's reading of the late Isaianic passages referring to a new era (eg. Isa. 65: 17, 66: 22) as 'reflect[ing] a mood that is later on echoed in a number of places in apocalyptic writings'. See his 'Jewish Apocalyptic Literature', in *Aufstieg und Niedergang der römischen Welt*, ii, ed. W. Haase (Berlin and New York: W. de Gruyter, 1979), 116.

[17] Cf. the comment by F. Cumont on this resentment of vanquished nations in 'La Fin du monde selon les mages occidentaux', *RHR* 103 (1931), 72: 'L'Asia, vaincue par les armes étrangeres, continua à lutter pour la suprématie à coups d'oracles.' On anti-Roman propaganda generally, see H. Fuchs, *Der geistige Widerstand gegen Rom in der antiken Welt* (Berlin: W. de Gruyter, 1938).

of foreign oppressors by identifying with the old symbol of a suffering servant of YHWH, who was himself purified and justified others through his vicarious suffering;[18] and finally, the group can transcend the threats of destruction confronting them via the human powers of the mundane world by focusing on the truths revealed by angelic powers and the realities of their supramundane world.[19] It is not without significance that, in formulating this native literary genre as the response to religious crisis, the biblical writer parallels not only the widespread phenomenon in the Hellenistic world whereby oppressed native groups projected the defeat of their enemy through reinterpreted prophecies when physical force was no realistic alternative, but he also parallels the contemporary Hellenistic genre of pseudo-prophecies.[20] His document is thus a product of its time and a distinctly native Jewish expression as well.[21] Indeed, if our earlier analysis is correct, the formulation of this pseudo-revelation is the achievement of professional 'calculators of the end' who used an ancient oracle to foment the Maccabean uprising— despite its realistic unlikelihood—at precisely this time. This would be a further propagandistic function of our text.

As regards the relationship between *traditum* and *traditio* within Dan. 10: 1-12: 10, one need only add this to the earlier form-critical observations: the core prophetic *traditum*—Jer. 25: 9-12—has been radically transformed. It is no longer an oral prophecy given immediately to a prophet by YHWH, with clear contemporary relevance. It is now a written prophecy read by a wise man and interpreted by an angelic intermediary, with relevance for a historical moment centuries later. A living divine word originally destined for public knowledge has thus been transformed into a coded message whose secret meaning is revealed to a special adept—who engaged in strict ascetic practices prior to his semi-mystical visions (cf. Dan. 9: 3, 10: 2-3)[22]—and through

[18] This ideological and organizational dimension comports with what social psychologists agree to be a crucial factor in the ability of so-called millenarian movements to cope with 'the special crises precipitated by prophetic disconformations or delays in prophetic fulfilments', and also crises precipitated by delegitimation or persecution. Cf. J. Zygmunt, 'When Prophecies Fail', *The American Behavioral Scientist*, 16 (1972), 250f.

[19] Cf. the parallel observations of J. J. Collins, 'Apocalyptic Eschatology as the Transcendence of Death', *CBQ* 36 (1974), 30.

[20] Cf. above, p. 485 n. 65.

[21] The revival of native traditions at this time has often been observed. Cf. the remarks of M. Hadas, 'Aspects of Nationalist Survival under Hellenistic and Roman Imperialism', *Journal of the History of Ideas*, 11 (1950), 131-9 (esp. p. 133). This even led to notable shifts in Roman historiography about 175 BCE. See F. Klingner, 'Römische Geschichtsschreibung bis zum Werke des Livius', *Die Antike*, 13 (1937), 1-19.

[22] See I. Gruenwald, *Apocalyptic and Merkavah Mysticism* (Leiden: E. J. Brill, 1980), 99.

him to his circle. Arranged around this core *traditum*, moreover, are the originally oral prophecies of Balaam, Isaiah, and Habakkuk. These, too, are correspondingly transformed into secret codes decoded by the *angelus interpres*. The exegetical *traditio* of these various texts thus takes place in an intermediate realm, between heaven and earth. The older divine word is sealed up; its meaning is beyond the natural ken of the faithful. Indeed, it is the very belief in the secret supernatural meaning of old oracles which constitutes the faith of this group—and to which they are faithful.[23] As in other instances, the *traditio* is a prolongation of the original divine *traditum*. Only now the overt meaning of this *traditum* has become covert, an esoteric symbol to be divined by agents of the divine. Hence, *traditio* is here both subversive and restorative: it subverts the meaning of the original text by transforming its exoteric content into an esoteric code, and thereby restores the *traditum* to a historical teaching.

2. As with other forms of inner-biblical exegesis, the *socio-historical context* of mantological exegesis is a significant form-critical dimension. Whether it is an event in the private life of an individual—like the symbolism of dreams, visions, or omens—or one in the public life of the nation—like the pronouncement of a prophetic oracle—the *Umwelt* plays a crucial role. It may be the context within which the symbolism is received and understood, or into which its meaning is projected, or in relationship to which the predictions or omens are confirmed or invalidated. Thus, a dreamer dreams with reference to concrete life-experiences; omens are found in the life-world and bear on it; and oracular predictions establish new temporal nexuses—linking a now to a then and projecting new social realities into the future. Mantological exegesis, then, not only arises out of a given situation in life, but characteristically opens up a new one to view. Indeed, apart from those cases where the exegesis is merely explicative, embellishing, or *ex eventu*, another socio-historical context is invoked—a counter-reality of promise or anticipation that is already lived proleptically in the present. Two socio-historical contexts are thus brought together by mantology, with the second one being consummatory of the first and previewed or pre-experienced in the present to different degrees. On the one hand, the proleptic fulfilment may merely provide short-range hope and expectation in a time of crisis; on the other, however, as is typically the case with apocalyptic programmes, the future vision disclosed through exegesis may provide a comprehensive cognitive structure and so the fundamental means of transcending the terrors of history. In the

---

[23] Typically, such groups regard themselves 'as the organizational link between the supernatural and earthly phases of the millennial drama, the bridgehead to the new future'; cf. Zygmunt, 'When Prophecies Fail', 265.

case of dreams, omens or visions, mantological exegesis unlocks ominous symbolism and projects the counter-reality into a variously determined future (the butler will be restored; some kingdoms will be destroyed and others will triumph; a time of consolation and cultic purity can be expected; and so on). In the case of oracles, however, which initially project a clear counter-reality, the general function of mantological exegesis is rather to verify and validate that new reality *ex eventu*, or to reapply the ancient words so that their sustaining hope will not be invalidated.

3. Rooted in social-historical realities, but nevertheless analytically distinct, is the *literary context* of mantological exegesis. With respect to the interpretation of dreams and visions, the first significant point is that our reports of them are part and parcel of native and cross-cultural literary conventions. Thus, however the interpretation of a king's dreams occurred *in situ*, the oneiromancies of Joseph and Daniel are preserved within literary narratives and in a highly stylized literary form, with close parallels to the dream-reports known from ancient Mesopotamia. This being so, it is not enough to say that these dreams are given a courtier setting by courtier-scholarly types.[24] It is rather necessary to add that the true life-setting of these dream-reports lies within the established literary conventions of such scholarly guilds. This point is reinforced by the formal literary consistency of the vision-reports in the Books of Amos and Jeremiah, or the vision-reports with mediating angels in the Book of Zechariah. Analysis of these cases suggests that the living experience of such prophets has been stylistically reformulated according to conventional forms.[25] This hypothesis helps to explain the highly patterned expression given to the experiences of these men, and requires the latter-day interpreter to be fully attentive both to the experiential life-setting or idiosyncratic imagery, on the one hand, and to the conventional literary form into which these have been poured, on the other. Certainly, this complex relationship between literary form and experience would be far more complex — and essentially unanalysable — if prophets actually experienced visions according to the conventional forms in which they were outlined in the schools by special virtuosi for their adepts. Such a possibility must not be dismissed outright; for comparable phenomena are well attested in the history of religions. For example, the frequently conventional nature of ecstatic visions reported by mystics belonging to traditional mystical circles in the Middle Ages has often been explained on the basis of

[24] Cf. above, p. 512 and n. 11.

[25] The same conclusion is suggested by the highly schematized form of the prophetic commission scenarios found in Exod. 3-4, Isa. 6, Jer. 1, and Ezek. 1-3. Cf. *Text and Texture*, 68f.

preconditioned expectations of certain schemata and imagery.[26]

The form-critical factor of literary context assumes further significance when we move from those cases of experiences secondarily reformulated into conventional literary patterns to those texts which are
literary in the first instance, or for whom literary context has become
a primary characteristic. The visions and interpretations in Dan. 9–12
are exemplary of the first type. As noted above, the revelations and
esoteric disclosures found in those chapters, while literarily realized
in a distinctly Israelite manner, are presumably nurtured upon the
widespread literary convention of pseudo-prophecies known from the
Hellenistic period. This being so, we are faced with a text or texts
whose fictive or imaginative character is the elemental setting of it, as
well as the controlling variable in analysing the place and function of
the exegesis therein. Where operative, this factor has two form-critical
dimensions of basic importance to the present discussion. First, the
literary framework of the given piece constitutes the intensive matrix
within which the text and its exegesis are functional, meaningful,
and potentially persuasive. More sharply put: the mise-en-scène of the
text and its contents (including the exegesis) establish a closed literary
context which attempts to be authoritative, coherent, and convincing
on its own terms. This consideration leads to the second point, which
concerns the ostensive socio-historical references *within* the literary
matrix. Mantological documents like Dan. 9–12, which are initially
literary products yet seek to propagandize about a non-textual or
social reality on the basis of privileged (i.e., revealed) information,
mark a trajectory from the literary to the social-historical spheres
since they seek to establish a new social–historical existence, or consciousness of existence, *on the very basis* of their literary conventions
and contents. They are thus texts which, for all their extra-literary
concerns, do not transcend their own literary context or character
and indeed remain profoundly dependent upon them.

These reflections may be contrasted with the second type mentioned
above, where the literary context *becomes* a primary characteristic for
textual analysis. What I have in mind here are those instances where a
series of conventionally formulated or reformulated vision-reports with
exegesis are anthologically grouped in one document, as in Amos 7–8,
Zech. 1–6, 9–12, or Dan. 7–12. Whatever the original status of each
vision separately, and whether they were gathered according to thematic
or stylistic associative principles, or were actually written as a literary
act in the first instance – a possibility which is stronger for the Daniel

[26] See G. Scholem, *On the Kabbala and its Symbolism* (New York: Schocken,
1965), 9, following G. A. Coe, 'The Sources of the Mystic Revelation', *Hibbert
Journal*, 6 (1907–8), 367.

materials than the Zecharian, though not out of the question for the latter – the fact is that we now have mantological anthologies which are intended to be read together.[27] Accordingly, the element of literary context expands from the literary conventions by which any piece has been stylistically realized, and through which it may now be apprehended, to the patterning of like pieces which can be read as one unit. Such redactional integrations or literary designs thus establish a notable *intertextual* context. The visions and exegeses may be read either successively or reflexively; and they may be analysed according to internal exegetic design or with cross-references to contiguous pieces. The presumed intent, particularly in Zech. 1-6 and Dan. 7-12, was to expose the readership to a cycle of exegetical texts bearing on their life-situation and, thereby, cumulatively to sponsor a new consciousness of the ominous nature of the times. For the author of the Zecharian cycle, the overall goal was to elicit a programme of restoration; for the author of the Daniel apocalypse, on the other hand, the communication of religious confidence and hope through understanding was of major concern.

4. The fact of living with divine predictions in the mind – that is, living mindful of their existence and their fulfilment or failure – points to a third form-critical dimension of mantological exegesis, its *mental matrix*. For particularly characteristic of mantology is the acute consciousness of the present-future horizon of the divine communications received. On the one hand, predictive communications, given in the present, express an as yet unrealized *future* fulfilment; on the other, the proleptic disclosure of a future means that the recipients of these communications already anticipate this final closure *in the present*. Of course, where the expected closure does not occur as predicted, exegesis may emerge in order to prolong the original divine voice. In fact, such prolongations of prestigious divine promises directly disclose a vital dimension of the cognitive commitment of persons in ancient Israel to the fulfilment of YHWH's words. Even more, they dramatize the attempts of later prophetic tradents, circles, and apocalyptic conventicles to decode present reality in the light of earlier forecasts, and to legitimate their hopes thereby. Such waiting, revising, and decoding are, then, the dynamic components of the mental matrix of mantological exegesis.

These features suggest a further consideration. To begin with, for all their initial esoteric obscurity, the resolution of the symbolism of

---

[27] Cf. the remarks of R. North, 'Prophecy to Apocalyptic via Zechariah', *SVT* 22 (1972), 50, that 'Zechariah's visions seem to have been composed interlockingly for private reading'.

dreams and omens occurs in a climate of wisdom and scholarship.[28] Typically, different scholars are consulted; they broach solutions presumably based on correlations and codes patiently collated in dream-books or tabulations of omens; and the recipient of the symbolic communication judges certain solutions to be rationally satisfying and others not so. As a result, in these cases at least, the inherent irrationality of divine communications in the Hebrew Bible—in the sense that they constitute autonomous divine acts, are quite impervious to human rationality as a manifest precondition, and impose solutions which are accepted because of the theological prestige of the divine communicator, not because of any inherent rationality—is countervailed by the rational procedures of their human interpretation.[29] Along this rational-irrational continuum, of course, the divine decoding of visionary symbols (e.g. Zech. 1-6), or the pre-emptive divine disclosure of ominous or oneiromantic symbols (e.g. Judg. 7: 9-15; 2 Sam. 5: 17-25), means that the interpretations, like their communication, are entirely dependent upon the divine will. They are thus irrational in the sense noted above and, in this respect, incite comparison with oracles. For while exoteric oracles provide divinely sponsored rational conditions and preconditions for their realization, and even evoke rational human efforts to apply them to different circumstances, these oracles remain absolutely dependent upon a sovereign divine action for their onset, nature and closure. Such, then, is the paradox for the mind that lives 'in the midst'—between the forecast and the finality of divine predictions.[30] Succinctly put, this paradox underscores the fact that divine oracles project rational structures upon time and history which inevitably lock their believing recipients into a doubly irrational position. On the one hand, the meaning-structures have been sovereignly imposed and are not rationally constructed; while on the other, the final realization of the oracles is out of all human control, all rational exegesis and scrutiny of their apparent sense notwithstanding.

The recipient of divine oracles, therefore, abides with both fateful resignation and cautious hope—with resignation, because the fulfilment of prophecies ultimately belongs to the giver of prophecies; and with

---

[28] Note the lists of scholars consulted in Gen. 39: 8, Dan. 2: 2, 10, 12, 48; 4: 2-4, 6; 5: 8-11, 14-15. The inquiries in Dan. 1-6 have been properly labelled 'mantic wisdom' by H.-P. Müller, in his 'Mantische Weisheit und Apokalyptic', *SVT* 22 (1972), 268-93.

[29] This understanding of rationality-irrationality in religion follows classical Weberian definitions and distinctions. Cf. the discussion above, pp. 236-56, with literature cited, and M. Weber, *Sociology of Religion* (Boston: Beacon Press, 1964), *passim*.

[30] For a comparative perspective, see the literary analysis of fictive endings and the sense of being 'in the middest' by F. Kermode, *The Sense of an Ending* (New York: Oxford University Press, 1975), esp. chs. 1-2.

hope, because the apparent failure of a prophetic word may yet be reversed by new divine revelations or by discerning human interpretations which will reapply or correctly elucidate the true intent of the original oracle. Indeed, it would appear that the double dimension of this hope—both its irrational and rational components—was the composite means for ancient Israelites, particularly in the post-exilic era, to transcend or deflect the onset of cognitive dissonance generated by apparently failed oracular predictions. As we have variously observed, the tight cognitive grip of this mental matrix cuts across various genres in this period: for example, the Jeremian oracle is revised by human and angelic beings in prophecies, visions, and historiography; failed prophetic pronouncements are reinterpreted in the deuteronomic historical traditions; and older prophetic promises are reappropriated in the proto-apocalyptic narratives of Ezek. 38-9.

Especially notable for their volume and force were the ways in which certain prophetic circles scrutinized the pre-exilic promises of First-Isaiah and reapplied them for later generations—thereby reconstructing new cognitive frameworks within which they found divinely sponsored hope and coherence.[31] Indeed, the intensity of this scrutinizing consciousness—fateful and faithful at once—is even more obvious in those situations where groups were formed, and even sustained themselves, under the aegis of reinterpreted prophecies.[32] Such is certainly the case among the persons who constituted the apocalyptical conventicles referred to in Dan. 9-12. For them, as repeatedly noted, a whole host of oracular snippets from the pre-exilic period provided both their framework of theological discourse and their coping mechanism in the face of cognitive dissonance. The fact that the true esoteric meanings of these ancient prophecies were divinely revealed, as well as a series of revisions of the original timetable (Dan. 12: 11-13), certainly inspired confidence in the apocalyptic hope projected thereby and provided resilience against its empirical disconfirmation. Indeed, from the social-psychological perspective, the frequent revision of the apocalyptical timetable underscores just how committed the faithful were to the oracular schemata as a fundamental means of cognitive orientation and consonance.

---

[31] Thus, a 'principal achievement of re-interpretation [of older prophecies] was that . . . [i]t expressed the faith that . . . history is not a series of happenings but a continuum of interventions of God's saving deeds ever increasing in power'; see P. Grech, 'Interprophetic Re-interpretation and Old Testament Eschatology', *Augustinianum*, 9 (1969), 264f.

[32] For an example of the interaction between Scripture, group organization, and historical experience in the development of apocalyptic ideology, see N. Dahl, 'Eschatologie und Geschichte im Lichte der Qumran-Texte', in *Zeit und Geschichte*, ed. E. Dinkler (Tübingen: J. C. Mohr, 1964), 3-18.

This leads to a final, though crucial, aspect of the mental matrix of mantological exegesis. For if the fundamental common denominator of all predictions—be they dreams, visions, omens, or oracles—is that they are divine communications expressing divine involvement in human events, this very factor establishes the dialectic ground of its own crisis. That is to say, in so far as the divine communications are taken to be providential revelations from the divine source of all history, failure of their predictive elements to materialize invites severe theological dissonance. Any review of the theological tensions associated with false prophecy bears this out. No doubt, the most acute manifestation of this theological crisis, and the one most needful of remedial exegesis, involves those groups whose entire historical vision was bound up with the fulfilment of particular (and often revised) oracles. Such groups not only lived with divine predictions in mind but, characteristically, with their exegeses in mind as well. This remarkable mental matrix is thus of major moment in the history of religions. It especially underscores the cognitive hold of oracular exegeses for those whose world-view is bereft of the immediacy of the divine presence—indeed, for those who live solely with exegeses and *their* promise of a return of the divine to history. And since present history is transcended by these people through an exegetically derived prolepsis into an anticipated future—for apocalyptical conventicles do nothing if they do not live proleptically—there is evident danger of antinomian eruptions. Immediate history and its norms, being destined to be swallowed by the imminent catastrophe, no longer retain their erstwhile authority. It is perhaps with this in mind that some late hand appended to the prophecies of Malachi, traditionally the last of the prophets, the admonition not to forget the Torah of Moses and its observance during the expected advent of Elijah, the precursor of a final redemption (cf. Mal. 3: 22-4).[33]

---

[33] J. Blenkinsopp, *Prophecy and Canon* (Notre Dame: University of Notre Dame Press, 1977), 122f., makes the converse and much more moderate point when he considers Mal. 3: 22-4 as a coda designed to harmonize more conservative impulses with eschatological ones which anticipate an all-Israelite restoration; i.e., 'observance of Torah . . . would not exclude the millenarian hope'. This messianic expectancy is particularly marked in Mal. 3: 1b-4, which speaks of those who 'desire' the 'coming' of the 'messenger' and 'abide the day of his coming'. Apart from this thematic feature, many commentators have noted that vv. 1b-4 are in the third person whereas vv. 1a and 5 are in the first, and so have considered the former unit to be a secondary interpolation. Cf. K. Elliger, *Das Buch der zwölf Kleinen Propheten*[4] (ATD 25; Göttingen: Vandenhoeck and Ruprecht, 1959), 205-7.

Epilogue

IT would appear that the questions raised in the Introduction have been answered. Among these was one which considered the possibility that early Jewish Biblical exegesis has antecedents in the Hebrew Bible. From the cumulative evidence of scribal, legal, aggadic and mantological exegesis, this possibility certainly seems to be a reasonable inference. Indeed, the broad range of stylistic patterns from many periods, together with their corresponding technical terms, strategies, or procedures, suggest that exegetical techniques and traditions developed locally and cumulatively in ancient Israel from monarchic times and continued into the Graeco-Roman period, where they served as a major reservoir for the Jewish schools and techniques of exegesis then developing.

But, however presumptive, this inference must remain historically inconclusive. For while many trajectories of exegetical form, terminology, and rationality can be discerned within the Hebrew Bible, and between it and the documents of early Jewish exegesis, such trajectories are in themselves no proof of definite historical relationships, and this for several reasons. First, despite the fact that a range of exegetical formulae are repeatedly found in the diverse legal corpora of the Hebrew Bible, or that a variety of deictic terms are commonly used in lexical or geographical explanations, it must be admitted that these similar usages may simply reflect parallel technical solutions to parallel textual problems.[1] Indeed this caveat is particularly pertinent given the gaps in our knowledge of the relations between ancient Israelite scholars, the frequently common nature of the terminology employed (like deictic הוא and זה,, or such particles as כן, או, כל, or רק), and the absence of explicit statements of historical affiliation. Moreover, if such considerations pose problems of judgement and analysis for exegetical data within the Hebrew Bible, they apply even more to apparent relations between it and early Jewish sources. To be sure, our study has disclosed many remarkable similarities in the logics of legal inference, deduction, or analogy found in the Hebrew Bible, the Dead Sea Scrolls, and classical rabbinic exegesis. But these materials only *suggest* trajectories of exegetical tradition over the course of centuries; the evidence is insufficient to *prove* historical dependence. Once again,

---

[1] S. Lowy, *Principles of Samaritan Exegesis* (Leiden: E. J. Brill, 1977), 211, has astutely stressed this important point – a caveat for all comparative exegesis.

these correlations may be the result of parallel solutions.[2] Conditions sufficient to offset such qualifications would include examples of uniquely worded or rarely used exegetical formulae, of complexly styled rhetorical-exegetical sequences, or of repeated patterns that also conform to established international conventions.

A second major reason to be cautious in the assertion of chains of exegetical tradition in ancient Israel involves considerations relative to the composite nature of biblical sources, and their extended and complex transmission. Thus, in due course, exegetical terms from one area or time could have been taken over by other exegetes at different times and with different ideologies. Scribes who recopied northern cultic, legal, or prophetic literature in Judaean scribal or other scholarly centres after the fall of Samaria may, for example, have taken over older terms or added to them, thereby producing conflated scribal traditions. Similarly, when the Covenant Code was reused and annotated by deuteronomic legists and draftsmen centuries later in Judaea, not only could older terms have been absorbed but, reciprocally, later usage may have been retrojected into the earlier sources at one or another point. Where such is the case, and the terms cannot be proved to belong to one stylistic family or another, our critical methods are virtually helpless in unravelling the preserved historical skeins. By the same line of reasoning, it is important to recognize that Ezra and his levitical colleagues, who appear after the exile with a whole exegetical tradition ready to hand, may have absorbed exegetical solutions from many

---

[2] Let us simply mention the argument *a minore ad maius*. Admittedly, there are many continuously used formulae from biblical to rabbinic times; cf. Jacobs, 'The *Qal Va-ḥomer* Argument'. On the one hand, it is certainly possible that rabbinic scholars were influenced by these rhetorical patterns from their close study of Scripture. Indeed, the second-century CE Palestinian teacher R. Ishmael actually mentioned ten instances of *qal wāḥōmer* in the Torah (see *Gen. Rab.* 92: 7; edd. J. Theodor and Ch. Albeck, *Midrash Bereshit Rabba*[2] (Jerusalem: Wahrmann Books, 1965), 145f. and notes). Moreover, it should be emphasized that a review of 'the argument from the minor to the major' in its diverse biblical genres and contexts (e.g. Gen. 44: 8; Exod. 6:12; 1 Sam. 23: 3; Jer. 12: 5; Prov. 11: 31; Esther 9:12), as well as the different terms and styles employed (e.g. 2 Sam. 12:18; 1 Kgs. 8: 27; Jer. 12: 5; Ezek. 33: 24; Amos 3: 3-8; Prov. 15:11; Job 15: 15-16) indicates a broad and even professional background for such 'inner-biblical' influence. Nevertheless, the possibility of independent genesis of parallel terms and forms must be considered, and R. Ishmael's remark may be a secondary legitimation of a later hermeneutical procedure. Regarding independent genesis, A. Kunst, 'An Overlooked Type of Inference', *BSOAS* 10 (1942), 976-91, has adduced a remarkable parallel to the rabbinic *qal wāḥōmer* argument in the Indian type of inference called *kimpunar*. He adds that in the absence of concrete proof of 'mutual influence' he prefers to consider the similarity of Jewish and Indian inferential procedures as 'an expression of a common human tendency to eulogize great things by comparing them with smaller, or to raise the value of small things by juxtaposing them with greater' (p. 991).

other tradents during the Babylonian exile, such that it is now impossible to isolate these from those which may have circulated in Ezra's particular exegetical milieu. Accordingly, it would be presumptive to go beyond the historical evidence and assume continuous or uncomplicated chains of exegetical traditions from before the exile, just as it would be presumptive, given the evidence, to assume continuous or uncomplicated chains of tradition from the post-exilic through to the early classical period half a millennium later.

Nevertheless, that an identifiable trajectory of exegetical elements can indeed be traced from the received corpus of the Hebrew Bible to the recorded texts of early Jewish exegesis is, in my judgement, a valid minimal conclusion. Put differently, there is no incontrovertible reason to doubt that the evidence of inner-biblical exegesis as reconstructed and analysed in this book reflects one part of a culturally integrated, 1,000-year-long spectrum of exegetical proliferation and development. During this long period, to be sure, new exegetical influences were felt as other exegetical traditions were lost or obscured. But, all told, it is hard to conceive that the exegetical practices of the early Jewish bookmen (סופרים), and the ancestral traditions referred to by the Pharisees and others, were not in some ways heir to exegetical techniques and traditions with roots in the ancient Israelite past. And if this is so, then our minimal conclusions have maximal implications as well; for they suggest in an unexpected way the validity of early Pharisaic claims that their exegetical tradition derives from biblical antiquity. But this claim aside, it is enough for us to have established the antecedents of this tradition in the diverse and sophisticated body of textual exegesis found in ancient Israel.

A second focal question raised in the Introduction also appears to have been answered. It dealt with the consideration of how an exegetical tradition endowed with religious dignity comes to be formed. Certainly, where this pertains to the phenomenon of the early classical and sectarian expressions of Judaism, many social and historical factors must be brought into view. Suffice it here, therefore, simply to refer to three fairly contemporary attempts to authorize and dignify a variety of exegetical achievements. Strikingly, a notion of 'two Torahs' plays a role in each. In early Pharisaic Judaism the ideology was put forward that, at Sinai, two Torahs were given to Moses, one written and public, the other oral and exegetical, continuously preserved and progressively disclosed by a chain of teachers and exegetes.[3] Corresponding to this remarkable notion is that found in the scrolls of the Qumran community, where the idea was expressed that the exoteric

---

[3] Cf. *Abot de-Rabbi Nathan*, ed. S. Schechter (corrected edn.; New York: Feldheim, 1967), Version A, ch. 15, p. 61; and *Sifre* Deut., 351.

Torah of Moses, and with it the exegetical traditions of other Jewish groups, were supplemented by a special esoteric exegetical dispensation revealed to the Teacher of Righteousness and preserved among the elected faithful until the final days when it would become the public inheritance of all Israel as well.[4] The two main differences between the early Pharisaic and the Qumranite solutions are that in the former the exegetical innovations of authoritative teachers are a continuous national inheritance stemming from a private revelation to Moses at the very origins of Israel's covenant life, and are meant for the public domain, while in the latter, by contrast, the proper praxis of exegesis is based on a new revelation of relatively recent vintage, and preserved by a closed, restrictive group that regarded itself as the true Israel and its sectarian commune as the only authentic Jewish covenant. The third interesting variation on this theme may be found in the Book of Jubilees, whose precise social roots are not altogether clear. In any event, the idea of 'two Torahs' appears in Jubilees again as complementary exoteric and esoteric components, the latter being the source of special theological and exegetical insights revealed by an angel to Moses at Sinai.[5] In addition, it is significant to observe that a number of exegetical traditions are authorized in the Book of Jubilees by their observance by the pious patriarchs themselves.[6] A comparable anachronistic retrojection of later exegetic praxes, and therewith their religious dignification through the prestige and authority of the patriarchs, are also found in early rabbinic sources.[7]

These preceding dynamics provide a valuable perspective on the phenomenon of inner-biblical exegesis, which equally sought to authorize its innovations and provide them with appropriate dignity. Indeed, the evidence of this concern as preserved in the Hebrew Bible shows a notable range of strategies of exegetical legitimation—themselves conditioned by diverse ideological groups and different literary considerations—and valuable insight into the real and projected sources of exegetical authority in ancient Israel. The relevant material may be conveniently assembled under three broad typological headings.

1. *Innovative and continuous revelations.* In this category may be put those instances whereby the formulae of revelation, and its authority, introduce exegetical supplements. In the area of legal exegesis, for

---

[4] Cf. 1Q S. 5: 7–12, 8: 8–16, 9: 17; and CDC 3: 12–16.

[5] See the observations of I. Gruenwald, *Apocalyptic and Merkavah Mysticism* (Leiden: E. J. Brill, 1980), 23f.

[6] *Jub.* 15: 1, 22: 1, 16: 20–31, 18: 18–19, 21: 1, 6–20, 32: 4, 27, 44: 4.

[7] For a detailed review, see J. Schultz, 'Two Views of the Patriarchs: Noachides and Pre-Sinai Israelites', in *Texts and Responses. Studies Presented to Nahum M. Glatzer*, edd. M. Fishbane and P. Flohr (Leiden: E. J. Brill, 1975), 43–59.

example, there are cases of revealed clarifications and extensions to the old Sinaitic corpus in Num. 9: 9-14, 27: 6-11, and 36: 5-12 – with the latter, as was shown, being a secondary revision under divine auspices of the exegetical supplement also given under divine auspices in Num. 27: 6-11. Remarkably, fundamentally polar positions on the role of blemished foreigners in the cult are each supported by divine revelations in the post-exilic period (Isa. 56: 1-8 and Ezek. 44: 9-31); and, one may add, the divinely authorized role of the Zadokites in Ezek. 44: 9-31 co-opts earlier priestly divine warrants in Num. 18 which appoint the Aaronid priestly family to the very same tasks and perquisites. Isa. 66: 18-21 further broadens the priestly and levitical base to all foreigners who will come up to Jerusalem, and this too in the name of YHWH.

In the main, aggadic exegeses may either make explicit use of revelatory dicta (as in Jer. 3: 1, Ezek. 33: 23-9, and Hag. 2: 11-14) or implicit use of earlier sources (as in Jer. 2: 3 and 2: 26, 34), without these revisions or transformations in any way colliding with the plain sense of the laws which serve as their basis. Of course, in some cases the aggadic hyperboles introduced under the auspices of divine revelation betray their power and danger (as in Isa. 58: 1-12 and Jer. 7: 21-2); but nowhere is revealed aggadic exegesis used to subvert the divinely revealed covenantal laws. One does, however, observe antithetical constructions in aggadic exegesis in the reuse of national and eschatological traditions. Thus, for example, the typology in Jer. 16: 14f.~23: 7f. contrasts the exodus with the anticipated restoration of the northern exile; the oracles in Isa. 19: 19-25 denationalize the old native Israelite tradition of the exodus from Egypt; and the topos of war in Joel 4: 10 reverses the scenario of universal peace in Isa. 2: 4~ Mic. 4: 3.

Innovative and continuous exegetical revelations also occur in the area of mantology. Thus, an old oracle is recorded and a revision of it is added in Isa. 16: 11-12 + 13-14; and Ezek. 38 announces by the 'oracle of YHWH' (v. 1) that oracles delivered in previous days 'by my servants the prophets of Israel' (v. 17) will soon some to pass. Similarly, the correct application of the old seventy-year oracle of Jeremiah, and many others, is revealed to Daniel in Dan. 9-12 by a divine messenger. Indeed, by that time, the Jeremian oracle was nearly half a millennium old, and its true application already indicated by other divine revelations (Jer. 29: 10; Zech. 1: 12-14, 7: 4-7; cf. 8: 14-19) and human speculations (2 Chron. 36: 21). Accordingly, the very preservation of these and other divinely revealed revisions of earlier oracles (like Isa. 16: 11-14) is as remarkable culturally as it is perplexing theologically. The tradents of biblical prophecy pass over these conflicts of divine interpretation without so much as a harmonizing comment. At the least, all this suggests that these tradents were not aware of all the texts now at our canonical disposal. Beyond this, the possibility that certain scholarly or traditionary circles may also have used the voice of divine authority or the power of ancient oracles in order to promote certain actions or attitudes must certainly remain an open question for the modern interpreter. The remarkable coincidence between the preserved interpretation of Jeremiah's oracle and major historical events is enough to elicit suspicion. A similarly justified 'hermeneutics of suspicion', to adapt Ricouer's well-known phrase, must also be applied to the above-noted cases of divinely revealed legal exegesis. The examples collected below further confirm the need for such a critical attitude.

2. *Pseudonymous or pseudepigraphic exegesis*. By this category it is possible to bring into collective review a variety of instances of exegesis which are authorized by a prestigious personality or narrative voice from the past, whether divine, human, or anonymous, and whether the procedure be one of interpolating comments into a pre-existent context, of adding prestigious introits to received laws or traditions, or of introducing exegetical revisions in the course of a total rewriting of received materials under the auspices of a prestigious name (like Moses in the Book of Deuteronomy) or omniscient narrator (like the Chronicler). As regards scribal exegesis, the label of pseudonymous exegesis refers, of course, to such lexical explications as occur at Lev. 19:19 and Deut. 22: 9, 11, to the variety of semantic and geographical comments incorporated into historiographical narratives, or to corrections and changes which replace religiously offensive or lexically obscure formulations. In all these cases the voice of scholarly tradents and exegetes has merged with the speaking or narrative authority of the surrounding context, so that it is now the latter which appears as the source of the words or phrases in question.

Comparable instances of pseudonymous legal exegesis may be found in Exod. 23:11b, 34: 21, and Lev. 25: 2-7, which purport to be the instructions of YHWH through his servant Moses; and in Deut. 20: 10-18, 22:1-3, and 22: 6, which purport to be the faithful repetition by Moses of divine instructions earlier received. For, despite their claim to be teachings of divine or Mosaic origin, these texts are actually exegetical in nature and legitimate their innovative comments via the prestige of YHWH and Moses. As a result, the old-new rules retain their divine aspect and the exegetical comments are theologically normalized. This human arrogation of divine or Mosaic authority is nothing short of remarkable, particularly when one bears in mind the transcendent nature of the lawgiver. Indeed, this factor makes the following two variations all the more notable for their slight betrayal of human exegetical processes. The first of these is Jer. 17: 21-3. In it, YHWH, speaking through the prophet Jeremiah, admonishes the people and in due course presumes to cite his own words from Deut. 5:12f. However, our analysis has shown that this is in fact not the case and the inner-biblical cross-reference is rather a tendentious utilization of divine authority to support the innovation of a series of substantive additions to the ancient laws of Sabbath observance. Of further interest is the case of Num. 15: 22-31. For, while adding various explications and exhortations to an older priestly law, as well as normalizing the latter's formulation and adducing a concluding supplement (cf. vv. 26, 30f.), the text does not purport to be an exegetical revision and presents its instructions as a self-contained divine teaching. Nevertheless, it is manifest that this exegetical legal discourse has betrayed its pseudepigraphical disguise; for it will be observed that in v. 22b the discourse abruptly and unexpectedly refers to commandments 'which YHWH spoke *to Moses*'—a remarkable discrepancy in light of the superscription(vv. 17-18a); for Moses is the implied speaker. Accordingly, it appears that an earlier human discourse has been subsequently given divine authority as part of other commandments which Moses is told to recite.

A comparable aggadic example occurs in the version of the Decalogue found in Deut. 5. For, while the text is introduced as a divine citation (v. 4 + לאמר at v. 5bβ), and the first-person divine voice is used from the outset (cf. v. 6), cross-references to the Decalogue found in Exod. 20 are introduced (vv. 12b and 16) and YHWH is abruptly referred to by another speaker at several points (vv. 11-12, 14-16). It may therefore be concluded that a didactic teaching voice is a major component of this document; and that its theological and ethical instructions have been subsequently authorized by a divine imprimatur.[8]. Among other instances of pseudepigraphic transformations in the domain of aggadic exegesis we may simply recall at this point the sermonic revision of Gen. 1 in Deut. 4:16-19 and the exegetical subversion of the divine attribute formulary of Exod. 34:6f. in Deut. 7:9f. Both cases are presented as the words of Moses, though both actually reflect the work of several strata of deuteronomic writers who utilized the authoritative voice of Moses for their own purposes.

Finally, a number of characteristic types of pseudonymity and pseudepigraphy in mantological exegesis may be noted. First, there are a number of cases of exegetical comments which supplement or transform the pre-existing context. Thus, among the many additions to the Book of Jeremiah one may observe a number of instances where a given historical description is supplemented by alternative phraseology in a parallel passage, with the result that new theological dimensions

---

[8] Similar considerations and conclusions apply to Exod. 20 as well. There too the opening divine voice (v. 2; cf. v. 5) abruptly shifts in vv. 7, 10-12.

are advanced which reflect later deuteronomic strata and their post-
exilic concerns.[9] One may add that these pseudepigraphic supplements
are comparable to other pseudonymous interpolations in the Book of
Jeremiah dealing with repentance (e.g. Jer. 18: 7-10),[10] and to the
pseudepigraphic prophetic sermons found in the Book of Chronicles.
In the latter, the historical descriptions preserved in the Book of Kings
are supplemented or replaced with orations which forewarn the people
and dramatize the consequences of repentance.[11] Quite certainly, these
new pieces reflect other theological concerns addressed to the post-
exilic community.

Another dominant mode of pseudepigraphic and pseudonymous
mantological exegesis involves the redactional collation of small collections of oracles of diverse authorship and their reassignment to a
prestigious prophetic personality of the past, or the composition of new
oracles in the light of those of a prestigious forebear and in imitation of
his concerns and style. These two features are by no means mutually
exclusive, and together characterize the Book of Isaiah as a whole. In
this work, not only have many components like the mini-apocalypse in
Isa. 24-7, or the apparently late oracles in Isa. 19: 19-25 and 35: 1-10,
been ascribed to the prestigious eighth-century prophet Isaiah ben Amoz
of Jerusalem, but also it is clear that the oracles collected in Isa. 40-55
and 56-66 frequently bear the linguistic and ideological imprint of this
prophet. The very fact, moreover, that Isa. 56-66 has also been shown
to adopt the language and hopes of Isa. 40-55 suggests that all this
material was gathered and stylized by the prophetic disciples of Isaiah

[9] For an analysis of the reworking of Jer. 37: 3-10 in 21: 1-7, 38: 1, 3-6 in
21: 8-10; and 21: 11b-12a in 22: 1-5, see Rofé, 'Studies in the Composition of the
Book of Jeremiah', *Tarbiz*, 44 (1974-5), 5-13 [Heb.].

[10] And cf. Jer. 26: 3-5, with similarities in 18: 7-10 and also 11: 7-8, 25: 4-7.
The parallel to Jer. 26: 3-5 in 7: 3, 5 has also been considered secondary. Most
moderns have recognized the contradictions between the conditional and unconditional prophecies in Jer. 7: 3-15. Representative is the position of J. Skinner,
Prophecy and Religion (Cambridge: Cambridge University Press, 1963; 1st edn.
1922), 170, who separated 7: 3-7 (conditional) from 7: 8-15 (unconditional) and
considered the former to be 'a supplementary composition by a Deuteronomic
commentator, such as we frequently find in the book'. By way of revision, I
would consider v. 4 part of the original unconditional prophecy: it links up with
v. 8 linguistically (cf. the verb *bāṭaḥ*, the noun *šeqer*), thematically (the Temple is
focal), and in mood (it is unconditional). The threat against the Temple concludes
in v. 14 (again with the verb *bāṭaḥ*). By contrast, vv. 3, 5-7 share similar terms
and themes; v. 15 introduces the analogy of the northern *exile* (vs. the analogy of
Shilo's destruction), and thus seems to be secondary as well. For a recent full
analysis of Jer. 7, see Rofé, loc. cit. 16-22.

[11] On this whole theme see S. Japhet, *The Ideology of the Book of Chronicles
and its Place in Biblical Thought* (Jerusalem: The Bialik Institute, 1977), 154-66
[Heb.]; cf. also my remarks, in *Enc. Miq.* viii. 949-62, s.v. *'tešûbāh'*.

and the tradents of the Isaianic corpus. It was undoubtedly felt that the voice of Isaiah of Jerusalem would give authority and force to the pronouncements and exhortations for later generations who would read them. For it can hardly be imagined that the post-exilic prophets who originally spoke the oracles in Isa. 40-66 suggested that they were merely repeating words that came down to them by prophetic tradition. Rather, the pseudepigraphy of the Book of Isaiah is a literary event for later generations who inherited the once spoken oracles.

3. *Attributive, pseudo-attributive, and non-attributive exegesis.* What is intended by this rubric are those instances of inner-biblical exegesis where a new interpretation is attributed to an authoritative historical source (textual or personal), although an examination of the latter indicates that some of these attributions are both spurious and tendentious in nature. The clearest examples occur in the areas of legal and aggadic exegesis. In the former, it may suffice here to recall such cases as 2 Chron. 30: 16 (cf. 35: 11), which refers to the fact that the priests sprinkled blood upon the altar after having received it from the Levites as being performed 'according to the Torah or Moses'—even though such praxes are unknown to our received Pentateuchal sources; or the case of 2 Chron. 35: 13, which refers to an act of 'boiling the paschal-offering in fire according to the law'—even though no such rule is found in the Pentateuch, and the Chronicler's formulation is arguably a harmonizing conflation. For a similarly remarkable instance of a legal-exegetical formulation presented as 'a statute of the Torah which YHWH commanded Moses', though the instructions are unknown in this form elsewhere, see Num. 31: 21-4. And finally, there is Deut. 12, a series of four distinct prescriptive units regulating the centralization of worship: (1) vv. 1-7; (2) vv. 8-12; (3) vv. 13-19; (4) vv. 20-8. In the third of these units there is found, after the introit, the phrase 'and there you will perform *all that I command you*' (v. 14b). This phrase clearly refers back to the major premisses of the first and second units, which emphasize the one legitimate shrine; for there follows the qualifying particle רק 'however', which elaborates the hitherto unstated *implications* of this injunction for private slaughter, together with an additional exegetical allusion to Lev. 17.[12] After this, unit (3) is repeated in vv. 20-8, with clarifying expansions and further allusions to prior priestly sources.[13] What is, however, particularly striking about

---

[12] Cf. the condensed analogy of *kaṣṣĕbî wĕkā'ayyāl* in Deut. 12: 15 and the protasis in Lev. 17: 13a.

[13] Deut. 12: 22 is an expansion of v. 15; and v. 23 is an allusion to Lev. 17: 14 (cf. v. 11). It is furthermore interesting that the priestly allusion in Deut. 12: 23 interrupts the sequence of vv. 22, 24, which is derived from vv. 15-16, where no expansion occurs. And, finally, the exegetical-paraenetic quality of unit four is

this fourth unit is the fact that a new exegetical distinction is drawn and the Israelites are told that *when* the borders will be expanded as promised *then* the rules of centralization and the permissibility of private slaughter will be in effect '*as I commanded you*' (v. 21aβ).[14] However, no such prior commandment was given. Presumably, this remarkable pseudo-ascription was introduced to legitimate the ensuing harmonization between unit (3), which enjoined private slaughter in the sacred land, and Lev. 17, which did not.[15] The new exegetical solution was thus that private slaughter was prohibited within the original boundaries but permitted in the promised new territories. But just how the biblical authors hoped to pass off this textual attribution and those noted earlier—assuming of course that their readers were aware of other formulations and that their ascriptions were not a pious fraud—is another matter. Perhaps such formulations as 'according to the Torah of Moses' or 'according to the law' in the preceding instances were simply meant to convey the elliptical assertion that these ritual acts were performed according to the divine law *as exegetically interpreted*.

No comparably generous interpretation can be invoked, however, in order to salvage the attributions found in Ps. 89 and 1 Chron. 28. In both of these cases of aggadic exegesis the attributions are clearly false. In the first example the psalmist purports to quote to YHWH, in the course of his prayer-petition, the very language of the divine dynastic promise to David in 2 Sam. 7 (cf. Ps. 89: 20). But, as we have seen earlier, there are numerous tendentious changes in the received psalm text which go well beyond any implicit sense of the language of 2 Sam. 7. A similar pseudo-attribution is to be found in the second example. There we find David's own citation of the divine oracle ('the Elohim said to me') to the effect that the reason he was not permitted to build the Temple was because he was a 'man of war' and 'shed blood' (1 Chron. 28: 3). However, these 'divine' words are not part of the original document and clearly serve here to explain this event on moral grounds. In 2 Sam. 7 there is only the barest of hints which may have triggered the Chronicler's aggadic exegesis (cf. v. 11). For this reason one must presume that his interpretation was derived from a more

marked by the motivation clause in v. 25b, which is introduced by a lemma cited from the previous verse. Cf. *lōʾ tōʾkĕlennû* in v. 25a and its antecedent in v. 24a, where it precedes a ritual regulation (as in v. 16).

[14] The introduction of the qualification in v. 21 by the phrase *kî yirhaq mimmĕkā hammāqôm* ('if the place is too far for you') was obviously of a technical nature, as can be seen from the fact that the exact terminology is used in Deut. 14: 24 to introduce the qualification of vv. 22f. (cf. Deut. 19: 8f.). It may be added that Prov. 7: 19–20 appears as a sapiential reuse of the regulation in Deut. 14: 24–5 (also compare Prov. 29: 24 with Lev. 5: 1).

[15] This harmonization was earlier noticed by A. Rofé, *Maboʾ le-Seper Debarim* (Jerusalem: Aqadamon Press, 1975), 20f.

comprehensive evaluation of the deeds of David.

It now remains to consider several instances where acts of exegesis are performed by prestigious individuals or recorded in narratives or liturgies *without* any attribution of the innovation to the rules and histories in the Torah. In some of these cases the exegetical innovations are simply embedded within a narrative, as in Josh. 5: 11f., which preserved a species of legal exegesis on the meaning of the phrase 'the morrow of the שבת', or in 2 Chron. 35:14, which includes 'fats' in connection with the proper paschal-offering. In other circumstances, the exegetical formulations of Ezra and his circle (Ezra 9), Nehemiah and his coterie (Neh. 10), and Hezekiah and his council (2 Chron. 30) all rest on their social-religious authority. Admittedly, Ezra has recourse to commandments known from the Pentateuch—though attributed to the 'prophets'—in the course of his discourse (Ezra 9: 10-12); and Nehemiah's new covenant ceremony and oath are done under the auspices of the ancient Torah (cf. Neh. 10: 1, 29f.). But in no respect are the exegeses in question (the formulation against foreign wives in Ezra 9: 1-2 and the conflation of sabbatical regulations in Neh. 10: 32b) directly attributed to the authoritative sources of the tradition. The case in Neh. 10: 32b is particularly notable in that other exegeses in that document do adduce the Torah for support (cf. v. 37). The exegesis of Num. 9: 10-14 in 2 Chron. 30: 2-3 does not even hint at the 'Scriptural' origins of its adjudication.

When the totality of inner-biblical exegesis is reviewed from the foregoing perspective, it appears that three sources of exegetical authority are affirmed or utilized in the Hebrew Bible: divine revelations; authoritative texts; and teachers of revelations or tradents of traditions. To the first sphere belong the diverse instances of new revelation given to Moses or the prophets in the areas of law, aggadic theologizing, and prophecy, as well as all those cases where exegetical comments are interpolated into an earlier original revelation or appended to it. To the second sphere belong those other instances of inner-biblical exegesis which are presented as normative regulations of the Torah of Moses, as frequently in the Book of Chronicles, or which are presented as the report or repetition of earlier divine words, as in the Book of Deuteronomy. And finally, in the last sphere belong the various instances of exegetical ratiocination performed by persons who were invested with the religious-political power to propound, interpret, and enforce the ancient divine teachings, as well as the anonymous exegetical work of liturgical and historical writers or tradents.

Naturally, these distinct sources of authority can and do come into conflict. As we have observed, such conflict may occur within any one of the three spheres, as is the case with the diverse divinely supported claims concerning the rights of Temple service (for example, the revelation to Moses regarding the Aaronides in Num. 18; to Ezekiel regarding the Zadokites in Ezek. 44; and to Isaiah regarding the foreigners in Isa. 56:1-8, 66:18-21). On other occasions the conflicts cross different spheres of authority (for example, the Chronicler's introduction of legal innovations often contradicts revealed Pentateuchal regulations). Significantly, these various contentions are each presented authoritatively, and while the context in each case indicates the attitudes of the tradents, only rarely did the final redactors attempt to establish unqualified hierarchical authority. For this reason the closing coda to the Pentateuch, in Deut. 34:10-12, is of great value. In these verses, the unrivalled superiority of the divine revelations to Moses is emphasized. Presumably such an exaltation was necessary in the face of rival revelations promoting alternative civil and priestly rules, such as we have observed. Similarly, Deut. 18:18 puts forward the ideal that all future prophets must be of the Mosaic type, which was particularly characterized by the fulfilment of oracles (v. 22). Quite possibly, this formulation was not solely intended as a handy principle for recognizing prophetic authenticity, but also served as a means of dissuading indiscriminate use of the authority of prophecy by apostates, revolutionaries, or self-serving advisers.[16] Moreover, even if this criterion could not in the event guide one to determine the authenticity of rival prognoses, it could at least be assumed that a prophet 'like' Moses would not put the covenantal instructions to Moses in jeopardy. This, however, was not a foregone conclusion. For, as we suggested in the conclusion to Part Four, eschatological enthusiasm may have elicited this very danger, and with it the corresponding admonition found in Mal. 3:22, which now serves as the coda to the entire prophetic corpus.

In concluding these reflections on the sources of exegetical authority in the Hebrew Bible, it is necessary to grapple with a difficulty noted or implied in other contexts, and ask: How did the exegetical guardians of ancient religious and historical traditions conceive of their task and understand their frequently intrusive activities? I pose this question sharply because the issue is vital and cannot be evaded, despite the meagre hope for a final or verifiable solution. What follows, then, is a digest of a spectrum of possibilities culled from earlier discussions.

1. At one end of the spectrum of possible attitudes towards the exegetical enterprise in ancient Israel is the *tendentious manipulation of authoritative names, rubrics, and teachings.* To this category belongs

---

[16] Cf. Deut. 13:2-19, 1 Kgs. 22:2-28, and Jer. 27-8, as well as the fact that the criteria of 'true' prophecy in Deut. 18:15-22 are preceded by a list of Canaanite divinatory practices and admonitions against these 'abominations' (vv. 9-14).

the strategic reuse of a *traditum* for specific religious or political ends. Here, the *traditio* functions as a means to promote certain ideas, or to validate them after the fact, and the exegetical tradents are fully alert to their manipulations of texts and textual symbols of social-religious power. For example, in our review of the occurrences of the seventy-year oracle of Jeremiah the remarkable temporal concordance between its various reinterpretations and such events as the return from exile, the rebuilding of the Temple, and the Maccabean revolt were noted; and it was wondered whether these successive interpretations were designed in anticipation of certain desired activities which could be reinforced by this oracle, or whether the reinterpretations are in fact legitimations after the fact. Obviously, no single conclusion for all the data is necessary; but the very nature of the biblical evidence gives solid grounds for a hermeneutics of suspicion on the part of the modern historian. Similarly, the back-reading of Solomon into the old divine oracle regarding the legitimate builder of the Temple, like the post-exilic promotion of Zadokite priestly supremacy by means of a new divine revelation, must be viewed from the perspective of tendentious manipulations of authoritative teachings. Such manipulations parallel the way the Babylonian priests of Marduk took political advantage of the ascendancy and invasion of Cyrus to promote their erstwhile legitimacy and power.[17]

The preceding examples shade off towards the tendentious ascription of many legal, aggadic prophetic innovations to YHWH, Moses, and David, as well as the political manipulation of Pentateuchal texts, such as occurs in Ezra 9. Nevertheless, due caution must prevail, for while the historian must always be mindful of the religious enhancement and benefits of power that accrue from the manipulation of sources, there is no explicit textual indication that the exegetes were fraudulent, impious, or disingenuous. Conceivably, the attribution to Moses of legal material which was believed to be *in the spirit* of Mosaic regulations, or the attribution to Isaiah of prophetic content which was seen to be *in the spirit* of this prophet's ancient oracles, were not considered to be a wrong use of authoritative names. By the same token, it is possible that the legal exegesis recorded in Ezra 9 was believed to be a legitimate extrapolation of the content and intent of old Mosaic regulations in new times. Accordingly, when all is said and done and the reasonable possibilities suggested, the profound temporal and cognitive distance separating every modern reconstruction of the mental reality of inner-biblical exegesis must be respected.

---

[17] See H. Tadmor, 'The Historical Background of the Edict of Cyrus', in *'Oz le-David* (Publications of the Israel Society for Biblical Research, 15; Jerusalem: Qiryat Sefer, 1964), 450–73 [Heb.].

2. Further along the spectrum of possible attitudes towards exegesis, one must reckon with the *non-manipulative amendment and elaboration of traditions*. This category is continuous with the preceding one; for by it one must directly confront the possibility that some ancient Israelites believed their exegeses to provide the true intent or meaning of ambiguous, problematic, or incomplete textual formulations. Thus, when Ezra's levitical colleagues determine the praxis of building booths on the feast of Tabernacles (Neh. 8:15), or when other teachers try to deduce the praxis of observing the jubilee-year regulations which ostensibly prescribe severe constraints for three consecutive years (Lev. 25: 20-2), one must assume devoted attempts to establish viable procedures *from out of* the received legal tradition. It probably would not be out of the question to see here, as also in the assorted interpolations and addenda found in the legal corpora, something comparable to the modern attempt to interpret rules in the light of the presumed 'intention' of the lawgiver. The paradox that legal exegetes in ancient Israel attempted to explicate the intention of divinely given regulations does not diminish the possibility that these human interpretations were attempts to state what the text was believed to imply *by means of responsible and authoritative exegesis*.

Another side of this non-manipulative exegetical reuse of traditions would involve those cases where a pious exegete sought to correct misimpressions generated by earlier laws, or where he simply read them in the light of normative piety and practice. It would thus probably be wrong to consider the Chronicler's corrective rereading of 2 Sam. 5: 21 as an outright manipulation of a legally problematic passage, rather than as a reading of it in the light of normative Pentateuchal practice, comparable to the treatment of earlier priestly formulations in Num. 15: 24. As the diverse texts of the legal tradition were increasingly scrutinized and read synoptically, there naturally developed attempts to render them cognitively and practically meaningful.

If these various reflections on non-manipulative exegesis in ancient Israel are accurate, one may suggest that hereby *traditio* attempts to serve the apparent intention of the text and the cumulative achievements of the tradition. From this perspective, moreover, exegetical creativity is a responsible service for the sake of the *tradition* and its *Vergegenwärtigung* in each generation. For, just as scribes ensure that the received textual artefact is reproduced responsibly for the sake of the memories and praxes of the historical community, so are the exegetes of the texts responsible for ensuring its meaningful, unambiguous, and normative contemporaneity. The individual talent of the exegete is thus subservient to the content and goals of traditional materials, and his expertise is the cumulative result of school traditions and a commitment to the values and content of the material in question.

If one were to formulate this posture in such a way as to contrast this exegetical attitude with that reflected in our first category, then it might be said that in non-manipulative exegesis the exegete is himself manipulated by the burden and direction of the traditions in his trust. Exegesis is thus a form of wisdom that mediates divine teachings *after* they have appeared.

3. While the evidence is meagre, it may nevertheless be possible to edge a bit further along our spectrum of attitudes and identify an exegetical standpoint that became dominant in the post-biblical era, *revealed exegesis*. Here it must suffice to isolate a small but valuable group of instances which indicate or suggest this reality – quite distinct from those legal, aggadic, or mantological interpretations which are introduced as a revealed word of YHWH. The reason for this restrictive sample is methodological in nature; for, as we have seen, the use of ascription of divine introits is sufficiently problematical and conventional in the Hebrew Bible to make the historian prefer reflective or even unselfconscious textual comments on the subject. Adopting this stance here, we may begin by recalling the repeated references found in connection with the dream interpretations of Joseph and Daniel which assert that the meaning of these symbolic communications is given by the God of Israel.[18] In addition, we may also recall the role of angelic mediators who reveal the interpretation of ancient oracles to Daniel.[19] The mantic and divinely guided exegesis featured in these texts thus complemented the role of Ezra as a mantic hermeneut of the Torah of YHWH, a point remarked upon in the conclusion to Part Two. It may now be added that this presentation of Ezra as one who 'enquires of the Torah of YHWH' (Ezra 7:10) is actually preceded by an indication that this scribe and priest of the law was also the recipient of 'the hand of YHWH' (v. 6) – a circumlocution used in late texts to indicate prophetic inspiration.[20] Ezra thus uniquely combined the roles of scribe and inspired legal exegete.

A final notable witness to this phenomenon of inspired legal exegesis in ancient Israel occurs at Ps. 119:18, where the psalmist prays: גל עיני ואביטה נפלאות מתורתך 'unveil my eyes that I may behold wonderful things *from out of* your Torah.' As it was this very psalmist who repeatedly requested instruction in the *received* Torah,[21] and even reused the ancient priestly benediction of divine grace as a prayer for instruction in the *existing* divine statutes (v. 135),[22] so is it reasonable to interpret

18 Gen. 41: 25, 32–3; Dan. 2: 28, 4: 5–6, 5: 11–12, 14.
19 Dan. 9: 21–2, 10: 1 (with the verb *niglâ*), 11, 21, 11: 2, 12: 4–13.
20 Cf. Ezek. 1: 3, 3: 14, 22, 8: 1, 33: 22, 37: 1, 40: 1.
21 Ps. 119: 12, 27, 33, 64, 66, 68, 73, 108, 124.
22 See above, p. 334 n. 50.

the petition for illumined vision in Ps. 119:18 as a plea for divinely inspired interpretation.[23] In all this the psalmist of Ps. 119 takes his stand at the intersection of two important streams of biblical tradition, and perhaps even establishes an exegetical accommodation between them. On the one hand an ancient and oft-repeated tradition of biblical wisdom referred to the core of natural and speculative knowledge as mysterious, as both hidden and 'wondrous' (cf. פליאה, Ps. 139:6; נפלאו, Prov. 30:18; נפלאות, Job 42:3). On the other, the deuteronomic tradition believed its Torah to be an immediately accessible wisdom (Deut. 4:6), neither distant nor 'wondrous' (נפלאת, Deut. 30:11).[24] Between these two poles is the attitude of the psalmist in Ps. 119:18, where the idea is conveyed that the Torah has wonders which are accessible *through exegesis*.

At this point one is bound to wonder whether the appropriation of the imagery of prophetic illumination in Ps. 119:18, corresponding to the use of the imagery of prophetic inspiration in Ezra 7:6, is merely an intensification of an attitude which derives from earlier times and which suggests that many ancient Israelite exegetes may have believed their textual interpolations or ascriptions to be the product of continuous divine revelations to the students of Torah; or whether Ps. 119:18 reflects an entirely new atmosphere, discontinuous with that reflected in Deut. 30:8 but continuous with the reality found in Dan. 9-10, where new divine revelations are also based upon inscribed words, and where the sage who engaged in prayer and ascetic practices receives divine illumination in the prophetic mode (Dan. 9:21, 10:12-19; cf. 8:16-19).[25] Be that as it may, it is nevertheless clear that the request for revelatory guidance in Ps. 119:18 is not a request for illumination into transcendent cosmic mysteries or the mysteries of the final days. The latter is what Daniel received from the angels Gabriel and Michael,

---

[23] Cf. the observations of M. Gertner in P. Kahle, *The Cairo Geniza*[2] (New York: F. Praeger, 1960), 100.

[24] Interestingly, when in this connection the deuteronomist derides the need to ascend to heaven for divine instruction (Deut. 30:12) he utilizes a topos found in the above-mentioned wisdom contexts (cf. Ps. 139:8; Prov. 30:4); and when he formulates this as a rhetorical question he is apparently further making use of the forms of wisdom instruction (cf. Prov. 30:4, and the whole range of divine questions in Job 38:4-39:30; 40:8-41:26). In this overall connection, a notable variation of the topos appears in Amos 9:2-3. By contrast with Deut. 30:11-12, which juxtaposes the near Torah with the distant heaven or sea, and with Ps. 139:6-9, which juxtaposes exalted divine wonders with the immediacy of the divine spirit, such that one cannot escape God in heaven, sheol, or the ends of the sea, the prophet Amos announces that on the day of the Lord no one could flee safely to heaven, sheol, or even the ends of the sea. He concludes his question-answer format with a doxology to the wondrous powers of the Creator (vv. 5-6). Cf. also the questions in 4 Ezra 4:5-8 and *1 Enoch* 93:11-14.

[25] See above, p. 508 n. 4.

and what a late glossator to the Book of Deuteronomy explicitly proscribed (Deut. 29: 28).[26] But such are not the concerns of the pious
sage in Ps. 119:18. What he wants are the 'wonders' of exegesis.[27]
Indeed, this point can be made quite clear by a further tracing of the
trajectory just drawn regarding 'wonders' and the Torah in the post-
exilic Book of Ben Sira. For in this remarkable collection the sage who
is referred to as both דורש התורה, an 'expositor of the Torah' (3:15),
and as one who 'pours out teaching as prophecy' (24: 33), is also
strongly admonished to be humble: 'For many are the mercies of God,
and he reveals (יגלה) his secret to the humble. Search not for what is
too wondrous for you (פלאות ממך אל תדרוש) and investigate not that
which is hidden from you. Meditate upon what is permitted to you, and
deal not with secret things' (3: 20-2).[28] As is clear from the original
context, and from early rabbinic citations and discussions of this
passage,[29] the inspired sage is advised to be an interpreter of the revealed

[26] I thus tend to interpret this well-known crux in the light of its preceding
context, which forecasts exile. S. R. Driver, *Deuteronomy* (ICC; Edinburgh:
T and T. Clark, 1895), 328, also understood the 'secret things' of Deut. 29: 28 as
relating to the future. It appears to me that this verse is an attempt to counter
intense calculations relating to the end of exile by shifting the focus to obedience
to the 'revealed things', the commandments of the Torah, which may have been
abandoned in despair or in the enthusiasm of expected restoration. If this is so,
Deut. 29: 28 plays the same admonitory function at the end of the Pentateuch as
does Mal. 3: 22-4 at the end of the Prophets (see above, p. 524 and n. 33). By
contrast, the Writings conclude with the fulfilment of a prophecy of exile and
ruin and announce the conditions for the onset of national restoration (2 Chron.
36: 20-3).

[27] The point was understood by the Targum, which produced a bilingual pun
on Heb. *niplā'ôt* (Aram. *pĕrîšān* 'wonders' plays on Heb. *pērûš* 'exposition').
Cf. Rashi ad loc.

[28] On the text-form of this unit, see H. P. Rüger, *Text und Textform im
hebräischen Sirach* (BZAW 112; Berlin: W. de Gruyter, 1970), 30f. Similar
terminology is also found in 39: 1-3. Here the wise scribe is more fully characterized as one who 'meditates' (*mitbônēn*) on Torah, who 'searches out (*yidrôš*)
the wisdom of all the ancients' and 'the secrets (*nistārôt*) of parables', and who
studies the ancient prophecies. In 3: 20-2, *hitbônēn* is used regarding the exhortation to 'meditate' on permitted wisdom, and *tidrôš* and *nistārôt* are used regarding the 'secret things' which one is not permitted to 'search out'.

[29] *b. Hag.* 13a; *yer. Hag.* ii. 7, 3; and *Gen. Rab.* 8: 2. On the texts, see *Midrash
Bereshit Rabba*, edd. of Theodor and Albeck, pp. 57f. and notes. The stimulus
for the talmudic passages is *M. Hag.* ii. 1, whose formulation is comparable to
gnostic speculations on origins. In this regard, see the remarkable explanation of
Tos. Hag. ii. 6 in terms of gnostic concerns provided by S. Lieberman, *Tosefta
Ki-Fshutah*, v, *Mo'ed* (New York: Jewish Theological Seminary, 1962), 1292-4.
Lieberman there cites from the *Evangelium Veritatis* 23:13-14, which provides a
striking parallel with *M. Hag.* ii. 1. In the light of such comparative evidence, the
polemical character of *M. 'Abot* iii. 1 seems obvious. E. E. Urbach, *The Sages:
their Concepts and Beliefs* (Jerusalem: Magnes Press, 1969), 165 n. 19 [Heb.], is
not, however, inclined to regard these questions about origins as necessary proof

Torah, and not one who speculates upon the פלאות of cosmological
origins and natural principles, as had become fashionable in the Hellenistic period.[30] Beyond this, it has been plausibly inferred from the
manner that Ben Sira refers to the heavenly ascension of Enoch (44:16)
and the throne vision of Ezekiel (49: 8), 'that Ben Sira was familiar
with some early kinds of apocalyptic or mystical traditions, and that
the above quoted verses from chapter iii were therefore an exhortation
directed to the general public to refrain from all kinds of speculations
which involved apocalyptic experiences'.[31]

It may be fitting to conclude these reflections with one final cluster
of texts which bear on the trajectory here under review. In the first two
of these, taken from hymnic expressions in the Qumran literature, a
remarkable conjunction of the topos of wondrous divine knowledge
and a reinterpretation of Ps. 119:18 are achieved.[32] In the one case a
doxological peroration near the end of the Manual of Discipline proclaims that God has caused the celebrant to be enlightened from the
divine source of knowledge, 'ובנפלאותיו הביטה עיני and my eye has
beheld the wonders of it' (1Q *S*. xi. 3; cf. lines 5–6); and in the second
the speaker acknowledges the gift of divine wisdom and rhetorically
asks 'איכ]ה אביט בלוא גליתה עיני [ho]w could I behold (these things)
if you did not unveil my eye?!' (1Q *H*. viii. 19; cf. x. 4–7). In addition
to this divinely guided understanding of cosmological and natural
mysteries, the members of the sect are graced, through their teachers
and their own diligent study, with the 'secret' meanings of the Torah
and the 'mysteries' of the ancient prophecies which are 'wondrous'
(להפלה, 1Q pHab. vii. 8). By contrast with this special divine benefaction to the elected few, Ps. 119:18 projects the shared Israelite ideals
and hopes of Torah piety as they were cultivated among sages of the
divine teachings. Indeed, the voice of the psalmist is not that of one
who delights in abstract speculations, but of one who is consumed by
the intellectual passion properly to comprehend and perform the
totality of the revealed Torah, that none of its commandments remain a
'secret' to him (v. 19). To that end the Psalmist requests new divine
revelations as the exegetical guidance that may be expected by all those
who are 'pure in practice, who follow the Torah of YHWH' (v. 1).

This brings me to the end. The whole phenomenon of inner-biblical
exegesis requires the latter-day historian to appreciate the fact that the

---

of gnostic speculations. But his assertion does not come to grips with the notable
similarities of literary style, question format, and speculative concern.
    [30] Cf. M. Z. Segal, *Seper Ben Sira ha-Shalem*[3] (Jerusalem: The Bialik Insti-
tute, 1972), 17 (Heb. pagination section).
    [31] Gruenwald, *Apocalyptic and Merkavah Mysticism*, 18.
    [32] Also noted by Gertner, loc cit. (above, n. 23).

texts and traditions, the received *traditum* of ancient Israel, were not simply copied, studied, transmitted, or recited. They were also, and by these means, subject to redaction, elucidation, reformulation, and outright transformation. Accordingly, our received traditions are complex blends of *traditum* and *traditio* in dynamic interaction, dynamic interpenetration, and dynamic interdependence. They are, in sum, the exegetical voices of many teachers and tradents, from different circles and times, responding to real and theoretical considerations as perceived and as anticipated. To retrace this substantial achievement is, then, correspondingly to encounter traces of ancient Israelite exegetical thinking in its attentive relations to textual contexts and historical memories, in its complex correlations of traditions and situations, and in its diverse interrelations between exegesis as action and exegesis as literary form. But, for all its sophistication and variety, we should not imagine that we have in this thinking and its achievements anything like the totality of ancient Israelite exegesis. Rather, what we have is sporadic, unsystematic, and contextual in nature, a corpus which hardly rivals the more complete, more stylized, and more theoretical achievements of classical Judaism. Nevertheless, it is just as surely false to imagine that the immediate ancient Israelite forerunners of Nahum of Gimzo and Hillel were the penurious orphans of Scripture. They were, on the contrary, heirs to a rich cultural patrimony, both substantial and scholarly, which had long since practised the arts of exegetical *traditio*. I believe the present book to be the first comprehensive proof and analysis of this fact.

Addenda

p. 57: Also note the replacement of *mĕʾazzĕrê zîqôt* in Isa. 50: 11 with *mĕbaʿărê zîgôt* in CDC v. 13; and of *nēṣer maṭṭāʿay* 'shoot of my planting' in Isa. 60. 11 with *šōreš maṭṭāʿat* in CDC i. 7.

p. 59: n. 38: On the sexual metaphor see also *Gen. Rab.* lxxxv. 4 and the (anti-Karaite) comment of Ibn Ezra at Exod. 34: 21.

p. 65: In other cases, inner-biblical repetitions may serve to indicate the presence of an explanatory gloss. For example, the manifestly redundant phrase *tiqvat ḥûṭ haššānî* ('strand of scarlet cord'; NEB) in Josh. 2: 18 is repeated more simply as *tiqvat haššānî* ('strand of scarlet') in v. 21. Presumably the more common term *ḥûṭ* ('cord') was used in the first verse to explain the noun *tiqvāh* (cf. Heb. *qav*; Akk. *qû*).

p. 72: The presumed piety of the patriarchs may have led some tradents to transform older citations into new theological assertions. Thus, it is arguable that in Gen. 14: 21 Abram swore by the god El Elyon, using exactly the same phrase as did Melchizedek (v. 19), but that later scribes revised this problematic formulation and prefixed the Tetragram to the divine name in the oath. In this way, 'El Elyon, creator of heaven and earth' is no independent (Canaanite) deity but merely the epithet of YHWH. This demotion of ancient gods to epithets (a shift not presumed in Exod. 6: 3) witnesses to a momentous conceptual breakthrough in ancient Israelite religious history. For a comparable phenomenon at Gen. 21: 33 see N. Sarna, 'The Authority and Interpretation of Scripture in Jewish Tradition', in C. Thoma and M. Wyschogrod (edd.), *Understanding Scripture* (New York: Paulist Press, 1987), 12.

p. 72: For a comparable technique, see below, *addendum* to p. 385.

p. 86: n. 20: For an example in the Qumran scrolls cf. the resumption of CDC vii. 13 at viii. 1. On different grounds, J. Murphy-O'Connor has contended that the prophetic material in vii. 13b–viii.1a is a later interpolation. See his 'The Original Text of CD 7: 9–8: 2 = 19: 5–14', *HTR* 64 (1971), 379–86.

p. 170: Various rules on sacrifice in the priestly and deuteronomic corpus exhibit generalizing comments preceded by the word *kol*. Cf. Lev. 21: 17–20, 22: 20–5; Deut. 15 21, 17: 1. Repetitions and syntactic awkwardness suggest that some of these formulations may be secondary expansions.

p. 245: In reference to the replacement of mantic qualities with wisdom, parallel transformation can be found in the references to
Joshua's investiture. In the first occurrence (Num. 27: 18)
Moses is told to 'single out Joshua son of Nun, an inspired man'
(lit. 'who has *ruaḥ*-spirit in him'); while in the recapitulation of
this account upon Moses' death (Deut. 34: 9) Joshua is described
as 'filled with the spirit of wisdom' (*ruaḥ ḥokmāh*).

p. 348: Cf. also the creative reuse of the attribute formulary in Prov.
16: 5–7, where it is part of a piece of rhetoric on divine providence (16: 1–9). It is striking that v. 7 notes that God may reward
a positive act by turning an enemy into an ally (*yašlīm*). This
terminology recalls the formulation of the attributes in Deut.
7: 10 (see p. 343). Thus, the wisdom tradition in Prov. 16: 1–9
has apparently incorporated older covenantal terms into its
matrix.

p. 350: n. 93: Cf. the idioms in *Gen. Rab.* xlviii. 7, lxviii, 10, lxxviii, 5;
and the idiom used by Ibn Ezra at Gen. 9: 18. Nachmanides
knows the typological idea to be ancient, for at Gen. 12: 6 he
introduces an expression of it with the remark 'As (the sages)
said' (cf. *b. Soṭ.* 34).

p. 384: The basis for this aggadic transformation can be more precisely
indicated. Whereas in Deut. 31: 5 Moses declaims that the
people should 'act (*va'ăśîtem*) in accordance with the entire
order (*kěkāl hammiṣvāh*) which I have commanded (*ṣivvîtî*) you'.
God now tells Joshua (Josh. 1: 7) that the people must be careful 'to observe (*la'ăśôt*) the entire Torah (*kěkāl hattôrāh*) which
Moses, my servant, has commanded (*ṣivvěkā*) you'. Thus, the
language of a military order has been reformulated as an injunction to obey the Torah.

p. 385: A comparison of 1 Kgs. 21: 1–9 and 2 Chron. 33: 1–9 is pertinent with respect to late sensitivity to 'the Torah of Moses'. In the
first context the historian refers to the sins of Manasseh and 'cites'
God's word to David *and* Solomon (!) that the nation will not be
exiled if they 'perform all that I have commanded them' (v. 8).
Presumably this apparent disjunction between the commandments of God and Moses was theologically problematic; for in his
rendition of Manasseh's sins the Chronicler not only cites the old
divine word but states that the people will not be exiled if they
'perform all that I have commanded them: all the Torah, and laws
and ordinances by means of Moses' (v. 8). By deleting the particle
vav, the Torah instructions (*and* laws etc.) are put in apposition
to God's command. There is no longer any potential theological
problem. For related revisions see above, pp. 72–4, 465–7.

p. 387: Something similar to this late ideological transformation occurs
in Ps. 106: 12. In that text (vv. 10–11) the destruction and elimination of the Egyptian foe through an act of divine salvation is indicated by language drawn from Exod. 14: 28–30. To this review of
magnalia Dei the psalmist adds: 'Then they (viz. the people)

believed in 'his words (*vaya'ămînû bidbārâv*), (and) sand his praise' (v. 12). The first half of this verse thus reworks Exod. 14: 31, which states that the nation 'believed in YHWH (*vayă'ă-mînû baYHWH*) and Moses, his servant' upon seeing the awesome power of the Lord at the sea. In part, this reformulation may be due to the implication that Israelite faith was only a consequence of the divine wonders. A more immediate factor may have been a desire to exalt the people's belief in divine prophecy. The act of national faithfulness in divine promises is thus used to counterpose the failure of the people in the desert to believe in the promises of the conquest ('they did not believe in his word', *lō' he'ĕmînû lidbārô*; v. 24b). The formulation that the people 'believed in . . . Moses' may have also provoked concern, with the result that the reference to Moses was eliminated. It may be added that the psalmist had a tradition in which a 'song' followed the wonders at the sea. He specifies that the song of praise was evoked by the preceding event. By this the psalmist indicates his understanding of the particle *'āz*: '*Then* Moses and the Israelites sang' (Exod. 15: 1).

p. 389: A related reworking occurs in CDC Ms. B xx. 16 f., which cites Hos. 3: 4 with the following adaptation: 'no king, nor prince, *nor judge, n[o]r any reprover for righteousness*'. The older references to sacrifice are replaced by 'judge', and the references to mantic instruments are replaced by an allusion to the community's own Teacher of Righteousness. The Targum also read 'teacher' at this place.

p. 446: n. 3: For the function of the textual comment in Ezek. 43: 3, see my remarks in 'Through the Looking Glass: Reflections on Ezek. 43: 3, Num. 12: 8 and 1 Cor. 13: 8', *Hebrew Annual Review*, 10 (1986), 63–75 (esp. p. 68).

p. 478: n. 52: This line of interpretation is already recorded in *Mekhilta de-Rabbi Ishmael, Pisḥa, Bo* 12. A fairly long collection of passages are noted, which suggests an established rabbinic tradition for investigating prophecies and the notation of their fulfilment elsewhere in Scripture.

p. 482: in reference to the Chronicler's reuse of Jeremiah's prophecy: Another linguistic point of contact between the several texts is the stem *šāmam*, found in Jer. 25: 21, 2 Chron. 36: 31, and Lev. 26: 32. Significantly, the Leviticus and Jeremian passages refer to the desolation of the land, whereas the text in Chronicles concerns the desolation of Jerusalem (vv. 17–19). Since 2 Chron. 36: 21 refers to the 'fulfilment' of the word of God to Jeremiah, that prophecy has clearly been reinterpreted and adjusted to a new object (the city).

p. 542: in reference to inspired exegesis in Psalm 119: The shift from a purely mantic perspective to a revelation of divine truth through the Law is clear from a thematic and verbal comparison of Ps.

119: 18 with Num. 22: 31. This line of development (with a resignification of the old mantic terms *baqqēš* and *dāraš*) is also evident from a comparison of Zeph. 1: 6 and 1QS v. 11. In the latter case, moreover, exegetical inquiry into the Law results in the knowledge of esoterica (*lāda'at nistārôt*)—these being, in *this* context, the hidden legal meanings (and applications) of the Torah, and reserved for the sectarian alone during the present Age. For these and related matters, see my forthcoming remarks, 'From Scribalism to Rabbinism: Perspectives on the Emergence of Classical Judaism', in J. Gammie and L. Perdue, (edd.), *The Sage in Israel and the Ancient Near East* (Winona, Ind.: Eisenbrauns, 1989).

Select Bibliography

ACKROYD, P. R., 'Some Interpretative Glosses in the Book of Haggai', *JJS* 7 (1956), 163–7.

—, 'The Chronicler as Exegete', *JSOT* 2 (1977), 2–32.

ALBECK, Ch., *Das Buch der Jubiläen und die Halacha* (Sibenundvierzigster Bericht der Hochschule für die Wissenschaft des Judentums in Berlin; Berlin, 1930).

—, *Mabo' la-Mishnah* (Jerusalem: The Bialik Institute, 1959).

ALT, A., 'Die Weisheit Salomos', *TLZ* 76 (1951), 139–44.

ALTHEIM, F., 'Das Alte Iran', in *Propyläen – Weltgeschichte* (Frankfurt-on-Main and Berlin: Verlag Ullstein, 1962), ii, 171.

ALTHEIM, F. & STEIHL, A., *Geschichte Mittelasiens im Altertum* (Berlin: de Gruyter and Co., 1970), 95–103.

ANDERSON, J. F., *The Bond of Being, An Essay on Analogy and Existence* (St Louis, MO.: B. Herder Book Co., 1949).

ANDERSON, R., 'Was Isaiah a Scribe?', *JBL* 79 (1960), 57–8.

ARTZI, R., 'The Glosses in the el-Amarna Documents', *Bar Ilan Annual*, 1 (1963), 24–57 [Heb.].

BACH, R., 'Gottesrecht und weltliches Recht in der Verkündigung des Propheten Amos', in *Festschrift für Gunther Dehn*, ed. W. Schneelmelcher (Neukirchen: Kreis Moers, 1957), 23–34.

BACHER, W., 'The Origin of the Word Haggada (Agada)', *JQR* OS 4 (1892), 406–29.

BAER, Y. F., 'The Historical Foundations of the Halakha', *Zion*, 17 (1952), 1–55 [Heb.].

BARNES, W. E., 'The Midrashic Element in Chronicles', *Expositor*, 44 5th Series, 4 (1896), 426–39.

—, 'Ancient Corrections in the Text of the Old Testament', *JTS* 1 (1900), 387–414.

—, 'Prophecy and the Sabbath', *JTS* 29 (1927–8), 386–90.

BARR. J., *Judaism—Its Continuity with the Bible*, The Seventh Montefiore Memorial Lecture, The University of Southampton (1968).

BARTHÉLEMY, D., 'Les tiqquné sopherim et la critique textuelle de l'A.T.', *SVT* 9 (1963), 283–304.

BEATTIE, D. R. G., 'A Midrashic Gloss in Ruth 2:7', *ZAW* 89 (1977), 122–4.

BEGRICH, J., 'Sōfēr und Mazkir', *ZAW* 58 (1940–1), 1–29.

—, 'Berit', *ZAW* 60 (1944), 1–11.

BEN SHAHAR, Z., 'From the Morrow of the Sabbath', *Beth Miqra* 77.2 (1979), 227–8 [Heb.].

BERGEN, R., *The Prophets and the Law* (Monographs of the Hebrew Union College, 4; Cincinnati, New York, Los Angeles, and Jerusalem: Hebrew Union College–Jewish Institute of Religion, 1974).

BICKERMAN, E., *Studies in Jewish and Christian History*, 2 vols. (Leiden: Brill, 1976).

BIDEZ, J., 'Les écoles chaldéenes sous Alexandre et les Seleucides', *Annuaire de l'Institut de Philologie et d'Histoire Orientales*, 3 (1935), 41–89 (volume offert à J. Capart, Université Libre de Bruxelles).

BIRAM, A., 'Corvée, *Tarbiz*, 23 (1952), 137–42 [Heb.].

BITZER, L. F., 'The Rhetorical Situation', in *Rhetoric: A Tradition in Transition*, ed. W. R. Fisher (Ann Arbor: University of Michigan, 1974), 247–60.

BLAU, J., 'Tradition and Innovation', in *Essays in Jewish Life and Thought Presented in Honor of Salo W. Baron*, edd. J. Blau *et al.* (New York: Columbia University Press, 1959).

BLAU, L., 'Zwei dunkle Stellen in Segen Moses (Dt. 33:2–3, 24–25), in *Jewish Studies in Memory of G. Kohut*, edd. S. Baron and A. Marx (New York: The Alexander Kohut Memorial Foundation, 1935), 91–108.

BLENKINSOPP, J., *Prophecy and Canon* (Notre Dame: University of Notre Dame Press, 1977).

—, 'Interpretation and the Tendency to Sectarianism: an Aspect of Second Temple History', in *Jewish and Christian Self-Definition*, ed. E. P. Sanders (Philadelphia: Fortress Press, 1981), 1–26.

BLOCH, R., 'Écriture et tradition dans le Judaïsme. Aperçus sur l'origine du Midrash', *CS* 8 (1954), 9–34.

—, 'Ézéchiel XVI: Exemple parfait du procédé midrashique dans la Bible', *CS* 9 (1955), 193–223.

—, 'Midrash', *DBS* v. 1263–81.

BÖHL, F. M. Th., *Die Sprache der Amarnabriefe* (Leipzig, 1909).

BOYER, G., 'De la science juridique et de sa méthode dans l'ancienne Mesopotamie', *Semitica*, 4 (1951–2), 5–11.

BREWER, J., 'Some Ancient Variants in Hosea with Scribe's or Corrector's Mark', *JBL* 30 (1911), 61–5.

BRIN, G., 'The Literary Composition of the Laws Dealing with the Sanctity of the First-born', *Tarbiz*, 46 (1977), 1–7 [Heb.].

BRUCE, F. F., 'Scripture and Tradition in the New Testament', in *Holy Book and Holy Tradition*, edd. F. Bruce and E. Rupp (Manchester: Manchester University Press, 1968), 68–93.

—, 'The Earliest Old Testament Interpretation', *OTS* 17 (1972), 37–52.

BRUNKEN, E., 'Interpretation of the Written Law', *Yale Law Journal*, 25 (1915), 129–40.

BUCHANAN, G., 'Midrashim pré-Tannaïtes, à propos de Prov., I–IX, *RB* 72 (1965), 227–39.

BÜCHLER, A., 'Family Purity and Family Impurity in Jerusalem before the Year 70 C.E.', *Studies in Jewish History* (Jews College Publications, *NS*, no. 1; London: Oxford University Press, 1956), 64–98 (the Adolf Büchler memorial volume).

CAQUOT, A., 'Ahiyya de Silo et Jeroboam Iᵉʳ, *Semitica*, 11 (1961), 17–27.

CARDASCIA, G., 'La codification en Assyrie', *RIDA*³ 4 (1957), 53–71.

CARROLL, R., 'Inner Tradition Shifts of Meaning in Isaiah 1–11', *The Expository Times*, 89, no. 10 (1978), 301–4.

—, 'Eschatological Delay in the Prophetic Tradition', *ZAW* 94 (1982), 47–8.

CASPARI, W., 'Über die Textpflege nach den hebräischen Handschriften des Sira', *ZAW* 50 (1932), 160–8; ibid. 51 (1933), 140–50.

CASSUTO, U., 'The Prophet Hosea and the Books of the Pentateuch', from *Abhandlungen zur Erinnerung an Hirsch Perez Chayes* [Heb.] (Vienna, 1933) 262–78; repr. *Biblical and Oriental Studies by U. Cassuto*, i, *Bible*, trans. I. Abrahams (Jerusalem: Magnes Press, 1973), 79–100.

CAZELLES, H., 'Une relecture du Psaume XXIX?', *A la rencontre de Dieu, Mémorial Albert Gelin* (Bibliothèque de la Faculté Catholique de Théologie de Lyon, 8; Le Puy: Éditions Xavier Mappus, 1961), 119–28.

CHILDS, B., *Isaiah and the Assyrian Crisis* (SBT 2. 3; London 1967).

—, 'Psalm Titles and Midrashic Exegesis, *JSS* 16.2 (1971), 137–50.

—, 'Midrash and the Old Testament', in *Understanding the Sacred Text. Essays in honor of Morton J. Enslin*, ed. J. Reumann (Valley Forge, Pa.: Judson Press, 1972), 45–59.

—, 'The Canonical Shape of the Prophetic Literature', *Interpretation*, 32 (1978), 46–55.

—, 'The Exegetical Significance of Canon for the Study of the Old Testament', *SVT* 29 (Leiden: E. J. Brill, 1978), 66–80.

CLEMENTS, R. E., 'Patterns in the Prophetic Canon', *Canon and Authority, Essays in Old Testament Religion and Theology*, edd. G. W. Coats and B. O. Long (Philadelphia: Fortress Press, 1977), 42–55.

COHEN, H. H., 'Legal Studies in the Book of Ezra', *Zer le-Geburot* [the Zalman Shazar Jubilee volume] (Jerusalem: Israel Bible Society, 1979), 371–401 [Heb.].

—, 'The Secularization of Divine Law', in *Jewish Law in Ancient and Modern Israel* (New York: Ktav, 1971), 1–49.

Collins, J. J., *The Apocalyptic Vision of the Book of Daniel* (Harvard Semitic Monographs, 16; Missoula, Mont.: Scholars Press, 1977).

DAUBE, D., 'Zur frühtalmudischen Rechtspraxis', *ZAW* 50 (1932), 148–59.

—, 'Some Forms of Old Testament Legislation', *Oxford Society of Historical Theology* (1944/5), 36–46.

—, *Studies in Biblical Law* (Oxford: The Clarendon Press, 1947).

—, 'Error and Accident in the Bible', *RIDA*² 2 (1949), 189–213.

—, 'Concerning Methods of Bible-Criticism', *Ar.Or.* 17 (1949), 89–99.

—, 'Rabbinic Methods of Interpretation in Hellenistic Rhetoric', *HUCA* 22 (1949), 239–64.

—, 'Alexandrian Methods of Interpretation and the Rabbis', in *Festschrift Hans Lewald* (Basel: Helbing and Lichtenhahn, 1953), 27–44.

—, 'Direct and Indirect Causation in Biblical Law', *VT* 11 (1961), 246–69.

—, 'Texts and Interpretation in Roman and Jewish Law', *Journ. of Jewish Sociology*, 3 (1961), 3–28.

—, 'The Influence of Interpretation on Writing', *Buffalo Law Review*, 20 (1970), 41–8.

DEISSLER, A., *Psalm 119 (118) und seine Theologie. Ein Beitrag zur Erforschung der anthologischen Stilgattung im Alten Testament* (Münchener Theologische Studien, 11; Munich: Karl Zink Verlag, 1955).

DELCOR, M., 'Les Sources du Deutéro-Zacharie et ses procédés d'emprunt', *RB* 59 (1952), 385–411.

DELITZSCH, F., *Lose- und Schreibfehler im Alten Testament* (Berlin and Leipzig: W. de Gruyter, 1920).

DODEWAARD, H. A. E., VAN, 'La Force évocatrice de la citation, mise en lumière en prenant pour base l'Évangile de S. Matthieu', *Bib*. 36 (1955), 482–91.

DÖRRIE, H., 'Zur Methodik antiker Exegese', *ZNW* 65 (1974), 121–38.

DRIVER, G. R., 'Glosses in the Hebrew Text of the Old Testament', in *L'Ancien Testament et l'Orient* (Orientalia et Biblica Lovaniensia, 1; Louvain, 1957), 123–61.

EERDMANS, B. D., 'Ezra and the Priestly Code', *The Expositor*[7], 10 (1910), 306–26.

EFRON, Joshua, 'Holy War and Hopes for Redemption in the Hasmonean Period', in *Holy War and Martyrology in Israelite and World History* (Jerusalem: Israel Historical Society, 1968), 7–34 [Heb.].

EISSFELDT, O., 'The Promises of Graces to David in Isaiah 55:1–5, in *Israel's Prophetic Heritage*, edd. B. Anderson and W. Harrelson (London: Fs. J. Muilenberg, 1962), 196–207.

ELIADE, M., *Patterns in Comparative Religion* (New York: Meridian, 1963).

ELMAN, Y., 'Authoritative Oral Tradition in Neo-Assyrian Scribal Circles', *JANESCU* 7 (1975), 19–32.

FESTINGER, L., RIECKEN, H., and SCHACHTER, S., *When Prophecy Fails* (Minneapolis: University of Minnesota Press, 1956).

FEUILLET, A., 'Les Sources du Livre de Jonas', *RB* 54 (1947), 161–86.

FICHTNER, Johannes, 'Jesaja unter den Weisen', *TLZ* 74.2 (1949), 75–9.

FIGULLA, H., 'Lawsuit Concerning a Sacrilegious Theft at Erech', *Iraq*, 13 (1951), 95–101.

FINKELSTEIN, J. J., 'Ammiṣaduqa's Edict and the Babylonian "Law Codes"', *JCS* 15 (1961).

—, *The Ox That Gored* (*TAPS* 71.2; Philadelphia: The American Philosophical Society, 1981).

FISHBANE, M., 'Varia Deuteronomica', *ZAW* 84 (1972), 349–52.

—–, 'Numbers 5: 11–31: A Study of Law and Scribal Practice in Israel and the Ancient Near East', *HUCA* 45 (1974), 25–45.

—, 'The "Sign" in the Hebrew Bible', *Shenaton. An Annual for Biblical and Ancient Near Eastern Studies*, 1 (1975), 213–34 [Heb.].

—, 'The Qumran Pesher and Traits of Ancient Hermeneutics', in *Proceedings of the Sixth World Congress of Jewish Studies*, 1 (Jerusalem, 1977), 97–114.

—, 'Torah and Tradition', in *Tradition and Theology in the Old Testament*, ed. D. Knight (Philadelphia: Fortress Press, 1977), 275–300.

—, *Text and Texture; Close Readings of Selected Biblical Texts* (New York: Schocken, 1979).

—, 'Revelation and Tradition: Aspects of Inner-Biblical Exegesis', *JBL* 99 (1980), 343–61.

—, 'On Colophons, Textual Criticism and Legal Analogies', *CBQ* 42 (1980), 438–49.

—, 'Form and Reformulation of the Biblical Priestly Blessing', *JAOS* 103 (1983), 115–21.

— and TALMON, S., 'The Structuring of Biblical Books, Studies in the Book of Ezekiel', *ASTI* 10 (1976), 129–53.

FOHRER, G., 'Die Glossen im Buche Ezechiel', *ZAW* 63 (1951), 33–53.

—, 'Tradition und Interpretation im Alten Testament', *ZAW* 73 (1961), 1–30.

—, 'The Origin, Composition and Tradition of Isaiah I-XXXIX', *ALUOS* 3 (1961–2), 3–38.

FOX, M. V., 'The Identification of Quotations in Biblical Literature', *ZAW* 93 (1981), 416–31.

FRAENKEL, J., 'Hermeneutic Problems in the Study of the Aggadic Narrative', *Tarbiz*, 47. 3–4 (1978), 139–72 [Heb.].

FRANKEL, Z., *Über den Einfluss der Palastinischen Exegese auf die Hermeneutik* (Leipzig, 1851).

FREEDY, K., 'The Glosses in Ezekiel I-XXIV', *VT* 20 (1970), 129–52.

FUCHS, Hugo, *Pesîq, ein Glossengleichen* (Breslau: H. Fleischmann, 1907).

FULLER, L., *Legal Fictions* (Stanford: Stanford University Press, 1967).

GALLING, K., 'Das Gemeindegesetz in Deuteronomium 23', in *Festschrift für Alfred Bertholet zum 80. Gerburtstag*, edd. W. Baumgartner *et al.* (Tübingen: J. C. B. Mohr, 1950), 176–91.

GEIGER, A., 'Ein alter Fehler in Nehemia 5, 11, *Jüdische Zeitschrift für Wissenschaft und Leben*, 8 (1870), 226–7.

—, *Urschrift und Übersetzungen der Bibel in ihrer Abhängigkeit von der innern Entwicklung des Judenthums*² (Frankfurt-on-Main: Verlag Madda, 1928).

GELIN, A., 'La Question des "relectures" bibliques à l'intérieur d'une tradition vivante', *Sacra Pagina*, 1 (1959), 303–15.

GERTNER, M., 'Psalm LXIX and Moshe Ben Aher', in P. Kahle, *The Cairo Geniza*·(Oxford: Blackwells, 1959), 98–105.

—, 'The Massorah and the Levites', *VT* 10 (1960), 140–72 (with excursus on Hos. 12, pp. 172–84).

—, 'Terms of Scriptural Interpretation: A Study in Hebrew Semantics', *BSOAS* 25. 1 (1962), 1–27.

—, 'Midrashim in the New Testament', *JSS* 7 (1962), 267–91.

GEVARYAHU, H. M., 'Colophons in the Books of Proverbs, Job and Ecclesiastes', in *Studies in the Bible and the Ancient Near East, presented to S. Loewenstamm*, i (Jerusalem: A. Rubinstein, 1978), 107–31 [Heb.].

GILAT, I. D., 'On the Antiquity of Several Sabbath Prohibitions', *Bar Ilan Annual*, 7 (1963), 106–19 [Heb.].

GINSBERG, H. L., 'The Oldest Interpretation of the Suffering Servant', *VT* 3 (1953), 400–4.

GOLDBERG, A., 'Shivuth Ve-di-oraitha Be-melekheth Shabbath', *Sinai*, 46 (1959), 181–9.

GOLDZIHER, I., *Die Richtungen der Islamischen Koranauslegung* (Leiden: E. J. Brill, 1952).

GOODING, D. W., 'On the Use of the LXX for Dating Midrashic Elements in the Targums', *JTS* NS 25 (1974), 1–11.

—, *Relics of Ancient Exegesis, A Study of the Miscellanies in 3 Reigns 2* (Cambridge: Cambridge University Press, 1976).

GORDIS, R., 'Midrash in the Prophets', *JBL* 49 (1930), 417–22.

—, 'Quotation as a Literary Usage in Biblical, Oriental, and Rabbinic Literature', *HUCA* 22 (1947), 157–219.

GRECH, P., 'Interprophetic Re-interpretation and Old Testament Eschatology', *Augustinianum*, 9 (1969), 235–65.

GRELOT, P., 'La Dernière Étape de la rédaction sacerdotale', *VT* 6 (1956), 174–89.

—, 'Soixante-dix semaines d'années', *Bib.* 50 (1969), 169–86.

GUILDING, A., 'Some Obscured Rubrics and Lectionary Allusions in the Psalter', *JTS* NS 3 (1952), 41–55.

GUNKEL, H., 'Der Micha-Schluss für Einführung un die literaturgeschichtliche Arbeit am Alten Testament', *Zeitschrift für Semitistik und verwandte Gebiete*, 2 (1924), 145–78.

HALLEWY, E. E., 'The Writers of the 'Aggada and the Greek Grammarians', *Tarbiz*, 29 (1959), 47–55 [Heb.].

—, 'Biblical Midrash and Homeric Exegesis', *Tarbiz*, 31 (1961), 157–69, 264–80 [Heb.].

HARAN, M., 'Studies in the Bible: The Idea of Centralization of the Cult in the Priestly Apprehension', *Beer-Sheva Annual*, i (University of Negev, Beer-Sheva; Jerusalem: Kiryat Sefer, 1973), 114–21 [Heb.].

—, 'The Law-Code of Ezekiel xl–xlviii and its relation to the Priestly School', *HUCA* 50 (1979), 45–71.

HARTMAN, L., 'Scriptural Exegesis in the Gospel of St. Matthew and the Problem of Communication', in *L'Evangile selon Matthieu, Rédaction et Théologie*, ed. M. Didier (Bibliotheca Ephemeridum Theologicanum Lovaniensium, 29; Gemploux: Éditions J. Duculot, SA, 1972), 131–52.

—, 'The Functions of Some So-Called Apocalyptic Timetables', *NTS* 22 (1975-6), 1-14.

HERTZBERG, H. W., 'Die Nachgeschichte alttestamentlicher Texte innerhalb des Alten Testaments', in *Werden und Wesen des Alten Testaments*, edd. P. Volz, F. Stummer, and J. Hempel (BZAW 66; Berlin: Topelman, 1936), 110-21.

HOBBS, T. R., 'Jeremiah 3, 1-5 and Deuteronomy 24, 1-4, *ZAW* 86 (1974), 23-9.

HOLM-NIELSEN, S., 'The Importance of Late Jewish Psalmody for the Understanding of Old Testament Psalmodic Tradition', *S.Theol.* 14 (1960), 1-53.

HUMMEL, H., 'The Old Testament Basis of Typological Interpretation', *Biblical Research*, 9 (1964), 38-50.

JACKSON, B. S., *Theft in Early Jewish Law* (Oxford: The Clarendon Press, 1972).

—, 'The Problem of Exodus XXI 22-25 (ius talionis)', *VT* 23 (1973), 273-304.

—, 'From *Dharma* to Law', *American Journal of Comparative Law*, 23 (1975), 490-512.

—, *Essays in Jewish and Comparative Legal History* (SJLA 10; Leiden: Brill, 1975).

—, 'Human Recognition and Divine Knowledge in Biblical and Tannaitic Law', *Shenaton ha-Mishpat ha-Ivri*, 16-17 (1979-80), 61-70 [Heb.].

JACOBS, L., 'The *Qal Va-homer* Argument in the Old Testament', *BSOAS* 35 (1972), 221-7.

JONES, D., 'The Tradition of the Oracles of Isaiah of Jerusalem', *ZAW* 67 (1955), 226-46.

KAMINKA, A., 'Neuste Literatur zu den Hagiographen', *MGWJ* 71 (1921), 289-91.

—, 'Expressions of Moses and the Psalms in Isaiah', *Lešonénu*, (1928-9), 40-3 [Heb.].

—, 'Bibelexegese', in *Encyclopedia Judaica*, v. 4. *Das Judentum in Geschichte und Gegenwart*, s.v. *Bibel*, VII (Berlin: Verlag Eschkol AG, 1929), 619-21.

KAPELRUD, A. S., 'The Date of the Priestly Code', *ASTI* 3 (1964), 58-64.

KAUFMANN, Y., *Toledot ha-Emunah ha-Yisra'elit*[4], 4 vols. (Jerusalem and Tel Aviv: The Bialik Institute and the Devir Co. Ltd., 1937-56).

KNIERIM, R., 'Old Testament Form Criticism Reconsidered', *Int.* 27 (1973), 435-68.

KNIGHT, D., 'The Understanding of "Sitz im Leben" in Form Criticism', in *SBL Seminar Papers*, ed. G. MacRae (Cambridge, MA: 1974), i. 105-25.

—, *Rediscovering the Traditions of Ancient Israel* (SBLDS 9; Missoula, Mont.: Scholars Press, 1975).

KOCH, K., 'Das Verhältnis von Exegese und Verkündigung an hand eines Chronik-Textes', *TLZ* 90 (1965), 659-70.

—, 'Ezra and the Origins of Judaism', *JSS* 19 (1974), 173–97.

KOENEN, L., 'The Prophecies of a Potter: A Prophecy of World Renewal Becomes an Apocalypse', in *Proceedings of the 12th International Congress of Papyrology*, ed. D. H. Samuel, (Toronto: A. M. Hakkert, 1970), 249–54.

KOENIG, J., 'L'activité herméneutique des scribes dans la transmission du texte de l'Ancien Testament, I, *RHR* 161 (1962), 141–74.

—, 'Sources, thaumaturges et scribes', *RHR* 164 (1963), 17–38, 165–80.

LANGLAMET, F., 'Israel et "l'habitant du pays", vocabulaire et formules d'Ex xxxiv 11–16, *RB* 76 (1969), 321–50, 481–507.

LAUTERBACH, J., 'The Sadducees and Pharisees', *Studies in Jewish Literature, Issued in Honor of Prof. K. Kohler* (Berlin: G. Reimer, 1913), 176–98.

—, 'Midrash and Mishna', in *Rabbinic Essays* (New York: Ktav reprint, 1973), 163–256.

LE DÉAUT, R., 'Apropos a Definition of Midrash', *Int.* 25 (1971), 259–83 [first appeared in *Bib.* 50 (1969), 395–413].

LEICHTY, E., 'The Colophon', in *Studies Presented to A. Leo Oppenheim* (The Oriental Institute; Chicago: University of Chicago Press, 1964), 147–54.

—, 'Two Late Commentaries', *AfO* 24 (1973), 78–86.

LEWY, I., *The Growth of the Pentateuch* (New York: Bookman Associates, 1955).

LIEBERMAN, S., *Hellenism in Jewish Palestine*[2] (New York: Jewish Theological Seminary, 1962).

LIEBREICH, L., 'The Songs of Ascents and the Priestly Blessing', *JBL* 74 (1955), 33–6.

LINDARS, B., 'Ezekiel and Individual Responsibility', *VT* 15 (1965), 452–67.

LIVER, J., 'The Literary History of Joshua IX', *JSS* 8 (1963), 227–43.

LOEWENSTAMM, S., 'The Death of the Upright and the World to Come', *JJS* 16 (1965), 183–6.

—, 'Exodus XXI 22–25', *VT* 27 (1977), 352–60.

LÖHR, M., 'Der Sprachgebrauch des Buches der Klagelieder', *ZAW* 14 (1894), 31–50.

LONG, B., 'The Stylistic Components of Jeremiah 3: 1–5,' *ZAW* 88 (1976), 386–90.

LOWY, S., 'Some Aspects of Normative and Sectarian Interpretation of Scriptures', *ALUOS* 6 (1969), 98–163.

—, *The Principles of Samaritan Bible Exegesis* (SPB 128; Leiden: E. J. Brill, 1977).

MASS, F., 'Von den Ursprüngen der rabbinischen Schriftsanlegung', *STK* 55 (1955), 129–61.

McCARTHY, C., *The Tiqqune Sopherim and Other Theological Corrections in the Massoretic Text of the Old Testament* (Orbis Biblicus et Orientalis, 36; Fribourg, Switzerland: Universitätsverlag, and Göttingen: Vandenhoeck and Ruprecht, 1981).

McKANE, W., *Prophets and Wise Men* (SBT 44; Naperville, Ill.: A. Allenson Inc., 1965).

—, 'Tradition as a Theological Concept', in *God, Secularization, and History; Essays in Memory of Ronald Gregor Smith*, ed. E. Long (Columbia, SC: University of South Carolina Press, 1974), 44–59.

—, 'Observations on the Tiḳḳûnê Sôpĕrîm', in *On Language, Culture, and Religion: In Honor of Eugene A. Nida*, edd. M. Black, W. Smalley (Approaches to Semiotics, ed. T. Sebeok, 56; The Hague and Paris: Mouton, 1974), 53–77.

MAINE, H. S., *Ancient Law* (New York: H. Holt and Co., 1877) [3rd American edn., based on 5th English edn.].

MANTEL, H., 'The Religious Reality in Judah and Neighboring Lands During the Exilic Period', in *Lectures During the Conferences on Historical Inquiry*, No. 16, 'The Place of the History of Israel in the Framework of World History' (Jerusalem: Israel Historical Society, 1973), 227–46 [Heb.].

—, 'The Dichotomy of Judaism During the Second Temple', *HUCA* 44 (1973), 55–87.

MARTIN, J., 'The Forensic Background to Jeremiah III 1, *VT* 19 (1969), 82–92.

MASON, R., 'The Relation of Zech 9–14 to Proto-Zechariah', *ZAW* 88 (1976), 227–39.

MELAMED, E. Z., 'Linguistic Forms Used Specifically for Divinity in the Bible', *Tarbiz*, 19 (1947–8), 1–18 [Heb.].

MERENDINO, P., *Das deuteronomische Gesetz* (BBB 31; Bonn: P. Hanstein, 1969).

METZGER, B., 'The Formulas Introducing Quotations of Scripture in the NT and the Mishna', *JBL* 70 (1951), 297–307.

MEYER, E., *Die Entstehung des Judentums* (Halle, 1896; repr. Hildesheim: Olms, 1965).

MILGROM, J., *Studies in Levitical Terminology*, i (University of California, Near Eastern Studies, 14; Berkeley: University of California Press, 1970).

—, 'Profane Slaughter and a Formulaic Key to the Composition of Deuteronomy', *HUCA* 47 (1976), 1–17.

—, *Cult and Conscience. The* Asham *and the Priestly Doctrine of Repentance* (SJLA18; Leiden: E. J. Brill, 1976).

MORAN, W., 'Gen. 49, 10 and Its Use in Ez. 21, 32', *Bib.* 39 (1958), 405–25.

MOWINCKEL, S., *Studien zu dem Buche Ezra-Nehemia* (Skrifter Utgitt av Det Norske Videnskaps-Akedemi i Oslo, Hist.-Filos. Klasse, Ny Serie, No. 7; Oslo: Universitetsforlaget, 1965).

MUFFS, Y., 'Reflections on Prophetic Prayer in the Bible', in *Erets-Yisrael*, 14 [H. L. Ginsberg *Festschrift*](Jerusalem, 1978), 48–54 [Heb.].

MÜLLER, D. H., 'Der Prophet Ezechiel entlehnt eine Stelle des Propheten Zephanja und glossiert sie', in *Komposition und Strophenbau* (Vienna: A. Hölder, 1907), 30–6.

NESTLE, E., 'Zu Daniel, 2. Der Gruelder Verwüstung', *ZAW* 4 (1884), 248.

NEUSNER, J., *The Idea of Purity in Ancient Judaism* (Leiden: E. J. Brill, 1973).

OLIVIER, J. P. J., 'Schools and Wisdom Literature', *JNWSL* 4 (1975), 49–60.

OLMSTEAD, A. T., 'Darius as Lawgiver', *AJSL* 51 (1935), 247–9.

ORR, A., 'The Seventy Years of Babylon', *VT* 6 (1956), 304–6.

OSSWALD, E., 'Zum Problem der *Vaticinia Ex Eventu*', *ZAW* 75 (1963), 27–44.

PAUL, S., 'Literary and Ideological Echoes of Jeremiah in Deuter-Isaiah', *Proceedings of the Vth World Congress of Jewish Studies*, i (Jerusalem, 1969), 102–20.

——, *Studies in the Book of the Covenant in the Light of Cuneiform and Biblical Law* (*SVT* 18; Leiden: E. J. Brill, 1970).

PEISER, F. E., 'Obadiah 6–7', *OLZ* 20. 9 (1917), 278.

PERELMAN, C., and OLBRECHTS-TYTECA, L., *The New Rhetoric* (Notre Dame and London: University of Notre Dame Press, 1969).

PERLES, F., *Analekten zur Textkritik des Alten Testaments* (Munich: T. Ackermann, 1895).

PETERS, J. P., 'Critical Notes', *JBL* 12 (1893), 47–8.

PETUCHOWSKI, J. J., '"Hoshi'ah Na" in Psalm CXVIII 25, A Prayer for Rain', *VT* 5 (1955), 266–71.

PHILLIPS, A., 'The Case of the Woodgatherer Reconsidered', *VT* 19 (1969), 125–8.

——, *Ancient Israel's Criminal Law; A New Approach to the Decalogue* (New York: Schocken, 1970).

POLOTSKY, H. J., 'Aramäisch *prš* und das "Huzvaresch"', *Le Muséon*, 45 (1932), 273–83.

POUND, R., 'Hierarchy of Sources and Forms in Different Systems of Law', *Tulane Law Review*, 7 (1933), 475–87.

PRAETORIUS, F., 'Pāsēq', *ZDMG* 53 (1899), 683–92.

PRINGSHEIM, F., 'Some causes of codification', *RIDA*[3] 4 (1957), 301–11.

RAWIDOWICZ, S., 'On Interpretation', in *Studies in Jewish Thought*, ed. N. Glatzer (Philadelphia: Jewish Pub. Soc. of America, 1974), 45–80.

RENAUD, B., *Structure et attaches littéraires de Michée IV–V* (Paris: Gabalda, 1964).

ROBERT, A., 'Les Attaches littéraires bibliques de Prov. I–IX, *RB* 43 (1934), 42–68, 172–204, 374–84; ibid. 44 (1935), 334–65, 502–25.

——, 'Le Genre littéraire du Cantique des Cantiques', *Vivre et Penser*[3] (1943–4), 192–213.

——, 'Les Genres littéraires', *DBS* v (1957), 405–21.

ROFÉ, A., 'The Strata of the Law about the centralization of worship in Deuteronomy and the history of the deuteronomic movement', *SVT* 22 (1972), 221–6.

——, 'Studies in the Composition of the Book of Jeremiah', *Tarbiz*, 44

(1974-5), 1-29 [Heb.].

SANDERS, J., *Torah and Canon* (Philadelphia: Fortress Press, 1972).

——, 'Adaptable for Life: The Nature and Function of Canon', in *Magnalia Dei, The Mighty Acts of God. Essays on the Bible and Archeology in Memory of G. Ernest Wright*, edd. F. Cross, W. Lemke, and P. Miller (Garden City, NY: Doubleday, 1976), 531-60.

——, 'Text and Canon: Concepts and Method', *JBL* 98 (1979), 5-29.

——, 'Canonical Context and Canonical Criticism', *Horizons in Biblical Theology*, 2 (1980), 173-97.

SANDMEL, S., 'The Haggadah Within Scripture', *JBL* 80 (1961), 105-22.

SARNA, N., 'Psalm 89: A Study in Inner Biblical Exegesis', in *Biblical and Other Studies*, ed. A. Altmann (Brandeis Texts and Studies; Cambridge, MA: Harvard University Press, 1963), 29-46.

SCHARBERT, J., 'Formgeschichte und Exegese von Ex. 34, 6 f und seiner Parallelen', *Bib.* 38 (1957), 130-50.

SCHECHTER, S., and TAYLOR, C. (edd.), *The Wisdom of Ben Sira, Portions of the Book Ecclesiasticus* (Cambridge: Cambridge University Press, 1899).

SCHOLEM, G., 'Revelation and Tradition as Religious Categories in Judaism', in *The Messianic Idea in Judaism* (New York: Schocken, 1971), 282-303.

SCHULTZ, A., 'Exegese im Alten Testament', *Zeitschrift für Semitistik und Verwandte Gebiete*, 3 (1924), 183-93.

SCHULTZ, F., *History of Roman Legal Science* (Oxford: Clarendon Press, 1946).

SEELIGMANN, I. L., *The Septuagint Version of Isaiah: A Discussion of its Problems* (Mededelingen en Verhandelingen, no. 9, van het Vooraziatisch-Egyptisch Genootschap, 'Ex Oriente Lux'; Leiden: E. J. Brill, 1948).

——, 'Voraussetzungen der Midrasch-Exegese', *SVT* 1 (1953), 150-81.

——, 'Investigations on the Transmission of the Massoretic Text of the Bible, I', *Tarbiz*, 25 (1955-6), 118-39 [Heb.].

——, 'From Historical Reality to Historiosophical Apprehension in the Bible', in *P'raqim, Yearbook of the Schocken Institute for Jewish Research*, ii, ed. E. S. Rosenthal (Jerusalem, 1969-74), 273-313 [Heb.].

——, 'Die Auffassung von der Prophetie in der deuteronomischen und chronistischen Geschichtsschreibung (mit einem Exkurs über das Buch Jeremia)', *SVT* 29 (Leiden: E. J. Brill, 1979), 254-84.

SEGAL, M. Z., *Parshanuth ha-Miqra*[2] (Jerusalem: Qiryat Sefer, 1972).

SHEPPARD, G., *Wisdom as a Hermeneutical Construct; A Study in the Sapientializing of the Old Testament* (BZAW 151; Berlin and New York: Water de Gruyter, 1980).

SIMONSEN, D., 'Ein Midrasch im IV. Buch Esra', *Festschrift zu I. Lewy's Siebzigstem Geburtstag*, edd. M. Brann and J. Elbogen (Breslau, 1911), 270-8.

SKEHAN, P., 'Exodus in the Samaritan Recension from Qumran', *JBL*

74 (1955), 182–7.

SLOMOVIC, E., 'Toward an Understanding of the Formation of Historical Titles in the Book of Psalms', *ZAW* 91 (1979), 350–80.

SMITH, M., *Palestinian Parties and Politics that Shaped the Old Testament* (New York: Columbia University Press, 1971).

—, 'Pseudepigraphy in the Israelite Tradition', *Pseudepigrapha*, i (Entretiens de la Foundation Hardt, 18, ed. K. von Fritz; Geneva: Fondation Hardt, 1972), 191–215.

SNAITH, J., 'Biblical Quotations in the Hebrew of Ecclesiasticus', *JTS* NS 18 (1967), 1–12.

SPIEGELBERG, W., 'Die sogenannte "Chronique Démotique" des Pap. 215 der Bibliothèque Nationale zu Paris', *Demotische Studien*, 7 (1914), 3–22.

STONE, J., *Legal System and Lawyer's Reasonings* (Stanford: Stanford University Press, 1964).

STREANE, A. W., *The Double Text of Jeremiah* (Cambridge: Deighton Bell and Co., 1896).

SWAIN, J. W., 'The Theory of the Four Monarchies; Opposition in History under the Roman Empire', *Classical Philology*, 35 (1940) 1–21.

SZLECHTER, E., 'Les Anciennes codifications en mesopotame', *RIDA*[3] 4 (1957), 73–92.

—, 'L'Interpretation des lois babylonniennes', *RIDA* 17 (1970), 107–15 (IIIe partie).

TEDESCHI, G., 'Insufficiency of the Legal Norm and Loyalty of the Interpreter', *Proceedings of the Israel Academy of Sciences and Humanities*, 1. 3 (1967), 1–22 (separate pagination).

TIGAY, J., 'An Empirical Basis for the Documentary Hypothesis', *JBL* 94 (1975), 329–42.

TOEG, A., 'Does Deuteronomy XXIV, 1–4 Incorporate a General Law of Divorce', *Dine Israel*, 2 (1970), pp. v–xxiv.

—, 'Exodus XXII, 4: The Text and the Law in the Light of the Ancient Sources', *Tarbiz*, 39. 3 (1970), 223–31 [Heb.]; ibid. 39. 4 (1970), 419 [Heb.].

—, 'Num. 15: 22–31; Midrash Halacha', *Tarbiz*, 43 (1973–4), 1–20 [Heb.].

TOV, E., 'Midrash-Type Exegesis in the LXX of Joshua', *RB* 85 (1978), 50–61.

TSEVAT, M., 'Studies in the Book of Samuel', *HUCA* 32 (1961), 191–216.

URBACH, E., 'The Exegetical Sermon as the Source of Halakha and the Problem of the Scribes', *Tarbiz*, 27 (1958), 166–82; repr. in *Gershom Scholem Jubilee Volume, on the Occasion of his 60th Birthday* (Jerusalem: Magnes Press, 1958), 40–56 [Heb.].

VERDAM, P. J., '"On ne fera point mourir les enfants pour les pères" en droit biblique', *RIDA* 3 (1949), 393–416.

VERMES, G., 'Bible and Midrash: Early Old Testament Exegesis', in *The Cambridge History of the Bible*, i, ed. P. Ackroyd, *From the*

Beginnings to Jerome (Cambridge: Cambridge University Press, 1970), 199–231.

VON RAD, G., 'The Levitical Sermon in I and II Chronicles', in *The Problem of the Hexateuch and Other Essays* (New York: McGraw-Hill, 1966), 267–80.

WACHOLDER, B. Z., 'Chronomessianism. The Timing of Messianic Movements and the Calendar of Sabbatical Cycles', *HUCA* 44 (1975), 201–18.

WANSBROUGH, J., *Quranic Studies, Sources and Methods of Scriptural Interpretation* (London Oriental Series, 5. 31; Oxford: Oxford University Press, 1977).

WEBER, M., *Law in Economy and Society*, ed. M. Rheinstein (Cambridge: Harvard University Press, 1954).

WEINFELD, M., 'God the Creator in Gen. 1 and the Prophecy of Second Isaiah', *Tarbiz*, 37 (1968), 105–32 [Heb.].

—, *Deuteronomy and the Deuteronomic School* (Oxford: Clarendon Press, 1971).

—, 'Sabbath, Temple Building and the Enthronement of the Lord', *Beth Miqra* 69. 2 (1977), 188–93 [Heb.].

WEINGREEN, J., 'Rabbinic-Type Glosses in the Old Testament', *JSS* 2 (1957), 149–62.

—, 'Exposition in the Old Testament and in Rabbinical Literature', in *Promise and Fulfilment: Essays Presented to S. H. Hooke*, ed. F. F. Bruce (Edinburgh: T. and T. Clark, 1963), 187–201.

—, 'The Case of the Woodgatherer (Numbers XV 32–36), *VT* 16 (1966), 361–4.

—, 'Oral Torah and Written Records', in *Holy Book and Holy Tradition*, edd. F. F. Bruce and E. G. Rupp (Manchester: Manchester University Press, 1968), 54–67.

—, 'The Deuteronomic Legislator – a Proto-Rabbinic Type', in *Proclamation and Presence, Essays in Honor of G. Henton Davies*, edd. J. Durham and J. Porter (Richmond, Va.: John Knox Press, 1970), 76–88.

WEISS, M., 'Studies in the Biblical Doctrine of Retribution', *Tarbiz*, 31. 3 (1962), 236–63; ibid. 32. 1 (1962), 1–18 [Heb.].

WEISS, R., *Studies in the Text and Language of the Bible* (Jerusalem: Magnes Press, 1981) [Heb.].

WESTERMANN, C., 'Vergegenwärtigung der Geschichte in den Psalmen', *Forschung am Alten Testament; Gesammelte Studien* (Theologische Bücherei, 24; Munich: Kaiser Verlag, 1964), 306–35.

WILLI, T., *Die Chronik als Auslegung; Untersuchungen zur literarischen Gestaltung der historischen Überlieferung Israels* (Göttingen: Vandenhoeck and Ruprecht, 1972).

WILLI-PLEIN, Ina, *Vorformen der Schriftexegese innerhalb des Alten Testaments* (BZAW 123; Berlin: Walter de Gruyter, 1971).

WRIGHT, A., *The Literary Genre Midrash* (Staten Island, NY: Alba House, 1967).

YOYETTE, J., 'L'Égypte ancienne et les origines de l'antijudaïsme',

RHR 163 (1963), 133–43.
ZEIDEL, M., 'Parallels between Isaiah and Psalms', *Sinai*, 38 (1955–6), 149–72, 229–40, 272–80, 333–55 [Heb.].
ZIMMERLI, W., 'Zur Sprache Tritojesajas', in *Gottes Offenbarung. Gesammelte Aufsätze zum AT* (TBü 19: Chr. Kaiser: Munchen, 1963), 217–33.

Glossary of biblical exegetic terms and expressions

אוֹ 525
אלה 448-9
אך 184, 184n., 185, 197-9, 260n
את 44, 48-50, 80, 101n., 193

בין
בינה 487-8
ויבינו במקרא 108-9

דרש
לדרש את־תורת ה׳ 245
הוא 44-6, 80, 447, 454, 461, 525
היא 44-5, 80
הם 447

וְ 199

זה 44, 51-5, 70n, 75n, 80, 454-5, 525

כ 213, 216, 298, 352-3, 362
כאשר 80n, 164, 216-17, 352, 362
כאשר . . . כן 216-18, 352
כל 175-6, 525

כמשפט 112, 209, 210, 210n, 211
כן 297-8, 374, 525
כן־תעשה (כן תעשה) 177, 178, 179, 181, 181n, 183, 199, 200

מן 63-4

פרש
לפָרֵש 100, 102
מְפֹרָש 108, 108n, 109n
פֵּרֵש 100
פִּשְׁרֵה 455
פתרונו 455
רק 73, 199n, 525, 533
שִׁבְרוֹ 456-7

שכל
להשכיל אל־דברי התורה 109
להשכילך בינה 488
שוֹם שֶׂכֶל 108-9

תעשה־כן 211n

Analytical index of contents and authors*

*Prepared by Bernard M. Levinson
  Names of authors cited in the footnotes or listed in the bibliography are not
indexed here.

Dream exegesis. *See* Oneiromancy
Dualism, 325
Dumuzi, 453–4
Dynastic succession oracle, 466–7.
 See also under David

Ea, 323
Ecclesiasticus. See *Ben Sira, Wisdom of*
Economic justice/oppression, 340–1
Écrits midrashiques, 287
Eden typology, 354, 368–71
Egypt(ian)
 in biblical oracles, 367–8, 460,
  476–7
 oneiromancy, 455–6
 post-exilic exegesis of, 115–20
 Vaticinia ex eventu, 474–6
EISSFELDT, O., 495
El Amarna glosses, 39
Eliezer (prophet), 403
ELIOT, T. S., 435
Eliphaz, 286
Ellipsis, legal, 224–5
Embedded form, 429–30
End-time, 356–7, 492, 495, 516.
 See also Former-latter things
Enemy from the north (oracle), 477,
  479–81, 515
Enlil, 323
Enuma elish, 323, 453
Epic of Gilgamesh, 454, 455
Errors, scribal, 38
Esarhaddon, 480
Eschatology, 354, 495
'Ēšdāt (fiery stream), 76
Esoteric/exoteric, 79, 484
 in mantology, 443–4, 506–11
 in post-biblical thought, 528
Esther, Book of, 503–5
Eunuchs, 257
Euphemisms. *See* Scribal corrections
Evidence, laws of, 188–9, 241–4, 254
Excision (*kārēt*), 92, 192–3, 198–9
Exegesis. *See also Angelus interpres*;
  Glosses; *Inclusio*; Interpolations;
  Redaction, exegetical; Vocabu-
  lary; *Wiederaufnahme*
 analogical, 257–50
 atomistic (legal), 266–7
 contradictory, of words, 61
 disrupts syntax, 62
 distinguishing *traditum* and *traditio*
  in, 10–11, 42–3, 283, 288–91
 etymological, 111

harmonizing, 221–8, 342, 529–30
 inner-biblical, 10–13
 as inspired, 539–42
 intention of, 536–43
 legal. *See under* Legal
 origins of, 3–5, 18–19, 282–3
 presented as Revelation, 4, 97,
  180, 258–60
 qualifying, 252–4
 relation of biblical and Rabbinic,
  3, 60–3, 525–7
 scholastic, 152–3
 synthetic, 250–2
 and social dissension, 142–3
 as unsystematic, 84, 233, 543
 social-historical setting, 15–17,
  62, 168–9
 as wisdom, 539
Exegetical
 authorization of innovations,
  256–65
 obscuring of temporal differences,
  226–8
 revision, aggadic, 285–91
Exile, 113, 389, 412. *See also* Community of the exile; Post-exilic
  community
 effect on exegesis, 263–5
 northern, 80, 361–2, 470
 and mantological exegesis, 471–4
 punishment for Sabbath violation,
  131–4
Exodus
 new, 375, 412–13
 as theomachy, 354–6
 typology, 358–68
Expiation, 190–3, 222–3
Extermination. *See* Ban
Ezekiel
 and Eden typology, 370–1
 failed prophecies in, 476–7
 on child-sacrifice, 185
 reform of Temple service, 139–43
 relation to prior law, 293–5
 and repentance, 390
 reuse of Zephaniah, 461–3
 Valley of Dry Bones, 449–52
 and vicarious punishment, 337–41
Ezra
 has exegetical tradition, 113,
  526–7
 and legal exegesis, 107–23, 126,
  261, 265, 535
 as priest-scribe, 26, 36–7

Index of scriptural and other sources